THE JEWS IN THEIR LAND
IN THE TALMUDIC AGE
(70–640 C.E.)

GEDALIAH ALON

THE JEWS IN THEIR LAND
IN THE TALMUDIC AGE
(70–640 C.E.)

Translated and edited by
GERSHON LEVI

Harvard University Press
Cambridge, Massachusetts
London, England
1989

This paperback edition, published by arrangement with the
Magnes Press, The Hebrew University, Jerusalem, reproduces
in one volume their two-volume English translation of Toldot
ha-Yehudim be-Erets-Yiśra'el bi-tekufat ha-Mishnah
veha-Talmud.

Library of Congress Cataloging-in-Publication Data

Alon, Gedalia.
   The Jews in their land in the Talmudic age, 70-640 C.E.

   Translation of: Toldot ha-Yehudim be-Erets-Yiśra'el
bi-tekufat ha-Mishnah veha-Talmud.
   Reprint. Originally published: Jerusalem : Magnes Press,
the Hebrew University, 1980-1984.
   Includes bibliographical references and indexes.
   1. Jews—History—70-638.   2. Jews—Palestine—
History.   3. Palestine—History—70-638.   I. Levi,
Gershon.   II. Title.
DS123.5.A713   1989   956.94'02   88-23495
ISBN 0-674-47495-3 (pbk.)

PREFACE

To the generations that came after it, the period of Jewish history we are about to discuss was especially noteworthy because it was the era that created Talmudic Judaism, thus enabling the people to survive for century after century in Diaspora, without a homeland of its own. Before very long, the liturgy of the synagogue would proclaim:

> Naught has been left us,
> Save only this, our Torah.[1]

Small wonder then, that the centuries in which the Mishnah and the Talmud were fashioned should come to be perceived as all of one piece with the subsequent generations of wandering and exile.

Indeed, that is exactly the view taken by our classic Jewish historians.

According to Graetz, the long period of exile began immediately after the Roman conquest in the year 70 C.E., so that the centuries we are going to study are simply Part One of that "history of suffering and of scholars" — his description of the protracted travail of the wandering People of the Book, a people of martyrs and learned authors, of persecutions and migrations.[2]

Graetz was undoubtedly a great historian. His "History of the Jews" shows that he was not unaware of political, and even of social factors. But these engaged his attention to a rather limited extent. His presentation is in the main literary-spiritual and biographical, especially in the period we are studying.

Even a historian like Dubnow, who explicitly proposed to give

---

1 [From the penitential hymn *Zekhor Berit Avraham* by Rabbenu Gershom of Mayence, ca. 960–1028 C.E.]
2 Part Three of his *Geschichte der Juden* is entitled: "Third Epoch — From 70 C.E. to 1780." See his introduction to Volume IV.

social history its due, was deflected from a realistic appraisal of life as it was in the Talmudic age, because he was in the thrall of the long-accepted way of looking at the era.[3] When he has finished describing the period, it stands before us with one major characteristic — as the time when a host of inner Jewish disciplines were fashioned, with the express purpose of keeping the Jews separate and apart from the world of the gentiles. Ordinances and prohibitions, laws and rituals were piled one upon the other, according to Dubnow, in order to create that "uniformity of behavior" which is so necessary for soldiers under attack, and on which they depend for survival.

This is not the way to discern the features of the complex society which we shall be examining. Later on we shall outline some criteria for evaluating the fundamental aspects of life in those times. But it should be stated at the outset that we shall begin our study by regarding the age as a *continuation* of the Second Commonwealth, expecting to find the Jews with all the attributes of a people dug in on its native soil; undergoing changes in its national, social and economic life; struggling to regain its freedom; trying with might and main to hold together its scattered limbs, to unite its far-flung diasporas around the central homeland, to strengthen them, and to fan their hopes for final reunification and liberation — a consummation that still appeared to be a practical possibility, perhaps just around the corner.

---

3 It must also be admitted that Dubnow was not really equipped to handle the source materials, nor to evaluate them.

CONTENTS

[vii]

Contents

Contents

[ix]

Contents

ABBREVIATIONS

A. *General*

Ant.	Josephus: Antiquities
Apion	Josephus: Against Apion
BASOR	Bulletin, American Schools of Oriental Research
CAH	Cambridge Ancient History
CIJ	Corpus Inscriptionum Judaicarum
CIL	Corpus Inscriptionum Latinarum
CPJ	Corpus Papyrorum Judaicarum
GLA	Stern: Greek and Latin Authors on Jews and Judaism
HUCA	Hebrew Union College Annual
JBL	Journal of Biblical Literature
JJCW	Alon: Jews, Judaism and the Classical World
JLTA	Alon: The Jews in their Land etc. (The present work).
JQR	Jewish Quarterly Review
JRS	Journal of Roman Studies
JW	Josephus: The Jewish War
Life	Josephus: Life
MGWJ	Monatschrift f. Gesch, u. Wiss. d. Judentums
PG	Patrologiae, Series Graeca
PL	Patrologiae, Eeries Latina
PW	Pauly-Wissowa
REG	Revue des études Grecques
REJ	Revue des études Juives
Tol.	Alon: Toledot ha-Yehudim etc.
Yishuv:	Sepher Ha-Yishuv, ed. S. Klein
ZATW	Zeitschrift f. Alttestamentliche Wiss.
ZDPV	Zeitschrift des Deutschen Palästina Vereins.

B. *Talmudic Literature*

ARN	Avot d'Rabbi Natan	Makh.	Makhshirin
Ahil.	Ahilot	Meg.	Megillah
Av.	Avot	Men.	Menahot
Av. Zar.	Avodah Zarah	Miq.	Miqva'ot
B.B.	Baba Batra	M.Q.	Mo'ed Qatan
B.M.	Baba Mezi'a	Naz.	Nazir
B.Q.	Baba Qama	Ned.	Nedarim
Bekh.	Bekhorot	Neg.	Nega'im
Ber.	Berakhot	NumR.	Numbers Rabbah
Bez.	Bezah	Orl.	Orlah
Bik.	Bikkurim	Par.	Parah
CantR.	Canticles Rabbah	Pes.	Pesahim
Dem.	Demai	Qid.	Qiddushin
DeutR.	Deuteronomy Rabbah	R.H.	Rosh Hashanah
EcclR.	Ecclesiastes Rabbah	RuthR.	Ruth Rabbah
Eduy.	Eduyot	Sanh.	Sanhedrin
Eruv.	Eruvin	Shab.	Shabbat
EstR.	Esther Rabbah	Sheq.	Sheqalim
ExodR.	Exodus Rabbah	Shevi.	Shevi'it
GenR.	Genesis Rabbah	Shevu.	Shevu'ot
Git.	Gittin	Sot.	Sotah
Hag.	Hagigah	Suk.	Sukkah
Hal.	Hallah	Taan.	Ta'anit
Hor.	Horayot	Tem.	Temurah
Hul.	Hullin	Ter.	Terumot
Kel.	Kelim	Tos.	Tosefta (the number in
Ket.	Ketuvot		parentheses is the page
Kil.	Kilayim		in Zuckermandel)
LamR.	Lamentations Rabbah	Yad.	Yadayim
Lev. R.	Leviticus Rabbah	Yer.	Yerushalmi
Maas.	Ma'aserot	Yev.	Yevamot
Maas.Sh.	Ma'aser Sheni	Zev.	Zevahim
Mak.	Makkot	Zuck.	Tosefta Zuckermandel ed.

Talmudic citations not specified as being from the Palestinian Talmud (Yer.) are from the Babylonian Talmud (Bavli).

PART ONE

PROFILE

Throughout, bracketed footnotes are Gershon Levi's.

CHAPTER ONE

THE TALMUDIC AGE

Some Definitions*

The designation "Talmudic" is used in this book as a convenient shorthand term for a period of time that covers almost six centuries — from the Roman destruction of Jerusalem (70 C.E.) to the Arab Muslim conquest (636 C.E.). In the broad perspective of Jewish history, what place should be assigned to these six hundred years?

The usual practice is to subsume them under the same heading as all the following centuries, lumping together everything from the Destruction of the Second Temple right up to modern times and calling it *"galut"* (exile). Hence the conventional trifold division of most Jewish history books:

1. First Commonwealth
2. Second Commonwealth
3. Dispersion.

This view is not entirely the invention of modern historians. It has its roots in the generation right after the Destruction.[1] For the concept "exile" is made up of a number of elements, not all of them geographical. Many a Tanna or early Amora is quoted by the Talmud as speaking of "our days, when Israel no longer dwells on its own soil", or using some similar expression whose intent is clearly to contrast the time of the speaker with the time when the Temple still stood in Jerusalem.

---

* [In the Hebrew original, which will from here on be called *Tol.*, this chapter and the next are simply two parts of a long "Introduction" (*mavo*). Since this is the one place where the author gives us a broad overview of his entire subject, it was thought best to incorporate his overture into the body of his work.]

1 ["Destruction" with a capital D will be used in these pages as an English equivalent of *ḥurban* — that is, the destruction in 70 C.E. of the Second Temple (and of Jerusalem, and of the Jewish commonwealth).]

Not much later we find Church Fathers habitually referring to the Jews as a people exiled from their country, thrust forth from their homeland, scattered among the nations, in thrall to strangers. One might even say that the formulation goes back to the very time when the Temple was burned down; that it was put into words by the perpetrator of that act himself. Addressing the last pockets of Jewish resistance in Jerusalem, the Roman commander Titus is said to have proclaimed: "Your people is dead, your sanctuary gone, your city at my mercy!"[2]

There is some truth in this view — namely, that the period of *galut,* the age of Jewish exile and dispersion began at that moment. But in a number of major respects this theory does not accord with historical realities. Granted that some manifestations of the time can be shown to foreshadow the Middle Ages; but in terms of its essential features the period should be classified under a different heading.

The category that suggests itself is *transition.* For these are the centuries that bridge the passage from Jewish *statehood* to Jewish *homelessness,* and embody that process of devolution by which Jewry in its entirety finally became a Diaspora people.

The Elements of Exile

Let us try to put this theory to the test by examining the period for the presence (or absence) of those elements which constitute exile. A people may be said to be in that condition when it *lacks* all or most of the following six attributes:

1) a state of its own;
2) a concentrated population making up a relative or absolute majority;
3) ownership of land, and a viable economic structure;
4) a leadership of its own;
5) hegemony over any Diaspora that may exist;
6) if occupied, an active political stance (including resistance and rebellion vis-àvis the occupying power).

---

2 Josephus Flavius, *The Jewish War,* VI:6:2 (349). [In this translation, citations from Josephus follow the English of the Loeb Classics. For readier reference, the numbered units of the Greek text have been added in parentheses.]

[4]

The Elements of Exile

Let us apply each of these yardsticks to the Jewish people as it was after the debacle of the year 70 C.E.

STATEHOOD

The Destruction put a final end to Jewish political independence, which had persisted in greater or lesser degree since the return from Babylon. In a political-legal sense, the country ceased to be the Land of the Jews. True, the Romans soon granted a form of national autonomy, but this was given as to an *ethnos* that lived in the Roman province of Judaea (or *Syria Palaestina,* as Hadrian renamed the territory after the Bar Kokhba Revolt, with the clear purpose of eliminating all mention of the Jewish presence.[3])

Nor can the Patriarch, along with the Sanhedrin, be considered to have symbolized any kind of territorial sovereignty. His was a socio-political sort of leadership, even though his jurisdiction was exercised most effectively within the borders of what had been the country of the Jews. So we must conclude that the element of statehood was distinctly lacking. Even the Emperor Julian ("the Apostate") who put forward the idea of rebuilding the Temple and restoring Jerusalem to the Jews, probably had no intention of reviving the Jewish State.

POPULATION

In two major wars fought against Rome — the struggle of 66–74 C.E. and the Bar Kokhba Revolt of 132–135 C.E. — the Jews suffered enormous losses. Both the sword and starvation took their toll. In addition much of the population was rounded up and deported, to be sold abroad as slaves. Then came political and religious oppression, which undoubtedly caused many more of the people to emigrate. But even after all this is taken into account, there are still no grounds for assuming that the Jews did not continue to form the majority of the inhabitants of Palestine, even though

---

3 Nevertheless, the name Judaea did persist for many years, used even by non-Jews. [For evidence, see Emil Schürer: *Geschichte des jüdischen Volkes im Zeitalter J.C.* I, p. 643, n. 1. English translation, revised and edited by Vermes and Millar, Vol. I, Edinburgh, 1973, T. and T. Clark Co., p. 514, n. 1.]

they were banished completely from Jerusalem and its environs after the fall of Betar.

To be sure, a steady deterioration of the Jewish position in the demographic mix of the country becomes evident from the end of the third century. The very efforts made by the Jews to maintain their economic and numerical positions reflect the continuing process that was squeezing them out. Nevertheless it can be safely said that they remained a plurality, outnumbering the Gentiles (Greeks, Syrians and Christians) on the one hand, and the Samaritans on the other.

As for the latter, it cannot be denied that relations with them continued to be unfriendly, as they had been throughout the Second Commonwealth. Still, there were those in both camps who regarded the others as coreligionists, followers of the same way of life — estranged, beyond doubt, but brothers nevertheless. There is every reason to suppose that in a number of political and military actions against Rome the two peoples acted in concert. Many of their contemporaries bracketed Jews and Samaritans together, and we may well be justified in doing the same. If we do, there seems little room for doubt that taken together they outnumbered all foreigners in the country, and constituted an absolute majority of the population.[4]

LAND OWNERSHIP AND ECONOMIC STRUCTURE

As we shall note in detail later, Josephus reports that the Emperor Vespasian decreed that all lands in Palestine were his personal property, and then ordered them to be sold. According to Eusebius, the Emperor Hadrian did the same thing about sixty years later, after the Bar Kokhba Revolt. These acts must have led to the alienation of considerable tracts of land previously owned by

4 [While he does not specify when the balance shifted, Alon seems to imply a Jewish-Samaritan majority well into the fifth century at least. For a somewhat different estimate, arrived at by a calculus based on averaging the population of towns and villages, see M. Avi-Yonah: *Biyemei Romi Uvizantiyon* (Hebrew) Fourth edition, Jerusalem, 1970; p. 25. In Avi-Yonah's own translation of his work, entitled *The Jews of Palestine, A Political History*, Schocken, New York, 1976, pp. 19, 132-133, 222 and 241. Also comp. *Tol.* II, pp. 260–262.]

Jews. Tannaitic tradition recalls that Jews were reduced to the status of tenant farmers and sharecroppers on land that had once been theirs.

It is also quite clear that in some areas which had become well-nigh *judenrein* (the Jerusalem district, for example) the new non-Jewish landlords were in complete possession. In addition, there is a strong probability that economic conditions in the middle of the third century resulted in a still further reduction in the ownership of land by Jews. An oblique illustration of how far this process had gone by the fourth century is the question raised by the Talmud: "Is most of the Land of Israel in Jewish hands or in Gentile hands?"[5] So it would appear that in this matter too there was a constant deterioration. And yet, in the final analysis, the sources at our disposal bear out the conclusion that no overwhelming decrease in Jewish land ownership in Palestine took place until near the very end of the period.

As for the general economic life of Palestine under the Romans, there is ample evidence that Jews followed a wide range of crafts, all of them productive. Especially noteworthy were the trades associated with the manufacture of clothing and utensils. From the middle of the second century Palestinian Jews were noted for the quality of certain of their products, namely linen clothing, dyed woolen fabrics and glassware. The first two played a major role in the country's export trade. But the products that had been associated with the land from ancient times — wine and oil — continued to dominate its commerce, and are still referred to in the middle of the third century as principal elements in the economy.

Admittedly, there are indications that in that very century — a bad time for all countries in the Roman Empire — the economic life of Palestinian Jewry was gravely weakened. This indeed seems to be the time when people turned more and more to petty entrepreneurial trade, and when many Jews went abroad "to earn a living" with the intention of returning home with "monies acquired in the lands beyond the sea." It is from this century that we have expressions denigrating agriculture as a means of earning one's livelihood.

Yet even when all these factors have been taken into account, it is

5   Yer. Demai II:1, 22c.

still the soil that remains the mainstay of the economic life of Palestinian Jewry throughout the period, whether through the cultivation of grapes, olives and flax, through sheep-grazing or surface mining of silicate-sand — or through the occupations involved in processing these crops into wine, oil, linen, wool, dyed-stuffs and glass.

LEADERSHIP

A short time after the Destruction, two central institutions of leadership came to the fore — the Patriarchate and the Sanhedrin. Between them they encompassed all the principal elements of the nation's life — religion, social relationships, economics, civil law and public law. These institutions began by winning the loyalty of the people. It was later that they achieved recognition by the Roman authorities, at first *de facto* but ultimately *de jure* as well.

The difference between the two institutions was this, that the Sanhedrin as High Court was decisive in matters of private law and religion, and loomed larger in the internal life of Palestinian Jewry; whereas the Patriarch took first place in social precedence and public law, so that it was of him that outsiders were most aware. Consequently both the Romans and the Jews of the Diaspora thought of the Patriarch as the representative of the nation, shorn though he was of all political power.

In order to satisfy ourselves that this central leadership can be regarded as the headship of a people ensconced in its own land, there is a question we shall have to consider: was not the authority of the Patriarch *ethnic* rather than territorial? After all, it is well known that his writ ran wherever there were Jews throughout the Roman Empire, and this was an authority recognized by the government. It might follow, therefore, that since the people had been deprived of its territorial existence in a politico-legal sense, the Patriarchate should be viewed as neither less nor more than the headship of the Jews in the Roman Empire, not necessarily connected with Palestine. That country just happened to be its seat for the time being, so to speak.

As a matter of fact, this view is not without its advocates. Juster[6]

6 [The reference seems to be to *Les Juifs dans l'Empire Romain*, Paris, 1914, vol. I, p. 393, where the Patriarch is described as "souverain sans

[8]

holds that since the Jews in the Diaspora could no longer settle their legal affairs as citizens *in absentia* of the now defunct Jewish State, their recourse to the jurisdiction of the Patriarch has to be viewed as direct and unmediated, a jurisdiction *ad personam,* so to speak. If we accept this view we cannot count the Patriarchate, or the Sanhedrin, as evidence for the continued corporate existence of the Jewish nation in its own land.

The theory has logic and legal clarity on its side, but it does not correspond with the realities. The sway of the Patriarch and the Sages (the Teachers of the Law) in the Homeland over the Jews in the Diaspora derives from the long-established hold of the Jewish authorities — the High Priest and the Sanhedrin — over the scattered Jewries abroad *before* the Destruction. That situation, which had prevailed during the Second Commonwealth, was itself a politico-legal anomaly. Jews who held Roman or Alexandrian citizenship should not, in all reason, have had the right to be judged under the law of the Judaean state. Nevertheless that was the way it was, a situation *sui generis* in the Roman world.

The same applies to the Patriarchate in its official relationship to the Diaspora. The Jews out there accepted the authority of the Patriarch because of the ties that bound them to the Mother Country. The position was this: basically, the Patriarchate was an institution intended for the Jews in their ancestral land. It was by derivation — that is, by virtue of the spiritual hegemony which the Mother Country exercised over its scattered children — that it served the Diaspora as well.

In any case, it is abundantly clear that the primacy of the Patriarchate over Jewry was based on the situation as it existed in the Land of Israel. For the more than three centuries during which the institution lasted, its authority over the people grew stronger, and it even acquired an aura of regality. But when the time came that the Roman Empire adopted Christianity and set about removing Jews from all public and quasi-public office, the fate of the Patriarchate was sealed. As a first step, it was shorn of official prerogatives. The final blow came with the abolition of the office

pouvoir territorial, chef en quelque sort spirituel de tous les juifs de l'Empire . . . *même* de ceux de Palestine."]

altogether following the failure of the Emperor Theodosius II to appoint a successor to Gamaliel VI.[7]

Even so, that did not mark the end of officially recognized central Jewish authority in Palestine. The Patriarchate was gone, but the Sanhedrin remained. We have clear-cut evidence, at least for the period immediately following the end of the Patriarchate, that the "*Sanhedra'ot* in the Land of Israel" had the same prerogatives vis-à-vis the Diaspora as had previously belonged to the Patriarchs, and that this arrangement continued to have Roman governmental sanction. On the other hand, it is safe to assume that the authority of the Sanhedrin, both in law and in fact, was much diminished, by comparison to what the Partriarchate in its heyday had been. But this only strengthens our view that the entire period is one of transition, during which the image of a people living in its own country becomes blurred and faded, but is not obliterated.

HEGEMONY OF THE HOMELAND

We have already referred to the leadership exercised by the authorities in Palestine over the Jews throughout the Roman Empire. Without entering into all aspects of that relationship, we would do well at this juncture to set forth some of the fundamental facts involved, the better to focus on the ties between Jewish Palestine and the most significant of all the Diasporas, the one lying *outside* the confines of the Roman Empire — the Jewish community of Babylonia.

The hegemony of Palestine over Jewish communities within the Roman Empire was expressed in the following ways: 1) *Religion:* The academies in Palestine had the last word on all halakhic questions. 2) *Law:* The Great Beth Din was the court of highest instance in matters of Jewish civil law. 3) *Judiciary:* In theory — and sometimes even in practice — Jewish judges in the Diaspora were appointed by the Patriarch. 4) *Communal Organization:* Through the agency of their "legates" — the *apostoloi* — the Patriarchs could appoint and dismiss leaders of Jewish communities abroad. 5) *Discipline:* The leadership in the home-country exercised religious supervision over the communities abroad, including the power to impose sanc-

---

7 [About 425 C.E. See *Codex Theodosianus*, XVI:8:29.]

tions. 6) *Support:* The Diaspora paid a tax to the Patriarch in the form of two drachmas (*aurum coronarium*) and later on supported the academies through the "levy of the Sages."

Most historians take the view that the authority of the Palestinian institutions was contested, and finally overcome, by the power of the great Jewish community of Babylonia. According to this reading, the two communities were engaged in a fairly balanced rivalry for the leadership of Judaism from the beginning of the third century to about the middle of the fourth. Then the Babylonians gained the upper hand, and Palestine was pushed right out of the picture. This view is certainly not without foundation, and is supported by a number of facts. But taken as a whole, it can be shown to be untrue. At no time up to the Moslem conquest did Babylonia capture the leadership. What is more, Babylonian Jewry remained in most respects *subject to Palestinian authority* up to the very end of the period we are discussing.

Obviously, certain factors tended to weaken the bond between the Land of Israel and the Jewish communities further to the east. The latter belonged to the Persian Empire of the Arcasides — and then the Sassanians — and were thus outside the Roman orbit. Besides, Mesopotamian Jewry had certain social and economic advantages by comparison with the various Roman Diasporas. It had whole districts with dense Jewish populations possessed of a sound economic structure, which included grazing and agriculture, as well as trade in farm produce. It also had the powerful institution of the Exilarchate, whose sway over the Jews of the Tigris-Euphrates basin can be attributed in part to the feudal character of Partho-Persian society. And then there were the great academies of Jewish learning that flourished from the beginning of the third century. All these factors tended to weaken the authority of Palestinian Judaism over the Jewry of Babylonia. No wonder the latter enjoyed greater independence than any other Diaspora community. Nevertheless, Babylonian Jewry was in many decisive respects still subject to the central institutions of the Mother Country — not only in legal theory, but in practical fact as well.

From the time when "Rav went down to Babylonia" and founded the academy of Sura, the Babylonian Jews drew most of their scholarship from the Land of Israel. The learned traffic between the two countries consisted largely in bringing the Torah of Palestine to the Jews of Mesopotamia, whose scholars yearned to go up and study at the academies in the Holy Land. This trend was deprecated by the authorities in Israel as socially and morally undesirable, since there were some Babylonians who actually abandoned their families, leaving wives and children in straitened circumstances.

Furthermore, even though the Babylonian academies themselves soon became great centers of learning whose scholars were on occasion bold enough to dispute legal traditions reported from the Palestinian yeshivot — nevertheless the arrival of an *igarta*, an official missive from the Palestine authorities, was enough to settle the matter. This held good throughout the entire period we are discussing, including the age of the Saboraim in the sixth century.

It is worthy of note that in the steady flow of correspondence between the two countries on matters of Jewish law and learning it is always, with one or perhaps two exceptions, the Babylonians who ask the questions and the Palestinian scholars who give the answers. This authority was not diminished even by those great Babylonian heads of yeshivot who claimed independence for Babylonia, and protested the outflow of scholars to Palestine. A good example is the case of Rabbi Judah, founder of the great academy of Pumbeditha. When he died, his institution asked the *Palestinian* authorities who should be his successor.[8]

As for the administration of Jewish Law, the Babylonians themselves admitted that their courts had only limited powers. The matter is put plainly in two well-known legal maxims quoted in the Babylonian Talmud: 1) "There is no power of judicial appointment (ordination) outside the Land of Israel."[9] 2) "The Jewish courts in Babylonia cannot impose monetary sanctions."[10] In effect, the latter principle excludes from judicature in the Diaspora any areas of law that rest on a full social consensus, leaving only such matters as would normally arise from contractual relations and business transactions. Even within that limited area, the *dayanim* in Babylonia were in theory the delegated representatives *(shelihim)* of the author-

---

8   Hor. 14a.
9   Sanh. 14a.
10 B.Q. 15b and 27b. Cf. Sanh. loc. cit.

ities in the Mother Country, an axiom from which the rule of "no ordinations abroad" naturally flows.[11] It is clear, therefore, that in Jewish legal matters the supremacy of the Land of Israel (which, as we have seen, was accepted throughout the Roman Empire) held good, albeit with some differences, outside the Empire as well. The same can be said for the recognition of the High Court in Palestine as the highest judicial instance.

It is apparent from historical evidence of the Amoraic period that the Babylonian Jews accepted this situation no less than, say, the Jews of Antioch. The relationship stands out most clearly in the well-known dependence of Babylonia on Palestine for determining the calendar, i.e., for the declaration of New Moons and leap-years. Granted, there were times when struggles took place between Babylonia and Palestine; when the younger community sought a measure of independence. Besides, Babylonia possessed that other headship — the Exilarchate — conscious of its Davidic descent, claiming to have authority on its own. One cannot gainsay that Babylonia was a special kind of Diaspora, with a special kind of status; in spite of which, one cannot deny that throughout our period Babylonia remained, like all the rest, under the effective authority of the Land of Israel.

POLITICAL RESISTANCE

A certain renowned modern historian of Ancient Rome once pointed out that none of Rome's subject peoples objected to her rule as vehemently as did the Jews. He was referring to the Jews in their own land before the Destruction of Jerusalem. Perhaps he did not go far enough. There were other peoples in both east and west, some of them, like the Greeks, great peoples with a long tradition of freedom, who not only bent their necks to the Roman yoke, but even let themselves become spiritually enslaved, going so far as to exalt Rome, and to ascribe divine status to her tyrant Caesars. For these admiring subjects, the sovereignty of Rome was as the kingdom of heaven, the Emperor entitled to be called "savior." Apart from a few scattered episodes of resistance and rebellion, this subjugation of the spirit prevailed throughout Imperial times.

11 B.Q. 84b.

By contrast, the Jews in Judaea expressed their detestation of Rome in every possible way from the very beginning of the Roman occupation. The formulations of this antipathy are instructive. For other peoples it was "Rome, eternal and divine"; for the Jews it was "Rome the Guilty" *(romi ḥayyavta)*. Elsewhere they spoke of *"Caesar divus"*, while Jews referred to "the kingdom of wickedness" *(malkhut ha-resha'ah)*. In contrast to the universal fawning on the Imperial master, the Jews equated Rome with the "wild boar" of the Bible (Psalm 80:14). In short, they protested unrestrainedly against the cruelty and depravity which the Roman legions brought with them wherever they went.

Why was this people unique in its rejection — even hatred — of Rome and her Empire? No doubt because of the Jewish religion, unique in thought and action, distinctive in its concept of social ethics. These fundamentals of Judaism made unthinkable any compromise with the Pax Romana, with the "heavenly order" which was Roman rule. What especially kept the Jews in a constant state of ferment against Rome was their demand for freedom — national as well as individual. How this must have sounded to the Romans may be guessed at, when we observe the measure of "freedom" they granted to local city councils, taking great care to restrict even that limited authority to the propertied class, while all other social strata counted for nothing. This process of delegating a little power, with all the fluctuations it underwent throughout the centuries of Roman rule deserves closer study; for present purposes let us simply note that it runs like a scarlet thread through the history of the Roman Empire.

As for the Jews in Judaea, with the exception of certain circles who were "close to the powers that be" *(mequravim la-malkhut)* they never willingly submitted to the Roman yoke. More than that, they never let up in their demand for freedom and equality for the depressed classes — at least, for every Jew. "We are seed of Abraham, and have never been slaves to any man." (John 8:33).

Did this antipathy persist even after the Destruction? Of course it did. All through the following centuries our sources are so full of expressions of it that there is no need to quote examples. To be sure, as time went on, and repressive actions by the Romans multiplied, people realized that there was little immediate hope for improvement.

[14]

But the attitude of antagonism to Rome and things Roman remained unweakened.

More than verbal manifestations of this hatred can be pointed out. Before the Destruction, opinion among the Jews was divided over the permissibility of paying taxes and excise duties levied by the Roman occupying power. The Zealots and their political allies declared all such payments forbidden, even on pain of death. Their opponents agreed that the Roman exactions had no basis in law, and that it was illegal for Jews to pay them, but held that it was allowable to commit that illegality because of *force majeure (ónes)*. So that both sides — in effect, the overwhelming majority of the people — refused to recognize the legitimacy of the Roman government.

This is the underlying reason why the publicans (tax-farmers) were held in such bad odor, a fact amply testified to by the Gospels. It was not only their strong-arm methods that caused these tax-collecting entrepreneurs to be shunned by the Jewish community. This unofficial excommunication was also an expression of popular contempt aimed at collaborators, willing servants of the occupying power who were deliberately helping the Romans strengthen their grip on the country. Indeed, an old pre-Destruction halakhah makes it permissible to take a false oath to "publicans and robbers".[12] The former are equated with the latter, because as far as the Jews were concerned, Roman taxes were devoid of any juridical basis, and were therefore out-and-out extortion.

This is the exact opposite of the Diaspora maxim formulated in Babylonia with respect to the Sassanian government: "The law of the sovereign is law for us" *(dina d'malkhuta dina)*.[13] It makes the Palestinian attitude all the more striking. And that attitude, so eloquent in what it tells us about the realities of the situation, carries over to the period *after* the demise of the Jewish State, even though there were Jewish leaders who sought to mitigate it. In spite of these efforts, the post-Destruction *gabbaim* (revenue agents) who took the place of the publicans were still treated by the Jews as semi-outcasts in the same class as robbers and extortionists, and therefore

12   Mishnah Ned. III:4.
13   Git. 10b.

disqualified from giving evidence or from sitting as judges. Here again, it was not only because of their unsavory methods of making money, but especially because they were lackeys of the Roman government. It took time before an effort was made to reach some measure of compromise, to legitimize in some degree the power that maintained order in the land.

However, the most pronounced expression of political resistance by the Jews is to be found in the series of revolts and insurrections that took place throughout our period.

Without doubt the greatest of these was the Bar Kokhba Rebellion. It was also the last effort of the nation as a whole to achieve its freedom through a war carried on exclusively by its own efforts. Even so, later insurrections more limited in their scope and goals — those in Sepphoris and elsewhere under Gallus (351 C.E.) for example — prove the persistence of political power and activity. Additional evidence is provided by our sources from the beginning of the second century onwards. They reflect the lively interest of the Jews in the relationships (and wars) between the empires of Rome (Byzantium) and Persia, and the hopes they aroused for a possible turn in the fortunes of the Land of Israel.

The latest political effort in this direction was made at the beginning of the seventh century, when the Persians conquered the country. The Jews of Palestine welcomed these enemies of Rome, giving them considerable military, and possibly also financial help. Finally, the messianic hopes and speculations common in those times should not be brushed aside as altogether unrealistic. It was only later that a clear-cut distinction came to be made between "this world" and the "days of the Messiah" — that is, between reality on the one hand, and hope deferred to the millennium on the other.

We have been discussing Palestinian Jewry's awareness of itself as a political force, capable of taking action. There is no gainsaying that in this respect too, the period shows a continuous process of weakening and diminution. But weakening and diminution do not necessarily add up to total disappearance. That was to come, but not until much later.

Whatever the nation had been able to salvage from its defeat and to preserve for succeeding generations had been salvaged and preserved only by dint of hard struggle. This involved an internal effort to create a new center of national leadership in the teeth of separatist and self-serving elements that had been present all along, even before the Destruction. It involved a closing of ranks in the face of "heretics" *(minim)* and "sects" *(kitot)* who challenged the religious identity of the people. It involved a united front against "informers" *(moserot)* and others who "separated themselves from the community" — that is, collaborationists who "associated with the ruling power."[14] It involved a struggle to maintain national unity by preserving the centrality and authority of the Land of Israel, despite tendencies toward fragmentation encouraged by the Roman authorities. It involved continuous tension with the gentiles. It involved prolonged grappling with those chronic conditions, political as well as economic, that kept driving people to emigrate. Finally, and not least, it involved an unrelenting struggle with the colonial administrators and the Roman government to preserve the religious and national character of the Jewish people.

About this last we have the testimony of the historian Dio Cassius. Describing Pompey's invasion of Judaea, he takes occasion to make some comments about the people of that country. It is a people, he says, that can be found everywhere among the Romans. "Though often repressed," he writes, "it has increased to a very great extent, and has won its way to the right of freedom in its observances."[15]

14 Sifre Deut. 357. Ed. Finkelstein, p. 425 f. Comp. below, p. 62, n. 18.
15 [*"Dio's Roman History"* translated by Earnest Cary, Loeb Classical Library, vol. III, p. 127.]

CHAPTER TWO

SIX CENTURIES IN REVIEW

Every attempt to break up historical time into chronological units has two purposes. One of these is to bring out the special characteristics of each time-segment. The other is the converse: to point up what is common to them all — in effect to show the general direction in which history seems to be moving, exposing at the same time the underlying changes which appear to alter that general direction.

Eras and Ages

This is an important undertaking, for it presumes to determine where the crossing-points of history are to be found; so that in fact it is laying down the ground-rules for subsequent historical study.

More often than not this task is also a very difficult one. Only rarely can we put our finger confidently on some decisive event that announces a turning-point in the historical process. Usually we lack the data which might have helped us to identify such crucial events, and shown us how, perhaps even why, they brought about some new historical reality.

Moreover, even when it seems that a dividing-line in history has been thrust under our very noses by some great dramatic event, we dare not jump to hasty conclusions. Further reflection may well lead us to conclude that the historical processes we have managed to discern actually straddle our imaginary boundaries.

Another problem that faces the historiographer is this: what criteria are to determine where he ought to close one chapter and begin the next? He might hesitate for a long time over whether to be guided by political change-overs, or social-economic processes, or shifts in the cultural and intellectual climate. Changes in one of these major areas of human life do not always conveniently produce simultaneous and equally decisive changes in the others.

These, then, are but some of the problems facing one who would diagram history's chapter headings. After careful consideration we are bound to conclude that the undertaking is normally a very difficult and risky business, and that any results must be treated as highly tentative.

But when it comes to the era in Jewish history that we are examining, the difficulty is even worse than usual, compounded as it is by the nature of our sources. To begin with, these include very little historical writing. The material is mostly literary: halakhic, homiletic-aggadic, commentary on older texts, religious apologetics, and the like. For certain time-spans even this kind of source material is wholly lacking, leaving us more or less in the dark.

Not only does this deprive us of hard knowledge about what went on in those years. It also flaws our ability to draw time-boundaries. It leaves gaping lacunae in our picture of the evolving historical process.

Secondly, the Hebrew literary works of the period, which constitute the bulk of our source-material, are extraordinarily difficult to date. This is true of the books themselves, for example the aggadic midrashim; and equally true of the underlying literary materials on which they are based. Such substrata had been cast into form before the books themselves were composed, or (in some cases) edited.

Finally, in the sources we do have there is a paucity of chronological data that can be connected with known events and personalities; and where such information exists, we are not certain about its reliability. For example, a tradition may ascribe certain words or actions to an individual — only to be contradicted by another tradition, which ascribes the same things to somebody else. Even in the absence of such contradictions, our own critical sense often makes us skeptical of the apparent evidence.

In short, then, the approximately six centuries we are studying can only be separated into periods on a basis arbitrarily agreed upon; and even then, with every kind of reservation. This said, let us now proceed to suggest such subdivisions.

If we were dealing with the history of the Jewish people as a whole, our task would be much simpler. We would cut the entire period into two, using as our chronological benchmark that time (at the beginning of the fourth century) when Christianity became the official religion of the Roman Empire. Prior to that event, everything that happened to the Jews of the Empire was conditioned and defined by the policy on the Jews laid down in pagan times, principally by Julius Caesar and by Augustus. It was a tradition and a policy of toleration. That it had its ups and downs during the course of the centuries goes almost without saying; there was, for example, a definite decline in the position of the Jews everywhere following the Destruction of Jerusalem. Nevertheless, their civil-juridical status, and even the way they were treated de facto, did not suffer any fundamental change. Their old basic rights remained untouched. They were still guaranteed the freedom to practice their religion; the right of assembly; their own courts; the right to be in touch with their national center in Palestine, and to subject themselves to its authority; and finally, their status as full-fledged citizens.

With the ascendancy of Christianity, bringing in its train the achievement of temporal power by the Church and the Christianization of the State, the position of the Jews began to be undercut. Action against them was taken at first by the clergy (the *episkopi*) and the populace responsive to their leadership; and then finally by the government, by means of Imperial legislation. To be sure, this change did not come about all at once. It took almost a century from the conversion to Christianity of Constantine the Great, followed shortly afterwards by the Council of Nicaea, until the publication of those Imperial rescripts that did so much to curtail the rights of the Jewish community, and to reduce the religious freedom and civil status of the individual Jew. During the intervening years, the aggressively Catholic image of the State became more and more pronounced, culminating in the official prohibition and vigorous suppression of all pagan religions and deviant Christian sects. But despite the time it took to get all this underway, the fundamental reality that was to set the process in motion was already present at the beginning of the fourth century.

However, we are not dealing here with world Jewry, but with the history of the Jews in one country — Palestine. That means that we must take account of other, more strictly local factors. Consequently, we shall have to divide our period not just into two, but into three sub-periods. The subdivisions we suggest are these:

Stage I: 70 C.E. (the Destruction) to 235 C.E. (Last of the Severan

Caesars, and shortly after the death of the Patriarch Judah I).
Stage 2: 235 C.E. to ca. 420 C.E. (Abolition of the Patriarchate).
Stage 3: 420 C.E. to the Arab conquest (636 C.E., Battle of the
Yarmuk; or 640 C.E., the conquest of Egypt).

Stage I: 70 to 235 C.E. Time of the Tannaim

This period witnesses the beginning and the culmination of that
process whereby the people grew accustomed to being led by the
Sages (the scholars, *"ḥazal"*) and the Patriarchs. The "Great Court
of Law", which was at the same time "The Great Academy" headed
by the Patriarch, became the central national authority.

Leadership by learned Sages was not an entirely new phenomenon.
Earlier, during the days of the Second Commonwealth, the influence
of the scholar-judges, the spokesmen of the Pharisees, had been decisive in matters affecting religious life. They had participated in the
Sanhedrin, and had played a role both direct and indirect in social
and political life. Of course they had shared power with the other
elements in the establishment, namely the High Priesthood, the
ordinary priesthood, and the leading families — in effect, the aristocracy. There were even times when the Sages were excluded by these
others from the national leadership, although it does not appear that
they ever lost their direct religious and moral influence over the
people.

Came the time when the Temple was destroyed, and the nation
was at a loss. It was then that the Sages, acting alone, created a
centralized and inclusive structure of leadership that was ultimately
to put the nation back on its feet, to give it solidarity, and to enable
it to survive. This achievement is usually explained in rather simple
terms, as though the other elements had defaulted, leaving the field
to the Rabbis. But things were more complicated than that.

According to the standard account, the Destruction of the Temple
put an end to the priesthood, since there was no role left for the
priests to play. But this overlooks the fact that the priests had
always had functions to perform outside the Temple. From time
immemorial they had served as judges and popular leaders; age-old
tradition endowed them with authority; and the people continued
to look up to them until the very last days of the Second Commonwealth.

[21]

Even after the Destruction of the Temple, the priests did not automatically lose their social importance, or drop their group cohesiveness all at once. Not even the Sages, for all their struggle against the élitist separatism of the priests in the generation after the Destruction, had any intention of overcoming the priesthood or of abolishing it, for reasons which need not detain us at this point. In any case, the concentration of national leadership into the hands of the scholars is not self-evident, nor did it take place without a struggle.

Actually, the element most favorably situated to share power with the Romans as they tightened their grip on Judaea was the upper classes, the men of wealth and family. After all, here as elsewhere, Rome was interested in delegating authority to people of substance, many of whom had co-operated with her before the war. True, there was no longer any question of national political appointment for Jews, but there was still local office in the towns and villages, and it would have been in the Roman interest to concentrate municipal authority in the hands of this class, the better to block the emergence of a Jewish national leadership led by the scholars. We do in fact have evidence of an intense struggle which took place after the Destruction between the Pharisaic teachers and those men of means who had "curried favor with the Government" *(nitqarvu lamalkhut),* and had sought power by grace of the Roman administration, and by exploiting the social-economic crisis. It was a struggle that lasted a long time, and deserves to be studied elsewhere in some detail.

That the Pharisaic teachers were able to gain the adherence of the vast majority of the people is due first and foremost to those *religious ideas* which sustained the national spirit and forged its strength to meet adversity. For many generations past the predecessors of these Sages had stood for those teachings in word and deed, and had nurtured a faith that was both visionary and practical, combining prophetic idealism with halakhic realism, messianic yearning with the needs and duties of the hour. It was a durable Torah which these schoolmen had left behind them, and it was accessible to everyman. So that when the state was brought down in ruins, and the nation was left to face confusion and chaos, it was only natural that the company of scholars — "the teachers of the people"

[22]

— should take upon themselves the task of reviving the nation by· means of its inherited religious vision, the faith of its fathers.

This is not to say that those teachers were in total agreement with one another in their attitudes towards Rome. The variety of political opinions and goals which characterized the people at large was faithfully reflected in the body of Sages. Before the Destruction, as afterwards, they had been divided on issues of war and peace, like everybody else in the country. The whole spectrum of partisan views was represented in their ranks; they too had their zealots, half-zealots, realist-moderates, outright pacifists, and even apologists for the Roman administration.[1] Nevertheless, there is a discernible main line, a normative point of view, to which the Pharisaic leaders gave expression. It was an amalgam of fierce patriotism with tender love for the people Israel; a mixture of hatred for Rome with an attachment to peace, of rebelliousness tempered with prudence, of impatient activism coupled with visionary messianism. Any one of these elements might come to the fore, depending on the needs of the hour.

The company of scholars also mirrored the varying social levels of the nation at large. The dominant element came from the plain people — artisans, small farmers, tenants — whose purposes ran counter to the social interests of the powerful. But the Sages also counted among their number other kinds of people — priests, rich

---

1 For example, R. Hanina the Deputy High Priest, who taught: "Pray for the welfare of the ruling power, since but for the fear of it, men would have swallowed one another up alive." (Av. III:2). Similarly, R. Jose ben Qisma chides R. Hanania ben Teradion for lecturing on Torah at public assemblies, at a time when this was expressly forbidden by Roman edict: "Brother, do you not know that this people (the Romans) are sovereign because it is God's will?" (Av. Zar. 18a).

These disputes are reflected in the famous argument recorded in the Talmud (Shab. 33b): "Rabbi Judah (bar Ilai) and Rabbi Jose and Rabbi Simeon (bar Yohai) were sitting together, and Judah ben Gerim (the son of proselytes?) was there as well. R. Judah brought up the subject of the Romans: 'What wonderful things this people has done! They have established market-places, built bridges, constructed bath-houses!' R. Jose kept silent, but R. Simeon spoke up: 'Whatever they have done has been only for their own sake. They have built markets so that they can house prostitutes; baths in order to preen themselves; bridges, so that they can collect tolls.'"

men, scions of old families; and their teachings sometimes echo ideas typical of the aristocracy and the wealthy.

If we want to learn the true nature of this band of teachers, we have only to read two or three chapters in the histories of Josephus Flavius, to discover that the Pharisees really were the party of the common people; close to the masses, loved and trusted by them. How the social scene had changed since the time of Ben Sira, that earlier sage (second century B.C.E.), who had written in gentle derogation of the ploughman, the builder, the smithy and their fellow-workers:

"Without them a city cannot be inhabited...
But they shall not be inquired of for public counsel,
And in the assembly they enjoy no precedence.
On the seat of judgement they do not sit,
Law and justice they do not understand."[2]

With their program of public study of the Torah, the Pharisees had changed all that, and had forged close bonds of affection and discipline between themselves and the mass of the people. Indeed, the social make-up of the company of Sages itself in the days of the Tannaim was utterly different from that of the learned fraternity of the "Scribes" *(soferim)* who had been the contemporaries and colleagues of Ben Sira. Poor men and artisans, some of them practising trades very low on the social scale; men of dubious pedigree or none at all — these were quite common among those whom we have come to call "The Rabbis", the Sages of Mishnaic-Talmudic times.

As for the Patriarch, he was originally the presiding officer of the High Court, and ex-officio head of the Academy. This qualified him to speak for the company of scholars, and entitled him to certain privileges and precedences. His standing in the society derived, therefore, from the powers vested in him by the Sanhedrin. But as time went on, his special status assumed greater prominence, so that he and the office he held developed into an independent element in the power structure, which then became a sort of diarchy.

Parallel with this internal development, the Patriarchate also promoted its own role as an external temporal power on a national

2 Ben Sira, end of Chapter 38.

scale, putting itself forward as spokesman for the nation vis-à-vis the Roman government. This could only have abetted the efforts of the Patriarchs to make themselves masters over the Sanhedrin. These processes characterize the first stage of our period practically from its beginning, and continue to its very end. They reach their high-water mark in the days of the greatest Patriarch of them all, Rabbi Judah I, *"Ha-Nasi"*, the redactor of the Mishnah.

Still another development, bounded for all intents and purposes by the beginning and end of the sub-period we have designated Stage 1, was *religious consolidation*. While the Temple still stood, and especially during the last generations before its Destruction, Judaism had produced a variety of sects and tendencies, each of them viable and capable of growth. As long as the vital powers of the nation had not been sapped, and the homeland was still able to nourish the centripetal forces that held the people together, Judaism could afford these sometimes wildly differing schools of thought (despite the sharp disagreements and clashes that they bred) without fear that internal strife might bring the roof down on everybody's head. But once the Temple had been destroyed, the very survival of the nation was at risk. Consequently a new process of spiritual-religious unification and consolidation set in, almost on the heels of the catastrophe.

One of the most notable of the pre-Destruction sects had been the Sadducees, and there are scattered references to their continued presence in the country until the Bar Kokhba Revolt. But thereafter — not a word. Even before the Revolt they had ceased to be a factor to be reckoned with. Granted, Sadducean ideas persisted, in a subterranean sort of way, into our period and beyond it, both in Palestine and in the Diaspora. But in terms of a recognizable social entity or organized sect, the end of the Temple sounded the death-knell of the Sadducees, and they vanished from the stage of Jewish history.

During the last several decades of the Second Commonwealth, another sectarian group had emerged — the Jewish Christians. This movement was born, and had its first growth, within the bosom of Judaism and the Jewish people. It was only later, shortly before the Destruction of the Temple, that the decision was taken under the leadership of Paul of Tarsus that Christianity should become a

[25]

Gentile faith. The processes set in motion by this crucial step did not reach their peak until many generations later.

In addition, there was a bitter struggle in progress throughout the second and third centuries between main-line (ultimately, Catholic) Christianity, and the Gnostic Christianity of Marcion and others. At issue were the Jewish foundations of Christianity, including the attribution of equal sanctity to the Old Testament, side-by-side with the New; belief in the God of Israel; and other articles of the faith. Thus, the beginning of our period coincides with the start of a double-edged process within Christianity: disengagement from Judaism, on the one hand; and on the other, incorporation within itself of the Jewish theological and prophetic heritage.

But for purposes of our present study we must turn our attention away from all that, and focus on the *Jewish* Christianity which rejected Paul and his doctrines. Its adherents were Jews who believed in Jesus — as prophet, teacher, Messiah even — but wanted to remain part of the Jewish people, to continue observing all the mitzvot most faithfully, and to keep apart from Gentiles and Gentile culture. These sectarians, whom Christians generally called *Ebionites,* and our Jewish sources dub *Minim,* were not expelled from the Jewish fold by the Sages before the fall of Jerusalem. But soon thereafter the Jewish leaders *did* declare them to be outside the community of Israel. In spite of this, there were continuing contacts between them and individual Jews — Sages as well — all through the second and third centuries. But the nation as a whole read them out of the fold, regarding them as a strange and dangerous element. The same can be said of certain other, less prominent dissenters, such as the Jewish Gnostic sects, traces of whose activities are discernable in Judaea during the days of the Tannaim.

Still another process of consolidation took place at the *social* level, involving the elimination of hereditary status, of privilege based on birth. The effects of this become noticeable towards the end of our period, with the erosion of social distinctions derived from family origin (*yuḥasin*). During Temple times, and for a while thereafter, there were circles for whom the family tree was of prime importance. These people tried to avoid marriages with "families of inferior status." But the social situation in later tannaitic times practically wiped out such distinctions, thus curing the nation of a serious social defect.

[26]

As for the priests *(kohanim)*, they began by trying very carefully to preserve their separate and exalted status; but gradually this too wore away, and they merged into the mass of plain Jews. To be sure, there were counter-tendencies; the people insisted on giving *kohanim* special rights, some of them real, some purely symbolic. There were even instances when priestly descent was successfully used to back up a claim to leadership.

Perhaps more important was the absorption into the body of Jewry of those elements in the population who were of dubious standing as a result of problems relating to the Jewishness of their ancestry, or to the matrimonial status of their forbears. Some of these elements had been declassed previously because of the stringent qualifications laid down by the priesthood. On the other hand, there were those whom the process of consolidation now excluded altogether from the Jewish fold, such as the descendants of foreign slaves called *netinim*, who had for generations been a lowly caste. The generalization we can make is that, during the first stage of our period, there was a growing tendency among the surviving Jews to drop such elements, while at the same time obliterating all distinctions among the rest of the people.

There were other social barriers which had developed among the Pharisees themselves, and which now withered away. The communal groups called *ḥavurot* which had been formed by some scholars so that they could be sure that their food was ritually pure and had been properly tithed, groups whose motivation had been to hallow every aspect of life, but which constituted potential forces for exclusivism and divisiveness — these groups disappear from view by the end of the first stage of the period we have undertaken to study.

But the most distinguishing characteristic of this time-span is the creation of a halakhic literature, fashioned out of that long chain of tradition known as the Oral Torah. The classic achievement is, of course, the Mishnah — the book which embodies the complicated process whereby the thinking of the nation about halakhah and law had been crystallized over the years. In its turn, this book was destined to serve as the basis for Jewish life and thought for many generations, in the homeland and in the Diaspora. During the next two or three centuries it became the foundation on which were erected

[27]

those all-embracing structures which we know as the Talmudim — the Jerusalem Talmud and the Babylonian Talmud. But that was to come. It is the Mishnah which here engages our attention.

Scholars are divided in their evaluation of the Mishnah. Some see it as a law book, a sort of codex; others view it rather as a source-book, a work of reference. It is hard to decide which opinion is right; the Mishnah seems to be both.

It should be recalled that the halakhah is oriented towards free decision-making on the part of the judges and religious authorities. The intention of the ancient halakhists was to teach and to guide, rather than to legislate; to express opinions, rather than to hand down decisions. While it is true that a number of rules of law were formulated in the academies as legal decisions in certain cases where conflicting opinions and practices made this necessary, nevertheless even these rules served only as guide-lines for the Sages, especially when the latter functioned as judges or decision-makers. So that, despite the demanding character of the halakhah, and its tendency towards a uniform and unifying way of life for the Jewish people and for the individual Jew, the halakhic process took place in an atmosphere of free decision-making.

The Sages were in origin and function essentially teachers of the meaning of the Torah. This makes it easier for us to understand the dual nature of the Mishnah, its amalgam of elements. In any case, the great achievement of Rabbi Judah Ha-Nasi and his academy served not only to harvest the creative work of preceding generations; it also functioned for generations to come as the foundation on which the whole house of Israel was to build its future.

Finally, this age of the Mishnah — the first stage in the history of our period — is characterized, as mentioned above, by the concentration of power into the hands of the Patriarch, and the subjection of the Sanhedrin to his authority. It was the time when, externally, Roman recognition of the Patriarch as supreme leader of the Jews reached its peak; and the same goes for Jewish acceptance of his authority. This may very well be connected with the economic upswing during the reigns of Antoninus Pius and the Severan emperors (138–235). Additional evidence of this prosperity has been provided by archaeological finds, especially in Palestine, where a number of beautiful synagogues built at the end of the second century and the beginning of the third, such as the one at Capernaum, have been uncovered.[3]

Another important factor was the friendly attitude of the Severan emperors to the Jews in general. In this connection there is an interesting bit of testimony provided by St. Jerome, who lived in Bethlehem at the end of the fourth century and the beginning of the fifth. In his commentary on a verse in the Book of Daniel *(When they shall stumble, they shall be helped with a little help...* 11:34) he notes that the stumbling may be taken as a reference to the sufferings of the Jewish people during the first century of the Christian era and well into the second. And what about the "little help"? Writes Jerome: "Some among the Jews interpret this verse as bearing on (Septimius) Severus (193–211) and Antoninus (Caracalla, 211–217) who were especially fond of the Jews."

Stage 2: 235–420 C.E. Age of the Amoraim

During the second stage of our period, the social-economic condition of Palestinian Jewry was governed in the main by the decisive changes that overtook the entire Roman Empire. In the years between the Severi and Diocletian (235–284 C.E.), rampant anarchy spread from one end of the Empire to the other, finally settling down into the order imposed by autocracy. That half-century of turmoil was marked by foreign wars on the eastern and western marches of the Empire, and by bloody internal struggles between rivals for the throne of the Caesars, a seat frequently left vacant by the assassination of the Emperor at the hands of the soldiery. Indeed, many of the Caesars reigned only briefly, some of them for less than one full year.

As a result, both agriculture and commerce suffered a severe decline, from which the Roman Empire never really recovered. The economic deterioration was accompanied by a steadily growing tax burden, along with other "temporary" levies on both cash and labor — such as the *angaria* [ἀγγαρεῖα] a species of corvée, or compulsory service. These factors speeded up the process whereby

---

3 [The recent excavations at Capernaum by the Franciscan Fathers V. Corbo and S. Lofredda suggest a later dating of that synagogue; see *Encyclopaedia of Archæological Excavations* (English) ed. by M. Avi-Yonah, Vol. I, Jerusalem 1975, p. 290.]

ownership of large tracts of land was concentrated into the hands of a few powerful individuals. On these huge estates, called *latifundia,* those who had been small farmers were converted into *coloni* — mere tenants, share-croppers. The *colonatus* was bound to the soil, subjugated to his landlord.[4]

At the same time, the lot of the urban citizen of means grew increasingly hard. It was his responsibility to collect the local taxes and to oversee the performance of forced labor — a burdensome chore. He was also drafted for a variety of municipal offices — *liturgia* [λειτουργία] — which he had to fulfill on pain of forfeiting his property, so that it was more a punishment than an honor. As a result, the middle class was gravely undermined.

Even the skilled artisans, organized as they were into associations of craftsmen, came collectively under government control. They were required to perform a certain amount of work for the state; and to the extent that individuals among them absconded, the group had to make good the deficit by their own labor.

All these developments, which tended to rigidify the social-economic structure by using the force of law to keep people in the class into which they were born, had their effects on Palestine in greater or lesser degree. Our Jewish sources offer ample testimony to the negative effects which this nascent feudalism had on the economic condition of Jews in that country. Time and again we read of Jews who "flee the country" leaving their property behind, in order to get away from the unbearable burden of fines, excises and exactions, and from the general depression caused by the heavy taxation.

One effect of the *liturgia* imposed on people of means was that many of them were forced to abandon their land holdings and move to Transjordan. The requirement that they serve on town councils (בולאות) and assume fiscal and personal responsibility for public services in towns and cities, and especially the exorbitant levies

---

4 A concomitant was the deterioration of the soil, and the abandonment of much farm-land in most provinces of the Empire. It has been traditional to say that the soil was overworked, and therefore became naturally exhausted. However, modern historians tend to put the blame on social conditions, which led to the abandonment of agricultural lands, and hence to the loss of fertility.

imposed on them by both civil and military authorities, became unbearable. Local wealth was constantly being eaten away by Roman demands for quarters and rations for the troops. This was especially true during the wars with the Persian Empire, and most particularly when Rome fought her campaigns against Palmyra.

No social or economic class was spared the sting of Roman power. The associations of craftsmen were subject to forced labor "under lash and rod." Our sources tell us how the soldiery would seize Jewish children as "sureties" with the intention of selling them into slavery against unpaid levies and imposts. It was at this time, in the third century, that the value of farming as a means of livelihood sank low. It appears that this too was when the loss of agricultural productivity made itself felt. In the opinion of many historians, the same thing was happening in other provinces of the Roman Empire.

The word for "farmer" now became almost synonymous with "tenant", indicating how far the process had gone. Then, in the eighties of the fourth century, the term *colonatus,* established in law some fifty years earlier by Constantine the Great, shows up in common official use in Palestine.

There are grounds for assuming that at this time there was a drastic reduction in land-ownership by Jews; and that gentiles from outside the country acquired tracts of major proportions. Simultaneously there was an increase in emigration by Jews in search of a livelihood. Many of them fully intended to return when they were able to. Other indications reveal a perceptible spread of the Samaritan population to certain districts outside Samaria, such as Caesarea, Lydda and Jamnia, with apparently negative effects on the position of the Jews in those places. Nor is it possible to ignore the fact that at this time Jewish highwaymen appear on the scene, operating in bands and as individuals, from whose depredations not even the Jewish population was immune. The causes of this phenomenon were clearly both social and economic.[5]

5 A number of the factors here noted had begun to manifest themselves earlier, towards the end of Stage I. This includes the stratification of social classes, and the obligations imposed on them by the government. It also includes the "urbanization" of Palestine. Emmaus becomes Nicopolis, Lydda is replaced by Diospolis, and in place of Beth Guvrin

Any evaluation of this period must also take account of the fact that it witnessed the first penetration into Palestine of Arabs, who came as marauding nomads. Explicit evidence for this is provided by Christian literature dating from this time. However, even earlier Jewish sources going back to the middle of the third century apparently refer to the same thing when they speak of "Sabaeans" breaking into a town, or mention armed brigands surrounding a city or a village.

Such raids occurred more and more often in the fifth and sixth centuries. They brought in their train another development: permanent Arab settlements that took root in territories adjacent to Palestine, and showed signs of becoming a political factor in Palestine, itself. Here we have the beginning of the "Kingdom of Ishmael" mentioned in midrashim prior to the Muslim conquest. Indeed, these Arab settlements paved the way for that conquest, which gave the coup de grace to the already weakened Jewry of Palestine.

Among the factors which enabled the Jewish people to survive in Palestine as long as it did, the steady flow of pilgrims and immigrants from the Jewish communities of the Diaspora should not be overlooked. They came from various parts of the Roman world — Egypt, Asia Minor, North Africa — as well as from Babylonia. Whether they came to visit or to stay, their presence did much to retard the economic and social deterioration of Jewish Palestine. In this connection, it seems hardly necessary to add that the annual contributions received by the Patriarch and the Sanhedrin from Jewish communities all over the world were of no mean significance.

This second stage of our period is marked by a separation between the two institutions of national leadership — the Patriarchate and the Academy of Scholars. At the end of the previous phase, the union of these authorities had reached its high point. The Patriarch himself — i.e. Rabbi Judah the *Nasi* — had been at one and the same time Head of the Academy *(Rosh Yeshivah)* and President of the High Court. Two administrative changes had given practical expression to this unification of powers: first, the office of *Ab Beth*

there stands Eleutheropolis. All of this signifies the displacement of the Jewish population, and an increase in the non-Jewish element.

Din had been abolished; and second, the power of appointing all judges, fellows of the Academy (*ḥakhamim*) and religious authorities had been concentrated into the sole hands of the Patriarch.

Then, approximately at the beginning of the second stage, these powers became separated. Alongside the Patriarchate we find the distinct office of *Rosh Yeshivah* who serves as Head of the Academy and as President of the High Court in Tiberias. As for the right to appoint judges and leaders, it is exercised by both the Patriarch and the Academy, independently of each other. This is the era when the Patriarch concentrated more and more on the political and administrative sectors. Yet it would be a mistake to view this development as a total split between the two centers of authority. The Patriarchs and the Sages maintained their interrelationship, and together formed one central leadership. It would be more accurate to speak of a diarchy, the two arms of which sometimes exercised overlapping authority, and of course found themselves clashing with one another from time to time.

This change undoubtedly signals the emergence of the learned scholars as the chief leaders of the people. The trend is of special importance in the context of community leadership in the towns and villages. To be sure, the learned class had already been playing this kind of role during the first stage of our period; but local leadership would appear to have remained, as heretofore, essentially in the hands of men of wealth and good family. Now, in the second stage, the balance shifted. Old habits of looking up to the propertied and the well-born did not vanish overnight; but more and more it became customary to look to the local scholar and teacher as community leader — *parnas 'al ha-ẓibbur.*

Another characteristic of this second phase of our period appears to be a shift in the attitude of the people to the Roman government. From the middle of the third century on we seem to have growing evidence of a wider acceptance of Roman rule as the inevitable reality. There were even those who insisted that all deference was due to the ruling power, and who condemned efforts to "cast off the yoke." Some even went further, and praised the Roman regime for providing all its subjects with the shield of the law and the maintenance of public order.

Granted, this attitude was not altogether new. Earlier, in the first phase of our period, voices had been heard praising the Romans for the way they fostered economic and technological progress, and for their socially useful public works.[6] But it is not until the second stage of our period that we hear the doctrine of make-peace-with-reality put forward so explicitly, and with such emphasis. For example: "The Holy One, blessed be He, adjured Israel not to rise up like a wall"—i.e. not to mount a military invasion of the Holy Land; or as one source puts it, the Jews are forbidden to rebel against the *'umot ha-olam*.[7] Equally forceful is the teaching that it is a mitzvah to go forth to greet a gentile ruler, and even to contract ritual impurity in paying him honor.[8]

The cultural achievement of this second stage is best summed up by the monumental work which marks its close: the Jerusalem (or Palestinian) Talmud. Like the Mishnah, which marked the close of the first stage, the Yerushalmi too is the distillation of generations-worth of complex spiritual and cultural activity. Like the Mishnah, it too represents but a fraction of the halakhic creativity and interpretive study of the age whose landmark it is. The Amoraim carried on from where the Tannaim had left off, and created many "Talmuds" based on the Mishnah. Only one such Palestinian Talmud has come down to us; but it is ample testimony to the spiritual resources of a people whose creativity did not slacken or dry up even at a time when the very foundations of society at large were crumbling.

Such, then, was the character of Stage II, otherwise known as "The Age of the Amoraim." We ought not to leave it without noting that it witnessed the break-up of the Empire into two parts, following the death of Theodosius in the year 395. When we enter Stage III, there already is an Eastern Empire, with its capital in Constantinople, and a Western Empire, with its capital in Rome.

Stage III: 420 to 640   Byzantine Palestine

Out of the six centuries this book deals with, these are the two about which we know least. Whatever information we do have for the several centuries after the completion of the Jerusalem Talmud is extraordinarily sparse. To be sure, some new sources have come

6   See above p. 23, n. 1.
7   Ket. 111a; Cant. R. II:18.
8   Yer. Ber. III, 6a.

to light in recent years, including literary works, inscriptions and archaeological finds. These data have helped us sketch an outline of the features of Palestinian Jewry at that time, but the picture remains vague at best, and aspects of it are still in doubt.

One major fact in the life of the Jewish people of that period is nevertheless quite clear: the Patriarchate was gone. Obviously, the loss of that institution must greatly have weakened the central leadership of the nation. The aura of regality, the sense of some surviving national dignity which had persisted as long as the princely office was in existence — this had now vanished. With it went much of the psychological hold which Palestine and its Jewry had had over the Diaspora, and a good deal of real authority as well. Nevertheless, some measure of central leadership remained.

Evidence for this is the continued role of the *sanhedra'ot*, which still exercised authority both in the country and abroad. Admittedly, the government now turned a baleful eye on the Jewish institutions, and expressly forbade the continued remittance of *demei kelilla (aurum coronarium)* which the Jews of the world had been accustomed to send in annually, at first to the Patriarchs, and later to the *sanhedra'ot* (429 C.E.). The Romans decreed that these monies were now to be paid as taxes to the public exchequer. But it seems that the Jews of the Diaspora still managed somehow to support the Palestinian institutions with their "taxes." We do know that the city of Tiberias (where the chief Sanhedrin had had its seat from the middle of the third century) continued to be an active center of Jewish leadership for the country as a whole and for the Diaspora, throughout the third stage of our period.

Another major feature of the time was the series of government decrees aimed at denigrating Judaism and undermining the position of the Jews. There were also Christian fanatics who went the government one better, and staged pogroms wherever they could.

As for anti-Jewish legislation, the process had already begun during the second phase of our period. We know, for example, that by an edict of the Emperor Theodosius II, the Patriarch Gamaliel VI was dismissed from his position (*praefectura*) for having violated a law which prohibited the building of new synagogues. Obviously, then, there was such a law, in Palestine as well as in the Diaspora.

From a Syriac Christian source we learn of a zealous monk called

Bar Soma who passed through Palestine at the beginning of the fifth century. Gathering up a band of the faithful, he led them in an attack on a synagogue in Transjordan. They burned the place down, along with all its sacred contents.[9] It may be noted in passing that such occurrences were not uncommon in the Roman Empire at that time. And anti-Jewish legislation was a growing phenomenon from the middle of the fourth century, although it only reached its crescendo in what we have chosen to call the third and final stage of our period. Yet there is one reservation that must be made: the situation was not uniformly bad everywhere, and there were places where Jews and Judaism were able to survive.

This brings us to the question of population. From the fourth century onwards, the Christian presence in Palestine becomes more noticeable — which is not to say that the gentile population increased. It seems that most of the new Christians were converts from among the pre-existing pagan population. Nevertheless, it is reasonable to suppose that among their number were Christians from other countries who had been drawn by religious motives to settle in the Holy Land. Either way, the growth of Christianity diminished the weight of the Jewish factor in the country. In spite of this, Christians remained a minority when compared with the combined numbers of Jews and Samaritans, as we pointed out above.[10]

The classical expression of Jewish spiritual creativity in this third and last phase of our period belongs to the realm of Aggadah. Of the literature in this genre that has come down to us, the major por-

9   The iron gates being opened, Bar Soma beholds the wealth of the sanctuary, but he allows nobody to take anything from the Jewish synagogue, so that all may be burned. See Nau: "Bar Soma de Nisibis," in *Revue de l'Orient Chrétien*, IIme Serie, 18me vol. 1913, pp. 383 ff.
[The Bar Soma Chronicle reports a Jewish defence force of 15,000 men (!) which causes Fr. Nau to remark: "Cette exaggération rend suspects les autres détails." One may agree, leaving unaltered the fanatical tone of the story and the Jew-hating reputation of the monk.]

10   [Supra, p. 6. Here however, the implication seems to be that this plurality persisted until the Arab conquest. This runs counter to the statement by Avi-Yonah ("The Jews of Palestine," p. 220 ff.) that in the fifth century "... a Christian majority was being created in Palestine for the first time in its history." Cf. *Tol.* Vol. II, p. 262, where Alon admits a Christian *plurality* in the sixth century, while estimating the Jews at that time at "over one fourth of the total."]

tion was committed to writing in these few centuries, much of it in its present form, such as the midrashim Genesis Rabbah, Leviticus Rabbah, Lamentations Rabbah and the like; while other elements created at that time have reached us as the sub-structure of works later edited and recast. Examples of the latter are the midrashim we call *Tanḥuma*.

There can be no doubt that Aggadah has its roots in much earlier times, and that the substance of most of the Aggadah in the books just mentioned goes back two or three generations and more. In fact, the leading Sages quoted in these books — that is, the great aggadic teachers — belong to the fourth century. Still, the gathering and editing of this literature, so that it was preserved for future generations, is the hallmark of the difficult years we are now describing.

In the field of halakhah, it seems that the principal activity of this period — one half of which, namely the sixth century, corresponds to the Age of the Saboraim in Babylonia — can also be classified as editorial. The purpose appears to have been juridical-practical: to cull legal decisions from the Yerushalmi and other sources; and to settle such points of law as had been left moot. From the point of view of legal literature, the age is best described by a term peculiar to it: *ma'asim (acta)* — which is to say, halakhic rulings.

It would be inaccurate to see this third and final stage of our period as an age that was more concerned with preserving the work of previous generations than with creating anything of its own. Indeed, there is an area of original spiritual creativity which is the special mark of these declining years. For this was the time when *piyyut* — the unique liturgical poetry of the synagogue — made its first appearance. In the *piyyutim* of Yannai, from all indications composed in the Land of Israel at the end of the Byzantine period, we discover this wonderful new literary genre already in full flower, combining halakhah, aggadah, prayer and art. It was to flourish for generations to come in many and varied forms, becoming a significant element in the blood-stream of Jewish life.

This phenomenon too must have had antecedents. It could scarcely have sprung up full-grown, a sudden revelation of the sixth century. It probably grew out of that prayer-poetry — possibly also secular songs — of which there is some evidence from the days of Tannaim and Amoraim. Its ancestry may even go back to the poetic arts of the

Second Commonwealth. Still, *piyyut* as *piyyut* did not appear on the scene until the end of our period. That was when it acquired the forms that were to characterize it for centuries to come; that was when it became an inalienable part of the Jewish heritage. It was as though a great period of Jewish history, about to move into the shadows, bequeathed a special legacy of its own to the generations that were to follow.

PART TWO

REBUILDING THE NATION

CHAPTER THREE

THE IMPACT OF THE GREAT DEFEAT

The Temple in Jerusalem was put to the torch on the Ninth of Ab, according to the tannaitic tradition, or one day later, if we take the word of Josephus. It took barely another month for the legions to complete the conquest of the entire city; they were finished by the eighth day of Elul. By order of Titus, the whole of Jerusalem was razed to the ground, except for the three largest towers, those named Hippicus, Phasael and Mariamne. Along with a portion of the city wall on the west, these towers were left standing to serve as head-quarters for the Roman garrison.[1] Thus ended, for all practical purposes, the war against Rome, a struggle that had lasted more than four years, and had been marked by extraordinary manifestations of valor, faith and martyrdom on the part of the Jews.

To be sure, there were still pockets of Jewish resistance holding out in such strong-points as Herodion, near Bethlehem; Machaerus, east of the Jordan; and above all Masada, overlooking the Dead Sea. Masada was not subdued until three years later, and then only after a prolonged siege that involved the entire Roman army of occupation. Such resistance shows that the fall of Jerusalem had not broken the spirit of the Jewish people, as is sometimes assumed. On the contrary, the amazing heroism of Eleazar ben Yair and his followers, the last defenders of Masada who took their own lives on the last night of the siege rather than fall into the hands of the Romans, is additional evidence that the Destruction of the Temple had not brought in its train a catastrophic failure of the national nerve. Apparently the Jewish people still retained enormous reserves of will and energy, such as emerged a couple of generations later in the Bar Kokhba Rebellion. These inner resources, operating both openly and beneath the surface of events, lay behind those strong,

---

1 JW VII:1:1 (1–2).

unremitting efforts that bridged the gap between the tragedy of tragedies — the Destruction — and the religious and national recovery that came after.

Nevertheless, the fall of Jerusalem meant that the war was over. The defenders of Masada, like those who followed a similar course elsewhere, could scarcely have believed that they had the remotest chance of holding out indefinitely against Rome, much less of defeating the imperial conqueror. The only possible objective of the last-ditch resistance seems to have been the one expressed by Eleazar himself in the speech attributed to him on that last awful night: to avenge the capture of the Holy City of Jerusalem, and the Destruction, and the desecration of the sanctuary. A like motive would appear to explain the uprisings of Jews in Cyprus, Cyrenaica and Egypt during the reign of Trajan in the years 115–117 C.E. The refugee zealots from Judaea could have hoped only to hurt and harass the power that had reduced Jerusalem to ashes; they could not conceivably have looked forward to any kind of victory.

The Draconian post-war policy of the Roman victors deprived the Jewish people of four pillars of their national existence: Jerusalem, the Sanhedrin, the High Priesthood, and the Temple.

Jerusalem

Far more than simply the capital, Jerusalem had been since the return from Babylonian captivity the "head and heart" of the country; "The City" — *ha-'Ir* — somewhat like the position of Rome as *urbs*. This situation had persisted throughout the period of the Second Commonwealth, regardless of the many changes in the political status of the country, and of Jerusalem itself.

It was as though the entire country had been compressed into the environs *(teḥum)* of Jerusalem; as though the whole socio-political existence of Judaea derived from, and was based on, the fact that it contained the Holy City. In the eyes of the world at large, in the eyes of the conquerors, and indeed for the Jews themselves, including the Jews of the Diaspora, the City symbolized both the Jewish State, and the life-source of the Jewish people.[2]

2 Comp. Philo, *In Flaccum*, chap. 7, para. 46 (In the Loeb Classical Library, Greek text and English translation by H. Colson et al; vol. IX, p. 274).

In this respect there is a difference between the Second Commonwealth and the First. Under the Monarchy, from David's capture
of the city onwards, Jerusalem served as the unifying center for the
diverse parts of the country, each with its own background and
socio-political identity. But after the Return, the City became the
very source and foundation of the religious, national and political
existence of the state. No doubt this was an outcome of the historical
development of the state under the Second Commonwealth. After
all, everything that had happened in Judaea after the return from
Babylonia had been organically connected with the reconstruction
and growth of Jerusalem, as well as with the unique religious polity
established by the returnees from the very start. In any case, there
can be no doubt that Jerusalem held this status vis-à-vis the rest
of the country, in spite of the occasional friction between the capital
and the provinces, and in spite of the separatistic tendencies that
showed themselves from time to time in various parts of the country.

It is worth noting in this connection that the political role of
Jerusalem, in the *administrative* sense, had changed in the last few
generations before the Destruction. From the time of Herod (or,
according to some opinions, following his reign) Jerusalem took on
the character of a Greek *polis* in relation to the rest of the country.
That is to say, the country as a whole lost its juridical identity in
an administrative sense, and became subject to the city it surrounded, resembling in this the stretches of countryside that made
up a Greek city-state, or the *territorium* of a *civitas,* to put it in
Roman terms. Viewed in this light, the order given by Titus to level
Jerusalem to the ground was simply the result of the special and
decisive role of the City in the existence of Judaea, and is seen to
be the logical consequence of the policy to dismantle the Jewish
State and to destroy the Jewish people.

The Sanhedrin

The second institution of Jewish government which the Roman
conquest swept away was the one that, since the Romans first came
to the Middle East, had been known as the Sanhedrin, or the Great
Sanhedrin. This body had undergone many changes during the era
of the Second Commonwealth, and there is a great deal about its
history that we do not know. We are not sure how it was consti-

tuted, who appointed its members, and other such basic questions.

A problem especially bothersome to scholars is whether there was one Sanhedrin or several (with different names, perhaps). Some historians posit the existence of a distinct Sanhedrin for religious questions, a second for dealing with legal and political matters, and a third confined to the municipal and communal affairs of Jerusalem. The scholarly debates about this problem stem in the main from the apparent contradictions between the tannaitic tradition on the one hand, and Josephus and the Gospels on the other. This is not the place to go into the details of this complex controversy. But we cannot avoid taking a stand on the question: "One Sanhedrin or many?" In my own opinion, the sources do not oblige us to assume that there was more than one such body. A single High-Court-Assembly could well have performed all the necessary functions. True, we might well wish that we knew more about it; that we had a clearer picture of the procedures that were followed in dealing with the various areas, whether judicial, political or ritual; that we knew the relative weight carried in each of those areas by the several constituent elements of the Sanhedrin, namely: the priests, the scholars (originally *soferim* — scribes), and the "elders" — i.e., the aristocracy.

At all events, we do know that the Sanhedrin served as a sort of representative national body, and that it was the highest authority in all matters of religion and law, including criminal jurisdiction. At the same time it gave top political leadership to the state, second only to the High Priest. These far-reaching powers were at their peak during those periods of the Second Commonwealth when there was no real monarchy in Judaea — in the years prior, shall we say, to Alexander Jannaeus, or perhaps Aristobulus. On the other hand, the later Hasmonean kings clipped the wings of the Great Sanhedrin, and there are grounds for thinking that Herod abolished it altogether, although it did recover after his death.

As for the people at large, they regarded the Sanhedrin as the very bastion of their freedom and autonomy. It was this that they cited in their complaint to the Roman Emperor against the autocratic tendencies of the last Hasmonean kings, especially the Herodians. So it is not surprising that when the Jews seized their independence at the start of the Great Rebellion, overthrowing the Prefect Cestius

Gallus and driving the Romans out of Judaea, they sought a juridical basis for their newly formed national coalition government by founding it on the Sanhedrin — allied, to be sure, with a "popular assembly".

Thus, when Jerusalem was destroyed, it was only to be expected that the Sanhedrin should be destroyed with it; the organic connection between the two made that inevitable. But even if that had not been so, the role which the Sanhedrin had played in the political and national life of the people during Temple times was sufficient to impel the Romans to get rid of it. They intended to stamp out the Jewish State; it was logical that they should stamp out the Sanhedrin as part of the process.

The High Priesthood

From the middle of the Persian period (that is, from the end of the fifth century B.C.E., following Ezra and Nehemiah), the *Kohen Gadol* comes increasingly to the fore as the chief leader of the people of Judaea. Aided by the Sanhedrin he becomes head of the religious life of the nation, especially in his role as guardian of the sanctuary. At the same time, he is charged with the administration of Judaean autonomy. Thus the High Priest fills the role of ruler of the people in its internal affairs, and is simultaneously spokesman of the nation in its external affairs, which is to say, in its relationships with the governing power. Of course, his internal functions — titular head of the nation, chief of the priesthood, guardian of the Temple — make it natural that he should be presiding officer of the Great Sanhedrin. That in fact was the situation, and it persisted beyond the Persian period, on through the years of Ptolemaic and Seleucid suzerainty over Palestine. The High Priesthood reached the apogee of its power and prestige in the days of the Hasmoneans. Even after the Hasmonean High Priests assumed the crown of royalty, the mitre which they also wore was not deprived of its lustre.

It remained for Herod to undermine the office, and to reduce its powers and its stability. He did so by dint of frequently dismissing the High Priest and appointing a new one. He also cast a shadow over the legitimacy of the High Priesthood by ignoring the hereditary principle which had for centuries governed accession to the post.

This process of downgrading the position continued throughout the period of the Roman Procurators of Judaea. The High Priesthood was thus weakened by forces external to the Jewish people, that is, by non-Jewish political factors, now Herodian, now Roman.

These factors were abetted from within by the moral deterioration that began to surround the office and to tarnish its image. The political stance of most of the last High Priests, their tendency to collaborate with the Roman power structure, played no small part in diminishing their standing and influence with the people at large. This reduction in power and prestige is tellingly revealed by the reduced role of the priesthood in the national government that was set up at the start of the war with Rome. To be sure, the *kohanim gedolim* appear as an important element in the coalition; but the High Priest is no longer head man, no longer ruler of the nation.

Nevertheless, the High Priesthood (along with the Sanhedrin) continued to be a factor of some weight in the public life of semi-autonomous Judaea all through the last days of the Second Commonwealth. The aura of both spiritual and temporal grandeur which had surrounded the office was never entirely dissipated. Obviously this held good among the Jews of the Diaspora; but it was true in Judaea as well. Witness the coins minted by Bar Kokhba, which bear on one side the legend *"Shime'on"*, referring apparently to Bar Kokhba himself — and on the obverse *"El'azar ha-Kohen"*, i.e. the High Priest.

The demise of the High Priesthood when the Temple was destroyed must be seen, then, as the loss of one of the mainstays of Jewish national, political and religious existence. That loss could not but leave behind it a great void in the life of the nation.

The Temple

As for the Temple, it had not been the sole center of Jewish religious experience during the days of the Second Commonwealth. There was also the synagogue, which had served as a focus of worship and instruction, of prayer and the reading of the Torah (later — of the prophets, too). As time went on, the scriptural reading came to be accompanied by *midrash*, that is homily, especially of an aggadic nature. The *midrash* added depth and dimension to both religious thought and religious experience.

But none of this detracted in the least from the great importance of the Temple. It continued to serve as the only center for the *collective* worship of the nation. More, the Temple was indispensible for the religious life even of the *individual* Jew, because only there could he practice the sacrificial rites that atoned for his sins, that freed him from ritual impurity, and that enabled him to fulfill other personal religious obligations. (Some opposition to the sacrifices appeared toward the end of the Second Commonwealth, but only in limited circles). The Temple continued to be the central "house of prayer," and even the synagogue service developed as a kind of accompaniment to what was taking place at the altars of the sanctuary. Indeed, certain basic elements of the liturgy still show, by name, by form and by content, that they came into the synagogue directly from the Temple.

Above all, the Temple was the focus of the great religious events in the life of the nation, such as the major pilgrimage festivals, especially Passover and Sukkot. Indeed, the journey to Jerusalem and to the Temple was essential to the proper observance of the holy days. For the individual Jew, these pilgrimages were the high point of his religious life; they were the strongest expression of his membership in the community of Israel, and contributed in no small measure to the sense of national solidarity. The Jews of the Diaspora, who made it their goal to perform the festival pilgrimage at least once in a lifetime, were thereby bound more closely to the ancestral homeland, and to their fellow Jews who still lived on its soil. So that, over and above its specifically religious function, the Temple was enormously significant as a cementing factor for the nation and its culture.

In this connection, an important role was played by the half-shekel sent in to the Temple annually by every Jew, whether he lived at home or abroad. As a matter of fact, the Jews of the Diaspora fought especially hard to maintain their right to make this contribution, a right which was sometimes attacked by Gentiles as "payment of a tax to a foreign country." The truth is that the funds were used not only for the Temple and the sacrifices; they also went towards the maintenance of Jerusalem's city-wall and towers, the repair of the aqueduct, and other such needs of the city.[3] Thus the

3   Mishnah Sheq., IV:2.

Temple served indirectly as a channel for financing the civil and defence needs of the capital city — hence, in effect, of the state itself.

The Temple was also an important element in the juridical structure of the country, at least during certain periods of the Second Commonwealth. The Jewish State was thought of as revolving around the sanctuary, and the sanctuary was looked to as the source from which the state drew its legitimacy. This was the way the Persian imperial authorities understood the status of Judaea during the last generations of their overlordship; and this, too, was the way their successors the Ptolemaids and the Seleucids, understood the matter. Internally, the same view is reflected in the Jewish conception of *where* the High Court belongs: the Sanhedrin sits in the Chamber of Hewn Stone. Indeed, when it is finally displaced from there, its authority and jurisdiction are somehow diminished.[4]

Another function of the Temple was that it provided a public forum for the dissemination of ideas, a sort of free academy where the people and the Sages heard one another out. Josephus tells us about Judah ben Sarifai and Mattithias ben Margalit, two Pharisees who urged their students to tear down the golden eagle which Herod had erected over the sanctuary during the last days of his life. We are told that these two used to lecture in the Temple every day, addressing a large assemblage of young men who would drink their words in eagerly.[5] Another who taught in the Temple regularly was Jesus of Nazareth. Later on, the apostolic community of Jewish Christians would gather in the sacred precincts, and some of their number would preach to the people there assembled. Much the same sort of thing is told of Rabban Yohannan ben Zakkai, whose custom it was to "sit and lecture in the very shadow of the sanctuary."[6]

But there was something far more important than any of this: the Temple was "the Tabernacle of the Lord," the dwelling-place of the *Shekhinah* of the God of Israel. It stood for everything that set the Jews apart from all other nations. Here was the very rock from

4 See Sifre, Shofetim, 154, Finkelstein 207.
5 Ant. XVII:6:2–3 (149 ff).
6 Pes. 26a.

which Israel was hewn, the center and focus of all that was bound up in the faith in Israel's God. Consequently, there was a strong belief among the people that the Temple was eternal, as indestructible as the nation itself; and this belief persisted right up to the Destruction. (We may disregard for the moment some traditions that tell of "signs and portents" predicting the end.) Philo of Alexandria informs his readers that the Temple cannot be destroyed so long as heaven and earth abide. This firm belief stiffened the resolve of the fighters and plain people of beleaguered Jerusalem, and kept them struggling against impossible odds up to the very last moment.

Thus the Temple was the hub of the Jewish religion and of the Jewish state, the fortress of the people's pride. It was probably for this very reason that Titus gave the order to have it burned down. There is, to be sure, conflicting testimony about this, and we need not go into the details at this point. Suffice it to say that Josephus describes a meeting of the Roman Headquarters Staff two days before the sanctuary was set on fire. According to this account, the Roman commanders were at odds about what to do with the Temple until Titus, who was presiding, settled the matter by deciding that it was to be spared. A directly contrary tradition has been preserved by Sulpicius Severus in his *Chronica*, a Latin-Christian text of the late fourth or early fifth century, which reports that the Temple was destroyed by explicit order of Titus, who intended thereby to strike Judaism a mortal blow.[7]

Which of these two reports shall we believe? Scholars remain divided in their opinions. My own view is that the Christian source is the more trustworthy of the two. That is to say, the Temple was destroyed not "by an accident of fate," as Josephus would have us believe, and not against the will of Titus; but on the contrary, by the deliberate and express decision of the Roman conqueror. No doubt the general may have held back for a while, as he discussed the pros and cons with his subordinates. But in the end, it is likely that the command decision was his. His purpose would have been

---

7 The report (Chronica II:30:4) apparently goes back to a passage that was dropped (suppressed?) from the *Historia* of Tacitus. For details see Bernays; *Gesammelte Abhandlungen*, vol. II, pp. 159–167 and 171–181. [and H.St. J. Thackeray in *Josephus*, vol. II, pp. xxiv ff.]

to destroy national Judaism, of which the Temple was a principal bastion.[8]

The Destruction of the Temple had consequences even graver than those mentioned above. Not only did it wipe out a symbol of national pride for Jews at home and abroad and tarnish their image in the eyes of the nations; not only did it shake the very foundations of the Jew's belief in his religion and in the future of his people; it cut deeper. It rendered *impossible* the practice of whole areas of his religion, especially in the field of communal ritual. With the altars gone, the nation was confronted by a gaping vacuum, one which the generation of survivors had to fill, and fill quickly, if the people as a people was to live on.

It is important to dwell on this point, because there are historians who tend to minimize the traumatic effects of the loss of the sanctuary on the feeling and thinking of the Jews who lived through it. This they do by underscoring the development of Judaism outside the Temple during the Second Commonwealth — the deepening of religious feeling, the role of the synagogue in broadening the scope of religion, the constantly increasing stress on the ethical motif. They are even able to point to an explicit tradition which seems to show how the Jews of the time were able to console themselves for the loss of the Temple, and how immediate was the transition to the new situation in which ethical living and the study of Torah were to cover the need for religious fulfilment.

> Once as Rabban Johanan ben Zakkai was coming forth from Jerusalem, Rabbi Joshua followed after him and beheld the Temple in ruins.
> 'Woe unto us!' Rabbi Joshua cried, 'that this, the place where the iniquities of Israel were atoned for, is laid waste!'
> 'My son,' Rabban Johanan said to him, 'be not grieved; we have another atonement as effective as this. And what is it? It is acts of loving-kindness, as it is said: *For I desire mercy and not sacrifice.*' (Hos VI:6)

---

8 See G. Alon: *Serefat ha-Miqdash*, in his *Mehqarim* vol. I, p. 206 ff. [English in *"Jews, Judaism and the Classical World"* p. 252; see above, *Foreword*, note 1. Hereafter this title will be abbreviated: *JJCW*; and will be the only reference cited for the essays appearing in it.]

Indeed, thus we find concerning Daniel, that greatly beloved man, that he was engaged in acts of loving-kindness all his days.[9]

Now, there can be no quarrel with the statement that the Temple worship was *not* the totality of Jewish religion during the days of the Second Commonwealth; it is a fact we have already emphasized. Hence, it scarcely needs to be said that Judaism was *not* at the point of bankruptcy even after the Temple had been destroyed. Nevertheless, the dimensions of the catastrophe, and the magnitude of the danger with which that disaster confronted the people ought not to be minimized or overlooked — certainly not by giving sweeping and inexact interpretations to texts like the one just quoted. All that the passage means is this: even without the altar and the sacrifices, religious purification and redemption from sin are not entirely out of reach, because there are other elements of the religion still accessible for such purposes.

What we have here is an extension of a much more ancient teaching attributed to Simeon the Just:

> "By three things is the world sustained: by the Torah, by the (Temple) Service, and by Deeds of Lovingkindness."[10]

And is not Rabban Johanan ben Zakkai himself authority for the statement:

> "Even as the sin-offering makes atonement for Israel, so does charity make atonement for the Gentiles."[11]

No; if we really want to get the feel of what it was like for those who experienced the Destruction, to plumb the depths of their pain and grief, their confusion and bewilderment — one step short of despair — we would do better to take a look at the three source-texts here offered:

The Sages taught: When the Temple was destroyed for the

9 *Aboth de Rabbi Nathan,* ed. Salomon Schechter, Vienna 1887, version A (= ARNA) ch. 4:5, p. 21. [Judah Goldin: *The Fathers According to Rabbi Nathan,* in Yale Judaica Series, vol. X, New Haven 1955, p. 34.]
10 Av. I:2 [Danby: *The Mishnah,* Oxford 1933, p. 446.]
11 B.B. 10b.

second time, large numbers in Israel became ascetics, binding themselves neither to eat meat nor to drink wine. Rabbi Joshua got into conversation with them, and said to them: My sons, why do you not eat meat or drink wine? They replied: Shall we eat flesh which used to be brought as an offering on the altar, now that the altar is in abeyance? Shall we drink wine which used to be poured as a libation on the altar, but is now no longer? He said to them: If that is so, we ought not eat bread either, because the meal offerings have ceased. They said: (You are right) we can manage with fruit. He replied: We should not eat fruit either, because we can no longer bring the offering of first-fruits. All right, they said, we can make do with other fruits. But, he went on, we should not drink water either, because we can no longer observe the ceremony of the pouring of water. To this they could find no answer, and he said to them: My sons, come and listen to me. Not to mourn at all is impossible, because the blow has fallen. To mourn overmuch is also impossible, because we do not impose on the community a hardship which the majority cannot endure ... This, rather, is what the Sages have ruled: A man may stucco his house, but he should leave a small space bare.... He may prepare a full-course banquet, but he should leave out an item or two.... A woman may put on all her ornaments, but let her then leave off one or two....[12]

The second source is Ezra IV, a book written originally in Hebrew, probably not more than thirty years after the Destruction. Its contents reflect ideas current at the time of the disaster, possibly even thoughts that had been jotted down then. Its whole thrust springs directly out of the sense of national tragedy and personal agony that weighed heavily on those who witnessed the Destruction of the Temple. Its author, clearly a gifted visionary from circles close to the Sages, offers us a vision of a widow-woman, keening for the loss of her

12 B.B. 60b; and Tos. Sot. XV:11–14. Comp. ibid. XV:10 (Zuck., p. 322): "R. Ishmael said: (Zuck: R. Simeon b. Gamaliel) 'From the day the Temple was destroyed it would have been proper for us to refrain from eating meat and drinking wine; but we have not so ordained, because the Beth Din ought not issue decrees that the people cannot abide by.'"

son, born to her in her old age, now dead on his wedding-night, expired under the wedding canopy:

> Thou foolish woman, why dost thou weep?
> Seest thou not the mourning of Zion, our Mother?
> For thou seest how our sanctuary is laid waste,
> Our altar thrown down, our Temple destroyed
> Our harp laid low, our song silenced,
> Our rejoicing ceased, the light of our lamp extinguished,
> The ark of our covenant spoiled, our holy things defiled
> The name that is called on us profaned.
> Our nobles are dishonored, our priests burned,
> Our Levites gone into captivity;
> Our virgins are defiled, our wives ravished,
> Our righteous are seized,
> Our children are cast out,
> Our youths are enslaved....[13]

A similar mood dominates the Syriac Book of Baruch, also written originally in Hebrew, in Palestine, around the same time as Ezra IV by someone close to those Sages we call the Tannaim. Baruch sits at the gates of the sanctuary and utters lamentation for Zion:

> Blessed is he who was not born,
> Or he, who having been born, has died.
> But as for us who live, woe unto us,
> Because we see the afflictions of Zion,
> And what has befallen Jerusalem.
>
> I will call the Sirens from the sea,
> And ye Lilin, come ye from the desert,
> And ye Shedim and dragons from the forests:
> Awake and gird up your loins unto mourning,
> And take up with me the dirges,
> And make lamentation with me.
>
> Ye husbandmen, sow not again;
> And, O Earth, wherefore givest thou thy harvest fruits?

13   Charles: *Apocrypha and Pseudepigrapha*, vol. II, pp. 604–605.

Keep within thee the sweets of thy sustenance.

And thou, vine, why further dost thou give thy wine;
For an offering therefrom will not again be made in Zion.
Nor will first-fruits again be offered.

And do ye, O heavens withhold your dew,
And open not the treasures of rain:
And do thou, O sun, withhold the light of thy rays.
And do thou, O moon, extinguish the multitude of thy light;
For why should light rise again
Where the light of Zion is darkened?

And you, ye bridegrooms, enter not in,
And let not the brides adorn themselves with garlands;
And ye, women, pray not that ye may bear.
For the barren above all shall rejoice,
And those who have no sons shall be glad,
And those who have sons shall have anguish.
For why should they bear in pain,
Only to bury in grief?
Or why, again, should mankind have sons?
Or why should the seed of their kind again be named,
Where this mother is desolate,
And her sons are led into captivity?
From this time forward speak not of beauty,
And discourse not of gracefulness.

Moreover, ye priests, take ye the keys of the sanctuary,
And cast them into the height of heaven,
And give them to the Lord and say:
"Guard Thy house Thyself.
For lo! we are found false stewards."

And you, ye virgins; who weave fine linen
And silk with gold of Ophir,
Take with haste all these things
And cast them into the fire,
That it may bear them to Him who made them,
And the flame send them to Him who created them,

Lest the enemy get possession of them.[14]

As we proceed to examine the halakhah, we will get a clearer picture of how deep was the void which the Destruction of the Temple created in the life of the people; how intense was the faith and the longing for its restoration "speedily"; and what efforts were made to maintain the observance of certain commandments connected with the sanctuary.

14   Ibid. pp. 485–486.

CHAPTER FOUR

JUDAEA UNDER ROMAN OCCUPATION

According to Josephus, the Roman siege of Jerusalem left 1,100,000 dead.[1] Tacitus suggests a somewhat smaller figure — 600,000.[2] But these numbers refer only to the casualties in Jerusalem. If we add the victims in other localities (Judaea, Galilee and Transjordan) for whom we find statistics scattered throughout the pages of Josephus, we shall have to increase the total by another 106,000; plus 37,500 more who fell in the mob attacks at Caesarea, Beisan, Ashkelon and Acre.[3]

As for prisoners, the number taken at the fall of Jerusalem is given by Josephus as 97,000. Again, we must add some 41,000 who had been captured earlier in other parts of the country and shipped off to the slave markets, or sent to hard labor on the galleys or in the mines; or presented (some of them) as gifts to pagan cities in the region, so that they could be employed to fight wild animals in the arena.

Now, we can scarcely accept these figures as exhaustive; but even as they stand they are frighteningly high. Taken at face value, they would lead us to conclude that the war left the country denuded of its Jewish population.[4]

---

1 JW VI:9:3 (420).
2 *Historia* V:1:13; Reinach, *Textes d'Auteurs Grecs et Romains Relatifs au Judaïsme*, Paris, 1895, p. 322.
3 Josephus makes additional scattered references to casualties for which no numbers are given. Later Christian writers, such as Alexander the Monk (5th or 6th century; see Migne, *Patrologiae Graeca*, 87:3, p. 4041) and Eutychios of Alexandria (Sa'id ibn Batriq, 877–940 C.E.; PG vol. 3, col. 984) relay a tradition which put Jewish losses at around 3,000,000. Account must also be taken of the lives lost in the civil war between the Zealots and other Jews.
4 There must have been Jews who left the country on their own initiative; some of them because they knew themselves to be marked men politically, and others who made the move because of economic reasons.

But the same figures can be looked at from another point of view. First of all, it can be safely assumed that the numbers are considerably exaggerated. Then too, it seems that many of the battle casualties were volunteers from other countries. Josephus implies that the rebels had hoped for support from their "brothers beyond the Euphrates," and had even made efforts to mobilize such support. Dio Cassius goes further. He states flatly that many fighters in the battle for Jerusalem were Jews from other parts of the Empire, as well as from Mesopotamia.[5]

Regarding the captives, it is fairly certain that many of them were redeemed — that is, bought and set free — by fellow-Jews, either in the market-places of Palestinian cities or in ports of entry abroad, where every organized Jewish community had a committee appointed for that very purpose. Certainly there were some who managed to regain their own freedom, and many of these no doubt found their way back to the land of Israel.

In sum, it can safely be said that the terrible war took a heavy toll, and that it was deliberate Roman policy to decimate the population so as to weaken the capacity of the Jewish people for resistance. But it can also be said without much hesitation that the policy was only partially successful; in proof of which one need only cite the massive uprising some sixty years later — the Bar Kokhba Revolt.

The Economy

A reading of Josephus' *War* leaves one with the impression that after the fall of Jerusalem Judaea was left "almost completely desolate."[6] And it is probably true that certain built-up areas were reduced to a shambles — Jerusalem almost certainly, as well as Jotapata and other places. For En Gedi we have the testimony of Pliny.[7]

On the other hand, most of the remaining sites that Josephus speaks of as having been destroyed during the war were not really

5 *History of Rome,* LXVI:4–6, fragment quoted by Constantinus Porphyrogentes, *Excerpta de Legationibus.* See Reinach, op. cit. p. 190.
6 See Graetz, *Geschichte,* 4 ed. IV, p. 9. So also S. Klein, *Neue Beiträge* [in *Palästina Studien,* Heft 1, Wien 1923, p. 1, where Galilee is described as "fast in eine Wüste verwandelt."]
7 *Historia Naturalis* V:73.

levelled, but only partially damaged. He himself reports that Vespasian rebuilt many of the cities that had been wrecked during the winter campaign of 67–68, proof that the Destruction was limited in scope and temporary in nature.[8] We might go further, and say that even those places most severely damaged were, to some extent at least, resettled by Jews. Even in Jerusalem itself, evidence for the presence of Jews in the years between the Destruction and the Hadrianic persecutions (135 C.E.) can be derived from early Christian traditions. This evidence is bolstered by an oblique reference in the speech of Eleazar ben Yair at Masada, as reported by Josephus.[9]

In any case, it is a certainty that Jewish-populated areas in the country were greatly reduced in size and number as a result of the war, particularly in the vicinity of Jerusalem. When Church Fathers such as Eusebius and Jerome report that certain places were uninhabited ruins in their time (Geva, that is Giv'at Sha'ul, Timna and others) it is reasonable to assume that those localities had been reduced to ruins during the War of Destruction, or at the latest, during the Bar Kokhba Rebellion.[10]

Damage to the productive capacity of the country was heavy, especially in the agricultural sector. Our sources do not give much in the way of specific details. But there are a number of passages in Josephus which describe how the Romans had a habit of "revenging themselves" on fields belonging to Jewish fighters, or even on farms of Jews who had fled without offering resistance. Burning houses and wrecking farm property was something the Roman soldiers did either for vandalistic pleasure, or because they had been ordered to do so, as a means of striking terror into the hearts of the people. True, some of the destruction derived from military necessity. Several times Josephus tells us how Titus cut down every single tree within a radius of 90 to 110 furlongs (12 km.) around Jerusalem for use in building siegeworks, so that the countryside was stripped bare. The Jerusalem Talmud, speaking of the situation after the Bar Kokhba Rebellion, says that "there were no olive trees left after Hadrian the Wicked had come and laid waste the

8   JW IV:8:1 (442).
9   "Hapless old men sit beside the ashes of the shrine, and a few women reserved by the enemy for basest outrage." *JW*, VII:8:7 (377).
10 Eusebius: *Onomastikon* s.v.; and Jerome: *Epistle to Paula*, § 108.

country."[11] We have every reason to believe that the situation was much the same in some parts of the land after the earlier War of the Destruction.

We must also take account of the fact that the Jews themselves sometimes practiced a scorched earth policy, in order to prevent the enemy from exploiting areas especially fruitful. Pliny, who took personal part in the war as an administrative officer in the Roman army in Judaea, describes some quite unusual groves near Jericho that produced a uniquely superior grade of balsam. He says that the Jews, despairing of their lives, began to destroy their own groves, while the Romans fought to save the trees.[12] Later Jewish efforts to protect the country's remaining trees — fruit bearing trees must have been the chief concern — are reflected in the halakhah, as we shall see.

Land Ownership

A much discussed statement by Josephus deals with the ownership of land in conquered Judaea.[13]

> About the same time (71 C.E.) Caesar sent instructions to Bassus (the Legate) and Laberius Maximus the Procurator to farm out[14] all Jewish territory. For he founded no city there, reserving the country as his property, except that he did assign to eight hundred veterans discharged from the army a place for habitation called Ammaus.[15]

11 Yer. Peah, VII:20a.
12 *". . . saeviere in eam Judaei sicut in vitam quoque suam: contra defendere Romani, et dimicatum pro frutice est." Historia Naturalis,* XII:25:113. Reinach, p. 276. Comp. Loeb Classics, *Pliny,* transl. by H. Rockham, vol. IV, p. 81.
13 *JW*, VII:6:6 (216–217).
14 Or "to sell"; the word is ἀποδόσθαι [See Thackeray's note on this in his translation ad loc. Following Schürer, op. cit. I⁴, p. 640 (Vermes and Millar, p. 512) he explicitly rejects "sell" as a possible meaning.]
15 Not the Emmaus in the low-country (Nicopolis) but the mountain-town near Jerusalem called Motza, or in the Bible *Hamotza* (Joshua 18:26), which supplied wood for the Temple's altar-fires (Mishnah Suk. IV:5) and which the Talmud identifies as *Colonia* (Suk. 45a; modern *Kuluniyeh*).
   [Alon here follows the identification proposed by Schürer in *Geschichte*

On the face of it Josephus seems to be saying that Vespasian claimed all of Judaea as his personal property. However, that is not what he means, although his choice of language is somewhat misleading. When dealing with land in conquered provinces, it is important to distinguish between such tracts as were declared the private property of the Emperor — i.e. his *patrimonium* — and other areas which were confiscated as property of the Roman State, i.e. *ager publicus,* or *ager publi Romani.* Even though the income from the latter went into the royal exchequer — the *fiscus* — and not into the treasury of the Senate (*aurarium*) the land in question was still public land. What Josephus is saying is that Vespasian declared all of Judaea property of the Roman State, and that he, the Emperor, as Head of State, had the power to dispose of its lands.

The comment that the Emperor founded no cities in the territory now becomes clearer. Had he done so, the citizens of any such *civitates* (or in local terms πόλεις) would, from a juridical point of view have become owners of the land. Thus, the fact that Vespasian founded no cities in Judaea, and even nullified the existing civic status of Jerusalem, was intended to demonstrate that all lands had become state lands, passing into control of the Roman administration *de facto* and *de jure.* The point is, we are not here dealing with a simple legal formality, a theoretical statement based on the Roman concept that all provinces become the property of the Roman State, and the title to their lands becomes vested in the Roman people, leaving the rights of the provincials confined to the *usufructus* thereof. There are scholars who claim that this juridical concept goes back to the days of the Republic, while some modern authorities hold that it was a new legal doctrine introduced under the Empire.[16]

At any rate, Josephus himself is evidence that in his time it was no mere theory, but a hard reality. He tells how Vespasian granted him certain properties "in the plain", in exchange for land that had been expropriated from him in Jerusalem because the site was

---

I[4] note 142, pp. 640–642; English translation by Vermes and Millar, pp. 512–13. Graetz agrees: *Geschichte* III, 2[5], pp. 544–5. See also Isaiah Press, *Encyclopedia of Palestine* (Hebrew) Vol. I, p. 24, 2nd edition, Jerusalem, 1951.]

16 Jones, in *Journal of Roman Studies,* vol. 31 (1941) pp. 26–31.

needed for quartering the Xth Legion.[17] The substitute lands he was given had undoubtedly been confiscated from other Jews, quite in the way we have been describing. In fact, if we want to grasp the intent of Vespasian's decree, we would do well to compare it with the land situation in other provinces that suffered a fate similar to Judaea's, such as Carthage after the Third Punic War (146 B.C.E.).

When the real-estate of a conquered province had been proclaimed *ager publicus,* some tracts were sold outright, either to Roman citizens or to indigenous provincials ("deserving" ones, of course, who had sided with Rome against their own people). But the major part of the confiscated land was leased out, usually for a term of five years. In this wise, even people who stayed put on land that had been theirs were converted from owners into tenants. We do hear of instances where the lease was to all intents and purposes a permanent one — but such cases were few and far between.

The usual practice was for the Roman authorities to lease very large tracts of land to *conductores* — large-scale operators who would subdivide the spread into plots, and rent them out to tenant farmers. These *conductores* made their profit by charging their subtenants somewhat higher rentals than they themselves had to pay the government for the master-lease. Naturally, such a favored position was a form of patronage, available only to those who stood in well with the Roman officials (*mequravim lamalkhut*). They could be expected to collaborate with the administration in exploiting the farmers, many of whom were tilling soil that had once been their own property. But if the Romans, or their favored lessees, decided to dispossess any of these farmers, they did not find it too difficult. The *conductores,* who functioned *de facto* as agents of the regime, could dispossess the quondam owners, whether arbitrarily or by legal pretext.

We must assume that this was the situation in conquered Palestine as much as anywhere else in the Empire. Tannaitic sources tell us about Jews who "rent, or receive, their ancestral fields from the gentile." The latter are apparently identical with the "new masters" who had been foisted onto the backs of the Jewish farmers in the capacity of purchasers or lessees of large blocs of land from the

17 "A large tract of land. . ." *Life* 76 (422–5).

Romans; and the term 'gentile' has to be read somewhat loosely — there were undoubtedly some Jews among them. It seems plausible that the *mesiqin* (sometimes *meṣiqin*)[18] mentioned in tannaitic literature were none other than *conductores,* gentile or Jew, who squeezed the heavy taxes out of the tenant-farmers, and sometimes pushed them right off their own land — all, of course, in close cooperation with the government, whose purposes they served so well. The Mishnah refers to *mesiqin* who seize fields as "a country-wide plague".[19] This fits in perfectly with the use of pretexts (non-payment of rent) or arbitrary action (renting to a new tenant).

Naturally, there were Jews whose land was confiscated outright by the Roman government itself. This was the treatment meted out to anyone suspected of anti-Roman activity. The process continued even after the fighting was over. After Vespasian had taken Beth Aris and Kfar Taba in "Idumaea", having killed ten thousand in the process and captured one thousand Jews whom he sold as slaves, "he expelled the remainder and stationed in the district a large division of his own troops, who overran and devastated the whole of the hill country."[20]

In general, the Romans made a habit of laying heavy hands on land and other property belonging to Jews. Josephus tells of "sons of the High Priests" and other Jerusalemites who took refuge with the Romans during the fighting.[21] Apparently these were members of the moderate party, who were ready to sue for peace. Titus ordered them to stay at Gophna until the fighting was over, at which time they would get their properties back. We gather from this that Jews who abandoned the die-hard rebels, or who threw in their lot with the Romans from the start, had a good chance of regaining their land. During the course of the war, says Josephus when speaking of the winter of 67–68, Jews who submitted to the Romans

18 E.g. Sifre Deut. 357, Finkelstein, p. 425 f. On the passage: *"The Lord showed him all the land"* (Deut. 34:1 ff) the Midrash has Moses surveying the country not only spatially, but in time as well. He foresees the land being tyrannized by the *"meṣiqqin . . . meṣiqim . . . meṣiqē Yisrael..."* See also Yerushalmi, Demai, VI:25b: "R. Yohanan says, they derived this from the *mesiqin. . ."* where the context clearly involves land seizure.
19 B.Q. X:5.
20 JW, IV:8:1 (448).
21 JW, VI:2:2–3 (114–115).

without a struggle would be settled in places distant from their own homes — in Jamnia and Lydda and cities of Transjordan.[22] Though these measures were regarded as temporary, it does not seem unlikely that many of these "new settlers", so useful and acceptable to the Romans, remained rooted in their new locations, becoming masters of properties whose original owners had either been slain, or taken prisoner, or had fled the country.

The war thus brought in its train major changes in the distribution of land ownership through: 1) the loss of ownership-title by those who remained on the land, and who could thus be thrown off their property at a moment's notice; 2) total confiscation from resisters and political undesirables; 3) government lease or grant to non-Jews (usually in the capacity of *mesiqin;* but occasionally as outright grantees), who would then clear the Jewish inhabitants right off the land; and 4) simple transfer of title from Jewish to non-Jewish owners.

On the other hand, one must reckon with the certainty that there were many pieces of land that had simply been abandoned. Here and there in tannaitic sources one finds references to "captives' property" (*nikhse shevui'im*), "abandoned property" (*nikhse netushim*), and "emigrés' property" (*nikhse retushim*).[23] These texts deal for the most part with the aftermath of the Bar Kokhba Rebellion, but it is not unreasonable to extrapolate from them back to the earlier War of the Destruction.

How did the people as a whole react to this situation? A partial answer can be found in the halakhah, to which we will turn in due course. For the present, suffice it to say that the Sages refused to recognize the title of the new owners, nor the transactions of their surrogates, Jewish or non-Jewish. Indeed they struggled, with some measure of success, to set right the complicated situation into which the conditions here described had plunged Judaea of the Jews.

Finally, it should be noted that certain properties were transferred directly to the personal estate of the Emperor himself, thus becoming officially incorporated into his *patrimonium*, to be managed by the royal household.[24] An example would be the balsam groves men-

22 JW, IV:8:1 (444); ibid. IV:7:6 (438).
23 Tos. Ket. VIII:3 (Zuck. 270); Yer. ibid. IV:29a; Bavli, B.M. 38b.
24 It seems that Vespasian was the first to set up the *patrimonium* as the

tioned above, which according to Pliny brought very large sums into the privy purse.

Taxes

Jews who continued to till the soil as tenant-farmers paid a high rental (*vectigal*), generally figured as a percentage of the crop, either in kind or in cash. But even those who retained title to their land, or were allowed after the war to purchase farms, or were lucky enough to get grants — Josephus, for example — even they had to pay an annual land-tax called *tributum soli*, again in kind or in cash. Only the favored few managed to get excused from this; such, Josephus tells us, was his own good fortune during the reign of Domitian.[25]

Practices concerning another tax — the head-tax — varied in different parts of the Roman Empire. In some places, people who paid the land-tax were exempt from the head-tax; elsewhere they paid both. It appears that the Jews of Judaea paid both taxes — except, of course, for the landless. In any case, the term "head-tax" should not be taken too literally. Scholars believe that it was not a fixed sum, levied equally on all, but rather a component of a variable personal tax — variable according to a man's property and income. We do not have detailed information on the way this was calculated; but there are sources that describe how heavily the head-taxes weighed on the people. A second century historian reports that the Jews of Judaea paid a capitation tax higher than that levied on the Empire's subjects in neighboring territories.[26] Similar evidence is provided by another source dating from the end of the second century, according to which the Palestinian Jews complained to Pescennius Niger that the heavy taxes were robbing them blind.[27]

Josephus speaks of a special Jewish tax, equal to two dinarii, which every Jew in the Empire had to remit annually to the treasury of the temple of Jupiter Capitolinus, the chief god of Rome. This

Emperor's personal account. See Pauly-Wissowa, *Realenzyklopädie der Klassischen Altertumswissenschaft*, vol. VI, pp. 2385 ff., art. *fiscus*.

25 See his *Life*, 76 (422, 425 and 429).

26 Appianos of Alexandria. (Reinach, p. 152).

27 *Historia Augusta*. (Reinach, p. 344; see Loeb Classics *Historia Augusta* transl. by D. Magie, vol. I, p. 447).

tax was intended by the Romans to take the place of the half-shekel per annum which every Jew had been accustomed to send voluntarily to the Temple in Jerusalem.[28] It has been suggested that this Roman enactment stems from the avarice for which Vespasian had a deservedly unsavory reputation.[29] The present writer feels that neither Vespasian's itchy palm, nor his desire to punish the Jews of the Diaspora for helping the rebels, is the fundamental reason for this Roman decree. Its real basis is a very old politico-legal concept according to which the gods of a conquered people came under Roman rule. In the War of the Destruction, the gods of Rome had emerged victorious; hence, those monies previously dedicated to the defeated Deity were now quite properly garnisheed on behalf of Rome's chief god.[30]

The same point is made by Dio Cassius, who adds that those liable for this tax were not only Jews, but also all who follow the ways of Judaism — which is to say, proselytes as well.[31] Suetonius takes us a step further. He reports that Domitian insisted on taking this tax even from Jews who had renounced their faith, and even from proselytes who gave up their new-found religion. (Life of Domitian, XII:2). We are given to understand that the Emperor was less concerned with the revenue than he was with the principle of the thing — degrading the Jews, putting them in their place.

From this passage in Suetonius we learn that there was a bureau in Rome called *fiscus judaicus* — a central Exchequer of the Jews, run by a commission — *consilium* — and headed by a *procurator*. Also extant is an inscription which mentions a *Procurator ad capitularia Judaeorum*.[32] More than likely, the only difference between the *fiscus* and the *capitularia* had to do with changes in the administrative method of accounting for the same thing — the two drachmas of the Jewish tax.

28 JW, VII:6:6 (218).
29 Michael Ginzburg, in J.Q.R. 1930, p. 281.
30 See Juster: *Les Juifs dans l'Empire Romain*. I:384.
31 Dio Cassius, LXVI:7; Reinach, op. cit. p. 194–5. Preisigke: *Sammelbuch Griechischen Urkunden* etc. 4429–4433. [See on this subject Tcherikover and Fuks: *Corpus Papyrorum Judaicarum*, Jerusalem-Cambridge, vol. I, pp. 80–83, vol. II, pp. 110 ff.]
32 *Corpus Inscriptionum Latinarum*, VI:8604. Also see Dessau, *Inscript. Lat. Selectae*, I: p. 330, no. 1519. Comp. Schürer, III, 117 note 62.

Ostraka and papyri discovered in Egypt in modern times have shed additional light on the subject. From the year 72–73 C.E. onwards, there is mention of *telesma Ioudaion* (tax of the Jews) in the sum of 8 Egyptian drachmas (= 2 Attic drachmas, or 2 dinarii). There is also mention of *timē dynarion duo Ioudaion* (the value of two dinarii of the Jews). Both these terms refer to the equivalent of the half-shekel which the Roman government exacted from the Jews after the Destruction of the Temple. These sources make it unequivocally clear that the tax had to be paid not only by adult males, but also by women and children — everybody between the ages of three and seventy.[33] There are scholars who contest the identity of this tax with the half-shekel. But we may agree with the majority, who hold that it is the actual *adrakhmon*.

A number of Egyptian documents mention, alongside the *aparchē*, still another *telesma* equal to one dinar — i.e. one-half the aforementioned tax. We cannot be certain about this, but there is a strong possibility that both the tax and its name are connected with the so-called *"terumot"* which Jews even in the Diaspora used to send in as a gift to the priests during Temple times.[34] In the immediate post-Destruction period, and especially during the days of Domitian, the government was very strict about collecting the Jewish tax. There in Rome sat the above-mentioned Procurator with his *Consilium*, casting his net far and wide throughout the Empire.[35] Jewish sources do not mention this particular impost; apparently it is included in the blanket appelation "taxes."

In a different class were the customs duties imposed on goods

33 Wiilcken: *Grundzüge u. Chrestomatie d. Papyruskunde*, 61. The Arsinoë Papyrus lists as payers of this tax 5 men, 6 women (one of them over 60) and four children aged 3 and up. See CPJ no. 421, vol. II, pp. 204 f.

34 Mishnah, Yad. IV:3 shows that heave-offerings (*terumot*) were part of religious observance in Egypt before the Destruction. See G. Alon: "Halakhah in Philo", JJCW, p. 89 ff.

35 According to Graetz in MGWJ, vol. I, p. 194, note 8, this council was composed of men who had been circumcised during the Bar Kokhba Rebellion, and had later taken measures to restore their foreskin, in order to escape the Jewish Tax. Graetz seeks to relate passages in tannaitic literature about such characters to remarks by Suetonius about similar types in Rome who went the same route. However, analogies like this are unreliable.

brought into the country. It seems that the amounts involved were not fixed by law, but were determined *ad valorem*. They were felt by the public to be very heavy indeed.

Tannaitic sources frequently speak of *"arnoniot."* These can be identified with the *annona militaris* which was levied on the local population to cover the costs of the military garrison, and to finance the civil administration in the occupied province. Jewish sources refer to *arnoniot* taken from the "dough vat" — i.e. baked bread — and from the flocks and herds. The fact is that this was standard operating procedure for the maintenance of Roman forces in every province of the Empire. The requisitions usually included wine, vinegar, oil, fodder, and clothing. In Palestine, where the Romans found it necessary to station a rather large army of occupation after the Destruction of Jerusalem, the Jews had a more than usually heavy burden to support. The following passage[36] gives some notion of how burdensome they found this *arnona*:

> Thus is it written in Deuteronomy by Moses our Master: 'They shall be upon thee for a sign and for a wonder, and upon thy seed forever; because thou didst not serve the Lord thy God with joyfulness and with gladness of heart, by reason of the abundance of all things; therefore shalt thou serve thine enemy whom the Lord shall send against thee, in hunger, and in thirst, and in nakedness, and in want of all things' (Deut. 28:46ff).
>
> *In hunger:* For example, at a time when one craves food and cannot find even coarse bread, the heathen nations demand from him white bread and choice meat.
>
> *And in thirst:* For example, at a time when one longs for drink and cannot find even a drop of vinegar or a drop of bitters, the heathen nations demand from him the finest wine in the world.
>
> *And in nakedness:* For example, at a time when one is in need of clothing, and cannot find even a wool shirt or a flaxen one, the heathen nations demand from him silks and the best *kallak* in the world.

36   ARN version A, chap. 20; Schechter, p. 71; Goldin, pp. 94–95.

No doubt this midrash is overstated; but its very hyperbole is an accurate reflection of how burdensome the Jews of the period felt the Roman *arnoniot* to be.

Finally, we must consider the service-tax, that is, the *angaria* and other kinds of forced labor. What the tannaitic sources call *angariot* consisted of work done by the subject or by his domestic animals in haulage, delivery of official goods and messages, and whatever else the local authorities required.[37] Hardest hit by this was the farmer. His animal was sometimes returned unfit for further work — if it was returned at all. True, under the law he was supposed to get his beast back. But suppose it had been overworked, or worked to death; what was he going to do? Usually it meant that he had lost his chief means of earning a livelihood.[38]

Other kinds of forced labor were chiefly road-repair and maintenance, and similar work required by the army and the police. The following, dating from a time not long after the Destruction, gives us an idea of what forced labor involved:

> Rabban Johanan ben Zakkai was going up to Emmaus in Judah and he saw a girl picking barleycorn out of the excrement of a horse. Said the Rabbi to his disciples: What girl is this? Said they to him: A Jewish girl. Said he further: And whose is the horse? They answered: It belongs to a bedouin horseman. Then said Rabban Johanan to his disciples: All my life have I been reading this verse, and not until now have I realized its full meaning: "If thou dost not know, O fairest among women (go thy way forth by the footsteps of the flock, and feed thy kids beside the shepherds' tents." *Cant.* I:8). You were unwilling to be subject to God, behold now you are subject to lowly bedouin; you were unwilling to pay the Biblically ordained head-tax of "one beqa per head" (*Exod.* 38:26), so

37 The word *angaria*, and the practice it connotes, both seem to be Persian in origin. At first it was confined to *cursus publicus*, but later came to include all forced labor of whatever nature.

38 Comp. Mishnah B.M. VI:3. See also Gemara *ad loc.* on 78b: "There is *angaria* that comes back, and *angaria* that does not." The reference in the latter phrase is to outright confiscation of the domestic animal, contrary to the interpretation suggested by Goldschmidt in REJ, vol. 34, p. 208.

now you have to pay fifteen shekels under a government of your enemies. You were unwilling to repair the roads and the streets leading up to the Temple, so now you have to repair the בורגסין and the בורגנין leading to the royal cities.[39]

We have no way of knowing where Rabban Johanan got the figure of fifteen shekels, or whether he calculated it as the sum of any specific components. It is more than likely that he simply picked on a good round number. But as far as forced labor is concerned, the text is an important and reliable source, even though there are no corroborative passages.

The *burgasin* mentioned in the text are the Greek *purgoi* — sentry-towers. The *burganin* are the equivalent of the Latin *burgi* mentioned in inscriptions, the earliest of which go back to the second century.[40] Since Rabban Johanan belongs to the first century, the tradition quoted here is therefore our earliest source attesting to the *burgi* as a fact of Roman life. It has been suggested that the word itself derives from the germanic *burg*.[41] And indeed, the inscriptions that refer to it come, as a rule, from Iberia and Gaul. However, as we now know, such *burganin* were to be found even east of the Jordan.

These structures were small watchtowers, erected near border strong points for the purpose of keeping an eye on the frontier. Those in the interior of the province served to police movement on the public highways. The passage quoted above from the *Mekhilta* refers no doubt to the latter kind.[42]

39   *Mekhilta de Rabbi Ishmael*, section *Bahodesh*, part 1, ed. Horovitz-Rabin, p. 203–4. [*Mekhilta*, text and translation ed. by Jacob Z. Lauterbach, Philadelphia, 1933. Vol. II, pp. 193–4.]
40   Publications of the Princeton University Archaeological Expedition to Syria, Leyden, 1929. Vol. IIIa, p. 132, Inscription no. 233.
41   M. Schwabe, in the Epstein Festschrift, pp. 273 ff.
42   References to "small towns of *burganin*" inhabited by Syrians come from as early as the period of Rabban Gamaliel. See Tos. Pes. I:27 (Zuck. 157); Yer. Av. Zar. I:40a; Bavli, Eruv. 64b; Lev. R. end of ch. 37. As a rule the *burgani* (watchmen, guards) were not Romans, but barbarians who performed para-military and para-police functions for the Roman military and civil authorities.

In this connection, we may quote a parallel passage:

> "They have made me a keeper of the vineyards (but mine own vineyard I have not kept)" (*Cant.* I:6). You yourselves did not keep the Temple properly, now you are become keepers of *burganin* in the exile."[43]

Persecution

Most historians pay no attention at all to religious persecution as an aspect of the struggle with Rome. But the sources we are about to quote indicate that during the War of Destruction and its aftermath, the Jews were under extreme pressure from the Roman *meṣiqim* (literally, "oppressors") to give up their religion. Granted, there is no basis for assuming that there were any official anti-religious decrees. But the evidence is almost conclusive that the Jews of Palestine (and of certain Diaspora communities as well) were in fact forced to undergo extreme suffering, and in some cases actual martyrdom, if they refused to give up the faith of their fathers.

This statement will no doubt be rejected out of hand by anyone familiar with the accepted historical tradition according to which Rome practiced tolerance towards all kinds of strange religions, Judaism in particular.[44] Even though she robbed the conquered peoples of their freedom and independence, it has long been known that Rome did not as a rule interfere with their freedom to practice their religions. This entrenched view has, in my opinion, led scholars to overlook sources which I believe point to religious persecutions in Palestine around the time of the Destruction of the Temple.

Without embarking at this point on an analysis of the tradition of Roman tolerance for Judaism, against which background we might be able to indicate those occasions when Roman rulers (or their legates) departed from that policy, we must at any rate distinguish between normal times, when tolerance was the rule, and exceptional periods of war and its aftermath, as in the case of the war of the

---

43　*Shir ha-Shirim Zuta*, ed. Buber, p. 14. S. Kraus: *Monumenta Talmudica*, p. 159, gets this wrong. [Originally vol. V, of *Monumenta Hebraica*, Wien-Leipzig 1914, this work is now available in a handy octavo photo-reprint, Darmstadt, 1972.]

44　Exception must of course be made for the Hadrianic persecutions connected with the Bar Kokhba Rebellion.

Destruction. In such turbulent times, Judaism was no longer protected by the shield of tolerance. If the Romans could practise the excesses of physical cruelty they did against peaceful civilians, old people, women and children, there is no reason to expect that they would have had the least concern for the religion of their victims.[45]

There is an additional consideration: the Palestinian Jews at that time of turbulence had no doubt been classified as *dediticii*, a kind of second class citizens.[45a] As such, they would quite properly have been deprived of certain rights, including the right to practice their religion. Thus, it was open season on the Jews, in law as in fact, during those days of the war and after it, until the time of defeat and conquest was past, and a reconstruction of sorts took place, and a kind of socio-legal status was worked out for Jews and Judaism in Palestine.

The parlous position of the Jews can be illustrated from a report by Josephus of an outbreak of violence in the Syrian metropolis of Antioch, during the time when Vespasian was in Judaea, that is to say, while the emperor-to-be was commander-in-chief in the Middle East.[46] It seems that the head of the Jewish community in Antioch — the Archon — had a son called Antiochus, who went to the

45 Compare the remarks of "his friends" to Vespasian about the atrocities against the Jews of Tarichaeae who were assembled in Tiberias, and either slaughtered or sold into slavery, to the effect that against the Jews there could be no application of the laws of war or impiety; they stand outside the law, and no measures taken against them are forbidden. JW, III:10:10 (532 ff.).

45a [The exact legal meaning of this term remains an unsolved problem, as pointed out by Ephraim E. Urbach in his review of *Toledot*, vol. I (in *Behinot*, no. IV, Mosad Bialik, Jerusalem 1953, pp. 61–72). Note also Salo Baron, in a remark not connected with the present work: "There is no evidence . . . for Mommsen's once widely accepted theory that, after 70 the vanquished Palestinian Jews sank to the status of half-free *dediticii*." (*Social and Religious History*, II, 103–104). Here, as elsewhere in the present volume, Alon seems to accept Mommsen's theory uncritically. However, in volume two of the present work he shows that he is aware of the problem. "The most difficult question (about the citizenship law of Caracalla) is the meaning of the word *dediticii*." Alon summarizes three conflicting opinions, including Mommsen's, and concludes: "My own view comes closest to that of A. H. M. Jones." See *Tol.* II, pp. 108 f.]

46 JW, VII:3:3 (43–53).

authorities and informed them that his fellow-Jews were plotting to set the city on fire. Among those informed against were "foreign Jews", apparently Palestinians who might very well have been in town to discuss some act of resistance. After the citizenry, enraged by these reports, had slaughtered the suspects, they decreed that the surviving Jews must offer sacrifices to the gods. Those who refused — and they were the majority — were put to death. The Roman governor of Syria provided a military detail to help force the Jews to violate the Sabbath. "Thus was the observance of the Sabbath done away with, not only in Antioch, but in all the cities of Syria."[47]

To be sure, Josephus also testifies that at a later date, Titus refused a request from the people of Antioch to banish Jews from their city. Their own native city had been destroyed, he argued, and there was no other place where the citizens would be willing to admit them.[48] He also refused to destroy the brass tablets on which the rights of the Jews were inscribed. All this may be true; but we must realize that public policy, designed for peacetime, is one thing, while the reality of wartime is quite another.

A sixth century Byzantine chronicler,[49] himself a native of Antioch, tells us that Vespasian erected a theater in Daphne, just outside Antioch, where once a synagogue had stood. Our chronicler reports that the Roman commander ordered an inscription placed over the entrance reading: "From the Spoils of Judaea" — and that he did so "to spite the Jews." The same general, ultimately Emperor, also erected an Odeon in Caesarea on the site of a synagogue.

Josephus Flavius, describing who and what the Essenes were, has this to say:[50]

> The war with the Romans tried their souls through and through by every variety of test. Racked and twisted, burnt and broken, and made to pass through every instrument of torture, in order to induce them to blaspheme their law-giver or to eat some

47 The rule of the halakhah is that all commandments may be transgressed when one's life is at stake, save only three: taking human life, performing forbidden sexual acts, and engaging in idolatry.

48 JW, VII:5:2 (109) Comp. corresponding passage in *Antiquities*.

49 Malalus (491–578). See portions of his chronicle edited by A.S. von Stauffenberg in *Römische Geschichte bei Malalus*, Books IX–XII, 1931.

50 JW, II:8:10 (152–3).

forbidden thing, they refused to yield to either demand, nor ever once did they cringe to their persecutors or shed a tear. Smiling in their agonies and mildly deriding their tormentors, they cheerfully resigned their souls, confident that they would receive them back again.

Elsewhere in the works of Josephus we read descriptions of a similar nature:

> Time and again ere now the sight has been witnessed of prisoners enduring tortures and death in every form in the theaters, rather than utter a single word against the Torah....[51] The facts have made all men aware that many of our countrymen on many occasions ere now preferred to brave all manner of suffering rather than to utter a single word against the Torah.[52] Has anyone ever heard of a case of our people (not, I mean in such large numbers, but merely two or three) proving traitors to their laws, or afraid of death? I do not refer to the easiest of deaths — on the battlefield — but to death accompanied by physical torture, which is thought to be the hardest of all. To such a death we are in my belief exposed by some of our conquerors, not from hatred of those at their mercy, but from a curiosity to witness the astonishing spectacle of men who believe that the only evil which can befall them is to be compelled to do any act or utter any word contrary to their laws.[53]

Without being able to interpret these passages in detail — especially the last one, veiled as it is in vague rhetoric — it seems to me that here we have evidence of unspecified but cruel religious persecutions in Palestine and in nearby provinces, carried out either by the Roman authorities or with their consent.[54]

51 *Against Apion*, I:8 (43).
52 Ibid. II:30 (219).
53 Ibid. II:32 (232–233).
54 Compare Josephus' speech to the defenders of Jerusalem before the conquest of the city's third wall (JW, V:9:4) (406): "The Romans ask you to pay the tax ... If you do, they will not destroy the city or interfere with the holy things. Your families will be free, your property will remain yours; and the holy laws will be preserved." The implication

A Jewish tradition about ruthless persecutions of Judaism in those days has been preserved for us by Jerome, in his commentary on Daniel:

> *And they that are wise among the people shall cause the many to understand; yet shall they stumble by the sword and by flame, by captivity and by spoil, many days.* (Daniel IX:33)
> The Jews relate this scripture to the time of the last Destruction, in the days of Vespasian and Titus. The meaning is, that many of the people will know God, and will be put to death for keeping the Torah.[55]

Taken in conjunction with the passages previously quoted, this comment would appear to offer significant evidence about the matter at hand. There is one more point to be made. The *didrachmon* ordained as a tribute to Jupiter Capitolinus was a grave insult to the Jewish religion. It forced every Jew to pay for the upkeep of idol worship, a thing abhorrent to Jewish belief and practice.

Morale

During the last three decades of the first century, almost everything that happened seemed designed to destroy the morale of the Jew, to make him turn his back on his people and his God. There were the religious clashes and persecutions just described; the bitter subjugation to Rome; the heavy tax-burden; the Destruction of the Sanctuary and the dashing of the people's hopes which had risen to fever-pitch during the resistance; and the inevitable mood of depression that followed as a reaction to the exalted messianic fervor which had fired the people to superhuman effort.

All this could only bring in its wake a wave of despair. Faith was undermined by the loss of the Temple, and the consequent dissolution of all those personal and communal aspects of the religion of Israel which depended on the altar. Spokesmen for the new

is, of course, that if the Jews do not submit, the holy laws will not be preserved.
55 *Patrologia Cursus Latina*, vol. XXV, p. 569. [Alon's attempts to prove that the Romans persecuted Judaism as a religion are rejected as "unacceptable" by Ephraim E. Urbach. See his previously cited review of *Toledot* vol. I, in *Behinot*.]

religion — Christianity — were not slow to point to this as proof that the old Torah and its mitzvot were now obsolete.

This ideological struggle between the old faith and the new must have been quite intense, and we may speculate on why our sources have so little to say about it. A faint echo does survive in some Talmudic passages, as in the story of the *"philosophos"* who functioned as a civil judge in the vicinity where Rabban Gamaliel lived. Discussing a point of law he said to the Rabbi: "Since the day that you were exiled from your land, the law of Moses has been superseded, and another Torah has taken its place."[56]

The weakening of morale which we have attributed to the generation that witnessed the Destruction can also be inferred from what took place later, after the fall of Betar. At that time there were "patrols of ex-Jews" in the service of the Roman authorities, hunting down Jews who were violating the Hadrianic decrees.[57]

Additional evidence is provided by the example of Elisha ben Abuyah, the renegade Rabbi who earned the epithet *Akher* — "The Other." Surely he was not the only Jew of his time to abandon both his religion and his people under the impact of tragic events. According to one tradition, Elisha lost his faith when he saw a swine make off with the tongue of Rabbi Ḥutzpit the Interpreter after the public execution of the Ten Martyrs.[58]

Certainly there were other Jews who witnessed equally shattering sights, with equal revulsion. Hence probably those references in tannaitic literature to Jews who "abandoned the ways of the community" and who "violated the Covenant", "rejected the Torah" — in short, who "threw off the yoke." Not all these references date from the reign of Hadrian. Rabbi Eleazar ha-Moda'i lived in the days of the Destruction; and he too speaks of those who "violate the Covenant of Abraham our Father," and those who "reject the Torah."[59] Therefore, there must have been noticeable desertions from Judaism in his generation. To be sure, such defections were

---

56 Shab. 116a-b. Instead of "Another Torah", unexpurgated Mss. of the Talmud read עָוֶן גִּלְיוֹן, a deliberate distortion of *Evangelion*.
57 Gen. R. chap. 82:8. Edition Theodor-Albeck, p. 985.
58 Qid. 39b; Hul. 142a.
59 Av. III:11.

not entirely unknown even in earlier times; but the motivations then were probably ideological.

Still another memory of the period between the Destruction (70 C.E.) and the Bar Kokhba Rebellion (132 C.E.) is preserved in the Tosefta: "Many who had obliterated their sign of the Covenant were circumcised in the days of Bar Koziba."[60] We shall not here attempt to establish when these acts of "de-circumcision" took place; but we can reasonably assume that it was prior to the outbreak of the Bar Kokhba Rebellion. No doubt this "violation of the Covenant" was related to the suffering being visited on the Jewish people, and to the wave of despair that came with it. Again we quote the Apocryphal Syriac Book of Baruch, written in Palestine in the generation of the Destruction: "For I have seen many of Thy people who have forsaken Thy Covenant, and thrown off the yoke of Thy religion."[61] The author is witness to a dejudaizing trend that becomes noticeable (dare we say, predominant?) after the Destruction of the Temple.

One thing is certain: A well-nigh superhuman struggle awaited those leaders and teachers who were destined to undertake the task of binding up the nation's spiritual wounds, of reuniting the people and putting it back on its feet.

Collaboration

Before the year 70, the Roman occupation authorities had left some elements of government in the hands of the local population. But now Judaea was placed under direct Roman administration, except of course for mixed cities on the fringe of Jewish Palestine, like Caesarea; and except for the little quasi-autonomous kingdom of Agrippa in northern Transjordan.[62] It was the Romans who now had to collect the taxes, and to enforce all other regulations to which the population was subject. The governing authorities of the province became responsible for public security, and for the functioning

---

60 Tos. Shab. XV:9 (Zuck., p. 133); comp. Yer. Shab. XIX:17a; and Yev. VIII:9a. See also Bavli Yev. 72a.

61 Baruch, 41:3; Charles, *Apocrypha* etc. vol. II, p. 501.

62 Its capital was at Banias, in the Golan, and its territory contained part of the Galilee, including Tiberias. Some scholars think that it extended to Sepphoris, but this remains unproven.

of local institutions. This included the administration of civil law, in all matters of any substance. Judges might be local people, but they were appointed and supervised by the Romans. It need hardly be added that criminal law was completely in Roman hands.[63]

In spite of all this, it seems more than likely that some shreds of local self-government survived the debacle. In many villages and small towns it would have been impossible for practical reasons to dispense entirely with local leadership. We must therefore assume that such leadership continued to function in a number of places, even if its authority was reduced, or its make-up altered. It seems logical that even for the collection of taxes the government had to appoint quite a few Jews. Although we have no explicit evidence of such appointees in the immediate post-war period, we do find frequent mention of them, under the title of *gabbai'im,* in the tannaitic literature of a generation or two later.

As for the imposts (*mekhes*) on land, crops and goods, the Romans had always farmed these out to tax-contractors, and they continued to do so during the Empire, although they had abandoned this method of collecting *personal* taxes after the end of the Republic. There can be no doubt that in Judaea many of these tax-farmers, or publicans, were Jews. The same applies to other petty officials — supervisors of the corvée, lower-level officers of the peace, even minor court functionaries. In other words, unimportant matters at the local level continued to be handled, as they had been before, by local native authorities who could, of course, be overruled at any point by the officials of the Empire.

Who, then, were the elements of the population that took charge of what was left of the society and its economy in the period right after the war, giving direction locally, and providing liaison with the Roman occupation? In the first instance they were men of means and social standing who had been leaders in their communities before the war. Many of them had retained much of their old status, for one of two reasons: either the town they lived in had not resisted the Romans (Sepphoris, for example); or else they had personally kept aloof from the rebels. Not all these personalities are

---

63 Compare Yer. Sanh. I:18a: "More than forty years before the Destruction of the Temple the Sanhedrin lost jurisdiction over capital cases."

to be judged negatively in terms of the national interest. Some of them had kept out of the war for good reason, and not merely because of economic selfishness. Afterwards, they were to constitute an element of strength in their communities.

They were not the only ones. There were others who had actually taken part in the resistance, but had not been caught by the Romans. Such men, even if they had lost all their wealth, still retained some of the prestige they had enjoyed in pre-war times.

But whatever the carry-over from the old regime, the situation as a whole was altered to its very roots. As we have already seen, the bitter struggle created economic havoc for the Jews of Palestine. Especially radical changes had taken place in the ownership of land, and these had far-reaching social implications. Land was the fundamental basis of economic life, for the individual as for the nation. Consequently, a new class of parvenus rose to the top of the social-economic ladder — the so-called *ba'alei-zero'a* (muscle-men), the *taqifim* (big wheels), who had seen the main chance and seized it. Add to them the outright collaborators, and you have a stratum of imposed leaders, from whose ranks most of the publicans, tax-agents and other willing servants of the occupation were no doubt recruited. These, the opportunists and the collaborationists constituted the unhealthy part of the post-war leadership — unhealthy for the nation socially, morally, spiritually and in every other way.[64]

64 Assuredly, it was not only newly-rich *arrivistes* who engaged in shady dealings and used their official connections for their private gain. There were equally corrupt characters who had been on the scene before the war, some of them from the upper echelons of society. We hear about certain members of the higher priesthood (dating back therefore to the days of the Temple) whose heavy hand was laid on more than one honest citizen. The testimony comes not only from tannaitic sources, but from Josephus as well. But perhaps the point can best be made by citing a passage from the Yerushalmi (Ta'anit IV, 69a):

> Why was Betar destroyed? Because its people lit lamps (to celebrate) following the Destruction of Jerusalem. But why did they so? Because prominent citizens (*bouleutin*) of Jerusalem would station themselves in the middle of the *medinah*. When they saw anyone going up to Jerusalem, they would say to him: 'We hear you are going to get yourself appointed magistrate (*archon*) or alderman (*bouleuton*).' He would answer: 'That is not my intention.' 'We hear you are going because you want to sell your estate.' He would answer: 'That is

This ugly social phenomenon was one of the first obstacles that faced the Sages in their attempt to restore the national and religious health of the Jews in Judaea, and it gave them a great deal of trouble.

Tannaitic sources do speak of "headmen" — lay leaders who exercised a beneficent authority over the community. But the same literature makes frequent mention of another type — those who gained authority only to abuse it, who grew fat on the troubles of the people, and battened on the national tragedy. Out of the many references of this kind, we need quote here only those that definitely date from the time of the Destruction, or at least can possibly be assigned to that period.

First, the following from the Mishnah at the end of the Tractate Sotah:

> Rabbi Pinhas ben Ya'ir says: From the time that the Temple was destroyed, *haverim* and freemen have been put to shame, and have walked with covered heads. Men of good deeds have grown feeble, while loud-mouths and men of violence have gained the upper hand. So now there is none to expound, to seek or to enquire. On whom can we depend? Only on our Father in heaven.

not my intention.' Then his colleague would say: 'Why do you bother with this fellow? Write out (a deed of sale) and I will sign.' This done, they would send the document to a member of his household with this message: 'If so-and-so comes to enter his estate, keep him out, because it has been sold to us.' When the victim learned what had happened, he would say: 'Would that I had broken my leg before ever I had set out for Jerusalem.' To this situation the scripture may be applied: *'They hunt our steps, so that we cannot go in our streets; our end is near, our days are accomplished.'* (Lam. IV:18) Nevertheless, they should not have celebrated, for it is written: *'He that is glad at calamity shall not go unpunished.'* (Prov. XVII:5).

In its present form, with its mention of *archontin* and *bouleutin*, this text can be dated no earlier than the beginning of the second century of the current era. But there is no reason to doubt the phenomenon it reflects — the use of public office for chicanery and selfish gain. Surely the passage echoes an old tradition, going back to the time of the Destruction. And clearly it does recall the tragic fate of those who withheld their help from Jerusalem, because they had suffered loss at the hands of certain of her dishonest officials.

Rabbi Pinhas ben Ya'ir lived, to be sure, in the latter half of the second century. But the Munich manuscript, the Lowe edition, and the *editio princeps* of the *'Ein Ya'aqov'* all read "Rabbi Eliezer the Great says..." — and he *does* belong to the generation of the Destruction.

Secondly, there is the following passage from the opening section of Esther Rabbah.[65]

> Abba Gurion of Sidon quoted five sayings of Rabban Gamaliel: When corrupt judges multiplied (i.e. unqualified ones, appointed by the occupation) false witnesses multiplied. When informers increased, spoliation of property increased. When effrontery grew rife, people were deprived of their dignity...

(Admittedly, there are versions of this which omit the attribution to Rabban Gamaliel, on which our dating here depends.)

A third passage, not without its obscurities, has been preserved in Aboth de Rabbi Nathan:[66]

> Rabban Johanan ben Zakkai used to say:
> Warn the young ones away from pride (of possessions; see note 67, below) and steer them clear of property owners, because these keep one far from Torah.... He used to say: there are five sins for which householders deserve to have their property taken from them (i.e. confiscated by the Romans): because they take usury, they suppress paid-up notes, they publically pledge charity and then don't pay the pledge... (another version reads: they transfer the yoke and the tax from their own shoulders and put it on the shoulders of the unhappy poor)... It is about these householders that Scripture speaks when it says 'Cursed be he that confirmeth not the words of this law to do them.' (Deut. 27:26)[67]

---

65 Midrash Abba Gurion, ed. Buber, p. 1.
66 ARN version B, 31; Schechter, p. 67.
67 The rendering of the Hebrew *ga'on* suggested here connects it with wealth used for ostentation, to lord it over other people. So too in Gittin 37a: "Rabbi Joseph took the verse 'I will break the pride (*ge'on*) of your power' (Levit. 27:19) and applied it to the *boula'ot* (town councils) of Judaea." On the same Biblical verse, see Sifra: (Behukotai ch. 5, ed. Weiss folio 111d): "Others say, 'I will break the pride of

Another text has an uncertain date of origin, but there is every reason to suppose that its main outlines can be applied to the period we are examining. The passage presents a clear-cut picture of a very unsavory social situation:

> When people began to concentrate on self-gratification, the honor of the Torah was cancelled out (Bavli: the laws were perverted, conduct deteriorated, and there is no serenity left in the world).... When respecters (Bavli: respecters of persons in court) increased, the commandment 'Ye shall not respect persons in judgement' (Deut. I:17) fell into disuse, and the commandment 'Ye shall not be afraid of any man' (ibid.) dropped out of practice, and people threw off the yoke of Heaven, and put themselves under the yoke of flesh and blood.... When those who force goods on householders became numerous, bribery flourished, and justice was perverted, and they went backward, not forward....
>
> When there was an increase of those (judges) who said: 'I accept your favor, I appreciate your favor', there was an increase of 'every man did what was right in his own eyes' (Judges XVII:6), and the whole country went bad, getting worse and worse. When 'every man did what was right in his own eyes', unworthy persons were raised to eminence, and the eminent were brought low. When ungenerous men and plunderers of the poor grew numerous, there was an increase in the number of the hard-hearted and the tight-fisted. When there was an increase in those of whom the prophet says 'Their heart is set upon their gain' (Ezek. XXXIII:31), there was a rise in the number of those of whom the prophet says' 'They call evil good, and good, evil.' (Isa. V:20). When these latter increased, the whole world was filled with 'woe' (ibid.). When there was an increase of those who strut ostentatiously, disciples became few and the honor of the Torah was set at

your power' applies to those high and mighty ones who were the pride of Judaea, like Pappus ben Judah, and Lulianos of Alexandria and their company." According to the Aggadah, they set up tables (*trapezin*) for silver and gold — for the rebuilding of the Temple — in the early days of Hadrian's reign. See Genesis Rabbah, LXIV, ed. Theodor, p. 710. For a detailed study of the meaning of *ga'on*, see Alon, *JJCW*, pp. 344 ff.

naught. When arrogant men became numerous, the daughters of Israel began to marry them, for our generation looks only to appearance.[68]

This, then, is how the tradition describes a social element newly come to power, an element domineering, arrogant and corrupt, contemptuous of the Torah with its doctrine of humility and righteousness, disdainful of the generations-old heritage of Jewish teaching, ready and eager to adjust to the sovereignty of "flesh and blood" — meaning, of course, to Roman rule. That the Romans abetted them goes almost without saying.

Judaea a Province

What was the legal status of Judaea in the years between the Destruction of the Temple and the end of the Bar Kokhba Rebellion in 135 C.E.? After Herod's son Archelaus had been exiled to Gaul by order of Augustus Caesar (6 C.E.), Palestine had been incorporated into the Roman Empire, except for the interval between 41 and 44 C.E. that marked the reign of Agrippa I. The administrative status of the territory was, however, unique. Judaea was treated neither as a separate province, nor as part of some other province, but as a sort of appendage to the Province of Syria. This relationship became apparent especially during periods of disaffection or threatened revolt in Judaea. At such times the Governor of Syria would arrive from his headquarters in Antioch, sometimes accompanied by a military force, and would intervene in the affairs of the country, for purposes of "pacification." The day-to-day administration was, however, in the hands of the Procurator (Josephus always calls him *"epitropos"* — i.e. *chargé*) who was a member of the equestrian order, and had his seat in Caesarea.

After the Destruction, Judaea became a separate province. (Whether or not the country was still under Syrian jurisdiction in certain matters remains open to discussion). Rule was now entrusted to a Legate of the Senatorial class, whose complete official title was *Legatus Augusti pro praetore Provincia Judaeae.* This styling for the Governors of Judaea occurs in Roman inscriptions dating from

68 Tos. Sot. XIV:3–4 (Zuck., p. 320); cf. also Bavli, ibid. 47b.

the period between the Destruction and the Bar Kokhba Rebellion, for example in no. 12117 of *Corpus Inscriptionum Latinarum,* for the years 107–109 (vol. III, p. 2054). After the year 134 (the crushing of the Rebellion) the title becomes *Leg. Aug. p.p. Prov. Syriae Palaestinae.*[69]

Another senior official served along with the Governor — a Procurator, who was in charge of financial matters. Josephus testifies to this set-up for the period immediately after the Destruction, when he speaks of the Legate Bassus, and his Procurator Laberius Maximus.[70] This testimony is supported by inscriptions, such as C.I.L. III:5776, for the period before Bar Kokhba, where we find *Procurator Augusti Provinciae Judaeae;* and entry no. 1369 of Dessau, *Inscript. Lat. Select.* The latter collection also provides a sample for the third century, which reads *Procurator Provinciae Syriae Palaestinae* (entry 1330).

Vespasian, departing from the usual Roman practice of stationing legions only in the frontier provinces of the Empire (as in Cappadocia, facing Armenia) garrisoned a permanent occupation force in Judaea, even though it was an interior territory. He assigned to this duty the Tenth Fretensian Legion (*Legio Decima Fretensis*) which had taken part in the war and in the mopping up. Its headquarters barracks were in Jerusalem, and its Commanding Officer was the Governor himself. In addition to the Tenth, there were other military units "scattered around in various places in the country", to quote Josephus.[71] Some of these units are named in a Roman Certificate of Military Service from the year 86, during the reign of Domitian. They turn out to have been auxiliary battalions of troops from faraway countries.[72] Auxiliary battalions made up of men from Caesarea and Sebastea (Samaria) who had been stationed in the country *before* the war, had been transferred by Vespasian to other provinces.[73]

Before we proceed to examine the emergence of the centralized

---

69 For the background of the name *Palaestina,* see Noth in *Zeitschrift des Deutschen Palästina Vereins,* 1939, pp. 62 ff.
70 JW, VII:6:6 (216).
71 JW, VII:8:1 (252).
72 C.I.L. 3, p. 857. See also Darmesteter in REJ I, p. 33 ff.
73 Ant. XIX:9:2 (366).

Jewish leadership in the post-war period, and the relationship between this process and the attitude of the Imperial authorities, we ought to take a brief look at what the sources tell us about political and administrative measures taken against the Jews in those days. There is, to begin with, what Suetonius says about the worsening of the Jewish tax situation under Domitian. We also know about Domitian's decrees against conversion to Judaism. To be sure, tradition has it that both these policies were directed primarily against the Jews in the Diaspora; still, they must have had some effect on the Jews of Palestine. These matters deserve attention; but we would prefer to take them up when we discuss the role of Rabban Gamaliel, since his activities tie in with the decrees of Domitian's last years. The same applies to the statement of Eusebius about efforts by Domitian to root out all survivors of the Davidic dynasty.[74] That too will keep until we come to the work of Rabban Gamaliel.

What we will take up here is a statement by the same Church Father that Vespasian, too, ordered a search for any Jews claiming descent from the House of David, "to make sure that the royal line of the Kingdom of Judah would be obliterated."[75] This statement, copied by many Christian historians who wrote after Eusebius, has been treated with scepticism by some scholars, like Juster (I. 225) and others.[76] They assume that it is simply an analogy from the evidence about the decree of Domitian, evidence which Eusebius had from the second century Hegesippus. When he attributes the same policy to Vespasian and Titus, Eusebius offers no evidence at all; hence, say these scholars, he made the whole thing up.

In the opinion of the present writer, it is far-fetched to claim that Eusebius "invented" the tradition connecting Vespasian with the decree against the Davidic dynasty. It is more likely that he got it from the same work by Hegesippus — the *Hypomnemata*. The reason he failed to mention the source, though he did so in connection with Domitian, is that in the latter case he had to refer to

---

74   Hist. of the Church, 3:8:9. Comp. Chronicle of Jerome-Eusebius, P.G. vol. 19, p. 551. = P.L. XXVII, p. 603.

75   Ibid. 3:12:2.

76   [Juster should not really be included, for he writes (ibid.): "...l'ordre *qui semble historique* donné par Vespasian de détruire la race de David..." Comp. Urbach, art. cit. in *Behinot*.]

Hegesippus because the descendants of another Judah — the brother of Jesus — were involved. Thus, even though we cannot accept this evidence unquestioningly, we cannot reject it out of hand either.[77]

In any event, it is reasonably certain that the Roman authorities were very anxious to prevent the rise in Palestine of influential men or circles who might become the focus of revolt. Nor can we altogether reject the possibility that there actually were such attempts at resistance. One scholar has proposed that an abortive uprising took place around 85–86.[78] His principal evidence comes from the Certificate of Military Service mentioned above. Ordinarily, such a certificate included the terms of honorable discharge (*honesta missio*) but the soldiers serving in Judaea that year got the certificate with no mention of discharge. They were given the rights and privileges to which soldiers are entitled at the conclusion of their period of enlistment — Roman citizenship, the right to marry, and so forth. But no discharge. This proves, according to the theory, that there was a rebellion, or at least rebellious agitation, going on at the time, so that it was necessary to prolong military service "for the duration."

One must perforce agree with Schürer that this theory "is far from proven."[79] It seems more likely that what we have here is connected with evidence in a Roman Certificate of Military Service dated November, 88 C.E., where it is stated explicitly that military units were being concentrated in Syria, apparently because of the threat of war with the Parthians, a situation that was chronic at that time. Perhaps, then, it was for the same reason that the units in Judaea, composed of soldiers from the western lands of the Empire, were kept in service.

---

77 Comp. Schürer, I, p. 661 (English: Vermes and Millar, p. 528).
78 Darmesteter, REJ., vol. I (1880), p. 37–41.
79 *Geschichte,* I p. 644. (English: Vermes and Millar, p. 515).

CHAPTER FIVE

POSTWAR LEADERSHIP:
RABBAN JOHANAN BEN ZAKKAI

The first twenty-five years after the fall of the Temple can be viewed as a time when the ground was prepared for a new form of central authority that was to give the Jewish people, both at home and abroad, a framework for its national spiritual existence in the absence of a Jewish State. The process involved the creation of a High Court (Beth Din) and a High Academy (Beth Midrash), and it centered chiefly around the activity of two personalities: Rabban Johanan ben Zakkai and Rabban Gamaliel II. Rabban Johanan was active in the first half of that quarter century — from the year 70 to about 80 or 85 C.E. Then Rabban Gamaliel took the lead.

Both ancient tradition and modern scholarship are agreed that Rabban Johanan marks the beginning of a new era in Jewish history. For it was he who established a Judaism able to survive and grow without a state, without those attributes and instrumentalities of nationhood which a political-territorial base normally provides for a people. Carried to its logical conclusion, this view maintains that when the Jewish people lost the very ground under its feet, Rabban Johanan stepped into the breach and by reformulating Judaism on a new basis — a spiritual instead of a territorial one — assured the millennial survival of the people and its faith.

This opinion is widely held, and there is a lot of truth in it. A great many historians and other writers do treat the religio-spiritual element as very nearly the only basis of Jewish survival after the Destruction. But this leads them to conceive of Jewry after the year 70 as a religious communion largely devoid of the attributes of peoplehood.[1] This is a view that can be maintained only by ignoring

1 For a thorough summary of the question, see the series of articles by S. Zeitlin, *"Judaism As A Religion"* beginning in JQR 1943, p. 1, and continuing in the following issues.

[86]

completely what the historical sources tell us, and by turning a blind eye on the very real social, demographic and ethnic factors which were clearly at work.

The trouble is, however, that we know altogether too little about those days immediately after the Destruction, so that it is hard to get a clear picture of Rabban Johanan's activities, or a precise idea of his role as leader and spokesman. Consequently, there is a tendency both to generalize and to simplify the man and his activities, as though he had stepped forward and transformed the people and its outlook at one stroke. The tendency is understandable, for we read into Rabban Johanan and his times much of what we know about the situation later on, or about events that were really shaped by personalities who came after him.

A sound estimate of Rabban Johanan's contribution to the founding of the new national center after the loss of the State, involves a careful study of the following three questions:

1) What was the origin of Yavneh? Was the Great Sanhedrin really established there immediately after the Destruction (or even slightly before it), by Rabban Johanan ben Zakkai, with the express permission of the Romans? If so, it would mean that the conquerors immediately granted to the Jews that semi-autonomous status which we encounter later on.

2) What exactly was the position of Rabban Johanan? Was he the leader (*nasi*), recognized as such by the people as a whole?

3) What were the public acts of Rabban Johanan and his Beth Din after they were established at Yavneh?

Before The War

Before we attempt to answer these questions, it would be well to see what the sources have to tell us about this man as he was earlier, before the Destruction. Unfortunately, not much — as is the case with a number of other great personalities of the pre-war generation. About his birth, his family, his youth and his middle years we are completely in the dark. There is, however, an instructive tradition repeated several times in the literature, to the effect that Rabban Johanan had served Hillel the Elder as the youngest of his students. This tradition makes for some serious chronological problems (it implies an astoundingly old age for Rabban Johanan);

[87]

nevertheless, we cannot dismiss it with absolute certainty.

Whatever the literal fact may be, Rabban Johanan was certainly at very least a spiritual disciple of Hillel. Like the gentle Babylonian, Rabban Johanan was characterized by a love of humanity, an attachment to peace, a realistic and activist approach to public affairs, a stress on intellectual inquiry, an insistence on humane conduct, and a deep religiosity. Add to all these an empathy for the common people, which finds expression in his halakhic opinions— and the resemblance to Hillel is fairly complete. So we must say that Rabban Johanan ben Zakkai, one of the first "Elders of the School of Hillel", was at least a spiritual descendant of the founder of that school, whether or not he ever actually sat at his feet.

This gives us some insight into the character and impact of the man. The study of his dicta also makes tenable the opinion that he shared something of that religious and ethical universalism which it seems was taught by the Hillelites both before and after Rabban Johanan, to the effect that Gentiles are eligible for salvation, for they can achieve the life of goodness, spiritual wholeness and eternal reward without becoming Jews. This contrasts with a more "nationalist" school of thought, according to which none of these things are attainable without full acceptance of Judaism.

We do know that Rabban Johanan was very active in public life before the Destruction, but it appears that he himself attached greater importance to his role as teacher and disseminator of Torah. In him are united the two main strands of Judaism as taught consistently by the Sages, from the earliest Pharisees to the last of their successors; namely: Torah and right action (*ma'asim tovim*); or to put it differently, study and involvement in the needs of the community.

As between these two fields of activity — between study and action — we sometimes find among the Sages a sort of specialization of function. There were those of whom it was said "they made their learning their career" (*toratam 'umanutam*). Such scholars eschewed public leadership and communal activity. By contrast, there were others who came to be known as "men of action" (*'anshei ma'aseh*) in the arena of public affairs. The distinction derived not solely from divergences in psychological make-up. It was also rooted in a philosophical difference of opinion, as shown by the famous debate

[88]

at Lydda on the question: which is more important, knowledge or action?[2]

Rabban Johanan ben Zakkai was one of the many Sages who were effective in both fields. In theory, he seems to have given the primacy to scholarship, as expressed in his well-known dictum: "Hast thou studied much Torah? Do not congratulate thyself. After all, it was for this thou wast created."[3] He was said to have trained many disciples during the days of the Temple, some of them great men who were destined to play important roles in reviving the people and the Torah after the Destruction. There is also the well-known tradition about his five famous students.[4] (Apparently the number five has significance. It seems to indicate a group *(ḥever)*, whether in the Beth Midrash or the Beth Din.)

The broad public influence of Rabban Johanan is reflected in the reputation gained by his academy in Jerusalem, to which "the great of the land" would come and listen to him or to his disciples. There is a tradition that he used to teach publicly on the Temple Mount, "in the very shadow of the Sanctuary."[5]

It is also reported of him that he neglected no branch of learning known to his day.[6] This included not only halakhah and aggadah. It also included "turnings (solar) and *gematriot*" as well as "parables." The former probably refers to astronomical data used in figuring the Jewish calendar; the latter represents a genre of "wisdom" literature with venerable credentials from the earliest days of the Second Commonwealth, rooted in the wisdom books of Bible and Apocrypha. This type of knowledge continued to occupy a respected place in the academies as late as the third century — witness the fabulist Bar Kappara.

Nor did Rabban Johanan ben Zakkai neglect mysticism and metaphysical speculation, which are referred to in our source-text[6] as "cosmology of the Creation" and "secrets of Ezekiel's heavenly chariot." This is supported by other tannaitic passages that tell how

2 Bavli Qid. 40b. See also Yer. Pes. III:30b.
3 Av. II:8.
4 Ibid. See also ARN, version A, chap. 14. Goldin, p. 74 ff.
5 Pes. 26a; Yer. Av. Zar. III:43b.
6 Sukkah 28a; ARN version A, ch. 14, Goldin, p. 74; version B, ch. 28, Schechter p. 58; Yer. Ned. V:39b.

two of Rabban Johanan's students, Rabbi Eleazar ben Arakh and Rabbi Joshua, discoursed in the presence of their teacher about the "heavenly chariot" — then as always a point of departure for theosophical speculation. It should be pointed out that apocalyptic literature pre-dates Rabban Johanan by many generations. However, such studies made their way into the academies of the scribes and Sages only in the last two generations before the Destruction. It was then that they gained acceptance as "Torah."

As for Rabban Johanan's participation in public affairs, the sources put greatest stress on his role as spokesman for the Pharisees in their struggles with the Sadducees. There is ample evidence to support the accuracy of this tradition, and there is no reason to doubt it. The record has Rabban Johanan disputing with the Sadducees on a matter of civil law (involving the relative status of a daughter and a son's daughter as heirs-at-law); on a question of priestly ritual (involving the Red Heifer);[7] and on a regulation which had been introduced by the Sopherim, and which the Sadducees, literalists that they were, refused to accept.[8]

These arguments with the Sadducees, most of them reported as face to face confrontations, show that Rabban Johanan was an important personage, and a leading spokesman for the Pharisees. This is especially apparent in his bold treatment of the High Priest. But it would in any case have been obvious that he was a man of authority in Temple times from the report that he abolished so ancient and entrenched a procedure as the ordeal of the bitter waters (Num. V:11–31).[9] (It should perhaps be noted that the corresponding passage in the Tosefta has Rabban Johanan not *abolishing* the ordeal, but merely reporting that it had *already* been abolished: "Quoth Rabban Johanan: Since murderers have proliferated, the ritual of the *'eglah 'aruphah* (Deut. XXI:1–9) has been discontinued . . . . Since adulterers became common, the ordeal of the waters has been dropped, for it was needed only in cases of doubt."[10] The text does not state specifically that the second sentence is also to be

7   B.B. 115b; and Tos. Par. III:8 (Zuck. p. 632).
8   Mishnah Yad. VI:6; Tos. ibid. II:9 (Zuck. p. 683); The issue is one of ritual contamination involving the books of the Scriptures.
9   Sot. IX:9.
10   Tos. ibid. XIV:1 and 2 (Zuck. p. 320).

attributed to Rabban Johanan, but it seems likely that it is. We do know that the ordeal was still in practice at the time of Queen Helena of Adiabne who died circa 56 C.E.)

The status of Rabban Johanan as one of chief leaders of his generation is made especially obvious by an official document that has come to light in modern times. It is a missive dealing with the clearing out of tithes, sent to all districts in Palestine, and bearing the signatures of Rabban Simeon ben Gamaliel and Rabban Johanan ben Zakkai, in that order: [11]

> "From Simeon son of Gamaliel, and from Johanan son of Zakkai to our brethren in the Upper South and in the Lower South and in Shahlil (?) and the seven districts of the Darom: Greetings! Be it known to you that although the fourth year [of the Sabbatical cycle] has arrived, the sacred [produce] has not yet been disposed of.... And it is not we who began writing to you, but rather our fathers who wrote to your fathers....

Another such letter includes the identical formula about who writes to whom:

> To our brethren in Upper and Lower Galilee, and to Simonia and to Obed Beth Hillel: Greetings!... And it is not we who began etc. etc....

Letters like these are, in effect, encyclicals sent out to various parts of the country. They show that, before the Destruction, Rabban Johanan ben Zakkai was Deputy to the Nasi Rabban Simeon ben Gamaliel. This important position helps to explain his leadership role after the War. [12]

It may also make us wonder whether there is substance to the suggestion that Rabban Johanan was a *Kohen,* a factor which, if true, might have contributed to his pre-war eminence. The sug-

11　Midrash Tannaim, Ki Tavo, p. 176.
12　[Urbach remains unconvinced: "There is no proof that Rabban Johanan ben Zakkai held any office whatsoever when he was in Jerusalem." (From his article "Class Status and Leadership in the World of the Palestinian Sages" (English) in *Proceedings of the Israel Academy of Sciences and Humanities*, 1966, p. 54.)]

gestion derives principally from a passage in tannaitic literature dealing with the red heifer.[13] However, it seems that the Tosaphist was quite right when he pointed out that said passage offers no real proof that Rabban Johanan was a *kohen*.[14] On the contrary, the sharp confrontations reported to have taken place between Rabban Johanan and the priests incline one to conclude that he himself was *not* a *kohen*. Had he been, it might have helped us explain the source of his prestige and prominence; as it is, we shall have to look elsewhere. Perhaps the letters quoted above imply that he came from a family that had already achieved eminence; that his forbears had sat in the Sanhedrin, and has signed official correspondence.

Political Views

In view of Rabban Johanan's prominence before the war, we must ask ourselves what his politics had been with regard to the insurrection. In the welter of conflicting parties, what stand did he take during the years between the outbreak of the revolt and that moment when he passed through the enemy lines on his way to see Vespasian (or was it Titus) at Roman headquarters? Unfortunately, we have no explicit evidence on this score. Even the spare aggadic traditions about his departure from the besieged city of Jerusalem have come down to us in variant versions. The best we can do is to survey the spectrum of opinion among the Pharisaic Sages, and try to see where Rabban Johanan ben Zakkai fits in.

Josephus, speaking in general terms, says that at the beginning of the revolt in the summer of 66 C.E. the Pharisees were among those who tried to quiet things down, and to talk the masses of the people out of joining the rebels.[15] Then he goes on to say that in the fall of the same year, after Cestius Gallus had been overthrown, many of the Pharisees saw no alternative but to join the fray. It is certainly

---

13 Sifri, Huqqat, 123.
14 Tosaphot on Menahot 21b, last entry on the page. [Alon's Hebrew editor, Shmuel Safrai, opts for the conclusion that Rabban Johanan *was* a *kohen*. See his "Reconsiderations Concerning Rabban Johanan ben Zakkai's Status and Achievements" in *Essays in Memory of Gedaliah Alon* (Hebrew), 1970, pp. 203 ff.]
15 JW, II:17:3 (411 ff).

possible to improve on so sweeping a statement, even without examining the subject in great detail. One can distinguish three tendencies among the Pharisees at that critical time:

1) *Pharisee-Zealots,* who hated the oppressive occupation and despised the cruelty of the Roman governors, and openly rallied the people to war.

2) *Moderates,* who might be dubbed National-Realists. Unlike the Zealots, they did not preach war as the only logical consequence of their patriotic ideology, but they were prepared to offer physical resistance in circumstances that seemed to promise some chance of victory. At the same time, they were no doubt capable of coming to terms with the Romans when such a step appeared either favorable, or on the contrary unavoidable. This seems to have been the thinking of the majority in the Pharisaic camp. It stands to reason that their number increased greatly after the first successes against Rome, at which point no doubt they took on important responsibilities in the national leadership. The outstanding representative of this position among the Pharisees was Rabban Simeon ben Gamaliel, whose political stance was close to that of Hanan ben Hanan, the Sadducee.

3) *The Peace Party,* who from the very start rejected the possibility of victory, and therefore made no effort at all to wrest freedom from the Romans. This grouping included some who even before the outbreak of war had had no faith in the ability of their countrymen to manage an independent state worthy of the name. Looking around them, they saw internecine violence, bloodshed, and civil disorder verging on anarchy, especially after the death of Agrippa the First when the Sicarii and their ilk came to the fore. Nor were the established institutions of the society, especially the High Priesthood and its hangers-on, calculated to inspire much confidence.

That there might have been a fourth grouping among the Pharisees at the time, who went still further and preached submission to Rome on religio-theological grounds — as did Josephus after he went over to the enemy — seems highly unlikely. The doctrine that Rome ruled the world because Providence willed it so, and that the Holy One had forbidden Israel to throw off the yoke until the coming of the millennium — these ideas belong to a later age.[16] True, Josephus

16 Av. Zar. 18a; Ket. 111a; Cant. R. II:18.

taught that Fate was on the side of the Romans — but that was after he himself had cast in his lot with them; and he was scarcely a spokesman for the Pharisaic point of view.

It would be even more far-fetched to suppose that there were any Pharisees at all who shared Josephus' awe of Roman grandeur, or his admiration for her *oeuvre civilisatrice*, to the extent of seeking shelter under her wings. The supposition is ruled out by everything we know about the world of the Sages — and of the Jewish people as a whole — both before the Destruction and after it.

As for Rabban Johanan ben Zakkai, he can certainly *not* be placed among the Zealots. But we cannot be sure that he belonged to the Peace Party either. The mere fact that he made a "separate peace" so to speak, does not prove that he had been a non-resister from the beginning. After all, there were many prominent people in the spring of 68 C.E. who chose to abandon the struggle because they found conditions within the walls intolerable. The Zealots had seized power from the legitimate government of the Sanhedrin (winter 67–68), and the extremists among them had taken to murdering their opponents. Jerusalem, as well as the country at large, was filled with bloodshed. No wonder this civil war caused many people to despair of holding out against the Romans.

The real story of Rabban Johanan ben Zakkai's exit from Jerusalem is hard to reconstruct, because the sources contradict one another. One version has him trying right at the start to persuade the Jerusalemites to stop the fighting and accept Roman rule. The idea seems to have been that the promises of the Roman commander could be relied on, and Jerusalem and the Temple could be saved, and Judaea restored to its semi-autonomous status quo.

Another source, however, describes Rabban Johanan as deciding to go out to the Romans only when it had become clear that the Zealots were adopting desperate and unrealistic tactics, and were bringing certain defeat down upon themselves. On this reading, Rabban Johanan would have to be counted with the middle party, the moderates; even though, unlike Rabban Simeon ben Gamaliel, he had not taken an active part in leading the revolt and even though he was one of the first to take the overt step of submitting to the Romans.

In the absence of any hard evidence on this question, we turn to a statement of Rabban Johanan's that throws at least a faint light on his attitude at the outset of hostilities. The passage occurs in two distinct sources:[17]

> Rabban Johanan ben Zakkai used to say:
> Do not rush to knock down heathen altars; you may have to rebuild them better than they were. What will you have gained if you knock down one of stone and are then forced to rebuild one of bricks?...

Apparently, this remark of his was made at the outset of the war, when the rebels had scored their first successes against Cestius Gallus. As Josephus reports, the Jews destroyed temples and altars in nearby cities that had heathen populations, especially in Galilee.[18] It would seem, then, that just when passions ran highest, Rabban Johanan warned against such actions, and called for moderation. Does the text also imply that, even at that early stage, Rabban Johanan saw that defeat was likely? If so, we would be justified in concluding that he was an out-and-out member of the peace party.

It is not, however, an unassailable conclusion. The remark may have been made after the event, and have been based on hindsight. It would then be incidental evidence that the Jews were indeed compelled to restore heathen temples they had wrecked.

Either way, what does emerge is that Rabban Johanan was a clear-eyed realist, who did not hesitate to warn his countrymen against the more feverish forms of patriotic passion. Another remark attributed to him illustrates the same attitude:

> If you have a seedling in hand, and are on the point of planting it, and someone comes to tell you that the Messiah has arrived, finish your planting first, (and then go to greet him).[19]

17 Midrash Tannaim, ed. Hoffman, p. 58; and ARN ed. Schechter, Version B, p. 66.

18 Compare what happened to the palace in Tiberias belonging to the family of Herod Antipas. It was sacked on account of its statuary representing living creatures. Josephus himself had intended to lead this action, but found it had already been carried out by Jesus ben Saffia, leader of the boatmen and other poor folk who had risen in rebellion (*Life:* 12 (66)).

19 ARN, version B, ch. 31, ed. Schechter, p. 67.

Going to Yavneh

After this attempt to fathom the political outlook of Rabban Johanan ben Zakkai, we return to the question: "What was the origin of Yavneh?"

The accepted view is that Rabban Johanan went to the enemy commander, whether Vespasian or Titus, with the express purpose of asking for the right to establish a center of Jewish autonomy in Yavneh along the lines of the great Sanhedrin as we know it. According to this tradition, the Roman officially sanctions the plan, whereupon Rabban Johanan proceeds to reorganize the High Court of Israel (that had formerly had its seat in Jerusalem) in the new location, albeit with jurisdiction somewhat reduced — exactly the situation we find existing a generation or two later.

There are two serious difficulties with this scenario. First, what made Rabban Johanan pick on Yavneh, of all places? It was not, after all, a center of Jewish population. For at least a generation before the Destruction, the majority of its people had been non-Jews. The suggestion put forward by a number of historians, to the effect that the place had already become the locus of an important Beth Din, and the home of several great scholars has no evidence at all to support it.

Second, the tradition that Rabban Johanan asked the Roman commander for "Yavneh and its Sages" — i.e. for the establishment of the Sanhedrin in that place — that tradition is mentioned in only one of the several sources that describe the famous encounter, namely in the *Babylonian Talmud,* which also adds that Rabban Johanan asked that "the dynasty of Rabban Gamaliel" be spared.[20] On these important matters the other sources are silent. Aboth de Rabbi Nathan, in both versions, speaks only of a request to instruct disciples, conduct regular worship, and the like — modest petitions indeed.[21] Even more striking is the fact that one account makes no mention at all of Yavneh. On the contrary, we are told that Rabban Johanan was incarcerated because he made so bold as to ask for

20 Git. 56a-b.
21 Version A, ch. 4, Schechter, p. 23; Goldin, p. 36.
    Version B, ch. 6, Schechter, p. 19.

the lives of the people who had survived the slaughter that followed the capture of Jerusalem.[22]

In short, a careful examination of what we know about the spring of 68 C.E. when Vespasian began his siege of Jerusalem, and what we know about the final months of the siege under Titus in the summer of 70 C.E., inclines us to reject the standard account, and to conclude instead that Rabban Johanan did not *choose* Yavneh: he was *directed* there by the Romans.

Yavneh is mentioned among those cities such as Ashdod and Lydda, as well as a number of locations on the east bank, which served the conquerors as places of *detention* for prominent citizens and groups of Jews who turned themselves in to the Romans during the war. Josephus tells us that Vespasian used these cities for that purpose in the spring of 68.[23] A little more than two years later we find Titus using Gophna as a place of protective custody for Jerusalemites who surrendered to him.[24]

Here, then, is evidence for the Roman practice of restricting the freedom even of people who accepted their authority. The conquerors kept them under surveillance. In this respect, Rabban Johanan was no different from anybody else. He too was detained, and sent to the half-gentile city of Yavneh which had already made its peace with Vespasian, and which was near the Greek-speaking "cities of the sea" — the coastal towns of Ashkelon and Gaza.[25]

Indeed, everything we know about the practices and policies of the Romans during their war with the Jews supports the conclusion that, at that juncture in the struggle, Rabban Johanan could scarcely have been granted so important a concession as the right to establish a new national center, even if only a "spiritual" one. Hence, if we

22 Lam. R. *(Ekhah Rabbah)* I:32. For the source texts, and a detailed comparison of them, see Alon, JJCW, pp. 296 ff.
23 JW, IV:8:1 (444); and IV:3:2 (130).
24 JW, VI:2:2–3 (115).
25 [Urbach rejects Alon's reconstruction of the origin of Yavneh as summarized in the foregoing and the following paragraphs, and as developed more fully in the essay in JJCW — almost in toto. See Urbach's review in *Behinot,* quoted earlier. Compare also his previously cited article in *Proceedings of the Israel Academy*: "He chose Yavne where there was a Beth Din (M. Sanh. XI:4) that was apparently under the administration of the sons of Bathyra, who were also acceptable to the Romans."]

give credence to that tradition which has him asking only for permission "to instruct his disciples," we will be dealing merely with an effort by Rabban Johanan to ameliorate the terms under which he was to be detained, so that he and his personal entourage might be permitted to observe their religion and to engage in the study of the Torah. On this hypothesis, we might say that since the Romans had good reason to regard Rabban Johanan as a prominent and influential individual who had been speaking up for compromise and accommodation, they would naturally have been inclined to grant his request, permitting him "to perform the mitzvot and to study the Torah."

As we have already noted, the version given by Lamentations Rabbah makes no mention at all of a bid for Yavneh. That silence, taken with the considerations mentioned above, points to the conclusion that the revived Sanhedrin seated in Yavneh did not come into being until later on, when the tensions of war-time had passed, and the severity of Roman rule had eased up a bit. What does seem probable is that the presence of Rabban Johanan, no doubt along with other important personages, attracted a number of Sages to Yavneh in the post-war period, especially from among those who had adhered to the "Peace Party" and were thus not under Roman suspicion. In this gathering of scholars, Rabban Johanan would naturally have emerged as the leader, given the eminence and authority that had been his in pre-war times. The Romans would no doubt have looked on with a tolerant eye, not interfering even when his newly founded academy grew in size and prestige, and began to function as a sort of informal "Great Beth Din" — *without,* however, any official status. So that when Rabban Johanan assumed for himself and his "court" authority in such *religious* matters as proclaiming the calendar of New Moons and Festivals — something formerly under the jurisdiction of the Sanhedrin in Jerusalem — the Romans did not intervene.[26]

Thus Rabban Johanan ben Zakkai gradually became the nation's

26 The conversations (reported in Bekh. 5a) between Rabban Johanan and the commander Controcos are no evidence that Rabban Johanan or his lawcourt had some official status. At best, they indicate the absence of government interference. Besides, these encounters are probably legendary.

leader in matters of religion, with his Beth Din taking over some — though by no means all — of the functions of the Great Sanhedrin that had formerly sat in Jerusalem, namely, those functions that regulated the public aspects of religious life.

There is no mention in our sources of any politico-legal status attaching to the Beth Din of Yavneh during the days of Rabban Johanan ben Zakkai. As we shall see, that Beth Din did not function as the central spiritual-national institution of leadership for Jewry, neither in the way in which the Jerusalem Sanhedrin *had* done before the Destruction, nor in the way in which the Sanhedrin of Yavneh *would* do later on. On the other hand, we must give Rabban Johanan, together with his colleagues, the credit for laying the foundations of what was to become the Sanhedrin reborn. The scope of his activities was limited both by external political factors and by internal social conditions in the years immediately following the war. What constitutes his historic greatness is the fact that he took the first steps. The time was one of transition; it cried out for new beginnings, and it found its leader in him.

Taking the Lead

We turn now to the second question posed at the beginning of this chapter. What position did Rabban Johanan occupy in the eyes of the public during his Yavneh days? Was he universally regarded as the spokesman of the people? Was his leadership widely accepted?

This question has been much debated by scholars, usually under the formulation: "Did Rabban Johanan serve as the *Nasi*?". Before we go any further, let it be understood that the question before us is not the technical one — that is, whether or not he bore the *title* of *Nasi*. The title itself may not yet have come into use. To be sure, tannaitic tradition explicitly dates the office back more than two centuries before the Destruction. According to the Mishnah, the *zugot* were a duumvirate of Nasi and Ab Beth Din.[27] At very least, the tradition assumes that Hillel the Elder and Rabban Gamaliel the Elder occupied the office of *Nasi*. Be that as it may, the question here is not about title, but about function. Did Rabban Johanan

---

27 Hag. II:2; also Tos. ibid. II:8 (Zuck. p. 235). See Bavli and Yerushalmi *ad loc.*

perform in some degree, however small, those duties which characterize the Patriarchate after him; that is, was he head of the Sanhedrin and leader of the nation?

The answer would seem to be a resounding yes. First of all there is the name by which he is known. "Rabban" — Our Rabbi — is an honorific that was never applied to anyone who was not a *Nasi*. In its Hebrew (rather than Aramaic) form, it comes out as *"Rabbenu"*, an appellation bestowed only on Rabbi Judah, editor of the Mishnah — "The Patriarch" par excellence. Further testimony is offered by Sherira Gaon, who states in his *Epistle* that the title goes with the office.[28]

Secondly, the enactment of certain *taqanot* is attributed to Rabban Johanan. Such authoritative action is ascribed by the tradition only to Patriarchs, or (before the Patriarchate) to whoever stood for the highest national instance at the time — to the *Zugot*, to High Priests (like Johanan the High Priest in the tractates Ma'aser Sheni and Sotah) or to Ezra and the "Great Assembly." (The exceptions are confined to local ordinances, or to such matters as the formulary texts of those legal documents known as *sheṭarot;* they have no bearing on the present argument.) What is more, the nature of some of the *taqanot* ascribed to Rabban Johanan — dealing with such matters as fixing the date of Rosh Hashanah — is such that they could only have been enacted by the leader of the High Court.

But quite apart from the evidence we have cited, there is inherent reason for Rabban Johanan to have assumed important responsibilities. After all, in the years before the Destruction he had served alongside Rabban Simeon ben Gamaliel in the highest echelon of national leadership, as we have shown above. In sum, everything points to the conclusion that Rabban Johanan stepped into the breach and took on the mantle during that time when the dynasty of Hillel was in eclipse, because it had become *non grata* to the Romans.

It seems, however, that Rabban Johanan's leadership in the emergency was not universally accepted. There were elements in the country that opposed him.

Foremost among these were the learned priests who had held

---

28 *Iggeret,* ed. Levin, appendix, p. 125 and p. 128.

important positions in the Temple. Their absence from the Academy of Yavneh under Rabban Johanan is conspicuous. No mention is made, for example, of Rabbi Sadoq or of his son Rabbi Eleazar, two priests who had been active members of Rabban Gamaliel's Beth Din, and personally very close to him. There is a similar silence about Rabbi Simeon son of the Deputy High Priest, a man frequently quoted on halakhic matters by Rabban Simeon ben Gamaliel.

A plausible explanation for the non-participation of these important *kohanim* in the endeavor at Yavneh might be that they refused to accept the leadership of Rabban Johanan. Perhaps they felt that they themselves ought to have been put in charge. After all, in pre-Destruction times it was taken for granted that the priests had first claim on public office. They had been an important and decisive element in the Sanhedrin, and they had played a major role in the government of national union during the early years of the war, after the overthrow of Gallus. Even in the post-Destruction years, the traditional status of the priests still maintained a hold over considerable segments of the people; nor did the *kohanim* themselves hesitate to demand their age-old privileges.

This view of the relationship between Rabban Johanan ben Zakkai and the priesthood, as a state of tension punctuated by occasional clashes, may be buttressed by certain citations from the Mishnah.[29] In the first of these:

> Rabbi Judah said that Ben Bukhri testified at Yavneh, that a priest who paid the shekel [*Temple-tax, from which he was exempt*] did not thereby commit a sin. Said Rabban Johanan ben Zakkai to him: On the contrary, any priest who did not pay the shekel was guilty of a sin. The only thing is, the priests interpret Scripture to their own advantage. The verse (Lev. VI: 16) 'Every meal-offering of the priest shall be wholly burned, it shall not be eaten' they expound as follows: If the Omer, and the Two Loaves and the Shewbread are ours [*i.e. paid for in part by our shekel*] how can they be eaten? [*Ergo, no tax.*]

In the second passage, Rabban Gamaliel is quoted to the effect

29 Sheq. I:4; Eduy. VIII:3.

that Rabban Johanan made a ruling contrary to kohanic practice. The case involves the widow of a priest, herself the daughter of a priestly family whose status was dubious. Is she eligible to marry another *kohen?* Said Rabban Johanan: "Ad hoc courts to rule on such matters should not be commissioned ... For the priests accept the rulings of such courts only when it suits them — i.e. only when they rule against the applicant."

What was at issue here can best be understood in the light of a tradition which is quoted in a number of places: [30]

> From the day that the Temple was destroyed, the *kohanim* have become very particular about themselves ... which is to say, they have become very fastidious about the purity of their priestly lineage, and very meticulous about the ritual purity of the food they eat.

Further on in the same chapter of Eduyot (Mishnah 7), we find Rabbi Joshua ben Hananiah reporting in the name of Rabban Johanan ben Zakkai that there were certain priestly families — apparently in pre-Destruction times — who imposed their will in the matter of priestly status, deciding which families belonged and which did not. "It is the like of these that Elijah will come to declare unclean or clean, to decide who is a *kohen* and who is not."

The same reaction to priestly hauteur may lie behind the tradition that Rabbi Hananiah ben Antigonos "held the Sages in contempt" (apparently in matters of ritual purity). He equated them with the *'am ha'aretz*, who is not trusted in such matters. We also have a citation from Rabbi Jose: [31]

> From the day that the Temple was destroyed, the *kohanim* have become very particular about themselves, and they do not entrust matters of ritual purity to the average person. [32]

Evidence of a state of tension between Rabban Johanan and the priests may also be adduced from the following episode, again dealing with the subject of ritual purity. [33]

30 See Qid. 30b, where the cross-references are listed.
31 Bekh. 30b.
32 Not mentioned in the corresponding passage in *Pesiqta d'Rav Kahana*. See ed. Buber, 12:2.
33 *ARN*, ed. Schechter, p. 56, A:12 and B:27. [Goldin, p. 71.] A variant of

"There was a certain man in Beth Ramah (ARN/B reads: a certain kohen in Ramath Beth Anath) who was said to preen himself on the strictness of his religious observance. Rabban Johanan ben Zakkai sent one of his disciples (version B has: Rabbi Joshua went) to investigate. Said the man: I am an important priest, and I eat *terumah* only in a state of ritual purity.... Said the disciple: you have never eaten pure *terumah* in your whole life."

(It is, of course, possible that this episode goes back to pre-Destruction times.)

There can be little doubt that this tendency of the priests to hold themselves apart was not directed solely at the person of Rabban Johanan. Basically it derived from the unique status that had been theirs, and from their assumption that authority and position still belonged to them. And yet this attitude of theirs seems to have vanished by the time of Rabban Gamaliel, not much more than a decade later. It would appear that the *kohanim* then placed themselves under the authority and leadership of Rabban Gamaliel, after having refused to accept that of Rabban Johanan ben Zakkai.

But the priests were not the only dissenters. A considerable number of Sages, prominent both before the Destruction and after, seem not to have participated in Rabban Johanan's Beth-Din-cum-Academy. Among them were such important personages as Rabbi Nehunya ben Haqaneh. This is all the more striking because he is specifically mentioned[34] as a disciple of Rabban Johanan; but that was probably before the Destruction. There is even a hint that Rabbi Nehunya settled in Emmaus rather than in Yavneh.[35] Both he and Rabbi Nahum of Gimzo fathered trends in *midrash halakha,* and both were teachers of Rabbi Ishmael and Rabbi Akiba; yet neither of them appears at Yavneh.

Others conspicuous by their absence were Rabbi Tarfon, Rabbi Dosa ben Hyrcanos (later to emerge as an ally of Rabban Gamaliel in his dispute with Rabbi Joshua ben Hanania), Nahum Ha-Madi,

---

this can be found in Midrash Hagadol to Levit. XI:35, ed. Rabinowitz, p. 241.

34 B.B. 10b.

35 Midrash Tannaim, ed. Hoffman, p. 175.

and many others. Then there is Rabbi Judah ben Baba (Abba?), who does show up in Yavneh later, when Rabban Gamaliel was in charge,[36] as does Yaqim ben Hadar (or Hadir)[37] and Hizqia, father of 'Aqash.[38] While we have no positive evidence to account for the absence of all these Sages from the Yavneh of Rabban Johanan ben Zakkai, we can reasonably conjecture that many of them opposed his leadership because they disagreed with his politics, and especially with his action in submitting to the Romans when he did.[39]

What is more, it looks as though some of Rabban Johanan's best disciples turned away from him. There is no mention of Rabbi Jose Hakohen at Yavneh until the time of Rabban Gamaliel.[40] Rabbi Simeon ben Nathanel, son-in-law of Rabban Gamaliel the Elder, also goes unmentioned, although perhaps he had died in the meantime. But what shall we say of Rabbi Eleazar ben Arakh, the favorite student of Rabban Johanan?[41] There is an explicit, if cryptic, tradition that he went off "to a place of pleasant waters" and "forgot his Torah." According to Aboth de Rabbi Nathan,[42] Rabbi Eleazar ben Arakh separated from his master on leaving Jerusalem, and went to Emmaus. That city was relatively undamaged during the War of the Destruction, for it had been taken by the Romans at the very beginning of their campaign. There is a reference in Midrash Tannaim to "Rabbi Nehunya ben Haqaneh of Emmaus."[43] Indeed, there are grounds for believing that Rabbi Nehunya founded an academy of sorts in that place. As for Rabbi Eleazar ben Arakh, it is related of him that "he often gave advice, and it turned out well."[44] He must therefore be accounted a "man of counsel," in some respects a public figure, like Rabbi Joshua ben

36 Eduy. VI:1.
37 Ibid. VII:5.
38 Bekh. 38a.
39 Büchler: *"Die Priester* etc.", p. 18; also M. Guttman (in his *Mafteaḥ haTalmud*) *"Ereẓ Yisrael baMishnah uvaTalmud,"* p. 98.
40 R.H. 17b.
41 Av. II:8–9.
42 Ed. Schechter, p. 59, version A, end chap. 14 [Goldin, p. 72]; version B, chap. 29.
43 Ed. Hoffman, p. 175.
44 Midrash Tehillim, I:19.

Hananiah, who is also spoken of later as "a man of counsel." In sum, it is reasonable to suppose that Rabbi Eleazar ben Arakh, unlike his fellow-disciples Rabbi Eliezer and Rabbi Joshua, refused to go along with their teacher's act of submission to the Romans; that he too went off and started his own academy; and was thereby reputed to have "forgotten his learning."

The next problem to be examined is the relationship between Rabban Johanan ben Zakkai and Rabban Gamaliel. A question immediately arises: why did not Rabban Gamaliel become the head right after the war? He was, after all, the son of Rabban Simeon "the *Nasi*," and should have been the successor in what had become a hereditary leadership.

Scholars have been pondering this question for a long time. An explanation commonly offered is that Rabban Gamaliel had not yet come of age at the time of the Destruction; hence, Rabban Johanan served as a sort of regent pro tem for the legitimate heir to the Patriarchate. However, it can be stated with some certainty that Rabban Gamaliel was an adult at the time in question. So we are forced to conclude that he was kept out of office by the Roman government. The tradition in Ta'anith 29a has Rabban Gamaliel being sought by the Romans; they may actually have intended to execute him. And the story in Gittin 56b, about the "dynasty of Rabban Gamaliel" preserves an echo of the belief that Rabban Gamaliel was in trouble with the Romans, and needed somebody to intercede on his behalf.

Furthermore, this view is made the more plausible by the tradition that his father, Rabban Simeon ben Gamaliel, was killed by the Romans at the time of the Destruction — a tradition, to be sure, of uncertain reliability; yet its core seems to have a solid basis. (See the relevant passage in the Epistle of Sherira Gaon). Nor is there anything in the writings of Josephus that does not square with this view. In any case, it is clear that for a long time Rabban Simeon ben Gamaliel was the leader of the embattled people, and that he never surrendered to the Romans. This makes it logical that the Romans would have sought to wipe out his heirs and descendants.[45] But whether or not that is so, they certainly kept the family of the *Nasi* from positions of leadership.

45 Reported in Ta'anith 29a.

This reading of the situation, taken together with the disagreement in political outlook between Rabban Simeon ben Gamaliel and Rabban Johanan ben Zakkai during the war, makes it highly unlikely that the two men worked together at Yavneh in intimate and friendly partnership. Add to this the fact that we have no record of Rabban Gamaliel participating in the academy of Rabban Johanan at Yavneh, except for one questionable source that lists the former among the disciples of the latter — questionable because the name is omitted from other versions of the same tradition![46]

Another point: two distinct sources tell us that Rabban Johanan had a Beth-Din at Beror-Hayyil.[47] We are forced to conclude that this was after the Destruction. The assumption is therefore inescapable that Rabban Johanan, towards the end of his life, left Yavneh and established himself in Beror-Hayyil, a small town nearby. This makes it seem likely that Rabban Gamaliel settled in Yavneh while Rabban Johanan was still alive — in other words, he displaced Rabban Johanan from the headship.

Of course it is possible to describe the relationship between the two men as a sort of idyll, with Rabban Johanan graciously stepping aside, and turning the leadership over to a man whose rightful patrimony it was.[48] But there is nothing in the evidence that forces us to accept this rather naive scenario. It is just as reasonable — perhaps more reasonable — to suppose that as soon as Rabban Gamaliel

46 B.B. 10b has Rabban Gamaliel among the disciples of Rabban Johanan; Pesiqta d'Rav Kahana 12:2 does not.

47 Sanh. 32b: "Seek out a fine Beth Din ... like that of Rabban Johanan b. Zakkai at Beror-Hayyil." Sifre Deut. 145 reads (ed. Finkelstein, p. 200) "Seek a Beth Din of fine judgment, like that of Rabban Johanan b. Zakkai, and that of Rabbi Eliezer." The second source is Tos. Maas. II:1 (Zuck. 82); also Yer. Ma'as. II:49b: "Rabbi Joshua went to see Rabban Johanan ben Zakkai in Beror-Hayyil."

48 The view of Wilhelm Bacher: *Agada der Tannaiten*, I, p. 74, and of Joseph Derenbourg: *Essai sur l'histoire et la géographie de la Palestine d'après le Talmud, etc.* Paris, 1867, I pp. 306 ff. [Dissent from the views of Bacher and Derenbourg, as well as from the analysis proposed by Alon, is expressed by Urbach in the paper previously cited from the 1966 Proceedings of the Israel Academy: "We do not know when Rabban Gamaliel attained leadership at Yavneh .... There is no foundation for the various conjectures advanced on this subject, be it the theory of Bacher and Derenbourg ... or that of Allon."]

found it safe to show himself in public, and to lay claim to his hereditary right of leadership, support rallied to him, and Rabban Johanan had to give up the office and move elsewhere, whether he liked it or not.

To be sure, the Mishnah in Eduyoth VIII:3 has Rabban Gamaliel citing a halakhic decree of Rabban Johanan — and acting on it. What is more, the decree seems to have been issued by Rabban Johanan in his capacity as President of the High Court, so apparently Rabban Gamaliel *did* recognize the legitimacy of such acts. But the facts in this case are not altogether clear; and besides, the case does not affect our hypothesis. We know more than one instance of Rabban Gamaliel's readiness to bow to rulings he had disputed, and to compromise with individuals with whom he had disagreed, when peace or the public interest were at stake. An outstanding example is his conduct when the majority voted him down, and put Rabbi Eleazar ben Azariah in the chair in his stead.[49]

Making Taqanot

Before we go on to consider the public acts of Rabban Johanan ben Zakkai at Yavneh, we must keep a number of points in mind. First, there is the constant difficulty of drawing conclusions from the absence of evidence (the well-known *argumentum e silentio* — in Talmudic legal parlance: "'We have not seen' is no proof at all") unless the argument is supported by some additional considerations. In the matter under discussion we find ourselves on this kind of thin ice, and our conclusions will have to be quite tentative.

Second, the tradition regarding Rabban Johanan's *taqanot* is rather blurred, and the sources do not always agree among themselves as to what should be attributed to him. Third, the very substance of some of these enactments is open to question, making it impossible to determine their purpose, or their importance.

Lastly, there are a number of *taqanot* which the tradition tells us were issued at Yavneh, without specifying just when. I prefer to postdate such doubtful cases to the period of Rabban Gamaliel, rather than to assign them to the time of Rabban Johanan ben Zakkai, as some historians tend to do.

49 Ber. 27b-28a; Yer. ibid. IV:7c-7d.

We return to our major theme — the achievements of Rabban Johanan. Of these, the greatest is undoubtedly the act itself of founding the Academy at Yavneh, along with the Beth Din that took over some of the functions of the defunct Sanhedrin, acting as its successor in the capacity of High Court. This achievement, limited though it was when compared to the importance that Yavneh was to achieve under Rabban Gamaliel, is nevertheless usually seen, and with every justification, as a historic breakthrough. It was a deed that completed the spadework and laid the foundations for what was to become the structure of central leadership for the entire Jewish people. And when we think of the adverse conditions under which Rabban Johanan ben Zakkai had to work, conditions both external and internal — the inimical Roman administration, the shattered morale and social disarray among his own people, the frightful economic situation — then we realize why he must be regarded as the first to have lifted the Jewish people up out of its ruins, and why his place in history is secure. It was his goal in founding the Academy at Yavneh to preserve the religio-spiritual basis of the national life, that is, the study of Torah; so that in the days ahead, it would be possible to revive the national-social life as well. At that difficult hour, when the people stood in grave danger of despair and extinction, clearly the most important task was to resuscitate the study of Torah. It was a deed equivalent to tying up the nation's vital nerve after it had been severed, or very nearly severed, so that it could continue not only to function, but even to develop.

The tradition does not tell us a single thing about Rabban Johanan's Academy at Yavneh, so that we do not really know how instruction was given there, or which branches of Torah-learning were cultivated. But we can be sure that Rabban Johanan put all the effort he could into the instructional aspects of his venture, because we do have evidence of his particular concern that the oral Torah might be forgotten.[50] (The reference is, of course, to the oral Torah as taught by the Pharisees). This fear of his was obviously a result of what he saw going on all around him after the Destruction. Besides, there is one source, albeit a late one, that speaks of his involvement with questions of spiritual-scholarly manpower — which

50 Mishnah Sot. V:2.

means that he was concerned about the training of duly ordained scholars to take care of the needs of the plain people.[51]

Now to the other aspect of Rabban Johanan's venture at Yavneh — the Beth Din that he founded there, and his acts as its President.[52] In this connection, the only evidence that the tradition has preserved for us deals with certain questions of religious observance, especially the calendar of Festivals and New Moons. All those other important matters that were dealt with later on by the High Court at Yavneh under Rabban Gamaliel, and which will be discussed in chapter 12, do not seem to have come up in the days of Rabban Johanan. In fact, the Beth Din in Rabban Johanan's Yavneh seems not to have dealt at all with any matters of civil law *(dinei mammonot)* nor to have imposed any sanctions on law-breakers.[53] It appears highly likely (as Professor Chayes has pointed out)[54] that in those days the High Court was barred from dealing with actual law-cases, because the Romans had taken away the judicial autonomy of the Jews, and had appointed their own courts and judges. Even though it is safe to assume that here and there, in matters of no great moment, the Romans did not prevent people in local communities from settling disputes among themselves in accordance with their own customs,[55] nevertheless the old jurisdiction of the Central Court, with its power not only to decide cases but also to legislate (for it was the highest national body) — all that was abolished by the post-war occupation. The same applies *a fortiori* to the disciplinary powers the Court had once exercised.

Concerning the actions taken by Rabban Johanan and his court, the traditions we can rely on best are those in the Mishnah (Rosh Hashanah IV: 1–4, Sukkah III: 12). Except for one passage, all these sources deal with the laws of Rosh Hashanah, especially with the method by which the New Moon of Tishri is determined. We know

---

51 Yer. Sanh. I: 18a.
52 No sharp distinction is to be made between the Great Academy and the Beth Din. In actual practice, the important scholars in the Academy were also the members of the court.
53 We do find rulings by Rabban Johanan in the area of property law (Ket. XIII: 1–2; and B.B. 89b). However, even if we were sure that these dicta are post-Destruction, they remain purely theoretical law.
54 REJ 39, pp. 39–40.
55 This explains Rabban Johanan's Beth Din at Beror Hayyil.

that all through amoraic times, and earlier in the tannaitic age, going back to the period before the Destruction, all New Moons were fixed by direct observation. On the twenty-ninth of each month an ad hoc tribunal sat awaiting the appearance of eye-witnesses — *edei ha-hodesh* — who would testify at formal proceedings that they had seen the crescent new moon, whereupon the court would make proclamation. According to the Geonim, this way of doing things persisted up to the year 670 of the Seleucid Era (359 C.E.) when the Patriarch Hillel IV finally made the mathematics of the calendar available to all.

It should be noted in passing that some scholars doubt the authenticity of this tradition. They argue that the *luah* as we know it was promulgated at a much later date; and there are grounds for such an opinion. But one thing is clear: no matter how long the calculation of the lunar-solar calendar had been known to the experts, and no matter how late in history that knowledge was made public, the ritual of taking eyewitness testimony continued long after the time of Hillel IV.

Naturally, it was the High Court in Jerusalem that originally had control of the calendar.[56] It was up to them to decide whether the month just ending would have twenty-nine days or thirty, depending ostensibly on when the witnesses appeared. It was their prerogative to declare a leap-year if spring was late in arriving. Their decision concerning the New Moon was notified to the nearby communities — in Syria and Mesopotamia — by messengers and by signal fires. However, it is certain that all this activity was, at least after the time of Rabban Gamaliel, strictly *pro forma,* because the authorities in charge were quite capable of reckoning the date in advance. Still, there was an understandable desire to hold on to traditional procedures of such solemnity, especially when they were so striking a symbol of the authority of the High Court.

Both the Geonim and the early Karaites report that Rabban Gamaliel the Younger — of Yavneh — was the pioneer in calendrical calculation. In fact, the Mishnah itself attributes to him a knowledge

56 For the pre-Destruction period, see the citation from Rabbi Josiah in the Mekhilta, Bo, end of section 2, ed. Horovitz-Rabin, p. 9 (Lauterbach, p. 22). For the time of Rabban Gamaliel the Elder, see Mishnah R.H. I:7.

of "reckoning." [57] Not many generations later there are references to individuals known as "calculators" who determined dates. And tannaitic literature is not without mention of rules-of-thumb governing the sequence of plain years and leap-years, of full months and "defective" months — all this despite the fact that visual evidence was still required.

There can be no doubt that immediately after the Destruction this matter of fixing the New Moons, on which the dates of the Holy Days depended, became a problem of utmost urgency. After all, Jews in every country needed to know, so it was only to be expected that the highest level of Jewish leadership should tackle the question at the earliest possible moment. As a matter of fact, this turns out to be the main subject of the *taqanot* which our sources attribute to Rabban Johanan ben Zakkai.

In this area there is a distinction to be made. Some of these pronouncements involved no halakhic innovations, and had no particular social significance, but simply took realistic account of the new situation brought about by the Destruction of the Temple. One example concerns the time of day when the witnesses to the appearance of the Rosh Hashanah new moon showed up. There had previously been a ruling that if they failed to appear by the hour of *Minhah* their testimony was not to be taken until the following day — "because one time the witnesses were slow to put in an appearance, and as a result, the Levites sang the wrong psalm!".[58] Obviously, with the Temple gone and the Levitical choir disbanded, the reason for the deadline had disappeared, and the testimony was acceptable all day long. (There is, to be sure, a tannaitic source according to which the taqanah in question predates Rabban Johanan.)[59]

In the class of new rulings which were simply the consequence of changed conditions, we can include the ordinance which forbade the eating of new grain for the entire duration of "Waving Day" — the 16th of Nisan.[60] In Temple times the prohibition had lapsed at whatever time the Omer was offered; but the offering was now in abeyance. (Here again, there is an opinion — Rabbi Judah's — that

57 R.H. II:8.
58 Ibid. IV:4.
59 See Tos. R.H. IV:3 (Zuck. p. 212).
60 See Levit XXIII:14.

no *taqanah* is involved, since the scripture itself can be so interpreted.)[61]

The same holds good for an enactment ascribed by the Talmud to Rabban Johanan, according to which the calendar messengers to Syria were despatched even on the Sabbath when it was a question of proclaiming the New Moon of Nisan or of Tishri, since the dates of imminent Holy Days depended on this information. Previously, when the Temple had stood, this need to notify had overridden the prohibition against travel on the Sabbath not just twice a year, but every single month, on account of the schedule of sacrifices. But now that the sacrificial system was gone, there was no further need to violate the Sabbath.[62]

A matter of greater importance, also connected with Rosh Hashanah, involves the sounding of the shofar on Rosh Hashanah when it coincides with the Sabbath. The previous rule had been that when such a conjuncture took place, the shofar was sounded in the Temple, though of course nowhere else. Now Rabban Johanan ordained that when the days coincided, the shofar was to be sounded in Yavneh — although still nowhere else.[63]

There are modern scholars who have drawn far-reaching conclusions from this act. According to them, it signified the abolition of the special sanctity of Jerusalem, thus opening the door for a fundamental new concept in Judaism: holiness is no longer attached to a place. In their view, the loss of the Holy City and its Sanctuary might have crippled the people of Israel and the Jewish religion. But no; thanks to Rabban Johanan the holiness of the Temple was transferred to wherever the leadership of Judaism had its seat.

Insofar as it relies on the halakhah under discussion, this view is based on a hasty and superficial look at the sources. The practice of sounding the shofar in the Temple when Rosh Hashanah fell on the Sabbath was undoubtedly connected with a very ancient halakhah which interpreted the command to sound the shofar as confined to the Temple anyway — even when Rosh Hashanah fell on a weekday!

---

61 Sifra, Emor, XI:10. Also, R.H. 30b.
62 R.H. 21b. Note, however, that the Mishnah I:4 reports this *without* attribution to Rabban Johanan.
63 Mishnah, R.H. IV:1.

It can be shown that Diaspora Jews, at least in Egypt, did not sound the shofar at all for as long as the Temple stood.[64]

An examination of the literature reveals two divergent approaches to the use of the shofar. One view connects it with the sacrifices (hence the close association with *mussafin*); consequently, when the day fell on the Sabbath, the shofar was used only in the Temple. According to this reading, Rabban Johanan was doing something boldly innovative when he sounded the shofar in Yavneh.

There is, however, another view that connects the sounding of the shofar with the High Court (originally in Jerusalem) — that is to say, with the body responsible for determining and proclaiming the dates of New Moons and Festivals.[65] If we follow this view, the *taqanah* of Rabban Johanan becomes simply the recognition of a fait accompli. Since the judicial body that proclaims the New Year is now resident in Yavneh (or wherever) then that is the place to fulfil the commandment, and to sound the shofar even on the Sabbath. On this showing, Rabban Johanan did not take any revolutionary step at all; nor did he "supersede the sanctuary in Jerusalem." As a matter of fact, our sources indicate clearly that it was the second view that lay behind his decision to sound the shofar in Yavneh. (It should be mentioned that there is a third halakhic approach, which reads the Torah's command to sound the shofar as overriding the Sabbath everywhere, quite independently of the Beth Din that makes the proclamation; so that Yavneh would have no special significance in this context.)[66]

---

64 See Alon: *On Philo's Halakhah* in JJCW, p. 89 ff.

65 Like the sounding of the shofar on Yom Kippur of the Jubilee Year, clearly an official court act. Comp. Yerushalmi Rosh Hashanah IV:59b. See also Bavli ibid. 30a: "The Jubilee is on the same footing as the New Year with regard to blowing the shofar and to *berakhot*, only on the Jubilee they sounded the shofar on the Sabbath in every Beth Din, whether or not it was the one in which the New Moon had been proclaimed; and besides, every individual was supposed to sound the shofar. Whereas on the New Year, they sounded it only in the Beth Din which had proclaimed the New Moon, and individuals were not obliged to do the same."

66 "The sounding of the shofar on New Year and the Jubilee overrides the Sabbath outside the Sanctuary for every man and his household." Bavli, ibid.

But Rabban Johanan did not merely defer to accomplished facts. He also took active steps to fill the vacuum which the Destruction of the Temple had created in the religious life of the Jewish people. His *taqanah* requiring that the lulav ceremony[67] be observed in "the provinces" throughout the seven days of Sukkot as a "reminder of the Temple" is a prime example of his concern for keeping certain of the Temple rituals alive, even though the Temple itself was gone.[68] This transfer to the home and synagogue of what had once been an exclusively Temple ritual, served to maintain a basic characteristic of the Feast of Tabernacles. It was the first step in a whole series of ordinances introduced later (in the days of Rabban Gamaliel) with the intention of preserving as many as possible of the major elements of the Temple service.

It may well be that another ordinance which the Babylonian Gemara attributes, via a *baraitha,* to Rabban Johanan ben Zakkai, was also designed as a "remembrance of the Temple." It is a ruling that the *kohanim* must remove their sandals before ascending the rostrum to bless the people.[69] If we were to regard this as implying that Rabban Johanan was responsible for a more far-reaching step —the transfer of the Priestly Benediction to every congregation— it would become especially relevant to our discussion. Before the Destruction the ceremony had been limited to the Temple. Graetz accepts the implication,[70] explicitly contrary to the view of the Gemara in Sotah (40a). However, there really is nothing to support this conjecture.

Two other ordinances attributed to Rabban Johanan deal with Temple practices which the Destruction rendered inoperative. Later on, when we take up the period of Rabban Gamaliel, we will examine a whole gamut of rituals which had been of the essence of the collective religious life, and seemed doomed to extinction by the Destruction of the Temple. When we do, we shall see how the Sages

67 Lev. 23:40.
68 Mishnah R.H. IV:3: "Beforetime the lulav was carried seven days in the Temple, but in the provinces one day only..."
69 R.H. 31b. Also Sot. 40a.
70 *History,* Hebrew edition, vol. II, page 160, note 6. [Actually, this view should not be attributed to Graetz. It is an interpolation by his Hebrew translator S.P. Rabinowitz.]

coped with this very grave problem. But for the moment, let us confine ourselves to a single generalization: the Sages made every effort to keep alive as many Temple ceremonies as possible. They wanted to preserve the continuity of Jewish religious life. The Destruction had left a vaccum behind it; they strove to keep its effects from spreading.[71]

On the other hand, there were Temple practices which simply had to be abolished. There were no more altars, no more sacrifices. To leave such requirements on the books could only have led to feelings of deprivation and guilt, destructive of religious morale. The two *taqanot* we are about to consider belong to this category; and there are traditions ascribing both of them to Rabban Johanan ben Zakkai. Even if the traditions prove to be mistaken, they bespeak nevertheless the reputation that Rabban Johanan left behind.

The first of these *taqanot* concerns the fruit of a four-year-old vineyard (see Leviticus XIX:24). The Mishnah of Ma'aser Sheni (V:2) records the way things were done while the Temple stood:

> The fruit of a vineyard in its fourth year was brought up to Jerusalem from a distance of one day's journey in any direction. And how far did this extend? From Elath[71a] in the south, Aqrabah to the north, Lydda to the west and the Jordan to the east.

The tradition explains that the reason for this requirement (which excludes the use of redemption money) was "to enrich (or decorate) the markets of Jerusalem with fruit." Now let us quote the Gemara:[72]

> Rabbi Eliezer had a vine in its fourth year east of Lydda, near Kefar Tabi (after the Destruction). He had a mind to declare it free to the poor, but his disciples said to him: Rabbi, your colleagues have already taken a vote on it, and declared it permitted, —

permitted, that is, to redeem the fruit, and not have to take it as is to

71 They had an additional motive: to emphasize their conviction that the situation was only temporary. "Speedily will the *Bet Hamiqdash* be rebuilt." (R.H. 30a).
71a [Location uncertain.]
72 R.H. 31b; Bez. 5a–b.

Jerusalem. Apparently, then, the halakhah quoted above from the Mishnah was declared null after the Destruction. There was no longer any point in bringing the actual fruits to Jerusalem. There were no more markets to enrich, no streets to decorate.

In the Talmudic context where this occurs, Rav Papa (5th century) attributes the nullification to Rabban Johanan ben Zakkai. But surely he is mistaken. The Talmud itself implies as much when it queries: how could the disciples of Rabbi Eliezer have referred to Rabban Johanan, their master's teacher, as his "colleague?" And as a matter of fact, the Tosefta puts the whole episode into clearer perspective.

> After the Destruction of the Temple, the First Beth Din said nothing on the subject (of fourth-year fruits); then the Latter Beth Din decreed that they be redeemed outside the walls. There was a case involving Rabbi Eliezer, who had a vineyard east of Lydda, alongside Kefar Tabi, which he did not want to redeem. Whereupon his disciple said to him: Now that they have decreed, you will have to redeem it. So Rabbi Eliezer had the grapes harvested, and he redeemed them.[73]

In this passage, the "First Beth Din" is almost certainly that of Rabban Johanan ben Zakkai, and the "Latter Beth Din" — Rabban Gamaliel's. An additional reason for post-dating the episode is that it comes from a time when Rabbi Eliezer already has disciples of his own.

True, the Mishnah in Ma'aser Sheni makes it clear that this *taqanah* permitting redemption of fourth-year fruits outside Jerusalem was issued before the Destruction. On the other hand, it is Rabbi Jose, author of the Seder Olam, a man with a talent for pre-Destruction historical detail, who testifies that

> after the Temple was destroyed, this ritual *(of redeeming the fruits)* was performed with a stipulation, and this was it: ' When the Temple is rebuilt, and may it be speedily, in our day, then things will go back to the way they used to be.'

The second of the two *taqanot* was related to the process whereby a proselyte enters the Covenant of Israel. The Gemara (Kerithoth

---

73 Tos. MaasSh. V:15–16 (Zuck. p. 96).

9a), quoting Rabbi Judah the Patriarch, lays down three principal requirements for conversion: circumcision, immersion, and the sprinkling of blood — that is, the blood of sacrifices on the altar.[74] It is quite clear that the sacrifices were not a sine qua non, since even the indispensibility of immersion was debated by Tannaim (specifically, Rabbi Eliezer and Rabbi Joshua).[75] Nevertheless, the requirement that the convert offer sacrifices had had its own special importance in Temple times. It had served to bind the proselyte to the Land of Israel and to the Holy Sanctuary by involving him in a pilgrimage to Jerusalem. Thus it had been a central and dramatic element in the process of becoming an adherent of the Jewish religion and a member of the Jewish people.

When the Temple was destroyed, a serious problem arose: what was the convert to do, now that there were no sacrifices? Hence the *baraitha* which the Talmud quotes:[76]

> Nowadays, a proselyte has to set aside a quarter (of a shekel or a denar) for his sacrifice of birds. (Rashi: In case the Temple is restored and the sacrifice becomes due.) Said Rabbi Simeon: As for this rule, Rabban Johanan ben Zakkai took a vote and abolished it, for fear the money might be diverted to some other purpose.

There is also a passage in the Yerushalmi[77] to the same effect:

> In these times, a proselyte must offer a quarter of silver for his birds. Said Rabbi Simeon: No, this was abolished by Rabban Johanan ben Zakkai, as a precaution against misuse.

However, the Tosefta reports the same abolition without attributing

---

74 Two offerings of turtledoves or pigeons, according to Sifre, *Shelaḥ* 108, ed. Horovitz, p. 108.

75 Yerushalmi Qid. III:64d: "It was taught, if a proselyte omitted either circumcision or immersion, it is the circumcision that is decisive — so says R. Eliezer. But R. Joshua says, immersion is also indispensible." Comp. Gerim, I:6. The report in the Bavli (Yev. 46a) that R. Joshua held immersion to be the *sole* indispensable requirement, seems to be based on a mistaken tradition.

76 R.H. 31b.

77 Yer. Sheq. VIII:51b.

it to Rabban Johanan![78] This in itself would not be enough to cast doubt on the tradition which is reported by both Talmudim, and which does connect Rabban Johanan with the abolition of the requirement. On the other hand, the implication of the text — *"nowadays"* — is that there *was* a time after the Destruction when the money substitute for the sacrifice was in force. But when could that have been, if it was Rabban Johanan who set the practice aside?

The solution seems to lie in the explicit — and different — version of the whole matter recorded in Sifre Zuta:[79]

> Rabbi Eliezer said: A proselyte is required (to set aside) the quarter for his birds. Rabbi Joshua said: He is not so required, since it may lead to error (through misuse).

This shows that the matter was still being debated in the days of Rabbi Eliezer and Rabbi Joshua. We must conclude, therefore, that it was not yet settled, and that it was resolved only later by *taqanah* in the time of Rabban Gamaliel.

We may note, as a postscript, how revealing this whole discussion is. It shows how keenly the Temple was missed in the years immediately after its Destruction, and how strong was the faith that it would be restored in the not too distant future.

---

78 Tos. Sheq. III:22 (Zuck. p. 179): "Rabbi Simeon says, he does not do it, for fear of misuse".
79 Ed. Horovitz, p. 283.

CHAPTER SIX

POSTWAR LEADERSHIP:
RABBAN GAMALIEL OF YAVNEH

Ten or fifteen years after the Destruction, the Academy and Beth Din at Yavneh were taken over by Rabban Gamaliel. The period of his leadership, from the eighties of the present era to the year 115 C.E., might well be described as the real Age of Reconstruction. It was a time that witnessed the establishment of almost all the elements of that political-juridical structure which characterized the life of the Jewish people in their own country — and to some extent in the Diaspora as well — throughout the remaining centuries of the Roman Empire, both East and West.

This was the time when the new institution of national leadership — the High Court headed by the Patriarch — became firmly entrenched. Its very real power over the Jewish communities in Eretz Israel grew steadily. Yavneh became almost what the Great Sanhedrin in Jerusalem had been — the seat of final decision on matters of law and halakhah. Local leaders were subject to the authority and supervision of Rabban Gamaliel. He, the Patriarch, travelled about the country on tours of inspection. The literature shows him — sometimes "Rabban Gamaliel and the Elders" — in Jericho, Lydda, Narvad, Kefar Uthnai, Tiberias, Acre, Akhziv, Ashkelon, and "Towns of the Samaritans."

Moreover, ties with the Diaspora were renewed and strengthened. Jews from abroad journeyed to Yavneh as "pilgrims", seeking guidance on both the theory and practice of Judaism. The voyages to Rome by Rabban Gamaliel and the Elders had as one of their purposes — or at very least, as one of their results — the establishment of closer communications with that important community at the seat of Empire, especially with regard to matters political.

This too was the period when the great *taqanot* affecting the religious life of Jewry were transmitted to the Jews of the Diaspora. It was also the first time since the Destruction that the disciplinary power of the authorities in the homeland was re-asserted over the scattered Jewish communities abroad. It also appears to have been the time when certain important rules of halakhah whose purpose was national and social were promulgated. The reference is to *taqanot* designed to keep the soil of Eretz Israel in Jewish hands, and to forestall the further penetration of non-Jewish elements into Jewish Palestine.

In the religious and cultural spheres, too, these years were rich in achievement. Centers for the study of Judaism proliferated, many of them accompanied by important *Batei Din* for the administering of Jewish law. Among these were Lydda, Peki'in, Bene Beraq, Sepphoris, Sikhnin — to mention only a few. The literature of the Halakhah began to grow, and we may date from this time the early recension of a number of tractates in our Mishnah, such as Middot, Tamid, Yoma and Eduyot.

It is also possible that Aquila's Greek translation of the Scriptures had its origin during the last days of Rabban Gamaliel. This version, written in Palestine and grounded on the Palestinian tradition of Biblical exegesis, aimed to provide a "home-grown" Bible translation for the Jews of the Graeco-Roman world.

It was at this time that Esdras IV and the Syriac Baruch, the last apocryphal books of Palestinian origin, were written. It was the period when Jewish religious life was given the form which has characterized it substantially down to the present day, especially with regard to those observances which had seemed doomed by the Destruction. This process included the editing of the essential elements of the liturgy, the fixing of the service for the Passover Seder, rules governing tithes and offerings, and the like. There also took place at this time the consolidation of the surviving religio-national forces, what with the extrusion of such far-out fringe groups as the various Judaeo-Christian sects, the Sadducees, and the Essenes.

Restoration of Autonomy

But it is probably correct to say that the most important thing that happened during this span of years was the restoration of a large measure of judicial autonomy to Jewish Palestine. If it is hard to imagine that any of the developments mentioned above could have come about without permission of the Romans, it is even more difficult to believe that the revival of the Jewish courts of law could have taken place without their approval. And as a matter of fact, our sources lead us to conclude with near certainty that it was Rabban Gamaliel who was officially recognized by the Roman government as the first post-war head of the Jewish nation in the Land of the Jews.

The Mishnah reports that Rabban Gamaliel "went to get permission from the Governor in Syria."[1] There are only two possible explanations as to what this unspecified permission involved:

1) It could mean "permission to go abroad," a usage common in the literature of the period (e.g. a disciple takes leave of his master before leaving the country — and asks leave to do so.) This interpretation makes sense, in the light of the standard practice in the Roman Empire. Any deputation sent by a *polis*, or by the *koinon* of a province, to Rome to see the Emperor or the Senate for purposes of lobbying, or of lodging a complaint, had first to get leave from the governor of the local *eparchia*.

2) The second possible explanation is the one which I prefer: Rabban Gamaliel went to get official appointment as Patriarch and leader of the Jews. This would have constituted the first step towards the *de jure* recognition of the Patriarchate — the beginning of that status which we find fully developed in the legal literature of the fourth and early fifth centuries (or, if we include non-legal literature, from the beginning of the third century onwards.) It is not argued here that Rabban Gamaliel achieved the full scope of authority that attached to the Patriarchate later; only that he made the beginning.

This assumption appears the more likely when set beside several other passages in the tradition. One of these tells of two Roman officers "sent by the Government to study Torah with Rabban Gamaliel."[2] These officials engage Rabban Gamaliel in argument about whether Jewish law discriminates against gentiles. Apparently, then, their mission was somehow connected with the proposal to give status to the Jewish courts.

Perhaps a similar connection explains the statement by Rabban Simeon ben Gamaliel, to the effect that "five hundred youngsters of my father's entourage were assigned to study Greek wisdom."[3] If we put that statement alongside another report that "there were those

1   Eduy. VII:7.
2   B.Q. 38a; Yer. ibid. IV:4b; Sifre Deut. 344, Finkelstein 401.
3   Sot. 49b; B.Q. 83a.

attached to Rabban Gamaliel's household who were given permission to study Greek, because they were needed for contacts with the Government," we will then have corroboration for our thesis that Rabban Gamaliel was recognized by the Roman authorities.[4] It may be added that the delegation headed by Rabban Gamaliel could scarcely have travelled to Rome, as it did, unless the Romans had recognized him and his Council of Elders as the official leaders of the Jewish people.

At this point, we confront a difficult question of chronology. If what has been said above is true, when did it happen? Just when did the Romans restore a limited measure of self-rule to the Jews of Palestine? Did it happen at the beginning of Rabban Gamaliel's emergence as leader — that is, in the days of Domitian? Or was it later, during the regimes of Nerva and Trajan?

Before attempting to answer this question, it is important to bear in mind that Roman recognition of the Patriarchate and the Sanhedrin, and of the jurisdiction of Jewish courts, implies an end to the status of *dediticii*, a position which the Jews had occupied since the Destruction.[5] That status, reserved for conquered subject peoples, deprived them of all collective rights as a matter of law, and to a large extent as a matter of fact as well. It was a status which was not, as a rule, intended to remain permanent; after a lapse of time, the *lex provinciae* would be declared in force, and jurisdiction transferred for the most part into the hands of this or that municipal unit — a *civitas* or a *polis* — which covered surrounding towns and villages declared to be part of its *territorium*. These extended municipalities, whether "free-cities" (*civitates liberae*) or "tribute-paying" (*civitates stipendiariae*), enjoyed varying measures of self-rule.

As for Jewish Palestine, neither the Flavian Emperors nor the two Caesars who followed them founded any cities there. Tiberias and Sepphoris had been cities before the Destruction, and all Trajan did was to give them back their old standing. However, it must have been possible to abolish the status of *dediticii* by granting religious and

4 Tos. Sot. XV:8 (Zuck. 322). It must be admitted that the term *"bet Rabban Gamaliel"* is often used as a generic name for the Patriarchate, not for a particular Patriarch. Indeed, the corresponding passage in the Yerushalmi reads *"bet Rebbi"* — undoubtedly a reference to the Patriarchate in general.

5 [But see above, p. 71, n. 45a]

judicial home-rule to a people without reference to a territorial entity. This, it seems, is what happened to the Jews of Palestine.

Still, the chronological question remains: when was this change of status granted to them? In my opinion, the sources at our disposal do not provide us with a conclusive answer. All we can do is examine the probabilities.

It seems to me unlikely that any of the Flavian Emperors would have taken such a step in favor of the Jews. One need only recall that all three of them struck coins celebrating the downfall of Judaea. The ones minted in Rome and in Palestine by Vespasian and Titus bore the legends *"Judaea Capta"*, *"Judaea Devicta"*. As for Domitian, he was still celebrating the defeat of the Jews in the years 85, 92, and 93, when he issued coins reading *"Judaea Capta"*.[6] One is tempted to go further, and to adduce the testimony of Suetonius and of Dio Cassius about the anti-Jewish decrees of Domitian, especially towards the end of his reign. The trouble is, we are not absolutely sure that what they say relates to the Jews of Palestine. According to Suetonius:[7]

> In the days of Domitian the collection of the Jewish tax (*the didrachmon*) was carried out with especial severity. Informers were encouraged to come to the *fiscus* and inform on individuals who practiced Judaism secretly, and also on those who sought to evade the payment of the tax levied on their nation, by concealing their Jewish origin. I myself remember a scene from my youth, when the Procurator, surrounded by a host of his assistants, subjected an old man of about 90 to a physical examination, in order to determine whether or not he was circumcised.

We can be sure that the severity of the tax collection had nothing to do with any government deficit. On the contrary, the exchequer in Domitian's time was quite well off. It appears rather that there was a drive against *converts* to Judaism; hence, the checking up on cir-

---

6 See Madden: *Coins of the Jews*, pp. 209–229; and idem: *History of Jewish Coinage*, pp. 183 ff. Also Narkis: Matbe‘ot Ereṣ Yisrael, Vol. II, pp. 144–47; and Rafaeli: *Matbe‘ot ha-Yehudim*, p. 141.
7 Vita Domitiani, 12 (Reinach, p. 333).

cumcisions.[8] This motive comes out strongly in the descriptions given by Dio Cassius of the executions ordered by Domitian in the year 95, which included among the victims his own near kin, the ex-consul Flavius Clemens.[9] The latter and his wife Domitilla were accused, along with many others, of "atheism" — another way of saying that they were involved in Jewish religious practices. Some of the accused were put to death. Others had all their property confiscated. Domitilla herself was exiled.

All things considered, then, we cannot be absolutely sure that Domitian's persecutions were aimed specifically at the Jews. It seems more likely that he was trying to stem the wave of conversions to Judaism that swept through Rome in his time, and continued afterwards. The highest reaches of Roman society were affected, including even members of the senatorial class.[10] And another thing: the tyrannical emperor obviously made use of the indictment for "atheism" as a handy means of getting rid of those members of the Roman aristocracy who were in his disfavor. At the very least, the accusation enabled him to confiscate their property. So Domitian's antipathy for the Jews of Palestine remains unproven.

Voyages to Rome

Our problem in chronology is further complicated, however, by interpretations that have been placed on the texts cited below. If the interpretations are correct, we would have proof positive that Rabban Gamaliel was recognized as Patriarch before the death of Domitian.

The passages tell of voyages made to Rome by Rabban Gamaliel

8 Tos. Shab. XV:9 (Zuck. p. 133) speaks of those who had tried to efface the effects of having been circumcised. It says that many of them were re-circumcised "in the days of Bar Coziba." For Graetz's conjecture on this, see above, p. 66, n. 35.

9 [*Dio's Roman History*, transl. by Earnest Cary, Loeb Classical Library, vol. VIII, p. 349] There is no foundation for the legend that grew up many years later, according to which Clemens was a Christian.

10 The same conclusion can be drawn from the coin minted by Nerva, with the motto *FISCI JUDAICI CALUMNIA SUBLATA*. This does not mean that the Jewish tax was abolished, but rather that an end was put to the situation whereby *Romans* could be denounced by informers as judaizers — and hence liable for the tax which was, both in intent and effect, a demeaning thing.

and the Elders — apparently on more than one occasion. Zechariah Frankel suggested that there were two such voyages, one near the end of Domitian's regime, and the other during the reign of Nerva.[11] Although the texts themselves are silent as to when these travels took place, Frankel thought to date the first trip during the reign of Domitian, by relating it to the following passage from Deuteronomy Rabbah (II:24):

> Once, when Rabbi Eliezer and Rabbi Joshua and Rabban Gamaliel were in Rome, the Royal Senate (*sanklitin shel melekh*) voted a decree which said that thirty days thereafter there were to be no more Jews left in the world. Now, one of the Emperor's senators belonged to the "God-Fearers." He sought out Rabban Gamaliel and told him about the decree. The Rabbis were greatly distressed, but the God-Fearer said to them: Be not dismayed; between now and the time when the decree is supposed to go into effect, the God of the Jews will surely take steps to help them. When twenty-five days had gone by, he revealed the whole thing to his wife. Said she: But twenty-five days have already passed. Said he: There are five days left. She, who was even more righteous than her husband, said to him: Have you not a poison ring? If you suck it, and die, the Senate will suspend sessions for thirty days on your account, so that the decree will lapse. He did as she said, and died. The Rabbis came to see her to show their sympathy. Said they to her: Alas for the ship that has sailed into the harbor without paying the fee. Said she to them: I know what you are saying, but the ship did pay the fee... She entered a chamber and brought out a box which contained his foreskin...

It has been suggested that the *sanklitos* in the preceding passage is none other than the martyred Senator T. Flavius Clemens, whose wife was the noblewoman Domitilla. If that is so, it would place Rabban Gamaliel in Rome in the year 95 C.E. The same theory would

---

11 Frankel: *Darkhe ha-Mishnah*, p. 84 (2nd ed., p. 87). See also Derenbourg, *Essai*, p. 336. [The suggestion is explicitly rejected by Graetz, who says "Ich kann... Frankels Ansicht nicht zustimmen." *Geschichte*, 3rd ed., Vol. IV, p. 110.]

relate the following passage in the Babylonian Talmud to the same aristocratic couple:[12]

> Once there was a Caesar who hated the Jews. He asked the most important men of the kingdom: what should a person do who has a painful growth on his leg? Should he cut it off and get rid of the pain, or should he leave it alone and suffer? They said, let him cut it off and live comfortably. But Qeti'ah Barshalom (literally: *The Cut-One, son of Peace*) said to him: No. In the first place, you cannot ever get rid of them all. It is written (*Zech. II:10*) "I have spread you out as the four winds of heaven." Now, what does that mean? If it intends to say, I have scattered them in every direction, then it ought to have read "*to* the four winds." But it says, "*as* the four winds." Therefore it means: Just as the world cannot abide without winds, even so can it not abide without Israel. And what is more, you, Sire, will come to be known as the "Cut off Kingdom" (*malkhut qetu'ah*). The Emperor answered: Truly, you have spoken well. However, the law is that whosoever bests the Monarch in arguments is to be thrust into a blazing furnace. They seized him and were about to lead him off to his death. A gentlewoman present called out to him: Alas for the ship that hath set forth for the harbor without paying the entrance fee. Whereupon he fell on his foreskin and cut it off (*qeta'ah*). Said he: I have paid the fee, I have crossed the bar. As they were about to cast him into the flames he was heard to say: All that I own I bequeath to Rabbi Akiba and his colleagues. . . A voice from Heaven was heard to call out: Qeti'ah Barshalom is summoned to life eternal. Rabbi (*Judah the Patriarch, when he was told this story*) wept and said: Some acquire eternity in a single moment, while others gain it only in the course of many years.

Unfortunately, this passage cannot help our problem in chronology. Even though it apparently contains elements of genuine historical memory, its present form must be dated at a time after the events it

---

12 Av. Zar. 10b. See Vogelstein und Rieger: *Geschichte der Juden in Rom*, Vol. I, p. 28.

purports to relate. It also contains several mutually contradictory strands woven together.[13] Apart from these considerations, it is also obvious that the aggadah combines two distinct and divergent traditions as to the meaning of the proper name *Qeti ah* — one of them, based on the phrase *malkhut qetu'ah*; the other, on the act of self-circumcision (*qeta'ah*). Still another reason for *not* connecting this aggadah with Flavius Clemens and the voyage of Rabban Gamaliel is the bequest to "Rabbi Akiba and his colleagues," rather than to Rabban Gamaliel, who was after all the Patriarch and senior member of the delegation. (Incidentally, there is no mention of Rabbi Akiba in the story quoted previously from Deuteronomy Rabbah). The conclusion must be that we have a late tradition which embodies the memory of an episode that actually took place; but just what took place, we have no way of knowing. Whatever it was, it was in no way connected with the problem under discussion.

Nor, indeed, does the story in Deuteronomy Rabbah give us anything to build on. Even if we disregard a number of points which call its authenticity into question, and ignore the lack of correspondence in details with the report of Dio Cassius about Clemens and his wife, there still remains the major divergence in the entire thrust of the two stories. According to Dio Cassius, there was no question of any anti-Jewish decree; it was Romans who were the target of persecution for being Judaizers or fellow-travellers. The aggadah, per contra, has the whole thing aimed solely at the Jews, with the God-Fearing *sanklitos* simply briefing Rabban Gamaliel and the others on the danger facing the Jews, and then nobly committing suicide, not because of any threatened sanctions against himself, but only to save the people.

Besides, the proposal that "there were to be no more Jews left in the world" does not fit in with the reign of Domitian. To be sure, a sixth-century Arab-Christian writer, Eutychios ibn Batriq, relates:

13 E.g. the use of the verse from Zechariah about the "four winds" is obviously a variant of a homiletical tradition quoted in the name of Rabbi Joshua ben Levi in Ta'anith 3b, where the context has not the remotest connection with Rome or with martyrs, but deals with a liturgical matter — the *gevurot* section of the Eighteen Benedictions. That seems to be where it rightfully belongs. Somehow, this bit of exegesis got tangled up in the *editio princeps* of the Talmud with the story of Qeti'ah Barshalom in Avodah Zarah. And note: it is missing from basic versions of the Talmudic text! See Rabinowicz: *Variae Lectiones* (*Diqduqe Soferim*) ad loc.

"Domitian treated the Jews badly, to the point where there was scarcely a Jew to be seen (in the Roman Empire) during his reign."[14] A similar statement is made in "The Acts of John".[15]

> Following the death of Vespasian, his son Domitian took the throne (sic). Apart from all his other wicked deeds, he denounced righteous and innocent people. When he discovered that the City of Rome was full of Jews, and he recalled how harshly his father had dealt with them, he decided to banish them all from the city. However, some of the Jews made so bold as to write him thus: Hail Caesar Domitianus, king of all the world! We the Jews petition and implore you not to banish us from your presence, O friend of humanity! Our conduct and our way of life is in accord with our customs and our laws, and we do no wrong. But there is an alien people newly risen up who do not comport well with any of the peoples, nor do they fulfill the commandments as the Jews do. They are not circumcised, they despise the generality of mankind — a people with no Torah... After this, Domitian looked with disfavor on the Christians, and ordered the *senatus consultum* to slay all who professed Christianity.

Doubtless all we have here is a late and highly colored recension of the tradition which echoed Domitian's clashes with the Jews, his antipathy for Judaism, and especially his opposition to the conversion of Romans to that faith. We find something similar in a late source dealing with Constantine, who is said to have expelled the Jews from all his provinces, and at the same time to have barred them from the cities.[16] Here, too, the picture is overdrawn — a way of describing Constantine's negative attitude to Judaism, but not to be taken literally. We do know that Constantine did *not* strip the Jews of their rights, much less expel them from the entire Empire. It is true that certain Caesars did ban the Jews from the City of Rome; Tiberius, for one, and Claudius for another.[17] But there is no evidence of their

14   *Annales.* Latin text in *Patrologia Graeca*, vol. 111, p. 985.
15   For the original text see *REJ*, vol. I (1880), p. 41.
16   *Historia Nestorianus* (in Arabic) XII century. Patrologia Orientalis, v. IV, 281.
17   For Tiberius, see Suetonius: *Life of Tiberius*; Tacitus, *Annales* 2; 82;

ever having been expelled from the Empire as a whole, nor as far as
Domitian is concerned, even from the City of Rome in his time —
except for the above-quoted Christian legend.

Finally, let us consider the varying traditions as to who accompanied Rabban Gamaliel to Rome. The report cited from Deuteronomy
Rabbah lists Rabbi Eliezer and Rabbi Joshua ben Hananiah as the
fellow-delegates. This is supported by only one other source — an
amoraic aggadah in the Yerushalmi.[18] All the other sources — early
tannaitic ones at that — always have Rabban Gamaliel accompanied
by Rabbi Joshua, Rabbi Akiba, and Rabbi Eleazar ben Azariah.[19]
One additional tannaitic source, which does not name those accompanying the Patriarch, reads: "Once when Rabban Gamaliel was
traveling at sea, his disciples being with him..."[20] This must also
refer to the second-named group, since Rabbi Eliezer and Rabbi
Joshua could scarcely have been called "disciples" of Rabban Gamaliel. On the other hand, it is almost a certainty that Rabbi Eleazar
ben Azariah and Rabbi Akiba could not have journeyed to Rome in
the year 95 C.E. as leaders of the High Court: Rabbi Eleazar was
probably too young at the time, and it seems very unlikely that Rabbi
Akiba, a late starter, had achieved recognition by then as an important scholar.

In the light of all this, we must assume that there was a *series* of
diplomatic missions to Rome; and that on the earlier ones the Patriarch was accompanied only by Rabbi Eliezer and Rabbi Joshua,
while on the later voyages Rabbi Eleazar ben Azariah and Rabbi
Akiba also joined the delegation. It seems to me, however, that since
all the tannaitic sources agree on Rabbis Joshua, Eleazar and Akiba,

Philo, as quoted by Eusebius; Josephus, *Antiquities* 18:3:5 (83). For
Claudius, see Suetonius' *Life of Claudius*, 25; and *Acts of the Apostles*,
18.2.
18   Sanh. VII:25d.
19   E.g. Mishnah, Maas. Sh. V:9; Tos. Bez. II:3; Sifre Deut. 43; and parallel
passages. See also Michael Higger: *Pirqei ben Azzai*, III:2, in *Mas. Derekh Erez*, p. 183 ff.; and the midrashic extracts in Ginze Schechter I,
p. 219. [The passage in Tos. Bez. is on page 204 of Zuck., but does *not*
mention Rome. However, that is because one word — *be-romi* — was
omitted by error from Ms. Erfurt. See Lieberman, *Tosefta Kifshuto*, vol. 5,
p. 955, ll. 44-5. The reference in Sifre is Finkelstein, p. 94].
20   Midrash Tannaim, ed. Hoffman, p. 172.

we should regard the non-tannaitic sources quoted above from the Midrash and the Yerushalmi as based on a divergent tradition, one which claims that the self-same delegation on the self-same trip consisted rather of Rabbi Eliezer ben Hyrcanos and Rabbi Joshuah ben Hananiah.

There remains one more text to be considered. We shall see that it tends to support the tannaitic tradition.

> The four species of plants used on Sukkot, what do they symbolize? The four righteous men whom the Holy One, blessed be He, placed in every kingdom to redeem the people, and to spread the knowledge of Torah. And these are they: In Babylon — Daniel, Hananiah, Mishael and Azariah. In Persia — Haggai, Zechariah, Malachi and Nehemiah. In Yavan (the Hellenistic world) — the four Hasmonean brothers, Judah the eldest having already lost his life. In Edom (Rome) — Rabban Gamaliel and Rabbi Joshua and Rabbi Eleazar ben Azariah and Rabbi Akiba.[21]

Since Rabbi Eleazar and Rabbi Akiba could scarcely have become national leaders during the lifetime of Domitian, we must relate all these passages to a journey — or journeys — during the reign of Trajan.

The sum of all this is that the story in Deuteronomy Rabbah — a relatively late midrash, in any case — cannot be brought to bear in determining when Rome granted official recognition to Rabban Gamaliel as Patriarch, and by so doing restored partial self-government to the Jews of Palestine. Whatever we can deduce from the data we possess points away from Domitian; indeed, makes all the Flavian Emperors unlikely sponsors of such an act.

But there is another possibility. Why could not the first official recognition have come from the local authority, without involving the Caesar himself? If we make that assumption, then the first stages of Jewish semi-autonomy could have developed even during the reign of Domitian! However, all this is speculative; we have no positive evidence. All that can be said is that it seems reasonable to associate this benign development in Judaeo-Roman relations with a time when

---

21 *Mishnat Rabbi Eliezer*, edited by Enelow, p. 103.

the Flavian dynasty was no more, and the wartime atmosphere had dissipated.

There is one thing which it is fairly safe to assume: the reconstruction of national life, and the rise of a central leadership, did not take place all at once, or as the result of any Roman grant. Organized Jewish life in Palestine was created by the Jews themselves. With the passing of time, the ruling power had to come to terms with the realities. It is clear that the Patriarchate as an institution was functioning, to the extent that circumstances allowed, before the Romans gave it their stamp of approval. The "permission" that Rabban Gamaliel journeyed to Syria to obtain simply carried his great undertaking one step further, thus strengthening it for the more than three centuries it was to endure.

We will assume, then, that Rabban Gamaliel asserted his leadership, albeit without official sanction, while Domitian was still alive. The ground having thus been prepared, the government finally took legal and political cognizance of a situation that had already come into being through the efforts and exertions of the country's inhabitants. The twenty-five years following the Destruction — the years marked by the leadership of Rabban Johanan ben Zakkai and Rabban Gamaliel II — should be seen as a period of reorganization, when the Jewish people pulled itself together, rebuilt its strength, re-established its ties with the Diaspora, and resumed the life of a people centered on its homeland, the Land of Israel.

All this entailed great effort and enormous struggle. Before we take up the events of the time, let us make a brief survey of the social and economic setting in which those events took place, and examine the administrative structure of the defeated and occupied country.

CHAPTER SEVEN

ERETZ ISRAEL BETWEEN TWO WARS

The assassination of Domitian in September of the year 96 brought to an end a dynasty that had restored "peace" to the Roman Empire. The Flavians had re-established an Empire-wide structure of law and order that dated back to Augustus Caesar, but had become rather shaky at the end of the Julio-Claudian period. At the same time, the assassination freed Rome from the yoke of a despotic tyrant. Whether this had much effect on the masses of subject peoples out in the provinces it is hard to say, but in Rome itself the upper classes could breathe free again. The accession of Nerva saw the Senate restored to a share of power, becoming what it once had been — a factor of consequence in the functioning of the *Imperium*. Trajan too (98–117) for all his dependence on the military, looked upon the Senate as a pillar of his regime.

As for the Jews, they certainly had no reason to mourn the passing of a dynasty whose founder Vespasian, and his son Titus, had been the destroyers of their land and their Temple. And while it is true that the coin struck by Nerva with the inscription *FISCI JUDAICI CALUMNIA SUBLATA* did not herald the end of the half-shekel tax on every Jew, nor signal any special affection for the Jewish people, it did nevertheless mark the end of an era of antipathy for Judaism, and of persecution directed against those attracted to it. Evidence of Trajan's freedom from the anti-Jewish feeling which had characterized the reign of Domitian is provided by the papyrus[1] which describes the adversary proceedings between the Jews and the Greeks of Alexandria before the Emperor. (The year was either 110[2] or 113–14 C.E.). The authors of this document make reference to the influence of Caesar's wife, Plotina on her husband Trajan, and also remind

1 P. Oxy no. 1242. [Comp. CPJ no. 157, vol. II, p. 82]
2 In the opinion of W. Weber; see Hermes, Vol. 50 (1915), p. 47 ff.

the Emperor that his *Consilium* is "full of Jews." The episode itself shows the ruler taking a stand free of Jew-hatred. In the event, his judgment went against the Greeks.

There was an administrative innovation implemented under Trajan which affected all the provinces, Jewish Palestine included. It was the introduction of *Curatores Civitatum* (in the Greek-speaking East — *Logistai*) — overseers appointed by the central government to supervise the affairs of every *polis* or municipal entity, whether autonomous or tribute-paying. This step marks the intrusion of the Imperial authorities into the affairs of local government, with an accent on municipal finances.[3]

Greater importance should no doubt be attached to the annexation of the small kingdom of Agrippa II, which included Trachonitis (Bashan) in northern Transjordan, along with a part of the Galilee. It has long been held that this took place in the year 100. More recently, historians have inclined to favor the year 93, towards the end of Domitian's reign. Equally noteworthy was the annexation of the Nabatean Kingdom, with its capital at Petra, in the year 105–6. It was known from then on as the Province of Arabia (*Provincia Arabia*).

Nor should the anti-Christian persecutions that took place throughout the Empire during Trajan's reign be forgotten. In Palestine, these persecutions sometimes affected Jews, since relationships between them and Jewish-Christians were still maintained. As a result certain Tannaim were sometimes caught "in the net of the *Minim*."

When we speak of the Eretz Israel of those days (or in Roman terms *Provincia Judaea*) we must distinguish between Jewish Palestine, and its periphery of Graeco-Roman towns. The first consisted of the inner heart of the country (exclusive of the "land of the Samaritans"). The periphery refers to those towns and trade-centers, mostly on the Mediterranean coast, but across the Jordan as well, in which there was, and had been for generations, a not inconsiderable Jewish minority. In these towns it was the gentile majority that set the socio-cultural tone, giving these centers a Hellenistic-pagan character.

The important thing about these cities, from an administrative

---

3 The original cause of this interference was fiscal mismanagement in the Hellenistic cities of the east.

point of view, is that they and their environs were organized after the fashion of a Greek *polis*, so that they were in effect self-governing localities. Their inhabitants had no direct contact with the provincial government. Their channel to the imperial authorities was provided via the institutions of local government, principally the *boulē* — the the Town Council — and the *archontes* — the municipal magistrates. The third organ of city government, the *ekklesia* — the Popular Assembly — was steadily whittled down during the Empire. Even where it survived, it was shorn of any real power. The last we hear of it is at the end of the third century C.E. Rome preferred to get rid of this somewhat democratic institution, and to put civic affairs into the hands of the propertied oligarchy.

However, these local authorities were not merely instruments for making sure that the citizen fulfilled his obligations to the State, such as paying his taxes, serving his turn on the rota for the maintenance of law and order, and the like. They were also possessed of considerable initiative and independence in the conduct of their own communal and civic affairs. They were in charge of the cultural institutions of the community, as well as of its economic concerns, including even the minting of coinage, and the levying of city imposts — *mekhes medinah.* What is more, they had a certain independence in the administration of justice, with city courts having jurisdiction over municipal ordinances and part of civil law. There is also some evidence for the existence of city police, with the power to enforce sanctions. The law administered in the courts was generally speaking Hellenistic-Greek, with an admixture of Semitic law, combined with certain principles of Roman law. For our purposes, this is important because of the legal interrelationships between Jews and gentiles in these Palestinian cities of mixed population.

As we have noted, the administrative profile of these cities was Hellenistic; but this by no means implies that their population was made up of Greeks. On the contrary, it is quite clear that real Greeks — that is, Hellenic families settled in the area since the days of the Seleucids and the Ptolomies, successors to Alexander the Great — were a small minority. Even Hellenizers, which is to say Semites who were totally acculturated to Greek mores and Greek values — even they were not so very numerous. The majority of the people of these cities were Syrians, a term which includes the descendants of the ancient Philistines and Phoenico-Canaanites. Most of these people, whether in villages, towns or big cities, still used the Syrian language in their daily speech.

How then can one account for the Greek character of these cities, most of them dating back to the age of the Macedonian conquest? In the first place, there was the strong influence which Hellenic civilization had been exerting on the Middle East ever since the days of Alexander the Great. But in the second place — and this is the telling factor, though it is usually overlooked — there was the administrative policy of the Hellenistic rulers in the East, a policy taken over by their successors the Romans. Both imperial powers preferred to withhold any real measure of self-government from their Asian subjects, except for those population centers which had absorbed a significant number of Greeks or Macedonians, and had organized themselves, both politically and culturally, on the model of the Greek *polis*.

In the light of this, we must view the influence of Hellenism on the Middle East not as the natural penetration of an attractive culture, but as an enforced acculturation, the gravitational pull of the powerful on their clients. Small wonder, then, that at a later stage we find both Jews and Christians making every effort to have their urban centers organized as proper Greek municipalities, even though we may be sure that neither Jews nor Christians had any special fondness for the Greek culture and life-style.

The Hellenistic cities of the East must have looked in their day like transplants from the Aegean, what with their theatres, amphitheatres, stadia, wrestling matches, boxing bouts — and as time went on, schools of rhetoric as well. The imitation of ancient Attica was complete. A second century C.E. inscription found at Aphrodisia of Caria in Asia Minor sings the praises of one Menander, who was the victor in many sports competitions at such places as "Caesarea of Straton", Neapolis of Samaria (Nablus), Scythopolis (Beth Shean), Gaza and Caesarea Banias. Again, at the beginning of the third century we find such games taking place at Caesarea, Ashkelon and Gaza. Indeed, some of these Asian-Greek cities had produced philosophers, scholars and rhetoricians of renown even before the Romans had penetrated into the area.

Public religious ceremonials in these places seem to have been mostly Greek-pagan, with here and there some surviving near-eastern cultic celebrations, like that of *maranas* in Gaza (*mar* = Baal).[4] Roman rites were practised too, and in these towns, so far from the Capitoline Hill, one could even attend Roman circuses.[5] Egyptian gods and goddesses were also worshipped in this area; the Tosefta mentions both Serapis and Isis,[6] and there is a papyrus that lists Palestinian cities where the cult of Isis was established — Ashdod among them. It is true, of course, that many of these Egyptian rites had long been practised in Rome itself as well as in the rest of the Graeco-Roman world. It must also be remembered that many of the Greek gods were originally Semitic deities dressed up in Hellenic names, like Aphrodite — really an alias for Ashtoreth, or Astarte.

It is difficult to say whether the Jews who lived in these cities were accounted citizens with full civil rights. We do know that a long and bitter struggle took place between the Jews and the "Greeks" of Caesarea over who should conduct the civic affairs of that port city. (Incidentally, it was Nero who finally settled that particular dispute by rendering a verdict against the Jews.) The question is no doubt connected with the status of Jews in cities throughout the Roman diaspora, and as to that, it seems clear that the situation varied from place to place, from time to time, and even from Jew to Jew. It is probable that the same variations existed among the Hellenistic cities in Palestine. At a later time we hear of Jewish *bouleutin* (city councillors) in Jaffa, for example; and there are other hints of Jewish participation in civic life. But that is later. At the end of the first century, or the beginning of the second, it is almost certain that the Jews had no civic rights whatsoever. After all, they were just filtering back into those cities from which they had recently been expelled, or had fled, or in which their brethren had been slaughtered in their thousands.

In these towns of mixed population the relationship between Jews and gentiles can be described, for the most part, as one of mutual antipathy, open or suppressed. We need only recall what the gentiles in these urban centers did to their Jewish neighbors during the War of the Destruction, and how they helped the Romans in the campaign

4　Coins minted by the cities are an important source of information about the deities revered there.

5　Tannaitic literature frequently mentions *Merculis* — that is, *Mercurius* (Mercury).

6　Tos. Av. Zar. V:1 (Zuck. 468).

against Judaea. This mutual antagonism was not simply the result of religious and racial differences. Political and economic factors were also involved. To a large extent the coastal cities had always controlled trade between Palestine and the other countries of the Mediterranean littoral. In the post-war period this commerce was still quite important in the economy of Palestine — and it would continue to be so. It is therefore no wonder that competition was sharp between the Jews, who were a decisive majority in the country, and the gentiles, who were concentrated chiefly in the trade centers, and whom the Jews were constantly trying to keep from spreading into additional areas.

The political factor probably had even greater weight than the economic. After all, the gentile population had been hand in glove with the Romans throughout the War against the Jews. It was a population that identified itself with the ruling power, as it had done earlier, when the Greeks were the masters. Not that these people loved Rome more. It was self-interest on both sides that made them political bedfellows. The imperial power was the only ally the gentiles had in their struggle against the Jews. Naturally, the Roman authorities welcomed the support of the gentile minority. It may be noted in passing that Herod had done the same thing, strengthening the non-Jewish element as a counter-weight against his Jewish subjects, of whose hatred for him he was well aware.

The latent animosity between Jews and gentiles usually came to the surface during periods of war, rebellion, and civil disturbance. But during more stable, peaceful times, natural normal relationships between fellow-residents of the same city were not uncommon. Economic co-operation between Jews and non-Jews during the tannaitic period is reflected in many source texts. As a result of such interaction, Jews are sometimes found appearing in non-Jewish courts of law, and by the same token, non-Jews can be observed making use of the Jewish courts. Similar co-operation existed in some places with respect to relief for the needy. There are references to a Jewish rule that in a city of mixed population "the poor among the gentiles are to be supported along with the Jewish poor." Contributions for that purpose were collected from Jews and non-Jews alike, and "Gentiles who are sick are to be visited equally with ailing Jews."[7] We also

7 Git. 61a, and Tos. ibid. V: (3), 4–5 (Zuck. 328).

hear of Jews accepting charity from non-Jews, although there were Sages who disapproved.[8]

But there were countervailing factors that militated against the full development of close ties, even in the economic sphere. The great trade fairs held at places like Akko (Acre), Gaza and Tyre had pagan rituals and sacrifices connected with them. They were often dedicated to one or another deity of the heathen pantheon, which was enough to keep many Jews from attending.

The same factor frequently inhibited Jews from taking part in civic functions and responsibilities. The pervasive paganism of community life tended to keep them away from the cultural and educational institutions of the cities they lived in, and especially from all gymnastic and sports events. Graeco-Roman theatres and similar places of public assembly were usually involved to some degree with the ritual of pagan cults. But even apart from all this Jews were not, by and large, attracted to the Hellenistic-Roman culture that permeated town life throughout the region. To be sure, the pull exerted by the world of the gentiles became stronger after the Destruction, and the danger of assimilation became very real. But the danger was countered decisively by the calculated efforts of the Jewish leadership.

The case of the Greek language was somewhat different. Jews who lived or traded in the urban areas had to familiarize themselves with Greek, and to acquire at least some knowledge of things Hellenic. Throughout the countries of the Eastern Mediterranean the language of international trade was Greek, and so too was the language of government and of city administration. No wonder, then, that the most noticeable use of Greek by Jews occurs in the urban centers of trade and government. This is illustrated by the discovery of an ancient Jewish cemetery at Jaffa, where the great majority of the epitaphs are in Greek.

Nevertheless, the inroads made by the foreign tongue and the alien culture were neither deep nor widespread. Here again, it is more than likely that the efforts of the Sages had a marked effect. In any event, there is no question of linguistic assimilation. The daily speech of the Jews continued to be Aramaic.

A closer look at the principal mixed cities, with special reference to their Jewish communities, will make the situation clearer.

8 Sanh. 26a; B.B. 10b.

The Mixed Cities

CAESAREA

This was the Roman headquarters in Palestine, and also the seat of the Procurator after the Destruction. Its older name was *Migdal Sharshon*, or the Greek *Stratonos Purgos* (Straton's Tower). It was Herod the Great who made the site important by building a Greek-pagan city complete with temples of the gods, and statues of Augustus and *dea Roma*. He also created a harbor bigger than that of Piraeus, and gave the new city its present name, after his patron Augustus Caesar.

Shortly before the Destruction, the city had a considerable Jewish minority numbering some 20,000 souls, fairly affluent merchants for the most part. It was against them that Nero had made his ruling in the struggle for control of the city administration. To that ruling Josephus attributes the outbreak of the Jewish revolt. Then, at the beginning of the War, the entire Jewish community was slaughtered by the townspeople, with some help from the Romans. As the War went on, and the Caesareans proved their loyalty to Rome, they got their reward. Vespasian elevated the town to the status of *colonia*, that is, a city suitable for the settlement of veterans retired from the imperial armies. Both on coins and in the works of Pliny, she is called *Prima Flavia Colonia Caesarea*. Vespasian also exempted the Caesareans from the head-tax; Titus, in his turn, from the property-tax as well.

This city was in its day a very important center of trade, due in large measure to the export shipping business. A number of Jewish sources dating from the amoraic period speak of "Caesarea and its environs" as "life-giving country", and comment: "The cost of living is low there; they have plenty of everything."[9] Even earlier, the importance of the place as a commercial center is taken for granted by the Sifre; it speaks of a man who went to Caesarea, where he needed ready cash of 100 or 200 zuzim.[10]

Although the Jewish community of Caesarea was wiped out at the time of Destruction, it was apparently reconstituted not long afterwards. Texts dating from tannaitic times mention a considerable Jewish population, while amoraic literature speaks later on of a big

9 Yer. Kil. IX:32c.
10 Sifre Deut. Ha'azinu, 306. Finkelstein, p. 338.

community with many scholars, a large studyhouse that had been in existence for many years, and an important Jewish court (*rabbanan d'keisarin, dayyanei keisarin*).

We have already noted that the Jews were a minority in the population before the Destruction, and it seems probable that they remained a minority after the reconstruction as well. But it is interesting to observe the testimony of the Yerushalmi regarding the third and fourth centuries, to the effect that of the three elements in the population of Caesarea — Jews, Samaritans, and Gentiles — no single one constituted an absolute majority.[11] The text in question deals with seventh-year produce, and declares it permitted in Caesarea, since Jews are presumed to be observing the Sabbatical year, and Gentiles are exempt from its provisions, and both together outnumber the Samaritans (who are bound by the rules of the Torah, but are suspected of laxity in observing them). Since, when there is no evidence to the contrary, the legal presumption follows the majority, therefore produce not identified is presumed to be permitted. A derivative conclusion is that none of the three had a majority. (There is evidence for the presence of Samaritans in Caesarea during the years immediately after the Bar Kokhba Revolt. They remained numerous in that vicinity up to the Arab conquest, and even beyond.)

Caesarea was also one of the places in which congregations of Christians had existed almost since apostolic times. Later, the *Episkopos* (Bishop) of Caesarea had authority over all Christian churches and communities in Palestine, Jerusalem included. A Christian theological academy, possessed of a very rich library, came into being in Caesarea around the beginning of the third century. One of the heads of this academy was Origen, who was in touch with the Jewish Patriarchate and with leading Jewish scholars on matters of Biblical exegesis, and who engaged them in theological argument. It was Jews who taught him Hebrew, thus enabling him to issue his *Hexapla*, which gives the Bible text in six columns: Hebrew; Hebrew in Greek transliteration; plus four Greek translations of the Hebrew, namely Aquila, the Septuagint, Symmachus and Theodotion. In the process, Origen mentions certain traditions, halakhic as well as aggadic, which

11 Yer. Dem. II:22c.

he says he learned from "Jews, or from those whom the Jews call Sages."

ASHKELON

This was a city where Greek influence had made itself felt quite early. It too was important commercially. Through its port passed much of the wine exported to foreign markets, a distinction it shared with the port of Gaza. Ashkelon was also connected with the manufacture of certain marine implements. The Mishnah refers to "grappling-irons of Ashkelon."[12]

To the best of our knowledge, relations between Jews and Gentiles in this town were never very cordial. At the beginning of the War of the Destruction, Jews from outside attacked the city twice. Meanwhile, 2,500 Jews living in Ashkelon were set upon and killed by their fellow-citizens; most of whom were Syrians.[13] Ammianus Marcellinus[14] includes the city in a list of five beautiful towns in Palestine (the others were Caesarea, Beth Guvrin, Neapolis, and Gaza).

There are not a great many source references to Jews in Ashkelon after the Destruction. But there is one mention of a visit by Rabban Gamaliel and his Council.[15] We also hear of a certain matron of Ashkelon, apparently a woman of means, whom Rabbi Joshua ben Hanania visited, apparently on some community business.[16]

AKKO

Another seaport (it was to play a role much later under the name of Acre in the campaigns of the Crusaders and of Napoleon) Akko had been a Hellenistic town for a long time. Claudius Caesar had elevated it to the status of *colonia*. At the start of the War of the Destruction, the city served as a Roman military base, where Vespasian concentrated his forces before invading the Galilee.[17] It was then that the people of Akko turned on the Jews of the town, slaughtering some 2,000 of them, and imprisoning the rest.[18]

12 Kel. XII:7.
13 JW. II:18:5 (477).
14 XIV:8:11.
15 Tos. Miq. VI:3 (Zuck. 658).
16 ARN, version B, Chap. 19. Schechter, p. 41–42.
17 JW, III:2:4 (29).
18 JW, II:18:5 (477).

However, the Jewish community must have been reconstituted soon afterwards, because there is record of several visits to Akko by Rabban Gamaliel. Indeed, as time went on the Jewish community seems to have grown considerably, until by the end of the Byzantine period, in the sixth and early seventh centuries, Jewish influence in the town was paramount. Tannaitic literature is ambivalent as to whether Akko is to be reckoned for halakhic purposes as "Land of Israel" or "foreign territory." Non-Jewish sources also treat the place as a border town between Phoenicia and the country of the Jews.

BETH SHEAN

It was known also as Scythopolis, and was renowned for the fertility of its surrounding countryside. Says the Talmud: "If the Garden of Eden be in the Land of Israel, then Beth Shean must be its gateway." The Mishnah refers to the famous "Beth Shean olives."[19]

Jewish-Gentile relationships in Beth-Shean were exceptionally cordial, and had been so for centuries, as testified to by the Second Book of Maccabees (12:29–31). In the second pre-Christian century when Judah, leader of the Hasmonean struggle, transferred the Jews of Transjordan and the Galilee to Judaea for their own safety, he left the Jews of Beth Shean where they were, because they had a "covenant" with their non-Jewish neighbors. This probably explains why, when Jewish rebels from outside attacked the city at the outbreak of the War of the Destruction, the Jews of Beth Shean remained loyal to their non-Jewish neighbors, and joined forces with them in defending the town.[20] But their loyalty proved to have been misplaced. Before very long, in a night of the long knives, the townsmen turned on the local Jews and slaughtered some thirteen thousand of them. Apparently this did not prevent the Jews from settling in the town again, for their presence is testified to in the tannaitic age.[21]

JERASH

This was one of the ten towns in Transjordan known as the Decapolis, and is famous to-day for its impressive archaeological

19 Eruv. 19a; Peah, VII:1.
20 JW, II:18:3–4 (466 ff.).
21 See, inter alia, Yer. Dem. II, 22c; Bavli, Meg. 24b.

ruins.[22] Its heyday was in the first and second centuries, especially after the Roman Empire annexed the Nabatean kingdom in the year 106. Jerash was on the road which the Romans laid down "from the borders of Syria to the Red Sea"[23] connecting Aqaba to Basra, and thence on to Damascus. This was not only a strategic highway; it was also a major trade route along which moved a great part of the merchandise from the Arabian Peninsula, as well as from India. So Jerash flourished as an important way-station for the merchant caravans coming through.

There were many Jews living in the city before the Destruction. Came the war, and the people of Jerash failed to follow the example of the other Hellenistic towns in the region. They did no harm to the Jews in their midst, who were free to stay or to leave.[24] As to what happened to the Jewish community later on, we have no information except for the archaeological remains of a synagogue, on which a church was built in the sixth century. However, the fact that there was no clash between the Jews and the other inhabitants gives us reason to believe that the community continued to exist. It is possible that Rabbi Joshua "Ha-Garsi", a disciple of Rabbi Akiba, came from Jerash.[25]

A striking fact about these mixed cities is that Jews came back to them so short a time after the War of Destruction. They were returning to the very towns from which they had been expelled, or in which their fellows had been slaughtered. This is eloquent testimony to the energy and will-to-live of a people that had just been through a devastating catastrophe.

We have seen that Vespasian declared Caesarea a *colonia*. In addition, he established two "new cities."

JAFFA

Jaffa was the first of these, and the reconstructed town was given the Roman name *Flavia Iope*. Before the War it had been a Judaean town with a preponderantly Jewish population. Then it was levelled

22 See Kraeling: *Gerasa* (1938).
23 A Roman inscription from the time of Trajan calls it: *viam novum a finibus Syriae usque ad mare rubrum.*
24 JW, II:8:5 (480).
25 Soferim, 5:2.

by the Romans, not once but twice. The first time was when Cestius Gallus destroyed it. Then, the Jews having regained the place, it was razed again by Vespasian himself in the late summer of 67 C.E. In the interval it served as the home port of the not inconsiderable Jewish fleet which fought full-fledged naval battles with the Romans, and successfully cut the sea-lanes between Egypt and the Syrian coast.[26]

After the War, Jaffa was rebuilt, but we have no information about a Jewish community at that time. However, the fairly recent discovery of a Jewish cemetery dating from the third century onwards indicates the prior growth of a Jewish population in this "port of Jerusalem." The epitaphs, 64 in number, are mostly in Greek, with a few in Hebrew and Aramaic. They show that many of the Jews buried here came from abroad — chiefly from Egypt and from Asia Minor.

However, if the following tannaitic passage dates from a time between the Destruction and the redaction of the Mishnah, and the sailors it refers to are Jewish, then it may well be that Jews lived in the port town during the second century: "If a man vowed to have no benefit from any sea-farers, he is permitted to have benefit from land-dwellers.... By sea-farers is meant, not such as sail only from Akko to Jaffa, but such as put out into the open sea."[27]

NEAPOLIS

This was entirely a creation of the Romans, founded by them at a site near Shechem called Ma'borta.[28] Their official name for it was *Flavia Neapolis* — roughly, "Flavian Newtown." The population included Romans, or at least Roman citizens — officials and members of the military. It is highly unlikely that there were any Jews there, at least not until centuries later during the Byzantine period, when a small number of Jews seems to have lived side by side with the Samaritans and Christians who by that time were the principal elements in the population.

The Jewish Heartland

We turn now from the Hellenistic-Roman periphery of Palestine to its Jewish inner core, beginning with administrative matters.

26 JW, II:18:10 (508); III:9:3 (427–8); ibid., 2 (416).
27 Mishnah, Ned. III:6.
28 JW, IV:8:1 (449).

The Jewish Heartland

During the period of Roman hegemony in Palestine — perhaps even earlier — Judaea was divided into administrative districts called by the Greek name *toparchiai*. Josephus enumerates eleven such districts, namely 1) Jerusalem, 2) Gophna, 3) 'Aqrabat, 4) Timna, 5) Lydda, 6) Emmaus, 7) Pella, 8) Edom, 9) 'En-Gedi, 10) Herodion, 11) Jericho.[29] Pliny the Elder, in his *Historia Naturalis* (V 15. 70) counts ten, and his list differs. He omits Pella (a mistake of Josephus') and rightly substitutes Betholethephene, which is Beth Netopha in the south.[30] Instead of Jerusalem he has "Orine", which stands for the Greek "Hill-Country." He leaves out Edom and 'En Gedi, and puts in Jaffa — apparently a mistake on his part. Anyhow, prior to the Destruction these districts, whichever they were, were run from Jerusalem by the Sanhedrin. It seems likely that each of the district capitals was the seat of a "small Sanhedrin" of 23 judges,[31] which was in turn responsible for the villages and small towns round about. Each small town would have its own "Seven Leading Citizens" (*shiv'a tovei ha-ir*).[32]

There is little doubt that the entire country was placed under direct and centralized Roman rule after the war. Our sources make no mention of these local districts, after the year 70 C.E. True, a vague and somewhat distorted memory of a system of administrative subdivisions persisted as late as the fourth century — witness Eusebius in his *Onomastikon*.[33] But essentially the facts had been forgotten, and for good reason. A process had been taking place since early in the third century, whereby one populated center after another had become "incorporated" as a *polis*, very often with a new name to go with the new status.[34] It seems probable that the process had covered most of the built-up areas by the time of the Arab conquest.

Nevertheless, there does seem to be evidence in a tannaitic source of the continuation of some sort of subdivisions into the second century:[35]

29 Ibid. III:3:5 (44–46).
30 Elsewhere, Josephus does list this as a "toparchy;" see JW IV:8:1 (445). For Pliny, see the Rockham Edition, II, p. 273, ff.
31 [Mishnah, Sanh. I:6].
32 [Meg. 26a].
33 See E. Z. Melammed in Tarbiz IV (1933), pp. 159–160.
34 See above, p. 135 and p. 31, n. 5.
35 Tos. Av. Zar. IV:(V):2 (Zuck. 466).

One should not take (out of the country) into Syria[36] necessities for subsistence, like wines, oils, or flour. But Rabbi (Judah) says: In my view, wine to Syria is all right, because thereby one reduces levity. And even as one should not carry to Syria, so too should one not carry (such foodstuffs) from one province (*heparchia*) to another. But Rabbi Judah permits it from province to province.

The commentators[37] explain the phrase "province to province" as a reference to two provinces on opposite sides of the Palestine–Syria border. But the plain sense seems to deal with two provinces *within* the Land of Israel. I prefer the plain sense, and suggest that the discussion deals with a temporary restriction that was placed on moving essential foods around [for commercial advantage?] during a period of shortages and want.

Be that as it may, for present purposes the passage shows us that the country was divided during the tannaitic period into *heparchies* rather than *toparchies*. (The term *heparchy*, in the sense of "district", is found in other parts of the Empire as well.) It seems reasonable to assume that around the middle of the second century these districts were also known as "*hegemoniai*", as when Rabban Gamaliel says "from one *hegemonia* to another."[38]

There can be no doubt that the Romans took direct control of all these districts after the war, although we have no information on how their government functioned at the local level. But our sources do give the impression that some form of local municipal government continued in the larger centers of population, especially those that had been what amounts to "county seats". It goes without saying that even these were treated as something less than fullfledged cities, but some civic responsibility was left to local leadership. (The internal life of Judaism within the Jewish community is a different matter, with which all this has nothing to do.)

Talmudic literature has a number of references to the "*boula'ot* in Judaea" or to the "24 *boula'ot* in Judaea (var.: in the south) that

36 So, despite the reading "from Syria."
37 On the corresponding passage in Bavli, B.B. 90b–91a.
38 Mishnah and Tos. Git. I:1 (Zuck. 323).

[146]

were destroyed."[39] A modern scholar has suggested that *"boula'ot"* in this context means "fortresses", "strongholds", by derivation from the Latin *vallum*.[40] He ties this particular tradition in with the War of the Destruction, during which the Romans levelled 24 strongholds. Without going into the matter in detail, it would be well to point out that the tradition in question cannot be dated from the Destruction, but belongs to a later period — most likely to the time of the Bar Kokhba Rebellion. Further, the term *boula'ot* has to be explained as derived from the Greek βουλαί plural of the word *boulé*.[41] This shows that recognized "town councils" persisted in Judaea after the Destruction. And since this was so in Judaea (in the geographical sense — i.e. in the south), we must conclude that the Roman authorities allowed some residual local self-government in Jewish Palestine after the Destruction of Jerusalem and the Temple. This is not at all surprising, because the Romans did exactly that in Syria and Transjordan during the period under discussion. In areas where there were few cities, they recognized town councils in the larger villages. Actually, this conforms to the practice in other parts of the Empire as well, during the time of the Caesars.[42]

Within that part of Palestine which was solidly Jewish, there were two cities which had been organized as Greek-style municipalities even before the Destruction. These two, Tiberias and Sepphoris, were destined to play a very important part in Jewish history during the Talmudic age.

TIBERIAS

The city had been founded by Herod Antipas, who named it in honor of the Roman Emperor Tiberius Caesar. According to Jerome, in his addenda to the *Onomastikon* of Eusebius, the site is that of the Biblical Kinnereth.[43] About the year 17 C.E. Tiberias was made the capital of the Galilee, replacing Sepphoris. Finally, around 61 C.E.,

---

39 Git. 37a; Yer: Ned. IV:38d and Shevu. III:34d.
40 S. Klein, in the Chayes Festschrift, pp. 279–284.
41 See G. Alon, JJCW, p. 349 ff.
42 See George McLean Harper, Jr.: "Village Administration in the Roman Province of Syria" in *Yale Classical Studies* I, 1928; esp. p. 112 and pp. 143–145.
43 See the Hebrew translation by E. Z. Melammed, no. 948, note 2.

the Emperor Nero ordered that it be incorporated into the kingdom of Agrippa II.

During the War of the Destruction, a minority of the Tiberians, mostly from the more affluent element, sided with Agrippa and the Romans. The majority joined the rebels, who were led mainly by the boatmen and other proletarians of the town. However, some people of wealth and family such as Joshua ben Saffiah, whose father was *Archon* of the *Boulé*, also threw in their lot with the rebels. When Vespasian finally subdued the city, he did not destroy it, perhaps out of consideration for his loyal satellite Agrippa; but he did order that the wall around the city be pulled down.

Tiberias had been a preponderantly Jewish city before the war, and it remained so afterwards. Visits made there by the Patriarch Rabban Gamaliel of Yavneh indicate the importance he attached to the place; it was here that he chose to make several pronouncements. Something of the economic importance of Tiberias may be gauged from the fact that it had a notable fishing industry, and that later on it became a center for the manufacture of glassware and pottery. We know that mats were woven locally, perhaps in sufficient quantity to reach foreign markets. There is explicit evidence dating from the second century that merchants out of Tiberias came to Rome on business trips, and even maintained a permanent way-station there. The evidence consists of two inscriptions in Greek, which refer to "*Station Tiberion*" — "Station of the Tiberians," who are also "citizens of Claudiopolis in Syria-Palesteini."[44]

SEPPHORIS

This had been the capital of the Galilee during the later years of the Second Commonwealth. Its people had been Jews — all, or almost all of them. Early in the war they had come out against the rebellion, and had made peace with the Romans. Still, there are indications that Sepphoris may have hesitated before casting in her lot with the invaders. Indeed, it may well have been the conduct of Josephus, contributing as it must have to the general anarchy, that

---

44 Cagnat: *Inscriptiones Graecae ad res Romanas* etc. I:111 and 132; also Schürer, op. cit., vol. II:221. While there is no clear statement that the merchant travellers were Jews, it seems from one of the inscriptions that the station was manned by Jews.

triggered the decision of Sepphoris to throw in the sponge. The indications and overtones may be derived from Josephus' own autobiography. But as he tells it, other factors seem to have been at work as well, not excluding rivalry between Sepphoris and Tiberias. Such internecine strife was a not uncommon feature of the war on other fronts, too.

After the war was over Sepphoris remained a very Jewish town. Its people sent questions about Jewish law to Yavneh, and were hosts to learned Sages. Rabbi Halafta, one of the important Tannaim, actually lived there on a permanent basis, and acted as the spiritual leader of the community.

Something must be said here about the generally accepted view that the people of Tiberias and Sepphoris, and of the rest of the Galilee too, were ignorant bumpkins, careless of the mitzvot, far removed from the teachings of the Pharisaic Sages, even opposed to them.[45] This extreme opinion is more widely-held than it is based on proof. To be sure, when Josephus tells of the founding of Tiberias by Herod Antipas, he says that the latter peopled the place with the "poor and ignorant" of Galilee, because nobody else was willing to live in a ritually defiling place, built over graves. But this would only show that the other Galileans were particular about the laws of ritual purity! What is more, in his autobiography Josephus portrays the Tiberians and the rest of the Galileans as loyal observers of the Torah. In chapter 12 of his *Life*, he has them offering tithes to the priests who came up from Jerusalem on behalf of the Sanhedrin. It is also reported elsewhere that the people of Sepphoris, in the generation after the war, took it upon themselves not to use a damp sponge in cleaning off the vegetables which they brought to market, since the moisture would make them receptive to ritual impurity.[46] But if there were two things that the genuine 'Am Ha-'Aretz had no use for, they were tithes and the laws of ritual purity!

Such bits of evidence, and others like them, are enough to make us discount the sweeping generalizations about the barbarous Galileans. We are forced to conclude that even though there were in Galilee, as in Judaea and elsewhere in Palestine, people who qualified as '*Amei*

---

45 The fullest exposition of this view is Büchler's *Der Galiläische 'Am-Ha-'Aretz*. See especially pp. 65, 212.
46 Tos. Makhsh. III:5 (Zuck. 675).

Ha-'Aretz — in the sense that they were "haters of the Sages" and "disdainers of the commandments" (especially commandments based on the oral law) — it is impossible to apply this characterization to all Galileans, to most Galileans, or even to a significant minority among them.[47]

In the matter of political boundaries, Büchler and others hold that Sepphoris was annexed to the kingdom of Agrippa after the war. The statement is based on two sources: one is the *Bibliotheca* of Photius, where we read that Vespasian extended the boundaries of Agrippa's kingdom.[48] The second is a *baraitha* in the Babylonian Talmud, as follows:[49]

> A (the?) steward (*epitropos*) of King Agrippa asked Rabbi Eliezer: What about a man like me? I have two wives, one in Tiberias and one in Sepphoris; and I have two sukkahs, one in Tiberias and one in Sepphoris. Do I go from one to the other? etc. etc.

The assumption is that both Tiberias and Sepphoris were within the area for which the royal steward was responsible. But that remains unproven. He could have had a sukkah (and a wife) outside the territory of his king. He could also have been a personal employee of the king, manager of his private holdings, and not a government official. Indeed, we know from Josephus' *Life* that the Princess Berenice owned properties as far away as Beth Shearim, well outside the realm of her brother Agrippa.[50]

Equally unproven is the theory that Joseph ben Simai, the "steward (*epitropos*) of the king" mentioned in the following *baraitha*, was an official of the government of Agrippa:[51]

> It once happened that a fire broke out in the courtyard of Joseph ben Simai in Shihin, and the men of the garrison of

---

47 For the learned character of some Galileans, note the many questions they asked Rabbi Eliezer about the laws of Tabernacles (Sukk. 28a.)

48 See Freese: *The Library of Photius*, SPCK, London–New York, 1920, Vol. I, p. 29.

49 Sukk. 27a.

50 Josephus: *Life*, 118.

51 Shab. 121a [The theory here controverted was advanced by Graetz in MGWJ XIII (1881), p. 484. Cf. Klein: *Neue Beiträge*, p. 66, n. 1].

Sepphoris came to put it out, for he was a steward of the king... (*This last phrase is absent from the corresponding version in the Tosefta.*)[52]

Be it noted that the context in which this passage occurs makes it plain that the men of the garrison were non-Jews, and so not likely to have been subjects of Agrippa. Then too, the steward mentioned — if such he was — did *not* live in Sepphoris. So all that can be safely said is that the case remains unproven.

52   Tos. Shab. XIII (XIV) :9 (Zuck. 129).

CHAPTER EIGHT

SOME ASPECTS OF THE ECONOMY

While it is not possible to document in detail the effects of the War of the Destruction on the economic life of Jewish Palestine, we can be reasonably sure that some sectors of the economy were gravely damaged, in certain cases irretrievably so. But there were other sectors that did recover from the wounds of war — wounds inflicted not only by the battles with Rome, but also by the fierce internecine strife between the Jewish parties. Nevertheless, even those branches of the economy that recovered did not escape unscathed.

We have already pointed out two general phenomena that had deep and lasting effects. One was the loss of title to many tracts of land, coupled with an increasingly heavy burden of taxation on real property. The other was the growing penetration of non-Jews into Jewish Palestine, and the resultant displacement of Jews.[1] The displacers included Roman soldiers who remained in the country as settlers after their discharge, whether on their own initiative or as a result of the government policy of colonizing conquered territory. We shall see how Judaism tried to counter the dangers which these two trends posed to the economic survival of the people. Along the same lines, we shall discuss those rules of the Halakhah intended to safeguard certain branches of agriculture which had been especially damaged by the long and bitter struggle.

There can be no doubt that not only the war itself, but also the depopulation that it brought in its wake what with flight and deportation and the abnormally high voluntary emigration, must initially have produced a disastrous effect on the economy. But after the immediate post-war trauma the nation began to get on its economic feet again. The negative effects of the war and its aftermath notwithstanding, the pre-war economic structure began to reassert itself. It had been wounded, but the wounds were not fatal.

1 See above, pp. 61 ff.

[152]

Agriculture

In a famous passage, Josephus explains the economic basis of the life of the Jewish people in its own land:

> Ours is not a maritime country; neither commerce nor the intercourse which it promotes with the outside world has any attraction for us. Our cities are built inland, remote from the sea, and we devote ourselves to the cultivation of the productive soil with which we are blessed.[2]

Josephus wrote this at the time we are discussing, about the year 100 C.E. His habitual use of the present tense notwithstanding, he is really describing pre-war Palestine. What, then, was the state of affairs *after* the war? A careful study of the sources shows us that even then, his description still held good.

During the Second Commonwealth most of the Jews were farmers. The fact is amply reflected in the literature of the Tannaim, both in details that reveal the realia of the times, and in the concepts that underly the Jewish law of property — what we would today call civil law. To illustrate the latter: a) security for payment of a debt is a plot of land owned by the debtor (*shi'abud qarqa'ot*);[3] b) a widow or a divorcee collects her marriage settlement (*ketubah*) only from land.[4] The transfer of moveables *agav qarqa* (as a concomitant to the transfer of real property) is a common instrument in commercial transactions.[5]

To make even clearer the role of agricultural pursuits in Jewish Palestine during the first centuries of the common era, and to emphasize the place that farm-land and the farmer held in the consciousness of the people, let us look at the following two passages:

> When the question was put: Who is rich? Rabbi Tarphon's answer was this: He who owns one hundred vineyards and one hundred fields, and has one hundred slaves to work them.[6]

2 *Against Apion*, 1:12 (60).
3 B.B. 44b.
4 See Ket. 69b and 51a. As the Tosaphist points out on the latter page (s.v. מקרקעי), this rule was set aside in Gaonic times. [Comp. *Sefer ha-Itur*, 43:4, and the Epistle of Sherira Gaon, 105. For the references to Gaonic literature the translator is indebted to Prof. S. Safrai.]
5 [Qid. I:5].
6 Shab. 25b.

The Rabbis of Yavneh were accustomed to say: I am one of God's children and my fellow-man is one of God's children. I do my work in the town, while he does his work in the fields. I go to my work early in the morning, and he too goes to his work early in the morning. He does not try to do my work, nor do I try to do his. Would you say that I do much and he does little? Have we not been taught: It is all the same whether a person does much or little, so long as he directs his heart to Heaven.[7]

In our context, the point of the first passage is not that Rabbi Tarphon interpreted riches literally rather than figuratively as did most of the other Sages. The point here is that when he wanted to measure possessions, it was natural for him to do so in terms of productive acreage.

Similarly, the point of the second passage is not that the scholars express an egalitarian attitude towards the workers, which of course they do. For our present purposes it is their assumption that "worker" means "tiller of the soil" which is significant.

The picture of the man behind the plough that comes to us from the literature of the period is that of the husbandman, the yeoman farmer who owns a small plot of land sufficient for his own needs, land which he works himself with the help of his own family. The evidence for such an image is even stronger during the preceding period, the time of the Second Commonwealth. And the age-old tendency of the small cultivator to cling to the family farm ("the field of his holding" — see Leviticus XXV: 25 ff.) through thick and thin clearly persisted after the Destruction. Both the halakhah and popular folk-custom wanted to see the farmer remain in possession of his ancestral piece of land.

Support for this statement may be found in the following two quotations from the literature of the halakhah:

A man has no right to sell his ancestral field so that he can get ready capital wherewith to buy cattle, or mobilia, or slaves, or to raise sheep and goats, or even to conduct business therewith.

7 Ber. 17a.

The only circumstance in which it is permitted is — if he has become penniless.[8]

Those appointed guardians (*epitropin*) for minor orphans may sell slaves (*from the estate*) in order to buy land (*with the proceeds*) but they are not at liberty to sell land in order to buy slaves.[9]

Popular custom expressing the same attitude of clinging to the family farm is revealed in the following tradition reported by the Yerushalmi:[10]

It was taught: 'We have eaten of the *qeṣiṣah* of so-and-so.' What is meant by *qeṣiṣah*? When a man sold off the field of his holding, his relatives would fill barrels with roasted grain and nuts, and would crack them in front of the children. The children would gather them up, chanting: So-and-so has been broken-off (*niqṣaṣ*) from his holding. (And when he got the farm back, they would do the same, but say: So-and-so has come back to his holding.)[11]

I see no compelling reason for consigning this tradition to pre-Destruction times, as Gulak does.[12] After all, many of the people still wanted to keep the plot of land their forbears had worked. The persistance of this tendency even after the end of the Second Commonwealth is revealed in the practice, still prevalent in tannaitic times, of "jointholding by brothers" — a way of keeping land in the family.[13]

How big was the average smallholder's farm? It is possible to make

8 Sifra, Behar 5 (ed. Weiss, p. 108b).
9 Git. 52a.
10 Ket. II:26b.
11 The sentence in parentheses does not occur in the version of this text found in *Sefer Metivot*, ed. B.M. Lewin, Jerusalem 1934, p. 7 (Hebrew).
12 *Le'ḥeqer Toledot ha-Mishpat ha-Ivri* etc. Jerusalem, 1929 (Hebrew), p. 42. On the contrary, the very difficulty he raises in his note (2): "How can the act of relatives opposed to the sale serve as proof that the transaction was consummated?" — seems to prove that the custom here reported is *later* than the original text. Surely the original meaning of the word *qeṣaṣah* is "contract", as in the Syriac *qiṣutha*. The whole picture at least conforms with what we know about our period.
13 Mishnah, B. B. IX:4. Also Yer., ibid. 17a.

an informed guess, using the hint given by Eusebius in his "History of the Church."[14] He quotes a report by Hegesippus to the effect that the Emperor Domitian was anxious to eliminate any possible descendants of King David. An informer told the Romans that two such descendants could be found living on a farm in Galilee — two grandsons of Judah, the brother of Jesus of Nazareth. The two were arrested and taken to Rome to stand trial before the Caesar. Asked about their property, they said that their total wealth consisted of farm-land valued at 9,000 dinars, measuring 39 plithar (the equivalent of 34 dunams) which they themselves cultivated by hand. It was their sole source of income; it enabled them to support their families and pay their taxes.

That gives us a figure to work with, at least for the Galilee, and for the end of the first century. Cutting the figure in half, since there were two of them, we may calculate that the run-of-the-mill small farm consisted of about 17 dunams. But plots a good deal smaller than that are treated by our sources as not entirely negligible. The evidence, pointed out by Gulak (op. cit., page 24), is to be found in the Mishnah:[15]

> No field shall be divided (between jointholders) unless each share is able to produce at least nine *qabin*. Nor should any garden-vegetable plot be broken up unless each portion can produce at least one half-qab.

The last measure, translated into area, comes to about 3750 square cubits, roughly equivalent to 1176 square meters. Whatever is to be made of this calculation, it is clear proof of the highly intensive scale of vegetable-farming practised at that time and in that place.

On the other hand, there is evidence that large estates were still being farmed in the country, as they had been before the war. It can be assumed that people with ready capital took advantage of the opportunity to buy up property that had been confiscated by the Romans, so that the trend was towards an increase in the number of big farms. But it was a slow process. Not until the third and fourth centuries did large-scale landholdings become the norm; and even

14 *Hist. Eccl.*, Book III, Chap. 20:1–3.
15 B. B. I:6.

then there were a considerable number of smallholders who still clung to their family farms.

There were also a lot of country-folk who earned their living by working land that belonged to somebody else. These tillers of the soil fell into several categories:

1) The *'Aris*: This kind of share-cropper emerged in the second century, and by the fourth century had become quite numerous. He had the use of the land, in return for which he had to give the owner a share of the annual crop — usually, it seems, one half. The most common type was the "temporary *'aris*" whose agreement ran for a year or two. But there were also "permanent *'arisim*" whose tenancy was protected; during their lifetime they could not legally be put off the land. It is possible that they were identical with the "hereditary *'arisim*" (*'arisei-batei-avot*) who could pass the right of tenancy on to their heirs. It is quite likely that most of these tenant-farmers were the original owners who had been forced by circumstance to sell their title, while retaining the right of continued occupancy; or original owners whose land had been confiscated from under them by the Romans, and sold to new owners who were not themselves farmers.

2) The *Ḥokher*: A tenant-farmer much like the preceding; however, the terms of his agreement stipulated that the landlord was to get a fixed quantity of produce annually, instead of a share of the crop. In this case too there is some mention, though it is not very frequent, of "permanent" or "hereditary" tenants.[16]

3) The *Sokher*: The simple tenant, who paid a cash rental. There is no record of him being anything but a fairly short-term lessee.

4) The *Shattal*: A hired planter, who contracted to prepare a piece of ground for cultivation. Like the *'aris*, he got one-half of the crop; but he was in a better position, because he was also entitled to half the value of his improvement of the land, and he could not be put off the farm until he got it. This type is mentioned explicitly only in the Babylonian Talmud.[17] Yet there are grounds for believing that it existed in an earlier period, and in Palestine, because the Tosefta

16   Yer. Git. V:47b.
17   B. M. 109a/b.

speaks of "a man who is entrusted with a field for the purpose of planting it."[18]

5) The *Sakhir*: The hired hand, who lived on the place for a fixed period, in return for room and board, and was paid off when he left. The minimum time seems to have been one week (*s'khir shabbat*) and the maximum term seven years (*s'khir shavu'a*). The norm, however, was apparently a three-year period, as in the following:

> "There was the case of a man who left Upper Galilee and was taken on as a *sakhir* by a landowner in the South for a period of three years."[19]

This term of service appears to have come down from antiquity, for the Torah refers to six years as "twice the service of a *sakhir*."[20] Biblical references to the three-year term abound, for example, "Three years as the years of a *sakhir*." (Isaiah, 16:14)

6) The *'Ikkar*: This has become the ordinary Hebrew word for "farmer." But it is clear that it applied in olden times to a species of agricultural worker who was in some way attached to the owner of the land. For this use of the word, a number of examples:

First, the Yerushalmi discusses the question: when an employer is in mourning, and must therefore refrain from his daily activities, how should his employees behave?

> The mourner's *'arisin* and his *ḥakhirin* and his *qabbalin* (contractors) continue their work; but his *'ikkarin* and *sappanin* (boatmen) and *gammalin* (camel drivers) do not do so.[21]

Apparently the *'ikkar* is a closer member of the master's household than the *'aris*.

Second, the Tosefta almost *en passant*, has this:

> ......a plot big enough to produce six half *kabin*, so that the *'ikkar* can run the plough in both directions.[22]

---

18 Tos. ibid. IX:17–18 (Zuck. 392).
19 Shab. 127b.
20 Deut. 15:18.
21 Yer. M. K. III, 82b.
22 Tos. B. M. XI:9 (Zuck. 395).

Third, the Babylonian Talmud, at a rather later time, speaks of "the *'ikkar* of Rav Zevid."[23]

Fourth, there is a fragment of a recently discovered Midrash:[24]

> Why were the Egyptians afflicted with the murrain? Because they made the Israelites work as *'ikkarin* for wheat and barley crops.

Finally, there is Biblical warrant for the use of the word in the sense of some kind of indentured farm-worker. One example occurs in Isaiah: "Aliens shall be your *'ikkarim* and your vinedressers."[25] Another appears in II Chronicles: "(Uzziah had) *'ikkarim* and vinedressers in the mountains and in the fruitful fields."[26]

7) The *Po'el*: He was an agricultural day-laborer; a seasonal worker more often than not, engaged at the time of harvesting one or another crop. Standards for his employment went back to old established custom. For example, it was understood that his workday was from sunrise to sunset. It was customary to give him his food, as well as the wage agreed on in advance. Over the centuries, the thrust of both law and custom was in the direction of protecting the farm-laborer's working conditions and his wages. As for his right to be fed, the following may be cited from the Mishnah:[27]

> It happened once that Rabbi Johanan ben Mathia said to his son: go out and hire us some *po'alim*. He went and made an agreement with them that he would provide them their meals. When he came back, his father said to him: My son, even if you prepare them a banquet worthy of Solomon in all his glory you will not have discharged your duty, for they are the sons of Abraham, Isaac and Jacob. So (if you want to protect yourself) go to them before they start work and get them to stipulate

23 Sanh. 26b.
24 Jacob Mann: *The Bible as Read and Preached in the Old Synagogue*, vol. I, Cincinnati, 1940, Hebrew section, p. רי״ח.
25 Isaiah, 61:5.
26 II Chron. 36:10 [English versions render variously "plowmen" or "husbandmen." See Isaac Mendelsohn in "Bulletin of American Schools of Oriental Research," October 1962, p. 34, n. 22.]
27 B.M. VII:1.

that they will not hold you responsible for anything more than bread and pulse.

There is a single Talmudic reference to *po'alim* who were paid no wage at all, but "worked for their meals."[28] One is tempted to guess that this practice was rare and confined to really hard times, if indeed it existed at all. We would need more evidence to be confident that it did.

There is also brief mention of a working arrangement in which the *po'el* appears as a kind of contractor: he agrees to be paid a lump sum for a job done, rather than to collect a daily wage.[29]

To what extent did slave labor figure in the agricultural sector of Jewish Palestine? Evidence that it existed has already been cited in Rabbi Tarphon's definition of a "rich man" (above, page 153). There is also a passage dating approximately from the period under study which tells of the many slaves who worked in the fields of Rabbi Eleazar ben Harsom, a wealthy landowner.[30] Other references can also be cited. The Mishnah speaks of slaves as part of the economic structure of a hamlet.[31] A third-century report attributed by Rabbi Isaac bar Nahman to Rabbi Joshua ben Levi refers to a case where a Jew bought an "*'ir*" (estate?) from a non-Jew, and the purchase included the slaves who were on the property.[32] And at the end of the same century there is mention of a "hamlet in Palestine" where the slaves refused to be circumcised.[33]

In spite of these scattered references, there are no grounds for thinking that the agricultural economy of Jewish Palestine was based on slave labor to any important extent. The episodes mentioned were not at all typical. What *is* common in our sources is the reference to slaves as personal servants of city-dwellers; or as managers of business enterprises; or as skilled workers and artisans. It was the town, not the countryside, that employed slaves.

Mention was made above of tenant-farmers, and of the fact that many of them were tenants on land that had originally been their

28 Ber. 16a; Yer. ibid. II:5a.
29 Tos. B. M. VII:1 (Zuck. 385); Bavli, ibid. 76b.
30 Yoma 35b.
31 B. B. IV:7.
32 Yer. Yev. VIII:8d.
33 Yev. 48b. See also Git. 40a.

own. Vespasian had decreed that all Jewish-held land in the country would henceforth be "state-land" (*ager publicus*). Although some of these tracts then passed *de jure* into other hands, the greatest number remained *de facto* in the possession of their original owners; only the latter now had to pay much higher taxes. Even the largest tracts that had been leased to "major tenants" of the state (basically an exercise in investment rather than in agriculture) remained for the most part in the possession (not the ownership) of the cultivators who had worked the land all along; and the middle-men gradually faded from the picture.

However, certain properties that had special economic value were appropriated as the *patrimonium* of the Emperor — that is, they became his personal property. Pliny informs us that this is what happened to the groves near En-Gedi, where the finest balsam in the world was grown.[34] They actually became a part of the *fiscus*, and that branch of the administration kept production going right up to the fourth century, no doubt by employing the skilled labor of the Jews who lived in the area. And En-Gedi was not the only place where "Caesar's Balsam" was cultivated. Even more important were the groves near Jericho, as well as those in the area of Zoar, south of the Dead Sea. It is highly likely that these groves too were incorporated into the *fiscus*, and that the main workers were Jews, cast now in the role of Caesar's tenants. Some support for this surmise comes from the tannaitic comment on a verse dealing with an earlier destruction: "Nebuzaradan the captain of the guard left of the poorest of the land to be vinedressers and husbandmen."[35] The Talmud comments in the name of Rabbi Joseph:

> 'Vinedressers' refers to the balsam-pickers from En-Gedi to Ramtha (Livias, facing Jericho on the other side of the Jordan). 'Husbandmen' refers to those who gather dyers' snails along the (Mediterranean) coast between Haifa and the Ladder of Tyre.[36]

Rabbi Joseph explains what happened at the time of the Babylonian

34 *Historia Naturalis*, XII:25:113; Rockham ed., vol. IV, p. 80. See above, p. 59.
35 Jer. 52:16.
36 Shab. 21a.

conquest in terms of what he himself witnessed after the Roman conquest. Then as now, he explains, the Jews remaining in the country were no longer freeholders, but *"coloni"*, so to speak, of the Babylonians.

Incidentally, in the matter of harvesting those molluscs for the dye-industry, we have it from Eusebius that the famous manufactories of Tyrian purple were under government control in the time of Diocletian, with a special procurator in charge. Most likely the same held good in the second century as well.

The main branches of agriculture in the early centuries of the common era were seed-crops and orchard husbandry, with cattle-grazing in third place. A detailed picture of the country and its productivity on the eve of the War with Rome is given by Josephus in the third chapter of Book Three in his "Jewish War." He describes Judaea, the Galilee, Samaria and Transjordan as very fruitful, intensively cultivated and thickly populated. That this continued to be the picture at least up to the end of the third century is reflected in rabbinic literature, which never tires of singing "the praises of the Land of Israel." Certain areas come in for special mention, among them the plain around Lydda, encompassing the environs of Emmaus, Timna and Bene-Beraq. Special admiration is also expressed for the Plain of Jericho, and for the adjoining flatland southward along the shore of the Dead Sea, through En-Gedi to Zoar. Also singled out are Rishpon; the Beth Shean Valley (called by Resh Laqish "the gateway to Paradise");[37] the Plain of Ginnosar west of Lake Kinneret; and the hills of Lower Galilee in the vicinity of Sepphoris.

Highly developed methods of cultivation were in use throughout the country, and in the surrounding region as well. Irrigation was widely practiced. A field dependent on it was called *"bet hashela-ḥin"*: the method itself was called *"shaqi."*[38] Artificial irrigation was used mainly for vegetable-plots and orchards, though sometimes for fields of grain as well, in order to increase the yield. Since fruit-crops were more profitable than cereals or vegetables, owners were inclined to convert fields into orchards by means of intensive irrigation. Rabbi

37 Eruv. 19a.
38 Tos. Shevi. II:4 (Zuck. 62).

Jose the Galilean tells us this quite incidentally in his parable on the verse: "The Egyptians said: What is this we have done, that we have let Israel go forth from serving us?" (Ex.: 14:5).

> This is like a man who inherited a field capable of yielding one kur, and he disposed of it for a small sum. The new owner went ahead and developed water-sources and planted trees and orchards. Then he who had inherited the land was furious with himself for having let his legacy go for so little. So was it with the Egyptians when they let the Israelites go, and then regretted it.[39]

But in spite of the attractions of fruit-growing, most farmers preferred to avoid single-crop agriculture. Prudence dictated a diversification of products, as clearly reflected in the following statement by Rabbi Johanan:[40]

> The Biblical benediction "Blessed be thou in the field" (Deut. 23:3) describes a situation in which your property is divided three ways: one third planted to cereals, one third olives, and one third vines.

Indeed, the production of cereals seems to have been sufficient for all domestic needs. That there may even have been a surplus for export in some years is indicated by a reference to the transport — and storage — of Judaean grain in places along the Phoenician coast, including Tyre and Sidon. On the other hand, in years when there was a shortage, grain could be imported from Egypt, as well as the north.[41]

Another important product was olive-oil, produced mainly in the Galilee.[42] This is echoed in a comment on Moses' blessing of the tribe of Asher: "Let him dip his foot in oil."[43]

Once the (Jewish) people of Laodicea in Syria needed a supply

39 Mekhilta, ed. Horovitz–Rabin, p. 87 [Lauterbach, p. 197 f.].
40 B. M. 107a.
41 Tos. Dem. I:10 and 13 (Zuck. 45 f.). Contrast with Yer. Dem. I:22a. [And comp. Lieberman, *Tosefta Kifshuto*, ad loc.]
42 Judaea was famous for its wheat, Galilee for its olives. See Sanh. 11b; Midrash Tannaim, p. 176. Also Josephus, JW II:21:2 (592).
43 Deut. 33:24. The territory of Asher was Western Galilee.

of oil, and they sent a buyer to Gush-Halav (Gischala). He came across one dealer with an enormous inventory worth eighteen hundred myriad dinars.[44]

Quite apart from the normal purposes of trade, the export of olive oil to nearby countries undoubtedly had a religious motive as well. The Jews of those lands had for generations refrained from using oil produced by gentiles. They therefore had need of oil processed in the Holy Land by their co-religionists. Josephus gives explicit testimony of this when he attacks John of Gischala for making what he calls excessive profits out of the sale of kosher oil to the Jews of Syria.[45] (To us it is reasonably clear that what really happened was that John had organized a marketing co-operative for the olive-growers of the Gischala region, and used the profits for strengthening the fortifications of the town against the impending Roman attack. The parallel passage in Josephus' *Life* has John sending the oil to the Jews of Caesarea Philippi, who had been detained by Agrippa II, and were thus prevented from raising their own crops.[46])

Viniculture has always been associated with the Land of Israel. At the period under discussion there is special mention of Sharon wine, Carmel wine, and the potent variety called Ammon wine. Later, during the Byzantine period, we find wine from the Land of Israel reaching distant parts of the Western Roman Empire, as far as Gaul. In Egypt it was regarded as a gourmet product, fit for the tables of

---

44 Sifre Deut. ad loc. It is incorrect to say that the country did not produce enough oil for export, as does Heichelheim in *An Economic Survey of Ancient Rome*, ed. by Tenney Frank, Baltimore, 1938; Vol. IV, p. 128. (See also p. 137, where he says the same thing about grain.) The conclusion is based on a misunderstanding of the rule quoted in Tos. Av. Zar. IV:2 (Zuck. 465; comp. B. B. 90b–91a) according to which it was forbidden to take such staples as oil, wine and flour out of the country. It is fairly certain that the rule stems from a time of abnormal scarcity, most probably the period following the Bar Kokhba Rebellion, when the country was badly depleted. Comp. Yer. Peah VII:20a: "Rabbi Simeon bar Yaqim said: When Rabbi Jose taught that the rule of leaving the 'forgotten produce' (for the gleaners: Deut. 24–19) does not apply to the olive crop, he was speaking only about the first days, when olives were scarce; for Hadrian the Wicked had come and made the whole country desolate."
45 JW, II:21:2 (591-2).
46 74f.

the rich. Such wines were often named after the port they were shipped from, like Wine of Ascalon, or Wine of Gaza. There is no reason to doubt that this was the situation in the preceding centuries as well.

A word should be said about the mention of "Wine of Italy" (*yayyin ha-italki*) in tannaitic literature. The term is puzzling, because the growth of the Empire was accompanied by the disappearance of Italian wines from the market. They could not compete with wine from the conquered provinces. Domitian tried to protect the Roman product by means of preferential decrees, but it did no good. How then did Italian wine get into the Mishnah?[47]

The answer is that it never really did. The phrase *yayyin ha-italki* (always in a quantitative context, such as "one *log*" or "a quarter-*log*") grew out of a misreading of words which originally had nothing to do with Italian wine. The important manuscript versions read *be-italki*— 'by Italian measure!".[48]

It therefore appears that this phrase, restored to its proper meaning by the correction of one Hebrew letter, has no connection with foreign trade, since it does not refer to a kind of wine, but to a kind of liquid measure: *log yayyin be'italki* yields the meaning: "one Italian measure of wine." The whole matter is connected with the penetration of the Roman system of weights and measures into the Middle East.[49]

47   Sanh. VIII:2. [cf. Rostovzeff: *Social and Economic History of the Roman Empire*, n. 199.]
48   [See for example the Cambridge Mishnah Manuscript edited by W. H. Lowe, 1883, Sanh. VIII:2. The reading there is supported by mss. Parma and Kaufmann and by other clear-cut cases of this linguistic usage in the standard Mishnah text, always meaning, "by Italian measure." Examples are: *shishim manah be-italki* = "sixty minas, Italian measure" (Shevu. I:2); and most tellingly, *midot ha-lah vehayavesh shi'uran be-italki* = "liquid and dry quantities are calculated by Italian measure" (Kel. XVII:1).

For the variant readings, and the light they throw on the passages in which they occur, see I.N. Epstein in Tarbiz, vol. V, p. 270; and S. Lieberman: *Tosephet Rishonim*, Jerusalem 1937, vol. I, p. 166 and vol. IV, p. 193; also idem. *Tosefta Kifshutah*, Peah, p. 184. These references were called to my attention by Professor Saul Lieberman.]
49   [The fact that one could refer to "one litra of meat as they weigh in Sepphoris" points to the lack of a standardized system of weights and

The notion that wine was imported into Palestine from Cilicia is based on a misunderstanding of the following tradition:[50]

> Rabban Simeon ben Gamaliel said: I myself once saw Rabbi Simeon ben Kahana (i.e. a priest) drinking *terumah* wine in Akko. He told me: this wine came to me from Cilicia.

It should be understood that this passage has no connection with trade or commerce. It is simply a case of the laws of *terumah* (heave-offering) being observed during the period of the Second Temple by Jews from the Diaspora.[51] They would bring their offerings to the Holy Land, and present them to a *kohen*. Later, a halakhic ruling dispensed with this practice, and undoubtedly put an end to such "imports."

That wine and oil were two of the chief products of the country is strikingly expressed in the following comment by the Palestinian amora, Rabbi Johanan:

> The sages taught: Public protest may be made even on the Sabbath when the prices of goods (crucial to the economy) have gotten out of hand. Rabbi Johanan explained: For example, linen fabrics in Babylonia, or wine and oil in the Land of Israel.[52]

Among the edible fruits which were an important part of the country's agricultural product, pride of place must be given to dates, some types of which were world famous. The date-palm was cultivated around Jericho; at Zoar, which was dubbed "date-city";[53] and in the valley of Beth Shean — where, incidentally, dates are cultivated again in modern times. The fruit was also produced in certain parts of the Galilee.

Figs too were an important food substance. The best varieties came from the "Plain of Lydda" (Bene Beraq) and the area of Ariaḥ. In

---

measures. The need for such a system must have been felt, and the imperial system would surely have been a logical choice.]
50 Tos. Shevi. V:2 (Zuck. 67); quoted in Yer. Hal. IV:60b.
51 See G. Alon, *On Philo's Halakhah*, JJCW, pp. 89 ff.
52 B. B. 91a.
53 Mishnah Yev. XVI:7.

Judaea the Keili strain was prized. It was only later that the Bostra fig was introduced into the country from the Transjordan.

Of course there were all kinds of other fruits. In the second and third centuries much was made of "The Fruits of Ginnosar," a lush plain bordering on the Sea of Galilee. Its fruits were prized for their juicy sweetness.

In the first centuries of the common era Palestine was involved in a great deal of agricultural give and take with the nearby countries of the Middle East, particularly with Egypt, Syria and Asia Minor. Products also came and went to and from lands of the Roman Empire even further afield, as well as countries to the east, in the Parthian sphere of influence. As a result, certain fruits and vegetables were introduced into the country from abroad, and soon became acclimatized.

Two economic activities somewhat related to agriculture were fishing and grazing. Fishing by Jews was centered on the Sea of Galilee. Tannaitic sources refer to the "Fisherman's Guild of Tiberias," which seems to have been a kind of co-operative.[54] Nearby was the port of Tarichaea (Salt-Town) called by the Jews Migdal Nunia (Fish-Tower). Both names, Greek and Semitic, reflect the main industry of the place — the salting and drying of fish for the foreign market. Two other fishing-grounds were the Bay of Akko (Acre) on the Mediterranean, and the River Jordan. Imports of fish were confined to special varieties, such as the "Fish of Elath," a port which had a considerable Jewish population right up to the Muslim conquest.[55]

A profitable business during the second century was the raising of sheep, goats and cattle. It was customary to send the animals out to pasture "from Passover until the autumn rains,"[56] although some domestic animals were kept out in the open all year around. Naturally enough, halakhic literature contains many references to shepherds and herdsmen.

A principal area for grazing was the Plain of Sharon, as it had

---

54 Tos. B. M. VI:5 (Zuck. 383; but a more explicit reference is Yer. Pes. 30d).

55 On the differing flavors of fish caught in different waters, cf. GenR. V:8. (The reading *Aspamia* should be corrected to *Apameia*, a reference not to Spain, but to Banias.)

56 Tos. Bez. IV:11 (Zuck. 208); Yer. ibid. V:63b; Bavli, ibid. 40a.

been since Biblical times. The table of organization for David's household staff includes: "In charge of the herds that grazed in the Sharon — Shirtai the Sharonite."[57]

There are other sources that locate grazing in the Sharon:

> One may buy from women (peddlers; i.e. without fear of stolen property): woollen garments in Judah; flaxen garments in Galilee; calves in the Sharon.[58]

Or, as an old saw puts it:

> Rams from Moab; sheep from Hebron; calves from Sharon.[59]

Several centuries later (about 400 C.E.) we have Jerome telling us that the Sharon Plain is a good place for raising sheep.[60]

Around Tiberias there seems to have been a poultry industry, involving the raising of baby chicks and fledgling pigeons for the market.[61]

Crafts

There were handicrafts that had an agricultural background; one of them was the manufacture of linen fabrics and garments. From the end of the second century onwards there is frequent mention in both Jewish and non-Jewish sources of flax-growing and linen-weaving. An important center of this industry was Beth Shean (Scythopolis). Its linen fabrics were expensive, and found their way to every part of the Roman Empire. An edict of Diocletian in the year 301, fixing prices for a whole range of products, shows "The Linen of Beth Shean" as the best and most costly cloth of its kind. The geographical treatise *Totius Orbis Descriptio*, written about the middle of the fourth century, also puts Beth Shean at the head of a list of those places from which linen textiles came:

> ...*in litore enim sunt hae: Scytopolis, Ladicia, Biblus, Tirus, Beritus, quae linteamen omni orbi terrarum emittunt et sunt eminentes in omnia habundantia* . . . . .

57 I Chron. 27:29.
58 Mishnah, B.Q. X:9.
59 Tos. Men. IX:13 (Zuck. 526).
60 *Onomast.* s.v. Also *Comm. on Isaiah*, 39:7. See P.L. vol. 24 (ed. Vallarsi), p. 365, par. 436.
61 B. M. 24b.

Crafts

(along the littoral — *i.e. of the Eastern Mediterranean* — the following places export linen goods in outstanding quantities to the whole world: Beth Shean, Latakia, Byblos, Tyre and Beirut.)[62]

Rabbinic sources also speak of "the fine linens that come from Beth Shean" and of the coarser garments that were made in Arbel, near Tiberias.[63]

It must be admitted that none of these sources deals with the immediate post-war period. However, there are two references which do bring us a little closer to the period right after the Destruction. One of them comes from Clement of Alexandria, towards the end of the second century. He chides people who indulge in a luxurious lifestyle. Coarse linen garments made in Egypt are not good enough for them; they have to deck themselves out in fabrics imported from the *land of the Hebrews* and from Cilicia.[64]

The second witness is Pausanias, who actually visited Palestine around the year 175. He makes a point of saying that linen-weaving was practised in Greece as well, and that the Greek product was not inferior to that of the Jews.[65]

Granted, these references come from late in the second century. But it seems reasonable to suppose that if this Jordan Valley industry had attained a world-wide reputation by that time, it must have been well on its way at the beginning of the century.

The importance of linen manufacture for our present study lies in the fact that at the time in question, Beth Shean was largely Jewish, and Arbel completely so; as a consequence of which, the industry nourished the cultivation of flax among the Jews of the Galilee. So it is not surprising to find Rabbi Hiyya at the end of the second century engaged in raising flax.[66]

62 Quoted in *Sefer ha-Yishuv*, ed. S. Klein, Jerusalem 1939, p. 166. [See Schürer, *Geschichte* II, p. 77, n. 205.]
63 Yer. Ket. VII:31c, where the cross-references are given. See also *Sefer ha-Yishuv*, p. 17; and Gen. R. XIX:1, ed. Theodor-Albeck, p. 170.
64 Bk. II:20:115; ed. Otto Stählin, vol. I, p. 170.
65 Pausanias, *Graeciae Descriptio*, Bk. V, sec. v, para 2. *Description of Greece*, with an English translation by W. H. Jones and H. A. Ormerod, vol. II, p. 403.
66 B. M. 85b.

Side by side with the export trade in linen garments, there was a certain amount of import of special types of clothing. Garments brought in from Dalmatia are mentioned in the literature.[67] It is also highly likely that the designs of imported fabrics were copied, and then produced locally. Thus, there were craftsmen called *"tarsim"* who wove linen fabrics after the fashion in the famous textiles of Tarsus, capital of Cilicia.[68] Indeed, so numerous were these craftsmen that they were organized into guilds or cooperatives. When the Romans arrested Rabbi Eliezer ben Partha and Rabbi Joshua ben Teradyon for teaching Torah, the former denied the charge. The arresting officers retorted: "If that is so, why then were the people calling you Master (Rabbi)?". He answered: "That is because I am a Master of the weavers *(tarsim)*."[69] To those who may doubt the authenticity of this report, it should be pointed out that then and later, the title *Rav* (Master) served in other Semitic languages too as the technical designation for the chief of a company of tradesmen or artisans.[70]

As a matter of fact, there is a record of two important towns where there were special synagogues for the guilds of *tarsim*. In the Yerushalmi we hear of a controversy that took place in such a synagogue at a time before the Bar Kokhba Rebellion. A parallel account in the Bavli enables us to place the synagogue in Tiberias.[71] In the same way, by putting together the story involving Theodos the Physician and a basket of human bones that was brought into the courtyard of a synagogue as told in the Bavli ("the synagogue of the *tarsim*") and as told in the Tosefta ("the synagogue of Lydda") — we discover a weavers' union in Lydda as well![72]

Our most explicit source for the existence of brotherhoods of artisans organized both for worship and for mutual aid is contained in the famous description of the Great Synagogue of Alexandria known as the *Diplostoon* (διπλόστωον; The Double Collonade).

---

67 Called *dalmatikon* in Kil. IX:7.
68 Yer. Kil. IX:32d.
69 Av. Zar. 17b.
70 About two generations later we find one Ben-Shila as Master of the Butchers in Sepphoris (Tos. Hul. III:2; Zuck. 504).
71 Yer. Sheq. II:47a; Bavli Yev. 96a.
72 Naz. 52a and Tos. Ahil. IV:2 (Zuck. 600).

Although the passage deals with a Diaspora community, it presumably reflects the practices of Palestine as well. As for chronology, the synagogue described probably stood until the anti-Jewish riots in Egypt during the reign of Trajan in 116–117. The description, quoted from Rabbi Judah, contains the following:

> ... (in the synagogue) the people did not sit at random, but rather grouped by trades: goldsmiths in their own section, silversmiths in theirs, blacksmiths in theirs, weavers (*tarsim*) in theirs. So that when a newcomer entered, he sought out the members of his own craft, and on applying to that quarter, received his livelihood.... [73]

It is highly likely that the "livelihood" he received consisted of either a job, or support for himself and his family until he (or the guild) found work for him.

Returning to sources dealing directly with Palestine, among the crafts mentioned are those connected with the manufacture of dishes and other such vessels. In the Galilee, the cruses of Shiḥin had a reputation, and Kefar Hananiah was noted for its cooking pots. [74] In Judaea, one finds mention of "pots of Lydda" and "of Bethlehem." [75] A good grade of earthenware wine-bottle was manufactured in the Sharon, obviously as an adjunct of the extensive wine-production which characterized that part of the country. [76] A late source testifies to the presence in Tiberias of a pottery-works, as well as a glass manufactory. [77] But it is true that vessels were *imported* from Rhodes during the time of the Second Commonwealth; and the practice did not stop completely even after the Destruction.

Copper was one of the country's natural resources, so it is natural that the trade of coppersmith is mentioned in the Mishnah. [78] The metal was mined in the south up to the end of the fourth century, for

---

73 Tos. Sukk. IV:6 (Zuck. p. 198); see also Bavli Sukk. 51b, and Yer. Sukk. V:55b.
74 Tos. B. M. IV:3 (Zuck. 383); Bavli, ibid. 74a; Shab. 120b; and Lam. Zuta I:8.
75 Mishnah Kel. II:2; Sifra, Shemini, VI:3.
76 B.B. VI:2, and Nid. II:7.
77 Midrash Tehillim 75b; see also Yer. Nid. II:50b.
78 Ket. VII:10.

example at Phaenon.[79] However, Jerome informs us that in his day the copper mines were no longer being worked.

According to Dio Cassius there were Jewish armorers who made weapons for the Romans. He says that they deliberately took to fabricating defective ones in the years leading up to the Bar Kokhba Rebellion. This sabotage had a double purpose — the product would be rejected by the Romans, and the Jews could keep the weapons and repair them for their own use.[80]

We have already noted the existence of organized guilds of Jewish artisans, and have suggested that one of their purposes was mutual economic support. The sources dealing with this subject are post-Hadrianic, but it is quite likely that they reflect the usages of an earlier generation. The Tosefta states:

> Wool-carders and dyers are within their rights in contracting with one another to share all business that comes to their town. . . .[81]

The economic-cooperative nature of these associations could hardly be put more plainly. Not only was it proper for the craftsmen to organize, but the courts would enforce the agreement of the trade association on each individual artisan. The Tosefta goes on to say: "Bakers may also make a mutual contract (*regi'ah*)." The latter term appears only in this context, although derivatives of it occur twice in the Yerushalmi.[82] Long afterwards, in the 11th–12th century, Rabbi Judah al-Barceloni elucidated this Tosefta by suggesting a sample text of a *regi'ah* contract in his formulary of legal documents:[83]

> We. . . the bakers (named herein) have made a *regi'ah* among ourselves that each of us will be assigned his own day in the market. . . and no one of us will bake on any day set aside for another. Whoso violates this agreement shall be fined such and such a sum, or shall suffer such and such a penalty. . . .

79 Eusebius, *Onomastikon*, s.v. (No. 922 in the Hebrew translation by E. Z. Melammed.) See also *De Martyribus Palestinae*, XIII, 1.
80 69, 12.
81 Tos. B. M. XI:24 (Zuck. 397).
82 Yer. Qid. IV:65d; ibid. B.B. III:13d.
83 *Sefer ha-Shetarot*, ed. Halberstam, no. 57.

This illustrates another purpose of the guild: the setting up of work-schedules. The Tosefta goes on to say:

> Donkey-drivers may contract among themselves that if the beast of any one of them dies, the group will replace it for him, unless the death be caused by the owner's own culpable negligence. And if he who suffers the loss says 'Give me the money-value of my animal and I will buy the replacement,' no heed is paid to him; but the guild replaces his donkey in kind...
> Boatmen may contract thus: we undertake to replace any boat that is lost, excluding cases of culpable negligence. If the owner sails outside the customary sea-lanes, and thereby loses his vessel, the guild is not required to replace it.

Here we have a third purpose for organizing: to provide mutual insurance for each man's tools of his trade.

These clues to the nature of the voluntary associations of craftsmen are enough to indicate that they were essentially economic cooperatives. This distinguishes them fundamentally from the Roman *collegia* of artisans, which were worship-brotherhoods and burial societies. Therefore there are no grounds for holding that the Roman model inspired the creation of the Jewish guilds. It is much more likely that the Jews were influenced by Hellenistic practices. The Greek trades-associations in the Middle East had clear-cut economic purposes, as is well-known. But at the same time, it must be borne in mind that workmen's organizations existed in the Semitic world long before the arrival of the Greeks. They left traces in the Babylonian and Assyrian Empires, and even in the Israelite Kingdom.[84]

The work-ethic of the Jews in the generations both before and after the Destruction is illuminated by a number of source-texts. One of these passages, in which the Sages of Yavneh equate the labors of the farm-worker with their own spiritual and intellectual exertions, has been cited earlier.[85]

In the Hellenistic-Roman world, physical labor was despised by the upper classes. Josephus was probably aware that he was expressing a contrasting view when he proudly described his fellow-Jews as

---

84 See Isaac Mendelsohn in *BASOR* 80 (Dec. 1940), pp. 17 ff.
85 Above, p. 154.

a people that loved work, particularly on the land.[86] He even claimed that this attitude and this ethic were absorbed by those Gentiles who, attracted to Judaism, became "God-Fearers", as such demi-proselytes were called.

Philo too declared that the love of labor was a specifically Jewish characteristic. According to him, the Biblical "six days shalt thou do work" (Exod. 31:15) is a positive commandment. Just as we are bidden to rest on the Sabbath, so are we bidden to work on the weekdays. Furthermore, in *"The Testaments of the Twelve Patriarchs"* Issachar says: "I know your sons will abandon husbandry and be dispersed among the nations."[87] This may very well be a viewing-with-alarm of the tendency to imitate the attitudes and values of the Gentile idle rich — a tendency that began to emerge toward the end of the Hasmonean period, the very time when the book was written. Finally there was pseudo-Phoklydes, another contemporary writer who regarded work not as a necessary evil, but as a positive duty.

As for rabbinic sources, Aboth de Rabbi Nathan has the following forthright statement:[88]

"Love work" — what does that mean? It teaches that... no man should hate work. For even as the Torah is meant to be a covenant, so was work given as a covenant; as it is written: 'Six days shalt thou labor and do all thy work.'

Version B of the same book contains this:

Great is labor; for it was only after the Israelites had performed manual labor that the Divine Presence rested upon them.[89]

In the Mekhilta of Rabbi Simeon bar Yohai, the same sentiment is attributed to Rabbi Eleazar ben Azariah, who lived at the very period we are discussing.[90]

These sources show us what underlay the Pharisaic work-ethic and its attribution of a certain sanctity to labor. Several principles are involved, the first of which is the social one: that is to say, every

---

86 *Against Apion*, I:12 (60).
87 Charles, *Apocrypha* etc., vol. I, p. 327.
88 Version A, Schechter, p. 44. Goldin, p. 60.
89 Version B, ed. Schechter, ibid.
90 Hoffman éd. p. 107; Epstein ed. p. 149.

person is to some degree responsible for maintaining the social order. Next comes the individual factor: idleness is thought of as destructive to character; the person who does no work is like a ship adrift, a prey to every passing wind; while at the same time work is a sovereign remedy against the trials and crises from which no one is exempt. Thirdly, work is perceived as a value in itself, a potential source of deep satisfaction, a distinctive mark of the human being — God's gift to man. Finally, work is seen as an indispensible prerequisite for reaching the higher levels of spiritual exaltation. It was a doctrine of the Rabbis that revelation and prophecy were available only to those who first engaged in manual labor, witness for example Moses or Elisha.

CHAPTER NINE

LOCAL GOVERNMENT OF JEWISH TOWNS

Most of what we can say about the conduct of local affairs in Jewish urban centers in Palestine during the generations immediately following the Destruction has to be based on informed guesses. That is because there is an unfortunate dearth of contemporaneous data. To the greatest extent our source material comes, on the one hand, from the days of the Second Commonwealth, or on the other, from the late tannaitic period. Indeed, some of the material is difficult to date at all.

Council of Seven

At one point in his *Antiquities* Josephus explains the "constitution" which Moses legislated for his people:

> Let each city have seven men exercised in virtue and the pursuit of justice, and to each magistracy let there be assigned two subordinate officers (ὑπηρέται) of the tribe of Levi. Let those to whom it shall fall to administer justice be held in all honour.[1]

Naturally enough, Josephus attributes to Moses the procedures with which he himself was familiar. In so doing, he makes it clear that at least during the Second Commonwealth it was customary for a Jewish town to be run by a group of seven. At times he speaks of them as judges: "If without any act of treachery the depositary lose the deposit, let him come before the seven judges and swear (i.e. to his own innocence)."[2] But it is clear from most of what he reports that the seven were a real policy-making town council, and that their magistracy was a function of their leadership. What he tells us about his own

1 *Ant.* IV:8:14 (214).
2 Ibid. 38 (287).

activities in organizing the Galilee before the Roman invasion supports this conclusion.[3]

As for Josephus, on his arrival in Galilee he made it his first care to win the affection of the inhabitants, knowing that this would be of the greatest advantage to him, however he might otherwise fail. He realized that he would conciliate the leaders by associating them with him in his authority, and the people at large, if his orders were in the main given through the medium of their local acquaintances. He therefore selected from the nation seventy persons of mature years and the greatest discretion, and appointed them magistrates of the whole of Galilee; and seven individuals in each city to adjudicate upon petty disputes, with instructions to refer more important matters and capital cases to himself and the seventy.

Josephus presents this as though the council of seven were a new idea, all his own. But what he himself says in *Antiquities* is evidence that it was a long-established practice. And although he underscores the judicial function of these councils, he does begin by calling them *archontes* — rulers, head-men. In the context just quoted he fails to mention the aides (Levites). This probably goes to show that they were *not* a long-established element in the municipal set-up. As for the role of the Levites in communal leadership, this is not the place for an extended discussion. Suffice it to say that there is some evidence for the employment of the Levites to enforce the judgements of the courts.[4]

3 JW II:20:5 (569–571).
4 The Sifre on Deut. 16:18 (Finkelstein, p. 25) expounds the words: *Judges and officers shalt thou make thee;* "*Officers* — refers to the Levites, who smite with rod and lash, as it is written: 'also the officers of the Levites before you.' (II Chron. 19:11)." The Talmud yields the following (Yev. 86b): "Said Rav Hisda, at first officers were appointed from the Levites only, as it is written: 'the officers of the Levites before you' — but now officers are appointed from ordinary Israelites." This seems to indicate that as late as tannaitic times it was still customary to use Levites as enforcement officers. However, one text that supports the version given by Josephus in *The Jewish War* is *Midrash Tannaim* which reads (ed. Hoffman, p. 95): "Judges means *dayyanim*, while officers means *shammashim* (assistants)."

Corroboration for the number seven as the norm for a Jewish town council is found in the Gospels. The early Christian community in Jerusalem chose exactly that number of leaders to conduct its affairs, no doubt in conformity with existing Jewish practice.[5]

The Mishnah speaks of "lesser" Sanhedria, consisting of 23 judges each (Sanh. I:6). Although there is no mention of such courts in Josephus, or in any other extra-Rabbinic source, the fact that they existed can scarcely be doubted. The situation seems to have been that these *sanhedra'ot* sat in the larger towns, and functioned as the local government for such towns and their environs. What the councils of seven did was to look after strictly local matters in the smaller centers of population.[6]

The evidence shows that the seven-member town councils continued to function even after the Destruction. Thus, a rule in the Mishnah forbids the people of a town to sell their synagogue unless it be for the purpose of buying something like a Holy Ark with the proceeds.[7] The principle involved is, that sacred things may not be converted to secular uses, but only to purposes of greater sanctity (*ma'alin baqodesh*). On this there is a remark by Rabba, the fourth century Amora: "The rule does not apply if the sale was made by the *seven councilmen* acting in concert with the town assembly, in which case there are no restrictions on what will be done with the place; the buyer may even turn it into a beer-hall without affecting the validity of the transaction."[8] This observation, even though it comes from Babylonia, doubtless rests on an old Palestinian tradition. It shows the citizenry, in meeting assembled, gaining power at the expense of the "seven leading men"; but it also proves the persistence of the seven-member council.

A passage in the Yerushalmi reads:

> Three on behalf of a synagogue are like the whole synagogue.
> Seven on behalf of a town are as the whole town.[9]

Although this dictum is reported without attribution, we may assume

5 Acts, 6:3–5.
6 After the year 70 C.E. small *sanhedra'ot* became defunct.
7 Meg. IIII:1.
8 Meg. 26a.
9 Yer. Meg. III, 74a.

that it is one of the many *baraitha* traditions which are not uncommonly quoted in the Yerushalmi without attribution. What the statement means is that a committee of three can be empowered to act for a whole synagogue, and a council of seven can represent a whole town.

Since we are here concerned with the generation of Rabban Gamaliel of Yavneh, it may be in order to suggest a possible contemporary reference to the seven-man council. The Syriac Baruch in chapter 44(45) has Baruch ben Neriah summoning to his death-bed "seven elders of the people," along with his own eldest son and his friend Gedaliah. He charges them to take care of the people after his death. The numbers involved may just possibly reflect the custom of having seven community leaders plus two aides, as described by Josephus.

Having thus more or less established that the seven-man local council was the norm in the last years of the Second Commonwealth and in the immediate post-war years, we must nevertheless hasten to add that it was never the exclusive practice. The very context in the Yerushalmi just quoted goes on to say:

> What do we conclude from this? We conclude that if the townspeople appoint their representatives, they may empower even one individual to act on their behalf; but if the council is self-appointed, no matter how numerous its membership, it cannot bind the community. Therefore, although seven is the normal number, that holds good only so long as the people of the town have not decided otherwise.

Elders and Archons

Furthermore, we must take account of still other evidence regarding the make-up of local governing bodies. Such evidence is to be found in the Book of Judith. Although the date of its composition cannot be determined with certainty, we can be sure that it was written well before the Roman penetration into Judea. From a number of passages in Judith, we get a picture of two elements in town governance: 1) The Elders (πρεσβύτεροι) and 2) the Head-Men (ἄρχοντες).[10] The number of the Elders is nowhere specified; while

10 6:15–16; 8:8–10; 10:6; 13:12.

the Head-Men are said to be three, which fits in with the three magistrates required by the Mishnah for adjudicating pecuniary matters (Sanh. I:1). Sometimes these Head-Men are called Elders as well, which leaves the impression that they belonged to both bodies.

On the basis of all this, it seems probable that the Elders belonged to a rather large advisory Council, which in its turn chose three of its members to be *archontes* — thus constituting an executive governing body. It would also appear that one of these three was usually made chairman, or chief magistrate (as in the case of Uzziah in the Book of Judith). The references in the Talmudim to "Shazpar, Head-Man of Geder", who was deposed from that position by order of Rabban Gamaliel, are consistent with this hypothesis.[11]

A careful examination of the tannaitic sources lends support to this theory, although the picture is not as clear as we would wish. The term "elders" is usually used in the sense of authorized or ordained religious leaders, but in one instance at least it has a purely community connotation, and means roughly "town fathers."[12] The Tosefta has the following:[13]

> How were the elders seated? They faced the congregation, with their backs towards the Sanctum.[14] When the Ark was put down, it faced the people with its back toward the Sanctum. . . The precentor stood facing the Holy Place, and so too did the people. . .[15]

On the other hand, we find a different usage to convey the same meaning — the use of *rosh* or *roshim* in the sense of "chief magis-

11 Yer. R.H. I, 57b; Bavli, ibid. 22a.
12 As used in Greek by the Jews of the Diaspora, "elders" very often means simply "leaders." The same holds good for the Aramaic *qeshisha* and *qeshishutha* as used in Dura-Europos about the middle of the third century C.E. The use of *zeqenim* to signify members of the High Court as well as "scholars of the Torah" is common in pre-Destruction times. However, this seems to have evolved from the older (Biblical) usage, which meant "heads of the tribes," "leaders of the people." The word seems to have retained its older meanings alongside its later ones.
13 Tos. Meg. IV (III) 21 (Zuck. 227).
14 The reference is to the Sanctuary in Jerusalem, or to the place where it had stood. A similar usage occurs in the Greek of the Apocrypha.
15 Tos. Sanh. VII 8–9 (Zuck. 426); see also Bavli Hor. 13b.

trate" or "town council." One such example is the Gemara in Rosh Hashanah 22a:

> It was taught: Rabbi Judah said, perish the thought that it was Rabbi Akiba who detained them (i.e. the witnesses to the new moon). Actually, it was Shazpar, the Head-Man of Geder who did it, whereupon Rabban Gamaliel sent word to have him removed from office.

The corresponding passage in the Yerushalmi reads: [16]

> Rabbi Judah the Baker said, perish the thought that Rabbi Akiba was excommunicated; no, it was the Rosh of Geder. Rabban Gamaliel sent word to have him removed from office.

A similar usage occurs in Pesahim (112a) where there is a report that Rabbi Akiba charged his son to follow three precepts, one of which was not to live in a town whose *roshim* are scholars.

All of this adds up to the same picture that we derive from the Book of Judith. It seems that the local town councils, after the Destruction as before, continued to consists of *zeqenim* (Elders) and *roshim* (Head-Men).

The relationship between these two bodies, it has been suggested, was that between a deliberative council and an executive committee; but it can also be viewed in another way. The Heads can be seen as the administrators of all secular matters, and as the liaison between the Jewish town and the Roman authorities; while the Elders looked after the spiritual and religious affairs of the community.

The existence side by side of *Heads* and *Elders* in the Jewish town over many generations points to a long drawn-out process in which the age-old institution of local Head-Men was challenged by the growing influence of Sages — that is, of men learned in the Torah. Sometimes the two worked together; sometimes they struggled against one another for leadership. The process had already begun during the Second Commonwealth; after the Destruction the field was left increasingly to the scholars. The dominance of the Patriarch and his High Court had a good deal to do with this development.

Yet the older institution did not altogether vanish from the scene,

16 Yer. R.H. I, 57b.

as the following sources indicate. First, Sifre on the verse "And ye came near unto me every one of you and said..." (Deut. 1:22).

The wording here indicates that they approached Moses in disorder. Further on it is written, 'Ye came near unto me, even all the heads of your tribes, and your elders' (5:20) — that is, the youngsters deferred to the Elders (*zeqenim*) and the Elders to the Heads (*roshim*) — but here all is in disarray, with the young ones pushing the Elders, and the Elders pushing the Heads.[17]

Obviously, the Elders here mentioned are part of the leadership, and the Heads are superior to them, which reminds us of the situation depicted in the Book of Judith.

However, a parallel version of this has Rabbi Ishmael, approximately in the generation we are dealing with, putting the Elders in a position superior to the Heads.[18] Then there is a puzzling passage in the Yerushalmi, which quotes Rabbi Joshua ben Levi:[19]

... as between a *rosh* and a *zaqen*, the *zaqen* takes precedence, for the man would not be a *rosh* had he not been a *zaqen* in the first place...

On the other hand, the *Halakhot Gedolot* has this:

.... as between a *rosh* and a *zaqen*, the *rosh* takes precedence over a *zaqen* who is not a *rosh*....[20]

The Yerushalmi seems to indicate that one had to be an Elder before one could become a Head; but the *Halakhot Gedolot* leaves the question open. Be that as it may, the Yerushalmi does stress the civic-secular role of the *roshim*. This is brought out even more strongly later in the same context:[21]

Rabbi Joshua of Sikhnin quoted Rabbi Levi to the effect that Moses, through his power of the Holy Spirit, foresaw that the people Israel was destined to become entangled (read להסתבך)

17 Sifre Deut. 20; ed. Finkelstein, p. 32.
18 Midrash Tannaim, ed. Hoffman, p. 11.
19 Yer. Hor. III, 48b.
20 Venice Edition, folio 125b; ed. Hildesheimer, Berlin, p. 502.
21 Yer. Hor. III, 48c.

with various kingdoms of the world, and that their *roshim* would bear the brunt of these encounters; therefore did he mention these leaders before the Elders.

This defines the role of the *roshim* quite clearly. It also explains why the Sifre, focussing in its day on the political problems of Jewry, gave those leaders precedence; whereas the Midrash Tannaim, having in mind the importance of the spiritual authorities, put the *zeqenim* first. It does appear that as the years passed into the second century, it was the Elders (the Sages) who took the leading role in *every* respect.

At the time of Rabbi Akiba the prominent civic leaders were not always learned in the tradition, as we have just seen. Many passages in Rabbinic literature contrast the "disciples of the wise" with the *"gedolim"* — big men, prominent citizens of wealth and power. At times one finds the two elements at loggerheads, with the civic leaders decried as "strong men" (*ba'alei zero'a*) whose actions are contrary to the public interest. But not invariably. Sometimes one finds them praised as followers of the Sages, as men who "devote themselves faithfully to the needs of the community." Some even dip into their private purse to support community institutions, especially those involved in social welfare. It was of such men that the Talmud spoke when it said of Rabbi Akiba and of Rabbi Judah the Patriarch that they "paid honor to the rich."[22]

Finally, a late reference which goes to show the persistence of a dual leadership. In the Tractate Soferim there occurs the following:

> He is praised at a feast at which there are present the twelve leading citizens and twelve scholars. (IX:10)

This double-tracked leadership was rooted to a large extent in the social-economic conditions of the time. Quite often it was the local "big men" who gained the upper hand. The struggle for leadership between the spiritually qualified and the financially able or socially powerful stemmed from two factors: a) Ancient tradition, which had always looked to men of property and good family, pitted against the rising influence of scholars and men of Torah; and b) The ability of people of means to finance public needs, including even local magis-

22 Eruv. 86a.

tracies, as against a tendency to seek judges from among the learned. In Josephus it is taken for granted that the judiciary comes from the upper crust — in Hebrew, *tuvei ha'ir*, in the Roman world, *optimates*. By contrast, the literature of the Tannaim talks about *mumḥin* — magistrates possessed of authorization from the High Court. Be it noted that neither the former nor the latter were allowed to accept remuneration.

This last fact created a problem for those who wanted to see the best in learning and character on the bench. The only possible solution would have been the provision of stipends for those engaged full-time in public work. As a matter of fact, there are traces in the century following Rabban Gamaliel of just such a development; Sages who function as community leaders begin to be supported out of community funds. To be sure, the problem was never fully resolved, but that is connected with the changing economic situation in the country.

The older custom of local government by local men of substance never fully disappeared; but it had been successfully challenged, and was clearly on the way out. Had it not been for a radical change in conditions in the Middle East as a whole, it would probably have died out altogether.

CHAPTER TEN

THE ORIGINAL SANHEDRIN: RETROSPECT

We have seen how the re-establishment of a central Jewish authority provided the focus for rebuilding national life in the Land of Israel after the Destruction. This central authority consisted of two elements: the High Court and the Patriarchate — at least until the latter was abolished early in the fifth century. The two institutions, and the varying relationships between them from the time of Rabban Gamaliel onwards, are a principal factor — perhaps even the determining factor — in the history of the several centuries after the Destruction.

The antecedent of the High Court set up at Yavneh was, of course, the Great Sanhedrin that had sat in the capital during the Second Commonwealth, especially during the last generations before the Destruction. Unfortunately for us, there is much about that original Sanhedrin that remains problematical and speculative. We do not really know how it began, or how it developed. We shall therefore focus more on its unitary nature and component elements; on its Presidency; its size; and its powers and functions.

There is clear-cut evidence to show that by the beginning of the Hellenistic period — that is, before the end of the fourth pre-Christian century — the Sanhedrin was on the scene, a representative national assembly with all the scope and power it possessed later on. It is scarcely less certain, if not quite so well attested, that this assembly existed even earlier, during the Persian period. Nor should we dismiss out of hand the evidence of the Chronicler for a still earlier time:[1]

> Jehoshaphat also appointed at Jerusalem some of the Levites
> and priests and heads of families of Israel to handle cases in-

---

1 II Chron. XIX:8–11 [Here the translator has deliberately followed the reading וַיָּשֶׁבוּ proposed by Alon in *Meḥqarim* I, p. 69. See JJCW, p. 78, and contrast Anchor Bible, II. Chron., p. 106].

volving religious matters and disputes, and they had their seat at Jerusalem. He charged them as follows: 'Thus you must do in the fear of the Lord, in truth and with utmost integrity. When any case comes before you involving any of your brothers living in their cities... look now, Amariah the chief priest shall be in charge of all cases involving religious rules, and Zebediah ben Ishmael leader of the House of Judah, in all civil cases; and the official bailiffs shall be the Levites."

To be sure, this passage mentions only one of the functions later carried out by the Great Sanhedrin — namely, the judicial one. It is therefore possible to view the body appointed by Jehoshaphat as no more than the forerunner of the actual Sanhedrin.

Tannaitic tradition takes the story further back, viewing the seventy elders with whom Moses counselled as the origin of the Sanhedrin. We cannot be sure that this tradition of an inter-tribal council is without foundation; on the other hand, there are no other grounds for identifying it with the later body, nor any evidence that such a council existed during the centuries of the monarchy.

The ups and downs of the Great Sanhedrin during the days of the Second Commonwealth must certainly have been closely connected with the varying fortunes of the nation. It goes without saying that the role of this national court-cum-council was determined by whatever power ruled the country, whether from without — Ptolemies, Seleucids or Romans — or from within — Maccabean Ethnarchs, Hasmonean Kings, Herodians. One thing is clear: Herod drastically reduced the powers of the Great Sanhedrin to the point of impotence. (A contrary view is put forward by Schürer and others, but I think that view is mistaken). Indeed, it is not impossible that Herod abolished the Great Sanhedrin altogether.[2]

Earlier on, King Jannai (103–76 BCE) had had his struggles with the Sanhedrin, and had seriously hobbled it, or perhaps even suspended it.[3] Here in my view, lie the roots of the fierce opposition between that king and the Pharisees, because the latter sided with the Sanhedrin against the Crown.

2 See Alon: "The Attitude of the Pharisees etc." JJCW, p. 39.
3 Alon, ibid.

Composition

Similarly, the fortunes of the Sanhedrin were determined to no small extent by the social history of the people. For example, the prolonged struggle between the Sadducees (oriented toward the important families and the upper priesthood), and the Pharisees (who included spokesmen of the common people and the country priests), was continually reflected in the composition of the Sanhedrin and in the positions it took. The same can be said for the ongoing tension between the "heads of the great families," men with economic power and social status, and their opponents the "scribes" and the "elders" — the teachers who expounded the Torah, and were regarded as spiritual and religious guides.

In any case, even though the societal elements that went into the make-up of the Sanhedrin changed as time passed, and the balance of forces within it shifted now this way now that, the institution persisted. There may have been times when its political and judicial powers were taken from it, and its status as a governing body was temporarily reduced; but it persisted.

The actual name "Sanhedrin" first appears in Josephus, in a context related to the reign of Hyrcanus II; that is, in the fifties of the first pre-Christian century. However, the institution is referred to by a number of names, around which revolve the principal problems that have engaged the attention of modern scholars. Let us therefore examine the nomenclature of the assembly as it appears in tannaitic literature; and then as it is to be seen in other, Greek-language sources, which for brevity's sake, we shall call "external."[4]

Tannaitic literature uses the following names: a) *The Great Beth Din in Jerusalem*; b) *The Great Beth Din in the Chamber of Hewn Stone*; c) *The Beth Din of Seventy-One*; d) *The Great Sanhedrin*; e) *Sanhedrin* (tout court). Sometimes the body is referred to obliquely without name, as when its members are called "the Elders" or "Elders of the Beth Din", or simply "the Sages."

The external sources show an even wider variety of designations:

---

4 There are four principal sources: a) The corpus of rabbinic literature; b) Josephus Flavius: *Antiquities, The War, Life,* and indirectly, *Against Apion;* c) Apocrypha, especially Macc. I, II, III, and Judith; d) New Testament, especially Acts and the four Gospels. There is also something to be learned from the works of Philo.

The Original Sanhedrin

a) *Sanhedrin*: b) *The Sanhedrin of the Men of Jerusalem*; c) *Gerousia* (γερουσία;) d) *The Gerousia of the People*; e) *The Gerousia of all the Children of Israel*; f) *Presbyterion* (πρεσβυτέριον — i.e. Council of Elders); g) *Elders of the People*; h) *Elders of Israel*; i) *Elders of Jerusalem*; j) *Elders of the Children of Israel*; k) *The Elders* (πρεσβύτεροι or γεραῖοι); l) *Boulé* (βουλή). This last is a usage of Josephus, who calls the council chamber *bouleuterion*.[5]

Adolf Büchler made use of this variety of names to buttress his argument that there were a number of different kinds of Sanhedrin, each with its own special functions.[6] He formulated this theory in order to cope with a striking contradiction between the rabbinic sources and those we have called external.[7] The tannaitic tradition, it was claimed, gives us a picture of the Sanhedrin as an entirely Pharisaic institution, composed exclusively of learned Sages. But the external sources show us the priests — particularly the upper priesthood — cast in an important (one might even say a paramount) role. Still more glaring is the difference between the two types of sources when it comes to the Presidency of the Sanhedrin. The rabbinic tradition calls this officer the *"Nasi"*, and makes him out to have been a learned judge — a Pharisee.[8] It is in accordance with this tradition that Hillel the Elder, and Rabban Gamaliel the First, and Rabban Simeon his son are said to have been each in turn *Nasi* of the Sanhedrin.

By contrast, the Greek-language sources always have the High Priest presiding at sessions of the Great Sanhedrin. That is the situation in the Gospels and in the Acts of the Apostles, at the trials of Jesus, of Stephen, of the Apostles, and of Paul.[9] So too in Josephus, as at the trial of Jacob, brother of Jesus, or the appearance of Herod before Hyrcanus II. Christian scholars have solved the contradiction

---

5   This list of names is far from exhaustive.

6   See his *Das Synedrion in Jerusalem*, Vienna, 1902.

7   See Schürer, *Geschichte*, 4th ed., Vol. II, pp. 237–267.

8   See Hagigah, Mishnah II:2 for reference to the five sets of *zugot*, ("pairs") of Sages: "The first of these held the office of Nasi, while the second in each case was Av Bet-Din — Presiding Justice." See also Tos. ibid. II:8 (Zuck. 235) and the relevant passages in the two Talmudim.

9   Even more striking is Acts 5:34, where Rabban Gamaliel is mentioned simply as "a member of the Council" — but *not* as its President.

by dismissing the tannaitic tradition out of hand. They have pronounced it a retrojection by the Rabbis, back to Temple days, of the institutions as they knew them at the end of the second century C.E. Büchler was quite right when he pointed out the lack of scientific objectivity that marks this solution. He demonstrated how these scholars were all too ready to abandon their customary canons of inquiry into the historicity of traditions, when it came to Jewish traditions. He proceeded to develop his own answer to the divergencies in the sources, by positing *three distinct institutions* in Jerusalem: 1) The Beth Din in the Chamber of Hewn Stone, a court that consisted solely of learned Pharisees, and dealt only with matters of religious ritual and the Temple cultus; 2) The Sanhedrin proper, which tried cases and imposed sanctions (but again, with special reference to offences against the Sanctuary); and 3) *The Boulé*, which was the governing body for the City of Jerusalem.

However, this theory of Büchler's is not well-founded. Such sources as we have lend no support to the notion of three co-existing high judicial or consultative bodies. We shall have to resign ourselves to the existence of one single Sanhedrin. It shows up, to be sure, under many names; but these testify to the vicissitudes which the institution had to undergo with the passage of time.

The problems created by our multiple and contradictory sources remain. Short of the discovery of some new evidence, the most promising approach to a solution is to examine the social elements that were represented in the Sanhedrin during the last several generations of the Commonwealth, and to study the power-struggle between them. At the same time, and as a corollary of that struggle, the question of the Presidency should be scrutinized.

First of all, let us not exaggerate the extent of the contradiction between the tannaitic sources and the external ones, as though the former spoke only of learned Sages in the Sanhedrin, while the latter knew only of priests, or "high priests".[10] The fact is that the tannaitic tradition is aware of the presence of other elements as well. An example, from the time of the last Hasmonean Kings, is the dispute

10 In Josephus and in the Christian scriptures, "High Priests" often means "important and powerful priestly families" and not necessarily the actual *kohen gadol*. Even rabbinic literature sometimes uses the term in this broader sense.

between Simeon ben Shetah and the Sadducees over a matter of law, which led to the Pharisees gaining control of the Great Sanhedrin.[11] From a later time, a generation before the Destruction, comes the account of a discussion about the Biblical form of capital punishment called *serefah*. The Mishnah explains that this was not actual burning, but Rabbi Elazar ben Zadok disagrees.[12] He claims that on one occasion the daughter of a priest was found guilty of adultery, and they literally "surrounded her with bundles of firewood and burned her." The Mishnah discounts this: "It was a court that did not know the law correctly." In the Gemara, Rav Yosef explains: "It was a court of Sadducees."[13] The case was undoubtedly tried before the Great Sanhedrin in Jerusalem; and the tradition quoted by Rav Yosef apparently means that the trial was held at a time when the Sadducees held a majority in that body.

That Pharisees and Sadducees sat side by side in the Sanhedrin, is testified to by the reference to Rabban Gamaliel the Elder in the Acts of the Apostles (5:34). It is a situation we run into again when the Sanhedrin of National Unity was constituted after the defeat of Cestius Gallus, at the beginning of the war against Rome. This, incidentally, is evidence of the Pharisees' policy of co-operation with "heretics" in the interests of preserving unity.

Even more to the point is the testimony of the Tosefta that the King's Torah scroll was inspected by the court of "priests and Levites, and of Israelites from families eligible to intermarry with the priesthood."[14] And still more explicit is the comment on Deuteronomy 17:8–9 which we find in the Sifre.[15]

> "The precept regarding the High Court envisages it as containing *Kohanim* and Levites. Does that mean that if these were not included, the court is disqualified? Not at all, for the Torah goes on to say: *'and to the judge who shall be in those days'* — which teaches me that the court is a valid court even without priests and Levites."

11 Meg. Taan., ed. Grossberg, p. 56.
12 Sanh. VII:2.
13 Ibid. 52b.
14 Tos. Sanh. IV:7 (Zuck. 421). There is no doubt that the reference is to the Great Sanhedrin.
15 Para. 153, ed. Finkelstein, p. 206. Comp. Midrash Tannaim, p. 102.

In other words, the halakhah was willing to forgo the presence of priests and Levites in the membership of the High Court, even though they were certainly called for *ab initio*, and were in fact usually present right up to the time of the Destruction. The priests no doubt kept insisting that their participation was essential. As long as the institution lasted they remained a factor to be reckoned with, even if their influence steadily diminished. In the meantime, the Sages in the Sanhedrin were constantly gaining ground at the expense of still another element — the "Elders", men of family and property and social standing whose importance went back to very ancient times.[16]

It is this state of affairs which is reflected in the frequent New Testament references to "the chief priests and the scribes," or "the chief priests and the elders of the people", or "the chief priests and the Pharisees", or "the chief priests and the elders and the scribes and the whole Sanhedrin", and the many permutations and combinations of these terms. All these wordings undoubtedly point to the varying human elements that made up the membership of the Sanhedrin.

To be sure, the oldest traditions gave the priests a decisive role in the Sanhedrin. As a result, the institution always remained physically attached to the Temple, as by an uncut umbilicus. The connection echoes in such phrases as "The Sanhedrin which meets near the Altar" (or "in the Chamber of Hewn Stone"); or in the maxim "When there are priests, there is *mishpat* (capital punishment); when the one does not function, neither does the other."[17] Given this background, and the continued presence of *Kohanim* in the Sanhedrin, it is not surprising that the body appeared to outside observers — including the Jews of the Diaspora — as a council surrounded by an aura of priestly sanctity, even after control had passed de facto to a Pharisee majority of Torah scholars. Hence, for example, the impression one gains from Philo that the priests were in charge of the highest judiciary — that is, the Great Sanhedrin.[18] Hence, too, the prom-

---

16 The Levites, a sort of "third estate", lost much of their importance as time went on, although the usual assumption that they disappeared entirely from any leadership role in the Temple worship, or in community service in the provinces, goes too far.

17 Sanh. 52b.

18 *De Special. Legib.* IV. See translation by Colson, Vol. VIII, sec. 190–192, p. 127.

inence of the "chief priests" throughout the Christian scriptures. The various elements within the High Court did not disintegrate and lose their separate identity. As a matter of fact, tannaitic literature speaks of a distinct "Beth Din of *Kohanim*" in Jerusalem one which occasionally disputed the opinion of the Sages, even in matters over which the Sanhedrin had jurisdiction. In much the same way we hear that the "sons of the high priests" had a sort of academy of their own for the study of civil law.[19] Nevertheless, the Sanhedrin held together as one single institution, though it undoubtedly carried within itself all the ingredients making for fierce internal struggle and ultimate break-up.

So the tannaitic tradition is *not* simply an anachronistic reading of post-Destruction conditions as the Rabbis knew them, back into the days when the Temple had stood. Just as the tradition preserved the memory of the once-powerful role of the priests and the Sadducees in the Sanhedrin, so was it justified in remembering that the Pharisaic Sages had taken a decisive part in the court and council during those last generations of the Second Commonwealth. The Rabbis held, in principle, that the priesthood — including the high priest — was *not* an indispensable part of the Sanhedrin, nor of its procedures. In this connection, it is worth noting that Josephus agrees with the rabbinic sources in picturing the Sadducees (practically synonymous with "the high priests") during the time of the Roman procurators as giving way reluctantly to the pressure of popular opinion in all matters of religious law, including even Temple procedures. If that was so, how much more likely would it have held good in matters affecting the Sanhedrin!

This leads us to the second major question, namely: who controlled the presidency of the Sanhedrin? Was it in the hands of the high priest, as would appear from the external sources, or was it the prerogative of the *Nasi*, a learned Sage of the Pharisees?

From what we have seen of the composition of the Sanhedrin, it is a logical assumption that no one of its elements was in complete control, at least not since the time when the Pharisees had successfully challenged the power of the priests. Secondly, none of the sources states explicitly that the high priest was an actual member of the

---

19   Mishnah, Ket. 1:5; XIII:1; R. H. I:7. Apparently the Pharisaic element also had its own "caucus".

Sanhedrin, and its permanent presiding officer. All we are told is that on certain specified occasions the high priest called the Sanhedrin together and took the chair. Does it not seem likely that the office he held was a separate and independent institution of government, so that he and the assembly were a kind of diarchy? A careful reading of all official documents from the time of the first Hasmoneans onwards allows of this interpretation. Consequently, the high priest could have had a perfect right, both in law and custom, to summon the Sanhedrin and even to preside over it, without being one of its members. It is noteworthy that the tradition which excludes the king from the Sanhedrin permits the high priest to be a member of that body.[20] This halakhah may well preserve the memory of a time when the high priest could hold a seat in the Sanhedrin, and even be its chief.

Perhaps this is what lies at the root of the dispute between Rabbi Judah and the Sages over the number of seats the Sanhedrin had had. They reckoned the total at 71; he said no, it was 70.[21] At issue seems to have been the status of the presiding officer. Was he a separate and distinct entity, or was he "a member of the House?" The Sages seem to be saying he was a regular member, with Rabbi Judah claiming he was not.[22] One is tempted to suggest that this difference of opinion is an echo of the constitutional problem that existed during Temple times, and was to recur in connection with the High Court at Yavneh.

The question before us has two aspects: 1) Did the Sanhedrin have a single presiding officer, or *more* than one? 2) Was there indeed originally such a thing *at all* as the "presidency" of the Sanhedrin, in a constitutional sense?

We have already suggested that it is unlikely that any one of the elements composing the Sanhedrin had control of it. This very fact,

20 The Mishnah rules both: "The King cannot judge" (Sanh. II:2) and "The High Priest can judge" (ibid. II:1). Compare Bavli, ibid. 18b. The two rules are strikingly juxtaposed by Maimonides in his *Mishneh Torah*, Hilkhot Sanhedrin, II:4.

21 Mishnah, Sanh. I:6.

22 See Louis Ginzberg: *"Perushim ve'Hidushim bi-Yerushalmi"*, vol. III, p. 217. He cites the Tosefta to prove that the issue actually was as stated above.

if fact it be, may explain why the sources contradict one another. It would allow us to view the high priest as *one* leader of the Sanhedrin, and the head of the Pharisaic party as another. If this be granted, then it is logical to suppose that the high priest took over when the agenda dealt with matters of state and public policy, while the *Nasi* or the Av Bet Din took the chair when the discussion concerned religious affairs, matters of substantive law, and whatever else was internally Jewish. As a matter of fact, all the sessions mentioned above that show the high priest presiding were cases with a political aspect, even though they seem on the surface to have been the trials of individuals. But when the subject before the house was purely halakhic, then Hillel and Rabban Gamaliel the Elder and Rabban Simeon Ben Gamaliel might well have presided.

We have no real proof that the *Nasi* had any official constitutional status in the Sanhedrin during the Second Commonwealth. On the contrary, it is much more likely that he was simply the de facto leader of his party, occupying no legally recognized office. Consequently, Rabban Gamaliel can be described in the Acts of the Apostles (5:34) simply as one highly respected member of the Sanhedrin, much as Josephus describes Shemaya (or Shammai). With the high priest it was slightly different; because he occupied an office with an importance of its own, there might have been a tendency to see his rôle in the Sanhedrin as more established.[23]

In this connection there is something to be learned from the "Revolutionary" Sanhedrin that was constituted as the sole organ of Jewish government at the beginning of the war against Rome. That Sanhedrin had no single head. Hanan ben Hanan and Joshua ben Gamla did not rule as high priests, nor were Rabban Simeon ben Gamaliel and Gorion ben Joseph given authority as Patriarchs.[24] Priests and laymen together formed the "governing committee" of the Sanhedrin. It is just possible that this was the pattern according to which the leadership of the Sanhedrin had actually functioned during the several generations preceding.

23 But note that the same "one among many" language is used of the high priest in John, XI:47–49. "Then gathered the chief priests (ἀρχιερεῖς) and the Pharisees the Sanhedrin. . . . . And one of them, Caiaphas, the high priest that same year. . ."
24 JW IV:3:9 (160).

Composition

This may well be the place to reject the view put forward by A. Kaminka, to the effect that the tannaitic tradition about the number of members in the Sanhedrin is purely speculative midrash.[25] This view is rather unconvincing, especially since no proof is advanced to support it. It ignores the corroborative evidence from Josephus, who tells us that when he was put in charge of the Galilee he established a council of 70.[26] Elsewhere, the same historian has the Zealots setting up a court of 70 judges to try Zechariah ben Baruch.[27]

There is another possibility: perhaps there were more than seventy men who were qualified to sit; but only seventy of them sat formally at any one time.

Another fact of some consequence is that though the body was considered a Jerusalem institution during the last generations of its existence, we can nevertheless detect among its members a goodly number who came from other Judaean cities, quite as though they were representing the provinces in a national assembly.

How did one become a member of the Sanhedrin? We cannot say with any certainty whether appointments were made by the high priest (or whoever else happened to be Head of State at the time), or whether members were co-opted by the Sanhedrin itself when vacancies occurred. The tannaitic tradition has it that the Sanhedrin filled its own vacancies from a pool of eligible candidates. But that is all the evidence we have.

The importance of the question derives from its bearing on the struggle between the Patriarch and the Sanhedrin in the post-Destruction era over who held the power of appointment. If it had originally belonged to the high priest, then the Patriarch could claim to be his legitimate successor. But if the old Sanhedrin had been the appointing authority, then the new High Court could claim the right.

25 *Zion* 1944, pp. 70–83.
26 JW II:20:5 (570).
27 Ibid. IV:5:4 (336). The tradition reports a council of 71 as the governing body of the Jewish community of Alexandria. So, too, a delegation of 70 appears before Varus in Caesarea according to JW II:18:6 (482). Comp. *Life*, XI (56).

The Original Sanhedrin

Scope

We proceed to examine the jurisdiction and functions of the Sanhedrin as they had been when the institution was at the height of its
powers. They can be summarized as follows:

1) The Sanhedrin was the highest authority for *settling doubtful
points* of religion and law. The Mishnah makes this quite clear in the
case of the "rebellious elder": "Both sides repair to the High Court
which sits in the Chamber of Hewn Stone, for from there teaching
goes forth to all Israel..."[28] The Tosefta is even more explicit:

> Said Rabbi Jose: At first there were no disputes in Israel, for
> there was the Court of Seventy-One in the Chamber of Hewn
> Stone, and Courts of Twenty-Three in all the towns of the
> Land of Israel... If any (judge) needed a ruling, he applied to
> the court in his town.. if they had heard (the law on that ques-
> tion) they told it to him; if not, he and the *mufla'* of that court
> proceeded to the court on the Temple Mount.. and if no (an-
> swer was forthcoming) both went on to the High Court in the
> Chamber of Hewn Stone.[29]

A similar procedure is reflected in the Book of Judith.[30] She tells
Holofernes that the people of Bethulia, having reached the point of
starvation, have decided to send a delegation to the *gerousia* in Jerusalem for dispensation to consume the produce and cattle that had
been set aside for tithes, heave-offerings and the like, which would
normally be forbidden.

Josephus gives a like description of Jewish court procedures:

> But if the judges see not how to pronounce upon the matters
> before them... let them send up the case entire to the holy city
> and let the high priest and the prophet and the council of
> elders (*gerousia*) meet and pronounce as they see fit.[31]

This is one instance where the high priest is enumerated as a separate element in the decision-making process, *alongside* the Sanhedrin.

28 Sanh. XI:2.
29 Tos. Sanh. VII:1 (Zuck. 425); ib. Hag. II:9 (Zuck. 235). See also Bavli,
    Sanh. 88b; Yer., Sanh. I:19c; Sifre Shofetim, 152 (Finkelstein 206).
30 XI:12–14.
31 Ant. IV: 8:14 (218).

As far as the "prophet" is concerned, this passage is not the only one in which such a person is referred to as a consultant in arriving at a judgement. No doubt the term is vestigial, a memory of much more ancient times. Since it was established that prophecy had come to an end shortly after the return from Babylonian exile, it was also held that this in no way detracted from the authority of the Sanhedrin as the final arbiter in matters of law and religious conduct. In the same way, the tannaitic tradition maintained that the participation of the high priest was not indispensable, either. With that the Book of Judith seems to agree; contrary to Philo, who gives the last word to the high priest.[32]

2) A second function of the Sanhedrin was that it not only answered *doubts* in matters of law, but also settled *disputed issues*. The Mishnah and the *baraitha* in the matter of the rebellious elder make this clear: "If he went back to his city and taught the law (in theory) as he had been accustomed to, he is not punishable; but if he actually directed people (to act on his rejected view), he is culpable." This shows that any local authority who gave direction contrary to the ruling of the Sanhedrin was punishable. A case is cited from pre-Destruction times (not an actual "rebellious elder") in which Akaviah ben Mahalalel differed with the majority on four points of law. They sent him a message: "Akaviah, give way!" But he wouldn't, and they put him under a ban, and he died unrepentant, and the court cast a stone at his coffin.[33]

Something similar is recorded from the time of Hillel, when Rabbi Judah ben Dorthai and his son Dorthai had to leave the Sanhedrin because they would not accept the majority opinion in a matter of ritual law involving festival sacrifices.[34]

The portrayal by Rabbi Jose of the "good old days" when there was brotherly unanimity among all the Sages does seem rather wist-

---

32 *De Spec. Leg.*, Book IV, 190; Colson transl., Vol. viii, p. 125-6.
33 Eduy. V:6.
34 Pes. 70b. Further on, Rav Ashi calls them *"perushim"* — separated. It seems clear to me that this means "separated from the Sanhedrin" despite the interpretation offered by Rashi and the Tosaphists that the two were sent to live in the Darom so that they would not be involved in the festival sacrifices. The trouble with that is, that the Darom is still part of the Holy Land!

fully unrealistic. However, the same tradition seems to be not entirely unfounded when it goes on to say: "But the time came when there were many disciples of Shammai and Hillel who had not sat long enough at the feet of their masters, and then disputes and divisions multiplied in Israel and the Torah became two Torahs".[35]

It is quite possible that Herod, by cutting down the powers of the Sanhedrin, did much to erode the tradition that the last word in halakhah rested with the highest institution of the people. But that cannot have been the primary cause for the growth of divisions of opinion. It should be kept in mind that the Great Sanhedrin gave decisions only in matters of which it was seized. It took no initiative in offering opinions on theoretical questions of law. What is more, the Sanhedrin hardly ever attempted to impose one single interpretation of the Torah on the whole people, except in a few specific instances when critical social and religious issues were at stake. For the Sanhedrin was basically an institution of government. The theoretical study and interpretation of the law was a matter for the schools more than for the courts.

According to Josephus, the Pharisees succeeded in winning the support of the masses because they "excelled at interpreting the Torah." The teacher (διδάσκαλος), the scholar (νομικός) and the scribe (γραμματεὺς)[35a] are the principal sources of the halakhah — hence the wide latitude and diversity, in practice as well as in theory, during the Second Commonwealth. Furthermore, the Sage is not necessarily the occupant of some officially recognized position; any person who devotes himself to the study of the Torah has the right to give his interpretation and to teach his opinion.

If nevertheless the result during the Second Commonwealth was in fact the development of a more or less normative halakhic consensus, that has to be attributed to the natural evolution of the attitude and thinking of the people at large. By a developing social process they created a religio-cultural unity out of diverse elements, able both to confront one another and to adapt to one another.

But it would be unrealistic to suppose that there were not times and situations which seemed to demand that diversity be curbed by

---

35 See above, note 29.
35a [For the Greek terms, see e.g. Matt. 23, verses 8, 35; and 22:34].

decision and free expression be replaced by discipline. "Teachers" and "Sages" were sometimes summoned to submit to authority. It was in the interplay between freedom of interpretation, and the limits set to that freedom at what were perceived to be times of crisis, that rabbinic Judaism was forged.

3) This brings us to a third function of the Sanhedrin — the imposition of religious disciplines. It appears that this power was invoked only when there seemed to be a danger that some new breakaway sect or religious movement was in the making. The following is an example from the days of the last Hasmonean rulers: (Mishnah Ta'anith III:8)

> Once they said to Honi the Circle-Drawer: Pray for rain. He said, bring your Passover ovens indoors (they were earthen, and could be washed away). He prayed, but no rain came. What did he do? He drew a circle and stood in the middle of it, and said: Master of the Universe, Your children have come to me, as to a member of Your household. I swear by Your Great Name that I will not stir from here until You take pity on Your children. Drops of rain began to fall. He said: That's not what I asked for, but rather rain that will fill the cisterns, pits and caverns. Whereupon it began to pour violently. He said: That's not what I asked for, but rather rain of grace, blessing and favor. Then it settled down to a moderate steady rainfall, until the people of Jerusalem took refuge on the Temple Mount. They came to him and said: Just as you prayed for rain, pray now for it to stop... Simeon ben Shetah sent to him, saying: Had you been anyone else but Honi, I would have put you under a ban. But what can I do? You pray to God, and He does what you ask, like a son who importunes his father. It is of you that Scripture says: 'Let your father and your mother be glad, let her that bore you rejoice.' (Prov. 23:25)

This tradition mentions Simeon ben Shetah (ca. 75 B.C.E.); but surely he acted on behalf of the Sanhedrin, as its chief or as one of its leaders. Their objection to Honi was that he presumed to have special "intimacy" with the Lord, and claimed that this gave him miraculous powers. The Sanhedrin and the Sages were opposed to such extreme pietists. They regarded them as misleaders of the people, verging on "false prophets."

Another notable example: Justin Martyr, in his "Dialogue with Trypho", reports that the Sanhedrin used to despatch emissaries to the Diaspora to counteract the preaching of Christianity to Jews. The same thing is reflected in Acts 28, 21: "And they said unto him (Paul) 'We neither received letters out of Judaea concerning thee, neither any of the brethren that came shewed or spake any harm of thee.'"

Even more explicit is the passage in Acts 9, 1–2: "And Saul.... went unto the high priest, and desired of him letters to Damascus to the synagogues, that if he found any of this way, whether they were men or women, he might bring them bound unto Jerusalem." To be sure, in this context the high priest alone is mentioned, and a little later on, (verses 14 and 21) it is "the high priests"; but we must assume that here as elsewhere the Sanhedrin was involved.[36] However, we do know that the Pharisees, who by this time constituted a large element in the Sanhedrin, were generally reluctant to be overly strict with dissenters. This is illustrated in the report of the trial of the apostles (Acts 5:34 ff.):

> Then stood there up one in the council, a Pharisee named Gamaliel, a doctor of the law, had in reputation among all the people, and commanded to put the apostles forth a little space; and said unto them, ye men of Israel, take heed to yourselves what ye intend to do as touching these men... And now I say unto you, refrain from these men, and let them alone: for if this counsel or this work be of men, it will come to nought; but if it be of God, ye cannot overthrow it, lest haply ye be found to fight even against God. And to him they agreed...

However, we do find the Sanhedrin intervening energetically in a matter that seemed to be fraught with serious consequences for Juda-

---

36 The role of the Sanhedrin as the instrument that bound the Diaspora to the mother country in religion and community affairs is also expressed in II Macc. 1:10, thus: "The people which is in Jerusalem and Judaea, and the Gerousia and Judah the Maccabee, to Aristobulus.... and the Jews who are in Egypt...." The subject is the institution of the new Feast of Hannukah.

ism. It was at the end of the Persian period, in a clash with the high priest's brother who had married the daughter of the Samaritan Sanballat, governor of Samaria. Josephus reports:[37]

> Now the elders of Jerusalem, resenting the fact that the brother of the high priest Yaddua was.... married to a foreigner, rose up against him.... They believed moreover that their former captivity and misfortunes had been caused by some who had.... taken wives who were not of their own country..... They therefore told Menasseh either to divorce his wife or not to approach the altar. The high priest shared the anger of the people.[38]

4) The Sanhedrin was also to some degree a legislative body. It had the power to enact *taqanot* (regulations) and *gezerot* (ordinances) of a semi-permanent nature. Although subsequent tradition usually attributes *taqanot* to the individual heads of the Sanhedrin — Simeon ben Shetah, Hillel the Elder, Rabban Simeon ben Gamaliel the First, and so on — nevertheless it can be taken as certain that these rulings were enacted by the Sanhedrin in concert with the *Nasi*, in the same way that the *Nasi*-in-Beth-Din of post-Destruction times promulgated rulings which were then accepted as binding by the entire Jewish people. To be sure, such enactments were regarded theoretically as mere glosses on the actual law of the Torah, purely temporary measures. In fact, however, they represent a broadening of the law. And since this interpretative power was entrusted to the Great Sanhedrin, we are justified in regarding it as at least a quasi-legislative activity.

5) Another function of the Sanhedrin was that of fixing the calendar. A number of tannaitic traditions (and there is no reason to doubt their accuracy) tell us that during the last few generations before the Destruction of the Temple, the High Court in Jerusalem had the duty of announcing the New Moons, and of deciding when there should be a leap year by the intercalation of an extra month into the lunar year. This was a very important responsibility, because it determined the dates of the festivals, and was thus one of the primary links between the mother country and the Diaspora.

37 Ant. XI: 7:2 (303).
38 Ibid. 8:2 (306 ff.).

In this context too, as in the preceding one, we sometimes find the *Nasi* mentioned alone; but it seems clear that he acted in conjunction with the Beth Din. As a matter of fact, the subject later on became involved in the jurisdictional dispute between the Patriarchate and the Sanhedrin.[39]

6) Still another area in which the Sanhedrin held, or acquired, an active supervisory role was that of the Temple cultus. In this connection one need only quote the Mishnah (Yoma I:5):

> The elders of the Court delivered him (the high priest) to the elders of the priesthood, and they brought him up to the upper chamber of the house of Abtinas. They adjured him and took their leave and went away, having said to him: 'My dear high priest, we are the messengers of the Court, and you are our messenger and the messenger of the Court. We charge you by Him who made His name dwell in this house that you change nothing of the procedures we have gone over with you. . . .

Here we see the Sanhedrin, at a time when its majority were Pharisees, exercising supervisory power to make sure that the crucial Yom Kippur ritual was carried out according to their teaching, and not according to the Sadducean priests. Similarly, the *priestly* jurisdiction of the Great Sanhedrin over the priesthood during pre-Destruction times may be seen from the following passage in the Mishnah (Middoth, V:4):

> The Chamber of Hewn Stone — there used the Great Sanhedrin of Israel to sit and judge the priesthood; and if in any priest a blemish was found he would clothe himself in black and veil himself in black and go on his way. . . .

A concrete example of this kind of sacerdotal involvement of the Sanhedrin during the last days of the Temple can be cited from Josephus. He tells us that the Levites of the Temple choir requested Agrippa II "to convene the Sanhedrin and get them permission to wear white-linen robes on equal terms with the priests." Agrippa did as he was asked, and the Sanhedrin granted its permission. Josephus, himself a *Kohen*, undoubtedly expresses the sense of outrage felt by his

39   See below, p. 318.

fellow-priests: "All this was contrary to the ancestral laws, and such transgression was bound to make us liable to punishment."[40] But it seems that the Sanhedrin, with its Pharisaic predilections, took the side of the Levites in this matter.

7) Elsewhere I have tried to prove — successfully, I think — that the Sanhedrin held exclusive jurisdiction in cases involving capital punishment, at least from the time of the Hasmoneans onward. It is true that we have many references to the competence of the "lesser Sanhedra'ot" in such matters, (comp. Sanh. I:4) but there was a fundamental assumption that those provincial courts derived their power from the High Court in Jerusalem; and I have argued that the local courts did not actually handle such matters during the last few centuries of the Jewish State. By contrast to the period of the ancient monarchy, there was a tendency during the Second Commonwealth to concentrate the higher criminal jurisdiction in the hands of the authorities in Jerusalem, a centralizing trend which can be observed in other respects as well.[41]

8) Moving from the judicial to the political, we find the Great Sanhedrin functioning as a kind of Senate — the highest political body representing the people internally.[42] We shall cite two areas in which this finds expression.

a) The consent of the Sanhedrin is required for the declaration of war: "The people may not be sent out to a war of choice (i.e. attack) save by decision of the court of seventy-one."[43] Shortly thereafter we find almost the same thing repeated: "He (i.e. the king) may order the people into a battle of choice by decision of the court of seventy-one."[44] The events described in II Macc. 13:13 seem to be an illustration of this very law in action. Antiochus Eupator, with his commander Lysias, marches against Judaea. Judah the Maccabee counsels with the *elders* (πρεσβύτεροι) on the proposition that the

---

40 Ant. XX:9:6 (218). There is no reason to follow Schürer in his interpretation of the "Sanhedrin" in this context as a council of priests.
41 Alon: *On Philo's Halakhah*, in JJCW, pp. 104 ff.
42 It is highly probable that the text *ḥever ha-yehudim* (חבר היהודים) inscribed on certain Hasmonean coins refers to the Sanhedrin, not to the people as a whole.
43 Mishnah, Sanh. I:5.
44 Ibid. II:4.

approaching enemy be attacked before they reach the mountains of Judaea and get into a favorable position to take the capital. It is decided to follow that very course — to mount a preventative attack; a decision on which the commander is required by law to have the consent of the Sanhedrin.

Something similar occurs in I Macc. 12:35. Jonathan convenes the elders of the people and lays before them plans to build strong-points in Judaea, to heighten the walls of Jerusalem, and to build a barrier between the Akra (held by the Greeks and their sympathizers) and the rest of the city, so as to isolate the garrison, and keep them out of the city proper. This source shows that military matters, including general defence activities, were within the purview of the Great Sanhedrin.

b) There is even one source according to which accession to the very highest offices of the State was controlled by the Sanhedrin: "Neither king nor high priest can be appointed save by consent of the Sanhedrin of seventy-one."[45] However, this source is probably nothing more than political theory, rather than the reflection of any actual situation.

9) The Sanhedrin represented the State externally as well, that is, in dealing with other peoples or with occupying authorities. The first clear-cut documentary evidence of this role is contained in an official communication from the Seleucid conqueror Antiochus III (ca. 198 BCE) in which he promises autonomy to the Jews in the Land of Israel, and exempts "the *Gerousia* and the priests" from paying taxes.[46] From then on we have many documents in which the Sanhedrin appears as the representative of the nation in foreign affairs. The Books of the Maccabees provide quite a number of examples:

a) The priests and the Elders go out to negotiate with Nicanor (I Macc. 7:3);

b) Jonathan is accompanied by delegates of the Elders and the priests when he visits the king on a political mission (ibid. 11:23);

c) King Demetrios addresses an official missive to "Simeon the High Priest, the Elders and the people of the Jews" (ibid. 13:26);

d) Jonathan, writing to Sparta about a treaty between the two

---

45   Tos. Sanh. III:4 (Zuck. 418).

46   Ant. XII:3:3 (142).

countries, opens with the formula: "Jonathan, the High Priest, and the *Gerousia* of the people..." (ibid. 12:7);

e) The Spartans address "Simeon, the High Priest, The Elders and the priests and the rest of the Jews." (ibid. 14:20);

f) Three members of the *Gerousia* go to Antioch to apologize to the Seleucid monarch for the popular uprising against Lysimachus, brother of Menelaus (II Macc. 4:44);

g) Delegates of "the *Gerousia* and the Elders" go to congratulate Ptolemy Eupator on his victory, bearing a gift from the Jews (ibid. 1:8);

h) Antiochus Epiphanes writes a letter "to the *Gerousia* of the Jews and the rest of the Jewish people" repenting of his persecutory decrees, and promising to convert to Judaism (ibid. 11:27; for our purposes, the legend itself is not important, but rather the channel of communication which is taken for granted).

The same situation holds good for the Roman period.

In sum then, the Great Sanhedrin in Jerusalem had broad jurisdiction and a wide range of powers. It is true that some of these powers were challenged from time to time, opposed and fought over. Nor are we sure that all of them were ever actually exercised to the full. But we *can* be sure that the institution occupied a place of enormous influence and prestige in the life of the nation. It was only natural, therefore, that efforts to revive national life after the Destruction should have concentrated on attempts to re-establish the Sanhedrin to whatever degree that was possible.

CHAPTER ELEVEN

THE REVIVED SANHEDRIN:
STRUCTURE AND PROCEDURES

Efforts to re-establish the Sanhedrin could begin to make headway only after the Flavian dynasty of Roman Emperors had come to an end, a quarter of a century after the Destruction of Jerusalem and the Temple. Not until then did the conquered people in its conquered land begin to retrieve some of its lost autonomy; some, but not all. It would have been too much to expect that the *status quo ante bellum* could have been completely restored. Let us see, then, what changes for the worse distinguished the revived Sanhedrin from its predecessor.

Even though Judaea under the Procurators had been de jure a conquered and subjugated province, it had nevertheless retained de facto a certain degree of political and administrative self-rule. In other words, prior to the War with Rome there had been a Jewish state; subject, but still a state. It was with the deliberate intent of symbolizing the abolition of that state that the Romans methodically burned Jerusalem to the ground. In a territorial sense, the political-juridical existence of the state had been based on its administrative center, Jerusalem. Therefore, the state could now be said to have ceased to exist.

As a consequence, the corporate entity known as "The Jewish People" in the Eretz Israel of Rabban Gamaliel, whether officially recognized or merely tolerated, could exist only as an *ethnos*, a socially and nationally distinct group with certain rights to administer its own internal affairs. And indeed, it was exactly as such that Jewry in Eretz Israel continued to exist for over three centuries, until those rights were drastically curtailed at the beginning of the fifth Christian century, when the Patriarchate was abolished by the Byzantine government.

The new, post-Destruction status within the Roman system is reflected in the fact that the institutions of Jewish autonomy, the Patriarchate and the Sanhedrin, were at no time identified with any particular place. Yavneh and Usha, Sepphoris, Beth-Shearim and Tiberias were all regarded as merely temporary headquarters of the Jewish authorities. The cities themselves derived no administrative importance from what was regarded as a chance circumstance. In this they were unlike Jerusalem which had been, and remained, a special place in a *juridical* sense.

What we have said about the very limited nature of post-war Jewish autonomy would be called into question if we were to accept the thesis that the Patriarch was responsible, within the Roman system, for collecting taxes in the Land of Israel, and that he had full power to determine the methods and procedures to be used for that purpose.[1] But the idea is without foundation. There is no reason whatsoever for doubting that the Romans themselves saw to the collection of taxes from the time of the Destruction and throughout the following centuries of their rule over the country. True, they made use of the Greek city-states in the Middle East for their own fiduciary ends; true, they sometimes harnessed local Jewish communities to the process; but the Patriarchate never had any role to play in the business.[2]

We return, then, to a consideration of the specific areas of jurisdiction which survived — or did not survive — the hiatus between the Destruction and the revival of the Sanhedrin. It is natural to begin with a key question: the power of the Court to impose sanctions.

Postwar Jurisdiction

A. DINEI NEFASHOT

Under this rubric are included all cases involving the possibility of capital punishment. As we have noted,[3] tannaitic tradition taught that the Great Sanhedrin held exclusive jurisdiction in such matters, and only by a delegation of its authority could lesser Sanhedra'ot (of twenty-three judges as described in Mishnah Sanhedrin I:10) be set up in provincial centers — if indeed they ever were.

A question much discussed by modern scholars is, to what extent did this authority actually function during the period when the Jewish State was under Roman occupation — that is, in the time of the

1 Hans Zucker: *Studien zur jüdischen Selbstverwaltung*, Berlin, 1936, p. 15.
2 See Alon: *The Strategoi* etc., in JJCW, pp. 458 ff.
3 Above, p. 203.

Procurators (roughly 6 to 66 C.E.)? Did the Romans permit the Sanhedrin in Jerusalem to exercise its capital jurisdiction during those decades? Some historians think that the Jewish High Court had the power to arrest the accused and hear the evidence, but that judgement and sentencing were in the hands of the Roman procurator. Others claim that the Sanhedrin could even pass judgement, but that its verdict and sentence were subject to ratification by the Roman authorities. Still others believe that even such ratification was unnecessary.

Some passages in Talmudic literature seem to support the view that the Sanhedrin was deprived of capital jurisdiction in the early days of the Roman occupation. For example, the Yerushalmi:

> More than forty years before the House was destroyed, the authority over *dinei nefashot* was taken away from Israel.

The Bavli, too, has a similar tradition, with Rabbi Ishmael son of Rabbi Jose quoting his father:

> Forty years before the Temple was destroyed, the Sanhedrin was exiled (sc. from its chamber) and met in Hanuta.[4]

R. Isaac bar Avidimi is said to have explained this to mean that they could no longer impose fines; but this is emended by R. Nahman bar Isaac to read: they could no longer impose the death penalty. One way or another, the historical situation seems to have been that the Sanhedrin continued to exercise capital jurisdiction right up to the Destruction, whether or not the Romans gave their legal approval.

But immediately after the Destruction that jurisdiction came to an end — once and for all. Be it noted that this was Roman practice throughout the Empire. From the days of the very first Caesars, capital punishment was taken out of the hands of even autonomous city-states (πόλεις). not to speak of subjugated areas. There is ample evidence of this from the second century onwards in the writings of the Church Fathers. Rabbinic sources also testify to the same effect:

> Scripture says, 'Ye shall come to the priests and to the Levites and to the judge who shall be at that time' (Deut. XVII:9) — from which I deduce, at a time when there is a (functioning)

---

4 Yer. Sanh. I:18a; ibid. VII 24b; and Bavli, Av. Zar. 8b.

priesthood, there is judgement (i.e. the power to impose sanctions); but when there is no priesthood, there is no judgement.[5]

The point is made even more explicit in the following tradition:

> Whence do we know that execution can take place only when the Temple stands? From the verse in Exodus (XXI: 14) 'Even from Mine altar shalt thou take him, that he may die.' It follows that if there is an altar you may put (a convicted person) to death; if there is no altar, you may not.[6]

Finally, the Bavli records a *baraitha* attributed to Rabbi Hiyya:[7]

> From the day that the Temple was destroyed, even though the Sanhedrin was abolished, the four modes of execution were not abolished. (Gemara) But wait! They were indeed abolished! His meaning is that Divine punishment is visited on the guilty offenders in ways that simulate the four modes of capital execution.[8]

These halakhic midrashim adduce halakhic reasons for the lapse of capital sanctions. But surely that lapse was the result of Roman coercion rather than of Jewish decision. Nevertheless, it is reasonable to assume that the halakhah had reasons of its own for regarding the competence of Jewish judicature as inherently diminished by the termination of Jewish sovereignty.

However, that is not the end of the matter. We still have to explain the eyewitness testimony of Origen who claims that in his day the Jewish Patriarch actually condemned transgressors to death.[9] He says that the Patriarch used to set up quasi-surreptitious courts and try capital cases.[10]

5 Bavli Sanh. 52b. Comp. Midrash Tannaim, ed. Hoffman, p. 102.
6 Mekhilta d'Rabbi Shim'on bar Yohai, ed. Hoffman, p. 126.
7 Ket. 30a.
8 This and the preceding traditions offer a historical memory that diverges from the one reflected in the passages cited earlier.
9 Origen, originally an Alexandrian, lived in Caesarea at the beginning of the third century. There he had many contacts with Jews, including Rabbis as well as people from the entourage of the Patriarch.
10 *Epistola ad Africanum*, 814, P.G. 11, pp. 81-2. Written about 240 C.E., it deals with the Book of Susannah. The extract is quoted in Schürer, *Geschichte*, II, p. 248, note 28.

Two widely differing interpretations of this passage in Origen have been put forward. Jacob Mann says that Origen could not have been right; after all, the bulk of the evidence points the other way.[11] So Mann theorizes that the courts actually tried capital transgressors. If the accused were found guilty they were given the lash, along with an announcement that they really deserved to be executed. Origen heard about this, but he got it wrong. That is Mann's theory, but it is totally unacceptable. There is no shred of evidence that the procedure he posits ever existed.[12]

Juster takes a diametrically opposite tack, and concludes from Origen's testimony that Rome looked the other way while Jewish courts continued to execute Jews found guilty of major sins against Judaism. And what is more, he would have us believe that the Romans continued to tolerate this practice all throughout the centuries of their rule over the land.[13]

I have no doubt that Juster's interpretation is equally wide of the mark. It seems to me more likely that Origen had heard of an instance — perhaps several of them — in which the Patriarch of his time had acted in what was judged to be a situation of extraordinary gravity, where individual Jews had committed acts which endangered whole Jewish communities. If in such essentially political crises the Romans turned a blind eye and allowed the Jewish leaders de facto freedom to discipline their own people, that does not mean that this was normally the case. Such things are conceivable, even as exceptions, only during the time of the Severan emperors (193–235 C.E.) when, as Jerome tells us, the position of the Jews in the Land of Israel was at its most favorable (see above, p. 29). Origen, learning of a particular case or cases, and unaware of the special circumstances, drew broadly general conclusions. But that is a far cry from normal legal procedure under the Romans, whether before the Destruction or after.

The idea that Jewish courts could apply sanctions outside the norms of Jewish law — taking upon themselves emergency powers, so to speak — is not without warrant or precedent. Rabbi Eliezer ben Jacob is quoted as having said: "I have heard that the Beth Din may

11 See *Hatzofeh le-Khokhmat Yisrael*, Vol. X, 1926, p. 201.
12 Comp. S. Katz: *Die Strafe im Talmudischen Recht*, 1936, p. 73.
13 *Les Juifs dans l'Empire Romain*, II, pp. 151–152.

inflict lashes and other punishments when the times make it needful, even though (such penalties are) not according to the law of the Torah."[14]

In sum, then, we have no reason to believe that at any time during the centuries dealt with in this book was capital jurisdiction by Jewish courts in effect. Apparent evidence to the contrary does not bear careful scrutiny.

B. CORPORAL PUNISHMENT

As the result of a thorough study of geonic responsa dealing with the imposition of corporal punishment by Jewish courts, it appears that there was divided opinion among the Geonim themselves as to the juridical status of this kind of penalty in their day.[15] Some held that the ancient code as prescribed in the Torah was still in force, both in the Land of Israel and elsewhere. Others however believed that such sanctions could properly be enforced only in the mother country, where the courts still exercised legitimate authority. Still others claimed that even in Eretz Israel legal corporal punishment had lapsed at the same time as capital punishment. The only vestige that had survived was a token substitute of post-Biblical origin called *makkot mardut*.

Perhaps this difference of opinion among the Geonim is foreshadowed, albeit indirectly, by a difference of opinion in the Mishnah:

Stripes (may be imposed) by a court of three judges. Rabbi Ishmael said (it requires a court of) twenty-three.[16]

In effect, Rabbi Ishmael was declaring this form of punishment defunct, since courts of twenty-three no longer existed. The majority of the Sages, however, held that the full formal punishment by flagellation as laid down in the Torah was still in force.

There is a good deal of evidence to show that Jewish courts did continue to impose physical punishment for many centuries to come. It is clear, however, that these stripes were not the Biblical "forty

---

14 Sanh. 46a; Yer. Hag. II 78a.
15 Aptowitzer in *Ha-Mishpat ha-Ivri*, vol. V, 1935-6, pp. 33–104.
16 Sanh. I:2.

lashes."[17] They were rather the informal — and a lot fewer — *makkot mardut*, which grew up as an instrument of community discipline, much as the various forms of excommunication.

C. CIVIL LAW

The complete lack of any reference to the functioning of Jewish courts in the area of civil law (*dinei mammonot*) during the post-Destruction leadership of Rabban Johanan ben Zakkai has been noted above.[18] The conclusion was drawn, and it is a highly probable one, that in the immediate postwar period the Romans denied any collective status whatsoever to the defeated Jews, treating them instead as *dediticii* — a mass of subjugated individuals with no group rights at all, much less the right to their own courts and judges.

On the other hand, during the following period — that of Rabban Gamaliel — we find Jewish courts dealing with the whole gamut of civil law. Rabban Gamaliel himself, and his colleagues in the revived Sanhedrin, including Rabbi Tarphon, Rabbi Ishmael and Rabbi Akiba, appear frequently as *dayyanim* (judges). Their generation also becomes a period of great growth in the theoretical development of Jewish law.

This revival of Jewish law and legal institutions is one of the most striking aspects of the national recovery after the Destruction. It seems fairly obvious that it was brought about by the steady efforts of the people and their leaders, culminating in a situation in which Jewish judicial autonomy had become the kind of accomplished fact that the Romans could not but recognize. When they finally did so, the Romans seem to have sent a team of experts to study the "Law of Israel." The context in which this tradition is quoted shows that the law in question was property law.[19]

At this period, as in later times, there were gentiles in the Land of Israel who appeared in Jewish courts as litigants against Jews. In such cases, the *dayyan* would sometimes follow Jewish law, sometimes the "laws of the gentiles."[20]

---

17 Reduced by the oral tradition to thirty-nine, and applied to specific transgressions; see Mishnah Makkot, chap. III.
18 See p. 109.
19 B.Q. 38a; Yer. ibid. IV:4b; Sifre Deut. 344, ed. Finkelstein.
20 Sifre Deut. 16, ed. Finkelstein, pp. 26-7; *Mekhilta deRabbi Shime'on bar*

However, there were two basic limitations on Jewish autonomy, even in civil matters. First, the Jewish courts had no exclusive jurisdiction; Roman judges were readily available for civil, as of course for criminal actions. In Roman legal theory the Governor of any province was the repository of Imperial power in his territory — at one and the same time head of government, commander-in-chief of the military, and bearer of supreme judicial authority. He would make the rounds of the principal cities under his rule in accordance with a regular court calendar, and sit in judgement on any civil actions pending. He was accompanied by legal experts called *assessores consilarii* or πάρεδροι.[21] It was these experts who actually made the decisions. At the same time, the governor (or procurator) was empowered to delegate his judicial authority to military officers, government officials, or even plain civilians.

It would be logical to assume that what held good throughout the Empire applied in *Provincia Judaea* as well. But there is no need to rely on logical assumption alone; it is confirmed by specific evidence to the same effect. For example:

> Thus would Rabbi Jonathan do when he saw some important personage (i.e. Roman official) arriving in his town: he would send him a gift as a mark of respect and honor. For he thought: what if some lawsuit involving an orphan or widow should be brought before him? At least I will have entrée to take the matter up with him.[22]

The context makes it plain that all this had nothing to do with government requirements, such as taxes, but rather with potential litigation. This passage, like so many others, reflects the reputation of Roman colonial officialdom for corruption and bribery; but what is more to our present point, it demonstrates the fact that Roman civil procedure was available under authority of the procurator.

Yohai, p. 155; B.Q. 113a. To be sure these gentiles came of their own free choice. Comp. a fourth century case, cited unhappily by the Church Father Chrysostom where both litigants are Christians, yet take their cause to a Jewish court: *Adversus Judaeos*, P.G. 48, Col. 847-8.

21   Called (in the singular) סנקתדרוס (συγκάθεδρος) by Jewish sources; see Sifre Deut. 27, ed. Finkelstein, p. 43.

22   Yer. Shab. I:3 c-d; ibid. Av. Zar. II, 41d.

Rabbi Jonathan belongs to the third century. But we have evidence, even if less clear-cut, dating from the Yavneh period:

> Imma Shalom, wife of Rabbi Eliezer and sister to Rabban Gamaliel, had a certain *Philosophos* living in her vicinity whose reputation was that he would judge without taking a bribe. They decided to test him, so she appeared before him with a golden lamp, and declared: "I want a share in my father's estate." He promptly ordered that the estate be divided (between her and her brother). Rabban Gamaliel said to him: "But in our law it is stated that where there is a son, the daughter does not inherit." The other answered: "From the day you were exiled from your land, the law of Moses has been removed, and another law set in its place, wherein it is written: a son and a daughter inherit equally." The following day Rabban Gamaliel brought him a Libyan ass, and said: "Look further on in your book, wherein it is written: I came not to destroy the law of Moses, but (most common versions of the Talmud read "nor") to add to it; and the law of Moses says clearly: when there is a son, the daughter does not inherit." His sister hinted broadly to the Roman, saying "Let thy light shine forth as a lamp." Rabban Gamaliel quickly rejoined: "The ass came and kicked the lamp over."[23]

Of course, what we are dealing with here is legend, not to be taken at face value in all its particulars; but it does preserve the memory of non-Jewish courts in the Land of Israel. The "philosophos" of the story was probably a citizen learned in the law who no doubt had been authorized by the procurator to act as judge even though he was a Christian, or a sympathizer with Christianity. It would also appear from this episode that government judges sometimes sought to apply Jewish law to cases affecting Jews. A few source texts illustrate these matters:

> Rabbi Tarphon taught: In places where you find courts of the gentiles, even though their judgements correspond to Jewish law, do not avail yourself of their services.[24]

23 Shab. 116, a-b. Comp. above p. 75.
24 Git. 88b.

A bill of divorce given under compulsion is valid if ordered by a Jewish court; but if by a gentile court, it is invalid. However, if what the gentiles do is — beat the man and say: 'Do what the Jews tell you!' then it is valid.[25]

A *halitzah* imposed on a man by a Jewish court is valid, but if by a gentile court it is invalid (unless) the gentiles beat him and said: 'You do what Rabbi N. told you'.[26]

These passages not only indicate the existence of Roman courts in the Land of Israel; they also show that the gentiles themselves sometimes forced Jews to obey the judgements of Jewish courts. There is a possibility that the gentiles referred to are the local courts of the Hellenistic cities in the region, for they too enjoyed a certain degree of autonomy in civil matters. But it seems more likely that real Roman courts and real Roman judges are involved.

Indeed, during the centuries we are studying it was Roman practice throughout the eastern provinces to offer a double-tracked system of procedure for civil actions. Litigants could choose to go to local courts to be judged by local laws, or they could have recourse to Roman judges administering Roman justice. That is why we find Greek writers urging the Hellenized citizenry to stay away from the Governor's judiciary, and to take their legal business to the tribunals of their own *polis*. They sound very like Rabbis warning their flock to stay away from the *'arkha'ot* of the gentiles. There must have been some competition between the jurisdictions, and no doubt there were times when the administration used its power to get preference for the Roman courts. The procurator or governor had wide judicial powers. He could find in terms of whatever system of laws he chose *ad hoc*.[27]

The second of the two basic limitations on the autonomy of the Jewish courts was the right of the Romans to overrule the Jewish judges. Though the evidence we have for this dates from the third century, it is not unlikely that the practice was established much earlier. One example dealing with a criminal offense, and one involving a civil suit, will illustrate how the Romans interfered in either

25 Mishnah, Git. IX:8.
26 Tos. Yev. XII:13 (Zuck. 256).
27 Mommsen, *Römisches Staatsrecht*, III, p. 749.

area when they chose to, on receipt of a complaint from a party un-
happy with the finding of a Jewish tribunal. The first case is from the Yerushalmi (Megillah III:74a):

> Rabbi Hiyya, Rabbi Jose and Rabbi Ami passed judgement on
> one Tamar (apparently sentencing her to corporal punishment
> for immoral conduct). She went and complained against them
> to the proconsul at Caesarea. Whereupon they wrote to Rabbi
> Abahu (who lived in that city and had access to the Roman
> governor). He sent them a cryptic reply, saying: We have al-
> ready appeased (i.e. sent tokens of esteem to) three *litorin* (i.e.
> ῥήτορες, legal rhetoricians) but Tamar bitterly persists (*tamar
> tamrurit betamrureha* — a play on words) despite our attempts
> to sweeten her; so the silversmith hath labored in vain.

It is scarcely conceivable that Rabbi Hiyya and his colleagues, who
were in their time the "judges of the High Court" that sat in Tiberias,
would have sentenced the woman unless they had official authority to
do so. We can only conclude that the Roman colonial administration
was in practice able to set aside procedures that were, in theory, perfectly legal.

The civil case is from the Bavli, Baba Batra 58a-b. Once Rabbi
Bena'ah passed judgement in a suit involving the law of property:

> Those who lost the case went to Government House (*bei malka*)
> and denounced him. Said they: there is a certain man among
> the Jews who separates people from their money when there
> are no witnesses, no nothing. As a result of this, the Rabbi was
> seized and put into prison.

Ostensibly, the complaint against the Rabbi was that he had been
unfair. He had acted contrary to Jewish law(!).

D. DINEI QENASOT

On the border-line between civil law (*dinei mammonot*) and criminal law (*dinei nefashot*), talmudic jurisprudence has a third classifi-
cation: cases involving monetary punishment (*dinei qenasot*). The
halakhah made a fundamental distinction between such cases and
ordinary civil matters by placing *dinei qenasot* outside the competence of all judges except those duly qualified by the Sanhedrin and

the Patriarch. As a corollary, such matters could not be heard by Jewish courts outside the Land of Israel.

What did the Roman authorities do about this during the period we are studying? Did they allow Jewish courts to sit in *dinei qenasot*, treating such cases as quasi-civil? Or did they forbid it, on the grounds that such matters are really criminal, from the point of view both of the act itself, and of the penalty?

The bulk of the evidence favors the first alternative. In other provinces of the Empire, for example, we find that the Romans did allow the local courts to impose fines; they simply placed a ceiling on the amount they could levy. And while we have the statement by Rabbi Isaac ben Avidimi declaring that the Romans deprived the Jews of jurisdiction over *dinei qenasot* forty years before the Destruction, we also have the correction by Rabbi Nahman bar Isaac, who says that the reference should be to *dinei nefashot* (Av. Zar. 8b). In other words, the tradition remembered that the Romans, at a time near the Destruction, restricted the Jewish courts to matters of civil law; but memory had become blurred as to the details. To clinch the argument that the restriction did *not* include *dinei qenasot*, we have an explicit case from the period between the Destruction and the Bar Kokhba Revolt. The Mishnah reports (B. Q. VIII:6) a matter that came before Rabbi Akiba. A woman, the plaintiff, had suffered nothing more that public embarrassment; Rabbi Akiba awarded her the clearly *punitive* sum of 400 zuz.[28]

The Jewish Court System Under Rabban Gamaliel

The set-up of the Jewish judicature after the Destruction, how the courts were structured, and to what extent they were controlled by the Sanhedrin and the Patriarch — these are among the most difficult problems facing the Jewish historian. Not that there is any difficulty from the point of view of legal theory as to the superior authority of the Sanhedrin with regard to the substance of the law. The High Court in Yavneh was regarded in this respect in the same way that the Sanhedrin in Jerusalem had been — as the supreme legislative and interpretative authority. But there is great difficulty in answering the following questions: To what extent did the Sanhedrin actually

28 Compare ARN, version A, III:4, Schechter, p. 15, Goldin, p. 27.

supervise the administration of justice in the country at large? Did the Sanhedrin have any power of initiative in appointing judges and setting up courts? On these points our sources are fragmentary, scattered, and not altogether clear; so much so, that a modern scholar came to the conclusion that there were no regularly organized Jewish courts in the land of Israel after the Destruction, until as late as the sixth century.[29]

If we are to make a systematic examination of these questions, we shall have to begin with the situation as it had been in pre-Destruction times. It will be recalled that the Mishnah reports that regional Sanhedrins of twenty-three were appointed by the High Court in Jerusalem (Sanh. I:1). Other texts indicate that smaller local courts were also appointed by the Great Sanhedrin, and subject to it. The Tosefta, for example, speaks of emissaries being sent from the Chamber of Hewn Stone to pick men fit to be judges.[30] A similar tradition is preserved in the Babylonian Talmud.[31] And then there is Josephus, doubtless acting on the authority vested in him by the Sanhedrin of Jerusalem, appointing seven-man courts in the towns of Galilee.[32]

What can we conclude on balance from the sometimes conflicting evidence? Apparently this: 1) the central authorities appointed, or at least ratified the appointment of, the local courts; and 2) the judges in such courts were local dignitaries. Yet it seems almost certain that de facto these courts came under the authority of the local town councils, and that the judges were considered part of the local administration. How are we to understand this apparent contradiction?

It was probably the resultant of centuries of pull and counter-pull between local authority and central government. In very ancient tribal times, it was the *'edah* (community, assembly) and the "elders of the city" who sat in judgement. With the rise of the monarchy, a strongly centralizing force was brought to bear. Then, during the Second Commonwealth, a certain balance seems to have been achieved between the two jurisdictions, local and central.

29 Chajes in REJ for 1899, No. 39, pp. 39–52.
30 Tos. Hag. II:9 (Zuck. 235) = Tos. Sanh. VII:1 (Zuck. 425).
31 Sanh. 88b. But the Yerushalmi (Sanh. I:19c and Hag. II:77d) implies that they were looking for candidates for the *High* Court.
32 JW II 569–571. However, perhaps Josephus' action was only an emergency measure.

After the Destruction, however, we find no more mention of any Beth Din under local control, and it begins to look as though the central authorities once again had to take charge of all the courts in the land. But curiously enough, for the tannaitic period, there is no evidence of this either — nothing to show that the Patriarch and the Sanhedrin had direct responsibility for the appointment of courts in the country at large, and for the supervision of those courts. The earliest explicit mention of the appointment of a *dayyan* by the Patriarch occurs in the late second or early third century in connection with the town of Simonia, when Judah I appoints Levi ben Sisi not only as judge, but also as community spiritual leader.[33] And that case is scarcely enough to generalize from, since all it involves is a recommendation made in response to a request from the local citizens.

This lack of firm data on whether there was a centralized or a decentralized court system may tempt us to conclude that there was no formal court system at all! Indeed, that very proposition was advanced by Chajes, as we noted above. He suggests that during the entire period dealt with in this book Jewish litigants made do with ad hoc arbitrators, who adjudicated matters on request. This is an erroneous theory; but curiously enough, it is supported by considerable evidence!

Take the Mishnah in Sanhedrin (III:1):

> Cases concerning property are decided by three judges. One litigant chooses one (judge), the other chooses one, and the two of them choose a third.

The tone here, and in the rest of this Mishnah, is unmistakable. The whole ambience is one of voluntarism, in which parties may under certain circumstances challenge one another's choice of judge; may interrupt the proceedings to ask that the panel be expanded; and other such informalities. The Sifre on Deut. I:12 reads:[34]

> (Moses says) 'How can I bear all by myself your troublesome bickering?' — from which we learn that when one of them saw his fellow gaining the upper hand at law, he would say.... 'I

---

33 Yer. Yev. XII:13a, and parallel passages in various midrashim.
34 Sec. 12, Finkelstein, pp. 19–20.

have new evidence to present' or 'I want a postponement until tomorrow' or 'I want *additional judges*.'

In fact, the Tosefta states flatly: "Judges may be added to the panel at any time until the case is closed."[35] Even more striking evidence of the informality of legal procedures in tannaitic times is the tradition that judges could withdraw in the middle of a trial.[36]

> Rabbi Judah ben Laqish used to say: if two appear for judgement (before a Sage) one of them being a powerful individual and the other someone easy and compliant, the Sage may say 'I will not take your case' — provided he has not yet heard their arguments; or even if he has heard them, but does not yet know who has the better case.

But in spite of these indications of a private and unofficial method of adjudicating disputes, careful study leads us to conclude that a *variety* of judicial "institutions" existed side by side after the Destruction. Some of them were public and formal; others were private and voluntary, although they too were governed by accepted rules. It is with the latter that the sources just cited are concerned.

In the Mishnah we learn first of all about the courts of three arbitrators chosen by the parties to the dispute. These three may be ordinary men, not appointed by any official body, or even learned in the law. Secondly, we discover that *dayyanim* were also available — learned jurists to whom the disputants could go if they so chose. In a sense, these scholars as well were only arbitrators (*borerin*) even if they had the *semikhah* of the Patriarch. They might have been qualified, but they had not been appointed.

This type of private, non-institutionalized procedure (*borerut*) for the settlement of disputes is first discussed in tannaitic sources by disciples of Rabbi Akiba, principally Rabbi Meir. Basing himself on this fact, Gulak suggests that the procedure originated after the Bar Kokhba Revolt, at a time when the Romans had outlawed the established Jewish courts.[37] To the extent that the Jews of Judaea did not

35 Tos. Sanh. VI:4 (Zuck. 424).
36 Tos. Sanh. I:7 (Zuck. 415); Bavli, ibid. 6b; Yer. ibid. I:18b.
37 Asher Gulak: *Yesodei Ha-Mishpat Ha-Ivri*, Dvir, Berlin 1922, Vol. IV, pp. 30–31.

use Roman tribunals, they had no other choice but to settle their legal matters before arbitrators, who were not necessarily bound by Jewish law, but could arrange compromises and "out-of-court" settlements.

In all likelihood the use of these informal procedures did become widespread in the wake of the Hadrianic persecutions after the fall of Betar. But it is almost a certainty that *borerut* existed earlier — at least in the form of seeking judgement from the single learned and trusted Sage. There is evidence for this even during Temple times, witness Luke XII: 13–14:

> Then one of the company said unto him, 'Master, speak to my brother, that he divide the inheritance with me.' And he said unto him, 'Man, who made me a judge or a divider over you?'

As for the Sages themselves, some sought to avoid involvement in litigation, while others regarded it is an important duty.[38]

In any event, alongside these voluntary and informal tribunals there still existed established public courts, with the power to summon litigants to appear before them, and the means to enforce their judgements. Proof of this can be found in the Sifre: on Deuteronomy:

> The words 'Ye shall not respect persons in judgement' (Deut. 1:17) are intended as a caution to him who is charged with appointing judges. Let him not say, 'This one has a fine appearance, I will make him a judge;' or 'That one is skilled in Greek, I will appoint him a judge.' The result might well be that the guilty would be cleared, and the innocent found guilty.

In the same source there is evidence that the courts had the power to compel appearance before them, and to enforce their findings:

> 'Judges and officers shalt thou make thee in all thy gates... and they shall judge the people." (Deut. 16:18). This means, that they may compel the people to judgement.
> 'When there is a dispute among men and they go to law, and they are judged' (Deut. 25:1) — that is to say, the litigants are forced to accept the judgement.[39]

38 Yer. Sanh. I:18a.
39 Sifre Deut. 17. Finkelstein, pp. 27–28; ibid. 144. Finkelstein, p. 196; and ibid. 286. Finkelstein, p. 302. On the court's power to compel, comp. Mishnah Git. IX:8.

The courts that had these powers were official public institutions. They were of two kinds: a) Lay courts (*shel hedyotot*); and b) Qualified courts (*shel mumḥim*).

a) LAY COURTS:

These tribunals consisted of three citizens appointed by the local authorities.[40] They were sometimes called "the three men of the kenesset."[41] They were associated with the local council, and represented a continuation of the age-old tradition of judgement by the "elders of the town sitting at the gate," or by the "*edah*-as-council."[42] Frequently these local judges were chosen from powerful local families, and their findings were at times out of step with the laws of the Torah and the views of the Sages. There is evidence of this from a number of sources dating from the second century onwards, of which we shall cite two. These texts show that there were local courts not connected with the Sanhedrin, courts that had nothing to do with the Sages:

> Rabbi Jose ben Elisha says: If you see a generation overwhelmed by troubles, look closely at the judges of Israel, for it is chiefly on account of their deficiencies that retribution is visited upon the world. This is what Micah the prophet means when he says (III:9–11) 'Hear this, I pray you, ye heads of the house of Jacob, and rulers of the house of Israel, that abhor justice, and pervert all equity; that build up Zion with blood, and Jerusalem with iniquity. The heads thereof judge for reward...' Nor will the Holy One allow His *Shekhinah* to dwell in Israel until all (such) judges and bailiffs have disappeared from Israel. (Shab. 139a)
>
> Rabbi Melai quoted Rabbi Eleazar ben Rabbi Simeon as follows: What is the meaning of Isaiah XIV:5: 'The Lord hath broken the staff of the wicked, the sceptre of the rulers'? It is this: 'The staff of the wicked' — refers to judges who allow themselves to become tools of their bailiffs; 'the sceptre of the

---

40 At this point, I diverge from Gulak. See his exposition, op. cit., pp. 38–39.

41 Tos. Sanh. I:2 (Zuck. 415) and its parallels.

42 [Comp. Deut. 21:19; Num. 35:24–25.]

rulers' — refers to scholars who use their influence to get their relatives appointed to the bench, even though the latter are unfit for the office. (Ibid.)

It is fairly obvious that the "judges" viewed with such distaste in these homilies did not come from the scholarly circles of the Sages. They must have derived their power — and their menace — from social forces *not* under the control of the Sanhedrin. Büchler surmised that texts such as those just quoted probably deal with appointees of the Romans, in the period just after the defeat of the Bar Kokhba Revolt "for as a rule, the *dayyanim* referred to in talmudic literature were scholars of the Torah."[43]

However, in my opinion the abuse of judicial power was not quite so ephemeral a phenomenon. It finds echoes in third century sources as well. It seems clear to me that what we are dealing with is "local" courts — locally appointed and locally dominated. And since power in towns and villages was frequently in the hands of men who had property and other means of influence, the way was open for the appointment of judges of less than impeccable character.

It is reasonable to assume that the Sages, led by the Sanhedrin, did everything they could to keep these *hedyotot* away from the seat of judgement, and to have legal matters handled by scholars versed in the laws of the Torah. There is evidence to support this conclusion, such as the rule which states: "One should not teach property law to an *am ha'aretz*."[44] In any event, the phenomenon of the "lay court" did not altogether disappear, though as time went on the central authorities gained almost complete control over judicature.

An important factor in the continued existence of these "citizen courts" was an economic one. No judge was allowed, *de jure* and *de facto*, to accept remuneration for his services. Therefore, in the same way that local town-councils were usually in the hands of wealthy citizens (since public service was unsalaried, and only the rich could afford it) — so too were locally appointed and locally functioning magistracies normally the preserve of the propertied. That is why the Sages themselves were constrained to find grounds for permitting the

43 A. Büchler: *Der Galiläische 'Am-ha-'Arez*, p. 189.
44 *Mekhilta d'Rabbi Shimeon bar Yohai*, on Exod. XXI:1; ed. Hoffman, p. 117, ed. Epstein–Melammed, p. 158.

appointment to judgeships of men of wealth, who could serve the public without salary, and without loss. The following tradition may illustrate the soul-searching involved in dealing with this problem:

> Scripture says: 'Let them judge the people at all seasons.' (Exod. XVIII:22) R. Joshua interprets this to mean that judges should be individuals free from work, *available* to judge the people at all times. Rabbi Eleazar of Modi'im says, people who are free from work *and* who occupy themselves with Torah — they shall judge the people at all times.
>
> Scripture says: 'Thou shalt provide out of all the people men of *ḥayyil*' (Exod. ibid. 21) — that is, men of means; 'such as hate pelf' — who, when sitting in judgement, hate to accept payment. So teaches Rabbi Joshua. But Rabbi Eleazar of Modi'im says, 'men of *ḥayyil*' means trustworthy men of their word; 'such as hate pelf' means, those who have little regard for their own money — how much the less for other people's.[45]

The difference of opinion voiced in these passages may well express a willingness on the part of Rabbi Joshua ben Hananiah to accept lay judges, unlearned in the law, provided they were able and willing to devote time to the service of the public. Rabbi Eleazar of Modi'im, on the other hand, insists that no one should be a judge who is not a scholar of the Torah.

The economic factor that kept the learned poor out of local judgeships, and thus threw the position open to wealthy ignoramuses, could have been overcome by providing salaries, or the equivalent, for judges. As a matter of fact, steps were taken in the days of Rabban Gamaliel to free the judge from economic dependence by having him housed and fed at public expense. This trend developed as time went on, so that ultimately the Sanhedrin and the Sages were practically in control not only of judicature, but of Jewish community life in general. But it need scarcely be added that the other tendency — the tradition of local independence — did not altogether die out. Local courts owing neither their appointment nor their allegiance to the Sanhedrin or the Patriarch continued to exist for many generations.

45 a) *Mekhilta d'Rabbi Ishmael*, Yitro, Sec. 2; Horovitz-Rabin, p. 199; Lauterbach, p. 184. b) *Ibid.*, Horovitz-Rabin, p. 198; Lauterbach, p. 183.

The old tug-of-war between the center and the periphery — between the "capital" and the "provinces" — still persisted.

b) COURTS OF QUALIFIED JUDGES

By the end of the tannaitic period there had emerged a type of trained judge — one who was *memuneh* (appointed) or *samukh* (ordained) by the Patriarch and the Sanhedrin to serve as *dayyan* and as halakhic authority.[46] A *dayyan* thus certified is referred to in the Talmud variously as *mumḥeh, mumḥeh lerabbim, mumḥeh lebhet din*, or *mumḥeh mipi bet din*. What distinguished any judge so qualified was his competence to impose sanctions (*kenasot*), a competence which underscores the public authority inherent in the office. As time went on — and as early as the tannaitic period[47] — it became acceptable for those qualified judges to try cases by themselves, although long thereafter that practice was still regarded with distaste by many Sages who remained faithful to the teaching of Rabbi Ishmael ben Rabbi José (Aboth IV:8): "Be not one who sits alone in judgement, for there is but One who sits alone in judgement."[48]

Another advantage accrued to the judge who had been duly qualified. He could not be held liable for losses resulting from judicial error on his part. This protected position is another evidence of his status as a public official.

It seems certain that the appointment or ordination of judges by the central Jewish authorities existed in the days of Rabban Gamaliel of Yavneh. The institution must be regarded as the very cornerstone of Jewish social and judicial autonomy; surely it came into being (or

---

46 The Yerushalmi states explicitly that the certification was called *semikhut* in Babylonia, but *minui* in the Land of Israel. See Yer. Sanh. I:19a.

47 Sanh. 5a: "If he had been duly qualified he may sit without colleagues." Comp. Yer. Sanh. I:18a.

48 Gulak (op. cit., Vol. IV, p. 86), thinks that the single-judge court developed at the beginning of the amoraic period. But apart from the tannaitic evidences just cited, there is the following, which takes us back to the days right after the Destruction: "Rabbi Simeon Shezuri says: My father's family belonged to the property owners of the Galilee. Why were their holdings wiped out? Because they used to try money cases without a colleague." (Tos. B.Q. VIII:14 (Zuck. 362); see Bavli B.Q. 80a). The point here is not that the practice was decried, the point is that the practice already existed.

was revived) along with the restoration of a measure of autonomy to the Jewish people living in their own land. If proof is required, one may point to the remark made by Rabbi Akiba to Rabbi Tarphon, after the latter had caused considerable financial loss by an erroneous ruling: "You are not liable, because you are a qualified judge, and qualified judges do not have to pay."[49]

However, there are grounds for assuming that the whole practice of "ordination", so familiar from the tannaitic and amoraic periods, had its origin in the generation immediately after the Destruction. This assumption is based on the fact that only after the Destruction do we encounter the title *Rabbi* as the standard honorific of a Sage who has been ordained. This is borne out by the famous Letter of Rav Sherira Gaon:[50]

> The designation *Rabbi* came into use with those who were ordained at that time (from the Destruction onwards), Rabbi Zadok and Rabbi Eliezer ben Jacob. The practice spread from the disciples of Rabban Johanan ben Zakkai.[51]

However, since we do not know how this business was handled *before* the Destruction, we have no way of knowing what new practices came into being *after* the Destruction.

It was stated above that ordination must have been in effect as early as the time of Rabban Gamaliel of Yavneh; but it remains to be shown whether it was the same in kind as the ordination so familiar to us from sources describing the situation at the end of the second and the beginning of the third centuries. In fact, there is a tradition that seems to say that it was not at all the same; that up to the middle of the second century ordination was transmitted privately from master to disciple, and was in no way centralized in the hands of the Sanhedrin and the Patriarch.[52] The tradition is reported in the Yerushalmi (Sanh. I:19a):

> Rabbi Abba said: Originally, each Sage used to ordain his own

49 Mishnah Bekh. IV:4.
50 Ed. B.M. Lewin, p. 125.
51 In the Gospels, Jesus is called "Rabbi" by his disciples; but there it is a form of address ("My teacher") not a title.
52 See G. Alon, "The Patriarchate of Rabban Johanan ben Zakkai," in JJCW, esp. pp. 341-2.

disciples, as when Rabban Johanan ben Zakkai ordained Rabbi
Eliezer and Rabbi Joshua, and the latter ordained Rabbi Akiba,
and Rabbi Akiba did the same for Rabbi Meir and Rabbi
Simeon.... But then they reconsidered and paid due deference
to the House of the Patriarch, declaring that if the Court ordained a judge without the approval of the Patriarch, the
ordination was null and void; while if the Patriarch ordained
without the consent of the Court, his act was valid. Finally they
reconsidered, declaring that the Court should not give *minui*
without the consent of the Patriarch, and the Patriarch should
not ordain without the consent of the Court.

Although this tradition comes to us from a rather late source, we
have no reason to doubt that it is, in the main, authentic. Besides, it
seems to be confirmed by the account of Rabbi Judah ben Bava, who
ordained five scholars (among them Rabbi Meir and Rabbi Judah)
"in a valley between Usha and Shafr'am," and was cut down by a
Roman patrol that came upon the scene.[53]

On the other hand, consider the following: Rabbi Judah ben Bava
acted in an emergency, at the height of the Hadrianic persecutions.
Both Patriarchate and Sanhedrin had been abolished, and ordination
had been declared a capital crime. Furthermore, even if we take Rabbi
Abba's tradition at face value, it may well be that the ordaining Sages
mentioned (who were all, be it noted, principal leaders of the Sanhedrin at Yavneh) had been delegated by the Sanhedrin to give ordination, and were *not* acting on their own. (Rabbis Eliezer, Joshua
and Akiba accompanied the Patriarch on his mission to Rome).
Careful attention to the language of the selfsame tradition bears this
out: "... they reconsidered and paid due deference to the House of
the Patriarch, declaring that if the Court ordained a judge without
the approval of the Patriarch, that ordination was null and void..."

I suggest that the ordination by "individuals" was really ordination "by and on behalf of" the Court, and that the whole thrust of
the statement by Rabbi Abba was to record a stage in the struggle
between the Sanhedrin and the Patriarch over the power to ordain.
Not only that, but it seems likely that even "originally" it was the
practice to get the consent of the Patriarch; the issue became, whether

53   Sanh. 13b–14a.

or not that consent was a *sine qua non*. As far as Rabban Gamaliel is concerned, it is on record that he did ordain:

> Scripture says: (Deut. 1:16) 'I charged your judges at that time...' Hitherto you were independent persons, but now you have become servants of the public. It happened that Rabban Gamaliel appointed Rabbi Johanan ben Nuri and Rabbi Eleazar ben Hisma to be seated in the Academy. The students did not notice anything (so unobtrusive were they). At eventime he (Rabban Gamaliel) entered and found them seated with the students. Said he to them: Is it your intention to let it be known that you do not seek to dominate the public? Be advised that (so far from that) heretofore you were your own masters; henceforward you are servants of the public.[54]

There are those who have explained this passage by suggesting that Rabban Gamaliel appointed the two men to be "overseers" at the Academy of Yavneh.[55] However, there are no grounds for making such an assumption.[56] The phrase used in our source-text always stands for *minui*, i.e. the elevation of a student to the status of a Sage, and to regular membership in the Sanhedrin. Since that status made one a "community leader," Rabban Gamaliel could speak of "domination."

This reading of the situation is supported by the version of the same episode in the Babylonian Talmud, which has Rabbi Joshua ben Hananiah asking Rabban Gamaliel to promote two of his disciples (the same two).[57] Rabban Gamaliel makes it his business to "seat them at the head" (another phrase equivalent to *minui*). Our conclusion must be that even in Rabban Gamaliel's day it was the Patriarch who effected ordination.

To what extent did the power over ordination actually make the courts everywhere in the country subordinate to the Sanhedrin and the Patriarch? After all, ordination only *qualified* the man to be a

54 Sifre Deut., 16; Finkelstein, p. 26.
55 Bacher, *Agada der Tannaiten*, Vol. I, p. 368; Zucker: *Studien zur jüdischen Selbstverwaltung*, Berlin, Schocken, 1936, p. 130; et al.
56 See Alon, *The Sociological Method* etc. in Meḥqarim, vol. II, pp. 222-3 (This essay does not appear in English translation).
57 Hor. 10a.

judge; it did not specifically *appoint* him to a court. And it is a fact that there is no reference in our post-Destruction sources to the despatch of *dayyanim* to local communities — not, that is, until the time of Judah I, and even then, only at the request of a community (who promptly discharged the man because they were not satisfied with his scholarship!).[58] So we are left without proof positive for the Yavneh period.

Nevertheless, we must assume that *minui* actually *did* bring in its wake an almost immediate appointment to one or another community. We know that this was the practice several generations later; but even at the time of Rabban Gamaliel it must have been the way things were done — an inference to be drawn from the episode quoted involving Rabbis Johanan ben Nuri and Eleazar ben Hisma.

It should be remembered that ordination was not the automatic result of a man's learning. Many a great scholar was never ordained; many lesser Sages were ordained because their services were required. In numerous instances, *minui* was given so as to qualify the candidate for appointment to a specific vacancy. There was a clear and present need; the qualification was, so to speak, *ad hoc*.

This means that the power to ordain gave the central authorities a large measure of control over the administration of Jewish law throughout the country. At the same time, it can be shown that no man could be imposed on a community without its consent. If a candidate was about to be ordained in order to go to a particular town, and it became known that the town did not want him, the ordination was withheld.

Side by side, then, with the locally-rooted tribunals, there was a system of courts deriving from the central institutions, and it was the latter system which gradually extended its power and influence. Most probably this happened not only because of the indirect control that went with the power to qualify judges, but also as a result of the *direct* supervision exercised by the Patriarch and the Sanhedrin. We hear of intervention by the *Nasi* in local affairs to the extent of dismissing community leaders and appointing others in their place.[59] We have mentioned the tradition that Rabban Gamaliel ousted Shazpar, the "head" of Gezer.

58 The episode of Levi ben Sisi in Simonia, referred to above in note 33.
59 Bavli, R.H. 22a; Yer. ibid. I:57b.

Structure and Procedures

To sum up, then: although the central institutions did not succeed in gaining complete control over Jewish judicature in the whole Land of Israel, Rabban Gamaliel was able nevertheless to get a firm grip over most towns and communities. In this way he strengthened the reign of Jewish law in the country, and made a major contribution to the national re-consolidation of his people, as it raised itself out of the depths of defeat.

The Authority to Interpret the Law

As we have seen, the Great Sanhedrin in Jerusalem had possessed the power to settle most questions of law. After the Destruction, that function was taken over by the Beth Din at Yavneh.

> 'If a matter be too difficult for thee in judgement... thou shalt arise and go up to the place...' (Deut. 17:8). 'And thou shalt arrive (there)...' (Deut. 17:9). The seemingly redundant phrase teaches us that the High Court at Yavneh is included.[60]

To this, Rabbi Zeira added: "For answering questions."[61] His point was that the Court of Yavneh did *not* have the power to exact the full penalty from the "Rebellious Elder."[62]

We have abundant evidence to show that the Court of Rabban Gamaliel functioned as the highest instance for deciding matters of halakhah. For example, Rabbi Zadok is recorded as having brought two questions of halakhic practice from Tiv'on in the Jezreel Valley to the Beth Din at Yavneh for decision; and a ritual decision made by the local authority at Sepphoris in the Galilee was overruled by

60 Sifre Deut. 152-3; Finkelstein, pp. 205-6.
61 Yer. Sanh. XI:30a.
62 *Zaqen mamre*, an elder who gives rulings contrary to the decision of the High Court. Based on Deut. 17:12, he exposes himself to trial for a capital offense. The Mishnah (Sanh. XI:2-4) limits this law, confining jurisdiction to the Sanhedrin in Temple times, and explicitly excluding the court at Yavneh. It is true that in the third century, when the Patriarch Judah II and his Beth Din made it permissible to use oils produced by non-Jews, and Rav opposed the step, his colleague Samuel said to him: "Eat, for if not I shall have you proscribed as a rebellious elder." But obviously, in that context the phrase was being used rhetorically; no real sanctions were contemplated — or indeed, possible. See Yer. Shab. I:3d and Av. Zar. II:41d.

Authority to Interpret

the Court at Yavneh.[63] From the same community a problem in the laws of circumcision was referred to Rabban Gamaliel.[64] Similarly, we hear of questions in halakhah being sent to Rabban Gamaliel from Kefar Aris[65] and from Kefar Segna in the Galilee.[66] The Jews of the Diaspora as well looked to Yavneh for religious guidance, even as they had looked to Jerusalem before the Destruction. From Tripoli on the Syrian coast a question concerning Sabbath observance was sent to Rabban Gamaliel at Yavneh. It is recorded in three distinct sources that from a place called "Assia" messengers went forth "to Yavneh on the three festivals" bearing requests for halakhic guidance.[67] "Assia" may be Asia Minor, but is more probably Etzion Gever (Aqaba) as proposed by Samuel Klein.[68] Eusebius refers to that Red Sea port as Αἴσια.[69] In any case, the place was outside the boundaries of the Holy Land.

Incidentally, it is a mistake to equate the custom of going to Yavneh on the three festivals with the old-time pilgrimage to Jerusalem. What we are dealing with is the custom of the Sages, members of the Beth Din and Academy, to foregather on holy days at the central meeting place. Thus it became customary, and remained so for centuries, for unsolved problems to be brought up on the festivals. It must be kept in mind that, as a general rule, many members of the Sanhedrin — perhaps the majority of them — did not live in the place where the High Court had its seat.

That the authorities at Yavneh in the days of Rabban Gamaliel exercised a considerable measure of supervision and control over the religious life of Diaspora Jewry is illustrated by the episode involving Theodos, leader of the Jewish community of Rome:

Rabbi Jose reported: Theodos of Rome had accustomed the

63 Tos. Nid. IV:3-4 (Zuck. 644); and Kil. I:4 (Zuck. 73).
64 Tos. Shab. XV:8 (Zuck. 133). There are variants that read "Simeon ben Gamaliel," a not uncommon switch.
65 Tos. Kel. B.M. XI:2 (Zuck. 589). Its location is uncertain.
66 Ibid. B.Q. IV:4 (Zuck. 572).
67 For Tripoli, see Tos. Eruv. IX:25 (Zuck. 150). For "Assia" see Tos. Hul. III:10 (Zuck. 504); Parah, VII:4 (Zuck. 636); Miq. IV:6 (Zuck. 656).
68 See *Jakob Freimann Festschrift*, Berlin, Heb. section, pp. 116 ff.
69 See his *Onomastikon*; Hebrew translation by E. Z. Melammed, nos. 133 and 229. It is probable that τῶν Ἡσιτῶν mentioned in the inscriptions at Beth Shearim were residents of that area.

[231]

Roman Jews to eat "helmeted kids" on Passover eve (*i.e. dressed after the fashion of Exodus XII:9*). They sent word to him that he was close to violating the prohibition against eating sacrificial flesh outside the Temple of Jerusalem, for the people were coming to call them "Paschal offerings."[70]

In the Talmudim it is recorded that the sages sent word to Theodos, saying: "Were it not that you are Theodos, we might very well have excommunicated you!"[71]

It is possible to date this contretemps before the Bar Kokhba Revolt by the fact that Rabbi Jose ben Halafta speaks of it in the past tense. But even without that clue we would have been inclined to date it somewhere near the time when the Academy at Yavneh debated whether it was permissible to eat helmeted lambs or kids on the first evening of Passover. The Mishnah reports that Rabban Gamaliel wanted to permit it, but the majority of the sages were opposed, and apparently they prevailed.[72] (The printed editions of the Bavli erroneously report that Simeon ben Shetach, who lived in the first century BCE, was involved in the rebuke to Theodos of Rome.[73] However, our basic versions, as well as corresponding passages elsewhere, all show that the communication came from "the Sages.")[74]

Supervision of the Communities

There is plenty of evidence to show that the Patriarch Rabban Gamaliel of Yavneh made it a practice to visit towns where there was a Jewish population of any size, and to instruct the people in matters both of law and of religion. Clearly it was the purpose of these journeys to inspect the communities and to cement their allegiance to the central authorities.

Some of the places he visited are specifically mentioned in the

---

70 Tos. Bez. II:15 (Zuck. 204): "What is a helmeted kid? One roasted whole, with head and shoulders placed within its entrails."
71 Yer. Pes. VII:34a; Bavli Ber. 19a.
72 Bez. II:7.
73 Ber. 19a (where the proximity to the episode of Honi, and the similarity in the phrasing, is undoubtedly the cause of the error).
74 See ms. Munich; and Pes. 53a; Bez. 23a.

literature: Akko[75] Ashkelon[76] Kefar Othnai[77] Tiberias.[78] An interesting reflection of this "circuit riding"[79] is found in the following:

> Once it happened that Shigabion, the head of the synagogue at Achziv, acquired a four-year-old vineyard from a Syrian non-Jew and paid for it; and he came and asked Rabban Gamaliel, who was *passing from place to place* (about the laws involved). Rabban Gamaliel answered: 'Wait until we get to our sessions on halakhah'...[80]

This shows that Rabban Gamaliel made regular swings around the country, visiting one community at a time.[81]

Of special interest are those traditions that reveal the Patriarch and the Sanhedrin (or a committee of its senior members) holding sessions in various parts of the country. Once the Sages were in a district where Samaritan villages were numerous, and they were served green vegetables, whereupon Rabbi Akiba immediately tithed them.[82] On another occasion, Rabban Gamaliel and the Elders were at table together in Jericho.[83]

This practice of holding meetings of the Great Sanhedrin (in the form of a select committee) away from "home" goes back to the days of the Second Commonwealth, as the following shows:[84]

> Once the elders were gathered in the upper chamber of Beth Gorio at Jericho, when they heard a heavenly voice proclaim: There is one present who is fit to be inhabited by the Holy Spirit — only the generation is not worthy of having that happen. At this point all eyes turned upon Hillel the Elder.

75 Mishnah Av. Zar. III:4; Tos. M.Q. II:15 (Zuck. 231).
76 Tos. Miq. VI:3 (Zuck. 658).
77 Mishnah Git. I:5.
78 Mishnah, Eruv. X:10. Tos. Shab. XIII:2 (Zuck. 128) etc.
79 There are no grounds for interpreting the last as a permanent move caused by persecution, despite Halevy: *Dorot Ha-Rishonim*, Vol. V, pp. 347-8.
80 Tos. Ter. II:13 (Zuck. 28).
81 Not as Halevy would have it (ibid. p. 348) that he was moving around the country to evade arrest by the Romans.
82 Tos. Dem. V:24 (Zuck. 56).
83 Tos. Ber. IV:12 (Zuck. 11).
84 Tos. Sot. XIII:3 (Zuck. 318 f.). Also Bavli Sanh. 11a; Yer. Sot. IX:24b; ibid. Av. Zar. III:42c.

It seems likely that these "sessions" of the Great Sanhedrin held outside its regular meeting-chamber were intended as a spiritual stimulus to the various localities where they took place, and perhaps also as a symbol of the bond between those localities and the central authorities. In any event these meetings appear to have taken up matters on the regular agenda of the Sanhedrin. What is more, they sometimes lasted for a considerable length of time. That, it seems to me, is the explanation for the way the following are phrased:

> Once it happened that Rabban Gamaliel and the Elders were seated at the home of Boethus ben Zonin in Lydda, engaged in a discussion of the laws of Passover...[85]

> Quoth Rabbi Eleazar ben Zadoq:[86] On one occasion the 14th of Nisan fell on the Sabbath day. We were seated before Rabban Gamaliel in the House of Study at Lydda[87] when Zonin, who was in charge of such matters, came in and announced that the time had come to get rid of all leaven. Father and I went to Rabban Gamaliel's house and we disposed of the leaven.

Here we have Rabban Gamaliel and the Elders away from Yavneh on Passover, but it seems to me that we ought *not* to draw any far-reaching conclusions from that. Let us *not* assume that the Romans had shut down the Sanhedrin, and that Rabban Gamaliel had been forced to move to Lydda.[88] All we need assume here is a temporary sojourn in another city, for the purposes outlined above. The fact that such visits were made even on Passover only proves that the Sanhedrin would leave home even on festivals — or perhaps especially then! Indeed, that may well have been the time when the Sages could make their greatest impact.

Renewal of Ties with the Diaspora

From the beginning of the third century through to the abolition of the Patriarchate in the fifth century, the official head of the Jews in

85 Tos. Pes. X:12 (Zuck. 173).
86 Ibid. II:11 (Zuck. 159).
87 But Bavli 49a reads: "at Yavneh."
88 Again contrary to Halevy, op. cit., pp. 335-6.

the Land of Israel (the *Nasi*) regularly sent out his legates (*apostoloi*) to the Jews of the Diaspora. The duties of these messengers included the collection of the "Jewish tax' (*aurum coronarium*) and inspection of the far-flung Jewish communities. Our most explicit sources in this connection are the writings of the Church Fathers, and the official entries in the Codex Theodosianus.[89] Origen tells us that these messengers used to carry with them circular letters (*encyclia*) from the *Nasi* and the Sanhedrin to the Jews of the Diaspora.

Communications such as these between the mother country and the Jewish communities abroad had been maintained for centuries, even before the Destruction. Tannaitic sources testify to the regular official correspondence between the authorities in Jerusalem and the Diaspora.[90] Messengers went not only to other parts of the Roman world; they also travelled to the domain of the Parthians. A fourth century writer says that these emissaries were leading members of the Patriarch's council.[91]

As we have noted above, Rabban Gamaliel made it one of his tasks to restore the ties between the homeland and the Jewish communities abroad. He himself, accompanied by senior Sages of the Academy of Yavneh, journeyed to Rome, apparently on more than one occasion.[92] And while he certainly had high-level diplomatic business to conduct, it was also part of his purpose to renew the bonds between the center of Judaism and the great Jewish community of Rome. It is recorded that the visiting dignitaries preached in the synagogue at Rome.[93] In a similar way, Rabbi Joshua ben Hanania answered 12 questions that were directed to him while he was in Alexandria.[94]

89 XVI, § 14; also Eusebius, in his commentary on Isaiah. The relevant passages are reproduced in Graetz, *Geschichte*, 4th ed., Vol. IV, note 21, page 441.
90 Tos. Sanh. II:6 (Zuck. 416) et passim.
91 Epiphanius: *Adversus Haereses 30.3*; Graetz, loc. cit.
92 Ma'as. Sh. V:9; Eruv. IV:1; Hor. 10a; Makk. 24a; Yer. Sanh. VII:25d; Deut. R. II:24.
93 Exod. R. XXX:6.
94 Mishnah, Neg. XIV:13; Tos. ibid. IX:9 (Zuck. 630); Bavli Nid. 69b. Some scholars believe with Zecharia Frankel, that the journey of Rabbi Joshua ben Hananiah to Alexandria took place during the reign of Hadrian — that is, after the death of Rabban Gamaliel. Their theory is based on what Flavius Vopiscus says in *Scriptores Historiae Augustae*,

It is much the same with the extensive travels undertaken by Rabbi Akiba. A list of the places he visited would have to include the "cities of the sea" (perhaps the Phoenician coast) where he dealt with halakhic questions;[95] Arabia Nabataea;[96] Zephyrion which is Cilicia,[97] where he gave a ruling on a matter of halakha;[98] Africa; Gallia (most likely Galatia in Asia Minor);[99] Mazaca, the chief city of Cappadocia;[100] Nehardea;[101] and Ginzak of Media.[102] In many of these places the record shows him rendering halakhic decisions and sometimes expounding on aggadah.[103]

There is scarcely any room for doubt that Rabbi Akiba had a specific reason for his extensive travels in foreign parts. It seems certain that he was on the business of the Sanhedrin, as its emissary. There are historians, to be sure, who agree with Graetz that this was a cover for more secret, urgent business — namely, preparations for the Bar Kokhba Revolt.[104] But this hypothesis remains pure speculation, without any support whatsoever in the sources.[105] In any case, the Mishnah explicitly places his journey to Nehardea during the lifetime of Rabban Gamaliel, which is to say, long before the Revolt.[106] It is a much more reasonable assumption that Rabbi Akiba journeyed abroad in the service of a program to re-establish the bonds between

namely, that Hadrian wrote a letter to a friend reporting that the Patriarch of the Jews had come to Egypt. These same scholars believe that Rabbi Joshua filled the position of Patriarch after the death of Rabban Gamaliel. However, the missive has been shown to be inauthentic, so the whole theory falls to the ground. Nor is there any proof that Rabbi Joshua acted as Patriarch. See *Darkhe Ha-Mishnah*, 2nd. ed., p. 88, note 3.

95 Yev. 98a. To be sure, R.H. 26a reads: "Rabbi said;" but other versions of the text read "Rabbi Akiba."
96 R.H. 26a.
97 Tos. B.Q. X:17 (Zuck. 368); Bavli, ibid. 113a; Sifre Numbers IV: Horovitz ed., p. 7; Sifre Zuta, p. 232.
98 Yer. Av. Zar. I:41b.
99 R.H. 26a.
100 Tos. Yev. XIV:5 (Zuck. 259); Yer. Ibid. XV:15d.
101 Mishnah Yev. XVI:7.
102 Taan. 12a; Av. Zar. 34a and 39a. Some versions read "Mar Ukba" but the correct reading is "Rabbi Akiba."
103 Gen. R. 33:7; ed. Theodor, p. 310.
104 [See *Geschichte*, 4th ed., Vol. IV, Chap. 8, p. 135.]
105 Comp. Halevy: *Dorot Ha-Rishonim*, Part I, Vol. V, p. 622.
106 Yev. XVI:7.

the mother country and its Sanhedrin, on the one hand, and the scattered Jewish communities of the Diaspora on the other.

Authority Over the Calendar

While the Temple still stood, it was the Great Sanhedrin in Jerusalem that managed the Jewish calendar. From its chambers word went forth whether the month was to remain 29 days long, or be extended to 30 days. Most especially, it was the Sanhedrin that promulgated Leap Years, adding a month at the end of the winter when necessary to keep the lunar and the solar cycles balanced.

After the Destruction this prerogative was taken over by the High Court at Yavneh (and subsequently at Usha and the other places to which it wandered). Control of the calendar was one of the important means of keeping the Jewish communities of the whole Land of Israel united around the national-religious center, wherever it might be located. Indeed, it was one of the centripetal forces, as it had been before the Destruction, in keeping the scattered diasporas bound to the ancestral homeland. Both in theory and practice, the Jews of the world turned their eyes to the Great Beth Din in the Land of Israel when they wanted to know when to observe the festivals and the holy days, the New Moons and the New Years.

But there is something peculiar about the sources that deal with this matter. They always make specific mention of the countries north and east of Israel — i.e. Syria and Mesopotamia. They never speak of lands to the south and the west, especially never of the great Jewish community of Alexandria. This holds good for the days of the Second Temple, as well as for the post-Destruction era. Any time there is mention of signal-fires, and messengers, and missives, they are always going the other way — never to Egypt.

This fact has led some scholars to suggest that the Jews of Egypt did not depend in calendrical matters on the decisions of the Jerusalem Sanhedrin, but managed these things in their own way. However, the suggestion is unconvincing. It is based entirely on the *argumentum e silentio*, which proves nothing. Nor are there any other grounds for the assumption. Besides, we have proof that the Jews of Alexandria *did* accept direction from the Old Country when it came to "the order of the festivals."[107]

107 Yer. Eruv. III 21c: "Rabbi Jose wrote to the Alexandrians: Even though

[237]

News of the promulgation of New Moons was passed on to the Diaspora in two ways: by signal fires, and by messengers. The Mishnah explains:

> Originally, they used to light signal fires. But when the Samaritans started interfering with this method, it was arranged that messengers should go forth.[108]

This Mishnah fails to say when the change took place. At first glance, it might appear that the Yerushalmi answers the question:

> Who abolished the signal fires? Rabbi (Judah I) abolished the signal fires.[109]

However, it strains credulity if we assign all references to the messengers in the Mishnah and *baraitha* to a time *after* Judah the Patriarch. What is more, it appears from certain tannaitic passages that the system of "messengers" was already well-established in the days of Rabbi Simeon ben Eleazar, or perhaps even in the days of Rabban Simeon ben Gamaliel, if we accept the reading of the Bavli.[110] Besides, the description of the signal fires can only refer to the time when the Temple still stood:[111]

> Whence did they kindle the signal fires? From the Mount of Olives (they signalled) to Sarteba, and thence to Agrippina etc.

It also seems rather far-fetched to suppose that, after the Destruction, the Jews could maintain signal fires deep into Syria (Beth Baltin). A much more reasonable interpretation of the tradition recorded in the Yerushalmi is that Judah I finally and officially put an end to the practice of signal fires; which is not the same as saying that it had been in full force up to that moment. It is quite within the bounds of possibility that the custom had been restored, off and on, whenever

we have communicated the order of the festivals to you, do not give up the custom of your fathers, of blessed memory" (i.e. in observing the extra days).

108   R.H. II:2.
109   Yer. R.H. II:58a.
110   Tos. Peah IV:6 (Zuck. 23); ibid., Ket. III:1 (Zuck. 263); Bavli, ibid., 25a; Yer. ibid. II:26d.
111   Mishnah R.H. II:4; Tos. ibid., II:2 (Zuck. 210).

conditions were favorable, within the country itself. Signal fires to the Diaspora had surely terminated with the Destruction. What Judah I appears to have done was to abolish the practice even within the country. Despite this official step, the custom did not disappear altogether. Rabbi Abahu, at the end of the third century, informs us that the bonfires were still being lit in the vicinity of Lake Kinneret[112] (out of nostalgia?). From the same context we learn that Safed continued the fires from its mountain top. These passages in the Yerushalmi support our hypothesis that the act of Judah I dealt only with flares within the country.

Notification about leap years had to be accomplished by means of letters. The Tosefta tells us how this was done during the days of the Temple:[113]

> Once Rabban Gamaliel and the elders were seated on the steps of the Temple Mount, with Johanan the scribe before them. To him Rabban Gamaliel dictated: Write! 'To our brethren of Upper Galilee and our brethren of Lower Galilee, peace abundant! We hereby make it known unto you...' (The missive goes on to deal with tithes)... 'And to our brethren in the Diaspora of Babylonia and of Media and of the remaining Diasporas of Israel, peace abundant! We hereby make it known unto you... that it hath seemed good to me and to my colleagues to add thirty days to the current year.'[114]

This method of notification by letter continued after the Destruction. Mar Ukba, a Babylonian Amora of the third century, is reputed to have found the originals of two such missives of different dates.[115] It appears that the Diaspora communities preserved these letters in their archives.

112 Yer. R.H. II:58a.
113 Tos. Sanh. II:6 (Zuck. 416); Yer. ibid. I:18d.
114 The Babylonian Talmud (Sanh. 11b) assumes that the above refers to Rabban Gamaliel of Yavneh. However, there is no doubt that Rabban Gamaliel the Elder is meant. In a *baraitha* resembling this, quoted in *Midrash Tannaim*, p. 176, the reading is: Rabban Simeon, the son of Rabban Gamailel the Elder. See above, p. 91, n. 11.
115 Yer. Meg. I, 71a.

The Halakhah states explicitly that leap years may not be proclaimed in the Diaspora.[116] On the face of it, this means that the decision to intercalate was reserved to the High Court in the Land of Israel. Immediately after the Bar Kohba revolt, an attempt to make independent calendrical decisions in Babylonia was launched by Hananiah, nephew of Rabbi Joshua. The attempt failed. The sources hint that Samuel, in Nehardea, tried his hand at the same thing in the third century, with no greater success. Still later, in the tenth century, long after the calendar as we know it had been published, making the Diaspora quite independent of the authorities in the Land of Israel, the issue came to the fore again. The famous polemic between Ben-Meir, the Gaon of Eretz Israel, and Saadiah ben Joseph, Gaon of Sura, dealt with this very subject. The former maintained that the Halakhah made the Jews of the Diaspora subservient in matters of the calendar to decisions and calculations made in the Holy Land. Saadiah's contention was that publication of the "secret of calendrical reckoning" had made all that a dead letter. However, anyone who examines the argument carefully must conclude that Ben Meir's case was not without merit.[117] It seems that the original Halakhah meant not only that the initiative must not be taken in the Diaspora; even the consent of the Sanhedrin, and even its request to the Diaspora to take action, had no validity. The only valid soil on which action concerning the Jewish calendar could be taken was the soil of the Land of Israel.

In the light of all this, it is most puzzling to read that Rabbi Akiba did exactly what is declared invalid. The matter warrants our careful attention, so we shall cite the passage in full:[118]

> Rabbi Akiba said: When I went down to Nehardea to ordain a leap year, there met me Nehemiah of Beth Deli,[119] and he said to me, 'I have heard that in the Land of Israel the Sages,

116 Yer. Sanh. I:19a; Ned. VI:40a.
117 For a discussion of this question, see Borenstein in the Sokolow *Sefer ha-Yovel*, pp. 19 ff. For the eighth century, see: Mann: *The Jews in Egypt and in Palestine under the Fatimid Caliphs.* Vol. I, p. 50 ff.
118 Mishnah Yev. XVI:7.
119 The Mishnah in the Yerushalmi reads: *Bedeli.* This Nehemiah was a Palestinian scholar who apparently migrated to Babylonia after the Destruction.

excepting Rabbi Judah ben Bava, do not allow a woman to marry again on the testimony of one witness.' I answered: 'That is right.' He said to me: 'You know that this country is in a state of confusion by reason of roving military units; tell them in my name that I had a tradition from Rabban Gamaliel the Elder that they may permit a woman to marry on the testimony of one witness.' When I returned and reported this conversation to Rabban Gamaliel (the Younger), he rejoiced and said: We have found a (supporting) colleague for Rabbi Judah ben Bava.

An early attempt to square Rabbi Akiba's mission with the monopoly of Eretz Israel on the calendar is found in the Babylonian Talmud.[120] Rav Safra quotes Rabbi Abahu about the episode of Hananiah, Rabbi Joshua's nephew. The latter migrated to Babylonia, and began proclaiming months and years like a full-fledged calendrical authority. The Sanhedrin sent two scholars after him. These waited until he had received them with full honours, and had praised them publicly. Then they began to goad him, contradicting his every ruling. He wanted to know why. Said they: "Because you determine months and declare leap years outside the Holy Land." He answered: "But Akiba ben Joseph did that very thing!" Said they: "Leave Rabbi Akiba out of this! He left not his like even in the Land of Israel!" Said he: "Well, neither did I!" Said they to him: "Those whom you left behind in the Land of Israel as mere striplings have grown up to be horned rams! It is they who sent us to you with this message: if he desists, well and good; if not, he shall be placed under a ban."

The Talmud seems to be saying that Rabbi Akiba could do what he did because he was the peerless scholar of his day, unmatched even in the Land of Israel. But, as Halevy points out, the journey to Nehardea took place during the lifetime of Rabban Gamaliel (and of Rabbi Eliezer, and of Rabbi Joshua ben Hananiah).[121] Are we to say that Rabbi Akiba was greater than these teachers of his? The fact is, the same tradition is reported in the Yerushalmi without that phrase about Rabbi Akiba, even though it has Hananiah boasting

120 Ber. 63a.
121 *Dorot* II, sec. 1, p. 192.

about his calendrical skill.[122] What is more, the Yerushalmi version contains the following:

> Said the Holy One, Blessed be He: I would rather have a small handful of scholars in the Land of Israel than a Great Sanhedrin outside the Land.

Going still further, Pirke d'Rabbi Eliezer has this:[123]

> Even when you have saints and sages outside the Holy Land, and nothing but a shepherd or a herdsman in the Land, it is the shepherd or the herdsman who is to promulgate the leap year. And even if you have prophets outside the Land of Israel, and only commoners and plain folk in the Land, the authority to proclaim the calendar rests with the commoners in the Land of Israel.

The tradition as recorded in the Babylonian Talmud makes no distinction between the mission of Rabbi Akiba (which was undoubtedly undertaken on behalf of the Patriarch and the Sanhedrin) and the action of Hananiah, who flouted the authority of the mother country, and arrogated the power over the calendar to himself. This is still another reason for doubting the authenticity of the Babylonian tradition.

So our problem remains. Graetz made an attempt to resolve it, but his solution is rather forced.[124] Basing himself on the reading of the Mishnah in the Yerushalmi he argues that Rabbi Akiba was simply the messenger of the court, carrying news of the step already taken by the Patriarch and the Sanhedrin. Graetz actually has textual support for his reading.[125] But his interpretation of that reading is far-fetched. The plain meaning of the word refers to the *action*, not to the announcement of it.

Not only that; the following two items cut the ground out from under Graetz's solution. First, there is the episode of Rabbi Meir:[126]

122 Yer. Ned. VII:40a; Sanh. I:19a.
123 Pirqe d'R. Eliezer, chap. 8.
124 *Geschichte*, 4th ed., vol. IV, note 21, page 441.
125 Lowe: *Mathnita*, ms. Kaufman and ms. Munich all read *le'ibbur*, not *le'abber*.
126 Tos. Meg. II:5 (Zuck. 223); Bavli, ibid., 18b.

"It happened that Rabbi Meir went to intercalate the year in Assia etc." This place, as we have said, appears to be Etzion Gever. Tannaitic tradition places it outside the boundaries of the Land of Israel,[127] claiming only that it had been promised to Abraham, and would become part of the Land "at the end of days." It was exempt from tithes, and from the restrictions of the sabbatical year. However, there are indications that its status was not altogether clear-cut.[128] There were circumstances in which it was regarded as quasi-Holy Land.[129] The entire question becomes complicated and it is not necessary to deal with its minutiae here.[130]

In any event, there is no way out of the difficulty in this instance by adopting Graetz's method and theorizing that Rabbi Meir was simply the bearer of information. Indeed, I.H. Weiss proposes the view that Rabbi Meir acted in deliberate defiance of the Patriarch, more or less after the fashion of Rabbi Joshua's nephew Hananiah.[131] But that view must be rejected. Even though the relationship between Rabban Simeon ben Gamaliel and Rabbi Meir was strained (see Horayoth 10b), there is no hint of that factor in the report of Rabbi Meir's journey to Assia. Nor is the incident related with any suggestion of disapproval (unlike the case of Hananiah).[132] In the absence of such condemnation, we can scarcely interpret one case of intercalation on foreign soil without reference to other cases of the same kind, such as that of Rabbi Akiba, not to speak of the following from the third century:[133]

> Rabbi Hiyya bar Zarnoki and Rabbi Simeon bar Yehozadak were on their way to intercalate the year in Assia. Resh Laqish met them. Said he: Let me go along and see how they do this thing: When they got there, they went up into the loft, and

127 B.B. 56a; Yer. Shev. VI:36a; Gen. R. XLIV:27.
128 Tos. Parah VII:4 (Zuck. 636).
129 See Meir Ish-Shalom in *Yerushalayim* (Lunz), vol. V, p. 48; and Alon in *Mehqarim* I, pp. 320–328. Not translated.
130 Tos. Ahil. XVIII:4 (Zuck. 616); Yer. Shev. VI:36c; see G. Alon: "Origin of the Samaritans in the Halakhic Tradition" in JJCW, pp. 354 ff.
131 See *Dor Dor* II, p. 226.
132 Halevy, Dorot, sec. 1, p. 195.
133 Sanh. 26a.

pulled the ladder up after them. (i.e. they realized from his questions en route that he was going to be difficult).

The story makes it clear that they were not simply bearing the announcement of an already promulgated leap year; they were actually going to carry out the entire procedure![134]

The solution proposed by mediaeval commentators, as well as by modern scholars, is to treat these episodes of calendrical proclamation outside the Holy Land as exceptions made necessary by emergency conditions.[135] The Sanhedrin and the Patriarch, it is suggested, were prevented from exercising their proper function, either by persecution or by war, so that the exception laid down by the Yerushalmi had to be followed, namely:

> The rule (that leap years may not be promulgated outside the Land of Israel) applies so long as it is possible for calendrical decisions and proclamations to be made in the Land. Should, however, conditions arise in which that is not possible, then years may be intercalated and proclamations be made outside the Land of Israel.[136]

But does this theory really explain Rabbi Akiba's journey? Historically speaking, what could have happened at the time that he went to Babylonia? It is true that the first Christian emperors interfered with the promulgation of the Jewish calendar — but that was a long time later.[137] It is also a reasonable assumption that the same sort of thing occurred during the Hadrianic persecutions — but Rabbi Akiba's journey took place almost two decades earlier. If we suppose that the trip in question happened during the "*polemos* of Quietus" (115–117 C.E.) — that will not hold up either, because Rabban Gamaliel had died by then, and we know that when Rabbi Akiba returned home, Rabban Gamaliel was still alive. Besides, at that time Babylonia was in an even worse state of turmoil than was Palestine.

To be sure, it is possible to interpret the remark by Nehemiah of

134 Ginzberg: *Perushim ve-Hidushim bi-Yerushalmi*, III, p. 131.
135 Tosafot on Yev. 115a, s.v. *"amar Rabbi Akiba;"* and Halevy, ibid.; Klein, in the Freimann Festschrift, p. 120; Ginzberg, ibid.
136 Yer. Sanh. I:19a.
137 Sanh. 12a.

Beth Deli (in the Mishnah) as meaning that "the whole world is in a state of confusion". But that will not do, because there is an explicit stress on "*this* country" (Mesopotamia), implying that conditions back in Palestine were comparatively peaceful. The reference to "roving bands" apparently has to do with nomadic Arabs whose incursions from the desert were a permanent feature of life on the borders of Babylonia, especially in Nehardea.[138] The risk of being taken captive by these raiders was constant.[139]

It is equally unlikely that the episode of Rabbi Meir took place during a time of emergency. Quite the contrary, the Rabbis on their way to Assia seem to be travelling in leisurely fashion. En route, they meet Jews peacefully ploughing their fields, and a travelling companion (Resh Laqish) returns to Tiberias entirely without incident.

I suggest a different approach to the problem. It seems to me that the proclamation of leap years outside the boundaries of the Holy Land was made in normal times, and by *authority* of the Sanhedrin and the Patriarch, for the benefit of the Jews in the Diaspora, and in order to strengthen the ties between them and the mother country. The despatch of members of the Sanhedrin for so important a function would certainly have served as a gesture of the esteem in which the Jews of the dispersion were held. It is even likely that learned scholars in the Diaspora were co-opted to take part in the necessary astronomical calculations, almost as though they were actual members of the Sanhedrin.

But I would go further, and suggest that fixing the calendar in the Diaspora was tied in with the *economic needs* of the Jews who lived there. The Halakhah recognizes such considerations as perfectly valid. It is laid down, for example, that the Sabbatical year may not be intercalated (twelve months without a harvest is enough!) nor may the following year, when new produce (this year's: *ḥadash*) may not be eaten until after the Omer offering. A leap year would prolong the shortage of food by one whole month.[140]

Based on the same principle, there is a rule that the extra month

138 B.Q. 83a and Eruv. 45a: "When R. Nahman said: Babylonia is classified as a border area, he meant Nehardea."
139 Comp. the capture of Samuel's daughters in Nehardea, and the capture of Rav Nahman's daughters, Ket. 23a.
140 Sanh. 12a.

is not added during a year of "hunger" (that is, following poor crops). The point is, to arrive as soon as possible at the 16th of Nisan, when "new" produce may be eaten.[141]

Bear in mind that the prohibition against eating this year's produce before Nisan 16th applies outside the Holy Land.[142] Therefore, in years when food was in short supply the Jews in the Diaspora would have an interest in postponing the intercalation. Nor ought it be surprising that their interests should have been taken into account. The tradition goes even further in connection with the intercalation of *months* (adding a thirtieth day). The standard rule is that months are not intercalated for economic reasons, although years are.[143] Nevertheless, even though it is explicitly stated that "since the days of Ezra there has been no case of a thirty-day Elul,"[144] it is also explicitly reported that:

> When Ulla came (to Babylonia) he said, 'We have intercalated the month of Elul' (that is, made it one day longer). Said he: 'I wonder whether our brethren in Babylonia realize what a favor we have done them.'[145]

The Talmud goes on to explain this. The purpose of the added day was to keep Yom Kippur from falling on a Friday (or a Sunday).[146] If it had so fallen, the Jews would have been confronted with two consecutive "full Sabbaths" — that is, non-cooking days. In the Land of Israel that would have been manageable, by preparing a meal of raw vegetables. But in the much greater heat of Mesopotamia, even raw vegetables would not keep for two days. Hence, the postponement of Yom Kippur by one day was a great boon to Babylonian Jewry.

But quite apart from such considerations, conducting the calendar procedure in a Diaspora community was a good way to stress the

141 Tos. Sanh. II:9 (Zuck. 417); Bavli, ibid., 11b–12a; Yer., ibid., I:18d.
142 Mishnah Orl. III:9; Qid. I:9; Bavli, ibid., 37a.
143 R.H. 20a.
144 Ibid., 19b, and elsewhere.
145 Ibid., 20a.
146 [That purpose, inter alia, is now served by a rule built into the Jewish calendar: *lo ad'u rosh* — i.e. Rosh Hashanah cannot begin on Sunday, Wednesday or Friday.]

fact that the Jewish authorities took serious account of their brethren who were domiciled abroad. The Halakhah does state:[147]

> Rabban Simeon ben Gamaliel and Rabbi Eleazar bar Zadoq say that intercalation of the year and other measures undertaken for the public welfare are enacted with the (implicit) proviso that the majority of the public receive them favorably.

It is a reasonable assumption that *from time to time* Patriarchs and Sanhedrin sought to extend this principle of public approval to Diaspora Jewry as well by going out to them and conducting the procedure in their very midst.

As for the law that calendrical procedures may not be carried out beyond the borders of the Holy Land — not even by authority of its High Court — it seems to me likely that this law was occasionally circumvented because of the needs of the hour. No doubt some legal device was found, such as the subsequent formal ratification of the act by the Beth Din in the Land of Israel, where in any case the theoretical calculation had already been performed. Actually, a solution something like that was proposed by the earliest Talmudic commentators.[148] Besides, a similar situation, where a leap year was declared by a legal device in the face of a rule to the contrary, is found in a *baraitha*:[149]

> The Rabbis taught: No year is to be intercalated because of needs foreseen for the coming year; nor may three consecutive years be declared leap years. Rabbi Simeon said: 'Once it happened when Rabbi Akiba was in prison (before his execution) that he intercalated three years, one after the other.' They said to him: (to Rabbi Simeon) 'What does that prove? In that case the court sat (for each one) and proclaimed each year at its proper time'.[150]

The point is, that Rabbi Akiba made the calculations and produced

147 Tos. Sanh. II:13 (Zuck. 418).
148 Tosafot on Sanh. 26a s.v. *le'abber*; Hameiri on Sanhedrin, p. 96.
149 Bavli, Sanh. 12b; Tos. ibid. II:8 (Zuck. 417).
150 [The translation of the foregoing paragraph depends on whether one follows Rashi or the Tosafot. For present purposes, however, it does not matter.]

the results de facto, while the court went through three separate formal procedures, declaring each year a leap year de jure.

Rabban Gamaliel and the Sages of the Sanhedrin in his day were willing to make this gesture of shared authority in the area of calendar management with the Jews of the Diaspora. Patriarchs and Sages of subsequent generations showed the same willingness — an index of the high value they placed on the interdependence of Jewry in the homeland and Jewry in the dispersion. They took the initiative in showing their interest in the needs of their brethren in the Diaspora, and in involving those Jews as partners in matters of mutual concern.

Financial Support from the Diaspora

Mention has been made above of the set, voluntary contribution with which the Jews of the Diaspora were in the habit of taxing themselves, and of submitting annually to the Patriarch. Roman legal sources, and other texts of the fourth and early fifth centuries, call these free-will offerings *aurum coronarium*. The term used by Epiphanius is an obvious rendering of the Jewish catch-phrase "heave-offerings and tithes" — *terumot u-ma'aserot*.[151]

These contributory "taxes" were collected by emissaries sent out by the Patriarch, according to the sources just mentioned. But there is a strong possibility that the Diaspora communities also remitted their dues in another way — by sending them in with their own messengers. Epiphanius claims that the role of Patriarch's messenger was filled by some of the leading Sages of the home country[152] — ranking members of the Sanhedrin:[153]

> These messengers (ἀπόστολοι) rank just below the Patriarch. They sit with the Patriarch and discourse with him, often for days and nights on end, in order to advise him on matters of Torah.[154]

It is doubtful whether these "apostles" of the Patriarch, or the

151 ἐπιδέκατα καὶ ἀπαρχαί See *Haeres.* 30.11.
152 Ibid. The lengthy passage is reproduced in Greek (with a Hebrew translation) in *Sefer Ha-Yishuv*, Vol. I, part 1, pages 68 to 72.
153 See Alon: *On Philo's Halakah* in JJCW, pp. 94-5, n. -).
154 S. Krauss: *Die Jüdischen Apostel*, in JQR (o.s.), Vol. XVII, pp. 370–383.

"tax" which they collected for him, are mentioned explicitly in Talmudic literature. To be sure, there are passages that can be construed as referring to delegates sent out by him for other purposes — for religious guidance and supervision, as we have just shown. Let us hasten to add that there is perfectly clear evidence in tannaitic and amoraic sources for the despatch of members of the Sanhedrin in order to gather contributions for the support of the central institutions in the mother country. But there is a sharp difference on this score between the Jewish sources and the Greek-Latin texts cited above. The latter speak of emissaries *of the Patriarch,* who gather funds *for the Patriarch.* The Jewish sources invariably refer to "our Rabbis" or "our Sages" or *ḥevraya,* or *ha-ḥaverim* (the collegium) on whose behalf the mission was undertaken and the monies collected.

A likely explanation for this is that to the governmental authorities — possibly even to the Jews of the Diaspora themselves — the Patriarch was the representative head of the Jewish institutions in the Jewish land, the leader of, and spokesman for what was left of Jewish autonomy. But within the Jewish community of the mother country itself, at least in those circles close to the scholars and teachers of the Torah, it was the Sages — the members of the Sanhedrin as a body — who were seen as the leaders. From the outside, it was the Patriarch who loomed large; within the country, it was the Sanhedrin collectively.

In this connection let us note a tradition dating from approximately the middle of the second century (probably from the time of Rabban Simeon ben Gamaliel). It points to the existence of a regular "campaign for funds". It is also our only indication of such activity outside the Roman Empire:

> It happened that Rabbi Dostai son of Rabbi Yannai and Rabbi Yose ben Kipar went down there (to Babylonia) to collect for the collegium.[155]

They ran into trouble with personnel of the Exilarch's staff, who wanted them to return the money!

Closer to home, and to the period we are examining, we have two traditions that tell of an established "campaign" for funds conducted

155 Yer. Git. I:43d; ibid. Qid. III:64a.

by important Sages who were close to the Patriarch. First, there is the story about Rabbis Eliezer, Joshua and Akiba who called on a philanthropic Jew in Syria named Abba Judah.[156] The three Rabbis went up to Ḥolat Antiochia[157] to collect for the collegium. One gets the impression that it was a regular stop on their itinerary. Once Abba Judah lost his property, and when the Rabbis came to town he was too embarrassed to see them. His wife said: "You still have one field left. Go sell half of it, and give our Rabbis the proceeds." He acted on her suggestion. The Rabbis prayed for him, saying: "May the Lord make your losses good." He went to plough his half-field, but his cow fell into a hole and broke her leg. When he went down to help her, he discovered a treasure. So Abba Judah was once again a wealthy philanthropist. When the Rabbis came around again he said to them, "Your prayer has borne fruit." They said: "Even though others gave more than you last time, we put you at the head of the list of contributors."

Although this story has all the marks of a legend, complete with a miracle for the benefit of the hero, we have no grounds for disqualifying the evidence it provides of regular trips to Syria by the aforesaid Sages to collect funds for the Academy. We also learn that the contributions were not in any fixed amount, but varied in terms of the capacity of the giver.

The second tradition touching this matter is also recorded in the Yerushalmi:[158]

> On one occasion the Sages were in need of financial help. They sent Rabbi Akiba (to solicit funds) accompanied by another of the Rabbis.

156 Yer. Hor. III:48a; Lev. R. V:4; Deut. R. IV:8. In the latter two versions, the protagonist is called "Abba Yudin." [Alon quotes in *Tol.* the entire long passage as it appears in the Yerushalmi. We have chosen to paraphrase, so as to focus on the element germane to our present purpose.]

157 The identity of this place remains conjectural. Some think it to be φάραγξ ’Αντιόχου a location in northern Transjordan mentioned by Josephus (see Horovitz: *Eretz-Yisrael u-Shekhenoteha*, note on p. 268). Others identify it with Οὐλάθο near Antioch, where Saturninus, governor of Syria, settled 600 Babylonians (according to *Antiquities,* XVII:2). See Kraeling in JBL, 1932, pp. 141–145.

158 Yer. Pes. I:31b-c.

In this instance, the place they went to is not specified.

It may be assumed that some part of the funds collected in this manner went towards the support of those members of the Sanhedrin whose resources were limited, especially those who held community office. This would have reduced the necessity of appointing only men of means to serve as judges in the local courts. However, the overall impression gained from the sources is that the funds contributed by the Jewish public were used, in the main, not for the support of individuals, but rather for the maintenance of the central institutions of Jewry, and for the funding of their activities both in the mother country and abroad.

It would seem, then, that Rabban Gamaliel and his High Court can be credited with establishing a format that lasted for generations, and that kept the Jews of the Diaspora involved in maintaining the central institutions of the Jewish people as a whole. It is a reasonable assumption that this format was based on the old half-shekel poll-tax which Jews had been sending to Jerusalem for centuries while the Temple stood, as a means of participating in the maintenance of the Holy City and the Holy Sanctuary. Rabban Gamaliel may very possibly have determined that the revived Sanhedrin ought now be entitled to receive the equivalent of this ancient tax.

We conclude this chapter with a few observations about the Stobi inscription (discovered in 1931 in Yugoslavia, at the site of the ancient capital of Macedonia) from which it appears that it was customary in the Diaspora to assign penalty payments to the Patriarch in Palestine. The words are inscribed on two pillars of the synagogue by the "father" (πατήρ) of the synagogue who had added several annexes to the building, and bear a date which Fr. Frey interpreted as 165 C.E.[159]

Of immediate interest is the clause: "If anyone wants to make innovations contrary to my decisions, he shall pay a penalty of 250,000 dinars to the Patriarch (τῷ πατριάρχῃ)." Frey expresses the opinion that this can scarcely mean the Patriarch in Palestine because the

159 Frey: *Corpus Inscriptionum Judaicarum*, pp. 504–507. See also Marmorstein in JQR, 1936-7, p. 382 ff.
[F. Heichelheim prefers the date 281 C.E. For this and other discussion, as well as updated bibliography, see now B. Lifshitz in the reprinted edition of the *Corpus*, Ktav, New York, 1975, pp. 76–77.]

latter did not attain any influence until the end of the second century, and then only in the east.[160] Consequently, the inscription must refer to "some local official" (*quelque fonctionnaire provincial*) whose duty was to look after synagogue funds.

This brings us squarely up against the question as to whether such "little patriarchs" ever existed in the provinces.[161] The hypothesis that they did is purely conjectural. So is Frey's assumption that the Patriarchate was without influence (and without recognition) until a time which would be equivalent to that of Judah Ha-Nasi. It is true that many scholars follow a similar line; some of them are willing to go back one generation to Rabban Simeon ben Gamaliel. But all these assumptions are unfounded.

In the same way, there is no basis for Frey's other supposition — namely, that the Patriarchs never had any influence in the countries of the Western Diaspora. We may therefore reasonably conclude that the Patriarch mentioned in the Stobi inscription is the actual *Nasi* in the Land of Israel. If the date suggested by Frey is correct, the incumbent would be Rabban Simeon ben Gamaliel.[162] In any case, the involvement of the Patriarch seems by then to have become a well-established procedure. It may have been introduced — or revived — at the time of Rabban Gamaliel of Yavneh.

160 Frey, p. 507. "Il n'est guère probable qu'il s'agisse du patriarche de Palestine, qui n'exerça quelque influence qu'à partir de la fin du IIe Siècle, et uniquement sur les pays de l'Orient."

161 The question arises particularly in connection with two passages in the Theodosian Code, in both of which the "patriarchs" of the Jews are mentioned in an apparently offhand manner:
(1) In Cod. Theod. XVI:8.1, quoting an order issued by Constantine in 315 C.E. the phrase occurs:
. . *Judaeis et maioribus eorum et patriarchis* etc. . .
(2) Ibid. 2 (330 C.E.) *Qui devotione tota synagogis Judaeorum patriarchis vel presbyteris se dederunt* etc. . .

162 [If Heichelheim is right, the inscription would be approximately contemporary with Judah (II) Nesia.]

CHAPTER TWELVE

MEASURES ADOPTED AT YAVNEH

The Destruction of the Temple removed one of the principal supports on which the practice of ancient Judaism rested. It was not only the sacrificial system that depended on the Sanctuary.[1] Involved also was the whole area of priestly and levitical offerings and to a great extent, the proper observance of the festivals. Had the Sages allowed themselves to be guided by the logic of events, they would have declared all these aspects of the Jewish religion obsolete, as a consequence of the fact that the very foundations had been pulled out from under them.

If they had indeed taken this logical step, their action would have had a grave corollary, and led to dangerous consequences. In the first place, it would have meant immediate recognition that the loss of the Temple was permanent. So speedy an adjustment would have meant acceptance of a Judaism forever cut off from the Holy Temple and from the Holy City of Jerusalem. But the Sages did the exact opposite. They affirmed — and taught the people to affirm — the faith that the Destruction was a phenomenon of now, not of eternity. "Speedily will the Sanctuary be rebuilt!". Tomorrow will the Temple be restored!" — that was their doctrine.

Had they done otherwise, and allowed whole areas of the religion to be uprooted, Judaism might well have faced a grave danger. One may wonder whether the abolition of the commandments of holiness-of-the-person (*tahara*) and holiness-of-days (festivals) would not have cut the ground from under the communal-ceremonial aspects of the faith, and so weakened the spiritual and national discipline of Judaism as a whole. It is quite true that personal and social morality — the ethical aspect of religion — had been gaining the upper hand

1   We shall not here deal with the question which has engaged the attention of some scholars: were there any instances of sacrifices being offered *after* the Destruction of the Temple?

[253]

throughout the years of the Second Commonwealth. More and more this side of Judaism had ceased to be dependent on its cultic aspects and on the rituals of the altar. Nevertheless, those rituals continued to serve as a binding force for Jewry as a whole, with its many and varying groups and sects and outlooks, both at home and abroad. The sense of oneness as a people fostered by the sanctity of shared ceremonials would have been badly shaken if these rituals had been abruptly abandoned. Bear in mind too that the Destruction of Jerusalem and the Temple had plunged the people into deep despondency, making them all the more vulnerable.

There is something else: nascent Christianity made much of the Destruction as proof of the truth of the new revelation. Indeed, the very fact that so many of the mitzvot were now no longer capable of observance was held up as proof that Judaism had come to the end of its road. It was now impossible to fulfil the commandments connected with the Temple. Hence, it was argued, the rest of the Jewish Law was finished, too.[2] And although I do not believe that *Gentile* Christianity played a significant role in Palestine at that time, either numerically or with respect to its impact on the Jewish population — it certainly did not evoke much reaction from the Sages — nevertheless, one may safely assume that it was a factor in the counter-thrust towards preserving these Jewish observances.[3]

In spite of all this effort to continue the tradition in the teeth of fundamentally changed circumstances — as though opposing will-power to reality — there was also another side to the coin. Rabban Gamaliel and his Beth Din showed themselves capable of facing up to new conditions, and of ordaining new forms of observance (one is tempted to say, new mitzvot) to make up for what had been lost.

Priestly Offerings

The tithe (*ma'aser*) which had been given to Levites and priests during Temple days,[4] as well as the heave-offering (*terumah*) and

---

2 Christian anti-Jewish polemics of the early second century make use of this argument. Comp. Shab. 116a: "From the day you were exiled from your land, the law of Moses has been superseded," etc.

3 [The *Jewish* Christians kept the mitzvot anyway!]

4 For many generations before the Destruction, the "First Tithe" was customarily given to the priests as well as to the Levites, as testified to by

first dough of the vat (*ḥallah*) which went only to the priests, had been intended to provide sustenance for those whose work kept them busy at the Temple. The same goes for "the shoulder and the two cheeks and the maw" and the "first shearing of the fleece" (Deut. 18:3–4) as well as the redemption-fee for the first-born. When the Temple was destroyed, the *kohanim* and the Levites no longer had any sacerdotal functions to perform, and by rights the priestly-levitical offerings should have become obsolete. But the Sages insisted that these "gifts" be continued, even though the people at large were reluctant to keep them up. Times were hard after the Destruction, and this was probably a factor in the popular resistance to tithing and the like. But times had been hard even before the Destruction, and it is probable that then too many people had balked at *terumot* and *ma'aserot*. In any case, the fact that the *kohanim* and Levites were no longer working at their priestly and levitical duties was surely a factor in the refusal by many country folk to pay the priestly "dues."[5]

The attempt to preserve something of the old priestly practices by eating ritually sanctified food, even though sacrificial meat was no longer available, is seen clearly in the following tradition involving one of the leading personalities at Yavneh.[6]

> Rabbi Tarphon was late in arriving at the academy. Rabban Gamaliel said to him: "What kept you?" Rabbi Tarphon answered, "I was busy with the Divine service" (*avodah* — he was a *kohen*). Rabban Gamaliel said to him, "You speak in riddles. Is there such a thing in our day as the *avodah?*" (Temple service). He answered, "Scripture says, 'I give you

Josephus and the Apocrypha. Even then there was an ongoing struggle on the subject between the Sages and the populace, as there continued to be *after* the Destruction. Over this, Rabbi Eleazar ben Azariah and Rabbi Akiba had a difference of opinion. See Yer. Ma'as. Sh. V:56b-c; and Bavli, Yev. 86a-b.

5 Büchler, in *Der Galiläische Am-ha-'Aretz*, pages 65, 212, maintains that these *amei-ha-'aretz* who disregarded the laws of tithes and of ritual purity appeared only in the Galilee, and only after the Bar Kokhba Revolt. He does not make out a convincing case. See Alon in JJCW, pp. 214–215.

6 Sifre Num. (Qorah), Sec. 116, ed. Horovitz, p. 133. Pes. 72b.

the priesthood as a service of gift' (Num. 18:7). The intent of this verse is to make the eating of hallowed foods outside the Sanctuary equal to conducting the hallowed rites inside the Sanctuary."[7]

It seems that Rabbi Tarphon wanted to stress the point; but he was not alone in this.[8] The same spirit pervades the halakhic ruling:

Even as the procedure in the Sanctuary requires (the priest) first to sanctify his hands and then to proceed with the sacrifice, so too does the eating of sacred foods outside the Sanctuary require him first to sanctify his hands, and then to eat.[9]

The survival of priestly and Levitical offerings into the post-Destruction era was not automatic — not the result only of natural conservatism in matters of religion. The Sages had to face it as a problem. They can be observed doing this when they discuss the verse: "For the tithe of the children of Israel, which they set apart as a gift unto the Lord, I have given to the Levites as an inheritance." (Num. 18:24)

That this law applies while the Temple stands, I known from the verse. How do I know that it applies as well when there is no Temple? From the use by Scripture of the (extra) word *lenahalah* (as an inheritance). Just as the laws of inheritance continue in force whether or no the Temple stands, so too is the First Tithe in force when the Temple stands and when it does not stand.[10]

We can see the Sages wrestling with this problem in the midrash on the verse: "And to the sons of Levi, behold I have given all the tithe

7 Comp. the following from Sifre Zuta, p. 293: "A person who gives *terumah* to one (*kohen*) who eats it under the prescribed conditions is accounted as though he had performed the service in the Temple; and so too is the priest who eats it in the proper fashion. Of Rabbi Tarphon it was said that he ate *terumah* in the morning and said, 'I have offered the daily morning sacrifice.' Then he ate terumah at eventide and said, 'I have offered the daily evening sacrifice.'"
8 After the Destruction priests became more punctilious than ever about their specifically priestly duties. See Qid. 78b.
9 Sifre, ibid. See also Sifre Zuta, ibid: "Even as the one requires the washing of the hands, so does the other."
10 Sifre Num. (Qorah) 119, ed. Horovitz, p. 146.

in Israel as an inheritance in return for their service which they serve, the service of the tent of meeting." (Num. 18:21)

> Perhaps then, since the service is no longer in effect, the tithe is no longer in effect? No; scripture says 'as an inheritance'; just as inheritance does not come to an end, so does the tithe not come to an end. Even though the Temple service has been discontinued, they still eat it. 'In return' for what? In return for what they did for Me in the wilderness.[11]

To be sure, it became the officially sanctioned practice after the Destruction — certainly from the middle of the second century and thereafter — to give the priestly offerings only to such priests as were themselves *ḥaverim*. There is a text for this in Sifre on Numbers:[12]

> (Scripture says) 'Ye shall give of it the heave-offering of the Lord to Aaron the priest' (Num. 18:28). Even as Aaron was a *ḥaver*, so too must his sons be *ḥaverim*. From this it was derived that the priestly offerings are given only to a priest who is a *ḥaver*.[13]

Indirectly, this rule is stated in the Mishnah in connection with the First Fruits, in the name of Rabbi Judah: "They may be given only to (a priest who is) a *ḥaver*, and as a favor."[14] We ought not to think of this as directed against the unlearned priests, but rather as intended to provide some income for those *kohanim* who gave service to the community by teaching Torah and providing spiritual leadership and communal guidance.

This thrust towards keeping Temple-centered rituals alive even after the Destruction of the Temple is most noticeable in the halakhah according to which the laws concerning firstlings remain in

---

11 Sifre Zuta, p. 197. But see Yerushalmi Sheq. VIII:51b: "In this (post-Destruction) age, one does not dedicate, nor evaluate, nor make sacrosanct nor set aside *terumot* and *ma'aserot*..." (all are activities connected with the Sanctuary). Perhaps what we have here is an ancient tradition at odds with the accepted one? Note that in the corresponding passage in the Bavli, Av. Zar. 13a, the phrase about tithes and heave-offerings is absent!

12 *Qorah*, 121. Horovitz, p. 149.

13 The same rule is stated in the Bavli. Sanh. 90b, where it is attributed to "the school of Rabbi Ishmael."

14 Bik. III:2.

force.[15] Actually, firstlings are classified in the Mishnah as "minor sacred things" (*qodashim qalim*) and are to be slaughtered "anywhere in the Temple court."[16] In all reason, therefore, the category should have been abolished. Yet it was continued; and when a firstborn animal, by accident or nature became unfit for the altar, it had to be eaten by a *kohen*.

Another of the "minor sacred things" that continued to be practised after the Destruction was the tithe on cattle.[17] But in this case, the Gemara records an amoraic tradition that the law was nullified, because it left too much room for error.[18]

The same applies to the Second Tithe. There is a difference of opinion about this between Rabbi Joshua ben Hananiah and Rabbi Ishmael. Rabbi Joshua claims that one is obliged to take the Second Tithe up to Jerusalem and eat it there, even after the Destruction.[19] On the contrary, says Rabbi Ishmael:

> One might think that a person should carry his Second Tithe up to Jerusalem (even) at the present time.... (but) Scripture says, 'Thou shall eat before the Lord thy God in the place which He shall choose.... the tithe of thy corn, of thy wine and of thine oil and the firstlings of thy herd and of thy flock.' (Deut. 14:23) Just as the firstling is eaten only when the Temple stands, so too is the Second Tithe eaten only when the Temple stands.[20]

Apparently the final decision in this matter followed the line taken by Rabbi Ishmael, although the commandment was not entirely annulled. Instead, the Second Tithe was "redeemed" by a money contribution, and so rendered available for ordinary consumption. This practice was followed throughout the days of the Tannaim and Amoraim in the Land of Israel.[21]

15 Mishnah Sheq. VIII:8.
16 Mishnah Zev. V:8 *et passim*.
17 Sheq. ibid. and Bekh. IX:1.
18 Bekh. 53a.
19 Mishnah Eduy. VIII:6.
20 Tos. Sanh. III:6 (Zuck. 419); Bavli, Mak. 19a.
21 Comp. Mishnah Ma'as. Sh. V:7; Tos. ibid. III:18 (Zuck. 92); Yer. IV:54d and III:54b.

Ritual Purity

The classic Halakhah on this subject, derived from a number of biblical passages, makes the laws of ritual purity applicable to the ordinary Israelite only in the context of the Sanctuary, and the eating of sacred foods. Thus one may not enter the Temple Mount or the holy precincts, or touch sacred foods, in a state of impurity; nor may one eat sacred foods in a state of incomplete atonement.[22] With members of the priestly clan it was otherwise. They were forbidden *ab initio* to allow themselves to become defiled. Consequently, the main body of these laws became obsolete with the Destruction — the more so since the "waters of purification" were no longer available. The ashes of the Red Heifer could no longer be prepared. Nevertheless, *kohanim* were still required to keep themselves in a state of purity.[23] What is more, priests still undertook the ritual decontamination of lepers, although to be sure the process could no longer include the sacrifice.[24]

> Rabbi Judah said: It was my Sabbath[25] and I stayed with Rabbi Tarphon at his home. He said to me, 'Judah, my son, hand me my sandal.' I gave it to him. He put his hand out the window and handed me a stick. Said he: 'My son, with this (stick) I purified three lepers.'. . . From this (episode) I learned seven *halakhot* . . . . (including the one that) the purification ritual is performed when the Temple stands and when it does not stand; within the precincts or outside them.

True, there was a halakhic trend even before the Destruction that sought to broaden the applicability of the purity laws to matters quite unconnected with the Temple, or with sacred foods or priestly offerings.[26] The normative Halakhah did not go along with such ideas.

22 [See Mishnah Ker. II:1].
23 There are a number of references to the excessive fastidiousness of the *kohanim* in matters of purity *after* the Destruction, comparable to their choosiness in contracting marriages. See Qid. 78b.
24 Tos. Neg. VIII:2 (Zuck. 628); Torat Kohanim (Sifra) Metzora I:13; Yer. Sot. II:18a.
25 Sc. "to give the lesson."
26 See G. Alon: *The Bounds of Levitical Cleanness*, in JJCW, pp. 190 ff. There is abundant evidence for the observance of the purity laws after the Destruction, especially in patristic literature.

Nevertheless, it persisted in maintaining some of the rules governing priestly purity and *terumah*. The motive was probably the one suggested above — "remembrance of the Holy Temple."

The Festivals: Sukkot

In the chapter on Rabban Johanan ben Zakkai, we referred to the following Mishnah:

> Beforetime the lulav was taken in hand the entire seven days (of Tabernacles) but in the provinces one day only. After the Temple was destroyed, Rabban Johanan ben Zakkai ordained that it should be taken the full seven days in the provinces, in memory of the Temple.[27]

In other words, the decision was taken to perpetuate what had been a purely Temple ceremonial, even though the Temple lay in ruins, in order to preserve one of the most inspiring and colorful aspects of the public celebration of the festival. The importance of this decision is all the more striking if our assumption is correct — and it probably is — that the lulav ritual was entirely confined to the Sanctuary, even on the first day, until almost the very end of the Second Commonwealth. Apparently the waving of the "four species" was closely connected with the Temple cultus, and with the circumambulation of the altar. The practice was therefore not observed in the Diaspora, nor even in Eretz Israel, during most of the days of the Second Temple.[28]

The *taqanah* whereby the lulav commandment in its full panoply — palm branch, citron, myrtle and willow — became a universal part of the observance of Sukkot after the Destruction was part of the general tendency to preserve the Jewish festivals in spite of the loss of the Temple. But it is only fair to add that an entirely different factor was also involved. By a natural process, which had already been at work some generations earlier, certain religious acts and customs had been moving over from the Temple to the Synagogue, from the realm of the altar and the priest to the everywhere and the everyman.

The extent to which the leaders of the survivor-generation looked toward the yearly round of festivals as a means of keeping the Jewish

27 Sukk III:12 = R. H. IV:3.
28 G. Alon: *On Philo's Halakha* in JJCW, pp. 133 ff.

people alive can be seen in a passage from the Syriac Baruch (Chap. IV:8)

> Remember the Torah, and Zion, and the Holy Land and your brethren and the covenant with your ancestors. And forget not the Festivals and the Sabbaths.

The Seder

The festive and solemn meal on Passover eve is a high point in the religious life of the Jew, an annual climax in the people's spiritual self-awareness.[29] It is freighted with collective historical memories of the birth of the nation, and its march to freedom. Faith in the future redemption and longing for it, the sanctity and radiance of the occasion, the intimate fellowship which binds all Jews to one another — all these are fully expressed in the Seder, and have come down to us much as they were in pre-Destruction times.

But in those early days, all these elements were centered on the ceremonial act of eating the paschal lamb. The essential components of the Seder as we now know it — the matzah and the bitter herbs — were at that time mere adjuncts to the shared eating of the flesh of the sacrifice ("Ye shall eat it with unleavened bread and bitter herbs"), as were the four cups of wine, served then as now. It would have been logical, therefore, for these concomitants of the Paschal lamb to have lapsed, along with the sacrifice to which they were attached. As a matter of fact, some later Talmudic Sages did say that eating matzah and bitter herbs nowadays is not a scriptural, but merely a Rabbinic obligation.[30]

The danger that such reasoning might have led to the total disappearance of the Seder may well have been in the minds of those Tannaim who taught that eating matzah is indeed a scriptural obligation:

> You might have thought that eating matzah on the first night is

29 Two peak experiences of a ceremonial nature in the Jewish year are the Seder on Passover eve, and the prayer service on Yom Kippur. In them is concentrated much of what it has meant over the centuries to be a Jew. The essence of Yom Kippur is purely religious, while the motif most clearly expressed in the Seder service is the sense of nationhood, the feeling of belonging to the Jewish people.

30 Pes. 120a; Mekhilta, Bo, VI, ed. Horovitz, p. 20; ed. and transl. Lauterbach, p. 47; Torat Kohanim (Sifra) XI:4, ed. Weiss, p. 100b.

merely voluntary; therefore does scripture state, 'They shall eat it with unleavened bread and bitter herbs.' That tells me for a time when the Temple stands; how do I know that it applies even when there is no Temple? From the (otherwise redundant) verse 'In the evening ye shall eat unleavened bread.' (Exod. XII:38)[31]

A principal element of the Seder as we know it is the Haggadah, or to be exact, the *Hallel* and the Haggadah. The first is the recitation of Psalms giving thanks for the emancipation and for the exodus from Egypt. The second is the retelling of the story, the remembrance of the past. That the Hallel was recited in Temple times we know for certain, from pre-Destruction sources. But about the Haggadah we have no exact evidence. It does seem reasonable to suppose that the practice of "telling about the going forth from Egypt" was also in existence at that time.

In any event, we are sure that an important element in the Haggadah as it has come down to us was formulated by Rabban Gamaliel of Yavneh. The Mishnah records, in the tenth chapter of the tractate *Pesahim*, a passage which is quoted verbatim in our Haggadah:

> Rabban Gamaliel used to say: Whoever fails to say (the scripture about) the following three things at Passover (Seder) has not done his duty; and these are they: the paschal lamb, the unleavened bread, and the bitter herbs... (and so on).

The Mishnah goes on to summarize the procedure at the Seder up to the meal, and ends with Rabbi Akiba's prayer for the redemption to come:

> So may the Lord our God bring us in peace to holy days and Festivals still ahead of us, happy to be rebuilding Thy city, glad to be taking part in the service of Thy Temple... (and so on).

It is an explicit prayer for the restoration of the Passover sacrifice, in a Temple rebuilt and on an altar restored.[32]

---

31 Pes. 115a, 120a, et passim.
32 The role of Rabban Gamaliel and his colleagues in establishing the post-Destruction Seder is reflected in other sources that speak of the special care they lavished on this *mitzvah*. See Tosefta Pesahim X:12 (Zuck. 173): "Once Rabban Gamaliel and the Elders sat together for the Seder in the house of Boethus ben Zonin at Lydda, and discussed the laws of Passover

But attachment to the Temple went further than that. We saw above how Theodos of Rome led his community in simulating the paschal sacrifice by eating "helmeted kids." And we noted that Rabban Gamaliel was actually in favor of the practice, but was overruled:

> Moreover, he gave three opinions... (including) permission to prepare helmeted kids for Passover. But the Sages forbid it.[33]

So it seems that Rabban Gamaliel tried to retain the sacrifice after the Destruction. Not the actual sacrifice, of course; that was impossible, since the proper slaughtering and sprinkling of the blood and burning of the sacrificial parts could be done only on the altar. But he did want to keep up whatever could still be kept up. Perhaps that explains what he said to his servant Tabi: "Go out and roast us the *pesaḥ* on the grill!".[34]

Based on this and a few other sources, some scholars put forward the idea that actual sacrifices — especially the paschal lamb — were offered *after* the Destruction. The idea must be rejected. Rabban Gamaliel was simply trying to keep alive whatever he could of the atmosphere that accompanied the ancient rite. He knew as well as anyone that there could be no real sacrifice without the altar. And as it happens, his approach to the matter was in the end *not* accepted by the majority, as we saw in the case of Theodos of Rome. However, from the disinterested testimony of a number of early Christian writers, it seems that the custom persisted in various Diaspora communities of eating some form of roast lamb or kid in observance of the Seder, something resembling those "helmeted lambs."

Two conflicting tendencies seem to have been at work with regard to the paschal lamb. On the one hand was the halakhic aversion to anything that gave even the appearance of offering sacrifices outside the Temple; on the other was the emotional clinging to the ancient rite.

---

all that night until cock-crow, when (the servants) came and carried the table away, and they all went off to the House of Study." Compare this with the all-night Seder in the Haggadah.

33 Mishnah Bez. II:7. See also Tos. ibid. II:15 (Zuck. 204): "What is a helmeted kid? A kid roasted whole, with its head and shanks placed with its entrails." See above, pp. 231–232.

34 Mishnah Pes. VII:2.

Hence, the majority opinion against helmeted lambs, on the one hand; hence on the other the following:[35]

> In places where it was customary to eat roast on Passover Eve, it may be eaten; where it was not the custom, it should not be eaten.

This, and other evidence of a simulated paschal offering may throw light on the following:[36]

> It happened in Bet Dagan in Judah that a man died on the Eve of the Passover, and they set about burying him. The men of the village entered (the cave) and tied a rope around the big stone, and then went outside and pulled. The women then entered and buried the corpse, and the men went off and prepared their Passover (lambs) for the evening.

First let us set aside the thought that this happened during the days of the Temple. The men could certainly not have made it from Bet Dagan to Jerusalem that same day. Apparently, therefore, they regarded a helmeted kid or a roast lamb as their paschal sacrifice, and were taking great care to eat it in a state of ritual purity, as though it were an actual sacrifice. As for the women, they could be excused from eating the roast under the circumstance; for them, the paschal lamb was voluntary, not obligatory.

The practice of eating roast on Passover Eve seems to have been prevalent in the Land of Israel during the days of the Tannaim. This is how the Mishnah records one of the questions which the son asks his father at the Seder:

> On all other nights we eat meat which has been roasted, stewed or cooked. But on this night, we eat only roast.[37]

Admittedly, the commentators (e.g. Rashi) associate this with the days of the Temple. But surely the plain meaning is that it deals with the time of the Mishnah itself. And we do have other evidence to show that many generations *after* the Mishnah the Jews of Eretz Israel and of ritually allied communities were still confining themselves to roast

35 Mishnah, Pes. IV:4.
36 Tos. Ahil. III:9 (Zuck. 600).
37 Pes. X:4.

on Passover Eve. The evidence comes from fragments of the Passover Eve liturgy discovered in the Cairo Genizah and published by Israel Abrahams. Here again we find the text of the child's questions (there are three of them — not four); and the question about roast meat is there, just as in the Mishnah. What is more, there is a special *berakhah* which reads as follows:

> Praised be Thou O Lord our God, King of the universe, who didst command our ancestors to eat unleavened bread, bitter herbs and meat roasted on the fire, that we might make mention of His mighty deeds. Praised be Thou, O Lord, Who dost remember the covenant.[38]

The attention which the Sages paid to the Passover Eve service after the Destruction, and their efforts to retain, in the atmosphere of the shared meal, the character of a "family offering,"[39] speak volumes about their determination not to allow the Destruction to sweep away the foundations of Jewish religious life, even if it sometimes meant acting as though the Temple still stood.[39a]

The Liturgy

Side by side with a reluctance to come to terms with the reality of the Destruction, the leaders of the post-Destruction era also showed a contrasting ability to take certain steps which can only be described as very realistic indeed. On the one hand, they revived rituals of mourning and remembrance which had fallen into abeyance since the return from Babylon; on the other hand, they sought to fill the void which the Destruction of the altars had left in the daily practice of Judaism, by frankly substituting prayer for sacrifice.

(1) First, the remembrance and the mourning. From the Book of Zechariah (VII: 3–5; VIII: 19) we know that the first (Babylonian) Destruction had been commemorated by four national days of mourning — the fast-days of the fourth, fifth, seventh and tenth months (17th of Tammuz, 9th of Av, 3rd of Tishri, 10th of Tevet). The prophet says

38 JQR., o.s., vol. X (1898), pp. 44, 47, 49; and p. 46.
39 They were helped by the fact that the rite had never completely lost its ancient quality of a family *zevaḥ*, even after it had become centralized in the Sanctuary. This can still be seen in the Samaritan paschal sacrifice.
39a The same is true of the Counting of the Omer.

that the Restoration of his times had annulled these fasts, turning them into "joy and gladness and cheerful seasons." It does seem that they were *not* observed during the Second Commonwealth.[40]

After the Destruction of the Second Temple the Sages saw fit to revive these fasts, with special emphasis on the Ninth of Av. We cannot take up here the origin of the liturgy for that day (the reading of Lamentations and *Kinot,* the prayer *Nahem,* etc.). Nor can we go into the evidence offered us by Church Fathers, especially those of the fourth century, about the heart-rending scenes at Jerusalem on Tish'a b'Av, when crowds of mourning Jews came up to the ruins of the Holy City to give vent to a grief which the passing of the years had in no way assuaged.

(2) The second, and perhaps more important way of coping realistically with the Destruction has to do with the liturgy. After all, Jewish worship had been centered on the Temple service — the "*Avodah.*" The sacrifices, together with the chanted psalms and prayers which accompanied them, had been the supreme expression of the bond between the people and its God. The Temple had also been the most exalted place where the individual could commune with his Maker, where he could bring his offerings and his prayers of thanksgiving or atonement, where he might utter his supplication or his confession. The Destruction of that Sanctuary left the Jew with an aching spiritual void, with an emptiness that cried out insistently to be filled somehow. The pain was felt by the individual Jew; it was felt collectively by the Jewish people as well.

This description of the need which the prayer-service filled sounds, on the face of it, as though the formal Jewish liturgy was first invented as a substitute for the sacrifices, right after the Destruction. And it has indeed been held, on the basis of certain traditions, that the "Eighteen Benedictions" (*Shemoneh Esreh*) actually *were* introduced by Rabban Gamaliel at Yavneh.[41]

The truth is, however, that *public, congregational* prayer had already become an important part of life in the synagogue many generations before the Destruction. Individual prayer, too, was not at all uncommon during Temple days. We must therefore ask ourselves just *what*

40 Doubt has been expressed as to whether this includes the Ninth of Av. See
  I. N. Epstein: *Mavo le-Nussah ha-Mishnah*, vol. II, pp. 1012 ff.
41 Weiss: *Dor Dor etc.*, vol. II, p. 67.

it was that Rabban Gamaliel and the Sages at Yavneh *did* do with respect to the prayers.

According to the sources we have, Rabban Gamaliel and his associates were responsible for three measures connected with the liturgy: a) Its format; b) The duty of the *individual* (not only the community) to say the set prayers; and c) the three-times-daily requirement. Let us survey each of these briefly.

a) Simeon Ha-Pakuli set forth the Eighteen Benedictions in their proper order in the presence of Rabban Gamaliel at Yavneh.[42]

This tradition seems to imply that the prayer originated at Yavneh. But in one of the sources where it occurs, a different tradition is immediately set forth, traced variously to Rabbi Johanan or to a *baraitha*:[43]

One hundred and twenty elders, among whom were many prophets, drew up the Eighteen Benedictions in a set order.

Rabbi Johanan is also cited as authority for saying that the Men of the Great Assembly "instituted for Israel blessings and prayers" etc.[44] And then there is the Yerushalmi, with this tradition:[45]

One hundred and twenty elders, including more than eighty prophets, drew up this prayer.

In order to arrive at some kind of historically sound conclusion about the Eighteen, also called '*Amidah*' and '*Tefillah*' (*the* prayer), we must first make certain distinctions. The six *berakhot* which provide the framework for the *Tefillah* on every occasion, whether weekday, Sabbath or Festival, must be viewed separately from the rest. These six are the opening three ("Praises of the Eternal"), and the closing three. The ancient names for the opening triad were '*Avot*' (God of the Fathers), '*Gevurot*' (God's Power) and '*Kedushat Ha-Shem*' (God's Holiness).[46] The closing three were called '*Avodah*' (The Service),

---

42 Ber. 28b; Meg. 17b.
43 Meg. ibid. Most mss. and *variae* attribute it to Rabbi Jeremiah or Rabbi Hiyya bar Abba.
44 Bavli, Ber. 33a.
45 Yer., Ber. II:4d.
46 Mishnah R.H. IV:5.

'*Hodayah*' (Thanksgiving) and '*Birkat Kohanim*' (The Priestly Blessing).

It can safely be said that these six were in use during the days of the Temple. Take this passage:[47]

> When Rosh Hashanah falls on the Sabbath day, the *tefillah* consists of ten benedictions, according to the School of Shammai, but according to the School of Hillel, of nine. When other festivals occur on the Sabbath, Beth Shammai say eight, since they require a separate one for the Sabbath followed by a separate one for the festival; but Beth Hillel say seven, with the festival theme introduced into the middle of the Sabbath benediction. (In discussing this) those of the School of Hillel said to those of the School of Shammai: were you not all present, O Elders of the School of Shammai, when Honi the Lesser led the congregation in prayer (on one such occasion)? He recited but seven benedictions, and all the people praised him.[48]

It can scarcely be doubted that these Elders of Beth Shammai and Beth Hillel were talking about an episode that had taken place before the Destruction. Apparently, then, the six basic benedictions must have been established liturgy even while the Temple still stood.[49]

But the same cannot be said for the petitionary prayers, originally twelve in number (they have grown to thirteen because of the Babylonian custom, which separated into two what had been one prayer for "The Restoration of Jerusalem" and "The Flourishing of David's House"). We have no real evidence to show that these supplications existed before the Destruction. However, the modern rediscovery of the Hebrew original of Ben Sira has lent some credence to the theory that the essence of these petitions goes back to the days of the Second Temple:[50]

> O give thanks to him who gathereth the dispersed of Israel...

47 Tos. R.H. IV (II):11 (Zuck. 213). See Lieberman, *Tosefta Kifshutto*, vol. 3, p. 320.

48 [The translation is here indebted to the commentary by Saul Lieberman, op. cit., vol. 5, p. 1062. The Honi of this passage has not been identified.]

49 On the prayers recited in the Temple by the *kohanim*, see Mishnah Tamid V:1.

50 Ben Sira 51:12.

...Who buildeth His city and His Sanctuary...

...Who redeemeth Israel...

Who causeth salvation to flourish for David's house...[51]

The view is widely held among scholars that the closing phrases of the petitions in the *Tefillah* were not original creations of Rabban Gamaliel at Yavneh, but were well known for many generations before the Destruction. One is inclined to agree.[52]

All this leads us to conclude that the tradition which connects Rabban Gamaliel with the arrangement of the Eighteen Benedictions must refer only to some form of *editing* this prayer or of *recasting* it into officially approved liturgical form. To be sure, one might readily suppose that he actually formulated those passages which reflect the changed situation brought about by the Destruction — "Return in mercy to Jerusalem," "Restore the service to Thy Sanctuary," "May our eyes behold Thy return to Zion," "Bring back our judges as of yore," "Gather the dispersed of Israel." But many of these could easily have been spoken before the Destruction, when people longed for the ingathering of the scattered brethren, and devoutly desired the accession of just judges and counsellors, instead of those they had to put up with under Herod, or under the Romans. However, we can drop our speculations. The Genizah has revealed that these passages were absent long after Rabban Gamaliel, and do not appear even later, in early mediaeval prayer-texts.[53]

b) The second liturgical measure attributed to Rabban Gamaliel is the individual duty to recite regular prayers:

Rabban Gamaliel says: Every day one should pray the Eighteen.

51 These sentences are missing from the ancient versions, so there has been argument about their authenticity. See ZATW 1909, pp. 287 ff. and Charles: *Apocrypha* etc. ad loc. [When the Hebrew text of Ben Sira was first published, its explicit reference to the Zadokite priesthood was advanced both as proof of the authenticity of this passage, and as an explanation for its suppression under the Hasmoneans. See Schechter and Taylor: *The Wisdom of Ben Sira*, Cambridge University 1899, pp. 35-6. Also M. Z. Segal: *Sefer Ben Sira Ha-Shalem*, pp. 356-7.]

52 Israel Levi went further, proposing a link between the Eighteen Benedictions and the Wisdom of Solomon. REJ XXXII (1896), pp. 161 ff.

53 Schechter in JQR, o.s. X, 654–9; Mann, HUCA, vol. 11, pp. 269 ff. and Finkelstein in JQR, n.s. XVI, pp. 1–43 and 127–70.

Rabbi Joshua says: The substance of the Eighteen. Rabbi Akiba says: If he is quite familiar with the Eighteen, let him pray so; but if not, the substance of the Eighteen (will suffice). Rabbi Eliezer says: He who makes his prayers fixed causes them to lose the quality of supplication.[54]

It is customary to interpret this halakhah of Rabban Gamaliel's as having two aspects: a) whereas before the Destruction, prayer as a duty was confined to public worship, it was now made incumbent on the *individual*; and b) a fixed form — *matbe'a shel tefillah* — was now established, that is, the Eighteen Benedictions.

It behooves us to look closely at these assumptions. And we shall actually find abundant evidence that individual prayer at set times *was* common practice in Temple times. Daniel prayed regularly three times a day.[55] The apostle Peter goes up on a housetop to pray "about the sixth hour."[56] And Cornelius, the Roman centurion and Godfearer, prays at home "at the ninth hour."[57]

But these are individual cases. Perhaps the general practice is reflected in the Psalms of Solomon:

> Happy the man whose heart is fixed to call on the name of his Lord.
> He riseth from sleep and blesseth God's name.
> When his heart is at peace he singeth to the name of his God,
> And entreateth the Lord for all his house,
> And the Lord heareth the prayer of every one who feareth him.
> (VI: 4–5. Charles, op. cit. II, p. 639)

(This may, of course, describe only the religious elite).

The Sybilline Oracle surely speaks of the generality of Jews when it says: "They rise early from their beds... and honor Him who alone reigns forever and ever."[58] And in the Wisdom of Solomon we read "...to make known that we must rise before the sun to give Thee

54 Mishnah, Ber. IV:3–4.
55 Daniel VI:11. Comp. Psalm LV:18.
56 Acts X:9 [At this point, *Tol.* reads 'in the Temple' — possibly a conflation with Acts III:1, where Peter and John enter the Temple "at the ninth hour, being the hour of prayer" — but not necessarily for individual prayer.]
57 Ibid. X:30.
58 Oracle III:591–593; Charles II, p. 389.

thanks, and must plead with Thee as light dawns."⁵⁹ Finally, the Letter of Aristeas implies that it was customary for Jews — at least, for many of them — to pray regularly every morning.⁶⁰

All this leads us to the conclusion that, if Rabban Gamaliel did indeed make solitary prayer obligatory, he simply took an existing practice and gave it the status of religious law. The practice itself was not innovated by him, but had already acquired a long and honorable history.

As for the *matbe'a* — the format of the prayer — Rabbi Joshua and Rabbi Akiba do not differ from Rabban Gamaliel in principle. They agree that the form is binding, but maintain that a person *may* condense and abbreviate the middle benedictions into one (as in "*Havinenu*").

That leaves Rabbi Eliezer, and it is not altogether clear what he is driving at. One can, of course, accept the prevailing explanation, which is simply that he rejects the very idea of a fixed form for personal prayer. It ought to be spontaneous, free and unfettered. The *matbe'a*, he seems to be saying, applies to public worship, not private. Regularity ('*keva*') is for congregations, not individuals.⁶¹

If that is what Rabbi Eliezer means, then it would leave him at odds with the main principles underlying Rabban Gamaliel's liturgical enterprise. The Eighteen Benedictions deal with the public need, the wants of the whole people. The fact that these prayers in no way address private concerns is precisely the point of making them a duty of the individual. It is unlikely that Rabbi Eliezer had any quarrel with that principle.

It seems to me that something like an interpretation offered by the Babylonian Talmud might better reflect Rabbi Eliezer's position.⁶² We could say that he accepts the principle of a fixed liturgy, but feels that each person should add a spontaneous element of his own. Also at issue here may be the question whether one must — or indeed

59   W.S. XVI:28; Charles I, p. 563.
60   [*Tol.* gives no reference. Perhaps 304-5 is meant: "In the early morning. . . as is the custom of the Jews, they washed their hands. . . and prayed to God."]
61   See most recently L. Ginzberg: *Perushim ve-Hidushim bi-Yerushalmi* III, p. 336.
62   Ber. 29b. Also Yer. ibid. IV:8a.

may — intrude his personal needs into those set petitions which are directed towards fulfilling the wants of the many. Finally, there is the question of the frequency of prayer: how many times a day? The sharp controversy between Rabban Gamaliel and Rabbi Joshua over the status of the evening prayer is well known, with Rabbi Joshua declaring it to be voluntary, thus reducing the daily statutory number to two.[63] This is not the place to go into the underlying basis of their disagreement. Elsewhere,[64] I have tried to show from very ancient sources that in Temple times there were varying customs — some prayed twice daily, and some prayed three times.[65] It would seem that Rabbi Gamaliel and Rabbi Joshua disagreed only in deciding between differing ancient customs. In the present context let it suffice to point out that in an early Christian work, "The Teaching of the Twelve Apostles" — written probably during the lifetime of Rabban Gamaliel of Yavneh — the author, undoubtedly reflecting a Jewish tradition, says that one ought to pray three times a day.

The Biblical Canon

It is a widely held view that the canon of Jewish Scripture was closed during the time of Rabban Gamaliel at Yavneh. At the same time, it is believed, the Books of the Apocrypha were not only excluded from Holy Writ, but were also declared forbidden reading. Attributed to the same enactment, or series of enactments, is the denial of sanctity to the Christian Gospels, and in the opinion of some, the finalizing of the official text of the Scriptures — the *Masorah*.

A basic source-text for at least one of these assumptions is contained in the Mishnah:[66]

> Said Rabbi Simeon ben Azzai: I have a tradition from the seventy-two elders, on the day when they made Rabbi Eleazar ben Azariah Head of the Academy, that the Song of Songs and Qohelet make the hands impure (*i.e. are canonical*). Said Rabbi

63 Ibid. Bavli 27b, Yer. IV:7c-d.
64 G. Alon: *"The Halakhah in The Teaching of the Twelve Apostles,"* Mehqarim I, pp. 284 ff. (Not available in English).
65 Contrary to L. Ginzberg, op. cit. Vol. III, p. 29, note 36. [But see Ginzberg's note there *in full*. Alon may have misunderstood the reference to "Hellenistic literature."]
66 Yad. III:5.

Akiba: Heaven forbid! Nobody ever disputed the sanctity of the Song of Songs, for the whole world put together is not worth the day on which the Song of Songs was given to Israel. All the other Writings are holy, but the Song of Songs is holy of holies! If they did dispute, it was (*no doubt*) about the book Qoheleth. Rabbi Johanan ben Joshua, son of Rabbi Akiba's father-in-law, said: It happened the way Ben Azzai described it; that was what they argued about, and that was the decision they took.

In another Mishnaic passage,[67] it is reported that Rabbi Simeon[68] cited three instances in which Beth Shammai gave lenient rulings, while Beth Hillel gave strict rulings. The first of these is: the School of Shammai declare that Qoheleth does not "make the hands impure," while Beth Hillel say that it does.

In the light of these reports, it seems we can conclude that it was at Yavneh "on that self-same day" — the day when Rabban Gamaliel was deposed — that the dispute was settled, and the canon of Holy Writ thereby closed. But we cannot let the matter rest there. This is not only because Rabbi Akiba questioned the tradition. We also have to contend with a variety of other traditions. For example:[69]

> All the Holy Writings make the hands impure. The Song of Songs and Qoheleth make the hands impure. Rabbi Judah says: The Song of Songs, yes; but there is dispute about Qoheleth. Rabbi Jose says: Qoheleth, no; but there is dispute about the Song of Songs.

The Tosefta gives us the following:[70]

> Rabbi Simeon ben Menasia says: The Song of Songs makes the hands impure because it was inspired by the Holy Spirit. But Qoheleth does not, because it is only Solomon's human wisdom.

Here we have Tannaim two generations after Rabban Gamaliel declaring that Qoheleth is *not* Holy Writ. Something similar occurs

---

67 Eduy. V:3; Tos. Ibid. II:7 (Zuck. 458).
68 Read so, although current texts have: Ishmael. The error is common; see Frankel, *Darkhe Hamishnah*, Warsaw 5683, p. 24; I. N. Epstein, op. cit. II, p. 1193.
69 Mishnah Yad. III:5. See Tos. ibid. II:14 (Zuck. 683); Bavli, Meg. 7a.
70 Tos. Yadaim, ibid.; Bavli, Meg., ibid.

with the Book of Esther at a still later period, when Rav Judah quotes the third century Babylonian Amora Samuel as saying that Esther does not render the hands impure.[71] There are also Fathers of the Church who claim that some Jews exclude Esther from the canon of Holy Scripture.

On the other hand, Fourth Esdras (XII:48) speaks of the *twenty-four* books of the Bible, from which we may infer that the term had jelled, so to speak, before his time. It would be too far-fetched to assume that the author would use the expression if it had only just come into being. Then too, Josephus talks of the *twenty-two* books which had been sacred to his people for generations and which alone are inspired. He must be referring to the Scriptures as we know them with Ruth attached to Judges, and Lamentations to Jeremiah.[72]

Nevertheless, it was still possible at as late a date as the War with Rome to discuss whether or not it might be better to "hide away" one of these books, as the Talmud reports:

> Rav Judah taught the name of Rav: There was a man whom we ought to remember gratefully, his name being Hananiah ben Hezekiah. Were it not for him, the Book of Ezekiel might have been hidden away, for (many of) its words contradict the words of the Torah. What did (this Hananiah) do? He had three hundred kegs of oil brought to him in a loft, and there he stayed until he had reconciled all the contradictions.[73]

Again, in this instance, it is unlikely that so momentous a decision as "closing the canon of Scripture" was taken on that famous "self-same day". What seems probable is that one of the books came up for discussion, but that neither the discussion nor the decision were looked on as major events. Hence it was possible for later Tannaim to disagree as to what the discussion had been about; and subsequently, an Amora could even propose dropping Esther from the Scriptures!

As for proscribing the Apocrypha, that notion appears to be based on the Mishnah (Sanh. X:1): "These have no share in the world to come... Rabbi Akiba says, one who reads in the 'external books'."

---

71 Bavli, Meg., ibid.
72 *Against Apion* I:8 (38). According to Josephus, Esther closes the canon. Later writings are not reliable.
73 Shab. 13b; Hag. 13a; Men. 35a.

On the meaning of those words, the Talmudim are in disagreement. The Bavli (Sanh. 100b) says they mean "books of the sectaries."[73a] But the Yerushalmi (ibid. 28a) explains the term thus: "Such as the books of Ben Sira and of Ben La'ana,"[73b] which seems nearer the mark. In any case, Rabbi Akiba's dictum should not lead us to believe that his contemporaries — the Sanhedrin under Rabban Gamaliel — took the major step of "outlawing" the non-canonical books. This is not only because, as we have shown, it is highly questionable whether they actually closed the canon at that time. More to the point is the fact that Rabbi Akiba had no intention of *banning* the apocryphal books. He used the verb '*qara*' in its technical sense, as it is employed for the *study* of Scripture ('*miqra*'). What he means is that anyone who treats the "external books" as inspired Scripture is thereby reducing the stature of Holy Writ; "for he who adds, diminishes."[74]

It appears, then, that the prohibition against according too much deference to the "outside books" was a long-established one; Rabbi Akiba merely advocated a stricter attitude on the subject. This resembles the way he came down hard on people "who warble the Song of Songs in public houses, as though it were some kind of popular ditty." (Admittedly, there is a different factor at work here; Rabbi Akiba was engaged in a struggle with those who regarded the Song as a secular piece of work.)

All in all, then, we find ourselves concluding in this matter of the Apocrypha, as we did with regard to the preceding points, that the Academy at Yavneh did *not* introduce new halakhah. What it did do was clarify — and in some instances ratify — older customs, precedents, rules and practices.

We must now consider the theory according to which the Beth Din at Yavneh denied Scriptural status to the Christian Gospels. It is a theory advocated mainly by Christian scholars.[75] This view would lead to some very important historical conclusions, if it could be convincingly demonstrated. Because if the Sages of Rabban Gamaliel's time

---

73a This is the correct reading, supported by all mss. The reading "Sadducees" in printed editions is the work of censors.

73b A similar passage in Eccl. R. reads: "Ben Sira and Ben Hogla." (XII:13).

74 Comp. Yer. Sanh. 28a: "The external books are for perusal, not for careful study. . . . . One reads them as one reads a letter. . ."

75 George Foote Moore: *Judaism*, vol. I, p. 87.

(ca. 100 C.E.) felt impelled to rule that the Christian Evangels were *not* Holy Writ, then it follows that these writings were then *widely current* among the people, and had gained considerable acceptance as at least a sort of holy writings.

However, this corollary — more accurately, this hypothesis — will not stand up to historical scrutiny. To be sure, there were at that time Jewish-Christians within the Jewish population, and one may posit the existence of a Gospel-text circulating among them in Aramaic (scarcely in Hebrew). But it is not conceivable that a "new Torah," containing polemics against Judaism, and filled with events and legends dating back only two or three generations, should have been regarded by many Jews as a holy book — except of course, by the actual Jewish-Christians themselves; and there is some doubt as to whether even they, at that early date, already considered their evangel as actual Holy Writ. But let us examine the sources on which the theory is based.

> The *gilyonim* and the books of the sectaries do not render the hands impure.[76]
>
> *Gilyonim* and books of the sectaries are not to be rescued (on the Sabbath) but are allowed to burn right where they are, along with their '*azkarot*' (Divine names that may be written on them).[77]

Those scholars who hold the theory above-mentioned interpret the word '*gilyonim*' to mean '*evangelyonim*' (the Gospels). Now it is true that the Babylonian Talmud mentions "*aven gilyon*".[78] Nevertheless, that is probably *not* the meaning in the present context. In my opinion, the term refers to a "sheet" of writing material (parchment) such as is sewn to others of the kind to make a scroll.[79] Basically, that is how the Talmud understands the word. That indeed is what Rabbi Judah makes explicit in his dissenting opinion:[80]

> The *gilyon* at the beginning of the book, and all the margins render the hands impure.

76 Tos. Yadaim II:13 (Zuck. 683); Bavli Shab. 116a; Yer. ibid. XVI:15c.
77 Tos. Shab. XIII (XII) (Zuck. 129):5; Bavli and Yerushalmi, ibid.
78 Shab. 116b (in uncensored versions). There is a play on words here.
79 Ginzberg in JBL 1922, p. 122, note 19, is prepared to grant the possibility that *evangelion* may be meant, but agrees that this has nothing to do with the Jewish attitude to these books. Only the '*azkarot*' are involved.
80 Tos. Yadaim II:11 (Zuck. 683).

The Ban Against Small Cattle

When the *baraitha* speaks of '*azkarot*', it means Divine names found in books of the sectaries — that is, in Torah scrolls and other scriptural works written *by the hand* of sectaries, and thus deprived of their sanctity.[81]

The Ban Against Small Cattle

A number of tannaitic sources lay down a halakhah that forbids the raising of sheep and goats in Eretz Israel. The *locus classicus* is the Mishnah:

> Small cattle may not be reared in the Land of Israel, but they may be reared in Syria and in the wilderness areas of the Land of Israel.[82]

Note that the prohibition is expressly limited to those regions where there are fields under cultivation. Something very similar is found in the Tosefta:

> Even though they said that small cattle are not to be raised in Eretz Israel (etc.)... How then shall I understand the verse 'Thou shalt not see thy brother's ox or his *sheep* gone astray' (Deut. XXII: 1)? Scripture speaks there of the uncultivated areas of Judaea, or of Kefar Emiqo.[83]

Baraitha quotations in the Babylonian Talmud preserve much the same traditions:[84]

> Small cattle are not to be raised in Eretz Israel; however, they may be reared in wooded areas... Small cattle are not to be raised in Eretz Israel, but may be raised in the Judean Wilderness and in the wilderness at the border of Akko.[85]

Elsewhere in tannaitic literature sheep-herders and goatherds, as well as people who make a business of breeding small cattle, are spoken

---

81 Ginzberg ibid. rejects the interpretation given by the Talmud, but his proof is insufficient. The case made out by Moore, op. cit., vol. III, p. 67, remains unconvincing.
82 Mishnah B.Q. VII:7.
83 Tos. B.Q. VIII:10 (Zuck. 362).
84 B.Q. 79b.
85 Talmud manuscripts read 'Emiqo' as in the Tosefta.

of with extreme disparagement. "Heathen and shepherds of small animals and those who raise the beasts need not be cast into a pit, but it is not necessary to help them out."[86] Or the following:

Traders at market-stalls and breeders of small cattle and people who cut down viable trees will never see a sign of blessing.[87]

What lies behind this enactment? What motivated the prohibition, and the stern condemnation of those who violated it? One of the most recent discussions of this problem is by Asher Gulak, in a paper published posthumously.[88] But before we take up the theory proposed by Gulak and examine the issues involved, we shall have to satisfy ourselves about the date when this prohibition was promulgated. It may well be that there is a relationship between the *period* when the ban was established, and the *purpose* it was meant to serve.

The sources provide us with two chronological guideposts — one early, one late. From what we are told about the days of Rabbi Judah ben Bava, it can be inferred that at a time just before the Bar Kokhba Revolt this halakhah was already firmly entrenched.[89] "Pious folk," we learn, were very meticulous about it, taking care not to maintain even a solitary sheep or goat; not even indoors, where it was spoken of as "a robber in the house."

On the other hand, it is recorded that the question was put to Rabbi Eliezer: What about raising small cattle?[90] He avoided giving an answer, as though the matter had not been definitely decided (the Tosefta says he would not give a ruling on a subject on which he had not been instructed). However, the very fact that the question was asked means that the ban was already in practice.

The same question was asked of Rabban Gamaliel, but there are two conflicting reports about his reply. According to one source, he answered that the last remaining sheep or goat of the flock may be kept in the house for up to thirty days.[91] That would put him on the

---

86 Tos. B.M. II:32 (Zuck. 375) and Bavli, Sanh. 57a. [For a note on this hyperbole, see the Soncino Talmud ad. loc.]
87 Tos. Bik. II:16 (Zuck. 102).
88 In Tarbiz, Vol. XII, pp. 181–189.
89 Tos. B.Q. VIII:13 (Zuck. 362); Bavli, ibid. 80a.
90 Tos. Yev. III:4 (Zuck. 244).
91 Tos. B.Q. VIII:12 (Zuck. 362). See Bavli, ibid. 79b–80a.

side of prohibition, with exceptions. But the Gemara recalls a tradition according to which he permitted the whole thing — and immediately asks: 'But the Mishnah teaches that it is forbidden!?' The difficulty is resolved by reinterpreting the conflicting traditions in this way: What they really asked him was not about *raising* cattle, but about *keeping* a single sheep or a goat, and he answered that it was permitted so long as the animal was not put out to graze with a flock.[92]

Modern scholars have tended to view the initial *baraitha* quoted by the Talmud ("Rabban Gamaliel says 'Permitted'") as historically sound.[93] The revision proposed by the Gemara is taken to be dialectic; that is, scholastic rather than historical. Very much the same interpretation is given to the version in the Tosefta. Pursuing this line, the same scholars conclude that the prohibition against small cattle was introduced a short time before the Destruction; but that after the catastrophe there was a tendency to relax the ban. This would explain what Rabban Gamaliel was about, and perhaps even enlighten us as to why Rabbi Eliezer hedged when asked about the matter. According to this theory the prohibition remained technically in force, but was mitigated by exemptions covering wilderness areas and wooded regions.

This view that the ban underwent a *process of dilution* underlies the proposal put forward by Gulak to explain the *origin* of the law. But before we examine his hypothesis in detail, we ought to consider additional tannaitic teachings which make shepherds — along with certain other untrustworthy characters — ineligible to be witnesses in any legal proceedings:[94]

> They added to the list (of those unfit to testify) robbers, herdsmen, extortionists, and all who are suspect where other people's property is concerned.

There are more tannaitic sources which treat herdsmen as no better than highwaymen when it comes to damaging what belongs to other people.[95]

92 Ibid 80a.
93 See the above-mentioned article by Gulak, p. 182.
94 Tos. Sanh. V:5 (Zuck. 423); Yer. ibid. III:21a; Bavli ibid. 25b.
95 E.g. B.Q. 96b: "For herdsmen and excise-collectors and tax-farmers repentance is difficult; yet they must make restitution to all whom they can identify as specific victims."

Gulak's theory is that the ban originated during the last generations of the Second Commonwealth, and was connected with the spreading movement of *rebellion against Roman rule*. The rebels, including people who had abandoned their small farms because of the exorbitant land taxes, probably took refuge in the forest and wilderness areas, keeping themselves alive by raising sheep and goats. He cites as a parallel the situation in Egypt, where many villagers fled the strong arm of Roman rule and took refuge in the wild regions and swamp lands of the Nile Delta. He mentions the Rebellion of the Shepherds (βουκόλοι) in Egypt in the year 172.

Reverting to Judaea, he turns to the case of Athronges the *shepherd* who led an uprising after Herod's death, and crowned himself king.[96] Josephus tells us that Athronges attracted a large following, men who were militarily well-organized. But their discipline soon began to deteriorate, and they took to plundering the countryside. If we postulate that, like their leader, they were mostly shepherds, we can conclude that they must have constituted a serious threat to the country's agriculture. Gulak goes on to surmise, that the *Pharisees*, essentially favorable to the small cultivator, and in all likelihood politically opposed to these violent rebels, would naturally have banned the raising of sheep and goats, and put herdsmen in the same category as highwaymen.

It seems to me that this theory of Prof. Gulak's does not stand up to analysis. It lacks real evidence, and is short on reasonable probability. Not only does it ask us to assume too much; the fundamental hypothesis which is its point of departure is also open to serious question. There is nothing to show that the ban was in existence during Temple times. It follows that there are no grounds for assuming that this law followed a course towards relaxing its restrictions, even if we agree that Rabbi Eliezer and Rabban Gamaliel were in favor of granting exceptions. Nor is there any basis for supposing that at first the prohibition was total, and only later was grazing in wild and wooded regions permitted.[97]

---

96 Josephus Ant. XVII:10:7 (278 ff.) [Herod died in 4 B.C.E.].

97 This scenario seems rather far-fetched. You start with a *total prohibition* before the Destruction; find yourself with opinions favoring its *total abolition* after the Destruction; and end up with a compromise law permitting the activity in some places. I think one must assume that the ban *never* applied to forests and wilderness areas.

The Ban Against Small Cattle

The Tosefta, a source much older than the Babylonian Talmud, yields a text much closer to the *other baraitha* in the Talmud where Rabban Gamaliel says, in effect, that the ban holds ("the dealer may buy and sell, just so long as he does not retain the last of the flock for more than thirty days"). It seems to me almost certain, therefore, that the Talmud does not offer a purely speculative emendation to Rabban Gamaliel's answer (so that he comes out upholding the ban), but bases its emendation on an actual alternative tannaitic tradition, much like the one in the Tosefta. That would mean that there were two conflicting traditions about what Rabban Gamaliel had to say in this matter. As for Rabbi Eliezer, his opinion remains unclear.

My own view is that this halakhah did *not* originate in Temple times, although it may possibly have been mooted in those early days. As halakhah it stems from the days of Rabban Gamaliel. However, it did not gain universal — or immediate — acceptance by the Sages, and certainly not by the common people. Rabbi Eliezer's refusal to give an answer was based on his unwillingness to take a stand on a halakhah so new, perhaps still not formulated or approved.

If this be so, then Gulak's entire theory has the props pulled out from under it. Political conditions as far back as the beginning of the Common Era can have had nothing to do with the matter. But quite apart from such considerations, it seems highly improbable that politics were involved at all with this halakhah. There is no shadow of proof that the rebels in Judaea went in for raising sheep and goats. We cannot argue by analogy from what happened in Egypt — where, by the way, there is no shred of evidence that the rebellious "shepherds" of the year 172 had ever been farmers! There remains the equally unwarranted assumption — which I find totally unacceptable on its own merits — that the Pharisees were opposed to rebellion against Rome. But this is the key to the proposed explanation of how this halakhah originated.

To be sure, Gulak seeks to bolster his theory by citing those tannaitic sources that couple herdsmen of small cattle with people who chop down viable trees.[98] He identifies the tree-choppers as rebels who sup-

98 See p. 278, n. 87. Also Tos. Suk. II:5 (Zuck. 194) : "The heavenly luminaries suffer eclipse because of four things: because of those who write spurious and scurrilous documents; those who give false witness; those who breed small cattle; and those who cut down viable (goodly) trees."

posedly destroyed their fruit-trees in order to deny them to the Romans. But there is no compelling reason to accept his interpretation. Quite the contrary: the fact that the tree-choppers are lumped together with false witnesses and market-stall vendors leads us to believe that none of this has anything to do with politics, but rather with the public interest and with damage to property. In this instance, the plain sense is the right sense. There are people who cut down their own fruit-trees to make use of the wood, or to clear the land for some purpose or other. The point is that their act is contrary to the public interest, and it is condemned on social and economic grounds.

So too with the halakhah against raising — and grazing — sheep and goats. It harms the public interest. The matter has nothing to do with politics, or with the Roman occupation, or with the resistance movement.[99]

From a different source we know about another regulation that was made much earlier, during the days of the Second Commonwealth, by the "Civil Judges of Jerusalem" for the protection of fruit-bearing trees:

> If an animal nipped off the growth on a young tree, Rabbi Jose says: The Civil Judges of Jerusalem used to rule that if it was in the first year of growth, the owner of the beast pays two pieces of silver; if it was in the second year he pays four silver pieces.[100]

It appears that even back then, they would fine anybody who let his animal do damage to trees. So much, then, for theories which connect the halakhah with the Roman occupation.[101]

My own view is that the halakhah as we find it is no older than the time of Rabban Gamaliel, and that it came into being for perfectly understandable social-economic reasons. Flocks of sheep and goats

---

[On *kitevei plaster*, see Lieberman: *Tosefta Kifshuto*, IV, p. 485, n. 2 and p. 856 (29).]

99 For the prohibition against cutting down trees, see B.Q. 91b. Also Mishnah Shevi. IV:10: "How much should an olive tree produce so that it may not be cut down? A quarter of a qab. Rabban Gamaliel says, it all depends on the kind of olive."

100 Ket. 105a. B.Q. 58b.

101 Another difficulty with Gulak's theory is that the ban on small cattle was introduced into Babylonia as late as the time of Rav (early third century). See B.Q. 80a.

were certain to damage crops in the fields and orchards — grain, vegetables, fruit-trees. This had become a particularly sensitive matter after the Destruction, because the war had wrought great havoc throughout the countryside, most especially to trees.[102] There was thus a crying need to protect all growing things, particularly those that the country needed most.

Furthermore, much had been laid waste during the fighting, and the easiest thing to do was to use it as pasture. Many husbandmen who had fled from the war probably returned to find their farms ruined, and turned to grazing as the course of least resistance.[103] We may therefore regard this halakha as an inducement to stay in agriculture, which the Tannaim looked upon as the mainstay of the national economy. The Tosefta reads:

> No man has the right to sell his ancestral holding... so that he
> may use the proceeds to go into raising small cattle.[104]

It is of course possible, as Büchler suggests, that the land-taxes had become unbearable, driving people to give up farming. But this does not seem to have been the principal motive for the flight from agriculture. The whole thing may become clearer if we take a close look at the nature of grazing as an occupation.

A number of sources point to the conclusion that it had become a *profitable* business. The Talmud quotes "If you want to get rich, go into the small cattle business."[105] And the Tosefta just quoted treats it as a form of investment.[106]

What brought this development about? I suggest that the production of wool and the manufacture of clothing may well have had something to do with it. Sources dating from the second century do point to the development of weaving, dyeing, and the making of clothes out of

---

102 Josephus J. W. passim [E.g. V:107-8; 263-4; 523.]
103 Perhaps many owners never came back. They might have been killed, or have died, or been sold as slaves, or fled abroad. The new owners may well have found cattle-raising the easiest way to realize cash income from their new real estate.
104 Tos. Arakh. V:6 (Zuck. 549).
105 Hul. 84b.
106 Tos. Arakh. ibid. "He might want to buy slaves, or merchandise, or small cattle..."

woolen fabric, as well as out of linen.[107] This may therefore have been another reason for the opposition of the Sages to sheep-raising. In defence of agriculture, which they regarded as the basis of the national economy, they took a stand against the allure of quick profits. To be sure, our sources speak only of the damage which the animals cause to crops. They make no mention of wool, or of goat-skin. On the contrary, some Tannaim even ask: Why did not the Sages ban heavy cattle as well? The answer given is, because one does not make a rule which most of the people cannot abide by: small cattle can be imported, but heavy cattle cannot be imported.[108] Still, none of this disproves our hypothesis that there was a demand for wool in commercial quantities to supply the growing textile industry.

Some historians think that the Rabbinic enactment against small cattle-breeding had little practical effect, but there is not enough evidence to support their opinion. It may be granted that the ban could scarcely have taken hold with the masses, and no doubt was observed almost exclusively by the very pious. But then, was any enactment (or law) ever observed to the letter by an entire population? As for the fact that sources reflect large-scale sheep-breeding at a later date,[109] there is nothing to show that the animals were not pastured in woods and wastelands. Further, the Babylonian Sages introduced the ban into their country as late as the third century; they would scarcely have done so had the prohibition been a total failure in Eretz Israel. But regardless of the effect of the original ban, it does show that the leaders of the day were concerned about the dangers which faced the economy of the Land of Israel.

As for the fact that Rabbi Eliezer side-stepped the issue, and that there are two conflicting reports about what Rabban Gamaliel said — all this simply reflects the state of affairs while the problem was still under discussion. Obviously, when it came to a proposal that was likely

107 [I am unable to identify any such sources with regard to the weaving of woolens. For linen, see GenR. XX:29, and above, p. 168 f. The closing paragraphs of Mishnah B.Q. are not explicit about an industry of woolen textiles. See nevertheless M. Avi-Yonah, *The Jews of Palestine* etc., pp. 22, 28, 59.]

108 B.Q. 79b; Tos. ibid. VIII:11 (Zuck. 362); Tos. Shevi. III:13 (Zuck. 64). Jerome also reports a shortage of heavy cattle in Palestine.

109 E.g. Yer. Bez. I:60a: "Wolves once killed 300 sheep belonging to the sons of Judah ben Shamu'a."

to have such far-reaching social and economic consequences, there must have been a good deal of heart-searching, much debate, and a lot of hesitation.

Restrictions on the Transfer of Property

Certain halakhot of tannaitic origin forbid the sale or lease of land or houses in Eretz Israel to non-Jews. Take for example the Mishnah:

> One may not sell them (trees) which are attached to the soil, but one may do so after one has cut them down. . . One may not lease houses to them in the Land of Israel or, needless to say, fields.[110]

Another prohibition covers the selling of slaves:

> If one sells his bondman to a gentile, or to anyone outside the Land of Israel, that bondman goes forth a freedman.

Indeed, the seller was penalized; he had to buy the slave back at no matter what the cost ("even a hundredfold") and set him free.[111]

Similar restrictions applied to large cattle

> Where the custom is to sell small cattle to gentiles, they may sell them; where the custom is not to sell them, they may not sell them. But nowhere may they sell them large cattle, calves or foals.[112]

As a matter of fact, it was even prohibited to let them have possession on a long-term lease. "They may not be given tenancy in fields or interim possession of a work-animal."[113] There was a penalty attached to the forbidden sale of a farm animal. It had to be bought back at whatever the price.[114] It is related that the Amora Resh Laqish once made a man buy back his camel at twice what he had sold it for. Clearly, then, the struggle to prevent the alienation of Jewish property

110 Av. Zar. I:8. Comp. Tos. ibid. II:8 (Zuck. 462 f.).
111 Mishnah Git. IV:6; Tos. Av. Zar. III (IV):16, 19 (Zuck. 464 f.); Bavli Git. 44a.
112 Mishnah Av. Zar. I:6; Pes. IV:3. Comp. Bekh. I:1: "If a man bought from a gentile the unborn young of his ass, or sold the like to him *although this is forbidden.* . ."
113 Tos. Av. Zar. II:8 (Zuck. 462 f.).
114 Git. 44a.

continued into amoraic times, when a pejorative nickname was pinned on a man who acted as a go-between in such transactions.[115]

The traditional explanation offered for these several restrictions is usually a religious one. Bondmen owned by Jews were taught to observe the mitzvot; how could they continue to do so if they were sold to gentiles? Beasts of burden would be put to work on the Sabbath, contrary to the fourth commandment.[116] As for the sale of land, one does to be sure find a national-economic reason for outlawing it: the words *'lo tehanem'* in Deuteronomy (8:2) are interpreted to mean 'thou shalt not give them *hanayah baqarqa* — a foothold on the soil.'[117] But even in this case, a religious reason is also given — to keep the land subject to tithing.[118] Nevertheless, we may conclude that the underlying motivation for all these prohibitions was the desire to forestall the permanent settlement of foreigners in the Land of Israel, by preventing them from acquiring land and other *economically important* property (a description which did not apply to ordinary moveables).

The Tannaim mentioned in connection with these halakhot are all disciples of Rabbi Akiba — Rabbis Meir, Jose, Judah, Simeon and Simeon ben Gamaliel. This fact might lead us to suppose that the restrictions in question originated in their time — that is, in the days following the Bar Kokhba Revolt. However, the very fact that all these authorities treat the *taqanot* in question as established realities, while at the same time they differ among themselves about some of the details, makes it seem more likely that the regulations came into being during the generation before them — in the wake of the Destruction. After all, that was when there was first seen to be a real danger that aliens in large numbers would settle in Judaea, and displace the Jewish people from its own soil.

---

115 Yer. Pes. IV: 30d. A ritual problem connected with this matter is much discussed by Tannaim and Amoraim. Can title to land in Eretz Israel pass out of Jewish hands to such an extent that the laws of tithing cease to apply? See for example Bavli Gittin 47a, and Yerushalmi Demai V: 24c. The question is not confined to the ritual problem. According to one amoraic opinion, title passes in every respect except the religious, so that the new owner may change the contour of the land at will. But a differing opinion claims that he acquires only the usufruct.

116 Git. 44a; Av. Zar. 15a; Yer. ibid. I: 39d; and Pes. IV: 30d.

117 Av. Zar. 20a; Yer. ibid. I: 40a.

118 Bavli, ibid. 21a.

It is certain that these *taqanot* remained in force throughout both the tannaitic and the amoraic periods. Around the middle of the third century we run into a problem created by the fact that in certain parts of the country the Jewish population had fallen off markedly, and numerous non-Jews had moved in. The Yerushalmi reports that Rabbi Simon owned fields at Har Hamelekh. He asked Rabbi Johanan (what he might do with them). The Rabbi said: 'Let them grow wild' (let them go to seed) — but do not lease them to a non-Jew.' He then asked Rabbi Joshua ben Levi, who permitted him (to lease), based on the fact that it was a place 'where Jews were hard to find.'[119]

Similar conditions undoubtedly prevailed in some districts throughout the post-Destruction centuries. The general trend toward the growth of non-Jewish centers of population in Palestine, especially from the third century onwards, must also have interfered with the strict observance of the *taqanot* regarding the sale and lease of property. Nevertheless, it can be stated without hesitation that these regulations played an important part in retarding the alienation of much Jewish property, and in preventing the influx of even larger numbers of non-Jews into the country.

---

119 Yer. Demai VI:25b. Comp. Av. Zar. I:40b ("a vine-nursery").

CHAPTER THIRTEEN

JEWISH CHRISTIANS: THE PARTING OF THE WAYS

The twelfth paragraph of the "Eighteen" Benedictions (*ve-lamal-shinim*) is referred to in Talmudic literature as "*Birkat ha-Minim*" — the prayer concerning the sectarians.[1] The same sources inform us that this part of the liturgy dates from the Academy of Yavneh:

> Simeon Hapakuli arranged the Eighteen Benedictions in their proper order in the presence of Rabban Gamaliel at Yavneh. Said Rabban Gamaliel to the Sages: Is there anyone that can formulate the *Birkat ha-Minim*? Up rose Samuel the Lesser and recited it.[2]

What was the nature of this "benediction"? As it appears in most Ashkenazic versions of the liturgy today, it says not a word about sectarians or Minim.[3] But there was a time when the *Minim* were explicitly mentioned.[4] Just who were they?

The Talmud uses the word frequently, and always in the sense of "sectarians" — Jews whose religious beliefs and practices set them apart from the rest of the people.[5] Some scholars hold that the term invariably refers to one or another kind of Jewish Christian, but that

1 Tos. Ber. III:25 (Zuck. 9) : "He includes the *Minim* with the *perushim*." (but read *poshe'im* = sinners) [This emendation was first proposed by J. Derenbourg, REJ XIV (1887), p. 31, n. 1. Lieberman in his Commentary on Tos. Berakhot, p. 53 (96) explicitly rejects it. He interprets *perushim* = 'separatists.']
2 Bavli, Ber. 28b; Yer. ibid. IV:8a. All mss. and early printings read as above. Any edition later than the 16th–17th cent. is likely to read "Sadducees," betraying the hand of the censor.
3 See Daily Prayer Book, ed. Singer, p. 50; or annotated edition by J. H. Hertz, pages 142–5.
4 Finkelstein in JQR, n.s. XVI, p. 156. The term survives in Sephardic rites.
5 Many explanations have been proposed for the meaning of the word "*minim*", but it remains obscure.

definition is difficult to maintain, since there are passages that cannot possibly be so construed.

However, when the field is narrowed down to the *Minim* of the Eighteen Benedictions, the definition becomes more plausible. For one thing, there is the evidence provided by several Church Fathers. The earliest to mention the subject is Justin Martyr, born a pagan at what is now Nablus at the end of the first century. In his "Dialogue With Trypho", written around the year 150, he says: "You Jews pronounce maledictions on the Christians in your synagogues." Of course this is too vague; there is nothing to show that he refers to *Birkat ha-Minim*.[6]

But more direct testimony comes from Epiphanius, who writes that the Jews denounce the *Nazarenes* in their prayers three times a day. Note that he speaks only of *Jewish* Christians (Nazarenes).[7] And Jerome, in his Commentary on Isaiah, Chapter 52, verse 4, says practically the same thing.[8]

That was about all we knew until 1925, when the question was settled by the discovery of Genizah fragments containing portions of the liturgy according to the ancient Palestinian rite. In these versions, *Birkat ha-Minim* reads like this:[9]

> May the apostates have no hope, unless they return to Thy Torah, and may the Nazarenes and the Minim disappear in a moment. May they be erased from the book of life, and not be inscribed with the righteous.

> (or)

> May the apostates have no hope, and mayest Thou uproot the wicked government speedily, in our day. May the Nazarenes and the Minim disappear in a moment. Let them be erased from the book of life and not be inscribed with the righteous.

The provenance of this text, which calls down wrath on the wicked

6 See S. Krauss in JQR, vol. V (1892–3), pp. 130–4.
7 His terms are unmistakable: "The Jews hate these *Nazaraioi* and pronounce them anathema morning, noon and evening." Justin, on the other hand, had mistakenly made it appear that the Jews denounced *Gentile* Christians as well.
8 Jerome's Latin and the Greek of the other patristic passages just mentioned, are readily available in Graetz's *Geschichte*, 4th ed., vol. 4, note 11, page 400. Also see Krauss, op. cit.
9 HUCA, vol. II (1925), p. 306.

(Roman) government — along with apostates, Nazarenes and *Minim* — leaves little room for doubt that we are looking at something very close to the original formulation as laid down in the days of Rabban Gamaliel.[10] The wording might give the impression that Nazarenes are one thing and *Minim* another; or that *Minim* is a generic term for schismatics. But that can scarcely be true; for why would Rabban Gamaliel have reacted to any heresy except one that posed a special threat in his own time? There was nothing new about non-Pharisaic sects like the Sadducees. They and others had been numerous in Temple days.

We must therefore assume that in this liturgical fragment, *Minim* and *Notzrim* are synonymous, and that both refer to the Jewish Christians. The assumption is borne out by Jerome, who writes that in his lifetime (4th to 5th centuries) there was a sect of Jews called *Minim* — *also known* as Nazarenes. He says they wanted to be both Jews and Christians, and so ended up by being neither![11]

Minim and the Sages

Before we outline the various kinds of Jewish Christians, and explain the differences between them, let us look at a few traditions on the subject dating from the time of Rabban Gamaliel. They may give us an idea of the extent to which Judaism in the first two centuries of this era experienced Jewish Christianity as a problem; and some notion of how the Sages reacted to it.[12]

---

10 It is possible that the memory of a connection between *Birkat ha-Minim* and the Nazarenes lasted into Gaonic times. See *Halakhot Gedolot*, ed. Hildesheimer, Berlin 5652, p. 27. The editor notes that his ms. contains a marginal note: *"Birkat ha-Minim* was introduced after Yeshua ben Pandera, when heretics became numerous." Also see Mahzor Vitry, p. 18, and Krauss, op. cit. p. 132. [The Gaonic passage may have eluded Ginzberg, or he may have doubted its authenticity. See his *Hiddushim*, vol. II, p. 271.]

11 *Usque hodie per totas orientis synagogas inter Judaeos haeresis est, quae dicitur Minaeorum et a Pharisaeis usque nunc damnatur, quos vulgo Nazaraeos nuncupant. . . sed dum volunt esse Christiani et Judaei, nec Judaei sunt nec Christiani* (Epistola 59).

12 [Most of the Rabbinic sources are collected in R. Travers Hereford: *Christianity in Talmud and Midrash*, London, 1903; see also J. Klausner: *Jesus of Nazareth*, translated from the Hebrew by Herbert Danby.]

The first passage is from the Tosefta; it also appears, with some variations, in both Talmudim:[13]

Blank writing surfaces (*gilyonim*) and books of the *Minim*[14] are not to be rescued (on the Sabbath) but should be allowed to burn right where they are, along with their *azkarot*.[15] Rabbi Jose of Galilee says: On a week-day, one should cut out the *azkarot* and bury them, then burn the rest. Said Rabbi Tarphon: May I lose my sons if I would not burn any such books that fell into my hands, *azkarot* and all! Indeed, if I were fleeing from a deadly pursuer, I had rather take refuge in a house of heathen worship than enter into the house of such as these. For the heathen do not know Him and (so) deny Him; but these do know Him, and (yet) deny Him. It is of them that Scripture says, 'Behind the doors and the posts hast thou set up thy symbol' (Isa. 57.8). Rabbi Ishmael added: If for the sake of restoring peace between man and wife the Torah ordains that the divine name, written in sanctity, be blotted out[16] — how much more should the *azkarot* of these *Minim* be blotted out, seeing that they sow discord and enmity and strife between Israel and their Father in Heaven! It is of them that Scripture says, 'Do I not hate them, O Lord, that hate Thee? Am I not grieved with those that rise up against Thee?' (Ps. 139:21).

The same question is the subject of a disagreement between Rabbi Ishmael and Rabbi Akiba in Sifre on Numbers:

Rabbi Ishmael says: The way to deal with books of the Minim is this: one cuts out the *azkarot* and burns the rest. Rabbi Akiba says: One burns the whole thing, because it was not written in holiness.[17]

13　Tos. Shab. XIII (XIV) 5 (Zuck. 129); Bavli, ibid. 116a; Yer. ibid. XVI: 15c. Cf. supra, p. 276.
14　That is, books of Scripture written by them.
15　Any divine names written therein.
16　In the ordeal of the bitter waters (Numbers 5:23).
17　*Naso*, sec. 16, ed. Horovitz, p. 21. From Git. 45b it would appear that books of Scripture written by heathen were not quite as undesirable as those written by *Minim*!

Something similar is embodied in the following tradition:[18]

> Once it happened that Rabbi Eleazar ben Dama was bitten by a snake, and Jacob of Kefar Sama came to heal him in the name of Yeshua ben Pantera.[19] Rabbi Ishmael would not permit it, saying: 'Ben Dama, you are not allowed!'[20] He answered: 'But I can prove to you that it is permissible for him to heal me.'[21] However, before he could manage to cite his proof, he died. Rabbi Ishmael exclaimed: 'Happy are you, ben Dama, because you have departed in peace without having broken down the barrier erected by the Sages...'[22]

The attitude of the Sages to the Jewish Christians at the beginning of the second century is further illuminated by the following:[23]

> Rabbi Eliezer was arrested by the Romans and charged with being a *Min*. They put him up on the stand (*bamah*) to be tried. The *hegmon* (governor? tribune?) said: 'How does an old man like you come to be involved in such matters?'[24] The Rabbi

18 Tos. Hul. II:22–23 (Zuck. 503); Bavli, Av. Zar. 27b; Yer. ibid. II, 40d–41a, and Shab. XIV:14d.

19 Origen reports that the heathen Celsus heard this name used by a Jew as early as about 178 C.E. (*Contra Celsum* I, ix, i 32-3.)

20 It had been ruled that the use of incantations for healing was forbidden on grounds of idolatry.

21 He proposed to argue that even idolatrous methods, if they proved efficacious, were permitted for healing purposes.

22 Curiously enough, it is Rabbi Ishmael who holds that even the most fundamental prohibitions, idolatry included, may be violated to save a life. Yet in the instant case he rules to the contrary! This paradox is pointed out by the Talmud, which proposes a solution: where the act is done in private, Rabbi Ishmael is permissive; but when it is public, and might set a dangerous example, he is strict about it. It may also be suggested that he viewed "faith healing" as more misleading than out-and-out idol worship.

23 Tos. Hul. II:24 (Zuck. 503); comp. Bavli, Av. Zar. 16b–17a.

24 The episode is connected with anti-Christian persecutions in Asia Minor and Syria during the reign of Trajan, when Ignatius, Bishop of Antioch, was sent to Rome, "tried" and thrown to wild beasts in the arena. The persecutions reached Palestine, too. Eusebius (Eccl. Hist. III:32) quotes Hegesippus: in the year 107 the Romans killed Symeon son of Clopas, a member of the family of Jesus, and leader of the Jewish Christian church in Jerusalem.

answered: 'I put my faith in the Judge.' Of course, he meant his Father in Heaven, but the *hegmon* thought he was referring to him. So he said: 'Since you put your trust in me — *dimus!* You are discharged.'[25] When Rabbi Eliezer left the stand he was upset because he had been arrested for *minut*. His disciples came to him to console him, but he would not be comforted. Then Rabbi Akiba entered and said: 'Rabbi, may I say something without giving offense?' He answered: 'Say on.' Said he: 'Is it possible that one of the *Minim* once told you something of their teaching that pleased you?' He answered: 'By Heaven, you have reminded me! I was walking once along the main street of Sepphoris, and I met Jacob of Kefar Sikhnin, and he told me a bit of *minut* in the name of Yeshua ben Pantera, and I enjoyed it!.. That is why I was arrested for *minut*, because I violated the Scripture that says: "Remove thy way from her, and come not near the door of her house." (Prov. 5:6)[26]

This tradition reveals, on the one hand, the fairly familiar relations that occasionally existed between some of the early Tannaim and some of the Jewish followers of Jesus — but at the same time, the growing alienation between the two camps, approaching the proportions of a halakah forbidding discourse with *Minim* in matters of Torah.

The latter aspect of the situation is reflected by Justin Martyr (*Dialogue With Trypho*, 38, 1) when he has the Jew express regret that he had ever gotten involved in the argument.

It were better had I listened to our Sages, who instructed us not to enter into discussion with any of you. I should not have made

25 The foreign word in the Hebrew stands for *dimissus* or *dimissio*. All that the Romans wanted at this point was submission to their authority. They were therefore ready to accept a verbal declaration like the above as tantamount to a renunciation of Christianity, and as grounds for dismissing the charge of subversion.

26 The Talmud goes into further detail. The 'bit of *minut*' which Rabbi Eliezer had enjoyed is said to have been something which the healer Jacob of Sikhnin had learned from Jesus himself. [It has been suggested that this Jacob might have been James son of Alphaeus, or James the Lesser. See Mark II:18 and XV:40.]

myself a partner to this dialogue, for I hear you utter many things that are downright blasphemous.[27]

Jewish Christian Sects

Now let us take a closer look at Jewish Christianity in its various forms. A number of Church Fathers between the first century and the beginning of the fifth tell us about the presence of these sects in the Middle East, especially in Palestine and the neighboring countries. To be sure, what they report about them is often quite confused. It is a safe assumption that the patristic writers were not especially familiar with these heretics, and consequently got the beliefs and practices of one sect mixed up with those of another. This holds good even in cases where the writers had seen those *Minim* with their own eyes, or had gotten first-hand reports about them.

As for the *history* and *development* of the Jewish Christian sects, the Church Fathers can hardly be expected to know the first thing about them. Because of this, and because of the dearth of other sources, we can get no clear picture of the doctrinal evolution of the various groups, of their shifting relationships with one another; or of the relations between all of them and the Jewish people, on the one hand, and the Gentile Christians on the other. Obviously, with the passing of the years none of these things remained constant. We might well wish that we knew more about their fluctuations.

Nevertheless, we are able to distinguish four separate kinds of Jewish Christians:

1) Ebionites A
2) Ebionites B
3) Notzrim (Nazarenes)
4) Gnostic-Syncretists

What all these had in common was their belief in the Messiahship of Jesus, and their Judaism. Even in the way they understood these two fundamentals they differed enormously from one another. But they all

---

27 Justin does not distinguish between Jewish and Gentile Christians, as we have noticed. But most late tannaitic sources that frown on contact with *Minim* refer to Jewish Christians.

agreed in acknowledging Jesus in some way, and in regarding themselves as Jews in both religion and nationality.[28]

To understand this phenomenon, which lasted for three or four centuries, we must review the earliest stages of Christianity, especially in Eretz Israel, during the years before these sects took shape.

We do not know enough about what went on among the believers during those formative decades between the death of Jesus and the end of the first century. The literary sources deriving from that period — the New Testament writings both canonical and extra-canonical — are not sufficient to give us a full picture of the emergence and spread of Christianity and of its early struggles, be it the external struggles (those with Judaism and with the gentile world, which includes the Roman authorities) or the internal ones (between the various trends within the nascent faith). But in spite of the dearth of direct evidence, it is still possible to outline a view of Christianity's first steps.

The first Christian community was centered in Jerusalem, although there were believers outside the Holy City and even outside the country, as far away as Damascus. The Jerusalem community was made up of local Jews, to whom were joined a number of coreligionists from the Graeco-Roman world who had settled in the capital. The latter were mostly Greek-speaking, and had long been accustomed to gather for prayer in synagogues of their own, according to their countries of origin.

The members of this early community of believers conducted themselves as Jews in every respect, adhering to all the mitzvot of Judaism, distinguishable from other Jews in one respect only — in their conviction that Jesus had been the Messiah, and that he was destined to reappear as the bearer of the ultimate redemption. Apostles like Peter and John, as well as other members of the congregation, went to the Temple every day to worship the God of Israel.[29] In the propagation of their beliefs, too, these people were fully Jewish. In Palestine, at any rate, they confined their preaching mainly to the Jewish community. In this attitude they were supported by the earliest traditions about

---

28 However, they did separate themselves from the nation when they opted out of the Rebellion against Rome in the year 68, and left the city for Pella. They also stood aside from the rest of the people during the Bar Kokhba Revolt.

29 Acts 3:1.

Jesus; he had instructed his followers to preach his doctrines to none but Jews.[30]

However, before long the new faith was being propagated among non-Jews as well. The man who did more than anyone else in this respect was Paul, *the* Apostle par excellence — although in fact he was neither one of the original Apostles, nor one of the original disciples. True, there were those who had preached the gospel in the Diaspora before him.[31] But it seems that most of the early Christians who had carried the message from Judaea to foreign lands had confined their efforts to Jewish audiences. Indeed, they disagreed with their fellow-believers who were already proclaiming "the good tidings of our Lord Jeshua" to the Gentiles.

At any rate, by the time Paul appeared on the scene there was precedent for a mission to the Gentiles. What he did was to make it a central principle of the new faith. It took him from one country of the dispersion to another in an intensive round of activity that occupied him from the forties to the sixties of the first century.

This was the first major issue that divided the early Christians, and it led to a sharp inner struggle. The question was, would Christianity continue to view itself solely as a religious movement within Judaism, as it had been in Jesus' day; or was it to become a religion for all men and nations? An even more serious question arose out of the first: did Gentiles who came to believe in Jesus have to accept Judaism and the Jewish way of life? This question was put forward especially by Paul and his faction. Ultimately, it was their victory that transformed Christianity into a Gentile religion.

For want of information we are unable to give a detailed account of the debates that must have raged on this issue. We do know, however, that it was Paul who swung the balance in favor of exempting Gentile believers from conversion to Judaism and from obedience to the Torah. The decision to this effect was first proposed by Peter as a "compromise," and was accepted by "the apostles and the elders" in Jerusalem.[32]

---

30   "Go not into the way of the Gentiles. . . but go rather to the lost sheep of the house of Israel." Matt. 10:5–6.
31   Acts 11:20.
32   Acts 15:20 — "But write unto them that they abstain from pollution of

However, that did not settle the problem. Three trends seem to have continued to make themselves felt: 1) The Pauline, which regarded the primary vocation of Christianity as a mission to the Gentiles, who were not only completely exempted from obedience to the Torah, but were actually *forbidden* to be circumcised or to observe the mitzvot. 2) The diametrically opposite doctrine, whose leading spokesman was Jacob (James), "brother of our Lord" and leader of the Jerusalem church. This group demanded that all non-Jewish believers undergo complete conversion to Judaism. James did not explicitly oppose Paul, but seems to have served as the focus of opposition to his teaching.[33] 3) Somewhere between the two extreme positions was a middle one, represented by Peter. It was a position of compromise, not marked by strict consistency; nor did it stand in open opposition to Paul. But whereas the latter worked chiefly in foreign lands as 'Apostle to the Gentiles,' Peter functioned principally in Judaea, as 'Apostle to the Jews.'

In the country of its origin Christianity, as taught by James, retained it original "primitive" character. In short, it remained Jewish Christianity. James himself, as we learn from Hegesippus (quoted by Eusebius) was a regular worshipper at the Temple, and was known among the Jews as a righteous man.[34]

It is a safe assumption that most of the Christians in Jerusalem — and in Judaea at large — were Jews. Indeed, it seems that even after the Destruction, the Jerusalem Church was made up principally of Jewish Christians. This is as good as confirmed by several Church Fathers who tell us that the bishops (*episkopi*) of the Jerusalem Chris-

idols and from fornication and from (meat that has been) strangled, and from blood."

33 It should be noted that Paul himself does not urge Jewish Christians to give up the Torah, despite the acerbity of his polemic with his Judaizing opponents (and despite his theology which taught that the Torah had become null and void with the appearance of the Savior; that indeed, the Torah had led to sin; and that Gentiles were forbidden to live by it). He does say that *Jewish* Christians should — or may — follow the Torah. Of course, it is possible that the latter statement was a matter of tactics, and *not* in accord with his fundamental convictions. The question calls for further study.

34 Eusebius, *Hist. Eccl.* II:33 (in the Kirsopp Lake translation, vol. I, p. 275); "He was called 'The Just' by all men." Comp. Josephus, Ant. XX:200.

tian community right up to the time of the Bar Kokhba Revolt were all circumcised Jews. On the other hand, the Destruction of Jerusalem did bring in its wake an increase in the number of Gentile Christians in Palestine.

It is against this background that we may now turn our attention to a brief analysis of the Jewish Christian sects:

1) *Ebionites A*

This group observed all the commandments of the Torah, practising circumcision and keeping the Sabbath and the Festivals. They followed the Pharisaic form of Judaism; they accepted the Torah, the Prophets and the Hagiographa as Holy Writ. When praying, they faced the Temple Mount in the approved Jewish manner. And not only did they regard Jerusalem as "God's Dwelling Place", but they also looked forward to its restoration, associating themselves in this with the whole of the Jewish people. Needless to say, their tongue was Jewish Aramaic, and their Scriptures — the traditional Hebrew Bible. They rejected Paul and his epistles, regarding him as a sinner who had led the Christians away from Judaism.[35]

They had a tendency to asceticism. They did not drink wine; we do not know whether they abstained from meat as well. Certainly they practiced a lot of ritual ablution. For one thing, it was a feature of their daily religious observance; for another, it was required after sexual intercourse. All these lustrations had a twofold purpose: purification in the Jewish sense (from impurity), and in the Christian sense (from sin).[36]

They recognized Jesus as a prophet, and as the Messiah; but they accepted neither his divinity nor his virgin birth. They taught instead

35 They spread the word that he was not a Jew by birth, but had converted because he wanted to marry the High Priest's daughter. When that didn't work out, he decided to take revenge on Judaism! Actually, Paul was at some pains to prove that he was "an Hebrew of the Hebrews" (Phil. 3:5), probably in order to counter the unfriendly stories set afoot by "The Jews" — that is, the Jewish Christians.

36 According to Epiphanius, the Ebionites were stricter in some matters than the Jews. They regarded physical contact with gentiles as contaminating; it required ablution. In this they agreed with Samaritan practice. But they called their meeting-houses "synagogues," not "churches." Their terminology of leadership was hybrid — both "elders" and *"archisynagogoi."*

that he was the son of Mary and Joseph, and a human being. But because he was a perfectly saintly man, one who had fulfilled the Torah in its every detail, he had been found worthy of becoming the Messiah — an achievement that would in theory have been possible for any man. Finally, they had an "evangel" of their own — a "Hebrew" version of the Gospel according to Matthew.[37]

2) *Ebionites B*

Justin Martyr (Dialogue XL) speaks of two schools of thought among the Jewish Christians. One of them keeps its distance from the Gentile Christians. The other fraternizes with them, and makes no demands on them to observe the Jewish way of life. It may be that Justin is referring here to the same two sects of Ebionites that Origen had in mind, when he distinguished between them on the basis of whether they accepted the Virgin Birth or not.[38] In any case, this was a sect of Jewish Christians who joined hands with the Gentile Christians, taking over from them, at least to some degree, a theology rooted in non-Jewish concepts — the idea of a God-Messiah. It seems to me that this is the group to whom an interesting bit of testimony applies: the report we have from Eusebius and Hippolytus that the Ebionites observe both the Jewish Sabbath and "the Lord's Day" (Sunday). I believe that this can only refer to these Ebionites of the second group.

3) *Nazarenes*

These too were observant Jews, but they accepted the Christological theology in toto. They believed in Jesus as the Son of God, born of the Virgin and the Holy Spirit. They accepted the Epistles of Paul. Theologically, then, they were on an equal footing with Gentile Christians.[39]

Probably what marks this sect out especially, is its antipathy towards the Jewish Sages — "the Scribes and the Pharisees." Jerome is our chief witness in this matter. When he comments on Isaiah VIII:14 —

---

37 A Christian tradition makes Theodotian and Symmachus (the translator) Ebionites. However, Epiphanius calls the latter a Samaritan convert to Judaism.

38 *Contra Celsum* VIII:61.

39 They too had a gospel of their own in "Hebrew" — that is, in Aramaic. Scholars differ as to whether this was an original, or a translation from Greek.

("He shall be for a sanctuary; but for a stone of stumbling and for a rock of offence to both the houses of Israel, for a gin and for a snare to the inhabitants of Jerusalem") — he says that the Nazarei apply this Scripture to the Schools ('Houses') of Shammai and Hillel "who interpret the Torah according to their own traditions and Mishnahs, and pervert the Scriptures. . . . . these two houses did not accept the Saviour, so that He became a stumbling block unto them."[40] This enmity seems to indicate that the Nazarenes were completely alienated from the Jewish People, despite their adherence to the mitzvot; for after the Destruction the only surviving Jews were Pharisees.

Some scholars hold that the "Nazarenes" were identical with the Ebionites B, since both believed in the Virgin Birth. But Origen states explicitly that both groups of Ebionites rejected the Epistles of Paul, while we know that the Nazarenes accepted them. I find it hard to believe that Origen was mistaken in a matter of this sort. I would also want some reasonably hard evidence before attributing to the Ebionites B that hostility to the Jewish Sages of which we have spoken.

4) *Jewish Christian Gnostics*

A fairly large number of sectarian groups in Palestine and the neighboring countries during the early years of our era can, from all appearances, be classified under this heading. We are in no position to catalogue the distinctions between them in detail. But we can point out four basic elements which they had in common. These were:

a) Adherence to the laws of the Torah, and to the Jewish people — at least, in their own opinion.

b) Belief in Jesus as Messiah, or as prophet (probably there were those who attributed superhuman, or even Divine, powers to him).

c) Gnostic elements, expressed, firstly, in the concept that the Messiah had been the embodiment of a primordial spiritual force which had originally resided in Adam, had passed over to the Patriarchs, and had finally been made manifest in the physical presence of Jesus; secondly, in a tendency to exalt the natural elements as then conceived: water, air, earth and fire (like the pseudo-Clementines — see below)[41]; and thirdly, in a strain of dualism, according to which

40 They derived 'Hillel' from '*ḥallal*' (profane); Shammai from '*ashmai*' (guilty?).
41 *Recognitiones* II 45, *Homilia* II 40.

the universe consists of two opposing principles, good and evil, locked in eternal struggle. The conflict can be resolved only on a higher plane — in the Kingdom of Heaven.

Some of these gnostic doctrines show affinities with mystical theosophy of the kind later exemplified by the *Shiur Qoma*. This is most apparent in the *Book of Elkesai* (see below). The visionary has a revelation in which he sees Jesus the Son together with the Holy Ghost, each of them in the form of a pillar 96 miles high. Other circles show the influence of pagan gnosticism and eastern Hellenistic mystery religions — not excluding some elements tinged with polytheism and the doctrine of multiple universes (αἰῶνες or *aeones*), just as we find among the Gentile Christian Gnostics. It may be that some of the Talmudic traditions relating to *Minim* refer to this particular species of sectarian.

d) The rejection of some part of the Bible. Two trends are discernable here. One of them is expressed in the Clementine literature, which includes two works attributed to Clemens Romanus, according to Christian tradition one of the first Bishops of Rome. These works, the *Recognitions* and the *Homilies*, both of them Catholic Christian, embody an older work, "The Preachments Peter" (Κηρύγματα Πέτρου) apparently written around the year 140 in Palestine by a Jewish Christian.[42] It speaks out on behalf of total observance of Judaism, and against merger with Gentile Christians; it carries on a polemic against Paul, although he is not mentioned by name.

This document originated with a sect whose adherents believed in the Torah, "which was present at Creation, and then was promulgated again at Mount Sinai." They accepted the Prophets as well; what they did reject was the sacrifices. To Jesus they attributed a dictum which is found in a Jewish Christian Gospel according to St. Matthew: "I am come to set aside the sacrifices." They taught, therefore, that the Biblical passages ordaining the sacrifices were not original parts of the Torah, but later interpolations.

Ephiphanius tells us of another sect that did not accept all of Scripture (he confuses them with the Ebionites). This group believed in the Pentateuch but rejected the Prophets and the Hagiographa, just

42 ["The two chief Clementine writings are both evidently the outcome of a peculiar speculative type of Judaistic Christianity." Quoted from F.J.A. Hort in *Encyclopedia Britannica*, ed. 1947, Vol. V, p. 797].

[301]

as though they were Samaritans. What is more, they villified the heroes of Jewish history after Moses and Joshua, including David and Solomon, not to speak of the prophets. Even in the Torah itself they rejected certain passages as "forgeries" — that is, not of genuine Mosaic origin.

5) *The Elkesaites*

Our knowledge of this sect comes chiefly from Hippolytus and Epiphanius.[43] Neither of them tells us anything about its original form, leaving room for sharp disagreement among contemporary scholars. The basic problem is, did these sectarians start out as Jewish Christians, or were they originally purely Jewish? The *Book of Elkesai* as cited by Hippolytus contains Christological passages, as noted above. It also records a liturgical formula recited by members of the sect undergoing immersion: "In the name of the Most High God, and in the name of His Son, the Great King." The question is, were these words original elements of the *Book of Elkesai*, or were they later additions?

As we have said, scholarly opinion about the Elkesaites is divided. Most experts believe that they began as a Jewish Christian sect, and that the Christological elements were not present in the original Aramaic version of the *Book of Elkesai*, but were added when the book was reworked into the Greek version.[44] According to Hippolytus, one Alcibiades, originally from Apamia in Syria, came to Rome at the beginning of the third century with a book he had gotten from a saintly man called Elkesai who in turn had received it from an angel. Brandt conjectures (and I think he is absolutely right) that some time during the second century the sect came into contact with Christians, and was drawn to Christianity. We learn from Epiphanius that much the same thing happened to the Ebionites and other Jewish Christians, along with the last of the Essenes. So that when some of the believers set

43 *Refut. Omn. Haer.* IX:13–17 and X:29; *Haer.* XIX; XXX:17 and LII.
44 In the exposition here offered I hew to the line laid down by Brandt, in his *Elchasai, Ein Religionsstifter und sein Werk*, Leipzig, 1912. Two summaries of his views are available, one of them in his work *Die jüdischen Baptismen*, published as a supplement to ZATW XVIII (1910), pp. 99–112; and the other in his English article in Hastings, ed., *Encyclopedia of Religion and Ethics*, vol. 5, pp. 262–269.

about spreading their doctrine among the Christians of Europe, it was only natural that they should insert Christological references into the Greek version of their book.

Elkesai "appeared" in Transjordan east of the Dead Sea in the third year of the Emperor Trajan, that is, in the year 100. He preached the observance of the Jewish way of life in its entirety, proclaiming himself a prophet. A saying of his transliterated into Greek is recorded by Epiphanius, whose attempt to explain it is wide of the mark. Two modern Jewish scholars have deciphered it quite correctly as a message in one of the most ancient of codes: *tashraq*, that is, the Hebrew alphabet taken backwards. Decoded, the message reads: "I shall testify on your behalf on the great day of judgement."

This self-proclaimed prophet explicitly urges his followers to face Jerusalem when they pray. An important element in his teaching is the atonement for sins through ritual ablution (clothed, and in running water). Brandt may be right when he suggests that this was intended as a surrogate for sacrifices, now that the Temple had been destroyed.[45] He may also be right in his interpretation of the following in the Book of Elkesai: "My children, follow not the sight of the fire... [G]o rather after the sound of the water." That this is an expression of antagonism to sacrifices is clear; but Brandt suggests that it was directed not so much at the offerings prescribed by the Torah as against the prevalent pagan sacrifices; and that it was a call to Gentile proselytes not to partake of them. (I am inclined to think that Elkesai was against sacrifice in principle, as were indeed many Jews *before* the Destruction — even before the birth of Christianity.)

Elkesai forbids immersion on the Sabbath. His doctrine contains some astrological elements and some gnostic influences, especially in his attitude to nature. But in broad terms it may be stated that this sect started life as a Jewish movement, and only later developed into something else.

Two items in Elkesai's teaching have special significance in terms

---

45 Brandt shows a fine sensitivity when he suggests that it was far from simple for Jews to conceive of atonement without sacrifices, and that many were unable to make the adjustment. One must certainly agree that the Destruction of the Temple left a painful void in the spiritual life of most of the people.

of Jewish history. One is a prophecy of his, uttered apparently in the year 116:

> Three years after Trajan conquers the Parthians there will be war among the Angels of Wickedness, and all the Kingdoms of Evil will be destroyed.

This is a prediction of the "end of days" connected with the war between Rome and Parthia, a motif which also occurs in tannaitic sources of the second century.

The second point concerns a ruling by Elkesai, as relayed by Epiphanius. According to this, one may violate the commandments under duress, and in time of persecution may even pay homage to idolatry in one's outward behavior, provided only that one remains inwardly true to the faith. As proof he cites the case of one Phineas, a *kohen* at the Persian capital of Susa in the days of the Emperor Darius, who was forced to bow down to Artemis, and complied in order to save his life.

Now, we know that Christian Gnostics permitted this course of action during the anti-Christian persecutions. Among Jews there were differing opinions. Some said: "Let them kill you, rather than transgress a single commandment." The Halakhah agreed with this if it was a time when Judaism as a whole was under frontal attack. At such times 'even the manner of tying a shoelace' was to be defended (Sanh. 74b). On the other hand, there were those who taught: 'Avoid martyrdom, save for the sake of three basic commandments;' and Rabbi Ishmael who said that it is always permissible to violate any law if one's life is at stake. (The tradition interpreted him to mean: in private, where there is no question of leading others astray.)

The historical question that arises is, what persecution prompted the teaching of Elkesai? If we follow the school of thought that sees the Elkesaites as *ab initio* Jewish Christians, then there is no problem: the persecution took place under Trajan, between the years 105 and 110, when Jewish Christians were hounded along with all other Christians. But if we accept Brandt's theory which would make the sect purely Jewish at that time, then the question remains unanswered. To be sure, Brandt offers the hypothesis that simultaneous with the anti-Christian persecutions, there were measures taken against the Jews as well. But there is no shred of evidence to support such a conjecture. On the other hand, just as Rabbi Eliezer was arrested for *minut* at that time, the same suspicions may have been levelled at the Elkesaites. I would like to suggest a different theory. As I see it, the matter may well have been connected with the "Polemos of Quietus." In the years 116–117, when the resistance movement in Judaea was quite active, is it not possible that the local Roman command imposed restrictive measures against Judaism without the sanction of higher authority? If that is indeed what happened, it would be additional evidence for the claim that at that time the sect was still an integral part of the Jewish people in its own land.

Summary:

What, then, prompted the Sages of Yavneh to place the Jewish Christians outside the Jewish fold? Why did they sometimes even regard them as worse than Christians who had never been Jews?

Up to the time of the Destruction, the Pharisees did not generally take any punitive measures against Jews who believed in Jesus, even though they did occasionally discipline them as sinners. It is true that, according to The Acts of the Apostles, the High Priest sent Saul of Tarsus to Damascus to take steps against the Jewish Christians. And Justin Martyr, in his *Dialogue with Trypho*, claims that the Sanhedrin in Jerusalem used to send delegates and missives to the Diaspora denouncing the Christians. But on the other hand, we do read in Acts that Rabban Gamaliel the Elder successfully defended the Apostles against the death penalty which the Sadducees and the High Priest wanted to impose.[46] Similarly, Josephus tells us how Onias ben Onias the Sadducee convened a Sanhedrin which condemned James, the brother of Jesus, to death, whereupon the "men of Jerusalem" — that is, the Pharisaic Sages — raised a bitter complaint. They took the issue to Agrippa II, and asked him to put a stop to such goings on. They went further, and lodged a complaint with Albinus, the new Procurator of Judaea.[47]

But there were two factors that caused the atmosphere to change radically. The first was that, in moments of national crisis, the Jewish Christians turned their backs on the national cause of the Jewish people. In a report relayed by Eusebius,[48] Hegesippus tells us how

46 Acts V:35–39.
47 Ant. XX (200).
48 Eccles. Hist. III:5:2–3.

the Mother Church in Jerusalem left the besieged city in the year 68, and went to Pella. And again, when the battle lines were drawn against the Roman occupation in the Bar Kokhba Revolt, the Jewish Christians refused to identify with the Jewish side.

Secondly, the Destruction of Jerusalem and of the Temple brought about a sense of national emergency and a consequent closing of ranks. It would seem that the nation could no longer afford the latitude previously allowed to a wide range of sectarians and schismatics. (This may also account for the disappearance of the Sadducees and Essenes.)[49]

Thirdly, as time went on, the Jewish Christian sects tended to intermingle with one another. And the Ebionites themselves split, as one wing (the Ebionites B) drew ever closer to the Gentile Christians.

It is therefore possible that the whole thrust of the *Birkat ha-Minim* was originally directed only against those elements who had joined hands with the Gentile Christians, and had diluted their Judaism to a considerable degree. There may have been no animus at all against the Ebionites A. If we look closely at the traditions which show some of the Sages of Yavneh (Rabbi Joshua, Rabban Gamaliel) in confrontation with *Minim*, we find that the latter always turn out to be folk who *dissociate themselves from the Jewish People*, especially from its hopes for the future. We read, for example, about Rabbi Joshua ben Hananiah standing in the Emperor's palace, when a *Min* (apparently a Jewish Christian) signals him to the effect that God has turned his back on the Jewish people (Hag. 5b).[50] Clearly, this doctrine of the rejection of the "old Israel" was an insurmountable barrier. A similar episode involves Rabban Gamaliel himself.[51] If we accept this view we will have an explanation for those incidents where we find Sages consorting with Jewish Christians during the second and third centuries. We will be able to assume that these were sectarians who had *not* given up their Jewish identity.[52]

---

49 [But perhaps some weight should also be given to intrinsic religious factors. Sadducees without the Temple were spiritually homeless; Essenes were exceedingly vulnerable to the new faith.]

50 Hag. 5b.

51 Yev. 102b.

52 A common juxtaposition in our sources is *"Minim* and informers." On the basis of this usage, many scholars have conjectured that Jewish Chris-

In any case, it is likely that the process of intermingling between these various sects created a situation in which the Jewish Sages could no longer tell them apart; and lumping them all together, read them out of the Jewish fold. The fact remains, however, that the "loyal" sects were never put on a par with the others.

What then was the purpose of *Birkat ha-Minim*? Most scholars believe that it was designed to keep the *Minim* away from worship in the synagogue, and they may well be right. But it is probably truer to say that that was the end result, rather than the original purpose. It is likely that the main intention was to make all Jews aware of the fact that the *Minim* were to be regarded as *apostates*, and could *no longer be called Jews*.

Whichever way we look at it, it will be seen that the Beth Din of Rabban Gamaliel at Yavneh took a fateful step, one that was to have far-reaching historical consequences. They declared in unequivocal terms that the Jewish Christians could no longer be considered part of the Jewish community nor of the Jewish people.[53]

tians made a habit of denouncing Jews to the Roman authorities, and that this led to bad blood, and finally to the anathema of *Birkat ha-Minim*. However, there is no real evidence to support this conjecture. The juxtaposition of terms does not necessarily imply any connection between them. Besides, as we now know, the original version of *Birkat ha-Minim* contains no mention of *malshinim*.

53 [The study of the Jewish Christians has naturally been affected by the discovery of new source-materials bearing on the subject. For examples, see "The Dead Sea Sect and Pre-Pauline Christianity," by David Flusser, in *Scripta Hierosolymitana*, vol. IV (1958), pp. 215 ff.; and "The Jewish Christians in the Early Centuries of Christianity According to a New Source," by Shlomo Pines, in Proceedings of *The Israel Academy of Sciences and Humanities*, vol. II, no. 13].

CHAPTER FOURTEEN

INNER TENSIONS: THE PATRIARCHATE AND
THE SANHEDRIN

We have seen what the leadership in Yavneh did after the Destruction to reorganise the social, economic, and religious life of the Jewish people, and what they achieved in the realm of the Halakhah. We have seen what they accomplished by tightening the link between the local communities in Palestine and the new national establishment, and by strengthening the bonds between the Diaspora and the Land of Israel, both in organizational and religious terms. We have also noted some of the difficulties they encountered. Their task was complicated by forces making for divisiveness, not the least of which was the inertia which resisted their efforts to organize a system of local courts responsible to the Great Beth Din at Yavneh.

But there were also problems of disharmony inherent in the very structure of the new national center. These were of two kinds, the one involving the connection between membership in the High Court and membership in the reconstituted Sanhedrin; and the other, the relationship between the Sanhedrin and the Patriarch. But before we go into these questions let us examine a different, though closely related matter.

We have already observed that in the field of judicature there were rival *Jewish* jurisdictions; that whereas full judicial authority was in theory vested solely in Sages duly qualified by the central High Court, there persisted nevertheless other courts, deriving apparently from *local* authorities. Such were the "Courts of Laymen" *(hedyotot)* and "Courts of Arbitrators" *(borerim)*. So that the attempt to centralize and control Jewish courts was not entirely effective. There was, it seems, a certain "freedom" of judicature, a system or lack of one which must have given rise to clashes and jurisdictional disputes from time to time. What is more, there was freedom to "teach" — that is, to give halakhic rulings. Here there was an ongoing tension between two polarities, namely: the full right of the individual Sage to give guidance, on the one hand; and the requirements of good order and centralized authority on the other.

The most striking expression of the freedom of the individual jurisprudent to rule according to his lights was the old tradition that even the unordained disciple could give halakhic direction. However, Judah I *reversed* the practice by proclaiming: "A student of the Law may *not* give a ruling."[1] This tradition fits in with the formula used by the same Patriarch when he granted ordination to Rav: "May he rule (in halakhah)? He may rule. May he judge (in torts)? He may judge."[2] The older practice is reflected in the Tosefta:

> Just as when a *kohen* who is not sober, yet goes about his priestly duties (*in violation of Leviticus* 10:8–9) with the result that all his acts are invalid and he himself has earned the punishment of death — so is it with a Sage or the *disciple of a Sage;* he may neither expound nor give rulings when in such a state.[3]

Indeed, we are told of a disciple who gave rulings in Sepphoris and in Ariah, and his rulings were followed. Later on, however, the same questions were submitted to the Academy at Yavneh, where one of the rulings was confirmed, but the other was struck down.[4]

Yet it appears that in earlier times — before the Destruction — the freedom to rule on questions of halakhah was an outstanding characteristic in the religious life of the Jewish people, and one of the factors in the development of the Oral Law in all its diversity. It is hardly necessary to add that this diversity entailed considerable risks. It is therefore logical to assume that the attitude of openess to variant teachings was balanced by a counter-tendency to fix limits within which the religious consensus would still be recognizable. It

---

1 Sanh. 5b: "It was then that they decreed: A disciple may not give a ruling unless he has permission (ordination?) of his teacher." Comp. Yer. Shevi. V:36c and Git. I: 43c: "Thenceforward it was decreed that no disciple should give a halakhic ruling. Rabbi Hiyya quoted Rav Huna as saying that if a disciple did nevertheless give a ruling, even though it was perfectly sound, his act was of no effect."
2 Sanh. 5a.
3 Tos. Ker. I:20 (Zuck. 563).
4 Tos. Kil. 1:3–4 (Zuck. 73).

may be further assumed that this tendency was especially strong after the Destruction, when the need for national unity was felt to be paramount.

These logical assumptions are borne out by what we read in the sources dealing with the period of Rabban Gamaliel. We find limitations being imposed on the freedom of the individual Sage to make his own decisions. To be sure, such limitations were only partial; some freedom of legal interpretation remained until the time of the Patriarch Judah I. Even after his time, residual elements of it still persisted.

The Mishnah makes it clear that not every disciple was considered "capable of deciding matters of law."[5] The *baraitha*, casting about for an example of a disciple who *was* capable, cites Simeon ben Azzai.[6] So we may conclude that the phrase means: a scholar who is actually of the first rank, but who has not, for whatever reason, been ordained nor appointed. This says only that he has not been formally "admitted"; but there is no question about his scholarship, or his years of study and attendance upon one or several great Sages. He might be described as a "candidate" waiting, so to speak, for an appointment.

This explanation is supported by another passage:

> Rabbi Judah ben Baba said: I am one of those who is capable of giving a ruling in matters of law.[7]

Apparently he made this statement at a time when he had not yet gotten his ordination, although he already had all the qualifications.

There is a case on record in which Rabban Gamaliel sought to take measures against Hanina, the nephew of Rabbi Joshua, for having given a ruling at a community in Lower Galilee called Simonia, although this Hanina was apparently not considered one who was "capable of deciding in matters of law."[8] Rabban Gamaliel sent a message to Rabbi Joshua: "Take your nephew in hand and

5 Hor. I:1.
6 Tos. Hor. I:1 (Zuck. 474); Yer. ibid. I:45d. The reading of the Bavli is "Simeon ben Azzai and Simeon ben Zoma." [For some reason these two great scholars were never ordained.]
7 Tos. Ter. V:10 (Zuck. 33).
8 Nid. 24b.

bring him to me" (ostensibly for punishment). However, Rabbi Joshua sent a return message to the Patriarch: "It was a ruling of mine that Haninah was quoting." Otherwise, it appears that Hanina would have been acting improperly.

It is highly likely that it was Rabban Gamaliel of Yavneh who was responsible for the restrictions placed on "the freedom to rule" in halakhic matters. One may safely assume that there had been some gestures in that direction even earlier, during the days of the Temple; but nothing more than gestures. The dictum, "Let no disciple give a halakhic ruling" was not expressed until the days of the Patriarch Judah I. But that was most probably the continuation, or rather the culmination, of a policy that was really set in motion by the grandfather of Judah I, the Patriarch Gamaliel of Yavneh.

The Sages and the Sanhedrin

We have noted the idyllic picture drawn by Rabbi Jose ben Halafta of the good old days when unity reigned in the household of Israel, because moot questions were settled once and for all by a vote of the High Court in Jerusalem. In the same context we read how the situation changed:

> But the time came when there were many disciples of the Schools of Shammai and Hillel who had not sat long enough at the feet of their masters. Then disputes and divisions multiplied in Israel.[9]

We are in no position to verify Rabbi Jose's tradition insofar as it deals with the generations prior to Shammai and Hillel. But we can certainly take his word for the situation that prevailed after their time. The question then arises, how did it really come to pass that so much difference of opinion in the field of halakhah developed, especially between the Schools of Shammai and Hillel?

In order to deal with that question, we must examine the composition and *modus operandi* of the Great Beth Din of Yavneh. In three passages in the Mishnah (two of which are identical) dealing with that famous "self-same day . . . when they seated Rabbi Eleazar ben Azariah" we hear that there were 72 members in the Sanhedrin,

9 Tos. Sanh. VII:1 and parallels (Zuck. 425).

approximating the 71 or 70 who had sat in the old Sanhedrin in Jerusalem.[10] But except for these passages, and except for that "self-same day," we have nothing to show that there were anything like 70 members of the body all through the period of the Tannaim and Amoraim. On the other hand, we do find *eighty-five* Sages seated before Rabban Gamaliel;[11] and a reference to *thirty-eight* Elders in the "Vineyard at Yavneh."[12]

The explanation is that the High Court did *not* sit at Yavneh in *fixed plenary* session. Many of its members lived in their own communities, where they served as heads of their own courts. Rabbi Joshua, for example, presided over a Beth Din at Peki'in; Rabbi Halafta at Sepphoris; Rabbi Hanina ben Teradyon at Sikhnin; Rabbi Akiba at Bene Beraq; and Rabbi Eliezer at Lydda, apparently even before he was put under the ban. Only a small number of the Sages made their homes in Yavneh, where they worked closely with Rabban Gamaliel.

This method of functioning, whereby the Sanhedrin could sit without its full complement, was not entirely new. It had been used from time to time, even before the Destruction, in the High Court at Jerusalem. But even apart from that, the High Court did not always sit as the Sanhedrin. Actually, it only went into plenary session when the need arose. When that happened, a number of Sages were summoned and a vote taken, all in terms of what the immediate situation required. The number of Sages "ordained" — that is, qualified to participate in a session should one be summoned — was usually in excess of seventy. Thus, it was possible for eighty-five to be present, although as a general rule less than seventy were summoned for a deliberation.[13]

There is another distinction which has to be kept in mind. The same men who sometimes sat as a Beth Din were at other times gathered together as an *Academy* of Law. This fact — that not all the qualified members of the Sanhedrin were normally assembled as a Court of Law, while *per contra* those Sages who *were* in

10   Yadaim III:5; and IV:2 = Zeb. I:3.
11   Tos. Kelim B.B. II:4 (Zuck. 592).
12   Sifre Huqat 124= ed. Horovitz p. 158.
13   How this applied in the days of the Commonwealth is a subject that requires further investigation.

residence at the seat of the Sanhedrin were generally engaged in academic discussion — this fact in itself helps to explain why there was an absence of decisions binding on the individual Sage, and scarcely any limitation on his freedom to follow his own opinion. As a rule, the Sanhedrin did not function as a decision-making body, except in the comparatively few instances when "they took a count and concluded." Hence the phraseology: "Patriarch So-and-So convened a Beth Din to settle a matter," or "to pass an ordinance." The Sanhedrin convened by Onias ben Onias, referred to above, may be viewed as a pre-Destruction example of the same procedure.

When such a convocation did take place, the decision was arrived at by a majority vote, and was thereupon binding on all the Sages, and indeed on all Jewry. More usually, however, moot questions of halakhah were debated in academic fashion, and individual Sages remained free to give direction in accordance with their own opinion, even if it ran counter to the opinion of the majority. This was a natural outgrowth of the tradition of free interpretation. *Torah* (literally = teaching) is acquired through the process of *hora'ah* (instruction). The Sage was in essence a *moreh* (teacher); it would not have made sense to deprive him of the right to interpret Torah in accordance with what he had learned from his teachers and concluded from his own studies.

The power to make binding decisions remained in reserve with the central body, to be invoked only when it appeared to the Sages that there was some national crisis, some urgent need for the High Court to intervene. Then the members of the Sanhedrin were summoned, and a vote was taken, and individual members were no longer free to rule as they saw fit. But in some instances even the vote of the majority did not totally eliminate minority opinions. There were times when dissenters simply absented themselves from the sessions where they would have been overruled. Such abstentions occurred not only after the Destruction, but before it as well.

What must be stressed is that in matters of halakhah it was not the vote that caused the view of the majority to prevail. Acceptance of the majority view in legal matters, even without a formal vote, was a general guide-line, rather than an abstract principle.[14] It left

14 Mishnah, Eduy. I:5–6.

one free, in specific cases where need arose, to fall back on minority opinions. Rabbi Judah formulated the principle thus:

> The reason for recording the opinion of one individual in dissent from the many is that the time may come when you may need it in a specific case, and it will be there to support a decision.[15]

It seems that there were times when the majority imposed its opinion even without a formal vote, because of some critical situation that seemed to call for an end to debate and controversy. Such struggles, where an individual or a small group were pitted against the Sanhedrin, and as a result major decisions were taken — such struggles were particularly characteristic of the generation of Rabban Gamaliel, the age of postwar reconstruction.

There is a tradition that one of the most important of halakhic decisions — to follow the School of Hillel in nearly everything — was made at Yavneh.[16] Even without the tradition we would probably have surmised as much. And in this instance there was no vote; the "house" did not "divide." Votes were taken on cases, not on principles. This instance is better described as the arrival at a consensus of major proportions, a species of "codification" whose purpose it was to shelve certain doctrines and practices that had existed for generations.

A question which occupied the Sages of the Talmud, and which we are in no better position to settle than they were, is this: why was the Hillelite view given the preference? Not, it can safely be said, because Rabban Gamaliel was a great-great grandson of Hillel. Even the fact that Hillelite halakhah is, in general, more "advanced" than the Shammaite, which tends to conservatism, does not explain the choice. In any event, the point must be made again: the decision at Yavneh did not entirely foreclose the option of the individual Sage to be guided in one or another case by the opinion of the School of Shammai.

The problem of the individual Sage in relation to the Sanhedrin comes into sharpest focus in the well-known tragic case of Rabbi

---

15 Tos. ibid. I:4 (Zuck. 455).
16 Yer. Ber. I:3b.

Eliezer ben Hyrcanus, whose banishment is described in both Talmudim.[17] It is possible (but it remains unproven) that this clash
had its roots in the Hillelite-versus-Shammaite controversy, for Rabbi
Eliezer was known to have Shammaite sympathies. This was an
instance when the Patriarch Rabban Gamaliel had the Sanhedrin
as a whole on *his* side against an individual who would not bow to
the authority of the established leadership. It appears that Rabbi
Eliezer was not alone in his resistance, for we read:

> Because of the stove of Akhinai there were a *great many*
> disputations in Israel.[18]

This was not the only instance when excommunication, or the threat
of it, was used as a weapon against a Sage who refused to accept
the rule of the majority of the Great Beth Din. The Mishnah tells
us (Shab. V:4) that Rabbi Eleazar ben Azariah's cow used to
go out on the Sabbath day with a guide-strap between its horns,
something of which the Sages disapproved. About this, the Yerushalmi preserves a tradition the authenticity of which we have no
reason to doubt:

> They said to him: Either betake yourself from our midst,
> or remove the strap. Quoth Rabbi Jose the son of Rabbi Bun:
> He did it in protest against their ruling.[19]

From all appearances, the use of the ban as a means of discipline
against Sages aroused their opposition. We learn that at Usha (the
successor to Yavneh) a rule was adopted: "No Sage shall be banned."[20]
The opposition which culminated in this ruling had most probably
originated in the days of Rabban Gamaliel.

Sanhedrin and Patriarch

Authority in the Jewish world after the Destruction was embodied
in two institutions: the Patriarchate and the Sanhedrin. The first
sharp clash between these two foci took place in the days of Rabban

17 Bavli B.M. 59a–b; Yer. M.Q. III:81d.
18 Tos. Eduy. II:1 (Zuck. 457). Note *Shir Hashirim Zuta*, ed. Buber p. 29:
    "On the day that R. Eliezer b. Hyrcanus took his seat in the Academy,
    each man girded on his sword."
19 Mishnah, Shab. V:4; Yer. Shab. IV:7c.
20 M.Q. 17a; Yer. ibid. III 81d.

Gamaliel. To understand the nature of the struggle, we must bear in mind that the Patriarch served in a triple capacity: 1) Leader of the nation and its spokesman; 2) President of the Sanhedrin; 3) Head of the Great Academy.

The combination of these three roles automatically gives rise to the question: wherein lay the fundamental source of his power and authority? Was it rooted in his own status as leader of the nation — "The Prince" so to speak — and therefore separate and independent from the Sanhedrin? Or was it derivative, flowing from his headship of the Sanhedrin, and therefore dependent on that body?

Beside this fundamental question, there are other, subsidiary ones. Regardless of its source, what was the *nature* of the Patriarch's authority? Was it a separate entity, an equal counterpoise to the Sanhedrin? Or was it merely a technical chairmanship, carrying in principle no separate weight of its own? If the Patriarchate *was* a distinct focus of authority, for how much did that authority count? Could it override the Sanhedrin? Was it equally balanced with that body? Or was it subject to the Sanhedrin's veto? These same questions apply not only to public affairs and judicial matters, but to academic procedures and conclusions as well.

The beginnings of an answer to these questions emerge from those sources which show the Patriarch as a kind of royalty, a sort of surrogate for the missing "King of Israel." We have such a tradition for a time as early as the Yavneh years:

> One may make a funeral pyre for kings (of their personal effects) ... One may do the same for Patriarchs, but not for ordinary citizens ... When Rabban Gamaliel died, Onkelos the proselyte burned more than seventy *maneh* worth in his honor.[21]

As for the status of the Patriarch in the Academy, suffice it to quote the following *baraitha*:

> 'The sceptre shall not depart from Judah, nor the ruler's staff from between his feet.' (Gen. 49:10) *The sceptre* — refers to the Exilarchs in Babylonia, who rule Israel with a firm hand.

21 Tos. Shab VII: (VIII): 18 (Zuck. 119) and parallels.

The ruler's staff — refers to the descendants of Hillel, namely the Patriarchs, who teach Torah to the multitudes.[22]

By contrast to the Exilarch, who is seen as a merely secular leader, the Patriarch in Eretz Israel is perceived as Head of the Academy too. The same applies to his headship of the High Court. Let us now take a look at the struggles between the Patriarch and the Sanhedrin for control of certain major spheres of authority. Some of these have already been described, such as the see-saw over the right to appoint or ordain Sages. That struggle ended in a compromise; it was finally agreed that the authority was to be shared by both institutions, each requiring the consent of the other.[23] In a different area, that of fixing the calendar, it seems that the Patriarchate jealously guarded its authority — witness the time when a leap-year was proclaimed while Rabban Gamaliel was in Syria on a diplomatic mission, but only on condition that he would approve when he returned.[24]

The fact is that the "Patriarch" (or whoever occupied the analogous position before that office existed) took primary responsibility for the calendar, even in Temple times. On the other hand, the Sanhedrin was never excluded from the picture. Indeed, whenever one or another Patriarch tried to claim sole authority in this matter, the Sanhedrin let itself be heard from. The texts of "Leap Year Missives" preserved in both Talmudim, as well as discussions among the Sages on this subject, reflect the ongoing problems of shared power.[25] In some of the documents, the Patriarch writes: "It appears proper to me;" in others he says: "It appears proper to me and to my colleagues."

In general, one finds this kind of variation in texts of documents going back to the Second Commonwealth. In some of them, the High Priest alone is mentioned; in others, he and the Sanhedrin; in still others, the Sanhedrin alone. If we examine references to official

---

22 Sanh. 5a. [The reference in *Tol.* at this point to *Bereshit Rabbah* is puzzling. Perhaps it intends to point out the tradition that Hillel was of Davidic descent. See Gen. R. 98:13, Theodor, p. 1259].

23 Vide supra, p. 227.

24 Mishnah Eduy. VII:7; Bavli Sanh. 11a.

25 Bavli ibid. 11a–b; Tos. ibid. II:4–5 (Zuck. 416); Yer. ibid. I:18d. Comp. Yer. Meg. I:71a.

enactments in tannaitic times, the same lack of uniformity is apparent. Sometimes it is the Patriarch and his Beth Din, as though referring to two partners sharing authority; sometimes the Patriarch alone; and sometimes the Patriarch seems to be included merely as one of the Sages.

This struggle was at the root of the clash between Rabban Gamaliel and Rabbi Joshua ben Hananiah over the intercalation of a month, as reported by the Mishnah.[26] A close look at the story reveals that what it describes was actually a confrontation between the Patriarch and the Sanhedrin. The former demanded recognition of his independent authority to fix the calendar. As a matter of fact, Rabbi Dosa ben Hyrcanos argued that the Patriarch was right, and succeeded in tipping the scales in his favor. Rabbi Joshua ben Hananiah gave in to Rabban Gamaliel, and even Rabbi Akiba submitted. The nub of the winning argument was that the Sanhedrin derived its authority from the Patriarch, and not vice versa!

A second clash between Rabban Gamaliel and Rabbi Joshua is reported in connection with a halakhah touching a firstling.[27] Here too we have a symptom of the underlying tension between the Sanhedrin and the Patriarch. Rabban Gamaliel takes severe disciplinary measures against Rabbi Joshua, thus adding to the accumulated resentment against the Patriarch which, as we shall see, finally led the Sanhedrin to depose him. At the same time, it should be kept in mind that the whole subject of *bekhorot* was an exceedingly sensitive one for the *Nasi*. It had been reserved by common consent as the special preserve of the patriarchal dynasty; hence it was given separate and specific mention in the formula of ordination. The Patriarch could delegate authority over *bekhorot* — or withhold it.[28] So there was special reason for Rabban Gamaliel's severity in this case.

---

26 RH. II:8–9.
27 Bekh. 36a.
28 Yoma 78a: "Once they asked Rabbi Eleazar: Does a scholar who is a Fellow of the Academy need special permission (from the Patriarch) to declare a firstborn animal fit for ordinary use? ... This was a matter reserved to the Patriarchs as a special distinction." See also Sanh. 5a-b, where Rabbah requests this special permission from the Patriarch Judah I, and gets it; while Rav also seeks that permission — and it is denied!

Before we deal with the "revolt" in the Academy, when Rabban Gamaliel was deposed, it is worth noting that there had already been several halakhic disputes in which Rabbi Akiba had sided with the Sanhedrin against Rabban Gamaliel. The Patriarch took umbrage at this:

> Rabban Gamaliel said to him: Akiba, why do you inject your-self into this contested issue? He answered: Rabbi, you your-self have taught us to interpret Exodus 23:2 to mean: 'Incline towards the many.' That is, even though you say thus-and-so, the halakhah follows the majority.[29]

In this instance, Rabban Gamaliel asked only that his opinion be given weight enough for the question to remain moot. He was not asking Rabbi Akiba to accept his opinion, but to allow that the question was still undecided. Rabbi Akiba, however, acting here as spokesman for the Sanhedrin, would not give the Patriarch's opinion weight equal to the majority of the Great Beth Din.[30]

The story of how Rabban Gamaliel was deposed from his office as Patriarch is related in both Talmudim with certain variations, some of them significant.[31] At issue was the right of members of the Sanhedrin to teach halakhah according to their own opinions, regard-less of whether the Patriarch agreed. The specific question over which the break came was whether or not the evening *tefillah* is voluntary or required. On this matter, the Mishnah quotes Rabban Gamaliel: "A person is to pray The Eighteen every day".[32]

Before we go further it should be observed that for the generations following the Destruction, there were certain areas of the halakhah that had become especially crucial, and one of these was the liturgy. Prayer had become central in the life of the people, and Rabban Gamaliel had taken some very important steps regarding it. It was

29   Tos. Ber. IV:12 (Zuck. 11); Bavli ibid. 43a. Comp. Tos. Bez. II:12 (Zuck. 204) and Dem. V:24 (Zuck. 56).

30   According to one tradition, Rabbi Akiba was put under a ban for detain-ing 'more than forty pairs of witnesses' who had seen the new moon, and were on their way to Yavneh. (Yer. R.H. I:57b). "R. Judah the Baker said: Heaven forbid! it was not R. Akiba etc." Comp. Bavli ibid. 22a. In this instance, the Patriarch máy have won the majority over.

31   Bavli Ber. 27b-28a; Yer. ibid. IV:7c-d, and Taan. IV:67d.

32   Ber. IV:3.

a sphere in which he must have felt it imperative to hold the reins of authority rather tightly. There were many other matters on which he differed sharply from Rabbi Joshua, but about which he saw no need to limit debate or insist on uniformity of practice. Here, however, as with the release of flawed firstlings and the proclamation of New Moons — issues where the prestige of his office was at stake — Rabban Gamaliel took his stand.

At first it looked as though the majority, like it or not, would have to bow to his will, as it had on two previous occasions. But then, his rough treatment of Rabbi Joshua led them to rebel. They deposed Rabban Gamaliel, and named Rabbi Eleazar ben Azariah to succeed him — in my opinion, because the latter was of priestly lineage. But the revolt did not last long; the breach was soon mended.

The reconciliation was spoken of as a gesture to the Patriarch "out of respect for his father's house." In modern terms, this means the Sages became convinced that it was in the public interest for the dynasty of Hillel to continue in office. But a problem and a question arise here. The problem concerns the language of the Mishnah. The day of the revolt is spoken of as "the day they seated Rabbi Eleazar ben Azariah in the Yeshivah."[33] But that phrase means only that he received his ordination. How is that possible, seeing that on the same day they made him Patriarch, (or at least head of the Academy)?

This problem was noted by Louis Ginzberg, who then pointed out that the accounts make no specific mention of the Patriarchate. He therefore suggested that Rabban Gamaliel was deposed only from the headship of the Academy, but *not* from his office as Patriarch.[34] This is a solution which I find myself unable to accept.

For one thing, there is evidence that the position of the *Nasi* really *was* involved.[35] Then, as to Ginzberg's argument that the scholars would not have dared interfere with the Patriarchate because the office was a quasi-governmental one, the objection can be dealt with. The Mishnah indicates that, for one reason or another, Rabbi

33 Zev. I:3; Yad. III:5 and IV:2.
34 *Perushim* etc. vol. III, pp. 190–197.
35 Ber. 27b: "(R. Eleazar) is rich, so that if it becomes necessary to pay court to Caesar, he will be able to do so."

Eleazar had not yet been ordained, and the Sages ordained him "on that day" with the express purpose of making him *Nasi*. By their very act they were refusing to recognize that office as constitutionally independent of their will. The Patriarch was to be regarded as one of their own, no more than *primus inter pares*. It might even be said that "that day" witnessed a constitutional crisis, in the course of which the Patriarchate was, in principle, abolished.[36] Hence the phraseology of the Mishnah, which makes no mention of the *Nasi*. The Romans may have felt the same way; they had recognized Rabban Gamaliel not because of his lineage, but because he was the head of the Sanhedrin.

So much for the problem of phraseology. Now to the question: what were the consequences of this crisis? The Babylonian Talmud reports a compromise in purely academic terms: Rabban Gamaliel was to give the lesson on two Sabbaths, and Rabbi Eleazar on the third.[37] The Yerushalmi reports an administrative-structural compromise: Rabbi Eleazar ben Azariah was to remain President of the Court (*Ab Beth Din*).[38] It might therefore be said that the latter position came into being as a result of the clash.[39] Against that, there is the report from Temple days which has Rabban Johanan ben Zakkai co-signing an official document along with Rabban Gamaliel the Elder;[40] and there are other indications of a pre-Rabbi-Eleazar President of the Court in the Beth Din of Rabban Gamaliel the Younger. So we cannot be positive about this question; but we can say that, as a result of the crisis, the principle of multiple leadership was firmly established — a duumvirate, or perhaps even a triumvirate *(Nasi, Ab Beth Din, Hakham)*.

The net effect of the compromise, then, was on the one hand to elevate Rabban Gamaliel above the Sanhedrin in his capacity as *Nasi* — *the* national leader; and on the other hand to give the status

36   A latent tension like this probably existed during the Second Commonwealth between the Sanhedrin and the High Priest.
37   The correct reading, although some versions have "one Sabbath" and "three Sabbaths."
38   So also Yer. Pes. VI:33a: "R. Eleazar b. Azariah remained the Number Two."
39   "R. Joshua was Ab-Beth-Din" (B.Q. 74b) no doubt refers to a local court. So too in the case of Aqavyah ben Mehalalel (Eduy. V:6).
40   Midrash Tannaim, ed. Hoffman, p. 176. See above, p. 91.

of President of the Court to the Sanhedrin's own elected chairman.
Another outcome of the dispute had its effect on the students of
the Academy:

> It was taught: On that day they dismissed the doorkeeper and
> allowed the students to enter the Academy. For Rabban
> Gamaliel had set strict standards of admission to the House
> of Study. But on that day they had to add many benches.[41]

At issue were differing definitions of the role of the Yeshivah. Was
it academic (for pure study) or practical (for the training of judges
and teachers)? It is a reasonable assumption that the Sages had
never accepted the right of Rabban Gamaliel to control procedures
in the House of Study.

The confrontation between the Sanhedrin and the Patriarch was
at bottom a clash between polarities: between freedom and the
need for order; between the collective idea and the leadership principle; between spiritual guidance and national discipline. The historic
situation played into the hands of Rabban Gamaliel. The Sages
recognized the national need, and restored their imperious leader to
power — but on the basis of a compromise.

The two opposites determined to work together: there would
be liberty, but it would be controlled; the "monarchy" would be
restored, but its power was to be limited; the national-political
leadership was recognized — but side-by-side with it a collective
religious leadership was to function, autonomous but related to the
other.

At the beginning of the third century the two elements of leadership began to drift apart, but they never became completely estranged. Indeed, they continued to co-operate with one another in some
measure for as long as both existed.

41 Ber. 28a.

PART THREE

RESISTANCE RENEWED

CHAPTER FIFTEEN

THE JEWRIES OF THE MIDDLE EAST

The twenty years from 115 to 135 of our era deserve to be called a major watershed in the history of the Jewish people. The reason is that those two decades are bracketed at either end by the last two massive attempts to cast off the yoke of Rome by force of arms. Viewed in the perspective of the centuries, the decisive turning point for the mother country (and consequently for the people as a whole) came at the later date, when Hadrian finally succeeded in crushing the Bar Kokhba Revolt (132–135). But for the great Diaspora Jewish communities of the time, located chiefly in the nearby lands of the eastern Mediterranean and western Asia, the critical juncture was passed two decades earlier during the regime of Trajan, when the Jews of Egypt and Cyprus and Cyrenaica and Libya and Mesopotamia rose up in arms against the rule of Rome (115–117).

It is true that our present study is centered on the history of the Jewish people in its own land. Yet we cannot ignore those bloody events in nearby countries. For one thing, the Jews of Judaea may not have been entirely uninvolved. And for another, there is every justification in the larger perspective of history for coupling the insurrections under Trajan in the teens of the second century with the revolt under Hadrian so soon thereafter in the thirties of the same century. Barely a couple of generations later the Mishnah, no doubt reflecting the popular memory, recalls these events as the last two parts of a single sanguinary process: "the *polemos* (war) of Vespasian ... the *polemos* of Quietus ... and the final *polemos*."[1]

But perhaps our perspective misleads us; and it may be that the popular memory tends to blur distinctions. Certain serious ques-

1 [Sot. IX:14. For the correct reading, see Lieberman, *Tosefta Kifshuto*, Sot. p. 767. Schürer was aware that "Titus" is an error; see his *Geschichte* I, p. 667, translation by Vermes and Millar I, pp. 533–4.]

tions of fact confront the historian who deals with the events of 115-7. Is there any real evidence of resistance activity in Judaea during Trajan's reign, while all that fighting was going on abroad? And if there is, can we be sure that whatever happened was all part of the same insurrection? Either way, we are compelled to ask where the motivating force for these outbursts of violence came from — from the homeland or from the Diaspora? As a corollary question, what about the nature and goals of the uprisings under Trajan? Was this essentially a politico-messianic movement, with the aim of ousting the Romans from the Middle East and establishing a "Kingdom of Israel" in Judaea and neighboring lands? Many historians, Jews and non-Jews alike, believe exactly that; from which it follows that the prime moving force came from the Land of Israel. According to this reading, the early decades of the second century witnessed a great movement of national liberation planned and directed, strategically and tactically, from the national center in Palestine. The majority of historians, however, while granting the nationalistic and messianic nature of these "wars of the Jews," do not believe that they were actually co-ordinated, much less that the Jews of Judaea were in charge.

It is possible, of course, that the causes for the uprisings in the various Diaspora countries are to be sought for in local conditions. If that be so, then whatever happened in Judaea would have to be seen as secondary, with the Jews of the homeland lending nothing more than a sympathetic hand to their brethren abroad.

We shall have to examine each of these problems briefly, before weighing all the available sources in an attempt to arrive at a reasonable picture of the events. But even before any of that, we must offer a brief survey of the Diaspora prior to the year 115, as a background to the explosions of that year.

As far as we know, the communities involved were those mentioned above: Egypt, Cyrenaica and Libya, Cyprus, Mesopotamia and Babylonia. (Actually, the only country to which we can devote much attention is Egypt, the largest of the diasporas and the one about which we know most.[2])

2 [The reader of English will be helped by Victor Tcherikover: *Hellenistic Civilization and the Jews,* transl. by S. Applebaum, Philadelphia-

EGYPTIAN JEWRY

According to Philo, there were one million Jews in Egypt in his day, 200,000 of them in the capital city of Alexandria.[3] It is estimated that the entire population of the country was seven or eight million.[3a] That would make the Jews about 12 to 14 percent of the total.

Outside the capital, it seems that the Jews were distributed fairly evenly throughout the country. They had settled everywhere "from the slope into Libya to the boundaries of Ethiopia," that is to say, in Lower, Middle and Upper Egypt.[4]

ORIGINS

Opinions vary as to what made Jews migrate from Judaea to Egypt, and not only to Alexandria, but to the provinces as well. Nevertheless, it is possible to list certain causes, even though we cannot determine their relative importance. The causes were:

1) Enforced migration, such as the transport of prisoners-of-war, slaves (sold and subsequently freed) and the import of soldier-farmers to serve as settled garrison troops. This applies to Ptolemy I (ca. 313 B.C.E.) and again to the period after the war with Rome (66–73 C.E.).

2) Voluntary expatriation for external political reasons; for example, the Jews who left for Egypt with Onias (160–150 B.C.E.) because they were opposed to the Seleucid occupation.

3) Flight for internal political reasons. Josephus tells us, for example, that after Jannaeus Alexander had won his war against

Jerusalem, 1959; Salo Baron: *The Jewish Community*, Philadelphia 1942, vol. I, pp. 75–117; and by Mary Smallwood: *The Jews in the Roman Empire*, Leyden 1980, chap. 10. The English translation by Vermes and Millar of Schürer's durable *Geschichte d. Jüd. Volkes* had at the time of writing not reached Vol. III, where a thorough survey is to be found on pp. 1–150. See also I. Fuchs: *Die Juden Aegyptens*, 1924; and I. Heinemann, *Antisemitismus*, in Pauly-Wissowa's Realenzyklopädie, Supplement V. Stuttgart 1931, pp. 3–43.]
3 [*In Flaccum*, 43, trans. Colson (Loeb Classics, IX, p. 327.]
3a [Excluding Alexandria, there is an estimate of 7 million by Diodorus Siculus (first century B.C.E.) 2:31:8, Loeb Classics I, pp. 103–5; and about a century later by Josephus of $7\frac{1}{2}$ million (JW II:385).]
4 [Philo, ibid.]

the Pharisees, 8,000 Jews left Judaea for Egypt;' and there is corroboration for this in the Aggadah.⁵ Similarly, in the civil disturbances that marked the last years before the Destruction, numbers
of citizens fled the country to get away from the Zealots and the
Sicarii. The refugees were either men of property, who feared
expropriation, or opponents in principle of those who were in
control.

4) Emigration for economic reasons. As Philo puts it:⁶

> So populous are the Jews that no one country can hold them,
> and therefore they settle in very many of the most populous
> countries . . . of Europe and Asia.

Actually, we do know that the natural increase of the Jewish
population of Judaea during the Second Commonwealth was so
great as to constitute a serious economic problem. But it must be
granted that, apart from this population pressure, there was the
attraction of Egypt's relatively greater economic opportunity. However, although this may have lured a certain number of Jewish
migrants to Egypt, it does not provide sufficient grounds for concluding, as some historians do, that "the Jewish bent for trade and
commercial skill" was the principal cause for the emigration of
Jews from their own country. We shall in due course examine the
assumption that the Jews of Egypt (and of other Diaspora communities) were to an inordinate extent merchants and traders; and
we shall show that this assumption is quite unfounded.

It should be added that from the time of the Hasmoneans, economic distress was experienced by certain circles because of the
unsettled conditions created by repeated civil disturbances and
foreign interventions. Emigration inevitably resulted from these
events, as it did from natural causes, such as the fluctuations in
rainfall to which the country had been prey since time imme-
morial.⁷

5   Ant. XIII: 383; JW. I:98; [Sot. 47b; Yer. Hag. II: 2, 7d.]
6   [*In Flaccum* 46; Colson, vol. IX p. 327.]
7   Apart from the many biblical "descents into Egypt," Celsus says there
    was a Jewish tradition that Jesus went to Egypt in search of work,
    and was employed as a day-laborer. [Quoted by Origen in *Contra
    Celsum* I: 2]

5) It is likely that the spiritual and national centrality of Eretz Israel in the consciousness of the Diaspora Jews played a role in the movement outward from Judaea of cultural emissaries. The religious connection was maintained not only by the pilgrimages from Egypt to Jerusalem, and by the exchange of communications between the two centers, but also by the flow into Egypt of Sages and teachers, who brought with them the literature that had been created in the homeland, as well as instruction in methods of interpreting the Torah. A case in point is the well-known legend told by Aristeas, who describes how 72 scholars came from Jerusalem to Alexandria to translate the Torah into Greek. Another example is the grandson of Ben Sirah, who translated (in Egypt) his grandfather's book of wise sayings, now called "Ecclesiasticus."

Some of these teachers and scholars probably returned to Judaea; others doubtless remained in Egypt. But they could hardly have constituted a statistically important element in the growth of the Jewish community.

6) Lastly, the Jewish population grew by the influx of converts to Judaism. This phenomenon existed throughout the days of the Second Commonwealth, and reached its peak towards the end of that period. Historians are divided in their view of this development. There are those who believe that the Jews deliberately set out to preach their religion to the pagans. Others deny the existence of any Jewish proselytizing efforts, and ascribe the trend towards conversion to direct contacts between Jews and non-Jews. The latter, they say, were attracted by the religious and moral example they encountered in dealing with Jews.

There is probably a measure of truth in both these views. But the fact itself — that there was a great wave of conversion to Judaism throughout the Diaspora, Egypt included, during the last pre-Christian century and the first years of the present era — is amply attested. It cannot be denied that there were also some desertions from the Jewish ranks. But these were numerically insignificant when compared with the movement in the other direction.

OCCUPATIONS AND ECONOMIC SITUATION

The little that we know about the economic pursuits of the Jews of Egypt derives from the chance survival of certain papyri. We are therefore in no position to describe the relative distribution of occupations. We can only catalogue the information that happens to have reached us for the period of the Second Commonwealth and for about a generation after the Destruction.

1) Professional soldiering: Jews followed the military career from Persian and Ptolemaic times right up to the Roman period.

2) Military colonization: This involved farming in strategic settlements whose manpower provided military reserves.

3) Police service: During the second century and the beginning of the first century B.C.E. we find Jews in Egypt in important positions of command in both the military and the police.

4) Farming: Most Jewish agriculturalists were tenants on government land, as were almost all farmers in Egypt.

5) Sheep and cattle raising.

6) Tax collecting: Some of this was on a fairly large scale. (It seems that this profession did not attract significant numbers.)

7) Others: This includes artisans and other skilled workers, including sailors. The papyri give the impression of small numbers, but Philo speaks in one breath of farmers, sailors, merchants and craftsmen.[8] And the Tosefta, in an often quoted passage, describes how the worshippers in the Great Synagogue at Alexandria were seated according to trades and occupations.[9]

> The people did not sit at random, but rather grouped by trades, with goldsmiths in their own section and silversmiths in theirs, blacksmiths in their part and weavers in theirs . . .

Elsewhere we are told that the Temple authorities in Jerusalem brought up skilled artisans from Egypt for the baking of the shewbread, the preparation of the incense, the repair of the golden flute and the fixing of the sacred brass pestle.[10] The range of skills involved gives us some idea of the occupations followed by Egyptian Jews.

8) Our list concludes with a small number of men of substance, probably merchants and ship-owners.

8   *In Flaccum*, VIII:57; [Colson IX, p. 335.]
9   Tos. Suk. IV:6, (198); also Bavli ibid. 51b and Yer. ibid. V: 55b.
10 Tos. Yoma II: 5–6, (184); Tos. Arakhin II:3–4, (544).

From the evidence at hand, therefore, it may be assumed that the economic condition of Egyptian Jewry was fairly sound, and that there were indeed those among them who were quite well off. But it must be stressed that there is no evidence whatsover that they turned to commerce in any appreciable numbers. Some of them no doubt *were* merchants; most likely, a normal proportion of the total.

COMMUNAL ORGANIZATION

Where there were Jews in considerable numbers, they organized themselves for community living. Sometimes this urge for social cohesion took the form of a special Jewish quarter. We know of such "Jewries" in Alexandria, Oxyrhynchus and Apollinopolis Magna. But we also know that Jews behaved similarly in other countries of the Diaspora. The Jewish quarter was the focus of Jewish life, but not all the Jews lived there, nor were they required to do so.

The synagogue was the center of Jewish community life. There the Jews congregated on Sabbaths and Festivals, as well as on other occasions. Some papyri show that there were synagogues in Egypt as early as the third pre-Christian century.

The Jewish communal authorities were, for the most part, chosen by election. The administrative structure of the communities followed that of the Greek city. This can, of course, be viewed simply as normal acculturation; but it seems to me that it may be connected with the demand of the Jews to have their *politeuma* (corporate entity) recognized on an equal footing with the Greek *polis*. The question deserves further study.

The principal community was that of Alexandria. Until the time of Augustus it was headed by an Ethnarch, whose position may be compared to that of the Patriarch.[11] Thereafter, according to one source, the community was led by a *gerousia*, a council, it seems, of 70 members; but Philo indicates that the office of Ethnarch persisted into Roman times.[12] On the other hand, there is indirect evidence that the *gerousia* existed early in the Ptolemaic era. But

11 Ant. XIV: 7:2 (117).
12 *In Flaccum*, 74; [Colson, IX, p. 343.]

why is it not possible that both these institutions — the Ethnarch and the council — functioned side by side throughout, even if we grant that there were changes in the balance of authority between them over the course of the years?[13] It is also possible that the Ethnarch and the *gerousia* had authority, not only over the Jews of Alexandria, but also over the whole of Egyptian Jewry.

CIVIL AND POLITICAL ISSUES

There are distinctions to be made under this heading which are frequently blurred — a confusion for which there are old precedents going back to Philo and Josephus. The subject should be viewed thus: The Jews throughout the Empire enjoyed religious autonomy, more commonly known as "special rights" or "privileges," which enabled them, legally and politically, to live "in accordance with their own laws." On the other hand, and at the same time, their civil status was that of citizens of the country they inhabited, or of the city-state (*polis*) if they happened to live in one.

The main significance of the autonomy was this, that it gave the Jews the right to organize into communities, and carried with it religious freedom, including exemption from certain obligations. Thus, they were excused on religious grounds from compulsory military service, and from appearance on Sabbaths and Festivals in court or in government offices.

A further aspect of this autonomy was the right to maintain Jewish courts as well as certain ancillary institutions connected with them. In Alexandria, for example, there was a Jewish registry of records. The scope of this judicial autonomy raises a number of questions. For example, did it include criminal jurisdiction? What sanctions were available to it? With these and related matters we shall not deal here, as they would take us too far from the subject of our present study.

There was still another right that the Jews of the Diaspora enjoyed: the right to maintain their bond with the religious and national center in the Land of Israel. This contact found its most striking outward expression in the *mahazit ha-sheqel* — the volunt-

13 Comp. Schürer, *Geschichte* III, pp. 77 ff.; and Bludau: *Juden und Judenverfolgungen im alten Alexandrien*, p. 16.

[332]

ary annual tax which each individual Jew throughout the world sent to the Temple in Jerusalem.

In general these rights existed throughout the Ptolemaic and the Roman periods, as they had earlier during the days of Persian suzerainty. The government of the day usually reaffirmed the Jewish status, although it is true that there were times when the rights of the Jews were temporarily suspended, as they were under the prefect Flaccus. But even apart from such episodes, the ruling circles in Hellenistic cities, especially those in Asia Minor, resented the autonomy enjoyed by the Jews, and made frequent efforts to have it restricted or abolished.

The civil status of the Jews in Egypt was the focus of a great deal of trouble throughout the Roman period. It remained a bone of contention up to the time of the Destruction, and probably afterwards as well, and was doubtless the main contributing cause of the repeated clashes between Jews and Greeks in Alexandria. The struggle itself will be reviewed in detail later. At this point let us simply state what appears to have been the essence of the problem.

As formulated by contemporary sources, the issue was: were the Jews of Alexandria citizens? Or were they resident aliens, not entitled to participate in the governance of the city nor to other rights of Alexandrians, insofar as these related, for example, to tax matters, to the penalties of the criminal law, and to the manner of acquiring Roman citizenship?

The issue affected not only the Alexandrian Jews; it bore in a large measure on the whole Egyptian Diaspora, especially on those Jews who lived in the provincial capitals. Even though such urban centers were not legally autonomous, still their citizens were possessed of certain special rights compared to the indigenous inhabitants of the countryside at large. What it boils down to is this: were the Jews to be classified as Egyptians, that is, natives devoid of civil rights, or were they to be counted as Greeks? Or perhaps the Jews did not fall into one single category, but were of several kinds, subject to change. These are questions we shall have to examine later.

RELIGIOUS AND CULTURAL ISSUES

Most Egyptian Jews were loyal to the faith of their fathers, in individual practice as in communal life. Of course, there were those whose attachment was tenuous, or was perhaps more a matter of abstract principles than of an actual way of life. Philo does mention certain Jewish intellectuals who were extreme allegorists and neglectful of the mitzvot. But there is no reason to suppose that there were many such Jews. Nor are there grounds for the theory advanced by Friedländer, who would have us believe that the Egyptian Jews and their brethren throughout the Hellenistic Diaspora were in general given to religious indifference and heretical-assimilatory tendencies. The contrary is the case. Religious feeling and discipline played a prominent role in the life of Egypt's Jews. They even produced movements of extreme pietists, including such self-denying contemplatives as the Therapeutae.[14]

The same can be said about their national feelings. It might be supposed that the Jews of the Diaspora, especially those of Egypt, regarded themselves essentially as nothing more than a faith community. However, the facts as we know them show that the Egyptian Jews, at any rate, thought of themselves as members of the Jewish people domiciled away from their natural home, the Land of Israel, with whose fate and whose people they identified. True, they did not always see eye to eye on political issues with their brothers in the homeland, but emotionally they felt themselves to be one people.

Naturally, such generalizations must be accompanied by a note of caution. It is only logical to assume that there were some Jews who were drawn, as time went by, into the cosmopolitan Hellenistic-Roman life of Alexandria, and who became integrated into the sophisticated social whirl and cultural ambience of that great metropolis. For such Jews, the ties with their people, whether in the Diaspora or in the old mother country, would undoubtedly have become rather tenuous. But these were the few. Most Egyptian Jews saw themselves, and were seen to be, a distinct religio-national

---

14 [Philo: *De vita Contemplativa;* Conybeare, F.C.: *Philo Concerning the Contemplative Life,* in JQR o.s. VII (1895) pp. 755 ff.]

entity, members of a people called "the Jews," united by common aspirations and by a shared community life.[15]

In the letter which he prepared for delivery to the Roman Emperor Gaius Caligula, the Jewish leader Philo describes how the Jews of Egypt saw themselves, in the following phrases:[16]

> Jerusalem is the mother city not alone of Judaea, but of most of the other countries as well, by virtue of the colonies settled in those places.

The point is that the Jews of the Diaspora are spoken of here as expatriates whose home country is Judaea, rather like those Greeks who live abroad in overseas colonies.[17] So that even from a political point of view, the Egyptian Jews regarded themselves as somehow citizens of Judaea. In fact, it seems that the Roman government shared that viewpoint to a very great extent, at least up to the Destruction. The school of thought represented by Mommsen suggests that this very principle lay behind the Roman willingness to extend autonomy to Jews everywhere in the Diaspora.

In another context Philo himself makes entirely explicit the sense of impermanence with which the Jews of his time regarded their residence in the lands of the dispersion:[18]

> When, having done penance, the Israelites will have gained this unexpected liberty, those who were but now scattered in Greece and the outside world over islands and continents will arise and post from every side with one impulse to the

---

15 See Alon in *Qiryat Sefer*, 16 (1939) pp. 158–160, or *Mehqarim* II, pp. 151–153 (not in JJCW).

16 *Embassy to Gaius*, xxxvi, 281 [Colson X, p. 143.]

17 Compare the attitude expressed in the following passage from *In Flaccum* VII, 46 [Colson vol. IX, pp. 327–329]:
"And while they (the Jews of the Diaspora) hold the Holy City where stands the sacred Temple of the Most High to be their mother city, yet those which are theirs by inheritance from their fathers, grandfathers and ancestors even further back are in each case accounted by them to be their fatherland in which they were born and reared, while to some of them they have come at the time of their foundation as colonists to the satisfaction of their founders."

18 *De Praemiis et Poenis*, 165, 168, 171 [Colson viii, p. 417 ff.]

one appointed place ... When they have arrived, the cities which but now lay in ruins will be cities once more; the desolate land will be inhabited; the barren will change into fruitfulness ... the enemies who rejoiced in the misfortunes of the nation ... will find that their misconduct was directed not against the obscure and unmeritable but against men of high lineage ...

Imbued with very much the same sense of living away from home is the legend related in chapter six of the Third Book of Maccabees. The Jews of Alexandria are supposed to have been assembled in the Hippodrome, under threat of massacre if they reject the royal edict to worship Dionysus. Eliezer the *kohen* utters a prayer, and here are some of the words put into his mouth:[19]

> King of great power, most high, Almighty God, who governest all creation with lovingkindness, look upon the seed of Abraham,[20] the children of Jacob Thy sanctified one, the people of Thy holy inheritance who are unjustly perishing, strangers in a strange land ... If our life has become ensnared during our sojourn in impious deeds, deliver us from the hand of the enemy ... Let it be shown to all the heathen that Thou art with us, Lord, and hast not turned Thy face away from us, as Thou hast said: 'Not even when they were in the land of their enemies have I forgotten them' *(Lev. 26:44)*.

Victor Tcherikover, to be sure, argues that the author of Third Maccabees speaks for a small minority of his contemporaries, a sort of "Zionist-nationalist opposition" in Egyptian Jewry.[21] I find it difficult to agree with him on this point. There does not seem to be any reason for supposing that the author of the book in question was anything but wholeheartedly in support of the struggle being waged by Alexandrian Jewry for full citizenship rights. The

---

19 [Moses Hadas, *The Third and Fourth Books of Maccabees,* Harper Bros. New York, 1953 (Dropsie College Apocrypha) p. 71; Charles, *Apocrypha and Pseudepigrapha of the O.T.* I, p. 171.]

20 [Comment by Hadas: "A manifest Hebraism, *zera avraham;* the opening of this prayer is very like the opening of the Amidah."]

21 V. Tcherikover: "Third Maccabees as a Historical Source" (Hebrew) in *Zion* X, pp. 17–19.

only ones he has anything against are those who are prepared to give up their Jewish religion for "material advantage;" who are willing to worship idols, if that will guarantee them citizenship. He has no quarrel with civil rights, only with turncoats.

This is not the place to analyze in detail the relevant passages in Third Maccabees. Suffice it to point out that the remarks quoted above from Philo are just as "Zionist." They are couched, to be sure, in a different style; but basically they express the same sense of Jewish peoplehood, the same attachment to the Land of Israel. This, from the same Philo who was in the forefront of the struggle to maintain the civic rights of the Alexandrian Jews!

The nature of that struggle must now be considered briefly. On the face of it, the Jews of Egypt were asking to eat their cake and have it. There is an apparent paradox in wanting to be recognized as an autonomous ethnic community on the one hand, and demanding full equality as citizens on the other. However, this seeming contradiction was met squarely by Philo, when he put the case for the Alexandrian Jews in the passage from *In Flaccum* quoted above.[22] From a religio-ethnic point of view, he declares, we Jews belong to Judaea, and our capital is Jerusalem. But from a social point of view, we are citizens of the city where we were born, and where our ancestors have lived for many generations, as long as the Greeks have!

The struggle of the Alexandrian Jews for citizenship rights was based in part on social and ethical considerations. They did not want to be treated as "natives," but rather as "free men" in their own home city; not as "barbarians," but as "civilized people." But it must be admitted that there was an even more compelling motive for their struggle — the very valuable privileges that went with citizenship. Citizens were exempt from the poll tax; they could receive municipal support when in need; they had certain priorities in matters of trade — to name some of the advantages.

The situation had another aspect. Citizenship status, and the resultant entree into municipal government, could help secure the autonomous institutions of the Jewish community, and ensure

22 See note 17.

freedom of religion to its members. It must be remembered that Jews in Alexandria and in other Greek cities had already had some unpleasant experiences in these matters during the Roman period. City councils had denounced Jewish autonomy and disallowed Jewish religious freedom. Membership on the city council would provide a strategic vantage-point for defending Jewish rights at the source, without having to go hat-in-hand to the governor, or to Rome.

Thirdly, citizenship status meant to the Jews that they could not be regarded as mere resident-aliens subject to the real masters of the city; that they would not be living where they did on sufferance, rather than as of right. This explains why the struggle for ethno-religious autonomy became confused in the literary sources (Philo and Josephus) with the struggle for citizenship, just as the distinction between the two issues was blurred in the actual confrontation.

LANGUAGE

It is well known that the Jews of Egypt, like those of other countries in the Hellenistic Roman world, adopted the Greek language as their own. They spoke it; they wrote in it; Greek even found its way into the synagogue, into the prayers and the reading of scripture. But a widely held view, according to which Greek took over the synagogue service in the Egyptian diaspora to the exclusion of all other tongues, cannot be accepted. The very many papyri and ostraka that have been found written in Hebrew and Aramaic dating from the Ptolemaic and Roman periods, both before and after the Destruction, show that these ancestral tongues were still in use in Egypt for literary purposes, for worship, and even for other needs.

These documents can be categorized as follows: a) fiscal accounts kept by Jews in Aramaic; b) epitaphs in Hebrew, including some inscriptions on the wrappings of mummies; c) snatches of Hebrew prayer, among them the famous Nash Papyrus, with its text of the *Shema* and the Ten Commandments;[23] d) fragments of

23 [The present consensus dates the Nash Papyrus at ca. 150 B.C.E. See Frank M. Cross in JBL (1955) p. 148, n. 3; and Moshe Greenberg in Encyclopedia Judaica XII, 833.

literary works in Hebrew,[24] and e) from the Byzantine period, circular letters on community matters.[25]

Actually, the use of Hebrew and Aramaic by Jews in other lands of the Hellenistic Diaspora, such as Syria and Asia Minor, is well documented. The subject deserves to be studied in depth, but we cannot enter into it, in the present context. We must content ourselves with noting that the phenomenon was continuous, rather than sporadic, although our documentation of it is richer for the generations after the Destruction.[26]

HELLENISTIC JEWISH LITERATURE

Most of the Jewish literature in Greek was produced in Egypt. This generalization applies to those complete books which have survived such as the works of Philo and the books of the Apocrypha, as well as to other works of which only extracts have reached us.[27] The chief exceptions are the works of Josephus Flavius; the *History* (now lost) by Justus of Tiberias; the original of Second Maccabees, which was written by Jason of Cyrene; and a few opuscula whose authorship is in doubt.

The literature can be classified as follows: 1) history and chronology, like Demetrius, Eupolymus, Artapanus; 2) historical legend, such as postscripts to the Book of Daniel, and possibly the *Letter of Aristeas;* 3) apologetics (anti-defamation); both poetic, like the Sibylline Oracles, and prose, as in Philo; 4) liturgy, exemplified by the works of Ezekiel the Poet; 5) religious philosophy: whether prose, like Aristobulus and Philo, and especially Pseudo-Phoklydes, or poetry, as in the *Wisdom of Solomon;* 6) homiletics (perhaps Maccabees IV); 7) a kind of hagiography, like Philo's *Life of Moses,* and his companion pieces on Abraham and Joseph; 8) halakhah, like Philo's *On the Special Laws,* and *On the Ten Commandments;* and 9) proverbs and apothegms.

---

24 Fuchs, op. cit. pp. 122–144.
25 Journal of Egyptian Archaeology, II (1915), 209 ff.
26 There are those who interpret this phenomenon as deriving solely from a nationalistic reaction to the Destruction; but I am not inclined to agree.
27 For a thorough survey of this literature, see Schürer, *Geschichte* III, pp. 424–716.

[339]

An examination of this body of writings shows that, whether written for a non-Jewish audience, or addressed primarily to Jews, it deals almost exclusively with Jews and Judaism.[28] Thus we may say that Hellenistic Jewish literature is essentially Jewish in purpose and scope. Of more general contributions to Greek culture written by Egyptian Jews (or for that matter, by other Jews of the Greek-speaking world) we have none — neither such works nor the mention of them, not in general philosophy, not in history, not in Greek philology, nor in the natural sciences, nor in poetry. There is no parallel among the Jewish authors to those Greeks who wrote about *Roman* history, or the history of other peoples.

This fact must be given great weight in any assessment of the cultural and spiritual attitude of Egyptian Jewry to Hellenism. We have grown accustomed to speaking of a symbiotic relationship between these two cultures, under the heading "Hellenistic Judaism." The man who, more than any other, symbolizes this blending is always taken to be Philo, the Jew of Alexandria. No doubt there is a strong element of truth in this view. Egyptian Jewry absorbed, to a greater or less degree, the cosmopolitan atmosphere of the Hellenistic world, with its Greek language, its acquaintance with Greek literature and its notions of social structure and ethical principles based on the philosophical schools of the Roman period.[29] But it would be a mistake to think of these as the chief determinants in the inner life of the individual Jew, or as the well-springs of any creativity he might have been blessed with. The factors of his acculturation remained, so to speak, external to him; or at most, as in the case of Philo, added certain elements to his personal world-outlook and to his creative drive. But for Philo as for his fellow-Jews these elements were secondary to what was central to their being — their Judaism.

Let us examine what the Jews of Egypt thought of themselves,

28 An exception would be Philo's essay, written apparently in his youth, "On the Eternity of the Universe." As for the Sibylline oracles, although their subject is the fate of the nations, their tenor is Jewish-religious.

29 Except for Philo, Egyptian Jewish writers do not as a rule show much breadth of familiarity with the classic literature of Hellas, nor depth of penetration into its world-outlook.

especially as expressed in the apologetic literature of the time, that is, those polemical writings in which Jewish authors defended Judaism and the Jewish people against various accusations. Some of these accusations were completely false, and could easily be dismissed. But there were others which turned out to be half-truths, so that explanations were called for. For example, the Jews were charged with separatism *(amixia)* — with keeping themselves to themselves. They would neither intermarry with Gentiles, nor sit down to eat with them. A corollary and more damning accusation was the charge of "hatred of mankind" *(apanthropia)*.

As far as the Jew was concerned, he was not embarrassed by these charges. He saw no need to be defensive about Jewish dietary laws and marriage restrictions. Even so thoroughly Hellenized a Jew as the author of *Aristeas*, justly thought of as a man who was eager to harmonize the two cultures — even he makes no bones about this Jewish exclusivism. Yes, it was so, and he was proud of it. Into the mouth of Eleazar the High Priest he puts the following, with reference to the dietary laws:

> Our lawgiver, being a wise man ... fenced us round with impregnable ramparts and walls of iron, that we might not mingle at all with any of the other idolatrous nations ... more especially because we have been distinctly separated from the rest of mankind (with regard to incest and homosexuality).[30]

We call such statements "apologetic," but the term is purely technical. The tone of this literature is almost aggressively proud. These Egyptian Jews know the worth of their Judaism, they are sure of its superiority to Hellenic culture, and they have no hesitation in saying so. This comes out in their rather naive claim that Hebrew civilization is older than the Attic. When Philo says that thinkers like Plato drew on the "philosophy" of Moses, he is merely summing up long-accepted ideas. Josephus is repeating a widely-held notion when he speaks of the greater antiquity of Jewish history. But the real nub of the Jewish anti-defamation

30 [Charles, *Apocrypha* etc. II, p. 107; comp. *Aristeas to Philocrates,* ed. and transl. by M. Hadas, New York, 1951. pp. 157, 161.]

literature is the claim that the value system and world-outlook of Judaism are superior to those of Hellenism (especially in the Helleno-Roman period).

In their controversies with Gentile authors, Jewish writers bore down on certain principles by which they themselves were persuaded that Judaism was the superior civilization. The fundamentals they stressed dealt with *religion, society* and *ethics.* They contrasted the pure monotheism of Jewish belief with polytheism, which seemed to them absurd and depraved. They pointed out how the discipline of the mitzvot imbued their own lives with depth and seriousness, compared with the superficial triviality characteristic of most of the life around them. The willingness of the Jews to suffer martyrdom for the sake of their religion made them wonder whether the Greeks knew of anything at all which so enhanced the value of *their* lives that it was more important than life itself.

There were other points which the Jewish authors brought up in this debate. Jewish sexual morality and the stability of Jewish family life they contrasted sharply with the casual promiscuity common among the general population. They also pointed an accusing finger at the widespread acceptance of infanticide as a means of getting rid of unwanted babies. They spoke of mutual aid among the Jews, of social solidarity and a low crime rate, contrasting these with the egotism and indifference to others which were taken for granted in the Hellenistic countries of the East at that time. They claimed that the Jews were not prone to that love of luxury and self-indulgence so characteristic of the upper classes in the world around them. In the Jewish community, they wrote, there was relative social equality. Indeed, in this literary polemic between Jews and Greeks in Egypt, the Jews proudly claimed to be loyal to the social ideals of the Hebrew prophets. It is not our purpose here to pass judgement on the validity of these claims. But it must be said that every one of them contains at least some measure of truth.

The Jewish literature of Hellenistic Egypt is shot through with these ideas. Philo frequently gives voice to them; they reverberate in the writings of Alexandrian Jewish authors whose works have *not* been preserved, but who are quoted liberally by Josephus

Flavius. Perhaps it would be best to present here a few extracts
from the Jewish apocalyptic writings called "The Sibylline Oracles,"
where some of these polemical points are couched in rather sharp
terms.

O race that delights in blood, crafty wicked race of godless
    men
Liars and double-tongued, immoral, adulterous, idolatrous,
Of wily devices, within whose heart is evil, a frenzied spur,
Snatching for yourselves, having a shameless mind!
For no man endowed with goods will give any part to another,
But miserable meanness shall be among all mortals,
And faith they shall never keep at all,
But many widowed women shall have other secret lovers
For lucre's sake;
And gaining husbands shall not keep hold of the rope of
    life . . .

But these diligently practice justice and virtue,
And not covetousness, which is the source of myriad ills to
    mortal men,
Of war and desperate famine.
But they have just measures in country and city,
Nor do they carry out robberies one against another,
Nor do they drive off herds of oxen, sheep and goats,
Nor does a neighbour remove his neighbour's landmarks,
Nor does a man of much wealth vex his lesser brother,
Nor does anyone afflict widows but rather assists them,
Ever ready to supply them with corn and wine and oil.
And always the wealthy man among the people
Sends a portion of his harvest to those who are in want,
Fulfilling the command of the Mighty God,
For Heaven hath wrought the earth for all alike.[31]
There shall be thereafter a holy race of God-fearing men,
In righteousness possessing the law of the Most High.
They shall dwell happily in their cities and rich fields,
Themselves as prophets exalted by the Immortal One,

31 Charles, II, pp. 379 and 383.

And bringing joy to all mortals.

For to them alone Mighty God hath given discreet counsel,
And faith, and an excellent understanding in their hearts,
In that they give not themselves to vain deceits,
Nor honour the work of men's hands ... such things as men
  with minds devoid of counsel do honour.
But they instead raise heavenward holy arms ...
More than any men are they mindful of the purity of
  marriage;
Nor do they hold unholy intercourse with boys,
As do the Phoenicians, Egyptians and Latins.[32]

These passages resound with the messianic conviction that the Jewish people is destined to lead the nations, and that it is qualified for that role by its moral superiority. The lines quoted are a prime example of the bold attack on the culture of the pagan Greek world, aiming at no less than the destruction of that culture. To be sure, the attack purports to come from within; it is put into the mouth of a pagan visionary. But its goal remains the enthronement of Judaism as the religion of mankind.

These basic elements, then: 1) belief in the superiority of Judaism and refusal to accommodate to the pagan world; 2) a messianic vision which promises victory to the Jewish religion and to its people; and 3) the sharp ongoing polemic with ancient culture, particularly that of the Greeks — all these were undoubtedly primary factors in the struggle of the Jews with the Greeks in Alexandria and elsewhere. They figure, too, in the attitude of the Roman ruling powers to the strife between the two communities. But before we get into the details of that strife, let us glance at the relationship between Egyptian Jewry and its own mother country.

TIES WITH ERETZ ISRAEL

We have already noted that the Jews of the Diaspora looked to the Land of Israel as their homeland. The missive from Jerusalem urging the Jews of Alexandria and of all Egypt to celebrate the new feast of Hanukkah (and purporting to date from the early days of the Maccabean era) reads in part as follows:

32   Ibid. p. 389.

God it was who saved all His people and restored to all their heritage and the kingdom, the priesthood and the holy way of life as He had promised to us in His Torah. For our hope is in God that He will soon have mercy upon us and will gather us together from under Heaven to the Holy Place.[33]

The clear implication of these words is that the Land of Israel, and the Kingdom of Judaea, and the priesthood — all now liberated from the foreign yoke — are the common possession of the entire Jewish people. Thus, although the Jews of the Diaspora were not themselves directly involved in the miracle of the liberation, they were in duty bound to join in the celebration of that miracle — Hanukkah — along with the Jews of the homeland.[34]

But we have been dealing with atmospherics. What about more palpable connections between the Diaspora and the homeland?

According to tradition, the Torah was translated into Greek in Egypt by Jews who came from Judaea for that specific purpose. From that time onward, Egyptian Jews translated Hebrew books, canonical and extra-canonical, and added them to the body of "scripture." An example is the translation of the *Wisdom of Ben Sira* (Ecclesiasticus) by the author's own grandson.

The above-quoted letter from Jerusalem to Alexandria contains the following passage:

Judah also collected for us all the reports and rumours that had been spread abroad due to the outbreak of the war. We still have them, and if you ever have need of them you may send messengers to us to get them.[35]

This letter is only one testimony among many to a close connection between Egypt and the mother country in matters of religious practice. The relationship is also underscored by the importance attached

33 [II Macc. 2:17; *The Second Book of Maccabees*, ed. by Solomon Zeitlin, transl. by Sidney Tedesche, Harper Bros. N.Y. 1954 p. 115; Charles, I, p. 134]

34 One might note here the enthusiastic reception which the Jews of Alexandria accorded Agrippa I as "King of the Jews" in 38 C.E. It was both a measure of their bond with the old country, and a contributing cause to the outbreak of violence that year.

35 II Macc. 2:14 [Zeitlin-Tedesche pp. 113–5; Charles I, p. 134.]

to the despatch of the annual Temple tax to Jerusalem. Philo waxes eloquent as he describes the ceremonial solemnity with which the half-shekel was collected, the emissaries were chosen and the contribution sent off to Jerusalem. He conveys the ardent emotion that accompanied the fulfillment of this mitzvah.[36]

From a number of sources we learn that there were Egyptian Jews who sent priestly offerings *(terumot u-ma'aserot)* to Judaea, although they were not really required to do so. Probably many of them also made the festival pilgrimages to Jerusalem. The existence in the Holy City of a "Synagogue of the Alexandrians" in the last few generations before the Destruction is probably connected with these pilgrims.[37]

Special importance attaches to the *political* co-operation between the Jews of Egypt and the Jews of the Land of Israel. There is the well-known story about Cleopatra's plan to annex the Judaea of Alexander Jannaeus. As it happened, her Commander-in-Chief was the Jew Ananias son of Onias.[38] He told her frankly that if she went ahead she would alienate all the Jews of Egypt.

The same holds good for the attitude of the Jews toward the expanding power of Rome. Josephus tells us that Jews — particularly Jewish military men — played a role in facilitating the Roman conquest of Egypt during the campaigns of Gabinius (57 BCE) and Caesar (47 BCE) in response to suggestions from Hyrcanus and Antipater.[39] And while it is probable that other political considerations of a more general nature entered into these decisions, there is no reason to discount the influence of Judaean political factors on the attitudes and actions of the Jews of Egypt.

JEWS VERSUS GREEKS

From the time of Caligula onward, the strife between Greeks and Jews in the city of Alexandria grew in intensity. Violent inter-communal clashes recurred, some of them quite bloody. There were adversary proceedings at the Imperial Court in Rome, with one set of

36 *De Spec. Leg.* I:xiv: 78, Colson VII p. 145; and xxviii: 144, Colson VII, p. 181. Compare *Legatio ad Gaium* xxxi: 216, Colson X, p. 113; Josephus Ant. XVIII: 9:1 (312).
37 Tos. Meg. III: 4 (224).
38 [Ant. XIII, 285, 287, 349, 354–355.]
39 [Ant. XIV: 99; 127–132.]

Alexandrians lobbying against the other. The accompaniment to all this was a drumbeat of verbal violence, as the two sides slashed at one another in a literary war of words.

Recent finds of papyri have provided us with some extremely important documents, adding a good deal to our knowledge and shedding considerable light on a number of problematical points connected with this struggle. On the other hand, these newly discovered sources are full of obscure passages, so that they bring with them not only new light, but also new mystification.

A proper examination of this complicated and drawn-out chapter in history would take us far afield. Scholars who have plunged into the detailed study of the sources, old and new, are by no means agreed in their conclusions.[40]

We do know that violent manifestations of the tension in Alexandria recurred over a period of some 75 years. Concerning the first of these eruptions, in the year 35 C.E. when Caligula was Emperor, we know quite a lot, because of two famous briefs by Philo: *Against Flaccus* and *Embassy to Gaius.*

The second clash, in a sense an aftermath of the first, took place at the beginning of the reign of Claudius. Our information about it comes from Josephus[41] and from certain papyri.

Some scholars argue for a third outbreak in the year 53, towards the end of the regime of Claudius. Their hypothesis, for such it remains, is based on papyrological evidence.

The next episode, according to the testimony of Josephus, took place in the year 66 C.E. It was an offshoot of the Jewish War against Rome which broke out in that year.[42]

Josephus also describes an incident following the end of the War of the Destruction, involving a political attack by the Greeks of Alexandria against the Jews. Finally, there is papyrological

---

40 For an analysis of the newer sources, see V. Tcherikover: *The Jews in Egypt in the Hellenistic-Roman Age in the Light of the Papyri;* Jerusalem, Magnes Press, 1963, 2nd ed. Hebrew, with English resume. [See now *Corpus Papyrorum Judaicarum* by Tcherikover, Fuks and Stern, Jerusalem–Cambridge Mass., The Magnes Press, Vols. I–III, 1957–1964.]

41 Ant. XIX : 278–279.

42 JW II : 487 ff.

evidence of a suit between the contending sides at the court of Trajan in the year 111 or 112, with an implication that the action had been preceded by a bloody clash.[43]

Even a cursory examination of this chain of events is bound to throw light on what followed: the ultimate explosion that can only be described as warfare (115 to 117 C.E.). However, before we can undertake that examination, we must first grapple with a rather elusive question. Did the enmity between Jews and Greeks in Egypt come into being only during the Roman regime? Or do its roots go back further, to the time of the Ptolemies?

Actually, we have no clear-cut evidence of violence between Jews and Gentiles in that earlier time. The pre-conquest polemical literature does, to be sure, reflect an undercurrent of antagonism in the area of culture and religion. But the few references to head-on disagreement in the second and first pre-Christian centuries seem to involve the governing authorities of the Ptolemaic regime, rather than the mass of the people. We get the impression that even then there were rumblings about the subject which was to become, in Roman times, a major *casus belli*: the civic status of the Jews of Alexandria. But we know nothing specific about what dispute may or may not have agitated the city before the Roman legions appeared on the horizon.

Almost all scholars trace the inter-communal turbulence in Alexandria to the beginnings of the Roman occupation of Egypt; indeed, they connect that turbulence with Rome's policy vis-a-vis her Greek and her Jewish subjects. But from that point of agreement they diverge sharply into two very different schools of thought about the nature and meaning of the events.

The majority view is that the Jews, who were helpful to the Romans when the latter conquered Egypt in the days of Gabinius and Caesar, remained loyal subjects at Rome. The Alexandrian Greeks, on the contrary, remained unreconciled; they hated their new masters. But they were powerless to give open expression to this enmity, so they took out their frustration on Jews.[44] As a

43   An apparent reference by Dio Chysostom to disturbances in the year 110 is inconclusive.

44   [For example: "The Alexandrines were in permanent opposition to Roman rule... Over against them stood the Jews, the 'good boys' of

matter of fact there are historians who explain the anti-Jewish "pogroms" altogether as veiled acts of rebellion against Rome.[45] This view of the matter has one main virtue. It offers a simple explanation for the fact that successive Roman emperors, in trials that were brought before them in Rome, decided in favor of the Jews, and imposed penalties on their adversaries, the delegates of the Alexandrian Greeks. After all, if the Jews were being attacked because of their loyalty to Rome, such an outcome was only to be expected.

But there are serious grounds for doubting the validity of this interpretation. To be sure, the Alexandrians had ample reason to regret their reduction to the status of "provincials," where once their metropolis had been the capital of a world power. But then, they were not the first citizens of a Hellenistic seat of government to whom that had happened. Actually, they were the last. What is more, from an economic point of view it may well be that Alexandria gained rather than lost by being incorporated into the Empire.

It is also true that the citizens of ancient Alexandria had a bad name when it came to civic unruliness. They were said to be prone to mob violence, a rascally rabble who enjoyed mocking and insulting foreign dignitaries, including Romans sent to govern them — even visiting Roman emperors themselves (in which respect they were rivalled by the people of Antioch in Syria).

But in spite of all this, we have no reports that the Greeks of Alexandria mounted or even attempted any real acts of rebellion against Rome throughout the entire period we are surveying. Nor do we have any evidence of anti-Roman sentiments on their part, open or covert, that would distinguish them from any of the other

the Empire ... to attack the Jews seemed a safer and less direct way of attacking the authority of Rome." H.I. Bell, *Antisemitism in Alexandria*, in J.R.S. 31 (1941) pp. 4–5.] Comp. Wilcken, *Zum Alexandrinischen Antisemitismus*, in the *Abhandlungen* of the Saxon Royal Society, Philological-Historical Division, vol. 27, 1909, pp. 786 ff; and I. Heinemann in his article *Antisemitismus* in supplement V of Pauly-Wissowa.

45 M. Rostovtzeff, *Social and Economic History of the Roman Empire*, Oxford 1957, [Vol. I, p. 117.]

Hellenistic cities of the east. Neither is there anything to show that these people harbored any special nationalistic feelings. The Alexandrians were loyal to the Roman emperors, certainly no less than the Jews were. It may be granted that their adulation — even deification — of the Caesars was insincere, and contained a goodly element of fawning flattery and hope of reward. But that does not prove that they were motivated by nationalism or rejection of the occupier, or longing for the political freedom which they had lost.

There is a totally different way of looking at the situation, one which sees the *Greeks* as Rome's favorite sons and collaborators. This view is given its fullest expression by Victor Tcherikover. He tells us that Rome, from the very beginning of her conquests in the eastern Mediterranean, had showered political favors on the Greeks, and made them partners in ruling over subject peoples, those with the lowly status of *dediticii*. This policy was applied in Egypt as well, when it too became part of the Empire.

But in this instance there was a special problem, because of the varied ethnic elements in the population. It was not always easy to differentiate between Egyptian subject-natives and Egyptian Greeks, properly members of the ruling class. As for the Jews, the Romans could take one of two options: either they could treat them as part of the ruling elite, like the Greeks; or they could classify them with the masses of natives. Whenever the Romans chose the latter course, the Jews were mortally offended, and fought against their status with every means at their disposal. Of course, says Tcherikover, we know that every Roman government from Augustus onward upheld the right of the Jews to religious freedom and juridical autonomy; but their civil status was exactly the same as that of all subject peoples throughout the Empire. In that respect, only one people enjoyed a special role as collaborators of Rome: the Greeks.

So it came about, according to this theory, that the Romans imposed the poll-tax on the Egyptian Jews, and divested them of whatever civic rights they had acquired under the Ptolemies. No doubt this did not happen all at once; the Romans applied their imperial logic by easy stages. But they were under constant pressure from their Greek allies who, as a consequence of their ongoing quarrel with the Jews, kept urging the authorities to deal harshly with them.

This analysis also has one outstanding virtue: it gives us a simple explanation for the disturbed state of Egyptian Jewry up to and including the bloody revolt under Trajan. It tells us that from the very beginning of Roman rule in the land of the Nile, the Jews there found themselves reduced to subject status. Their consequent resentment against Rome was intensified by the Destruction of Jerusalem, and fed by messianic hopes and Zealot-inspired angers. All this rage came to a boiling point in the great second-century uprising against Rome, and against those who were regarded as her lackeys and helpers — the Greeks of the Hellenistic diaspora.

This interpretation of the data is, as we have pointed out, useful. But it does give rise to certain fundamental questions. It would be a good idea to examine them carefully.

For one thing, there is the attitude of Philo and Josephus. If Roman rule was so bad for the Jews, why is it that these two leading Jewish writers of the time lavish so much praise on the Emperors of Rome, whom they speak of as defenders of the Jews against the Greeks? And they do this even in contexts where they cannot be suspected of having any axe to grind. To be sure, what the Romans were defending was probably the *religious* autonomy of the Jews, those "special rights" against which the Greeks were always agitating. But that drives us to the conclusion that the Roman rulers repeatedly recognized that the Jews (everywhere in the Empire) were entitled *not* to be regarded as *dediticii* — conquered, subjugated natives. Furthermore, when we find Augustus and other successive rulers turning down petitions from autonomous Greek municipalities in Asia Minor who wanted to put a stop to the Jewish practice of sending the half-shekel contribution to Jerusalem, it becomes a bit difficult to speak about an imperial policy of keeping the Jews in their place, and about the Greeks as accessories to it.

Then too, if the Romans began a process of downgrading the status of the Jews, and the Greeks kept pressing them to follow that process through to its logical conclusion, how explain the fact that emperors repeatedly ruled against the Greeks when these issues were contested at the imperial court? Furthermore, many leading historians ascribe to Rome, quite rightly in my opinion, an ongoing policy of treating the Jews as a useful element in the structure of the Empire, at least up to the war of 66.[46] Unless we agree with that assessment of Roman policy, we will find it difficult to explain Rome's persistent maintenance of Jewish rights in other parts of the Hellenistic world, such as Asia Minor, in the teeth of constant anti-Jewish pressure from the overseas Greeks.

Indeed, the occurrence of such pressures at about the same time in countries that had been under Roman rule for many generations makes one wonder whether the Roman conquest of Egypt had anything at all to do with the deterioration of the Jewish position there. Is it not possible that we are dealing, at least partially, with a *general movement* throughout the Middle East of Greeks against Jews? Might not such a movement have been generated by Greek resentment against the imperial confirmation of the special rights of the Jews?

Perhaps we shall not be far from the truth if we assume that it was Roman strategy to maintain an even-handed policy between these two competing client peoples, the Greeks and the Jews. Because of the roles these peoples played in the great Empire, it was perhaps in Rome's interest not to come down too heavily on the side of one or the other, but to hold a balance between the two.

This reading of the situation would seem to be the one best calculated to explain Roman conduct up to the year 66 C.E., when the Jewish War broke out. It would even illuminate the shifts in Rome's tactics, including her actions with respect to the violence in Alexandria. If the assumption is correct, we would have evidence of divided counsels within the ruling circles in Rome itself; we might also gain some insight into the divided counsels within Jewry, both at home and abroad.

It is rather difficult to envisage the Greeks of Alexandria and Egypt as partners of Rome in ruling the country of the Nile. We know that the Alexandrians petitioned Augustus to let them have

46 In this respect, there was another people that played a similar role, and the analogy between the two is striking. Both Greeks and Jews had large and widely scattered diasporas; both were in a sense dependent on Rome for protection; and both had reason to be loyal to the Empire.

a senate (*boulē*) which would have symbolized the autonomy of this, the Empire's second city. The Emperor turned them down. When the question arose again during the regime of Claudius, he too said no. It makes little difference whether there had been an Alexandrian Senate under the Ptolemies. The point is that neither the conquering Caesar nor any of his successors were willing to grant the Alexandrians the institution of self-rule for which they so ardently lobbied — not until Septimius Severus, over 300 years after the conquest.

Actually, all Augustus did for the Alexandrians was to leave them in possession of whatever limited rights they had had under the Ptolemies. He certainly gave no sign of making them partners in the governing establishment. Nor should it be forgotten that Egypt was unique among the provinces of the Empire, in that it was under the direct control of the Emperor through his prefect — a sort of "crown colony" if the anachronism be permitted. That makes it all the more unlikely that there was any plan to share power with the Greek residents (although the latter undoubtedly enjoyed certain hereditary privileges, and probably manned much of the bureaucracy). It is well known that, contrary to the practice elsewhere in the East, the Ptolemies did *not* found Greek-style cities, but rather settled Greeks in the countryside. This remained true of the Romans, until approximately the year 200 C.E.

But we have left unanswered the question whether Greek-Jewish animosity had its roots in earlier, Ptolemaic times. The absence of specific information gives us only the thin ice of an *argumentum e silentio,* against which there is the probability that at least the politico-legal dispute *does* go back that far. Besides, Josephus claims that the debate had been going on since the city was founded.[47] Thus, while the evidence is not conclusive, we cannot discount the possibility that dissension between Greeks and Jews in Alexandria predated the Roman conquest.

As to the etiology of that dissension, we have presented two schools of thought that agree in tracing the trouble to the Roman conquest, and then take diametrically opposite views of what fol-

47   JW II: 18:7 (487).

lowed. One view sees the Greeks attacking because the Jews took the side of Rome. The other view has the Romans oppressing the Jews, with the Greeks lending a willing hand. We have tentatively suggested a middle view: the Romans found the quarrel brewing, and played one side off against the other, in accordance with the shifting interests of empire.

We must now leave these preliminary generalities, and look at the events themselves.

Under Gaius Caligula

In the year 38 of the present era the Alexandrians began a series of hostile acts against the Jews. They were aided and abetted by the Roman prefect Flaccus, who at first played his hand behind the scenes, but then revealed his position quite openly. The events were triggered by the visit of Agrippa I, to whom the Jews of Alexandria gave a right royal welcome.[48]

The subsequent rioting and bloodshed is described by Philo. But we are left to wonder what the Greeks (and their principal supporter, the prefect) had in mind. Were they out for some fundamental change in the status quo? Were they attacking the religious autonomy of the Jews? Their claim to citizenship? Perhaps even their right of residence?

First, the Greek mob placed statues of the Caesar in the synagogues. This makes it appear that they were demonstrating against the old entrenched Jewish religious privileges (which included exemption from emperor-worship). But there is no conclusive proof that they expected to get these privileges permanently abolished.

Second, we know that the mob tried to drive the Jews out of one of the two main city districts where Jews lived, and to chase those who lived in areas scattered around town into the one remaining "Jewish neighborhood." This would constitute a direct attack on the Jewish freedom of residence (*katoikia*) in the city of Alexandria.

---

48 "But jealousy is part of the Egyptian nature, and the citizens resented a Jew having been made a king just as much as if each of them had thereby been deprived of an ancestral throne." Philo, *In Flaccum* V: 29 [Colson, IX, p. 319.]

Thirdly, there was the order issued by Flaccus, in which he characterized the Jews as "foreigners, but newly arrived." It may have been his intention to quash thereby the Jewish claim to full citizenship. If so, then it proves that this was one of the issues at stake. On the other hand, the phrase used by Flaccus may have been intended to show that the Jews should not even be treated as resident aliens *(katoikoi)* with the right to live and conduct business in the city. If that was the meaning of his order, then its intent was to back up the attempt of the local Greeks to confine the Jews to one sector of the city.

In any case, the evidence from Josephus and from papyri dealing with the first days of Claudius makes it fairly clear that the dispute evolved into an argument over citizenship rights.[49] After Flaccus was dismissed from office, the new prefect allowed both Jews and Greeks to carry their cause to the Imperial court in Rome. The process is described by Philo in his "Embassy to Gaius." When the Emperor asked, "What have you Jews got to back up your claim to citizenship (the apparent meaning of *politeias)*?" and the Jewish representatives stood up to present their case — Caligula turned his back on them and walked out!

UNDER CLAUDIUS

About three years later, the same issue was adjudicated at the court of the Emperor Claudius. Josephus tells us that when Claudius was proclaimed Caesar after the assassination of Caligula, the Jews of Alexandria armed themselves and turned in revenge on the Greeks of the city.[50] Learning of this, the new Emperor first directed his prefect to restore order; and then, or soon thereafter, he issued the following edict:[51]

> Having from the first known that the Jews in Alexandria
> called Alexandrians were fellow-colonizers from the very

---

49 The events under Claudius were merely an epilogue to the riots of the year 38. As for Philo, I believe that he too was concerned about *municipal* civic rights, although he is not entirely specific about this point.

50 Ant. XIX: 5: 2 (278).

51 Ibid. 281 ff.

earliest times jointly with the Alexandrians and received equal civic rights *(ises politeias)* from the kings as is manifest from the documents in their possession and from the edicts; and that after Alexandria was made subject to our empire by Augustus their rights were preserved by the prefects sent from time to time, and that these rights of theirs have never been disputed; moreover, that at the time when Aquila was at Alexandria, on the death of the ethnarch of the Jews, Augustus did not prevent the continued appointment of ethnarchs, desiring that the several subject nations should abide by their own customs and not be compelled to violate the religion of their fathers; and learning that the Alexandrians rose up to insurrection against the Jews in their midst in the time of Gaius Caesar, who through his great folly and madness humiliated the Jews because they refused to transgress the religion of their fathers by addressing him as a god; I desire that none of their rights should be lost to the Jews on account of the madness of Gaius, but that their former privileges also be preserved to them, while they abide by their own customs; and I enjoin upon both parties to take the greatest precaution to prevent any disturbance arising after the posting of my edict.

Josephus goes on to relate that Claudius also sent the following message to be promulgated in all parts of the empire:

Kings Agrippa and Herod, my dearest friends, having petitioned me to permit the same privileges to be maintained for the Jews throughout the empire under the Romans as those in Alexandria enjoy, I very gladly consented, not merely in order to please those who petitioned me, but also because in my opinion the Jews deserve to obtain their request on account of their loyalty and friendship to the Romans. In particular, I did so because I hold it right that not even Greek cities should be deprived of these privileges, seeing that they were in fact guaranteed for them in the time of the divine Augustus. It is right, therefore, that the Jews throughout the whole world under our sway should also observe the customs of their fathers without let or hindrance.

I enjoin upon them also by these presents to avail themselves of this kindness in a more reasonable spirit, and not to set at nought the beliefs about the gods held by other peoples, but to keep to their own laws. It is my will that the ruling bodies of the cities and colonies and municipia in Italy and outside Italy, and the kings and other authorities through their own ambassadors, shall cause this edict of mine to be inscribed, and keep it posted for not less than thirty days in a place where it can plainly be read from the ground.

The second of these two documents proves that it was not only in Alexandria that the Jews had to struggle for their rights, at least on the political front. From other parts of the empire, too, they had to invoke the aid of Claudius Caesar, just as in an earlier generation Jews had had to appeal to Augustus Caesar because Greek municipalities were attempting to undermine Jewish rights.

The same edict also contains the Emperor's warning to the Jews against insulting other religions. This shows us that the Jewish war of words against paganism was probably a contributing cause to the clashes between them and the Greeks. To put it plainly, one senses resentment against Jewish missionary activity.[52]

But it is the first of the documents quoted above from Josephus which seems to have most to tell us about the issues between the Greeks of Alexandria and their Jewish fellow-townsmen. The edict purports to deal with a) citizenship (Claudius rules that the Jews are full citizens); and b) autonomy. Somehow, the latter subject seems to get entangled with the first. The Emperor talks in the same breath about equal citizenship and about the right of the Jews to observe their own religion and elect their own ethnarch — as though these two areas were one and the same! That would be enough to make us suspect the authenticity of this document. But there is more to it. The genuineness of the version in Josephus is challenged by evidence much more compelling.

The evidence is contained in a papyrus in which is recorded an official communication from Claudius on subjects of concern to the

---

52 Note also the implied bargain with the Jews: the government will back them, but it expects loyalty in return.

Alexandrians. Included are rulings concerning the very matters dealt with in the supposed edict quoted by Josephus. The problem is that the rulings he gives differ rather widely from those set forth in the papyrus. The relevant passages are presented herewith:[53]

> With regard to the responsibility for the disturbances and rioting, or rather, to speak the truth, the war against the Jews, I have not wished to make an exact inquiry, but I harbour within me a store of immutable indignation against those who renewed the conflict. I merely say that, unless you stop this destructive and obstinate mutual enmity, I shall be forced to show what a benevolent ruler can be when he is turned to righteous indignation. Even now, therefore, I conjure the Alexandrians to behave gently and kindly towards the Jews who have inhabited the same city for many years, and not to dishonour any of their customs in their worship of their god, but to allow them to keep their own ways, as they did in the time of the late Emperor, the divine Augustus, and as I too, having heard both sides, have confirmed. The Jews, on the other hand, I order not to aim at more than they have previously had and not in future to send two embassies as if they lived in two cities, a thing which has never been done before,[54] and not to intrude themselves into the games presided over by the *gymnasiarchoi* and the *kosmetai*,[55] since they enjoy what is their own,

53 [Tcherikover, Fuks and Stern: *Corpus Papyrorum Judaicarum*, published for Magnes Press, the Hebrew University; Cambridge Mass. 1960; Vol. II, p. 43.] Comp. H. Idris Bell, *Jews and Christians in Egypt*, Oxford University Press, London 1924, pp. 29 ff.

54 The passage is a difficult one. On the face of it, the Emperor seems to be complaining because the Jews have sent their own deputation, alongside the representatives of the Alexandrian Greeks. But then, how could he say that such a thing had never happened before? Three years earlier that is exactly what *had* happened at the court of Caligula (and the same thing would be repeated later under Trajan and Hadrian). Because of this difficulty, there are scholars who suggest that there were two Jewish delegations, one Liberal and one Orthodox, with the latter opposing full citizenship. I find this rather far-fetched.

55 This clause is also somewhat obscure. The translation given here is favored by most scholars, including Bell and Tcherikover. Another

and in a city which is not their own they possess an abundance of all good things. Nor are they to bring in or invite Jews coming from Syria or Egypt, or I shall be forced to conceive graver suspicions. If they disobey, I shall proceed against them in every way as fomenting a common plague for the whole world. If you both give up your present ways and are willing to live in gentleness and kindness with one another, I for my part will care for the city as much as I can, as one which has long been connected with us.

Obviously, these two documents contradict one another in a fundamental way. The version relayed by Josephus has Claudius recognizing the full civic equality of the Alexandrian Jews, whereas the papyrus shows the same emperor reminding the Jews that they are tolerated aliens in a foreign city. Not only that; they are warned to keep out of municipal sports events, participation in which was a symbol, and to a large extent a requisite, of full citizenship.

To be sure, the two documents agree in reasserting Jewish *religious* rights. Even so, it must be noted that the version given by Josephus is couched in language highly favorable to the Jews, while the papyrus, although it calls the Greeks to order with a show of even-handedness, is worded in a manner that must have fallen harshly — even offensively — on the ears of the Alexandrian Jews.

For the discrepancy between these documents, two different kinds of explanation have been offered. One way out is to deny the authenticity of the edict reported in *Antiquities*. According to this view, Josephus drew on Jewish literary sources which had dressed up the original edict by adding clauses favorable to the Jews. The result is an unreliable version from which it is no longer possible to disentangle the underlying original text.

A particular adherent of this view is Victor Tcherikover.[56] He espouses it not only because it explains the contradiction between

---

possibility, "let them not seek election as *gymnasiarchoi* and *kosmetai*." The *agones* had to do with election to office.

56 See his *Hellenistic Civilization and the Jews,* pp. 318 ff.

the two sources, but also because it answers problems inherent in Josephus' text itself. For one thing, the issues of citizenship and religious autonomy are not differentiated. Then there is the mention of the office of Ethnarch, which has nothing to do with the matter at hand. Other such questionable points are raised by Tcherikover, so that his final analysis is: the real edict is the one reflected in the papyrus. Claudius merely reaffirmed the religious autonomy of the Jews; their claim to citizenship he denied outright.

In my own view, however, the second line of explanation seems to make better sense: the two imperial pronouncements differ because they were issued at *different times*. The document quoted by Josephus was written very shortly after Claudius ascended the throne of the Caesars, to which high office he was helped in no small measure, as is well known, by Herod's grandson Agrippa I. Indeed, the edict itself makes mention of this great and good friend of the new emperor.

The epistle to the Alexandrians, as we have it in the papyrus, was written about half a year later, by which time Agrippa had already left Rome. It may be assumed that by now Claudius had a somewhat different view of the matter (perhaps certain important Romans who were part of the pro-Alexandrian lobby had brought their influence to bear). The thought is supported by Claudius' reputation for changeability, as reported by Tacitus.

Those who hold this view also point to subsequent anti-Jewish actions by this emperor: his expulsion of them from Rome, his edict forbidding them to assemble in synagogues, his abolition of the Judaean monarchy when Agrippa I died in the year 44 (on the pretext that the heir to the throne was not yet of age, although Agrippa II was 17 years old).

But I do not think that it is necessary to provide so much detail to prove that this particular emperor changed his mind. The fact is that the whole question of Jewish rights, civic or religious, had been very much in the balance for many years. The attitude of the emperors on this issue depended on their evaluation of the respective role of the Greeks and the Jews in the structure of the empire. In Rome, where policy was formulated and decisions were taken, there was an almost continuous political reappraisal: were the Jews a positive and desirable element (in official language "loyal and friendly")? Or were they, on the contrary, rebellious and subversive?

These opposing formulations occur over and over again in both official and literary documents of the period up to the War of the Destruction (and afterwards as well). So it seems altogether probable that the very question we have been examining was under constant debate in Rome among officials and makers of policy at the highest level. The varying results of this debate were felt by Jews in the Hellenistic cities of the empire — Alexandria included.

To put the matter differently, there were two lines of imperial policy in almost continual tension. One school of thought sought to bolster the position of the Jews vis-a-vis the Greeks; the other believed it was in Rome's interest to give the upper hand to the Greeks, at the expense of the Jews.

From this point of view, there is nothing surprising about Claudius' shifts of policy, any more than there is in other changes in the imperial treatment of the Jews from the first contact between Rome and Judaea to the end of the Second Commonwealth — and afterwards as well. Claudius himself explains, in his first pronouncement on the subject, why he is favorable to the Jews; it is because of their loyalty and friendship to Rome. Later, for reasons no longer clear to us, he takes the opposite tack, and against a background generally antagonistic to the Jews, he rules against them in the matter of Alexandrian citizenship.[57] Such an about-face was possible because the question of citizenship for the Jews of Alexandria had never been settled in law. No official ruling on the subject had ever been handed down.

57 The sharp reversal by Claudius is pinpointed by the diametrically opposed arguments advanced in the two documents before us. In the edict he justifies his affirmation of civic rights for the Jews not only by his intimacy with Agrippa and Herod, but also by the friendship and loyalty that the Jews have shown to Rome. In other words, she can rely on them — everywhere in the empire. But in the epistle, where he warns the Jews not to push for civic rights, he threatens that if they do, they will be regarded as a plague — everywhere in the empire. This echoes the line of those who had always regarded the Jews as an unreliable, rebellious element throughout the Roman world.

This means that the two conflicting pronouncements by Claudius get us no nearer to the truth about the citizenship question.[58] So, leaving that question temporarily in abeyance, let us first examine some very unfriendly language used by Claudius in his epistle to the Jews of Alexandria, words which contrast sharply with the phraseology in the earlier edict about "the friendship and loyalty to Rome shown by the Jews." In the later document Claudius warns the Jews of Alexandria not to

> bring in or invite Jews coming from Syria or Egypt, or I shall be forced to conceive graver suspicions. If they disobey, I shall proceed against them in every way as fomenting a common plague for the whole world.[59]

This enigmatic passage may have a bearing on the relationship between Judaea and the Diaspora, and hence it may be crucial to our understanding of the events of the years 115–117. But what does it mean? There are those who say that Claudius was hinting at Jewish Christians, who may have been coming into Alexandria to preach the new faith. I find this hard to believe.

Others suggest that the emperor was echoing fears expressed by the Alexandrians that immigration might make the Jewish community too powerful. That may be so. But there is a third possibility, and it seems to me to be the right one: the emperor meant actual armed men brought in to reinforce the Jews of Alexandria in their struggle with the Greeks of the city. Such cadres would

---

58 The extent to which the emperor was willing to disregard the truth can be seen from his statement (in the papyrus) that the Jews had *never before* sent a delegation of their own to Rome! (We can dismiss the notion that there were *two* such delegations; the idea is totally without foundation.) What seems to have happened is that the Greeks argued that the Jews *had no right* to send spokesmen, and when the emperor decided in favor of the Greeks he quoted from their brief, without too tender a regard for the truth. If indeed this is the way things were done, it may also help explain the irrelevant mention of the Ethnarch in the earlier edict, when the shoe was on the other foot. In both cases the emperor first decided which side he would favor. The resultant document then quoted selectively from the brief presented by the winning side.

59 See above, p. 358.

have come from the provincial towns of Egypt, and *from Syria,* which in Roman terms included Palestine.[60]

But even if it be granted that Claudius was warning the Jews of Alexandria against bringing in such reinforcements, what could he have meant by his threat "to proceed against them . . . as fomenting a common plague for the whole world" (i.e. the whole Roman empire)? Either the warning applies to the immediately preceding words (if the Jews bring in outsiders) or it applies to the epistle as a whole (if the Jews do not do everything that the emperor commands). I suggest that the first interpretation is the correct one; and that the phrase about the "common plague" echoes an anti-semitic cliché current at the time. A similar phrase occurs in a papyrus fragment recording a hearing before Claudius, the date of which is not certain. It is part of the so-called "Acts of the Pagan Martyrs," which provide a fragmentary record of three cases heard at Rome before the emperor.[61] Representatives of the Alexandrian Greeks brought the charges, presented their arguments, lost the cases — and paid with their lives.

The fragments that deal with "The- Acts of Isidoros and Lampon" show these Alexandrians arguing before Claudius as he sits with the senators comprising his *consilium,* in the presence of the empress and a group of noblewomen. The Alexandrians denounce Agrippa. Claudius complains about the killing in Alexandria of Theon, a friend of his, and refers to Isidoros as "the son of a harlot." Isidoros, unwilling to swallow the insult, retorts that he is nothing of the sort, but a gymnasiarch of the great city of Alexandria; and adds that Claudius himself is the unacknowledged

60 In support of this interpretation one may cite a similar clash between Greeks and Jews at about the same time in the city of Antioch, as reported by the sixth century chronicler Malalas. He says that thirty thousand Jews rushed up from Tiberias to support their brethren in Antioch. With all due allowance for Malalas' notorious exaggerations, it still remains probable that there is a kernel of truth in his story that the Jews of Antioch had help from outside. The fact is that Malalas is now generally thought to be credible on matters touching his birthplace Antioch, where, in addition, he seems to have had access to official records.

61 [*Corpus Papyrorum Judaicarum,* Vol. II, 1960, entries 154 to 159, pp. 55–107.]

son of the Jewess Salome. The upshot of the whole matter is that the Alexandrian delegates are condemned to death.

There are those who suggest that this episode took place in the year 53 C.E. when Agrippa II was in Rome. If so, then there must have been a fresh outburst between the Jews and the Greeks in Alexandria around that time.

But there is no reason why this document should not be connected with the hearing that took place in the year 44 C.E., at the beginning of Claudius' reign. If that is so, then we would want to pay special attention to a Berlin papyrus published in 1930.[62] In it, Isidoros accuses the Jews of trying to "foment disturbances" *(tarassein)* in the whole world. He also argues that the Jews, like the Egyptian natives, are payers of the poll-tax. Agrippa denies this, and says that it was never true at any time.

If the case of Isidoros was indeed tried in 44 C.E., then the menacing phrase used by Claudius in his epistle becomes all the more understandable. The time came when the emperor wanted to signal to the Jews that they had better not get out of line. In the time-honored manner of official discourse he used a phrase that had been part of a brief filed in his chancery not long before. Perhaps this was intended to convey the following message: "Your enemies have argued that you are a source of unrest throughout the empire. If you push too hard I may have to see things their way." If this is what Claudius meant by his threat, it may also throw some light on the general tension between Jews and Greeks in the Hellenistic cities throughout the Roman empire.

It is also significant that the Jews (represented by Agrippa) and the Alexandrians are shown in the Berlin papyrus disagreeing on whether the former are liable for the poll-tax. That is just another way of arguing whether or not they were citizens. The verdict seems to show that the emperor agreed with the Jews.[63] If that is

---

62 See Uxkyll-Gyllenband in the *Sitzungsberichte* of the Prussian Academy, Philosophical-Historical Section, 1930, pp. 665 et. seq. [Comp. CPJ, II, entry 156c.]

63 Those who think the Alexandrians were executed because of their insolence are on the wrong track. The report of their "brave" impertinence is obviously nothing but legend. Nobody ever went so far as to call the emperor "Jewish bastard" to his face. The simple explanation

so, then the Berlin fragment testifies to the authenticity of those Claudian documents quoted by Josephus, including the passages which aver that the Jews had civic rights.[64]

Whether or not the Jews of Alexandria ever really had such rights remains, nevertheless, an open question. Before the Letter of Claudius had come to light,[65] most historians thought that the Jews had full rights, and that the Greeks wanted those rights revoked. After 1924, when Bell published the text of the papyrus, opinion swung to the other extreme. Most scholars took at face value the statement by Claudius that the Jews were (and had been) mere resident aliens ("in a city not theirs"). However, what we have been suggesting here is that Claudius' epistle be read *in the light* of his earlier edict, as set forth by Josephus. We have attempted to show that the newly discovered document is evidence of a *reversal* in Roman policy, rather than objective testimony about the situation that had prevailed before that time.[66]

There is, then, no definite proof that the Jews of Alexandria were citizens of that city; nor is there — prior to the rescript of Claudius — any definite proof that they were not. In the absence of such proof, the reasonable conclusion seems to be that from the time of Alexander until the middle of the first century of our era the issue was never decided with any finality. It remained moot under the Ptolemies, and continued to be debatable under

---

is, that the Alexandrians brought suit against Agrippa (and the Jews) — and they lost. This would not be the only time when spokesmen for the losing side were executed.

[On the phraseology in the brief, compare Tcherikover in *Corpus Papyrorum II*, p. 68: "The sentence about the Jewish intention of provoking troubles throughout the world has its exact parallel in the letter of Claudius."]

64 See above, p. 356.
65 Above, note 53.
66 In support of this interpretation, it may be pointed out that when Claudius refused to grant a *boulē* (senate) to the Alexandrians, he said that they had never had one. But many historians believe that they *did* have such a council under the Ptolemies, until Augustus came along and abolished it. All of which goes to show how unreliable are statements made by the emperor when he is out to make a political point.

the Romans. Hence the wrangling over it between the Greeks and the Jews.

But in the midst of all this lack of definition, there are certain things which can be noted with reasonable certainty. For one thing, the Jews were never classified as "natives." At a minimum, their status was somewhere between that of the Hellenes and that of the Egyptians. Therefore, whether or not they had *full* rights, they had *some* rights. Secondly, whatever their status, it was not automatically acquired by every immigrant who came to Alexandria and joined the Jewish *politeuma*. Thirdly, even among the old families there were categories of citizenship. When Josephus speaks of Jews who enjoyed the rights of "Macedonians,"[67] he is letting us know that there was a privileged elite whose ancestors had served in the military forces of the Ptolemies, thereby winning rights which their descendants still enjoyed in Roman times, as the papyri show.

On the other hand, belonging to the ephebate — that is, having been educated in the *gymnasia* — was also an important qualification for citizenship. Did that keep the Jews out? It seems not. First of all, there were not a few Jews who qualified as *epheboi*. Then too, such an educational background was not absolutely *sine qua non*. There seems to have been a lower grade of citizenship, available even to those who were not enrolled in the *phylae* and the *demes*. This too was a source of contention between Jews and Greeks.[68]

Finally, there is the theory that posits that it was legally impossible to be a member of the Jewish community *(politeuma)* and a citizen of Alexandria at one and the same time.[69] The theory is without foundation, and must be rejected.

Having thus canvassed the question in most of its aspects, we seem to have demonstrated that any blanket generalization in this matter is probably wrong. We cannot say that the Jews of Alexandria, as a class, were ever possessed of civic rights. By the same token, we cannot say that no Alexandrian Jews ever were.

---

67 E.g. JW II, 487 ff; Ant. XII: 8; Apion, II: 35.
68 See Cambridge Ancient History, vol. X, pp. 295–296.
69 Engers, M. [in *Klio*, vol. 18 (1923), pp. 79 ff.]

EGYPTIANS AND JEWS

In this investigation of the background behind the events of 115–117, there remains one question which we have not yet raised. If we could know where the native Egyptian population stood in this tension, rivalry and bloodshed between the Greeks and the Jews in Alexandria, we might be able to estimate what role, if any, was played by the local populace when "disturbances" gave way to "uprising" during the regime of Trajan.

We have no unequivocal evidence to show whether the antagonism between Greeks and Jews was confined to those two peoples, or extended to all other gentiles. On the one hand, the drive of the Jews for full citizenship, and against being considered "natives," could scarcely have endeared them to the Egyptians. On the other hand, the rejection of the Jews by the Greeks might well have driven the former closer to the "barbarian" natives. But we do not know.

Or take the religious issue. The attitude of the Jews towards all pagans could easily have generated resentment among both Hellenes and Egyptians, drawing these peoples together in a shared antisemitism. It would be interesting to find out which factor predominated. But we simply do not know.

Nevertheless, there are historians who are prepared to assume that the Egyptians played a marked antisemitic role in the struggle. They call to witness Josephus, who lays stress on the Egyptian background of Apion, Lysimachus and Chaeremon, the leading antisemitic propagandists of his day.[70] The same historians also quote Philo, whose negative attitude to the ancient religion of Egypt can be demonstrated.[71]

But the evidence in both cases must be called into question. Josephus, for one, made no secret of his purpose in writing. He was a propagandist, an apologist. He wanted to defend the Jewish people against calumny, so with one eye on his Greek readers, he set out to prove that antisemitism was foreign to the Hellenic spirit. He wanted to show that its principal spokesmen were "bar-

---

70 *Apion*, I:223.
71 [E.g. *Sac.* 48, Colson II, p. 131; *Quod. Deus* 174, Colson III, p. 97.]

barians" who had insinuated themselves into the world of Greek culture; they were not "true Hellenes."

As for Philo, there· are times when he can be found admiring Egyptian culture.[72] Therefore, we should be careful not to make too much out of his abstract allegorical hermeneutics. True, in his system of symbols the religion of the Pharaohs is a metaphor with negative connotations. But this does not necessarily have anything to do with actual relations between the two peoples in his own day.[73]

It is possible that some light may be thrown on our problem by an analogous situation in a different country, under a different political system, at about the same time. Seleukia, on the banks of the Tigris, was then under Parthian rule. Following the collapse of the short-lived little "state" of Anilai and Asinai in Babylonia, a considerable number of Jews arrived in Seleukia in search of refuge.[74] They found that they had stumbled into a long-standing state of tension between the local native Syrian population and the local Hellenistic element. The Jews lined up with the natives, thus giving them the upper hand.

But not for long. The Greeks worked on some of the more prominent Syrians and won them over, and the balance shifted. Then both pagan elements in the population turned on the Jews, and the result was a bloody pogrom. This account, which comes from Josephus, shows that in his view, at any rate, the native population had no fixed loyalties. In the struggle between the Greeks and the Jews they might throw their weight now to one side, now to the other. Quite probably the situation in Egypt was not very different.

72 [Perhaps *de Leg.* 138, Colson X, p. 71.]
73 It is not uncommon to find III Macc. 3:8–10 quoted to prove that it was the Egyptians who were the real Jew-haters: "The Greeks of the city . . . were distressed for them (the Jews) . . . Some of their neighbors and friends and business associates offered pledges to protect them." But this passage merely contrasts the *citizenry* with the *king,* and proves nothing about the Egyptians.
74 Ant. XVIII:9:9 (374 ff.).

ALEXANDRIA IN THE YEAR 66

At about the same time that the Jews in Jerusalem were driving out the Roman garrison and, in effect, declaring war on Rome, the Jews in Alexandria were involved in some very bloody clashes which brought the Roman army into action against them, and led to a very heavy loss of Jewish lives. The question arises as to whether this was another in the long series of inter-community clashes between Jews and Greeks, or was rather, as most historians think, an integral part of the Jewish Revolt against Rome. It behooves us, therefore, to examine the account of the event as reported by Josephus:[75]

At Alexandria there had been incessant strife (*stasis*) between the native inhabitants and the Jewish settlers over the special status bestowed on them by Alexander the Great, and late confirmed by the Ptolemies and the Romans ... They *(the Jews)* were continually coming into conflict with the Greeks ... On one occasion when the Alexandrians were holding a public meeting on the subject of an embassy which they proposed to send to Nero, a large number of Jews flocked into the amphitheatre along with the Greeks; their adversaries, the instant they caught sight of them, raised shouts of "enemies" and "spies," and then rushed forward to lay hands on them. The majority of the Jews took flight and scattered, but three of them were caught by the Alexandrians and dragged off to be burned alive. Thereupon the whole Jewish colony rose to the rescue; first they hurled stones at the Greeks, and then snatching up torches rushed to the amphitheatre, threatening to consume the assembled citizens to the last man. And this they would have done had not Tiberius Alexander, the governor of the city, curbed their fury. He first, however, attempted to recall them to reason without recourse to arms, quietly sending the principal citizens to them and entreating them to desist and not to provoke the Roman army to take action. But the rioters only ridiculed this exhortation and used abusive language on Tiberius. Understanding then that nothing but the in-

75 JW II: 18:7 (487 ff.)

fliction of a severe lesson would quell the rebels, he let loose upon them the two Roman legions stationed in the city, together with two thousand soldiers who by chance had just arrived from Libya, to complete the ruin of the Jews. Permission was granted them not merely to kill the rioters, but to plunder their property. . . .

Finally, Josephus goes on to say, the governor took pity on the Jews, and called off his troops. But the Alexandrians, who had joined the fray, continued to pillage, until the Romans had to separate them by force from the corpses they were looting.

As noted above, most historians take it for granted that these disturbances were political, brought on by the spread of Jewish nationalist ferment from Judaea to Egypt. This seems logical enough, and appears moreover to be implied by Josephus himself when he ties these riots in with contemporary attacks on Jews in Syrian towns, attacks which were clearly related to the revolt in Judaea. It is also highly probable that Jewish Zealots from Jerusalem appeared in Alexandria at that time intending to stir up popular feeling against Rome, and to enlist volunteers for the Jewish forces back home, who were then bracing themselves for the expected counterattack by the Roman army. There is a hint of such activity in Josephus' report about the pogrom in Antioch, provoked by Antiochus, the renegade son of the head of the Jewish community. He went to the authorities and told them that the Jews were planning to burn the city down. "He (Antiochus) also delivered up some *foreign Jews* as accomplices to the plot."[76]

However, a straightforward reading of the reportage by Josephus leaves the distinct impression that the immediate and obvious cause of the violence was the long-standing hatred between the Greeks and the Jews in Alexandria. The role of the governor — as always with governors — was to mediate between the sides and to restore law and order. It is clear that the trouble started when Jews tried to participate in a public meeting of citizens, and the Greeks protested their presence. The clear implication was that the Jews had no right to be there; they were *not* citizens. And this was the basic issue on which the sides joined battle.

76 JW VII:3:3 (47).

To be sure, there are specific aspects of the situation, such as the attitude of the Jews to the governor (himself a renegade Jew) and their passionate reaction to the events as they unfolded, an attitude and reaction which may be traceable to the waves of patriotic fervor emanating at that particular moment from Jerusalem, where the standard of revolt against Rome had been raised. It is quite possible that this revolutionary ardor contributed to the first incendiary outburst by the Jews against the crowd in the amphitheatre. But in the last analysis, the episode in its entirety must be seen as one more act in the protracted drama that pitted Jews against Greeks in the urban centers of the Hellenistic world.

AFTER THE DESTRUCTION

Not long after the end of the Jewish War against Rome, the Greeks of Alexandria made representations, first to Vespasian and then to his successor Titus, to have the Jews of their city deprived of the rights of citizenship *(dikaia ta tas politeias)*.[77] The Greeks of Antioch lobbied in a similar vein. However, both emperors rejected the idea, refusing to take away the ancient rights of the Jews. It was their view, according to Josephus, "that those who had taken up arms against them and engaged in battle with them had paid the penalty; but it was not right that those who had done no wrong should be deprived of their existing rights."[78] In another context Josephus tells us that the initial demands of the Antiochans were even more extreme: they wanted the Jews expelled from their city.[79]

So it seems that shock waves from the Destruction spread through the region, and that Jews in the Hellenistic Middle East found themselves in a truly precarious position. From all appear-

---

77 Ant. XII:3:1 (124). [The Greek phrase is rendered by Alon *"mishpat ha-ezrahut"* (Tol. I, p. 230). Aryeh Kasher, in his work "The Jews in Hellenistic and Roman Egypt" (Tel Aviv 1978, Hebrew with extended English summary) renders "the rights of their community" (p. 257). Kasher takes Alon's distinction between civic equality and group autonomy to its ultimate conclusion, and argues that the struggle was *only* about the latter. His thesis is that *politeia, politeuma,* etc. always mean communal self-rule, not "individual citizenship."]
78 Ant. ibid.
79 JW VII:5:2 (109).

ances the Hellenes in the Greek-speaking cities took it for granted that the Jews were now stripped of the protection of the law. It was the emperors, Josephus tells us, who refused to go along with that notion. To be sure, there are modern historians (e.g. Mommsen, Weber, Fuchs) who hold that the Jews of the Diaspora *did* suffer the same legal consequences of the defeat as did the Jews of Judaea, that is, they became *dediticii,* conquered subjects who no longer enjoyed any corporate rights, but were considered individual adherents of a religion, people of indeterminate legal status whose right of association was doubtful. But there are others, such as Juster, who completely reject this view,[80] claiming that the status of the Jews in the Diaspora was not changed by the Destruction, neither de jure nor de facto.

It is here suggested, however, that even if Juster is objectively right, the legal and political position of the Jews in the dispersion was now at least potentially undermined. Although the Destruction may not have had any immediate consequences for the status of the overseas Jews, such consequences were nevertheless implicit in the new situation; they were simply postponed for several generations, as by a delayed reaction. This suggestion is put forward purely as a hypothesis, but it is decidedly worth investigating, even though such an investigation would be hampered by the lack of reliable sources.

In any case, it is clear that during the immediate postwar decades the Jews of Alexandria retained their collective autonomy. They were able to send their own independent delegation to a hearing before Trajan more than 40 years after the Destruction, as we shall soon see. What then of their civic status? There are those, like Weber, who think that all Egyptian Jews now had to pay the head-tax *(laographia),* even those who were previously exempt. There is no proof for this statement. We are equally at a loss to know whether the heavy poll-tax imposed by the Romans on the defeated Jews of Judaea applied also to Jews throughout the empire. The evidence that it did is not conclusive, and the question remains open.[81]

80 [He calls it "thèse sans fondement." For the references, see Jean Juster, *Les juifs dans l'empire Romain,* Paris 1914, Vol. II, pp. 19 ff.]
81 [For a recent survey of the literature on the "Jewish tax" see Menahem

THE ZEALOTS

The background of the uprising under Trajan also includes the activity of certain Zealots who escaped from Jerusalem during the last days of the siege and made their way to Egypt. Once more it becomes necessary to examine the report of these events by Josephus:[82]

> Moreover, at Alexandria in Egypt after this date many Jews met with destruction. For certain of the faction of the Sicarii who had succeeded in fleeing to that country, not content with their escape, again embarked on revolutionary schemes, and sought to induce many of their hosts to assert their independence, to look upon the Romans as no better than themselves, and to esteem God alone as their lord. Meeting with opposition from certain Jews of rank, they murdered these; the rest they continued to press with solicitations to revolt. Observing their infatuation, the leaders of the council of elders, thinking it no longer safe for them to overlook their proceedings, convened a general assembly of the Jews and exposed the madness of the Sicarii, proving them to have been responsible for all their troubles. 'And now,' they said, 'these men, finding that even their flight has brought them no sure hole of safety — for if recognized by the Romans they would instantly be put to death — are seeking to involve in the calamity which is their due, persons wholly innocent of their crimes.' They accordingly advised the assembly to beware of the ruin with which they were menaced by these men and, by delivering them up, to make peace with the Romans. Realizing the gravity of the danger, the people complied with this advice, and rushed furiously upon the Sicarii to seize them ... Nor was there a person who was not amazed at the endurance and — call it what you will, desperation or strength of purpose — displayed by these victims.

Stern: *Greek and Latin Authors on Jews and Judaism*, Vol. II, Jerusalem 1980, pp. 129 f. This work will hereinafter be cited as GLA.]
82 JW VII : 10 : 1 (409 ff.).

The outcome of these events, according to Josephus, was that the Temple of Onias was shut down, and its sacred vessels confiscated. The Romans wanted to make sure that it would not serve as a focus of Jewish insurrection. This in itself is prima facie evidence that the sicarii had an influence on certain elements, at least, of Egyptian Jewry, something which can be inferred from the account of Josephus himself.[83] Indeed, the same conclusion can be drawn from the analogous situation in Cyrene, where the Zealots drew considerable support from the lower classes, while the more solid citizens informed against them to the Romans. Anyone reading Josephus' account of how the leading members of the Jewish community of Alexandria reacted to the inflammatory propaganda of the sicarii will probably assume that these agitators found a more sympathetic audience among the poorer Jews. In fact, it is generally thought that the same kind of division along class lines marked the inter-party strife among the Jews in Judaea and Jerusalem during the war against Rome.

After that war, the "War of the *Hurban,*" was there a fundamental change in the Jewish attitude towards Rome? Did the bitter and protracted struggle breed implacable hatred and a spirit of revolt? That is a question we shall try to deal with when we describe the uprising under Trajan. At this point let us do no more than take note of the bonds between the Jews of Alexandria and the mother country. A personal symbol of those bonds is Rabbi Joshua ben Hananiah, whose visits to the Egyptian community and whose discussions with the Jews there on matters of halakhah and aggadah have left their mark on the tradition.[84] It is even possible that the Jews of Alexandria continued their long-standing practice of sending tithes for the poor and offerings for the priests up to the Holy Land.[85]

---

83 A similar inference can be drawn from the fact that the Roman government suspected the Jews of Rome and Alexandria of helping the insurrection (in Cyrene) of the sicarius Jonathan the Weaver, with money and arms.

84 Neg. XIV: 13; Tos. ibid IX:9 (630); Bavli Nid. 69b.

85 Mishnah Yad. IV:3 mentions the need for Egypt to send in the Poorman's Tithe during the Sabbatical year.

TRIAL BEFORE TRAJAN

The so-called "Acts of the Pagan Martyrs" include a partial record of a hearing held at the court of the emperor Trajan about 111–113 C.E.[86] Spokesman for the Alexandrian delegation was one Paul of Tyre, obviously a professional pleader. The Jews were represented by a certain Sopatros of Antioch. Caesar's wife, Plotina, and most of the senators in the *consilium* gave the impression of being sympathetic to the Jewish side, and Trajan himself upbraided the Alexandrians for having treated the Jews cruelly. This caused Hermaiskos of the Alexandrian delegation to wonder aloud why the emperor was taking the part of "the impious Jews," and to suggest that the Senate was "full of Jews" (many senators may indeed have been "God-Fearers" — i.e. sympathizers with Judaism). The papyrus claims that at this point the bust of the god Serapis which the Alexandrians had brought with them broke into a sweat, causing many Romans to panic and flee into the hills.

The document, which is fragmentary, leaves the impression that the Alexandrians lost this case too, and that their representatives paid the usual penalty. But this is not stated explicitly, so perhaps Trajan relented and granted them pardon.

What was at stake in this trial? Perhaps the perennial issue of *isopoliteia* — civic equality for the Jews— was again being contested, as Weber suggests.[87] Or perhaps this time the Alexandrians had raised their sights, and wanted the religious autonomy of the Jews abolished, or at least curtailed.

In any event, the document seems to indicate that there had been violence in Alexandria around the end of the first decade of the second century. There is additional evidence for this in an oration by Dio Chrysostom at about the same time.[88] Furthermore, a modern student of numismatics has suggested that symbols on Alexandrian coins of Trajan's 14th year (110–111 C.E.) may echo

---

86 P. Oxy 1242 = CPJ II, no. 157, pp. 82 ff.
87 "Eine Gerichtshandlung vor Kaiser Trajan," in *Hermes*, 50 (1915) p. 47.
88 *Dio Chrysostom*, translated by H.L. Crosby (Loeb Classics), Vol. III, p. 264, xxxii: 95.

rioting between Greeks and Jews, and possibly commemorate an imperial judgment on the matter.[89]

However, it is highly unlikely that either of these sources has anything to do with the Jewish question. The very fact that neither Chrysostom nor the coins give the slightest hint of the Jewish presence makes it probable that what they do echo is some widespread general unrest in a city known for its turbulence. How this relates to a trial in Rome can only be guessed at. It is possible that, under cover of the rioting and bloodshed which characterized the empire's second city, some sort of pogrom actually did take place.

CYRENE AND CYRENAICA

What we know about the Jews of Cyrene (in northern Libya) during the Hellenistic era amounts to not much more than the fact that they were there.[90] Josephus remarks on the movement of Jews from Egypt into Libya and Cyrene during the days of the first Ptolemies.[91] His citation from the geographer Strabo shows that they had been there for generations. And the Egyptian connection may turn out to be significant when we describe the uprisings under Trajan.

That the community was important in the days of the Hasmonean ruler Simeon (142–135 B.C.E.) is apparent from the First Book of Maccabees — else why would the Roman Senate have included Cyrene among the places notified about Rome's treaty with Judaea?[92] Furthermore, from the fact that a large work by Jason of Cyrene underlies the Second Book of Maccabees, there are several conclusions to be drawn. The first is, that by the second pre-Christian century the Jews of Cyrene had become suf-

---

89 J. Vogt, *Die Alexandrinischen Münzen,* Stuttgart, 1924, part I, p. 85.

90 [The studies of Shimon Applebaum have shed more light on the picture, through his use of analogy with the Egyptian situation, and his accumulation of archaeological and epigraphic data. See his *Greeks and Jews in Ancient Cyrene* (Hebrew, Jerusalem 1969; 2nd revised edition, English, Leiden, 1979). References herein will be to the English edition.]

91 Apion II:94.

92 I Macc. 15:23.

ficiently well-established to produce first-class literature. Secondly, they were completely at home in literary Greek; and thirdly, they had close emotional and spiritual ties with their ancestral homeland, and were in intimate contact with their fellow Jews in Eretz Israel. The fact that Jason wrote his account of the Maccabean struggle so soon after the events, coupled with the warmly partisan tone in which he tells the story — surely these are evidences of his attitudes and commitments, and probably those of his fellow Cyrenean Jews as well.

The Romans conquered Cyrenaica in 95 B.C.E. Writing ten years later the Greek geographer Strabo, according to a quotation by Josephus, divided the population of the province into four groups: 1) citizens *(politai);* 2) farmers *(georgoi);* 3) resident aliens or metics *(metoikoi);* and 4) Jews.[93] What this does not tell us is whether the Jews had the status of citizens or metics; surely they must have been one or the other. But in any event, the quotation from Strabo does indicate that they were organized as a distinct element in the population, with their own *politeuma.*

Actually, we are afforded a glimpse of this community organization by an inscription found in modern times in the city of Berenice (Benghazi). It is dated early in the reign of Augustus, possibly 21 B.C.E.[94] The purpose of the inscription was to record a public vote of thanks to the Roman governor, and the stele bearing it was placed in the civic amphitheatre, an indication that the Jews had access to that place. Twice the declaration mentions the *politeuma* of the Jews. It refers to Jewish public assemblies *(synodoi)* on Sukkot, and to lesser ones on New Moons. The inscription lists nine archons as leaders of the Jewish community.

But there were darker days ahead. Trouble between the Jews and the Greek cities of Cyrenaica broke out during the regime of Augustus, according to Josephus Flavius.[95]

---

93 Ant. XIV: 7:2 (115).
94 [For the text and comment, Schürer III, p. 78, note, pp. 78 ff. where the suggested date was 13 BCE. Reconsideration, REG 62 (1949) pp. 284 ff. has settled on 24/5 C.E. Applebaum, op. cit. pp. 160 ff. knows of an earlier inscription (8–6 B.C.E.) and a later one (56 C.E.)]
95 Ant. XVI:6:1 ff. (160 ff.).

The Jews of Asia and those to be found in Cyrenean Libya were being mistreated by the cities there, although the kings had formerly granted them equality of civic status *(isonomia);* and at this particular time the Greeks were persecuting them to the extent of taking their sacred monies away from them...

The reference is, of course, to the half-shekel for the Temple in Jerusalem, collected annually by the community from each Jew.

The Jews sent a delegation to Rome to complain, with the result that Agrippa was able to write "To the Leaders and Council and People of Cyrene," reminding them that Augustus had previously instructed the governor *not* to allow the blocking of the sacred monies destined for Jerusalem. Specifically, the Greeks were not to invoke the usual grounds for such action — namely, that the money had not been taxed. Agrippa further ordered the cities of Cyrenaica to give back the funds they had already confiscated.

The fight put up by the Jews of Cyrenaica for the right to send their gifts to the Temple is evidence of their close ties to the mother country. The New Testament makes this even plainer. The presence in Jerusalem of Simon of Cyrene, who was compelled to carry the cross, is one such indication.[96] Apparently he was a member of the Cyrenian congregation in the holy city.

Then there arose certain of the synagogue of the Libertines... and of the Cyrenians and the Alexandrians...[97]

Josephus reports that in the aftermath of the siege and fall of Jerusalem some of the more extreme Zealots tried to continue the war from abroad. A certain Jonathan came to Cyrenaica, and

96 Matt. 27, 34; Mark 15, 21; Luke 23, 26.
97 Acts 6, 9. It seems that these synagogues served Jewish pilgrims from various countries in the Diaspora, some of whom stayed on in Jerusalem for a considerable time. Compare the inscription of Theodotus, discovered (1914) in excavations at Jerusalem, for which see Frey, *Corpus Inscrip. Jud. II.* no. 1404, pp. 332–335; and S. Klein in *Yediot* of the Institute of Jewish Studies, Vol. II, Hebrew University, 1925, p. 24. [There is an excellent photograph of the inscription in the Westminster Historical Atlas of the Bible, Phila. 1945, p. 87.]

having gained a following as a sort of messianic wonder-worker, led a flock of the poorer Jews into the wilderness. The Jewish community leaders denounced this Jonathan to Catullus, the governor of Libya, who attacked Jonathan's unarmed followers and practically wiped them out.[98] Jonathan escaped, but was ultimately captured.

In these circumstances, Catullus saw his own opportunity. By inflating the whole situation, he could make himself appear as the victor in another "Jewish War." He therefore got the captive Jonathan to implicate the leaders of the Jewish community in the uprising, and then had some 3,000 of them executed.[99]

On the basis of these reports by Josephus we may conclude that on the one hand, there were many Jews in Cyrenaica, as there were in Egypt, who were receptive to anti-Roman messianic-revolutionary ideas brought to them by Zealots from *Judaea Capta;* while on the other hand such ideas were frowned upon by the organized Jewish communities in these countries, especially by the community leaders. The latter sought to keep the peace, which meant preserving loyalty to the established power of Rome.

We may sum up by noting that both in Alexandria and in Cyrene there was a prolonged struggle between the Jews and the Greeks, dating at least from the beginning of Roman rule. This struggle had a dual focus: the civic rights of the Jews, and their religious privileges. In Cyrene an additional issue was the right of the Jews to send their yearly contribution to the Temple in Jerusalem. There is some evidence, at least for Alexandria, of renewed strife between the protagonists shortly before the outbreak of major hostilities. Reasoning from these facts, it is possible to argue that it was the conditions inherent in Jewish life in the Diaspora that provided the lethal brew out of which came the final big explosion.

On the other hand, we have noticed the emergence among the Jews in both Egypt and Cyrenaica of nationalist movements of a

98 JW VII : 11 : 1–4 (437 ff.); Life 76 (424).
99 Catullus also extracted a "confession" involving many important Jews in Alexandria and Rome, Josephus among them. The historian, who had been adopted into the Flavian clan, is able to report that both Vespasian and Titus cleared him of the accusation.

pronounced political character, nurtured by activists who had survived the battlefields of Judaea. We must therefore bear in mind the possibility that this too may have been a factor in fuelling the final conflagration.

THE JEWS OF CYPRUS

About the Jews on the island of Cyprus our information is very scanty indeed. It is only because the Roman Senate included Cyprus among the states and principalities notified about the treaty with Judaea in 139 B.C.E. that we are able to infer that the island already had a sizeable Jewish community by that time.[100] Indeed, we have to wait until the days of Gaius Caligula for the next clear-cut reference, an allusion by Philo in the documents related to his mission to the court of the mad emperor.[101]

But it is from the *Acts of the Apostles* that we really get a sense of the size and importance of Cypriote Jewry.[102] Paul and Barnabas preach the word "in the synagogues of the Jews" at Salamis (the large city which was to be the focus of violence in the following century). Perhaps they found other communities to visit as well, for the two apostles went through "the whole island to Paphos" (at the opposite end).

Jewish influence on Cyprus must have been strong during the first century, because the governor, Sergius Paulus, was a "God-Fearer," — that is to say, a sympathizer with Judaism. According to *Acts* there was a Jewish "false prophet" called Elymas bar Yeshua who had the governor's ear. Paul engaged Elymas in a struggle for the governor's soul.

Finally, there is an implication elsewhere in *Acts* that Jerusalem had a Cypriote community or synagogue, just like Cyrenaica and other Diaspora communities.[103]

As for the Jews of Mesopotamia, we shall deal with them separately, when describing the events themselves. What happened there on the fringes of Parthia was different both in cause and in

---

100 I Macc. 15:23.
101 *Embassy to Gaius* 282; [Colson X, p. 143.]
102 Acts 13:4 ff.
103 Ibid. 11, 20.

nature from what took place in the lands of the Roman Empire proper.

Let us therefore now focus on those events to which this chapter has been an introduction — the uprisings which embroiled the Jews of most of the Diaspora with the Roman Empire during the years 115 to 117 C.E.

CHAPTER SIXTEEN

DIASPORA AFLAME
(115 C.E.–117 C.E.)

What we know about the warfare between the Jews in the Diaspora, and their Roman rulers and Greek neighbors during the regime of the Emperor Trajan, derives from three principal kinds of sources: a) narratives by historians; b) inscriptions in public places; and c) papyri.[1] This material, especially the literary and papyrological, is at times rather baffling. However, by assembling all the data, and fitting one piece to another, we can obtain at least a partial picture of the disturbances, of their intensity, of their extent, and of their thrust.[2]

---

1   [The papyri are among the many that have, since Alon's time, been collected, annotated and translated by Tcherikover, Fuks and Stern in *Corpus Papyrorum Judaicarum*; see vol. II, pp. 225 ff. under the heading "Jewish Revolt Under Trajan," which is described as "one of the most significant events in the history of the Jews under Roman rule." See also Tcherikover's *The Jews of Egypt in the Light of the Papyri* (Hebrew) which stresses that the revolt was "a real war, involving battles, victories and defeats" (English resumé, p. xxii).
  For updated bibliography on these events, consult Schürer, *History of the Jewish People*, ed. Vermes and Millar, Vol. I, Edinburgh 1973, pp. 529–534; see especially Alexander Fuks: "Aspects of the Jewish Revolt in A.D. 115–117" in *Journal of Roman Studies*, Vol. 50 (1960) pp. 58 ff.; and Smallwood: "The Jews in the Roman Empire," 1980, Chapter XV.]

2   [Jewish sources (i.e. Rabbinic literature) contain very scanty references to Trajan. Even these are largely legendary, and cannot seem to get the Emperor's name straight (variously "Turgeinos" or "Trakhinos"). Whether this is attributable to the almost total extinction of the Eastern Mediterranean Diaspora, whose survivors might otherwise have left us some record of the catastrophe; or is the result of it having been overshadowed so soon thereafter by the trauma of another tragedy in the homeland itself under Trajan's successor — the Hadrianic persecutions and the Bar Kokhba War — must remain a matter for speculation.]

[382]

Narrative Sources

Our principal narrative reporters are the Roman historian Dio Cassius (ca. 155–230 C.E.) and the Church Father Eusebius (ca. 260–339). The former was a member of the Roman governing class, a senator and the son of a proconsul. He himself served at one time as a consul. The passage from his *Roman History* dealing specifically with the Jewish insurrections under Trajan happens to have been lost, but we do have a summary prepared by the eleventh century monk Xiphilinus. In this "Epitome" of Dio's work we find a description of the difficulties encountered by the Roman Expeditionary Force in Mesopotamia (117), and then the following:

> Trajan therefore departed thence, and a little later began to fail in health. Meanwhile the Jews in the region of Cyrene had put a certain Andreas at their head and were destroying both the Romans and the Greeks. They would eat the flesh of their victims, make belts for themselves of their entrails, anoint themselves with their blood and wear their skins for clothing; many they sawed in two, from the head downwards; others they gave to wild beasts, and still others they forced to fight as gladiators. In all two hundred and twenty thousand persons perished. In Egypt too they perpetrated many similar outrages, and in Cyprus, under the leadership of a certain Artemion. There also two hundred and forty thousand perished, and for this reason no Jew may set foot on that island, but even if one of them is driven upon its shores by a storm

Nevertheless, the tradition did remember enough to blame the destruction of the famous Great Synagogue of Alexandria on "the wicked Trajan" (Yer. Suk. V: 55a–b). Other Rabbinic references are: *Mekhilta de R. Ishmael* Beshallah II, (Horovitz-Rabin p. 95, Lauterbach transl. I, p. 216); LamR, I: 48 and IV: 23; Bavli Taan. 18b.

Most of these passages are excerpted in *Tol. I,* 4th ed. p. 360, where it is also implied that the mention in Git. 57a of the destruction of "Kefar Sikhnaia of Egypt" echoes the events of 115–117 C.E. However, the implication must be rejected as being too far-fetched. We do know of a village called Sikhnin — but in the Galilee. Long ago S. Klein suggested that *Mitzrayim* here is a misreading for *minim* or *notzrim.* See his *Beiträge zur Geschichte Galiläas,* Leipzig, 1909, p. 30, note 1. In 1931, the village of Sakhnin still had 200 Christians in a total population of 1,891.]

[383]

he is put to death. Among others who subdued the Jews was Lusius, who was sent by Trajan.[3]

In dealing with this report, our initial task is to straighten out the sequence of events. One's first impression is that the insurrections broke out at the end of Trajan's life, just when he was withdrawing from his disastrous campaign in Mesopotamia. That would be in the year 117 C.E. Indeed, this very passage has misled some historians into postdating the disturbances in Cyprus and Egypt, so that they become an *outcome* of Trajan's failure in Asia. According to this view, the Jews in North Africa and elsewhere took advantage of the Roman entanglement in the Middle East to launch their own military venture against Rome.[4]

However, a careful reading of the passage just quoted does not really reveal any temporal or causal sequence. It seems safe to say that Dio simply intended a general survey of the wars that filled Trajan's last days. Actually, as can be seen from the account by Eusebius which we are about to quote, it appears that the Jews in Cyrenaica and Egypt revolted *before* the outbreaks in the Tigris-Euphrates valley, where a large Roman force became bogged down, and ultimately retreated before the Parthians.

Another thing: Dio implies that the insurrection broke out first in Cyrenaica. This seems to disagree with the report by Eusebius. On the other hand, in the main outlines of his narrative the Church Father does support the Roman historian. Eusebius writes:

> In the course of the eighteenth year (115 C.E.) of the reign of the Emperor a rebellion (*kinesis*) of the Jews again broke out and destroyed a great multitude of them. For both in Alexandria and in the rest of Egypt and especially in Cy-

---

3   [*Dio's Roman History,* LXVIII:32; edited and translated by Earnest Cary, vol. VIII, pp. 421 ff., comp. Stern, GLA II, no. 347.]

4   Ferdinand Gregorovius: "Der Letzte Kampf," in Ellbogen: *Gestalte und Momente,* Berlin 1927, pp. 74–100. On the other hand, R.P. Longden in *Cambridge Ancient History,* Vol. XI, p. 250, thinks that the news of rebellion in Palestine fanned the resistance which the Romans were already encountering in Mesopotamia, into open warfare. Dubnow, Hebrew version II, p. 23, thinks the Jewish rebellion in Mesopotamia caused the uprising in Egypt and Cyrene.

rene, as though they had been seized by some terrible spirit of rebellion, they rushed into sedition against their Greek fellow citizens, and increasing the scope of the rebellion (*stasis*), in the following year started a great war (*polemos*) while Lupus was governor of all Egypt. In the first engagement they happened to overcome the Greeks, who fled to Alexandria and captured and killed the Jews in the city; but though thus losing the help of the townsmen, the Jews of Cyrene continued to plunder the country of Egypt and to ravage the districts in it under their leader Lukuas. The Emperor sent against them Marcius Turbo with land and sea forces including cavalry. He waged war vigorously against them in many battles for a considerable time and killed many thousands of Jews, not only those of Cyrene but also those of Egypt who had rallied to Lukuas, their king. The Emperor suspected that the Jews in Mesopotamia would also attack the inhabitants and ordered Lusius Quietus to clean them out of the province. He organized a force and murdered a great multitude of the Jews there, and for this reform was appointed governor of Judaea by the Emperor.[5]

It seems likely that the uprisings in Egypt preceded those in Mesopotamia; and that they began at least as early as those in Cyrene. But as Eusebius continues his narrative, one gets the impression that it was the Jews of Cyrene who first defied the Romans; that it was they who went so far as to appoint a "king"; and that the Egyptian Jews took their cue from them. This would take us back to the year 116, when *stasis* (disorder) gave way to full-fledged *polemos* (war). In any event, it seems from what Eusebius says that the disturbances in Egypt assumed major proportions as a result of the entry into that country of Cyreneian Jews led by Lukuas (probably the same man as Andreas). Apparently, then, it was these Jews who were the standard-bearers of the uprising, at least at its most critical stage.

However, the testimony of neither Dio Cassius nor of Eusebius

5 Eusebius: *Ecclesiastical History*, Bk. IV, II:2; [transl. by Kirsopp Lake, Vol. I, pp. 305-7.]

enables us to determine the actual starting-point of the rebellion. Merely as a suggestion, let us focus on an ambiguous passage in the account by Eusebius. Lake's translation skirts the ambiguity by rendering ... "but though thus losing the help of the townsmen, the Jews of Cyrene continued to plunder the country of Egypt ..." It would be equally valid to translate: "The Jews of Cyrene, having lost the help of the Jews of Alexandria, now arose and led by Lukuas, plundered the land of Egypt."

The suggested interpretation is this: The Jews of Cyrene carried on the fight for as long as their co-religionists in Alexandria were able to hold the line of their own front. However, when the latter were swamped, and could therefore no longer help out, the Cyreneian rebels had no choice but to make their way to Egypt, and to join forces with the rebels there. That seems to be what Eusebius intended. The corollary is that the Jews of Alexandria initially provided backing for the rebels in Cyrene.[6]

Is this corollary supported by anything else we know? A little further on we shall try to shed as much light as possible on the position taken by the Jews of Alexandria, and on what ultimately befell them. At this point, however, let us merely note that Eusebius seems to be informed by a historical tradition that traced the uprisings to the Jews of Alexandria. According to this view, they were the very instigators of the subversion against Rome, and the supporters of rebellion in other countries of the Empire. We have already seen how Catullus, governor of Cyrenaica in the years after the Destruction, extracted a trumped-up confession from Jonathan the Weaver implicating the Jews of Alexandria in the riots that took place in his territory at that time.[7]

This whole line may have been deliberate policy, calculated to counter the claim of the Jews of Alexandria that they were not the aggressors, but that the Greeks of the city had attacked them first. We shall have to deal with that issue in connection with the whole complex of questions relating to the genesis and thrust of the Jewish uprisings. For the present, however, let us examine the

6 The other possible interpretation — that the Alexandrian Jews helped by keeping Roman troops tied down on their "second front" — seems far-fetched.

7 Above, p. 379.

theory that the differences between Dio Cassius and Eusebius stem from the fact that each of them relied on divergent traditions about these events.[8] According to this theory, Dio based himself on anti-Jewish Hellenistic sources, while Eusebius drew his account from an Alexandrian-Jewish tradition. Now, it is quite reasonable to suppose that Dio's account comes from tendentious gentile sources, especially in the light of his exaggerations and his tales of barbaric atrocities perpetrated by the Jews. But the converse — that Eusebius used Jewish sources — does not follow. The mere fact that his version is free of such horror stories scarcely proves anything but his own lack of gullibility.[9] I therefore prefer to interpret his ambiguous phrase in the manner I have suggested.

CYRENAICA

A number of inscriptions that have come to light in recent years, some in Greek and some in Latin, have added to our picture of the impact of the Jewish uprising in Cyrenaica.[10] These include the text of edicts issued by Trajan's successor, the Emperor Hadrian, ordering the rebuilding of the temple of Hecate in the city of Cyrene, after it had been wrecked and burned during the "Jewish disturbance" (*tumultus* in Latin; *tarachos* in Greek). Also to be restored are "the baths with porticoes, ball courts and other connected buildings which were razed and burnt down during the Jewish *tumultus*." There is also record of the repair of "the highway between Apollonia and Cyrene which had been overturned and smashed up during the Jewish disturbance."

The fact that the inscriptions speak only of a "Jewish disturbance" might be taken to imply civil unrest rather than outright warfare against the government. And it is also possible that shrines and temples were destroyed as the result of religious zealotry, and

---

8   For example, Wilcken in *Die Bremer Papyri,* no. 2 in the *Abhandlungen* for 1936 of the Prussian Academy of Sciences, Philological-Historical Section [p. 14, note 4.]

9   I am puzzled by the suggestion of some scholars that Eusebius had a pro-Jewish bias.

10   *Archäolog. Anzeiger, Beiblatt z. Jahrbuch des archäolog. Inst.* 1929, pp. 400, 412, 421, 423. [For an extensive survey of archaeological and epigraphic evidence, see Applebaum, op. cit. 1979, pp. 269–294.]

roads torn up out of rage and spite. But it is equally possible that these acts of destruction came about in the course of a full-blown insurrection, and as a by-product of it.[11] Take for example the report of a contemporary witness, Appian of Alexandria, regarding the destruction of the Temple of Nemesis, dedicated to the memory of Pompey:

> Caesar could not bear to look at the head of Pompey when it was brought to him but ordered that it be buried, and he set apart for it a small plot of ground near the city which was dedicated to Nemesis, but in my time, while the Roman emperor Trajan was exterminating the Jewish race in Egypt, it was devastated by them in the exigencies of war.[12]

Dio Cassius also reports the ruination of this memorial to Pompey, and adds that it was restored by Hadrian.[13]

An intriguing, if somewhat cryptic passage occurs in the *Onicritica* of Artemidorus, a Greek author of the late second century C.E.

> There are some dreams that cannot be solved before the events come to pas ... Of that kind was one in which a *stratopedarches* (camp prefect) saw written upon his sword the letters *iota, kappa* and *theta*. Then there came the Jewish war (*polemos*) in Cyrene, and the fellow who had seen the dream distinguished himself in the war, and this was what the above mentioned dream had signified: by the *iota* were meant the Jews (*Ioudaiois*), by the *kappa* the Cyreneans (*Kyrenaiois*), and by the *theta*, death (*thanatos*). However, before it came to pass, this dream was unresolvable, but when the event happened, it was very manifest.[14]

11 Contrary to the view of Tcherikover, *The Jews of Egypt etc.* 2nd edition, p. 177. It seems more probable that the highway was torn up in order to interfere with Roman troop movements. [But more recently Applebaum, op. cit. p. 260 has expressed the conviction that religious fervor really was the motive for the extensive destruction.]

12 *Historia Romana,* I. [Appian's *Roman History,* ed. and transl. by Horace White, vol. III, p. 393 ff.; comp. Stern GLA II, no. 350, p. 187.]

13 *Dio's Roman History,* [ed. and transl. by E. Cary, LXIX:11:1, vol. VIII, p. 445.]

14 [Stern, GLA II, no. 396, p. 330 f.]

Cyrenaica

Note that Artemidorus speaks of a Jewish "war" (*polemos*), unlike the inscriptions cited above. He uses a term more suited to large-scale rebellion against the government than to rioting between elements of the colonial population. Still, the word is not strictly limited in its meaning. In his letter to the Alexandrians Claudius had referred to the conflict between the Greeks and Jews of that city as "the *stasis*, or rather to speak the truth, the *polemos* against the Jews."[15] Apparently, then *polemos* can also describe civil disorder of major proportions, and the difference between it and *stasis* (or *tarachos*) is purely a matter of degree.[16]

There is another problem raised by the dream. The letters *iota* and *kappa* make it appear that the struggle was between the Jews and the Cyreneans. However, there is a manuscript version of the same story in which there is no *kappa*, nor any mention at all of the Cyreneans, making it consistent with the fact that the war was between the Jews and the Romans — as indeed it was.

Still another ambiguity involves the *thanatos*. Whose death is meant? Juster, commenting on the published version of Artemidorus, thought that the word applied to the defeat facing the Roman commander and his troops (not to speak of the Cyreneans).[17] However, in the manuscript version only "Jews" and "death" are mentioned, so that the dream must have been about the final extermination of the Jews of Cyrenaica. It seems that this version is the correct one. Otherwise, how could the Roman com-

---

15 Above, p. 358.

16 [Nevertheless, Alon usually takes careful note of the terms used by his sources. These run the gamut from "disturbances" and "disorders" to "rioting," "the troubles," and "war." In *Aegyptus* 33 (1953) pp. 155–6, Alexander Fuks showed rather convincingly that the *official* Roman designation for the events of 115–117 became *tumultus* (or the Greek equivalent *tarachos*); comp. CPJ II, p. 257 and ibid. p. 251. This looks like the familiar unwillingness of governments to dignify rebelliousness and insurrection with the name "war." But Applebaum, op. cit. pp. 308–9, presents evidence to show that a *tumultus* was legally more serious than a *bellum*. When the Senate declared a *tumultus*, all leaves were cancelled, and even civilians could be drafted. This may throw some light on the mobilization of civilians referred to below p. 392.]

17 *Les juifs dans l'empire romain*, II, p. 186.

mander, who was to distinguish himself in action, have been supposed to have dreamt of his own death? It seems obvious that all this is a reference to the ultimate downfall of the Jews. Perhaps we can connect it with the evidence provided by Eusebius: when the Jews of Alexandria could no longer help them, the Jews of Cyrenaica had to fall back before the pressure of Roman arms, and to cross the border into Egypt.

LIBYA

For the fighting in Libya, the fundamental source is the *Chronicle* of Eusebius, as transmitted by the Latin of Jerome.[18] (All the later sources derive from him.) Now, Eusebius refers to "the Jews of Libya who rose up in war and turmoil (apparently Eusebius had written *polemos kai stasis*) against the Greeks among whom they lived," to quote the Armenian version. But where that version reads "Greeks," Jerome renders *alieni genae gentilium pars* — i.e. pagan gentiles. Orosius, writing in the year 418 C.E., says:

> The Jews waged war on the population throughout Libya in the most savage manner, and the country was devastated to such an extent by the killing off of its husbandmen that it would have been left entirely without inhabitants, had not the Emperor Hadrian brought in settlers from outside, and settled them on the land.[19]

Additional testimony to Hadrian's role in re-colonizing Libya is given by Eusebius,[20] and confirmed by coins which celebrate that emperor as *Restitutor Libyae*.[21] It may, however, be necessary to caution that none of this proves that Libya underwent the kind of devastation that Cyrenaica appears to have suffered.

CYPRUS

As far as source material for events on the island of Cyprus is concerned, we really have very little to add to the report quoted

18 *Chron. (Hieron.)* ed. Helm, p. 196; Ed. Karst (Armenian) p. 219.
19 *Historia adversum paganos*, 7:12.
20 Ibid.
21 See Wieber *Untersuchungen zur Geschichte d. Kaisers Hadrianus*, p. 120.

above from Dio Cassius,[22] other than the very brief generalization drawn by Jerome from the *Chronicle* of Eusebius:[23]

The Jews killed the gentiles in Salamina, the chief town of Cyprus, and destroyed the city.

The Armenian version of the same sentence says "Greeks" instead of "gentiles," and the same is true for the Syriac chronicles. It need scarcely be added that these differences are not accidental, but reflect differing viewpoints. They have a bearing on the question as to whether the Jews fought only against the Greeks, or against *all* the pagans.

An inscription found in Beirut may possibly echo the fighting on Cyprus. It is dated 116 C.E., and mentions one Valerius Rufus, tribune of the Seventh (Claudian) Legion, who was despatched by Trajan on an expedition to Cyprus at the head of one *vexillatio* (detachment).[24]

Although the Christian sources speak only of the capital Salamis, it is obvious from the number of casualties reported by Dio, and from the subsequent exclusion of Jews from Cyprus, that the fighting spread all over the island. There are, incidentally, inscriptions proving that by the fourth century at the latest Jews lived on Cyprus again.[25]

EGYPT

Eusebius says that the war spread throughout the entire country, a statement supported by the papyri. These documents also afford us an intimate glimpse into the world of the upper class Greeks in Egypt. They take us backstage with some of the local officials, giving us a frank look at their concerns. They record certain Roman troop movements. They echo some of the economic and populational consequences of the fighting.

There is one fact reflected in the papyri which has puzzled most

22 Above, p. 383.
23 Above, p. 384.
24 Dessau, *Inscriptiones Latinae Selectae* VII:2, 9491. See also Pauly-Wissowa 23, 1285.
25 [For evidence of renewed Jewish settlement on Cyprus in the third and fourth centuries, see Stern, GLA II, p. 389.]

historians. Apollonius, a district commissioner from central Egypt, and clearly a civilian, takes part in the fighting as the commander of a military unit! It was Wilcken who finally suggested that the Romans were so hard pressed by the Jews that they had to mobilize civilians to reinforce their legions: [26]

> Aphrodisius to his dearest Herakleios, greeting. I have learnt from men who arrived from Ibion today that they had travelled with a slave of our lord Apollonios; the slave was coming from Memphis to bring the good news of his victory and success. I have therefore sent to you specially that I may know with certainty and make festival and pay the due offering to the gods. You will do well, dear friend, to inform me with speed . . .

That the success referred to in this letter must have been a victory in battle over the Jews is clear from another letter addressed to the same *strategos* by his wife Aline. She writes to her husband Apollonius: [27]

> I am terribly anxious about you because of what they say about what is happening and because of your sudden departure. I take no pleasure in food or drink, but stay awake continually night and day with one worry, your safety. Only my father's care revives me, and as I hope to see you safe I would have lain without food on New Year's Day had my father not come and forced me to eat. I beg you to keep yourself safe, and not to go into danger without a guard. Do the same as the *strategos* here, who puts the burden on his officers.

Among others worried about the welfare of Apollonius was his mother, Eudaimonis, who writes:

26 For Wilcken's suggestion, see *Die Bremer Papyri*, p. 17. Tcherikover agreed, *The Jews in Egypt*², p. 172. Apollonios was on active duty as *strategos* of the district of Hermoupolis; Herakleios was his major domo. The document is Pap. Giss. 27 [CPJ II 439, pp. 239–40. For the suggestion that civilians were called up because it was a *tumultus*, see note 16 above.]

27 P. Giss. 19 [CPJ II, no. 436, 233 ff.]

... with the good will of the gods, above all the invincible Hermes, may the enemy not roast you ... [28]

This remark is a vivid reflection of the ferocity with which this particular struggle was fought, and reminds us of the atrocities reported by Dio Cassius. To be sure, we are dealing here with the natural tendency of an old mother, worried for the safety of her son, to exaggerate the dangers at the front. There must also have been current some rather wild rumors about the fiendish behavior of the Jewish fighters.[29]

We can get some idea of the scale on which the Jews in Egypt attacked, of the losses they inflicted and the extent of the territory that came under their control, from the following passage from the *Roman History* of Appian of Alexandria:

> When I was fleeing from the Jews during the war *(polemos)* which was being waged in Egypt and I was passing through Arabia Petraea in the direction of the river, where a boat had been waiting in order to carry me over to Pelusium, an Arab served me as guide at night. When I believed us to be near the boat a crow croaked, just about daybreak, and the troubled man said: "We have gone astray." And when the crow croaked again, he said: "We have gone much astray." Then I became disturbed and looked for some wayfarer. I saw none, since it was early morning and the country was in a state of war. When the Arab heard the crow a third time, he said rejoicing: "We have gone astray to our advantage and we have gained the road." I only laughed, thinking we would gain the wrong path again, and despaired of myself as we were surrounded everywhere by enemies, and it was

28 P. Giss. 24 [CPJ II, no. 437, pp. 325 f.]
29 [We have enough letters by Eudaimonis to have enabled Fuks to characterize her as "an irascible old lady" who was given to the use of rather extravagant expressions. "The only thing we can safely say is that the war was conducted ruthlessly on both sides." See *Aegyptus*, 1953, p. 135; and CPJ II, p. 236. Comp. the remarks by Stern about Dio's "strongly-colored tale of atrocities committed by the British rebels under Boudicca against the Romans;" as well as Dio's story concerning "the Egyptian rebels in the Delta in 171 C.E. who ate the body of a Roman centurion." (Stern, GLA II, p. 387).]

not possible for me to turn back because of those behind from whom I was fleeing. However, being at a loss, I followed and gave myself up to the augury. Being in such a state, I unexpectedly perceived another river very near to Pelusium, and a trireme sailing to Pelusium. I embarked and was saved, while the boat which awaited me at the other end of the river was captured by the Jews.[30]

The seriousness with which the governing authorities and the Greek-speaking population of Egypt viewed the Jewish threat comes out strongly in a papyrus written apparently by a resident of Hermopolis in Central Egypt, and containing a report on developments up to that moment.[31]

The one hope and expectation that was left was the push of the massed villagers from our district against the impious Jews; but now the opposite has happened. For on the 20th(?) our forces fought and were beaten and many of them were killed . . . now however we have received the news that another legion of Rutilius arrived at Memphis on the 22nd. . . . and is expected (here).[32]

This document, bearing as it does the earmarks of a situation report from the field, is especially important because it testifies to the participation of Egyptians in the fighting. Among the "massed villagers" there were no doubt a good many natives, and most historians have concluded from this that the Egyptian population fought alongside the Greeks against the Jews. We plan to examine that question later; but let it be said here that one papyrus scarcely seems evidence enough for so sweeping a conclusion. Indeed, a careful reading of the document shows that this was an exceptional situation. It really sounds as though the authorities were voicing the desperate hope that perhaps, after all, the Egyptian natives

30 [Stern, GLA II, no. 348, pp. 185 f.]
31 P. Brem. I [CPJ II, no. 438, pp. 236 ff.]
32 This would probably have been the XXIInd (Deiotariana) or the IIIrd (Cyrenaica) both in Egypt at the time under command of the prefect Rutilius Lupus; and would therefore refer to a time before that prefect was replaced by Marcius Turbo.

could be brought in on the Graeco-Roman side. The case recorded was probably a local phenomenon, duplicated no doubt in a few other places where the peasants were particularly loyal to their Greek and Roman masters; but probably the exception rather than the rule.

Another document which has a bearing on this question (that is, who were the principal targets of the Jewish *tumultus*?) is a papyrus dated much later, in the year 199–200 C.E. It is a letter addressed to the Emperor Septimius Severus and his son Caracalla, and it justifies a request on behalf of the people of Oxyrhynchos in the following terms:

> They also possess the goodwill, faithfullness and friendship to the Romans which they exhibited in the war against the Jews, giving aid (*soumachesantes*) then and even now keeping the day of victory as a festival every year.[33]

Of course we are struck by the fact that the victory was still being celebrated two generations after the event. But the point relevant to our discussion is the apparent evidence that the Egyptian peasantry took part in the fighting against the Jews.

But this evidence must be taken as inconclusive. For one thing, provincial capitals like Oxyrhynchos were largely Hellenic in population, even as they were the seat of completely Greek-style civic institutions. Besides, even if the people of the town included non-Hellenic Egyptians, the document before us would not prove that this element in the population bore arms against the Jews on a countrywide scale. Actually, it tends to prove the contrary. The case of Oxyrhynchos, one might say, was so exceptional that it became grounds for an argument for special privilege.

WAR DAMAGE

The war caused extensive destruction to land and property in the countryside, as witnessed by certain other documents.[34] A postwar survey of rural land and farm buildings remarks on "open

33 Pap. Oxy. 705; [CPJ II, no. 450, pp. 258 ff.]
34 [The papyri dealing with war damage are now conveniently grouped in CPJ II, no. 443 et seq.]

lots in which there are farm buildings burned by the Jews."[35] Another document refers to "properties . . . waste and disused from . . . the Jewish disturbance *(tarachos)*."[36] A papyrus written apparently in August of the year 118 C.E. contains a reference to ruined villages, and to a state of "want."[37]

In one letter which has come to hand, we find two men asking to be excused from the obligation of providing supplies for the *epistrategos* on the grounds of hardship "due to the Jewish troubles *(thorubous)*."[38]

The devastation left by the war comes through especially in two letters from Apollonius, *strategos* of Apollonopolis Magna, to the prefect at Alexandria. These letters date from the beginning of the reign of Hadrian, Trajan's successor:

> To Rammius Martialus, the mighty prefect, from Apollonius, strategos of Apollinopolis-Heptakomias greeting! I attach a copy, prefect, of the application for leave which I previously submitted, in order that, by your favor, you may grant me sixty days to put my affairs in order . . . (*the second letter repeats the greetings, and after some lacunae, goes on to say*:) . . . for not only are my affairs completely uncared for because of my long absence, but also, because of the attack of the impious Jews, everything I possess in the Hermoupolite nome and in that metropolis needs my attention. If you accede to my request, and I am able to put my affairs in order as far as possible, I will be able to approach the duties of my office with a more tranquil mind.[39]

Many years later the economic effects of "the Jewish disturbance" still weighed on the country. The document quoted above referring to waste and disused farm properties (note 36) comes from the year 151 C.E. And we have records of requests made by Egyptian farmers asking to rent "crown lands" at the specially reduced rate fixed by the edict of the Emperor Hadrian. Wester-

35 Pap. Oxy. 707; [CPJ II, no. 447, p. 255.]
36 B.G.U. 889. [CPJ II, no. 449, p. 257.]
37 Ibid.
38 Pap. Brem. II [CPJ II, no. 444, pp. 249 ff.]
39 Pap. Giss. 41 [CPJ II, no. 443, pp. 246 ff.]

mann explains this step as a government attempt to restore to cultivation land which had become waste as a result of the Jewish war under Trajan, by providing an incentive to potential farmers. This fits in with the measures Hadrian took to recolonize Libya at the same time, and for the same reason. Both Wilcken and Rostovtzeff view Hadrian's edict in the same light.[40]

ALEXANDRIA

If it were not for some recently discovered papyri, we would be at a loss to describe, even by way of conjecture, what happened in Alexandria during the Jewish *tumultus*. It will be remembered that Eusebius, in his *Ecclesiastical History*, begins by telling how the Jews fell upon their Greek neighbors, in Alexandria as well as in the rest of the country.[41] In his *Chronicle* he writes: "The Jews of Libya rose up against the Greeks ... as did the Jews of Egypt and Alexandria ... The Alexandrine Greeks proved victorious." To which should be added, from the Armenian version of the same source:

> Hadrian caused Alexandria to be rebuilt, it having been destroyed by the Jews.[42]

Since it was the Greeks who wiped out the Jews in the last bloody encounter, this statement can only mean that it was the latter who started the whole thing. It should be remembered, however, that gentile authors made the Jews responsible for the entire war, from start to finish.

Despite this, in the Latin version of Eusebius this particular sentence comes out a little differently:

> ... caused Alexandria, which had been destroyed by the Romans to be rebuilt.[43]

40 Westermann in *Journal of Egyptian Archaeology*, vol. II (1925) pp. 173 ff.; Wilcken, *Die Bremer Papyri*, p. 84; [Rostovtzeff, *Social and Economic History of the Roman Empire*, I, p. 367 f.] Probably mention should be made in this context of papyri which speak of assigning title to land previously owned by Jews; see CPJ II nos. 445, 448.
41 Above, p. 385.
42 *Chron. (Hieron)*: Helm p. 197; Karst p. 219.
43 Helm, ibid.

It was this version which guided the later Christian chroniclers. Even so, it is possible that Jerome copied Eusebius incorrectly, but we cannot be certain that that is what happened. Eusebius may actually have written that Alexandria was laid waste by Roman (and Greek) soldiers in their war against the Jews. Nicephorus Callistus, whose work is basically Eusebius rewritten, says explicitly:

> the Hellenes who had fled from the cities of Egypt in the most cowardly manner (*scil.*: *to Alexandria*) now unexpectedly fell upon the Jews, who were conducting themselves peacefully, and thought themselves safe and secure. Taken by surprise, they were caught and put to the sword.[44]

Latin and Syriac chroniclers who derive from Eusebius tell a similar story.

The fact is, that if we were to rely solely on these narrative sources we might well doubt whether the Jews *ever* initiated any attack on the Alexandrians, or ever participated in clashes with their non-Jewish neighbors. Indeed, the most striking point made by Eusebius in his *Ecclesiastical History* is that the Greek refugees from the Egyptian provinces attacked the Jews of Alexandria and slaughtered them.

It may therefore be assumed that Eusebius' contrary generalization pinning on the Jews the blame for starting hostilities in Alexandria, is simply the logical outcome of his commitment to the historical doctrine which seeks to explain the whole outbreak by the theory that the Jews everywhere in the empire went berserk at one and the same time. From the evidence at our disposal this is not what happened. The "troubles" varied in their nature from one Jewish community to another, and took different courses in different countries.

But Eusebius was not the only one to remain faithful to this formula. Historians long after him were still fitting themselves into the same Procrustean bed. Thus in the twentieth century H.I. Bell could write:

> It seems that the presence of the Roman garrison held the

44 PG 145, pp. 940–941.

Jews of Alexandria back from getting into the fight at the very start, even though our sources indicate the opposite.[45] And that "opposite" is even more explicitly upheld by Weber, who writes that the Jews attacked the Greeks, and that the latter defended themselves and beat them back.[46] However, it does now appear from a recently published papyrus that there *was* some rather serious rioting in Alexandria during the first stage of the war.[47] The document is internally dated: the thirteenth of October, in the 19th year of the Emperor's reign — only it fails to state which Emperor. Since, however, the style of script indicates the second century, I think Tcherikover is right when he concludes that the emperor must be Trajan.[48] That would mean that the document was written on the 13th of October 115 C.E.

The papyrus is, to be sure, defective; but on a number of essential points it is clear enough. In the first place, it is obviously an edict emanating from the prefect Rutilius Lupus in Alexandria, with copies distributed to the principal cities of Egypt (the one we have comes from Tebtynis). Secondly, there is almost no doubt that it is directed against the Greeks of Alexandria, reproving them for having caused disturbances:

> I know that they are few, but they are supported by many more, and paid by the powerful ... I know that most of them are slaves; that is why their masters are blamed. I therefore bid them all not to simulate anger for the sake of profit. Let them not trust in my indulgence.

The prefect goes on to speak of a judge who has been sent by the emperor to investigate these disorders, and refers to the claim of those being reproved that they themselves had been hurt.[49] Finally, and most important of all:

45 Bell, *Juden und Griechen im römischen Alexandreia*, 1926, p. 39; also idem JRS 1941, p. 15.
46 Weber, *Röm, Herrschertum und Reich im zweiten Jahrhundert*, 1937, p. 125.
47 P. RuMil. *Melanges Boisacq*, 1937, p. 159 [CPJ II no. 435, pp. 228 ff.]
48 Tcherikover, *The Jews in Egypt²*, [p. 166; see also CPJ loc. cit.]
49 Whether this means that the Jews were accused of being the aggressors is not entirely clear.

Some of these errors could perhaps have had an excuse before the battle between the Romans and the Jews, but now...

From this it appears that at the very beginning of the *tumultus* there had been a clash between the Roman military and the Jews, although it is not clear whether it refers to Alexandria, or only to the Egyptian countryside. It also seems that the Roman soldiery had attacked the Jews and punished them.

There may be additional evidence from the field of numismatics that something untoward was going on in Alexandria at that time. In his study of Alexandrian coinage, Vogt observes a falling off in the number of coins minted during the period beginning 114/115. He conjectures that this may be connected with the "Jewish war."[50] If he is right, we have added proof that there was rioting in Alexandria at the very earliest stages of the uprising.

But the question remains: who started the fighting? Does the intervention of the Roman army prove that the Jews were the aggressors? Of course, they may have been. Certainly, if the Jews did attack, their target must have been the Greek population, as shown by the edict of Rutilius Lupus just cited. But is it not equally possible that the clashes began with the Greeks provoking the Jews, and then the Roman troops being let loose against the latter — which is just the way things went when Flaccus was prefect, and to a certain extent also during the reign of Nero? At any rate, it is clear that the Greeks took the Roman action as a green light for a pogrom on the Jews, so that the prefect had to issue the above-mentioned edict, and the emperor found it necessary to order an investigation by a magistrate.

Considerable light is shed on events in Alexandria during the war years 115 to 117 and immediately thereafter by the papyri sometimes known as "The Acts of the Alexandrian Martyrs."[52] They deal with a trial before Hadrian, Trajan's successor, in which the Greeks were accused of having provoked tension in the city by theatrical mockery of the "Jewish King" Lukuas-Andreas.[53]

It seems to me that something important is established by these

50   J. Vogt, *Die Alexandrinischen Münzen*, p. 92.
52   [CPJ II, 158a–b, pp. 89–99.]
53   See Tcherikover, *The Jews in Egypt*,[2] p. 163 ff.

documents: namely, that the Roman authorities did not attribute anti-Roman subversion to the Alexandrian Jews. They were not accused of involvement in the rebellion that had won the allegiance of most Cyrenean Jews, and had been widely supported by the Jews of the Egyptian countryside. The document before us shows the Emperor chastising the Greeks for imputing such disloyalty to the Alexandrian Jews. This runs counter to the testimony of Eusebius, who would have us believe that the Jewish rebels chose a "king," and that all or most of the Alexandrian Jews rallied to his banner. But with the papyri now in our hands our conclusion must be that during Trajan's reign relations between Greeks and Jews continued to be pretty much what they had been for many decades. That means that it was still the Greeks who were constantly picking quarrels and provoking trouble.

Another important point arises from these papyri. Antoninus, spokesman of the Alexandrian Greeks, accuses the prefect Lupus of failing to forward certain letters of theirs to the Emperor, letters in which they had complained

> that the prefect had ordered the impious Jews to transfer their residence to a place from which they could easily attack and ravage our well named city ...

The Greek word here translated as "transfer their residence" (*proskatoikein*) presents certain difficulties. I cannot agree with Tcherikover's suggestion that it refers to the creation of a new Jewish district for newcomers who had come to Alexandria to help their brethren resist attack, or to find refuge themselves from the violence in the provinces.[54] I am more inclined to read this passage as part of an effort to get the Jews out of Alexandria altogether. The Alexandrian Greeks may have thought that the Romans would do for their city what they did for Cyprus — expel the Jews completely in the wake of the great insurrection. (That is exactly what the Roman commander Lusius Quietus did in Mesopotamia, as we shall see.)

This interpretation runs along the same lines as the suggestion put forward by Weber, to the effect that "in the year 117 A.D.

54 Ibid., p. 165. [Cf. CPJ II, p. 98.]

the Romans may have promised the Greeks that they would expel the Jews from Alexandria."[55]

Finally it should be noted that in the trial before Hadrian the Greeks lost their case, and their representatives paid with their lives (hence the name "martyrs"). The point is that Hadrian found the Jews of Alexandria *not* guilty of rebellion against Rome.

Another significant point is that, although this was *after* the debacle, the Jews of Alexandria still had their officially recognized community organization (*politeuma*) and were still able to send a delegation to Rome.

But if the great Jewish community of Alexandria was not utterly obliterated, in the juridical-political sense, by the *tumultus* of 115–117, it was indeed shattered in every other sense — demographically, economically, socially. The same can be said, and with even greater emphasis, about the rest of Egyptian Jewry.

With characteristic hyperbole the aggadic tradition relates the words of Genesis, chapter 27, verse 22, to the death-blow suffered by Alexandrian Jewry:

> *The voice is Jacob's voice, but the hands are Essau's*: this refers to the Emperor Hadrian[56] who slaughtered in the city of Alexandria two times sixty myriads, which is twice as many Jews as made the original exodus from Egypt.[57]

The Yerushalmi attributes to Trajan himself the massacre of the Jews of Alexandria —

> so that the sea ran red with blood as far as Cyprus... 'Twas then that the horn of Isaac was torn away, nor is it destined to be restored until the son of David comes.[58]

---

55 *Hermes*, vol. 50 (1915), p. 86, n. 3. He admits, however, that in actual practice the prefect simply forbade the Jews to move into gentile areas.

56 Even though the final stages of the insurrection took place during the early years of Hadrian's reign, the text here should obviously be emended to read "Trajan," [as proposed by Graetz, *Geschichte* IV p. 426. In the context, the Bavli has Vespasian as the destroyer of Beitar!]

57 Git. 57b.

58 Yer. Sulk. V 55b; comp. LamR. I: 45, IV:22; EstR. Proem B.

That last phrase may be an indication of the high value which the Jews of the mother country placed on Alexandrian and Egyptian Jewry. Alternatively, it is possible to regard this aggadah as an echo not alone of the events in Alexandria, but also of the *"polemos* of Quietus" in the homeland. In my own view, however, this passage is a compression of deep feelings arising out of both the Trajanic insurrection and the slightly later Bar Kokhba Revolt. Such an emotional-historical conflation is not uncommon; early Christian sources accord the same treatment to the very same two events in Jewish history.

There is another tradition which may well be an echo of the catastrophic events in Alexandria:

> Rabbi Eliezer the Great said: There are two streams in the valley of Yadayim, one running this way and the other that way. It was estimated by the Sages that (at one time) they ran red, two parts water to one part blood. A Baraitha tells: for seven years the gentiles fertilized their fields with the blood of Jews, it being unnecessary for them to use ordinary fertilizer.[59]

Most scholars relate this passage to the Bar Kokhba War, and identify the "valley of Yadayim" with the "Valley of Beth Rimmon."[60] The difficulty is that R. Eliezer the Great was no longer alive at the time of the Bar Kokhba War! This leads to the conclusion that the aggadah just quoted refers to the Trajanic *tumultus,* and that the "Valley of Yadayim" means — the Delta of the Nile.[61]

---

59 Git. 57a.
60 Graetz, *Geschichte* IV, note 16.
61 A conclusion buttressed by the vocalized reading *yadei yam* (arms of the sea) in Gaster's edition of the *Ma'aseh Bukh,* p. 48. [The identification with the Delta had already been made in 1851 by Nahman Krochmal in his *Moreh Nevukhe ha-Zeman* (Hebrew, ed. Ravidowicz, London-Waltham 1961, p. 107); and by S.D. Rapoport in 1852 in his *Erekh Milin,* s.v. "Alexander Tiberius." Graetz explicitly rejected the idea, preferring to see in the midrash under consideration a mixture of traditions deriving from both the Trajanic War and the Hadrianic persecutions.]

Support for construing the aggadah in this way may come from what seems to be another version of the same tradition: [62]

> R. Eliezer the Great applied the verse *O God, the heathen are come into Thine inheritance* (Ps. 79:1) to the Emperor Hadrian, who came and seized Alexandria of Egypt, in which there were one hundred and twenty myriads of people, and talked them into assembling in the Vale of Yadayim, where that nation (the Greeks?) would not have the upper hand over them. They went out and stood in the Vale of Yadayim, and he posted fifty thousand swordsmen at their rear and butchered them until not one was left alive; as Scripture says, *They shed their blood like water*. (ib. verse 3). And the Sages added: Three streams of blood flowed at that time from the Vale of Yadayim into the Mediterranean, and those who assayed the sea-water found three parts of blood to one part water.

What stands out in this tradition is that it shows the Jews entrapped by guile, then overwhelmed and destroyed by a sudden onslaught. This agrees with the account given by the church historian Eusebius, except that in his version the attackers are the Greek civilians rather than the Roman military. The passage in the Yerushalmi which describes the Great Synagogue of Alexandria ends with the words: "Who destroyed it? The wicked Trugeinos (Trajan)."[63]

The downfall of the Jewish community of Alexandria is echoed in the last words of the following Baraitha:

> In the Land of Israel two practices (*in a man's family*) are proof presumptive that he is a *kohen*: the lifting up of the hands,[64] and the taking of a share in the distribution of the priestly gifts at the threshing-floors. In Syria the first presumption also obtains, up to the (geographical) limits reached by the calendar heralds of the Sanhedrin; but the second does not obtain. The rule for Babylonia is the same as for Syria.

---

62 *Seder Eliahu Rabba*, Vienna 1902, ed. M. Friedmann, p. 151.
63 Yer. Suk. V:55b–c; comp. JLTA I, p. 171.
64 Blessing the people: Num 7: 22–27.

Rabbi Simeon ben Eleazar (*Bavli*: ben Gamaliel) adds: originally, the same held good for Alexandria, *when there was a Beth Din there.*[65]

TRAJAN'S PARTHIAN WAR

The Jewish involvement with the Roman forces in the Tigris-Euphrates valley arose out of the great war mounted against Parthia by Trajan towards the end of his reign, and out of the Roman conquests in Armenia, Mesopotamia and Babylonia. In order to obtain some understanding of the Jewish role in the drama, we must try to form a picture of these great campaigns, despite the many unsolved problems that continue to bedevil this chapter in Roman history. Even the chronological aspects of these large-scale military operations are still under scholarly review. We shall adopt the conclusions of most present-day historians, who have been led by the newer epigraphical and numismatic evidence to conclusions at some variance with those of such classical historians as, for example, Theodor Mommsen.

The main elements in the currently favored view can be found in the following essays:

1) The article *Lusius Quietus* by E. Groag, in Pauly-Wissowa, Realenzyklopädie, vol. 26, pages 1874 to 1890; 2) *Notes on the Parthian Campaign of Trajan* by R.P. Longden, in the "Journal of Roman Studies," vol. 21 (1931), pages 1 to 35; and 3) *Trajan in the East* by R.P. Longden, in the Cambridge Ancient History, vol. II, pages 237 to 252, and 858-9.

The revised chronology proposed in these essays has the Parthian War beginning in the year 114, rather than in 115, as Mommsen had thought. Indeed, this reading places Trajan in Syria as early as October 113 C.E., making preparations for the campaign. The whole time-table looks like this:

> 114 — Conquest of Armenia and northern Mesopotamia (Nisibis and Singara put up no resistance. It seems the latter place served as the capital of an Arab kingdom.) King Mannus flees.

---

65 Tos. Peah, IV:6 (23) and Ket. III:1 (263); Yer. Ket. II:26d; Bavli ibid. 25a.

115 — Conquest of Adiabene and southern Mesopotamia.
115–116 (winter) — Conquest of Ctesiphon.
116 — Trajan reaches the Persian Gulf (conquest of Edessa).
116 — Peoples in the conquered territories rebel, and are suppressed. Roman forces begin to withdraw. Dura Europos.

The massacre of the Jews of Mesopotamia by Lusius Quietus is to be placed at the end of 116 or the beginning of 117.

It is highly unlikely that Trajan's intention was to conquer all of Parthia, and then go on in the footsteps of Alexander the Great and reach India — even though that ambition is perhaps hinted at by the *Historia Augusta*. On the other hand, it is clear that it *was* his purpose to stabilize and make secure the boundaries of the empire; and where that purpose seemed to call for the outward expansion of those boundaries, he was ready to depart from what had been post-Augustan policy, and push the frontiers out. Thus we have the two Dacian wars with Decebalus (101–3 and 105–7).

The more immediate cause that set things moving in the East was the Armenian question. The Parthians exercised suzerainty over the Armenian kingdom, and had the right to appoint a member of their own Arceside dynasty to its throne. However, this right had been limited by a treaty concluded with Rome during Nero's reign in 63 C.E. Under this agreement, appointment to the throne of Armenia became dependent on ratification by Rome.

In the year 110 the Parthian king Pacorus died, and was succeeded by his brother, Chosroes. The latter promptly removed his nephew Axidares from the throne of Armenia, and appointed another nephew, Parthamasiris, in his stead — without consulting Rome. Thus the treaty was violated, and Trajan had a perfect excuse to intervene.

As things developed, it became clear that Trajan had no intention of restoring the status quo, because in the event he turned Armenia into a Roman province. What the larger imperial plans were is probably illuminated by a glance backwards to a time some eight years earlier, when Trajan had annexed the Nabatean kingdom, as though preparing the ground for his advance into Asia. The most reasonable explanation for this activity in Western Asia seems to be a Roman drive to secure the trade route to India via the Indian Ocean, the Red Sea, Nabataea, the Land of Israel and Syria. Evidence for this is the new Roman highway connecting Aqaba to Damascus.[66]

The fact of the matter is that Roman trade relations with India rose to a peak during the course of the second century. This was one of the reasons why Trajan established a Red Sea fleet. It may also explain why an Indian delegation showed up in Rome in the year 107.

In the light of all this, it is not beyond the bounds of possibility that Trajan's campaigns against the Parthians were designed to put Rome in firm control of the best trade routes with India. To accomplish that, he would have to conquer Mesopotamia and Babylonia as far as the Persian Gulf — which is exactly what he proceeded to do.[67]

At first, the war went well for the Romans. Then, in the campaign of 115, they began to encounter stiffer resistance. But it was in the year 116 that things really turned sour. Word reached Trajan who was encamped on the Persian Gulf that all the conquered territories in his rear had risen up in rebellion. Aided apparently by Parthian forces that had penetrated the Roman rear from the direction of Media, subject peoples now showed their hand, cutting down Roman garrisons or putting them to flight.

In these circumstances, the Romans despatched three counter-insurgency forces. One of these was under Lusius Quietus, a Moor who had risen to command rank since the early days of Trajan's regime, and had participated in the Dacian campaigns. The second was led by Appius Maximus Santra, prefect of either Mesopotamia or Assyria. The third was commanded by S. Erucius Clarus and Julius Alexander. Maximus fell in action. Clarus and Julius Alexander subdued Seleucia and levelled it, while Lusius Quietus crushed Nisibis and Edessa.

---

66 For the inscription on one of the milestones, see Dessau, *Inscriptiones Latinae Selectae*, no. 5834. Comp. JLTA I, p. 143, n. 23.

67 Even after the annexation of Nabataea most trade with India still had to pass through Parthian territory. Besides, Malalus claims that the Parthians had attacked Syria not long before Trajan's campaign, and there is some evidence to support this. See the map in CAH vol. 11, p. 104.

The narrative sources at our disposal tell us that this anti-Roman uprising was widespread throughout the Middle East. It seems that all the subject peoples in the region turned on the Romans at one and the same time. One wonders whether the Romans had been behaving badly in those areas which Trajan had already annexed to the empire. The fact is that even "Greeks" — whether settler-families from the Aegean or thoroughly hellenized locals — joined the revolt. For example, Seleucia on the upper Tigris, a very Greek metropolis in Asia Minor, had to be reconquered. Further evidence of this antagonism is the inscription in the temple at Dura Europos, where we read that the Romans burned the place down, and the Greeks welcomed the returning Parthians with open arms.[68]

Another matter which should catch our eye (because it may throw some light on the subsequent encounter between the Jews and Lusius Quietus) concerns reports about the tactics used by that general in dealing with Nisibis and Edessa. He is said to have palavered with the rebels, come to an agreement with them on the peaceful cessation of hostilities, and then brought up his troops by stealth during the night and massacred his unsuspecting enemies the next day.

Finally, it should be remembered that in the area in which Nisibis and Edessa were the main urban centers, the Jews were numerous and influential. Josephus describes the former city as having been a "Jewish stronghold" in the first century.[69] It continued to be an important Jewish community into the second century; and the same holds good for Edessa.

As for Adiabene, which played a major part in the anti-Roman uprising, its royal family were no longer Jews.[70] But its population was still heavily Jewish, as we learn from the Syriac *Chronicle of Arbela*.[71] Note also the reference in the speech by Agrippa II (put

68 *Excavations at Dura Europos*, edited by Rostovtzeff, Brown and Welles. 1937.
69 Ant. XVIII: 9:1 (312) and 9:9 (379).
70 Even though some scholars think the contrary. The dynasty that had embraced Judaism during the reign of Claudius had all settled in Judaea. See Gregorovius in Ellbogen, op. cit. Graetz leaves the matter in doubt (*Geschichte* vol. III note 23).
71 Baumstark, *Geschichte d. Syrische Literatur*, pp. 134–5; Sachau, *Die Chronik von Arbela*.

into his mouth by Josephus): "You expect our brethren from Adiabene to fight for us."[72] Josephus also says that he sent an Aramaic version of his *Wars* to Adiabene.[73]

MESOPOTAMIAN MASSACRE

We must now examine the all too meagre sources that deal with the fate of Mesopotamian Jewry, and try to suggest solutions to the problems connected with this chapter in the history of the Jewish people. To begin with, there are words previously quoted from the *Ecclesiastical History* of Eusebius:

> The Emperor suspected that the Jews in Mesopotamia would also attack the inhabitants[74] and ordered Lusius Quietus to clean them out of the province. He organized a force and murdered a great multitude of the Jews there, and for this reform was appointed governor of Judaea by the Emperor.[75]

According to this, Quietus attacked the Jews at a time when they were not fighting the Romans at all. It was just that the Emperor felt uneasy about them, so he ordered a preemptive strike. Furthermore, the suspicion that the Jews might attack the other inhabitants is itself peculiar, considering that the other inhabitants, Greeks included, had all lined up against Rome!

Another thing apparent from Eusebius' account is that Trajan had not ordered the extermination of the Jews but rather their expulsion from the province; so that Quietus really exceeded his instructions. According to Nicephorus Callistus, he did this by using sneak tactics. "He arrayed his forces secretly, and then suddenly fell on the Jews."[76] One recalls that the same use of treacherous deception was attributed to Quietus in his pacification of Nisibis and Edessa.

72 JW II : 15 : 4 (388).
73 Ibid. I : I : 2 (6).
74 This seems to be the meaning of the phrase   ἐπιθήσεσθαι τοῖς αὐθότι The Syriac translation so understood it. But the intention may have been "(suspected) that. . . they would join with those in other countries."
75 Bk. IV : 2 : 2; Lake, I, pp. 305–7.
76 PG 145. Groag: ". . . Wenn die Angabe des Nikephoros Kallistos der sonst auf Eusebios zurückgeht, auf guter Uberlieferung beruht." Pauly-Wissowa, vol. 26, p. 1882.

But there is a discrepancy between the Eusebius of the *Ecclesiastical History* and the Eusebius of the *Chronicle*. The latter reads:

> Trajan ordered Lusius Quietus to root out the Jews, who had revolted in Mesopotamia, from that province. Quietus mounted an attack on them, and killed countless thousands of them.[77]

According to this version, then, the Jews in Mesopotamia actually *did* take part in the anti-Roman uprising. This, indeed, is the traditional view of the Syriac chroniclers (as of the Latin and the later Greek-Byzantine historians). One of the Syriac writers adds some vivid detail. Pseudo-Dionysius of Telmachre says:[78]

> He (Quietus) slaughtered many myriads of them, so that the streets and houses of the cities, and the highways and pathways of the countryside were filled to overflowing with unburied corpses.

But there is another very important source, written not long after the events themselves, which has a serious bearing on the role played by the Jews in the Mesopotamian clashes. At the same time, it may help explain the tactics of Quietus. The source is the Lexicon of Suidas, which says:[79]

> Trajan decided to expel the people, if possible; if not — to crush them, and thus to put an end to the great presumptuous wickedness.

It has been shown that this is a citation from the *Parthica* of Arrian, and that the "people" referred to are the Jews of Meso-

---

77 Chron. (Hier) Helm p. 196, Karst p. 219. The first edition of the *Chronicle* was finished in the year 303. The revised version, from which both Jerome and the Armenian derive, can be dated about 325. We are not sure whether the second edition was simply a continuation, or was a rewritten version. As for the *Ecclesiastical History*, it was written in 311–12, and given its final form in 325.

78 ed. Chabot, vol. 1, p. 123.

79 ed. Adler, vol. I, p. 400, s.v. Ἀτασθαλία and vol. IV, p. 53, s.v. παρείκοι.

potamia.[80] According to this, the Emperor's orders were to expel the Jews, if possible; but if they resisted, to kill them. That made it easy for Quietus to report that, for whatever reason, he had not found expulsion practicable, so that his only choice was to take the Jews by surprise and massacre them wholesale, as reported by Nicephorus.

At the same time, the citation from Arrian speaks of putting an end to "the great presumptuous wickedness." This can well mean that the Jews *were* participants in the anti-Roman uprising, which agrees with Eusebius' *Chronicle*. True, Arrian can be interpreted as making reference to "the great wickedness" of the Jewish *tumultus* in Cyrene and Egypt, so that his words would be in accord with the Eusebius of the *Ecclesiastical History*. This would make the Emperor's strike at the Jews of Mesopotamia a purely preemptive one. However, the most likely reading of the events is that the Mesopotamian Jews joined in with all the other conquered peoples of the region in the general uprising against the Roman legions.

Of course, there was a difference. The other peoples were punished severely by the Roman military action which suppressed their rebellion. The Jews paid an additional penalty: they were massacred later on, *after* the pacification described by Dio Cassius.

It should also be noted that in certain areas the Jews were the predominant element in the population, so that it was easy to single them out as the chief rebels. To be sure, they could have had their own special reasons for being anti-Roman; and an additional stimulus would have been the news of what was happening to their brethren at the opposite end of the fertile crescent. But there is nothing in our sources to indicate any specifically Jewish uprising of any size in Mesopotamia, or any direct connection with the fighting in Egypt, Cyrene and Cyprus.

It seems most likely that the Jews of Mesopotamia joined the general population in the wholesale attacks against Trajan's expeditionary force. At the same time, Trajan was badly stung by the distinctly *Jewish* warfare going on far to his rear. He therefore gave the orders which resulted in the massive slaughter of Meso-

80 P.W. vol. 26, pp. 1880–81; *Philologus* 74 (1917) p. 82.

potamian Jewry. This may also be the background for that version of events — perhaps the official one — which spoke of a purely Jewish revolt having taken place after the wider one had been put down.

CHAPTER SEVENTEEN

THE WAR OF QUIETUS

Our sources for events in Judaea during the days of Trajan are so clouded by uncertainty that there are historians who doubt whether anything at all happened there, beyond a certain amount of tension caused by the fighting in the Diaspora. The problem, apart from its intrinsic importance, also bears directly on the question that arose at the beginning of this volume: was the war against Trajan part of a movement with messianic pretensions? Was its aim to throw off the yoke of Rome and re-establish, in one form or another, a Kingdom of Israel? If so, the Jews of Judaea could scarcely have been uninvolved.

In order to deal with such questions, it would be best to examine the sources for this episode in Jewish history, or those that appear to have some connection with it. They can be divided into four groups: a) traditions which refer, or seem to refer, to actual warfare in Judaea; b) inscriptions which seem to indicate that something was going on at the time; c) stories about Pappus and Lulianus and "The Martyrs of Lod," plus a report by an early Christian writer about Quietus in Jerusalem; and d) certain data regarding oppressive acts by the Roman occupying authorities which may be connected with the matter under examination.

NARRATIVE TRADITIONS

During the war of Vespasian they banned the custom of the wearing of a crown by the bridegroom, and the beating of a drum (*at wedding processions*). During the war of Quietus they abolished the bridal crown, and ordered fathers not to teach their sons Greek ...[1]

1 Sot. IX:14. Regarding the reading "Titus" in the current editions of the Mishnah, see above, Chapter XV, note 1, p. 325.

The tradition here recorded does not specify where the said "war of Quietus" took place, so that Schürer could assign it to Mesopotamia.[2] But there are several reasons for rejecting his suggestion. The Mishnah is a Palestinian document; it would scarcely record an event from outside Judaea without saying so. Secondly, the reference occurs between "the war of Vespasian" and "the last war" (that of Bar Kokhba), both Palestinian events.[3] Finally, an ordinance against Greek would have been altogether out of place in the Tigris-Euphrates area.[4]

A second tannaitic tradition comes from the *Seder Olam Rabbah* :[5]

> ... From the war of Vespasian to the war of Quietus — 52 years; from the war of Quietus to the war of Ben Kosiba *(Bar Kokhba)* — 16 years. The war of Ben Kosiba itself three and one-half years...

(It is perhaps worth noting that the same report, in substantially the same language, occurs as a quotation from Seder Olam Rabbah in a Gaonic document.)[6]

This tradition, to be sure, contains a slight chronological discrepancy. The earliest possible date for the outbreak of the "war of Vespasian" is 66, and the year of Trajan's death is 117, so

2 Schürer, *Geschichte*, I, p. 667 [Vermes and Millar I, pp. 533–534.]
3 Groag in P.W. vol. 26, pp. 1874 ff.
4 All other traditions, deriving from other periods, about the proscription of the Greek language and 'Greek wisdom' are explicitly rooted in Eretz Israel. Thus, a tradition dealing with the feud between the princely brothers Hyracanus and Aristobulus, and the consequent invasion of Jerusalem by Pompey, says:
> ... when the Hasmonean kings fought against one another ... it was then that they said: cursed be he who teaches his son Greek wisdom (Sot. 49b et passim).

The same applies to the ordinance against "the tongue of the gentiles," one of the 18 *gezerot* which, it is generally believed, were adopted during the tense years that preceded the War of the Destruction.
5 ed. Neubauer II, p. 66 ed. Ratner p. 145; comp. *Me'or Einayim* by Azariah dei Rossi, chap. 19, and Schürer I, p. 669 [Vermes and Millar I, p. 534, n. 94.]
6 Ginzberg, *Ginze Schechter*, II, p. 249; *Otzar ha-Geonim*, Sot. p. 275.

that the maximum possible interval would be 51 years, not 52. Still, that does not invalidate the essential core of the recollection. So much for Jewish sources. We move on to narratives compiled by non-Jews. In the "Life of Hadrian" attributed to Spartianus there is the following passage : [7]

> On taking possession of the imperial power Hadrian at once resumed the policy of the early emperors and devoted his attention to maintaining peace throughout the world. For the nations which Trajan had conquered began to revolt; the Moors moreover began to make attacks and the Sarmatians to wage war, the Britons could not be kept under Roman sway and Egypt was thrown into disorder by riots and finally Libya and Palestine showed the spirit of rebellion.[8]

Although this text speaks only of "the spirit of rebellion," the inclusion of Palestine with Egypt, the Moors, and the Sarmatians suggests that some overt acts of violence are meant.

Nor can we dismiss out of hand the evidence of the Armenian historian Moses of Koren, who writes : [9]

> ... When the Egyptians and the Palestinians saw this (*i.e. an attack by the Parthians and Armenians against the Romans after the death of Nerva*) they refused to pay the Roman taxes. At that time Trajan became Emperor, and after pacifying the whole of the West (*a reference to the Dacian Wars*) he proceeded against the Egyptians and the Palestinians. Having subdued these, he went on to fight the Parthians.

Even though he has got the chronology wrong, and we may doubt the accuracy of his statement that the Parthians attacked the

---

7   In *Scriptores Historiae Augustae,* [ed. and trans. by David Magie, London, 1922, Vol. I, p. 15.]

8   [The date and credibility of the *Historia Augusta* have been discussed at length by historians. For a resume of the current state of opinion, see Stern, GLA II, pp. 612 ff.]

9   Moses von Chorene, *Geschichte Gross Armeniens,* aus dem Armenischen übersetzt, by Lauer, p. 115.

Romans before Trajan's campaign, his words show that there was a tradition in the Middle East about warfare in Judaea during Trajan's time.

Another possible reference to disturbances in Eretz Israel at the time in question is found in the work of Michael Syrus who writes that at the end of Trajan's reign the Jews in Egypt rebelled and chose themselves a king named "Lumpusuas" who led them to Judaea. Then Trajan sent Lusius against them and he destroyed myriads of them; therefore was Lusius made *hegmon* of Judaea.[10]

Now, it is obvious that Michael has confused the events in Judaea with what happened in Mesopotamia, and has confounded both with what occurred in Egypt.[11] Nevertheless, at the core of his version stands a collective memory of some sort of insurrectionary activity in Judaea, and that counts for something. For the rest, we may be properly skeptical about his story that the rebels came to Judaea from the outside. That may be no more than interpretive embroidery on his part.

An even more garbled version of this Middle Eastern tradition is related by Eutychios ibn Batriq.[12] He says that in the days of Trajan the Jews returned to Jerusalem. Trajan came and slew many of them. He was opposed by a rebel called "the Babylonian." Trajan fought against him and fell in battle.

EPIGRAPHIC EVIDENCE

In 1895 a Roman inscription was found on Mount Zion in Jerusalem.[13] The short Latin text, which is defective but can be fairly easily reconstructed, reveals a dedication

> to Jove for the welfare and victory of the Emperor Trajan etc. etc. ... and the Roman people ... by a detachment of the IIIrd Legion Cyrenaica.

The titles that accompany the emperor's name show that the inscription comes from the year 116, or early in 117. Since at that

10   ed. Chabot, IV, p. 105.
11   See Groag, P.W. 16, p. 1889.
12   *Annales,* PG. vol. III, pp. 986–987.
13   Palestine Exploration Fund, vol. 25 (1896) p. 133.

time the IIIrd Cyrenaica was stationed in Egypt (and continued to be until the year 125, when it was transferred to Arabia) the presence in Jerusalem of a detachment (*vexillatio*) indicates that something was going on that created a need for reinforcements there.[14]

I suggest that another Roman military inscription, which turned up in 1930 during building operations in the Armenian quarter of Old Jerusalem, may also be dated to this time. It mentions a temple erected within the military camp of an African contingent, and devoted to "Geniu Africe."[15] There can be little doubt that the shrine in question was erected by troops from Africa. The problem is: when?

It seems to me reasonable to assign this inscription to the last days of Trajan, and to identify these troops as the Moorish tribesmen whom Lusius Quietus had commanded in Parthia, and had brought with him to Judaea when he took over as prefect.[16] The identification seems all the more likely in the light of their bad Latin — *Geniu Africe* instead of *Genio Africae*.

I am much more hesitant about suggesting that another inscription discovered fairly recently be dated to the years we are discussing. It appears to be the epitaph of a Roman soldier called Bitius Crescens. The number of years he lived is no longer legible; but it is stated clearly that he took part in "the wars in Dacia, Armenia, Parthia and Judaea."[17]

When this text was first published, it was assumed that "the war in Judaea" meant the Bar Kokhba War; and the truth is that most

14 It may be pointed out that from the year 70 on, the regular garrison of Judaea was the Xth Fretensian. Elements of that legion took part in the Parthian War: see *Inscrip. Lat. Select.* no. 2727.

[On the other hand, it may be suggested that these troop movements are not conclusive proof of military activity in Judaea. Perhaps the detachment of the IIIrd was simply filling in as replacement for those elements of the Xth that were in action on the eastern front.]

15 *Revue Biblique*, 1931, pp. 191–4

16 Comp. Spartianus, *Life of Hadrian*: "He (Hadrian) deprived Lusius Quietus of the command of the Moorish tribesmen who were serving under him, and then dismissed him from the army." v:8 (Magie, p. 17).

17 *L'année Epigraphique*, 1929, p. 45, n. 167.

second century Roman inscriptions, when they speak of war in Judaea, do mean the Bar Kokhba Revolt (132–135). The difficulty here is that Crescens fought in the Dacian campaign at the very beginning of the century, and that would make him a very old sweat indeed. It was not normal for a Roman soldier to serve for more than 25 years. Even if he started as a very young soldier in the *Second* Dacian War (105–107), it would still be stretching things for him to have been in action against Bar Kokhba. I therefore suggest, albeit tentatively, that the entire military career of this Roman soldier was confined to the reign of the Emperor Trajan, and that the fighting he took part in in Judaea was a real *pulmus shel qitos.*

Since we have quoted inscriptions which deal with the setting up of shrines in Jerusalem, it will be instructive for us to examine an early Christian tradition dealing with "the abomination of desolation," a statue reputedly set up on the site of Jewish Holy Temple. Bar Salibi, a Christian Syriac writer, quotes a fragment of a commentary on Matthew by Hippolytus (third century):

> It was not Vespasian who set up the statue of a god in the Temple, but rather the legion which Traianus Quintus, a Roman commander brought, had set up an image of a deity there. It was called Koré.[18]

The fragment from Hippolytus is rather obscure, and opinions have varied as to its meaning. The translation here offered rests to a considerable extent on the interpretation first suggested by Clermont-Ganneau in *Receuil d'Archéologie Orientale,* and then developed more fully by Krauss in his *Monumenta Talmudica.*[19] There are those who hold that the Traianus Quintus mentioned in this passage is the commander of the Xth Legion mentioned by Josephus.[20] However, we know that that commander was posted out of the country before the fall of Jerusalem, and replaced by another officer.

This business of the "abomination of desolation" attracted a

18 *Scriptores Syri,* ed. Sedlacek, second series, vol. ci. p. 17.
19 R.A.O. vol. VI, p. 199; *Monumenta Talmudica,* p. 117–118.
20 JW III:7:31 (289).

lot of attention from early Christian writers.[21] They wanted to know when it happened, and who was to blame. Some pointed a finger at Pontius Pilate (a statue of Caligula?); others blamed Titus; still others thought it was Hadrian.[22] However, when Hippolytus absolved Vespasian from guilt in this matter, we may be sure that it was not because he loved this particular Caesar more; but rather to indicate his belief that the act was not tied to the War of the Destruction, but belonged to another period in history.

We are left to conclude that the thing happened in connection with a different war, and a different commander; that "Traianus Quintus" is actually "Quietus"; and that the name Traianus derives from the regnant Caesar.[23] If this is so, then the old Christian tradition fits in with the evidence of the inscriptions. Pagan temples went up in the Holy City — in this case a shrine to the goddess Κόρη (= Persephone), who is perhaps identical with Artemis.[24] Putting all this evidence together — the Jewish traditions, the Roman inscriptions, the Christian memories of idols in the holy places, and the general tradition that such acts usually aroused violent resistance, we emerge with the strengthened assumption that some sort of uprising took place in Judaea during the consulship of Lusius Quietus.

Together with these sources I would include the puzzling Mishnah in Tractate Ta'anit:

> On the seventeenth of Tammuz the Tablets (*of the Law*) were shattered; that was the date on which the daily sacrifice was discontinued; on which The City was breached; and on

21 The *shiquts meshomem* (*shomem*) of Daniel 11:31 and 12:11. In Jewish tradition it was also identified with Roman acts of desecration; see Taan. 28b.

22 See Jerome on Daniel 11:31. For the theme in patristic literature, see *Revue Biblique*, 1936, pp. 53 ff.

23 Krauss (op. cit.) suggested that "Traianus" was one of the names of Lusius Quietus; but later he backed off, in REJ 80, pp. 117-8. To my mind, he should have stuck to his guns.
   [Mary Smallwood came to a similar conclusion: "Traianus Quintus is easily recognizable as Quietus, the legate being confused with the emperor who appointed him." Historia XI (1962) p. 506.]

24 As demonstrated by Clermont-Ganneau, RAO III, 186-8.

which Apostomus burned the Torah and set up an image in the Sanctuary.[25]

To be sure, the Yerushalmi does report that there were two versions of this text, one read *he'emid* (he set up) and the other read *hu'amad* (it was set up).

According to the latter version, it was the image of Menasseh. According to the other version, with the verb in the active voice, Apostomus set up his own image.[26]

But if we focus on the Mishnah text itself, there can be no doubt that the correct reading is *he'emid*, supported by our principal versions; which is to say that Apostomus set up the statue (but certainly not of himself).

All sorts of solutions have been proposed for the identity of this mysterious character. There are those who suggest that he was the Roman soldier who, according to Josephus, set fire to the Temple. But that fellow put up no image. Schlatter, on the other hand, proposed the reading *"apostatis"* — and detected the presence of Elisha ben Abuya![27]

I would rather connect this mishnaic tradition with the one recorded by Hippolytus, and identify the culprit as an officer of Quietus' headquarters command. And while we are speculating, I would hazard a further guess, and suggest a possible connection with one *Posthumius*, whose name occurs in a recently discovered inscription as procurator and adjutant to Quadratus, consul of Syria in 115–117.[28] But this, as we have said, must remain in the realm of speculation.

PAPPUS AND LULIANUS

The tradition that two important men, Pappus and Lulianus

25 Taan. IV:6.
26 Yer. ibid. 68d.
27 [Apparently he changed his mind, not about the reading, but about the identity of the "apostate," because his 3rd edition states: "Die Beiziehung von Mi. Taan. 4.7. (*sic*) in der zweiter Ausgabe war ein Irrtum . ʒ . der Apostat war Menelaus." (!) (*Geschichte Israels,* 3te Aufl. 1925, p. 452).]
28 *Syria,* 1939, pp. 53–59.

(perhaps Julianus) were put to death by Trajan, is found in a number of sources, both tannaitic and amoraic. The most frequently cited comes from the Sifra on Emor:

> Now when Trugeinos killed (*sic. ms. Rome; current editions*: "when Mareinos caught") Pappus and Lulianus his brother at Laodicea, he said to them: if you are of the people of Hananiah, Mishael and Azariah, let your God come and rescue you ... It was reported that before he had left that place there arrived messengers from Rome who split his skull open.[29]

It is almost a certainty that this tradition is based on the fate of Lusius Quietus, who was executed by order of the Senate in the early days of Hadrian's reign. The switch of names from the legate to the emperor who appointed him is, as noted above, a not uncommon phenomenon.

There is, however, a problem created by the appearance of Pappus and Lulianus at a *later* date, in a tradition which has them handling the affairs of pilgrims on their way to Jerusalem rather later, during Hadrian's reign.[30] Graetz made an elaborate effort to dispose of the contradiction by stressing the printed version over the manuscript ("caught" rather than "killed"). To do so, he had to argue that the phrase in the Bavli "even so he killed them on the spot" is a later interpolation. He also had to posit a mix-up between Laodicea and Lod, and between this case and the two other martyrs of whom we know little — Shemayah and Ahiah.[30a]

Unfortunately, the solution proposed by Graetz does not hold up. The text he rejects ("killed") cannot be so lightly set aside, supported as it is by so many solid versions.[31] So that we are left

---

29 Sifra, IX:5, ed. Weiss 99d; Taan. 18b; Semahot VIII:15, ed. Higger, p. 164; EcclR 3, et passim.

30 GenR. LXIV:8, ed. Theodor-Albeck, p. 710.

30a *Geschichte* IV, pp. 411–414, n. 14; see also Megillat Taanit XII; but the whole episode is lacking in the leading mss; see Lichtenstein in HUCA VIII, p. 272.

31 Yalkut, Yitro 247a; Midrash Hagadol Vayyikra ed. Rabinowitz p. 560; Ma'aseh Bukh ed. Gaster, p. 17.

with the contradiction between the two traditions about Pappus and Lulianus unresolved. The baraita has them martyred in Laodicea in the last days of Trajan; the Midrash[32] shows them still active during the reign of Hadrian.

The tradition that these men were martyred during the reign of Trajan seems to be preserved in certain other sources, such as the following from the Sifra:[33]

> *I will break the pride of your power* (Lev. 26:16). Some say this verse refers to those dignitaries, the pride of Israel, Pappus and Lulianus and Alexandri and his associates...

Add to this the passage in the Yerushalmi:[34]

> Is not the 12th *(of Adar)* the Day of Tirion? R. Jacob bar Aha said, the Day of Tirion was abrogated. It was the day on which Pappus and Lulianus were put to death. (Bavli: The Day of Traianus ... they set it aside, because on that day Shemayah and Ahiah were killed.)[35]

Just what the "Day of Tirion" means is one of the more arcane puzzles in Talmudic literature, and a host of surmises have been put forward for its solution. It seems to me that we can only assume that the day originated as some sort of celebration for the removal of that bête noire of the Jewish people, Lusius Quietus, the appointee of "Traianus", with whom his name became entangled. The Yerushalmi passage quoted above reports that Pappus and Lulianus were put to death at the same time; whereas the Sifra, like Genesis Rabba, preserves a variant tradition that has them surviving well into Hadrian's reign.

Another tradition that deals with these two men is recorded elsewhere in the Yerushalmi: It concerns the rule that one may perform most forbidden acts if, by so doing, one saves a life, in-

---

32 See note 30.
33 Sifra V: 2, ed. Weiss 111d.
34 Yer. Taan. II 66a, Meg. I: 70c.
35 Sic, not *aḥiv* ("his brother"); see Dikduke Soferim; note ′ח Because of the interchange of names between the two Talmudim, it has been suggested that Shemayah and Ahiah are really Pappus and Lulianus; but the identity is far from proven.

cluding one's own — but only in private. When, on the other hand, one's behavior may set an example for others, and may thus have historic consequences, one must suffer martyrdom:

> In public, however, one must refuse to violate even the least of the commandments, though one's life be at stake. There was the case of Pappus and Lulianus, to whom they handed water in a colored glass (*making it appear that they were partaking of a heathen libation*) but they refused it.[36]

In sum, it can be said that while the traditions about these martyrs are far from clear, they do at a minimum support the other evidence tending to show that there was more than mere tension in Judaea during Trajan's last years — there was a genuine disturbance, a real *pulmus*, ruthlessly though it may have been suppressed.

ACTS OF REPRESSION

In the Tractate *Shabbat* we learn indirectly of certain prohibitions enacted by the Roman authorities in Judaea:

> Rabbi Eliezer says: if he had not brought the circumcision knife before the Sabbath he must bring it openly on the Sabbath. But during *sakanah* (danger-time) he conceals it in the presence of witnesses.[37]

In the same context, the Bavli quotes a Baraïta:

> He brings it openly, but he must not bring it concealed — this is Rabbi Eliezer's view. Rabbi Judah said, quoting Rabbi Eliezer: "During the *sakanah* they used to (ms.: *we used to*) bring it concealed, having shown it to witnesses."

---

36 Yer. Shevi. IV: 35a; Sanh. III:21b; comp. EcclR. IX:I, where the mention of "the shame of Pappus and Lulianus" helps to becloud the issue by implying that they *did* behave badly. I should add that in my opinion "the martyrs of Lod" belong to a later time, though we are completely in the dark about them.

37 Mishnah, Shab. XIX:1; Bavli ibid 130a. [The point is that the commandment to circumcise on the eighth day takes precedence over the commandment to observe the Sabbath, and this must be shown demonstratively. When concealment is unavoidable, let there at least be witnesses.]

Now, as a general rule *"sakanah"* refers to the Hadrianic persecutions connected with the Bar Kokhba Revolt in the thirties. But in this instance that will not do, because by then Rabbi Eliezer was no longer living. We are forced to conclude that in this case the *sakanah* was the *pulmus shel qitos.*

To be sure, it is possible to cast doubt on this line of evidence. For one thing, the phrase about the *sakanah* may be a later addition to the ruling of Rabbi Eliezer. And as for the Baraita, the accuracy of Rabbi Judah's quotation may be called into question. The truth is that Rabbi Judah frequently testifies to what happened during the Hadrianic *sakanah.* Nevertheless, it would be rather arbitrary of us to reject Rabbi Judah's statement without a shred of evidence against it.

It is also true that Büchler expressed some doubt as to whether there was religious repression of the *sakanah* type during the consulship of Lusius Quietus.[38] But we have already pointed out that the Romans, though normally tolerant of licit religions, were quite ready to suspend all such rights when faced with rebellion, actual or putative.

We may apply a similar line of reasoning to the following passage in the Tosefta: [39]

Rabbi Jose said: (Zuck: *Rabbi Joshua said:*)
On one occasion four Sages met secretly with Rabbi Eleazar ben Azariah in Sepphoris . . .

The secrecy of the meeting shows that it took place during a time of danger. On the other hand, Rabbi Eleazar ben Azariah was no longer alive during the Hadrianic persecutions. That leaves us only the time of Quietus.

We could go on to other traditions whose *dramatis personae* would lead us to assign them to the same period. Let us confine ourselves to one more.

The well-known tradition about the execution of Rabban Simeon and Rabbi Ishmael has given rise to a great deal of difficulty and discussion, because the identity of these martyrs is not at all clear.

38   JQR os. XVI (1904) pp. 155–156.
39   Kel. BB II:2 (591).

In my opinion, the tradition has mixed together two separate events: the deaths of Rabban Simeon ben Gamaliel the Elder and Rabbi Ishmael the Kohen, both of whom died in the War of the Destruction, and the later execution of two Sages with similar names, Rabbi Simeon and Rabbi Ishmael (not the colleague of Rabbi Akiba) who lost their lives in the War of Quietus.

I suggest that these events in Judaea at the end of Trajan's reign became blurred in the people's memory because of their proximity to both earlier and later catastrophies of greater magnitude. They were overshadowed by the earlier War of Destruction under Vespasian and Titus, and the later War of Bar Kokhba under Hadrian. Tradition tended to assign the lesser violence in between to one great war or the other.

It seems to me that our sources support this statement as it applies to the case under discussion.

> When Samuel the Little lay dying he uttered this prophecy: Simeon and Ishmael will meet their deaths by the sword, and their colleagues will die violently, and the people will be plundered, and great troubles will follow thereafter.[40]

Now, at first blush, one might say that Samuel the Little was talking about the Bar Kokhba War; but then, why would he fail to mention such outstanding martyrs of that war as Rabbi Akiba, Rabbi Haninah ben Teradyon and the rest? Furthermore, there is another passage about Samuel the Little which bears on the date of his death:

> When Samuel the Little died ... Rabban Gamaliel and Rabbi Eleazar ben Azariah eulogized him. And at his death he uttered the prophecy etc. ...[41]

Since, then, Samuel the Little died before Rabban Gamaliel and before Rabbi Eleazar ben Azariah, he must have died long before the Bar Kokhba Revolt. We would then be justified in relating his deathbed statement to the War of Quietus.

As a last word on the subject, it may be said that the appoint-

40 Tos. Sot. XIII:4 (319): cf. Bavli Sanh. 11a et passim.
41 Semahot, VIII:8, ed. Higger, pp. 152–3.

ment of Lusius Quietus as governor of Judaea with the rank of consul was scarcely likely to have been simply a reward for his ruthlessness in Mesopotamia. Trajan was obviously either suppressing an uprising, or nipping one in the bud.[42]

TRAJAN AND THE JEWS : CONCLUSIONS

When we embarked several chapters ago on our study of the Jews during the reign of Trajan, in the Diaspora as well as in the Land of Israel, we raised certain broad questions. These questions we must now attempt to answer, as we summarize what we have learned.

1. The battles fought by the Jews in Egypt, Cyrenaica and Cyprus were fierce and bloody. In economic as well as demographic terms this prolonged fighting had grave consequences for the general population as well as for the Jews themselves. But it was the latter who were damaged beyond recovery. The abrupt decline of Egyptian Jewry can be dated from this point in history.

2. In the Tigris-Euphrates valley the anti-Roman resistance was general, not specifically Jewish. The Jews simply participated, along with the rest of the population. Apparently, too, an attack on the Roman rear by a Parthian force had a lot to do with making things difficult for the invaders. But the subsequent massacre of the Jews by Lusius Quietus was an entirely separate matter. The Jews were singled out, and subjected to special punishment.

3. There *was* an uprising in Judaea, but it was aborted. Had

---

42 [It cannot be said that this conclusion, repeated by Alon over and over in this chapter, represents a consensus. Baron, for example, differs: "Palestine Jewry's participation in the uprising against Trajan appears ever more questionable." (*Social and Religious History*, 1952, Vol. II, p. 370). On the other hand, Mary E. Smallwood comes to a conclusion remarkably similar to Alon's. She subjects the Greek and Latin sources to a rigorous re-examination, dissects the archaeological evidence, and cites the Talmudic and midrashic sources (via translations) in an article entitled "Palestine in 115–117 A.D." (Historia, vol. II, 1961.) Her conclusion: "The general picture that emerges from this investigation seems to be that there was more than mere unrest and a threat of revolt in Palestine towards the end of Trajan's reign. The evidence suggests that an actual rising began, which military force was required to suppress."]

it taken on anything like the proportions of the war in the Diaspora, this *pulmus shel qitos* could not have become so blurred in the popular memory. Nor would it have been possible for the people to rise again a bare 15 years later in the Bar Kokhba Revolt.

4. As for the sequence of events: our studies show that the fighting began in Cyrene, then spread to Egypt and Cyprus, Mesopotamia came later; Judaea last of all.

5. The most difficult questions concern the *causes* of these outbreaks, and the *war-aims* of the Jews. The fact that these explosions followed one another in such rapid succession over so wide an area has made it appear likely to many historians that they were all rooted in the same cause, and all directed towards a single aim. According to this reading, we are confronted with a general and widespread uprising of the Jewish people against the Roman Empire, a movement of messianic dimensions that aimed to restore the kingdom of Israel. Those who hold this view claim that the destruction of the Temple in Jerusalem had fundamentally altered the attitude of the Jews of the Diaspora to Rome. The old loyalty to the power that had for so long guaranteed them their rights was now changed to hatred and a thirst for revenge. All that was needed was an opportunity; and when Rome became embroiled in the Great Parthian War, her legions concentrated on the eastern front — that opportunity was at hand. There are even some who claim that all the fighting was centrally co-ordinated — from Judaea.

It seems to me that a careful study of the sources leads to more modestly framed conclusions, somewhat as follows:

a) The disturbances in Egypt, Cyrenaïca, Lybia and Cyprus were the result of the long-standing tensions between the Jews and their Greek-speaking neighbors in those countries. The Destruction had made matters worse by weakening the social and political power of the Jews, thus emboldening the Hellenes to try to deprive their old rivals altogether of their civil rights. As a rule the Roman government kept a watchful eye on the situation and refused to let this happen. But the two antagonists did keep at each other.

b) The intervention of the Roman military when things got out of hand led to situations when Jews found themselves fighting

Romans as well as "Greeks". As for the native populations, the Jews had no quarrel with them. It seems there were times when the latter helped the Jews, and other times when they fought against them.

c) In any event, when Jews refused to lay down their arms, even though confronted by Roman troops, the struggle developed into a nationalist war. Zealot elements from Judaea fanned the flames of resistance to Rome, something which is hinted at in rabbinic sources.[43] If we were sure that there really was a "king of the Jews" (Lukuas) as reported by Eusebius, the nationalist or messianic aspect of the uprising would be confirmed. But the fact that Dio says nothing of this nature counts against it, even though there is something in one of the papyri about a "king of the mime and the scene."[44] I would guess that the gentile historical tradition, whether by design or in all innocence, awarded a royal title to the Jewish military leader, and thereby pinned an anti-Roman political label on the movement right from the start.

These varying undercurrents in the Trajanic uprisings — the social aspects represented by the long struggle with the Hellenes, and the political aspect that developed out of fighting with Roman soldiers — gradually became intertwined. Nor can there be much doubt that the Jews disagreed among themselves as to the nature of the struggle and its aims. It is obvious that the Jews of Alexandria were most reluctant to be drawn into an anti-Roman movement. This could scarcely have been unknown to the local authorities, as well as to their superiors in Rome itself.

The "Hellenic" citizens of Alexandria took advantage of this Jewish hesitancy, both by accusing the Jews in their city of disloyalty to Rome, and by mounting an enormous and tragic pogrom against them. The evidence shows that the imperial power knew what was going on. It also shows that this once proud community was shattered beyond all hope of recovery.[45]

---

43 Mekhilta de Rabbi Ishmael, Beshallah, II, ed. Horovitz-Rabin p. 95, Lauterbach, I, p. 216.

44 [CPJ II, no. 158a, p. 89, cf. commentary ibid. p. 95.]

45 [The issues dealt with by Alon in this summary are far from settled. His handwritten notes bear the date "Winter 5706" (1945–46). It was not long thereafter that more archaeological and epigraphic data

Conclusions

began to emerge from Cyrenaica and Libya, partly as a result of World War II bombardment, partly because of postwar British occupation. Especially the degree of destruction to which pagan temples had been subjected, which was now more clearly revealed, taken together with the *mass movement* of Jews from Cyrenaica into Egypt described in the sources, led to some reconsiderations. The direction of the movement was towards Jerusalem. Were these Jews embarking on a "long march" to the homeland, scorching the earth behind them? Quite possibly, suggests Alexander Fuks of the Hebrew University in his article "Aspects of the Jewish Revolt in A.D. 115–117" in the *Journal of Roman Studies*. Vol. 50, 1960, pp. 98 ff. "Physical damage, especially in Cyrenaica, but also in Egypt and Cyprus, was so thorough and extensive that one might suppose that the Jews did not intend to go on living in these countries. And in fact, the Jews of Cyrene left their country, leaving scorched earth behind. Was this *trek* (italics added) only a first stage in leaving the Diaspora? Was Judaea the final destination of the rebels?"

As for the motives of the Jewish rebels, here too Fuks finds the evidence suggestive rather than conclusive. "The objectives of the Jewish war can only be guessed at. Annihilation of the pagans and their holy places seems to have been an objective in itself, and not merely incidental to fighting."

The proposition is put more forcefully by Shimon Applebaum of Tel Aviv University. "The decisive universal factor was psychological — the messianic aspiration derived from the destruction of the Temple, and the activist ideology of which the Sicarian is an example." (*Greeks and Jews in Ancient Cyrene,* Leiden, 1979, p. 331). At the same time, Applebaum can point to evidence of an agricultural crisis in North Africa, so that the *tumultus* there can be described as "a movement by radicalized agrarian zealots with the aim of marching on Eretz Israel" (ibid. p. 328). A certain strategic pattern can also be reconstructed from hints in the papyri, such as the battle at Memphis, the Jewish ship at Pelusium, and even the fighting in Mesopotamia. The aim would have been to seize "control of the route from Babylon to the Red Sea and the approaches to Sinai and Judaea." Attractive as this theory is, Applebaum is aware of the difficulties it involves when looked at against the much wider geographical canvas on which the uprising took place; not to speak of the staggeringly quixotic nature of the whole undertaking from a purely military point of view. "It is hard to think ... that the insurgents hoped to overthrow the entire Roman Empire at one blow; their immediate objective seems to have been Eretz Israel" (ibid. p. 335). As for the situation outside of Africa — "the position in Cyprus is obscure" (p. 331). It must be admitted that there is a good deal about the Jewish *tumultus* which continues to remain obscure.]

[429]

CHAPTER EIGHTEEN

THE RIDDLE OF HADRIAN

During the summer of the year 117, while in the field with his armies on the eastern front, Trajan was stricken with a fatal illness, and died on his way back to Rome.[1] His successor to the throne of the Caesars was his ward, Publius Aelius Hadrianus.

The first fifteen years of Hadrian's reign present the historian of the Jews with a bewildering array of events — and of knotty problems. It was a time when Rome had to come to terms with the failure of her last great effort to extend her sway over those ancient lands of the Middle East which had been the cradle of civilization. Might she have perceived the Jews as a major factor in frustrating that effort? Their role in Mesopotamia, in North Africa and in Cyprus would certainly have been interpreted that way. And is it possible that survivors of the fighting in those lands had made their way to Judaea — which might account for the fact that the disturbances there came after they were over in those other countries? And did unrest in Judaea continue to simmer right up to the outbreak of the Bar Kokhba Revolt?

There can be no doubt that the decisive event of the time in Judaea was the Bar Kokhba War — "the last *polemos*". The question with which it confronts the historian is the biggest enigma of all. How could a people so recently bled white in the war of the Destruction summon up the reserves of strength, not to speak

---

1 [In the published version of Alon's Hebrew lecture notes, this chapter opens with several pages of tentative schematization forecasting his planned treatment of the entire balance of the period. (Tol. I, p. 265 ff.). His handwritten notes indicate that this was the beginning of the academic year, and he probably felt it was desirable at this stage to reorient his listeners, but in the circumstances, the editor-translator has felt justified in omitting those pages.]

of morale, with which to recapture Jerusalem and to hold the
Roman Empire at bay for three whole years?

Undoubtedly the way to deal with these problems is to analyze
the Bar Kokhba War itself; to study the sequence of events, the
victories and defeats, the battlefields and the battles themselves,
the make-up and strength of the opposing forces, the degree of
popular support behind the rebels, the attitude of the nation's
leaders — and so on. However, we shall learn even more from
a study of the *prehistory* of the Revolt; its immediate causes, to
be sure, but also the events of the preceding years. That includes
the uprising in the Diaspora, the related *"Polemos shel Quietus"*
in Judaea and its aftermath early in the reign of Hadrian. All of
these may be connected with the final big explosion, whether as
causal factors, or as *early warning* signals.

As a matter of fact, there are historians who take the two decades from 115 to 135 as a single unit, as if to say: we are dealing
here with one last mighty effort by the Jewish people to cast off
the yoke of Rome, and to establish the kingdom of Israel, the
hoped-for reign of the Messiah.

But we will refrain from such sweeping generalizations. Our
purpose is, rather, to see what we can learn in detail about the
events themselves, and to subject each development to critical
analysis. Only then will we be able to fit the results together into
a picture of the whole — if indeed our venture succeeds, and we
are at all able to arrive at such a result.

Since we have already examined the uprisings under Trajan in
some detail, we can now turn our attention to the reign of Hadrian.
And we must begin by asking: what was his policy in Judaea?
What turn did events take after the liquidation of the *polemos
shel qitos*? Basically, this is the famous question historians have
been mulling over for quite some time: what was the nature of
Hadrian's presumed promise, and what effect did it have — the
promise to rebuild Jerusalem? (which may or may not have included a promise to rebuild the Temple as well).

Detente and Appeasement

The first act of the new emperor was to reverse the expansionist
policy of his predecessor. Not only did he wind up the Parthian

War; he ordered the withdrawal of Roman forces from the newly conquered territories of Mesopotamia, Assyria and Armenia, and stationed them on the old boundaries of the Empire, on the banks of the Tigris-Euphrates. Armenia reverted to its previous status; Mesopotamia and Assyria became Parthian satrapies once again.[2]

Hadrian was not unfamiliar with the political and military picture in the Middle East. He had had an important command in that arena, and had been appointed governor of Syria during Trajan's Parthian War. Why he decided to reverse Roman policy so suddenly and so fundamentally, as soon as he had the power to do so, has been the subject of much discussion. Two factors probably underlying his decision have been given prominence. The first is economic. The prolonged foreign wars conducted by Trajan had put an intolerable burden on the Roman treasury, particularly in the eastern provinces, and the economy was beginning to show the strain. This factor is especially stressed by Rostovtzeff.[3]

The second reason for Hadrian's reappraisal has to do with the rebelliousness of the conquered populations. As the Romans advanced into Asia and overran new territories, they left behind them unfriendly and insurgent peoples, a constant threat to their lines of communication. Meanwhile, still further to their rear were the Jews of Egypt and Cyrenaica and Libya, Cyprus and Judaea, whose uprisings made it necessary to detach much needed troops from the main theater of war. Add to this the fact that there was increasing tension throughout Europe and Africa, with rumblings along the Danube, as well as in Britain and Mauretania.

Having liquidated the hapless Parthian War begun by his predecessor, Hadrian set about restoring peace to his domains. This involved him in the rebuilding of Alexandria, the recolonization of Libya, and the remission of land taxes for areas under reclamation. These and similar measures were, of course, necessitated by the *tumultus judaicus,* with the aftermath of which Hadrian now had to cope. Naturally, the first thing he had to do was to mop up any remaining pockets of resistance. But the question that

2   On the basis of an inscription found in Dura Europos, some historians think that Trajan had already begun the Roman withdrawal.

3   [*Social and Economic History of the Roman Empire,* I, p. 355 ff.]

should really interest us is: once that was over, what was Hadrian's attitude towards the Jews of Egypt?

When we examined the sources dealing with the uprising in North Africa and Cyprus, we came to the conclusion that the most likely root-cause of that "Jewish war" was the long-standing animosity between the Jews and the Hellenic populations in those countries. To be sure, the intervention of Roman authorities and Roman soldiery in those clashes, frequently on the side of the Hellenes, led many Jews to see Rome as the enemy, and there were those on the Jewish side who welcomed the opportunity to fan the flames of revolt against the power that had destroyed the Temple. But the original nature of the struggle as a rivalry between two client peoples of Rome, — each with its own far-flung Diaspora — was not entirely lost sight of at the seat of imperial power. The Romans were still capable of ruling against the Hellenes, and of finding in favor of the Jews.

An example of this is the trial held before Hadrian, probably in 118 C.E.[4] It seems obvious to me that the verdict there was in favor of the Jews. But even those who find it more evenhanded will have to admit that the Imperial Court retained its cool objectivity, by refusing to go along with the attempt of the Hellenes to have the Jews excluded from Alexandria.

Hadrian's balanced policy towards the Jews was undoubtedly based on his understanding of the fact that the *tumultus* had not been basically anti-Roman. The policy also conformed to his general line of pacification, and the restoration of the status quo ante. And while we have no reason to ascribe philo-Judaic attitudes to this emperor, it is clear that his willingness to restore Jewish autonomy and to re-establish the *politeuma* in Alexandria immediately after the fighting stopped — these indicate a willingness to open a new page in the relationship between Rome and the Jews. At the very least, they were to be included in the new program of detente between the Empire and her subjects — the *Pax Justitia Felicitas* which was now on the agenda.

In Judaea itself the accession of Hadrian found the country in the grip of the ruthless Lusius Quietus. While it is true that we

4   [CPJ II, no. 158a–b, pp. 88–99.]

lack unequivocal information about his term in office, it seems certain that those who lived through it regarded his regime as intolerably oppressive. One need only recall our demonstration above that the persecution of Jewish religious practice by Quietus included a ban on circumcision, to appreciate the relief with which the Jews learned that the new Emperor had replaced their draconic governor, having first relieved him of the Moorish troops who formed his praetorian cohort.

It is not to be assumed, however, that the dismissal of Quietus was motivated primarily by Hadrian's desire for a change of government policy in Judaea. The Moor was fired, in the first instance, because he was suspected of conspiring against the new Emperor; and also because Hadrian felt that he had to get rid of Trajan's "old guard" — the top commanders who had been carrying out that Emperor's expansionist policy. For it must be remembered that at the beginning of his reign Hadrian was not completely secure on the throne. There were others with imperial ambitions, and the general from Morocco seems to have been one of them. In the event, his ambition cost him not only his job as governor of Judaea; it cost him his life as well.

He was not the only one. Three other great commanders who had been Trajan's right-hand men — Nigrinus, Celsus and Palma — were executed by order of the Senate, no doubt on instructions from Hadrian. The ostensible charge was that they had conspired to assassinate the Emperor. Perhaps so. However, it is also true that they constituted, actually or potentially, a strong focus of opposition to the new Emperor's dramatic shift away from the policy of imperial growth.

But whatever lay behind the dismissal of Quietus, the result for Judaea was surely an end to repressive military government and religious persecution. It is even likely that Hadrian welcomed the opportunity to introduce a more benign administration, in conformity with his general policy of the relaxation of tension and the search for peace.[5]

---

5   There is no basis whatsoever for the assumption by W.D. Carroll (*Bittir and its Archaeological Remains,* Annual of the American Schools of Oriental Research, V, 1925, p. 81) stating that Hadrian

REBUILDING JERUSALEM

More than that; certain sources indicate that the new Emperor took a major step in the direction of appeasement in Judaea. These sources speak of an imperial decree ordering the rebuilding of Jerusalem and the Temple, and tell of Jews streaming towards the Holy City from other parts of Judaea, and from countries in the Diaspora, quite as though a "Declaration of Hadrian" had been issued, just like the proclamation of Cyrus the Great half a millenium earlier. In these texts, there is an echo of the days of Zerubabel, as if the ancient "Return to Zion" from Babylonia were being re-enacted.[6]

Now, none of these sources is unequivocally reliable. Some of them are clear and explicit, but they date from a time long after the events described, and their tone is rather legendary. Others date from a time quite close to the events, but their meaning is somewhat ambiguous. The result is that historians differ widely in their interpretation of the material. There are two mains lines of interpretation, and they are diametrically opposed to one another.

Most Jewish scholars are willing to overlook the ambiguities of the early sources, and accept the tradition about the promise to rebuild the Temple.[7] This reading of the situation was most fully developed by Graetz, as follows: Hadrian, anxious to restore tranquillity to the Empire as soon as possible, began to negotiate with the Jews who were still embattled in the Diaspora. In their terms for the cessation of hostilities, the Jews included a demand for the restoration of their state and the rebuilding of the Temple. Hadrian agreed, and issued the necessary decrees; but under the influence of the Samaritans (and of the Jewish-Christians) he went

balanced his withdrawal from the newly conquered territories by tightening up Roman rule in the rest of the Empire.

6   See, e.g. S. Klein, *Eretz Yehudah,* 5699, p. 161.

7   Some Jewish scholars date this event even earlier — during Trajan's regime; e.g. Joel, *Blicke in der Religionsgeschichte,* Breslau, 1880, I, 15–25; and more recently Finkelstein, in *Akiba, Scholar Saint and Martyr,* New York, 1936, pp. 313–316; see the review-essay by Alon, *Tarbiz,* X, 5699, p. 271, n. 65. The principal argument against this dating is that it would place the promise in Trajan's last years, when the Jewish *tumultus* in the Diaspora was at its height. In the circumstances the whole thing seems politically impossible.

back on his promise. As we shall soon see, this follows the line of the story related in Bereshit Rabbah.

But before we examine that midrash, let us take a critical look at the assumptions which underlie the view developed by Graetz.[8] Does the nature of Roman-Jewish relations at that juncture make his theory plausible?

We have already expressed our view that the Jewish uprisings in the Diaspora during Trajan's reign did not originate as a political movement directed against the Empire, and never became totally committed to that aim. It is therefore difficult to envisage political negotiations between the Jewish insurgents in the Diaspora and the Roman Emperor with respect to the future of Eretz Israel. Secondly, by the time Hadrian came to power the back of the insurgency had just about been broken — even though there was still some fighting in Egypt, and some disorder in Judaea. It hardly seems likely that the defeated Jews were in any position to make demands on Hadrian, or that he had to resort to any diplomatic measures, when he was after all in a position to dictate terms to the defeated rebels.

A diametrically opposite view of the situation is espoused by most non-Jewish historians. In their view, the sources that tell of promises by Hadrian to rebuild Jerusalem, and maybe even the Temple, are pure fiction. The thing never happened.

In the face of this flat contradiction we have no choice but to examine the most important sources, and to weigh up the probabilities. Let us begin with the tradition recorded in Genesis Rabbah.[9]

> In the days of Rabbi Joshua ben Hananiah the Roman government decreed that the Temple should be rebuilt. Pappus and Lulianus set up tables from Akko to Antioch and provided for the *olim* from the Diaspora. Those Cuthim then went and said to the Emperor: Be it known now unto the king that if this city be builded and the walls finished, they will not pay tribute, impost or toll. (*a verbatim quote from*

8   *Geschichte*, vol. IV, pp. 120–125; and note 14, p. 408.
9   GenR 64 Theodor-Albeck, p. 710.

Ezra IV : 13). Said he to them: What is to be done, seeing that I have already issued the decree? Said they to him: Send to them and say: either change the site of the Temple, or enlarge it by five cubits, or diminish it by five cubits. Then they will of themselves abandon the venture.

A throng of Israel had congregated in the Vale of Beth Rimmon when the letters of the Emperor arrived. The people began to weep. Then a spirit of revolt began to sweep through the assemblage. Some said: Let a Sage stand forth and calm the people. They said: Let Rabbi Joshua ben Hananiah stand forth, for he is a great *askolastika* of the Torah.

Rabbi Joshua arose and expounded this parable: Once a lion ate of his prey, and got a bone stuck in his throat. Said the lion: If anyone can get the bone out of my throat, he will get a reward. There came an Egyptian heron, who stuck his beak into the lion's throat and pulled out the bone. Said the heron: Give me my reward. Said the lion: Be off with you! Go and boast that you entered the lion's mouth and got out of there safely! So is it with us Jews. We ought to be satisfied that even though we got entangled with the Romans, we got disentangled without coming to harm!

An analysis of this tradition yields the following points: Genesis Rabbah was probably composed in the fifth century — that is, some three hundred years after the events we are discussing. There are no linguistic elements in the text that would lead us to suspect a tannaitic substratum; on the contrary, it seems certain that the text in its present form contains no elements older than the fourth century. In style and tone, the whole passage has a distinctly legendary ring.

As for the content of this midrash, it breaks down into the following elements: a) The imperial edict to rebuilt the Temple. b) The role of Pappus and Lulianus. c) The animosity of the Cuthim. d) The revocation of the imperial order (as the result of intrigue). e) The ensuing agitation among the Jews, allayed by Rabbi Joshua.

The text does not say when the imperial order was supposed to have been issued. But it is obvious from everything else we know that it was supposed to have happened in the early days of Hadrian's reign.

As for Pappus and Lulianus (Julianus?) we have already met these two in connection with the *pulmus shel qitos*. The present text shows them implementing Hadrian's order. We noted above that the older, i.e. tannaitic, sources can only be taken to mean that they were seized and put to death under Trajan; so that the older sources are completely at variance with the tradition we have cited here. (Graetz tried to solve the problem by reading the older texts in such a way as to allow for the escape of the two men from Roman custody at the beginning of Hadrian's reign, but his solution does not work. See above, Chap. 3, note 31.)

Another point on which attention should be focused has to do with the "tables" which Pappus and Lulianus set up in Phoenicia and Syria for the *olim* from the Diaspora. What were they for? Graetz suggests that they were "foreign exchange" centers, where monies from various countries could be converted into Roman specie to go towards rebuilding the Temple. However, his suggestion does seem rather farfetched. To be sure, "tables" (*trapezin*) in the Rabbinic literature of the time do usually refer to banking operations. But the most likely meaning in the present context is that these two wealthy citizens offered *loans* to Jews out of the Diaspora on their way to settle in Jerusalem.

So it appears that we have before us a combination of two distinct traditions, one of them dealing with the rebuilding of the Temple, the other describing a movement towards the resettlement of Jerusalem. The distinction between these two is not mere pedantry. It will prove instructive when we examine Christian texts of a later time.

The next point for us to investigate is the identity of those spoilers, "the Cuthim". It has been suggested that these were the Jewish Christians. They had a vested theological interest in blocking the restoration of the Temple and its altars; they had, so to speak, bet their religious commitment on the termination of the Old Covenant. According to this view the Midrash, by applying the term "Cuthim" to the Jewish Christians, instead of the more

[438]

usual "Minim," deliberately used the standard epithet of opprobrium for the Samaritans, in order to make it plain that the former, like the latter, were outside the pale, even though both observed the mitzvot of the Torah.[10]

But this notion must be rejected: there is nothing to support it. Without even entering into the question as to what might have been the attitude of he Jewish Christians towards the project of rebuilding the Temple, the decisive fact is that the text speaks of *kuthai*, a term which never means anybody but Samaritans. The real question we should consider is whether or not the tradition about Samaritan malevolence is based on historical reality. Certainly it is possible. The sanctity of Mount Gerizim versus Mount Moriah had always been the chief bone of contention between Jews and Samaritans. It would have been natural for the hostility of the latter to be aroused by any plan to rebuild the Jerusalem Temple.

However, the trouble with this scenario is that it recurs so often in the Jewish tradition. The plot goes like this: the powers that be conceive some good intention regarding Jerusalem and its sanctuary. Enter the devious Samaritans with Iago-like slanders which they whisper into the ears of the authorities — and the benevolent designs of the government are abandoned. In fact, the episode just cited from Bereshit Rabbah uses a verbatim extract from the Book of Ezra (IV : 16) going all the way back to the rebuilding of Jerusalem in the days of Zerubabel. In the same way, a scheming Samaritan is blamed for the fall of Beitar; and Samaritans are said to have lobbied with Alexander of Macedon to get the Temple at Jerusalem dismantled.[11]

We must realize, therefore, that we are dealing with a very ancient phenomenon — Jewish anti-Samaritan prejudice. To be sure, the mirror image of this bias — a strong anti-Jewish tone — colors all Samaritan chronicles. But that does not make this evidence any more admissible. We shall have to discard it, even though what it says sounds historically quite probable.

The same treatment will have to be accorded the clever strate-

10   Joel, op. cit. pp. 42–46.
11   Yoma, 69a; Meg. Taan. IX.

gem imputed to the Samaritans. It must be dismissed as legend, pure and simple.

What about the agitation among the people, and the role of Rabbi Joshua in calming it down? This may well contain an element of historical truth. It conforms to what we are told about this Sage in other contexts. It is true that Rabbi Joshua appears often in aggadic literature as the prototype of a "wise and thoughtful man of counsel."[12] He is frequently shown appearing before Hadrian himself, arguing skilfully as the advocate of Judaism and the Jewish people, defending them successfully against the Emperor and against the "Minim." So it is quite possible that in the text before us, his name is simply used as that of a folk-hero. On the other hand, actual historical sources portray him as a man admirably suited to step forward and sound the warning against ill-considered impetuosity. His reputation spoke of his sagacity, his political moderation, and his profound humanity. These attributes coupled with a certain homespun quality, made him likely to be listened to, the right man to calm the distraught crowd.

Nevertheless, we can scarcely ignore those elements of style and content which point to a literary composition late in provenance and legendary in flavor. First of all, the people are congregated together in the Vale of Beth Rimmon *before* the arrival of the message from the Emperor. What were they doing there? Did they have to assemble en masse, and in a given place, in order to receive the royal message? Secondly, is it not curious that the Vale of Beth Rimmon recurs as the locus of a number of tragedies in the Hadrianic period? It is there that the people are summoned by the Emperor and then massacred; there too certain Sages gathered "in the last stages of the Hadrianic persecution" to declare a leap year.[13] We must therefore reckon with the possibility that Beth Rimmon was the traditional mythic site for all such dramatic episodes.

In the third place, the aggadah quotes members of the public — obviously "moderates" — proposing that some sagacious person

12 Tos. Sot. XV: 3 (321).
13 Yer. Hag. III; 78d.

be found to quiet the throng. The choice falls on Rabbi Joshua ben Hananiah, who is introduced as an *"askolastika* of the Torah." There is a certain contradiction here — a Torah-scholar is not necessarily the worldly-wise person that had been called for. However, it may be that the word *askolastika* has the meaning of σχολαστικός in late Greek — i.e., "advocate."

Incidentally, if we were able to accept this text as historically reliable, it would show that the rebellion against Rome came from the broad mass of the people, and that the role of the Sages was to moderate the popular passion — which may well have been the case. Indeed, this passage might then have shed some light on aspects of the Bar Kokhba Revolt, about which we know too little. Would it then be correct to say that at that later date the masses again led the way? And that *some* of the nation's leaders — i.e. of the Sages — fell in behind them? Yes, we might be able to talk about these things if we were able to accept the aggadah as a historical source. Unfortunately, however, as we have already indicated, its value for this purpose is dubious. It seems to be a literary contrivance, out of a much later time; and the word *askolastika* is a rather late usage.

To sum up: The most that we can derive from the midrash is this: at one point the Roman government promised to rebuild the Temple but then reversed itself. The Jews were very upset by this, and there were signs of revolt in some quarters, but the would-be rebels were cooled down by Rabbi Joshua ben Hananiah and his colleagues. All the rest of the details are either legend, or at best dubious.

CHURCH FATHERS

We now turn to our second source of information, the Church Father Epiphanius. He was born in Palestine early in the fourth century, in a village near Beth Guvrin. There is an old tradition that he was born a Jew, and baptized at an early age, but there is no truth in that story. He was undoubtedly born a Christian.

As a youth he went down to Alexandria, and returned to the land of his birth about the year 335. He founded a monastery at Beth Guvrin and became its head. In 367 he was invited to Cyprus, where he was appointed Metropolitan (chief bishop) of the whole island, with his seat at Costanza, the former Salamis. There he wrote his books, the most important of which is the *Panarion*, a polemic against heresy.

The works of Epiphanius contain an enormous amount of old historical material, including a good deal about the Jews and Judaism, especially about the Land of Israel. Some of this material relates to his own times; some of it goes back to early generations. But his work has a serious fault: he is not a careful compiler. He gets things mixed up, and sometimes adds imaginative passages of his own. He is neither a creative historian nor a reliable copyist, and certainly his insight and his respect for the truth do not rate very high. His testimony, therefore, cannot be taken at face value, but must be examined with a critical eye. Despite all this, his writings cannot be disregarded, for they are a vast storehouse of reports and traditions about many things, not only the Jews. In one of his books he tells the following story:[14]

> Continuing his journey, Hadrian wended his way towards Egypt. ... He passed through Antioch and went on to Caelo-Syria and Phoenicia, arriving in Palestine, which is Judaea, in the forty-seventh year after the destruction of Jerusalem. It was the second year of his reign when he went up to Jerusalem, the famous and much-praised city which had been destroyed by Titus the son of Vespasian. He found it utterly destroyed and God's Holy Temple a ruin, there being nothing where the city had stood but a few dwellings and one small church ... Hadrian decided to restore the city, but not the Temple. In charge of the rebuilding he appointed a pagan, Aquila the translator from Sinope in Pontus, whom we have mentioned previously. The rebuilt city was to be called *Aelia*, after the Emperor himself.

Those historians who deny the whole story about Hadrian's intention to rebuild Jerusalem point out that Epiphanius, when he talks about Hadrian's travels in the Middle East can only mean

---

14 *Peri Metron kai Stathmon* ("On Weights and Measures") (In the Bible), PG vol. 43, pp. 260–261, ed. Dindorf, vol IV, pp. 17–18. Epiphanius wrote the book in the year 392.

the Emperor's long journey to Syria, Egypt and Palestine, from 129 to 131. What is more, Epiphanius connects the rebuilding of Jerusalem by Aquila with the name "Aelia" which is to say, the renaming of the capital as "Aelia Capitolina." Now, we have the word of Dio Cassius for the fact that the renaming was decreed by Hadrian while he was on that long trip, in the twelfth or thirteenth year of his reign rather than in the second. Indeed, Dio believes this decree was the proximate cause for the Bar Kokhba Revolt.[15]

However, I do not think we can brush off Epiphanius and the tradition he records in quite so cavalier a manner. For one thing, his sources told him that Hadrian had appointed Aquila to supervise the rebuilding of Jerusalem. We have the word of Jerome, on the one hand, and of the Rabbis on the other, that Aquila translated the Bible into Greek under the direction of his teacher Rabbi Akiba (the Jewish sources also mention Rabbi Eliezer and Rabbi Joshua). And since quite some time had passed, according to the tradition received by Epiphanius, between the time Aquila the pagan arrived in Jerusalem and his conversion to Judaism — after he had first become a Christian — it becomes impossible to date his arrival in Jerusalem at the year 130 (Akiba was executed no later than 135).

The only possible conclusion is that Epiphanius combined two different traditions connecting Hadrian with Jerusalem. The first of these told about the appointment of Aquila to supervise the rebuilding of the city in the year 117 — and whatever else that tradition may have said, we no longer know. The second strand was an account of the building of Aelia Capitolina. As we have already pointed out, it was common in Epiphanius' time to attribute the Bar Kokhba Revolt to the early years of Hadrian's reign. It was therefore natural for him to weave the two strands together,

15 Those who discount Epiphanius have a quite reasonable explanation for his date "47 years after the Destruction." They attribute it to his having transferred the Bar Kokhba Revolt to the beginning of Hadrian's reign. This chronological error is common among early Christian writers, Jerome among them, and can also be found in rabbinic literature.

thus compressing events that were in reality more than a decade apart.

In the composite which results, there is a phrase which calls for attention. "Hadrian decided to restore the city, but not the Temple." This proves, I should think, that the relevant portion of the original could not have dealt with Aelia Capitolina. It would be ridiculous to suppose that the Jewish sanctuary would be placed in a pagan city dedicated to the Capitoline Jupiter. Furthermore, Dio Cassius tells us that Hadrian ordered a pagan temple erected on the very site of the Temple Mount — and this, before the revolt. Under such circumstances, what would be the point of stressing "but not the Temple"? (It must be admitted that the tradition known to Epiphanius may not have been aware of the facts described by Dio). We must also consider the possibility that this portion of Epiphanius derives from a source that deliberately stressed the fact that Hadrian had *not* promised to rebuild the Temple — because a tradition was current that he had!

In the light of this possibility we should examine a Syriac chronicle emanating from the 8th or 9th centuries:[16]

> In the 12th year of Hadrian's reign, Aquila the translator became well-known. He was the son of the Emperor's brother-in-law. At that time the Jews were about to build Jerusalem and its Temple. When Caesar appointed Aquila to oversee the work, the latter met the disciples of the Apostles...

Note that, in contrast to Epiphanius, this chronicler places Hadrian's edict and appointment of Aquila in the year 129. Could it be that he wanted to synchronize the event with the "correct date" for the building of Aelia, for which he had what he considered dependable information? But note too: he says it was *the*

---

16 *Chronicon ad annum Dominum 846 pertinens,* in Brooks: "Corpus Scriptorum Christianorum Orientalium, Scriptores Syri, Chronica Minora," Paris, p. 184. This chronicle reaches the year 846, so it was written in the 9th century. However, it is the consensus of scholars that everything in it after 784 is a later addition; hence it must have originated in the eighth century. See Hasse: *Altchris.liche Kirchengeschichte nach orientalischen Quellen,* 1925, p. 178.

Jews who were about to build Jerusalem; so it could not have been the Aelia Capitolina project. He also says the Jews were going to rebuild the Temple as well — and Hadrian had put Aquila in charge of both projects.

This source serves to buttress our argument that there was a Christian tradition that at one time Hadrian was involved in a plan to rebuild Jerusalem for the Jews, with Aquila in charge of the project. The main thrust of this tradition was no doubt to tell the story of Aquila, the translator of Scripture, from a Christian point of view. After all, his first step away from paganism had been into Christianity, under the influence of "the disciples of the Apostles." (His later "desertion" to Judaism was explained as the result of his dabbling in astrology, which led to his being excommunicated).

There is, or was, another Christian work in which the appointment of Aquila by Hadrian is reported. When in 1898 the British scholar Fred Conybeare published two manuscripts, one from Vienna and one from Vatican, containing two ancient dialogues, he proposed that they were based on an older, lost work written in the second century by Ariston of Pella, called "The Dialogue of Jason and Papiscus", a work on which Eusebius drew for his description of the Bar Kokhba Revolt.[17] Conybeare thought that the second dialogue — the one between Timothy and Aquila — reproduced the lost source most faithfully. While other scholars regard this theory as unproven, they do agree that these dialogues contain material from the earlier work by Ariston.[18]

The following passage is quoted from the second dialogue, the one between Timothy and Aquila:

> This Hadrian was a man with a great thirst for knowledge. He therefore wanted to see for himself all the lands under his rule. When he arrived at Jerusalem and found the city utterly desolate ... he took Aquila, a pagan, and entrusted to him the task of rebuilding the city.

17 Conybeare: "The Dialogues of Athanasius and Zachäus and of Timothy and Aquila," in *Anecdota Oxoniensia,* Classical Series, part VIII, [Oxford 1898, p. 91; comp. Eusebius, *Eccl. Hist.* IV:6:3.]
18 Bardenhewer: *Geschichte der altchristichen Literatur,* I, p. 187.

Conybeare compares this story in detail with the account given by Epiphanius; and while one may disagree with his judgement on some points, it is highly likely that he is right when he says that the dialogue here quoted was not taken from Epiphanius, but that both of them drew from a common source. Nor should we be put off by the fact that the author of this dialogue connects the appointment of Aquila with the Bar Kokhba Revolt, and places the Hadrianic persecutions *before* the reconstruction of the city.

> Hadrian ... found the city desolate, therefore (sic! ?) he was angry with the Jews and seized them and took them to the market in Hebron where he sold them as slaves ... at the price of four for a measure of barley ...

The chronological confusion should not prove surprising; it is characteristic of most of the Christian writers. We find it in Epiphanius and in the Syriac chronicle, as well as in the dialogues here quoted. But that should not mislead us into discarding this tradition as altogether worthless. Let it therefore be noted that this dialogue states that "Hadrian began to build the city and its walls, but *not the Temple*." That is approximately what we heard from Epiphanius.

Another early Christian chronicler, Alexander the Monk, writing probably around the middle of the ninth century, says:

> When (Hadrian) went to the Holy City and saw it in ruins, except for one small Christian church, he gave orders that the whole city be rebuilt, save for the Temple. When the Jews heard of this they streamed thither from every direction, and before long the whole city was rebuilt. But once again an evil spirit entered into them and agitated them, and they rebelled against Rome. They set over themselves a commander called Bar Kokhba ... [19]

We have no way of knowing where Alexander got his information. But he does say explicitly that Hadrian's decree led to the settlement of large numbers of Jews in Jerusalem, and in his opinion this concentration had something to do with the outbreak of the Bar Kokhba War. In any event, it is clear that this settlement, if

19 *De Inventione Sanctae Crucis*, PG. 87 III, 4044–4045.

it took place, could have had no connection with the foundation of Aelia Capitolina in the year 130 (or possibly 135).

From the tenth century bishop of Alexandria, Eutychios, also known as ibn Batriq, we have a very similar report:[20]

> Hadrian came to Jerusalem and found it in ruins except for one Christian church. He gave orders that the city be built around the Temple. When the Jews heard of this they hastened to Jerusalem from every city and every land, until Jerusalem was filled with them. And when their numbers grew great, they made Bar Kokhba king etc. etc. ...

When he published a translation of the passage just quoted, the French scholar Clermont Ganneau pointed out that it must be based on sources no longer available to us.[21] But as we have just seen, Eutychios is not the only one who tells it in almost exactly the same way. Almost all oriental Christian chroniclers do.

So much for those sources whose account of what happened is clear and straightforward, but whose date of composition is long after the events themselves. What these sources net us is about as follows:

a) It was widely believed among Christians in the Middle East that at one time Hadrian had ordered the reconstruction of Jerusalem as a Jewish city (by contradistinction to the pagan city which he actually did rebuild there at end of his reign). Some of the sources connect the project with Aquila. Most of them exclude the Temple from the plans, but some of them include it. It seems that the most widely disseminated Christian tradition spoke of the rebuilding of the city alone, to the exclusion of the Temple.

While it is reasonable to assume that most of the Christian accounts that have come down to us were derived from a common source — whether it was the lost Dialogue between Jason and Papiscus, or some other work — nevertheless, the fact that no one of them was itself written any earlier than the fourth century, and that there is so much disagreement between them, and such confusion about details — all this reduces their credibility more than

---

20 PG III, p. 986–987.
21 Receuil d'archéologie orientale, VII, p. 159 f.

somewhat. Still, I would not say that they are completely without historical value.

b) The second thing we have learned is that there was also a Jewish tradition about a plan in Hadrian's time to rebuild the Temple — a plan which was subsequently revoked. There seem to have been two strands to this story, one about the city of Jerusalem, the other about the Temple itself. In this case, too, the source is a late one, and the obviously added elements woven into the texture of the story are not calculated to inspire confidence in the historicity of the whole.

BARNABAS

Now let us turn our attention to sources of the second kind — closer to the events, but cloudier in their meaning. The first of these is an early patristic document known as the Epistle of Barnabas. Most scholarly opinion dates this work, written apparently in Alexandria, to the early years of the second century. It purports to be a letter, after the style of the Pauline epistles, by a member of Paul's own circle.[22]

The main purpose of Barnabas is to counter any Judaizing tendencies among the Christians of his day (he himself is clearly a gentile). In this respect, he carries the Pauline doctrine much further. Paul conceded that the Torah and the commandments had been a valid part of the Old Covenant; they had been replaced by the crucifixion. But Barnabas argues that the mitzvot, indeed the whole halakhah, had *always* been a perversion of the Divine word, close to idolatry. The Sabbath and circumcision, the sacrifices and the Yom Kippur fast — these had never been intended as anything but allegories — spiritual symbols. By taking them literally, and turning them into observances, the Jews had forfeited their right to the Covenant, which had passed to the Christians.[23]

22 [For an updated summary of the conflicting views about the date, authorship, country of origin etc. of the work, see Klaus Wengst in *Theologische Realenzyklopadie*, Berlin-New York, 1980, Vol. V, pp. 238 ff. He says that nobody now believes that Barnabas was the real author.]

23 See Alon: "The Halakhah in the Epistle of Barnabas" (Hebrew) in his *Mehqarim*, I, pp. 295–312, or *Tarbiz*, XI, pp. 23 ff.

Epistle of Barnabas

Our present interest in Barnabas is in the context of the search for sources dealing with Hadrian and the rebuilding of Jerusalem. In this respect, the following may prove relevant:[24]

> I will also speak with you concerning the Temple, and show how the wretched men *(the Jews)* erred by putting their hope on the building, and not on the God who made them, and is the true house of God. 2. For they consecrated him in the Temple almost like the heathen. But learn how the Lord speaks, in bringing it to naught, "Who has measured the heaven with a span, or the earth with his outstretched hand? Have not I? saith the Lord. Heaven is my throne, and the earth is my footstool, what house will ye build for me, or what is the place of my rest?"[25] You know that their hope was in vain. 3. Furthermore he says again, "Lo, they who destroyed this temple shall themselves rebuild it."[26] 4. That is happening now. For owing to the war it was destroyed by the enemy; at present even the servants of the enemy will build it up again.[27] 5. Again, it was made manifest that the city and the temple and the people of Israel were to be delivered up. For the Scripture says, "And it shall come to pass in the last days that the Lord shall deliver the sheep of his pasture, and the sheep-fold, and their tower to destruction."[28]

There can be scarcely any doubt that verses 3 and 4 refer to something that was happening at the time the epistle was written. The trouble is, the author is too vague about it, leaving room for

24 Epistle of Barnabas, XVI:1-5, in "The Apostolic Fathers" edited and translated by Kirsopp Lake, I, p. 397.
25 The quoted verses are slightly different (inexact?) quotations from the Septuagint for Isaiah 40:12, 66:1.
26 The Septuagint for Isaiah 49:17 indicates a very different reading of the Hebrew text, a reading the sense of which agrees with Barnabas. Nevertheless, his quotation again does not faithfully reproduce our LXX.
27 So most versions of the Greek text. But the Codex Sinaiticus has a reading which can only mean, "at present both they *(the Jews)* and the enemy *(the Romans)* will build it." This would have to refer to the order of Hadrian to rebuild the Temple.
28 Enoch, 89:56.

all kinds of conflicting interpretations. Almost all modern Christian scholars reject the idea that these verses refer to a plan to rebuild the Temple at the beginning of Hadrian's reign. On the other hand, only a small number of them think that Barnabas is talking about the "Temple of the Spirit" — i.e. the Church Universal, which gentile Christians were then counting on to replace the old Jewish Temple.[29]

To be sure, this interpretation fits in nicely with the entire outlook of the author. After all, his main point is that no physical structure can serve as God's house; those who destroyed the visible Temple — i.e. the Romans — will be the very ones to build the new sanctuary, the spiritual one. Who are "the servants of the enemy"? The Christians.

However, this theory has been rejected by Christian scholars themselves, who point out two main objections. First, the verses quoted by Barnabas cannot by any stretch of the imagination be made to refer to anything but the actual physical Temple. Secondly, it is scarcely conceivable that the author would call the Christians "servants of the enemy." Although he does mean gentile Christians, the gulf between them and the very pagan Rome of his day was still vast. The phrase would have been simply too incongruous.

Because of these objections, most recent scholarship assumes that the "temple" mentioned in the Epistle of Barnabas means the pagan temple of Jupiter which Hadrian ordered built at Aelia Capitolina (as he renamed Jerusalem) in the year 130 (or 135).[30] But we will have to confess that this solution is not much better. Even if we ignore the reading of the Codex Sinaiticus, it is more than a little difficult to force the text into the procrustean bed of this interpretation.

Perhaps the best approach to this problem is to put oneself into the position of the author of this epistle. He wanted Christians to believe that the old Temple in Jerusalem, even when it had stood there, had had no value; and that there was no point in looking forward to its restoration. Just imagine how he would have reacted

---

29 See Bardenhewer: *Geschichte der altchristliche Literatur* Vol. I, p. 93.
30 See Schürer, I, 672, trans. Vermes and Millar, I, p. 536, Windisch, *Handbuch zum Neuem Testament*, pp. 388–390; Stählin, *Geschichte der griechischen Literatur*, II : 2, pp. 1230–1.

to the news that the Romans were putting up a temple to Jupiter (or planning to put one up) on the Temple Mount! Would he not have pointed to this as proof positive that the Jewish Temple was finished once and for all? Indeed later on, when Bar Kokhba had been defeated and Jerusalem destroyed for the last time, that was exactly the line taken by Christian authors. One after another they reasoned that the fate of the Jewish sanctuary proved that the old Israel had been rejected, and Christianity had emerged triumphant.

The failure of "Barnabas" to make the same argument is striking. Even more startling is his need to invoke the prophecy from Enoch about the *ultimate* downfall of the people and the city and the sanctuary. Apparently things were not going his way, and he needed to shore up his belief by a prophecy of things to come.

I think, therefore, that the most likely explanation is this: the author of Barnabas found himself in a quandary about an event that upset his deepest beliefs. So he tried to prove to himself — and his readers — that it had all been foreseen, and that it would not last. There were prophecies still to be fulfilled (he urged) showing that present events were merely a temporary aberration. In any event, (he said) neither holiness nor the Shekhina had ever dwelt in the Temple; and ancient prophecies tell us that it will ultimately be destroyed forever. So the hope of the Jews that it will be rebuilt is really meaningless.

The event that would fit all this most exactly would be a decree by the Emperor Hadrian ordering the rebuilding of Jerusalem. The prospect would excite eager anticipation among the Jews, but trepidation and dismay among the Christians. The author of the Epistle sets out to allay the alarm in the Christian ranks, as we have demonstrated. To be sure, he speaks haltingly, because events seem to be going the other way. But his faith buoys him up.

This interpretation comes close to the position adopted by Veil, who wrote the chapter on Barnabas in Hennecke's work on the New Testament Apocrypha.[31] He is practically alone among mo-

31 "Barnabasbrief" in Hennecke, *Neutestamentliche Apokryphen*, 1924, pp. 503–504. See also Schlatter: *Die Tage des Trajan und Hadrian,* 1897, pp. 61 ff, (except that Schlatter dates Hadrian's building decree to 130, and the Epistle of Barnabas to 131).

dern Christian scholars in interpreting the passage quoted as a reference to the Jewish hope for the rebuilding of the Temple. Indeed, Veil thinks that the whole purpose of the Epistle of Barnabas was to counter the danger to Christianity represented by the prospect of the Jerusalem Temple being restored. There was a noticeable "judaizing" trend among Christians at the time, and Veil thinks it was due to, or abetted by, the rising barometer of hope for the future of Jerusalem.

But there is a serious difficulty with this reading of the situation. If it was the prospect of the restoration of Jerusalem that caused so many Christians in Egypt to go over to Judaism, and if it was against *this* lure that the author of the Epistle was taking up the cudgels — why didn't he come right out and say so? Why did he spend most of his ammunition on attacking Jewish ceremonials, and say so very little about the Temple?

In order to deal with this difficulty, I would suggest that the Epistle was written at a time when Christianity was undergoing persecution, perhaps locally. We know that at such times Christians often adopted Jewish observances, whether as a cover to avoid discovery (without necessarily giving up their Christian beliefs), or because they were genuinely attracted to the Jewish way of life. Those were the circumstances, I suggest, that prompted the writing of the Epistle.

As for the inclusion of his remarks about the proposed restoration of the Temple, I suggest that they were a kind of insertion or afterthought, as though the news had reached him while he was writing. He thought it best to comfort his Christian readers about this surprising turn of events by proving to them from Scripture that there could not be a *genuine, lasting* re-establishment of the Jewish Temple. (Interestingly enough, the same line of argument would be called into service again several centuries later, when Julian the Apostate announced his intention of restoring the Temple. Then, too, Christian writers declared that it would not be the real thing, but only a pagan Temple.) If the Epistle is read in this way, the "servants of the enemy" turn out to be none other than Jewish builders, working under Roman orders.

THE SIBYLLINE ORACLES

The second early source bearing on our subject is one of the Sibylline Oracles, where these famous lines occur:[32]

> And after him shall reign a silver-helmed man;
> He shall have the name of a sea (*Adria-tic*).
> He shall be a most excellent man, and shall understand
>   everything.
> And in thy time, most excellent, most noble dark-haired prince,
> And in the time of thy scions, all these days shall come..

These cryptic lines can only be a prediction of the messianic age, confidently expected during the reign of Hadrian (the pun on his name is transparent). And the poet must have been a Jew. The question is: when could he have written these words? The answer given by most Jewish — and some gentile — scholars is: early in the reign of Hadrian.[33]

In strong contrast to this praise of Hadrian, treating him like a second "Cyrus the Great," is the unsparing castigation in another oracle written after his death.[34] The impression conveyed is of vast hopes overwhelmingly betrayed. Some overt act must have been involved, something connected with the Land of Israel. Perhaps there is a connection here with the prophecies of Elkesai, predicting "birth-pangs of the Messiah" in the year 116–117, to be followed by the redemption.[35] The *polemos shel qitos*, both in the Diaspora and in Judaea, could certainly have been perceived as the "pangs;" and the initial acts of the new Emperor in reversing

---

32 Sibyl. V: 46–50, Charles: *Apocrypha and Pseudepigrapha*, II, p. 398. The 14 books of Sibylline Oracles which we possess, written in Greek hexameters and purporting to be the prophecies of a pagan oracle, are for the most part Jewish works of various periods, with some Christian additions. For the principal literature, see Charles, op. cit. Vol. II, pp. 368–376; Geffcken, *Komposition und Entstehungszeit der Oracula Sibyllina* (1902); and the artic'e by Rzach in Pauly-Wissowa, second series, semi-volume IV, pp. 2117–2164.

33 ["...the extravagant praise of Hadrian would be inexplicable in a Jewish writer, except in the earlier years of his reign, before the revolt of Bar Kokhba." Charles, op. cit. Vol. II, p. 373.]

34 VIII: 50–64. See Stählin, *Geschichte d. Griechische Lit.* II:2, 1219.

35 See *JLTA* I, p. 304 f.

the trend of warfare and persecution might well have led many Jews to the thought that the age of the Messiah was at hand at last. Apparently great hopes were aroused; all the deeper, then, was the disappointment.

TANNAITIC SOURCES

Largely because of the chronological factor, there are several tannaitic traditions that may have a bearing on our question.

> Rabbi Simeon ben Azzai said: Once some bones were found in the Wood Chamber *(of the Temple)* and some Sages sought to declare Jerusalem impure. Said Rabbi Joshua to them: It would be a shame and a disgrace to declare our House impure! Where, after all, are the dead of Noah's flood? Where are the victims of Nebuchadnezzar's siege? (Where are those who fell in the last war?)[36]

Since Rabbi Joshua appears here as a mature authority, able to stand up to the majority, it is argued that the episode must have taken place after the Destruction. And because Rabbi Joshua did not live to see the Bar Kokhba War, it is therefore argued that the episode must have taken place early in the reign of Hadrian, when at least a beginning could have been made on the reconstruction of the Temple.

In my opinion, the argument is not convincing: I believe this tradition deals with an event in pre-Destruction Jerusalem. One need only refer to the Mishnah: [37]

> Rabbi Joshua testified about some bones that were once found in the Wood Chamber of the Temple, concerning which the Sages said that the bones are collected one at a time, and everything remains clean.

Obviously both passages deal with the same episode, something which was past history for Rabbi Joshua. In the course of defending the views of his predecessors, he added the war dead of his own generation.

36 Tos. Edu. III:3 (459); also Bavli Zev. 113a, where the last sentence in parentheses is not found.
37 Edu. VIII:5.

A somewhat similar line of reasoning is based on the biography of Ben Zoma, who lived between the Destruction of the Temple and the Bar Kokhba War:

> Ben Zoma beheld throngs on the Temple Mount, and exclaimed: Blessed be He who created all these to serve me.[38]

Without disagreeing with the probable life-span of Ben Zoma, one must nevertheless point out that this passage proves nothing about the reconstruction of the Temple. At most, it suggests an increase in the population of Jerusalem.[39]

In the same way, the Mishnah which says that Ben Azzai discovered a document in Jerusalem does not prove anything about the reconstruction of either the city *or* the Temple.[40] Both before that time and since, documents have turned up in ruined buildings.

THE CHRONICLE OF ARBELA

Another source which has to be drawn into our discussion is the Syriac *Chronicle of Arbela*. It purports to be the biography of Noah, fifth Christian bishop of Arbela, the principal city of Adiabene in Mesopotamia.[41] The detail relevant to our present purpose is that the Jewish parents of Noah are said to have migrated to Jerusalem at a time which must have been early in the reign of Hadrian. One is greatly tempted to combine this hint with the tradition in Bereshit Rabbah about "*olim* from the Diaspora", and with the quotation from Ben Zoma about throngs in Jerusalem — and to speak about large-scale Jewish activity in the Holy City.

However, these and similar indications fall short of proof positive. The whole question boils down to the issue: were there any Jews at all in Jerusalem between the Destruction of the city in

---

38 Tos. Ber. VII:5 (16). There are no grounds for suggesting that Ben Zoma lived until after the Bar Kokhba War, as S. Klein does in *Eres Yehudah*, p. 136.

39 The corresponding passage in Ber. 58a reads *al gav ma'aleh har habayit*, which does suggest building. But the reading is questionable in the light of mss. and variae. Besides, the Yerushalmi reads: "Ben Zoma saw throngs *in Jerusalem*."

40 Yev. IV:13.

41 The standard reference on this document is Sachau: *Die Chronik von Arbela*, 1915.

the year 70, and the end of the Bar Kokhba War in the year 135? Most historians tend to think not. Josephus speaks of the reduction of the entire city to rubble in the last months of the summer of 70, with the Xth Roman Legion sitting on the ruins, and converting the once proud capital into an army encampment.

It is true that Josephus himself puts into the mouth of Eleazar ben Yair, a few years later at Masada, a reference to a remnant of Jews in Jerusalem:

> Hapless old men (who) sit beside the ashes of the shrine, and a few women reserved by the enemy for basest outrage.[42]

But we must bear in mind that those lines were composed with a purpose — to emphasize the absolute ruination of Jerusalem. We may therefore make allowance for some exaggeration, and assume that there was a small Jewish community in Jerusalem until the fall of Masada.

On the other hand, the Church Father Eusebius tells us that the Christian congregation of Jerusalem was revived right after the Destruction, and that its members were circumcised Jews and its bishops Jewish-Christians, and that this continued to be the way things were until after the Bar Kokhba War.[43] It stands to reason that if Jewish Christians managed to move back into ruined Jerusalem, there were at least some Jewish Jews who did the same.

But not only does this stand to reason. Early Christian sources say so quite explicitly. Eusebius, Jerome, and Theodoretos of Kyros (Syria 393–465) in their comments on Isaiah VI: 13 (*And if there be yet a tenth in it*) all apply the verse to the last two destructions of Jerusalem — the one by Titus, and the one by Hadrian. For, as they explain, a small number of Jews resettled in Jerusalem after the Destruction in the year 70—"yet a tenth"—until Hadrian came after the Bar Kokhba War and destroyed the city and its Jewish community completely. Eusebius is also responsible for the statement that myriads of Jews and Christians lived in Jerusalem between the years 70 and 135.[44]

For the record, we must mention another Syriac source, by a

---

42 JW VII: 8: 7 (377).
43 Eusebius, *Hist. Eccles.* IV: v, Lake, Vol. I, pp. 302 ff.
44 Eusebius: *The Theophania* (Syriac), ed. Lee, London 1842.

ninth century writer, who says that the Jews "flourished in Jerusalem during the reign of Trajan (sic!)". But the passage has all the earmarks of outright legend, contributes nothing to our purpose.[45]

WAS HADRIAN IN JUDAEA IN 117?

Whether or not the new Emperor managed to squeeze in a visit to Judaea and Egypt on his way to Rome in 117 to take over the reins of power, is a matter of some dispute. The answer depends a lot on what we think of the reports that he did, by Epiphanius and others; and what, on the other hand, we think he could have accomplished in the less than two months between the day he became Emperor (August 7th) and the day he sailed for Rome (early October). Wilhelm Weber made a detailed study of the question, and was unable to come to a definite conclusion.[46] Later, in his article in the Cambridge Ancient History, he makes no mention of the subject at all, and by that silence appears to be voting against the journey.[47] In short, from the evidence available to us at present we can neither affirm definitely that Hadrian made the trip, nor can we positively deny that he did so.

SUMMARY

In beginning our discussion about Hadrian's early policy in Judaea, we pointed out that there are two conflicting views on whether he ever promised to rebuild the Temple. Some accept the Jewish tradition that he did, while others dismiss the whole story as pure and simple legend. But before we sum up the matter we should note that there are also some scholars who occupy a sort of middle ground. These scholars would claim that the Jews got their hopes up for the restoration of Jerusalem (and the Temple) without really having anything substantial to go by.[48] As Gray says:

45 Moses Bar Cepha: ed. Nau, in *Revue de l'orient Chrétien*, 1914, p. 226.
46 *Untersuchungen zur Geschichte des Kaisers Hadrian*, 1907, pp. 50–60.
47 *Cambridge Ancient History*, [Vol. XI,] pp. 313 ff.
48 See Ismar Elbogen in the (unfinished German) *Encyclopedia Judaica*, Vol 7, p. 779; or the corresponding Hebrew *Eshkol*, Vol. I, p. 713. Comp. W.D. Carroll, in AASOR, V, p. 81: "Hope leaped high in their hearts — hope that was baseless."

It is possible that (Hadrian) held conferences also with de-putations from the Jewish leaders, and that the Jews were deceived regarding the real character of his intentions . . .[49]

That formulation — "it is possible" — characterizes almost every aspect of the problem that has engaged us in this chapter. And it is perfectly true that all the sources put together do not suffice to give us a solid, reliable explanation of Hadrian's Jewish policy. But to dismiss these sources and traditions, obscure and confused though they be, as having no historical value at all, is no solution either. The suggestion that there was a strong subjective factor at play is quite attractive. The intensity of Jewish hopes, not necessarily grounded in reality, may well be helpful in explain-ing some of the texts that have reached us.

In the absence of clear-cut evidence, I would present what is, in my opinion, the most probable reading of the events.

Hadrian, true to his chosen role as *Restitutor* of the war-ravaged lands in the East; bearing the Jews no malice, and at the same time anxious to strengthen, both demographically and economically all countries facing the border with Parthia — decided to restore Jerusalem. It should be borne in mind that the ruin of that city 47 years earlier had meant to a large extent the ruination of *Pro-vincia Judaea*. For Jerusalem had served as more than the political and spiritual capital of the Jews; it had been at the same time the economic center of the country as a whole.

Indeed, the geographical location of the city had probably been a factor in its importance from time immemorial. Major inland trade-routes passed that way, and intersected there. The water-shed route, running along the height of land and connecting the Southland with Samaria and Galilee and thence to Syria in the North, ran through Jerusalem or very nearby. The east-west road connecting the Jordan Valley with the Coastal Plain also came close. And even though the Romans established their administra-tive and military headquarters at Caesarea on the coast, that port city had not been able to function as the legal and practical gov-ernmental center of Judaea, for two reasons. First of all, it was

49   American Journal of Semitic Languages, Vol. 39 (1923), pp. 248–256.

[458]

Summary

located off to the side, on the western periphery of the country; and secondly, the population there was largely gentile, and in no way representative of the majority of the governed. Jerusalem, organized as a *polis*, had served the earlier Roman administrations well, in keeping this border province soundly organized in the face of the Parthians who were, so to speak, just over the eastern horizon. Now, with Jerusalem still a wasteland forty-seven years after the Destruction, the eparchy of Judaea was like a body without a head.

The Emperor, I suggest, was thoroughly receptive to these reasons of state — political, strategic, economic. He felt no enmity towards the Jews, no feelings of vengefulness, as shown by his treatment of their co-religionists in Alexandria. He probably envisaged the reconstitution of Jerusalem as a *polis*, and its revival economically. It would have to be populated by Jews, since these were the majority inhabitants of the southern regions (the Darom, the Negev) and of the Galilee.

However, he probably had no intention of restoring the semi-independence that had been Judaea's before the Destruction. No doubt he meant only the rehabilitation of Judaea as an eparchy, not as a state. And it is even more unlikely that he intended to rebuild the Temple. But it is only natural that the Jews pinned grander hopes on this promising new ruler. In the mind's eye of the people, Jerusalem and the Temple were inseparable, as they had been for a millennium. Therefore, as the wish became father to the thought, word spread that the Temple was about to be restored.

It seems that that was not at all what Hadrian had in mind. But as things turned out, he put off even the rebuilding of Jerusalem. Why? Was it perhaps because of the kind of outside interference that the Jews suspected? Or was it after all due to their own over-enthusiasm? In any case, one need scarcely be surprised ference that the Jews suspected? Or was it after all due to their was a chance for the anti-Jewish lobby in the Senate and outside of it to bring its influence to bear on him directly, he might well have reappraised his original plans. We saw something similar happen to Claudius, when within the space of one year he did a complete about-face in his attitude to the Jews of Alexandria!

Perhaps, then, this will serve as an explanation for what happened at the beginning of Hadrian's reign. It must be admitted, however, that it does nothing to solve another riddle that continues to haunt historians who are unwilling to accept facile or prejudged solutions: what happened between Hadrian and the Jews about fifteen years later to turn them into such sworn enemies? That remains an enigma.

CHAPTER NINETEEN

THE HADRIAN YEARS:
SANHEDRIN AND PATRIARCH

Hadrian ruled the Roman Empire for fifteen years (117–132) before the Bar Kokhba War broke out. We might have expected our sources to give us some inkling about the state of the nation during that short prewar period, some premonition, some awareness of what made that decade-and-a-half a road to war. But no. The literature is abundant, but it leaves us with the impression that life pursued the even tenor of its daily routine. There is much halakhah and aggadah echoing from the academies, but it requires a very sharp ear indeed to detect the reverberations of what was going on beneath the surface.

Because something must have been going on. Is it at all conceivable that so fierce a fire-storm could have burst suddenly on a completely tranquil land without the least sign of warning? Or is it not rather more likely that the embers of rebellion had been smouldering in Judaea all along? Perhaps we can guess what went on in the minds and hearts of the people after the Jewish uprisings in the Diaspora had been liquidated, and the "War of Quietus" in Judaea itself had been suppressed. Perhaps, too, we can gauge the mood of the Jews after the bubble of expectation had burst, and the hope for the restoration of the Temple had turned out to be a mirage.

What we sorely miss at this point is the report of a witness — even a biased one, even one offering less than a full and frank disclosure, — someone, say, like Flavius Josephus. With all his faults, his often infuriating digressions and omissions, he has at least left us some idea of the forces at work during another pre-war era — the forces that shaped the political, religious and social life of Judaea during the 22 years that led up to the First War with Rome (66–72). Occasionally his history even lights up sharply

[461]

the elements of the gathering storm, as with a sudden flash of lightning.

But the Hadrian years have bequeathed us no Josephus. The literature is fairly abundant; but it is, after all, the literature of the schools. To be sure, the Sages were close to the people Their world was no ivory tower, and their recorded concerns reflect much of the reality of the times. But it is inevitable that we miss much of the picture, especially as concerns the life of the small farmer class at one end of the social spectrum, and of the wealthy and worldly elements at the other. We will therefore have to sketch the period in rather broad outline, and try somehow to understand it even in the absence of the kind of detailed information we might have preferred.

WHERE WAS THE SANHEDRIN?

Because of certain sources, coupled with the general consideration that life under Quietus must have been particularly uncomfortable in the southern regions of the country, Graetz and a number of other historians have argued that the Sanhedrin must have moved to the Galilean town of Usha at the very beginning of Hadrian's reign.[1] It is here contended that, even on general grounds, the theory creates more problems than it solves; and the sources prove, on closer examination, to be unreliable.

For one thing, everything else we know points to the conclusion that the process by which the Jewish population of the country shifted northwards did not really begin until *after* the Bar Kokhba War. This theory would imply that it began much sooner, thereby contradicting the view (of which these scholars themselves are the chief proponents) that there was massive Jewish activity in Jerusalem at the beginning of Hadrian's reign.

In the second place, if it were proven that such a move did indeed take place, our thinking about the Bar Kokhba Revolt would have to be revised. Either we would have to see it as a Galilean movement, organized and conducted from the north; or, if it was

---

1   [Graetz: *Geschichte*, IV, p. 131]; Halevy: *Dorot Harishonim*, Vol. I, Part 1, pp. 426, 575. More recently S. Klein, in the article "Akademien" in the (unfinished German) *Encyclopedia Judaica*, [Vol. I, 1176] takes the same stand.

rooted in the south, as an uprising led by revolutionary circles who had neither sanction nor backing from the Sages who constituted the Sanhedrin. Perhaps enough has been said to make it unnecessary to take up all the implications of such a hypothesis.

As for the sources on which the aforementioned historians rely we must look at them carefully.

The first of these is the famous tradition recorded by the Babylonian Talmud in the name of Rabbi Johanan about the wanderings of the Sanhedrin.[2] It says plainly that the Sanhedrin was exiled from Jerusalem to Yavneh, from Yavneh to Usha, from Usha to Yavneh, from Yavneh to Usha (again), from Usha to Shefaram... and so on. That would seem to be pretty clear-cut evidence that the Sanhedrin moved to Usha twice, moving back to Yavneh the first time, which would not have been likely after the Bar Kokhba War; so it must have been before. It certainly sounds as though Graetz and the others were right.

But there are reasons for regarding the text as suspect. First of all, there is a Palestinian version of the same tradition, to be found in Bereshit Rabba — and it records only *one* move from Yavneh to Usha.[3] Secondly, even the Babylonian tradition does not record the back-and-forth movement to Usha in important versions of the text.[4] These two reasons seem sufficient grounds for discrediting this witness.

The second source which is supposed to support the theory is the phrase describing Rabbi Ishmael, who died before the Bar Kokhba War, as one of those who "went to Usha".[5] But this proves nothing. Gatherings of members of the Sanhedrin were held at various places in the country throughout the tannaitic period, as we pointed out above.[6]

A third piece of evidence cited in support of the early move to Usha is the report about the two Roman officers who studied Jewish law at the academy of Rabban Gamaliel. The version in

---

2   R.H. 31a–b.
3   GenR 97, Theodor-Albeck p. 1220.
4   See *Dikduke Soferim* IV p. 88.
5   B.B. 28b.
6   JLTA I, pp. 233 f.

the Sifre reads: "they went to Rabban Gamaliel at Usha".[7] Since he was the Patriarch, that seems rather convincing.

But first, we have to recall that Rabban Gamaliel almost certainly died before Hadrian became Emperor. And then, we have to look at the proposed evidence. The identical tradition is found in two other places — and in neither of them is Usha mentioned at all![8]

So it seems, on both the evidence and the argument, that we must agree with those scholars who maintain that the Sanhedrin did *not* move to Galilee until after the Hadrianic period.[9] In fact, the most reliable sources indicate that throughout the reign of Hadrian the Sanhedrin sat either at Yavneh or at nearby Lod (Lydda). We have a number of references to meetings of the Sages at Yavneh during this time, and to decisions taken there.[10] We also have references to gatherings — and votes taken — at Lod.[11] In fact, there are even instances where the identical discussion — or decision — is assigned by one tradition to one meeting-place, and by another tradition to the other.

How did Lod get into the picture? Possibly for no special reason, other than the fact that it was deliberate policy of the Jewish leaders to meet in important centers of population as a means of strengthening their relationship with the local communities. In this instance there may have been an additional factor: Rabbi Tarphon, at that time presiding over the Great Beth Din, had his home in Lod.

7   Sifre Deut. 344, ed. Finkelstein p. 401.
8   B.Q. 38a; Yer. ibid. IV:3, 4b. [Even the reading in Sifre is doubted by Finkelstein, who suggests (Proc. of Am. Academy for Jewish Research, 1934–35, p. 115) that "Usha" is "nothing more than a slip of the pen for Yavneh."]
9   [See Büchler: *Der Galiläische Am ha-Arez,* pp. 28–9. Alon's ms. gives no specific reference; in the one here cited, Büchler merely finds the "sources uncertain".] See also Ginzberg: *Perushim ve-Hidushim,* vol. I, p. 159. As for the meeting at Sepphoris in secret of four important members of the Sanhedrin (Tos. Kel. B.B. II:2, (591), referred to above, this has no bearing on the question, since it deals with an emergency situation, when the Sanhedrin was probably homeless.
10 Ber. 63b; Shab. 33b; Mekhilta, Beshallah, V: 106, Lauterbach I, 135.
11 Tos. Yad. II:16 (683); Tos. Miq. VII:10 (660–1); Tos. Ber. IV:16 (10).

In mentioning such meetings, whether at Yavneh or at Lod, the sources speak of the attendance of varying numbers of Sages, usually ranging between thirty-two and thirty-eight. As we already know, it was not customary for the entire membership of the Sanhedrin to attend regular sessions, even on those rare occasions when a matter was to be submitted to a vote. Perhaps this explains the references to a council of five, a sort of standing committee of Sages.[12] It appears that this arose from the fact that there was no fixed assemblage of members of the Sanhedrin, making it necessary for the Patriarch to have a compact commission available at all times.

THE PATRIARCHATE

We do not know exactly when Rabban Gamaliel died, but it was almost certainly before Hadrian became Emperor. The most likely date is a few years before the death of Trajan (although there is no date we can propose that does not raise some questions).

The departure of Rabban Gamaliel was followed by a hiatus of some thirty years in the dynasty descended from Hillel the Elder. Why this should have been so — why Gamaliel II was not followed in the Patriarchate by one of his sons — we are not told. Was his firstborn son Simeon too young at the time? The possibility must be considered. Yet there may have been other factors as well. Perhaps the dynasty was still somewhat shaky; perhaps the tensions that had temporarily unseated Rabban Gamaliel had not been forgotten. In any event, it is clear that leadership passed for the time being out of the hands of his family.

Who then took the helm? Graetz suggests Rabbi Joshua ben Hananiah. There is no reason to reject his idea; but there is no irrefutable way of confirming it, either. Halevy offers a different suggestion: until Hadrian's time, it was Rabbi Eleazar ben Azariah; then — Rabbi Akiba.

I have no idea how to answer the question with any finality. But I do think that during most of Hadrian's reign Rabbi Tarphon

---

12 In one case called explicitly "the five Sages of Lod". (Yer. Bez. III: 62a). See also Naz. 44a ... "he asked Rabbi Joshua ben Elisha and the four Sages who were with him."

served as presiding officer of the Sanhedrin, though not as actual Patriarch. I base this on the fact that he is referred to in the sources a number of times in terms usually reserved for the Patriarch.[13]

There is reason to believe that a principal factor in propelling Rabbi Tarphon and Rabbi Eleazar ben Azariah into the leadership was the fact that they were kohanim. In addition, both these scholars were men of considerable means, something which was of no small importance, because the leader was expected to fund many of the expenses of the Sanhedrin, and to defray the costs of "diplomatic" representation to the Roman authorities.

THE WORLD OF THE SAGES

The focus of activity for the Sages, especially for those who had been granted ordination and who functioned as leaders in local communities, was the Sanhedrin.[14] The location of the Sanhedrin was the town where the Patriarch happened to live, since he was its presiding officer.

The Sanhedrin had a twofold function; it was both a Court and an Academy. On the one hand, it took decisions and issued rulings; and on the other hand, it engaged in learned discussion and exposition of the Torah.

But it would not be correct to say that Court and Academy were identical bodies, with merely a change in role. The need for the High Court — *Bet ha-Din ha-Gadol* — arose only when questions were presented, by individuals or communities, especially from the provinces or from the Diaspora. When that happened, a court was convened (*"moshivim bet din"*), the size of its membership determined by the circumstances. The question was examined in all its aspects, and a decision taken. The same procedure was followed when the needs of the moment called for action, particularly in the area of religious practice.

---

13 E.g. "R. Tarphon and the Elders". Three times the Yerushalmi calls him *rabban shel kol yisrael* or *avihen shel kol yisrael*. See Alon: "The Patriarchate of Rabban Johanan ben Zakkai", in JJCW p. 231 f.

14 In what follows I have relied almost exclusively on sources emanating from the actual period under discussion. In the few instances where this is not so, and conclusions have been drawn by analogy from earlier or later times, I have made it a point to say so explicitly.

For the most part, it was the Patriarch who set in motion the procedure for convening a High Court. Consequently it would seem that he was in a position to exercise considerable influence over the resultant decisions in matters of halakhah. All he had to do was to appoint a majority of members whose views approximated his own. But in fact he was not independent of the Sanhedrin as a whole, since halakhic questions submitted to the High Court were always finally considered by the full membership of the Sanhedrin.

Thus when major questions arose, or there were matters to be settled which were in dispute, a plenum of the Sanhedrin was summoned for the purpose of taking a vote (*minyan* = counting). In such cases not all members were always on hand: some were unable to attend, others did not *want* to attend.

It appears almost certain that such *minyanim* could not be held without the participation of the Nasi; but the decision was by vote of the majority. Nevertheless, the principle of majority rule was challenged at times by Patriarchs who claimed authority to act independently, or to overrule the Sanhedrin.[15] Generally speaking Patriarchs were unsuccessful in asserting such authority, apart from certain areas which were readily ceded to them by common consent as their special preserve. Most of the Sages resisted the patriarchal effort to rule, although a few did favor granting them special powers.

One of the problems constantly on the agenda during the years between the War of the Destruction and the Bar Kokhba War was whether the individual Sage was bound by the halakhic decision of the majority. As we have already noted, once a *minyan* had spoken none of those present could give a contrary ruling. But what of those who had not been present, and so had not taken part in the voting, but had on the other hand received a variant ruling on the matter from their teachers? The famous instance of

15 See Tos. Taan. II:5 (217) = Eruv. 41a: "During the lifetime of R. Gamaliel his decisions were accepted as authoritative. After he died, Rabbi Joshua sought to set his rulings aside. Up rose Rabbi Johanan ben Nuri and said: As I see it, the body follows after the head. While Rabban Gamaliel was alive, the halakhah followed his rulings. Now that he is gone, do you seek to abrogate his words?"

Rabbi Eliezer ben Hyrcanus is a case in point. He refused to yield his minority opinion on a ritual matter, and was in consequence banished from the company of his colleagues.[16]

His case illustrates two things. It shows the freedom of spirit (no heavenly intervention allowed!) and freedom of debate that characterized the Sages, on the one hand; and on the other, the power of the majority in limiting the freedom of the dissenting individual, no matter how important a man he was — not his freedom to debate, but his freedom to make rulings contrary to those of the majority.

The truth is, however, that only in a few matters did the majority invoke this power. In most cases the individual Sage was left free to follow the teachings of his own masters, and the interpretations of the Torah that he favored. It is a remarkable fact that even the Destruction had not made it imperative to insist on uniformity in religious behavior. In actual practice, however, individual Sages voluntarily restricted their own freedom of judgement. The maxim *yahid ve-rabim*: *halakhah ka-rabim* ("one versus many: the law follows the many") served not only to determine the decision of a court or other deliberative body. It frequently served also as a self-imposed brake on individuals, who felt themselves conscience-bound not to "violate the opinion of their colleagues".

There were of course instances where one Sage or another was adamant in his opinion, and refused to accept the decision of the majority. In the more extreme of such cases the rebel was brought to book by being placed under a ban (*niddui*) which meant that he was shunned by his colleagues for a time. There were various degrees of shunning, depending on the gravity of the offense. But no one was immune, not even the most prominent. The punishment, though not often used, was extremely effective.

The availability of measures such as these helped maintain a certain broad unity in the spiritual life of Eretz Israel in the period between the two wars.[17] But other centripetal factors were oper-

16 B.M. 59b.
17 It would not be difficult to cite instances of the enduring tolerance, even respect, for the dissenter, as reflected in e.g. the following: "The

ative as well. The power of appointment — *minui* — was vested solely in the Sanhedrin and the Patriarch. This appointment (later called *semikhah* — ordination) gave its recipient the authority to act as judge and leader of a community. It made him a full member of the Sanhedrin, and a "Fellow" in the Academy (*hushav ba-yeshivah*). There were, to be sure, learned but unordained "students" capable of expounding the law: but it was appointment that gave their teaching the full stamp of authority. In this way the Sanhedrin acted as a focus for the legal and religious life of the nation.

THE GREAT ACADEMY

The Sanhedrin had a second function. It served as the highest academy for the study of the Torah in all its aspects. Our sources for the period under review give us only the sketchiest outline of the procedures followed for dealing with any given topic. It seems that the study sessions were presided over by the Patriarch who opened the discussion, in which all the Sages participated. Present also in the outer ring were students (*talmidim*) usually more numerous than the Sages themselves, listening intently to the exposition (*derashah*) by the Nasi or by one of the Sages, and to the give and take that followed.

But these regulars were not the only *talmidim*. Behind them stood members of the public, temporary *talmidim*, auditing the discussions at will. They stood outside the railing (*l'ahore ha-gader*) whereas the regular disciples sat on benches. These latter could speak up, with permission of the chair, to ask questions or to suggest answers. But they did not have the right to hold a discourse of their own, nor to bring up any subject not already on the floor.

It was stated above that the Nasi was officially the presiding officer of the Academy, and that it was his privilege to deliver the opening discourse. But he was not always available for that role, nor was it customary for him to monopolize it. Even in Yavneh it was the right of every Sage appointed to the Sanhedrin to deliver a *derashah*. And a good case can be made for the assertion that

disciples of R. Eliezer (*under ban at the time*!) said to R. Joshuah ben Hananiah: We have already followed the instructions of our Old Master!" Yer. Ber. III:5d.

the Sages at Yavneh took turns in delivering the main discourse, especially on Sabbaths, when a large public audience of townspeople was in attendance. It is probably true that the Patriarch could give the lesson whenever he chose to claim the right; and that it was his prerogative to set the topic and open the discussion whenever he was present. But he was away from home a great deal of the time; and even when he was present he frequently deferred to other Sages.

It is also clear that even though the *Bet ha-Midrash* functioned more or less without interruption, not all its fellows lived in Yavneh or were in regular attendance at the sessions. Many of the famous "Sages of Yavneh" conducted academies and law-courts in their own communities. There were some who appeared in Yavneh only once in a while, either to vote on some moot question or to sit in on a discussion that was underway in the Great Academy.

THE FESTIVALS

There is ample evidence to show that it was customary for the members of the Sanhedrin to assemble on the three pilgrimage festivals — Pesah, Shavu'ot and Sukkot — at Yavneh or at Lod. This explains why Jews from the Diaspora would send delegations to Yavneh on these three festivals seeking answers to halakhic questions.[18] The presence of so many Sages in one place at one time made it likely that these Jews would find the answer to their problem.

It is well known that this continued to be the practice in Eretz Israel for many centuries, and that it also took root in Babylonia, where it was known by the Aramaic designation *rigla*. The custom itself appears to have originated in Yavneh. We shall quote some of the evidence. First, a tradition about one Rabbi Judah ben Nahman, who refuted Rabbi Tarphon in a matter of halakhah.

> Rabbi Akiba looked at him and saw that his face was radiant. Said Rabbi Akiba to him: You are radiant because you bested the old Sage. I wonder whether you will live long. Said Rabbi Judah bar Ilai: That happened on Pesah, and

18 Tos. Par. VII:4. (636).

when I came back on Shavu'ot I asked: Where is Judah, Nahman's son? I was told: He has passed away.[19]

This practice of assembling on the festivals gives point to the remark of Rabbi Judah about the (apparently crowded) sleeping arrangements in the Sukkah:

> Said Rabbi Judah: We used to sleep under the bed, in the presence of the Elders, and they never indicated any disapproval.[20]

The Great Academy was not the only one that drew "pilgrims" on the three festivals. Students journeyed to other, less famous academies throughout the land, in order to spend the day within the orbit of their learned masters. Hence the well-known aphorism: "One should pay one's respects to one's teacher on the festival."[21]

But there were Sages who frowned on this practice. As far as they were concerned, a man's proper place on the festival was at home with his wife and family. One of those who objected was Rabbi Eliezer, who reproved his disciple Rabbi Ilai when the latter came to spend the festival with him at Lod.

> Rabbi Eliezer used to say: I reserve my praise for the so-called lazy ones, who do not leave their homes on the festival. For Scripture says: "You shall rejoice, *you and your household*." (Deut. XIV:26).[22]

THE LIFE OF STUDY

How did that society produce its Torah Scholars? How did they get their education?

Those students whose ambitions led them in that direction, and for whom the normal level of learning which characterized the average lad proved insufficient — such young fellows would become dedicated scholars as soon as they began the regular study of the oral tradition. Some of them — but these were the exception

---

19 Sifre Num. 148, ed. Hurvitz p. 195; Men. 68b.
20 Mishnah Suk. II:1.
21 R.H. 16b.
22 Suk. 27b; Yer. ib. II:53a.

to the rule — remained at home, studying with their first teacher. The vast majority became wandering scholars, moving "from town to town, and from one city to the next", so that they could sit at the feet of certain Rabbis who were reputed to be great teachers. The aphorism cited in the Mishnah gained wide currency:" "Wander afar to a place where Torah is to be had."[23]

On the other hand, there were Sages who would travel about and lecture in one place after another to groups of students as well as to the general public. When a learned scholar arrived in town, those interested would assemble in his presence, sit on the ground, and give him their attention. Many of these listeners were former students who had left home at some previous time — having obtained the consent of their wives — for varying periods of study, extending sometimes over many years. The Talmud tells of Hananiah ben Hakhinai who was away from his home studying Torah for twelve consecutive years during the early decades of the second century, without once visiting his wife and daughter.[24]

Better known is the story of Rabbi Akiba, whose wife Rachel gave him permission to stay away for 12 years, and then for another 24, while she struggled to maintain herself in lonely grass-widowhood.[25] But these cases must be regarded as exceptional. Periods of marital separation for purposes of study, which required mutual consent, were without a doubt usually much briefer.

How did students of the Torah support themselves? There were those who had independent means. Some married with the stipulation that the wife would provide while the husband studied, as in the case of Joshua, Rabbi Akiba' son.[26] Others worked at all kinds of jobs to earn their keep, like Hillel, who managed on one *tropaik* per day.[27] So too, Rabbi Akiba worked as a gatherer of sticks (or straw), so that he could continue his studies.[28] Apparently it was not uncommon to see a student trudging along from one town to the next with "a leathern sack (*n'od*) of flour on his

23 Av. IV : 14.
24 Ket. 62b; comp. GenR XVII : 3.
25 Ket. ibid.
26 Tos. Ket. IV : 7 (264); Yer. ibid. V : 29d.
27 Yoma 35b.
28 ARNA Chap. 6 (Goldin, p. 42).

shoulder" — his source of sustenance as he sought out teachers at whose feet he could sit.

The famous warning to anyone who aspired to a life of learning, with its description of the austere lot of the scholar, was doubtless meant for the hard times that followed the Bar Kokhba War, but it was probably not altogether untrue during the decades that preceded it:

> This is the way of (studying) the Torah: bread and salt shalt thou eat; water doled out by measure shalt thou drink, and upon the ground shalt thou sleep, living a life of privation while thou toilest in the Torah.[29]

There were three main areas of study: a) *halakhot;* b) *midrash* or *talmud;* and c) *aggadot.*

The first of these consisted of rules of law, stated categorically, without reference to their basis in Scripture, or even in any system of general principles. This discipline had a practical aim — it was action-directed. Its intention was to teach people what to do.

The second branch — *midrash* (investigation) or *talmud* (study) was more theoretical. It involved the analysis of scriptural texts by various methods of interpretation (hermeneutics or exegesis) in order to derive new halakhot or to discover the underlying principles of existing halakhot. This discipline also included analysis of traditional halakhot without necessary reference to their scriptural basis. This branch of study relates to practical halakhah, but only indirectly — insofar as it provides the theoretical legal tools with which the halakhist can deal with specific practical questions.

The third branch of study — aggadah — must be defined negatively, since it is a catch-all term covering everything *not* halakhic. Thus it includes theology, religious philosophy, ethics, aphorisms, historical legends — and much else.

One can discern two main currents within aggadah. The first springs from the reflections of individual Sages, spoken perhaps in the limited circle of their chosen disciples. It takes the form of brief nuggets of wisdom, or pithy comments on biblical phrases. The second current obviously originated in the public arena, that

29 Pirke Avot VI:4.

is, in the synagogue or in the house of study when it too served as a place of public worship on Sabbaths and festivals. Here the Sage might combine teaching with preaching, dealing with questions of the moment while expounding the biblical texts, holding the attention of his audience by means of parables and popular folk-sayings. Aggadah thus represents an amalgam of introspective thought — as an end in itself — with homiletics, as a means of public instruction.

No doubt every student tried to learn something about each of the three main areas of study; but the majority most likely concentrated on one branch at the expense of the others. There were some who specialized in memorizing decisions, without learning the process of reasoning on which these conclusions had been founded. Such walking compendia of legal traditions were called *"tannaim"*, in one limited meaning of the word. Of the more repeat-by-rote types the Sages said: "These memorizers bring destruction to the world."[30]

In addition to the three disciplines we have just described, there were two rather peripheral fields of study: a) astronomy, plus the mathematics connected therewith; and b) cosmogony. The first of these was undoubtedly related to determining new-moons, leap-years, and the other features of the Jewish solar-lunar calendar. To quote Eleazar ben Hisma, who lived at the very time we are discussing: "The calculation of orbits (*tequfot* = turnings, probably solstices and equinoxes) and *geomatria* — these are ancillary studies."[31]

The second field of study, treated as peripheral by the mainstream of Pharisaism, involves metaphysical religious speculation, based primarily on the creation chapters in Genesis, and on the *Ophanim* vision described in the opening chapter of the Book of Ezekiel. Very few students went in for this type of study. The most widely quoted tradition in this regard is the one about the four who "entered the garden" (*pardes*), but only one emerged sound in body and mind.[32] Lest it be thought, however, that the

30 Sot. 22a.
31 Av. III:18. [*Geomatria* only later acquired the meaning of "numerical word-play".]
32 Tos. Hag. II:3–4 (234); Bavli, ibid.

[474]

subject was ignored or forbidden, it should be noted that Rabbi Joshua ben Hananiah discoursed on it in the presence of Rabban Johanan ben Zakkai, that Rabbi Akiba did the same before Rabbi Joshua, and Rabbi Hananiah ben Hakhinai recited on the subject in the presence of his teacher, Rabbi Akiba.[33]

Our sources do not give us a clear picture of the nature of this type of speculation, or enable us to determine its relationship to the oriental-Greek theosophy we call Gnosticism. But I would venture the opinion that its roots go back to indigenous Jewish thinking during the several generations that preceded the end of the Jewish Commonwealth.[34]

The designation *talmid* — student, or disciple — was not limited to the young. Many a mature and accomplished scholar with an academy of his own where a host of younger students sat at his feet, still retained the status of *talmid* — just so long as he had not been ordained.[35] After all, ordination was not always evidence of exceptional learning; considerations of public policy (such as the need to send a leader to a particular community) were also a factor. Among the great "students" of the generation before the Bar Kokhba War were the three Simeons — Ben Azzai, Ben Zoma, and Simeon the Yemenite.[36]

Study was not confined to the *bet ha-midrash* (study-house) or even to the synagogue. Learning went on in the open air — in the fields, by the wayside, "under the fig-tree", or "the olive tree"; at the city gate, even in the market-place[37] — until the Patriarch Judah I (died ca. 220 C.E.) pronounced the *shuq* no fit place for the study of Torah. Apparently, then, it was not an uncommon sight in the larger towns before the Bar Kokhba War to see a Sage expounding to his students out in the open, with nothing to prevent any passerby from joining the audience and getting a taste of learning. Obviously, the Torah was intended to be available to every-

---

33 Tos. ibid. II:2; Bavli, ibid.
34 [See now the definitive works of **Gershom** Scholem, especially *Major Trends in Jewish Mysticism* and *Jewish Gnosticism, Merkabah Mysticism and Talmudic Tradition.*]
35 Qid. 49b and Sifra, *Hova,* VII:3.
36 E.g. Qid. 20a.
37 M.Q. 16a.

one. No wonder that, over the span of several centuries, observers from Philo and Josephus to some of the Church Fathers remarked on the high level of knowledge of their religion prevalent among the Jews of their day.

ATTENDING THE SAGE

Study by itself was not enough to make a *talmid*. He also had to be in constant attendance — quite literally — upon his master, as though he were the teacher's son, or apprentice, or manservant. This was not solely a matter of propriety — of the honor and respect due to the Torah embodied by the Sage, or of the deference due to scholarship. Such propriety could have been served when occasion arose, in the house of study or in the synagogue. But the steady unremitting attendance on one's teacher — at his table, in his home — had an underlying educational purpose. It was a way of gaining a fuller insight into his teachings, of absorbing every nuance of his world-outlook. The living example of the Sage was an indispensable supplement to his oral instruction, more effective perhaps than his discourses in the *bet ha-midrash*.

This full-time service of the master by his disciple created a unique bond between them compounded of intimacy and distance, awe and collegiality, respect and affection — such as has not been unknown elsewhere between special teachers and special students. In the Jewish houses of study it was the rule rather than the exception. The student sought to become the faithful spiritual heir of his teacher in every respect, while enlarging and deepening his own learning and wisdom.

In the light of this, one can understand the boundless admiration with which the Sages speak of their teachers, even though they themselves were often the greater scholars. The text for this is "For all things come from Thee, and of Thine own have we given Thee" (I Chron. XXIX:14). For whatever the student had achieved, he regarded himself as indebted to his teacher. Thus, Rabbi Akiba mourned extravagantly for his teacher Rabbi Eliezer,[38] who in turn had spoken in deepest admiration of his own teacher, Rabban Johanan ben Zakkai!

38 [ARNA Chap. 25: "I have many questions, but now there is no one left to answer them." See Goldin p. 110, and note 27.]

The duty to wait upon the personal needs of the Sage is stressed repeatedly, generation after generation. In the second century, our present focus of attention, it is Rabbi Akiba who puts the idea in the strongest possible terms: "He who does not minister to the Sage does not deserve to live!" and "he has no share in the world-to-come!"[39] From the period *after* the Bar Kokhba War we find the following thought:

A person may have learned the Scriptures and rehearsed the Oral Law; but if he has failed to wait upon scholars he is accounted an *'am ha-aretz* (boor).[40]

The shared and rather austere life of master and disciples was most suited to small groups, such as were to be found in provincial towns. It was an even more appropriate mode for the itinerant teacher, accompanied by a handful of devoted disciples. Such groups usually held their meagre possessions in common, and shared in the preparation of meals, which they took together. One baraitha compares the relationship between master and student to that between father and son, or between brothers who have chosen to keep their legacy undivided.[41]

We may perhaps be justified in citing an example from a time several generations before Rabbi Akiba — the example of Jesus and his disciples. His conduct towards them no doubt reflects in some measure what was customary between a teacher of the Pharisees and his *talmidim*. He sits down to eat with them; there is a shared concern for the food and lodging of every member of the group. The way they minister to him conforms in most respects to what is prescribed by the tradition.

In the larger established academies this duty of the student took on regularly organized forms about which we are informed in some detail. Just as the Festivals were the occasion for large general assemblies of Sages and their students, so was the Sabbath the day for the *havurah* — the intimate circle of one Sage and his students, often joined by some of the local townspeople.

39 Yer. Naz. VII:56b; ARNA Chap. 36, Goldin p. 152.
40 Ber. 47b; Sot. 22a.
41 Eruv. 73a.

The role of an important disciple on one such occasion is described in the following:

> Rabbi Judah said: It was my Sabbath, and I stayed with Rabbi Tarphon at his home. He said to me, 'Judah, my son, hand me my sandal.' I gave it to him . . .[42]

This episode, Rabbi Judah tells us, taught him seven halakhot. As for us, it teaches us that the senior disciples took turns in ministering to the Sage. There can be no doubt that that is what "my Sabbath" means. Elsewhere, Rabbi Akiba tells us, "It was my Sabbath with Rabbi Eliezer and Rabbi Joshua. I kneaded a vat of dough for them (for the Sabbath)."[43] The custom persisted into amoraic times, as witnessed by episodes remembered by Rabbi Hoshaya and Rabbi Dimi.[44]

One more word about this type of spiritual apprenticeship. It had a lot to do with establishing norms of custom and halakhic practice not only in scholarly circles but further afield, among the people at large.

42　Tos. Neg. VIII:2 (628); Sifra, Metzora I:13; Yer. Sot. II:18a; [comp. JLTA I, p. 259. Note 25 there should be deleted.]

43　Pes. 36a.

44　Yer. Shab. III:5d; IV:7a; Bavli, ibid. 38b and 74a.

CHAPTER TWENTY

THE HADRIAN YEARS:
SAGES AND COMMUNITY

We now turn our attention to the role of the scholars in public life at the local level. This applies especially to those who were officially appointed to be leaders of communities; but it includes as well those learned *talmidim* who for one reason or another had not been granted *semikhah*, but who were nevertheless active in giving spiritual guidance and religious instruction. The decades before Bar Kokhba were especially rich in outstanding personalities, many of whom had already been active during the lifetime of Rabban Gamaliel, while others rose to prominence after his time.

The list includes such men as Rabbis Eliezer ("The Great") Joshua ben Hananiah, Eleazar ben Azariah, Tarphon, Ishmael, Akiba, Eleazar of Modi'in, Halafta, Haninah ben Teradyon, Johanan ben Nuri, Jose of Galilee, Judah ben Baba, Johanan ben Baroka, Judah ben Bathyra, Simeon ben Nanas, Simeon ben Azzai and Simeon ben Zoma. All these men were prominent during the period under consideration, and were among those who shaped the tannaitic age and gave it its distinctive character.

It would be logical to start a study of the age of the tannaim by discussing the ideas of the men who gave the age its name. That, after all, is their legacy to all the generations that came after them, as expressed in terms of values, of beliefs, of religious teachings. Nevertheless, we shall postpone our treatment of these fundamentals, and deal with them when we survey the literature of the years between the Destruction and the Bar Kokhba War. Here we propose to deal with the activity of the Sages in public life, as distinct from their more purely academic role in the *bet ha-midrash*. Of course, this will involve us in a consideration of one aspect of their *Weltanschaung*, namely the social and ethical principles by which they were guided.

Actually, this may turn out after all to be the best approach to their thought-world. For it was their ideas about interpersonal relations and social behavior that formed the most direct point of contact between their world-outlook and the mass of the people. It was in this area that their doctrines took on living form and became embodied in the life of the ordinary Jew.

It was pointed out above that as a rule each of the "Sages of Yavneh" lived in his own home-town, journeying from time to time to the Great Beth Din. But the literature indicates that many of them maintained their own local Beth-Din-plus-Academy. We know that Rabbi Eliezer (and Rabbi Tarphon) did so in Lod; Rabbi Akiba in Bene Beraq; Rabbi Joshua in Peki'in (of the South); Rabbi Halafta in Sepphoris; Rabbi Hanina ben Teradyon in Sikhnin. There also seem to have been (at this time) academies of a sort in Tiberias and in Beth Shearim. Rabbi Ishmael's academy was somewhere in the South, possibly in Kefar 'Aziz.[1] All these academies served not only the towns in which they were situated, but the surrounding areas as well.

Sages such as those just listed, assisted by their disciples, performed the following functions at the local level: 1) the resolution of halakhic problems, when such arose; 2) the supervision of community procedures in religious matters; 3) the adjudication of legal disputes; and 4) the teaching of Torah to the public at large.

With regard to the second function, it should be pointed out that the more direct responsibility for such procedures was in the hands of the lay leaders, the *roshei ha-k'nesset*. It should be noted further that ordinary guidance in matters of religious custom and practice could be obtained from *talmidim* and from middle-level scholars known as *safraya* (*soferim*, scribes). The exact meaning of this latter designation has not been established, but I think that the evidence, though admittedly sparse, is enough to give us a general idea of who they were.

First, there is a tannaïtic tradition rooted in the period we are studying:[2]

Rabbi Joshua says: From the day that the Temple was

1 Mishnah Kil. VI: 4.
2 Mishnah Sota IX:15. The text here followed is that of the Cambridge Ms. ed. Lowe, 1883.

destroyed the Sages began to be like *safraya*, and the *safraya* became no better than *talmidim*, and *talmidim* sank to what had been the level of ordinary people, and ordinary people became like pagans.

Another such passage comes from the Babylonian Talmud:[3]

> Rabbi Hiyya bar Abba was asked: If one listened (*to the beginning of the sections of the Hallel*) but did not give the responses, what is the law? He answered: The Sages, the *safraya*, the leaders of the people and the expounders, all state that he has fulfilled his duty.

I do not think that these *safraya* were the teachers of little children, as Rashi would have it, even though it is likely that many of them also served in that capacity. My interpretation is that they were practical guides in religious matters, and probably supervised the prayer services and the Torah readings in the synagogues.

The local *batei din* exercised considerable power in their own communities. According to one tradition, there was a time when they organized Sabbath meals for the entire citizenry:[5]

> In former days the agents of the Beth Din used to take up positions at the entrance to towns (*during Sabbatical years, when regular harvesting was forbidden.*) Anyone coming in from the countryside with agricultural produce would find it taken away from him; the agents would give him back enough for three meals, and the rest would be stored in the community sheds. During the fig season, agents of the Beth Din would hire workers to pick the figs, and press them into fig cakes, which were put into storage. When the grape season arrived, grapes were similarly picked, trodden in a wine-press, and the result stored in casks. The olive crop in its turn was treated in the same way, and the oil stored under community auspices. Distribution of these food sup-

---

3   Suk. 38b, according to the reading of Ms. Munich. This conforms to citations of this passage by Alfasi and the Rosh.

4   And all the commentators, following him. [So also Danby; *Mishnah*, p. 308.]

5   Tos. Shev. VII:I (72).

plies to the people of the town was made every Friday, to each according to the needs of his household.

It would be a mistake to read this as meaning that the local Beth Din had any enforcement powers of its own. Quite the contrary; it must be assumed that this efficient distribution system could only have been worked by the lay authorities. But if the executive powers were entirely in the hands of the town council, the Sages were nevertheless able to initiate and to supervise, even though their authority was only moral and religious, rather than legal.

As for the third function — the adjudication of disputes — a brief survey of this matter was presented in a previous chapter.[6] There we observed the tension between the lay tribunals controlled by the local councils and rooted in the ancient tradition of judgment by the elders of the town, as against judicature by Sages officially appointed by the Patriarch and the Sanhedrin. Some of these "ordained" judges functioned as free-floating jurisprudents, available on request to litigants or to local councils to sit on specific cases. The judgments of these Sages were accepted by the parties as well as by the local authorities, who were apparently prepared to see to it that their decisions were enforced.

In their judicial capacity these Sages also acted in a supervisory and administrative role. Thus, they not only appointed guardians for minor orphans; sometimes they themselves became executors, or acted *in loco parentis*. This role was inherent in their appointment by the Patriarch and the Sanhedrin, and is expressed in the maxim: "Rabban Gamaliel and his Beth Din are the fathers of orphans."[7] Similarly, it seems that there were times when physicians had to get permission from the Beth Din to practice their profession.

REACHING THE MASSES

Finally, there was the function of disseminating Torah to the public. The very fact that anyone could attend the discussions at the many *batei midrash* scattered throughout the country, or could listen in to the give-and-take between a Sage and his disciples in

6   JLTA I, p. 214 ff.
7   B.Q. 37a.

some public place, no doubt served as an indirect way of reaching many of the plain people. But the Sages went further, and conducted regular programs of adult education, targeted at the average man. These programs included both halakhah and aggadah.

During the several weeks preceding each of the festivals, public discourses on the halakhah connected with that festival were delivered in the synagogues as well as in the academies.[8] On ordinary Sabbaths too, halakhic subjects were dealt with, and not only on the practical level, but also theoretically.

That the Sabbath *derashah* (discourse) had been appended to the public reading of the Torah and the Prophets since olden times can readily be seen from the writings of Philo and from the Christian Gospels. The custom continued throughout the tannaitic and amoraic periods. In theory, anyone could give the *derashah*, but in practice it was usually delivered by a Sage. The chief content was normally aggadic, but it was customary to include some halakhic elements.

As we have noted the synagogue was not the only place of public instruction on Sabbaths and festivals. The *bet ha-midrash* served the same purpose. The sources show that these academies were "in session" continuously, by night as well as by day. They were open to anyone who chose to come and listen, or study.

Halakhah, then, was never entirely absent from the public discourses on Sabbaths and festivals. But the chief content, as we have noted, was aggadah. The Sages used these opportunities to convey their reflections on matters religious, national, moral and social. They would speak in a popular style, using simple language, without talking down to their listeners. They did not try to sugarcoat their more difficult ideas, nor to dilute their convictions. They were uncompromising in the demands they made on their audience.

These popular discourses of the Sages included denunciation of social evils together with encouragement to stand fast in the face of persecution. Their listeners were exhorted to love God, and the Torah, and their people, and to be willing to make sacrifices for all of these. The longed-for "days of the Messiah" they heard depicted in glowing colors — that future redemption which

8   Sifra, Emor XVII : 12; comp. Meg. 32a.

is to usher in a new world from which all evil and wickedness will have been banished, a world purified of all that is mean and corrupt.

It was these words of comfort, holding out the promise of salvation and nourishing the hope for a better world, which formed the main burden of the Sabbath discourses. Looking back at the glorious past of Israel, at the age of Patriarchs and Prophets and Kings, they looked forward to the promise of a glowing future. The idealized picture of the people's ancient heroes offered models worthy of imitation, particularly by the young. At the same time, these Sabbath discourses did not avoid the burning issues of the day. The Sages took their stand on the political and social questions that were in everybody's mind, and told their listeners explicitly what they thought people should do,

A number of sources show us that at these popular Sabbath lectures, attendance was not limited to men. There were women in the audience as well. And among those in attendance were folk who did not have enough education to understand what was going on but who were considered praiseworthy merely for being present: [9]

> Whoso enters the synagogue and listens to the words of Torah, even though he understand them not — he will be granted his reward.

Writing towards the end of the amoraic period, the learned Church Father Jerome says, not without a touch of irony, that crowds of Jews used to flock to hear the discourses of the Sages, even when they did not know a single verse of the Scriptures. It seems to me that that very point is made by the following Baraitha from the very period we are discussing: [10]

> Once Rabbi Johanan ben Baroka and Rabbi Eleazar ben Hisma went to pay their respects to Rabbi Joshua at Peki'in. He asked them: What new thing did you hear at the academy today? They replied: We are your disciples; it is you who must teach us. Said he: Just the same, no session

9   [I have been unable to find the source for this. —Ed.]
10   Tos. Sot. VII:9 (307); Yer. ibid. II:18d; Bavli Hag. 3a.

[484]

could have passed without some new word being spoken. Whose Sabbath was it? They answered: It was the Sabbath of Rabbi Eleazar ben Azariah. And what text did he expound? They said: He spoke on the passage: *"Assemble the people, the men, the women and the little children."* (Deut. XXI:10). He raised the question: If the men came to learn, and the women came to listen, what was the purpose of bringing the little children? He gave the answer: it was so that those who brought them might be rewarded for doing so. Then Rabbi Joshua said to his two disciples: You had a lovely jewel in your hands, and you almost deprived me of it.

At first glance this passage seems to take feminine ignorance for granted. But a second look shows that the women *did* understand what was being said — *lishmo'a* implies comprehension.

There is other evidence from the period before the Bar Kokhba War, that women were not excluded from the learning process. Not only did Beruriah, Rabbi Haninah ben Teradyon's daughter, express independent opinions in matters of halakhah;[11] another Jewish matron held her ground against Rabbi Eliezer in an argument about aggadah.[12] To sum the matter up, we may refer to the opinion of Ben Azzai, "A person should teach his daughter Torah."[13]

THE SAGES AND THE TOWN COUNCILS

In a previous chapter of the present work we quoted a source which showed the Patriarch removing from office the head of a town council who went against the express wishes of the Jewish authorities in Yavneh.[14] However, this should not lead us to suppose that the Sanhedrin and the Patriarch exercised direct control over the actual day-to-day functioning of the communities on the local level. As we have already observed, the Sages freely and voluntarily co-ordinated their activities with the local lay author-

11 Tos. Kel. B.M. I:6 (579) and B.Q. IV:17 (574).
12 Yer. Sot. III:19a.
13 Mishnah Sot. III:4. (Rabbi Eliezer disagreed.)
14 JLTA I, p. 181.

ities. But it was the latter who were the real civic administration, even with respect to judicature and religious institutions.

In spite of this, the local Sage, who derived his status from an outside source — the Sanhedrin and the Patriarch — could play an important role in the conduct of civic affairs on the local scene by working with the lay authorities of the community. The question arises: what were the dimensions of that role during the period we have under examination in this chapter — the pre-Bar Kokhba years of Hadrian's reign?

To begin with, it should be noted that the Jewish small town or village was fundamentally a democratic social unit. Nothing in law or custom gave any man special privileges over any other. The local council was selected by *anshei ha-'ir* — the men of the town. Constitutionally, so to speak, everyone had a voice, anyone could be chosen. Neither wealth nor family status were supposed to have anything to do with it. That was the underlying principle.

In practice, however, there were factors which operated counter to this basic democratic tenet. Old traditions die hard; and despite the power that had been gained by the common people during the years of social stress and strain preceding the War of 66–74, the idea that leadership belonged to men of family and property had survived, especially in the provinces. There can be little doubt that the old aristocracy and the newer merchant oligarchy had been favored, and therefore strengthened, by the Herodian monarchy and subsequently by the Roman colonial regime, up to the very outbreak of hostilities.

Secondly, following the Destruction, the Roman occupation authorities intervened directly in Jewish municipal life on behalf of those elements in the local population who had taken pro-Roman positions during the struggle. That this was in the political interest of Rome is obvious; it is also consistent with Roman imperial policy throughout the years. Everywhere in her empire Rome gave short shrift to democratic tendencies, and sought to back the economically strongest elements among her subject peoples. Although this policy was not completely successful in Judaea, especially once the Jews had recovered from the immediate wounds of war, and had resumed some semblance of normal living —

still, the more prosperous elements retained some of their power. Thirdly, there was the question of taxes and imposts of various kinds. Although in law the Romans still held each subject personally responsible for his taxes and other obligations to the state, there was in fact an aspect of collective responsibility, and this fell on the shoulders of the town councillors. Any deficit in what was due to the authorities had to be covered somehow, often out of the pockets of the leaders. The corruption for which Roman provincial administrators were notorious only compounded the financial risk, and made it all the more necessary to pick men of independent means to manage the town's affairs, so that they might shield the community by the power of their purse.

A fourth factor militating against the practical application of the egalitarian principle in municipal leadership was the fact that this position had to go unpaid and unrewarded (though there must have been dishonest individuals who knew how to turn public office into a means of personal gain). This was enough to keep the average hard-working citizen from accepting a place on the town council.

Lastly, there was the problem of providing for the needy. To be sure, social welfare was well organied, and everybody contributed his share. But the share of the wealthier citizen was greater than the average; and when there were unexpected needs the members of the council, who organized both the collection and the distribution, were expected to make up the shortage out of their own pockets. So that in spite of the underlying principle of equality, the factors we have enumerated combined to put men of means, more often than not, in charge of the town councils.

As a result of this situation, the literature of the times reflects a certain amount of friction between the Sages and the prominent citizens who more or less controlled public life during the years after the Destruction — a condition which was to repeat itself after the Bar Kokhba War. It was only to be expected that there would be those who would misuse their position and public office to the detriment of the weaker elements in the population, as we pointed out in an earlier chapter.[15]

15 JLTA I, 78 ff. note 64.

But to what socio-economic class did the Sages themselves belong? The answer varies widely. Some of them were actually quite wealthy, as for example Rabbi Eliezer, Rabbi Tarphon, Rabbi Eleazar ben Azariah and Rabbi Ishmael. Objectively there was nothing to prevent such men from serving in the office of *rosh ha-'ir* — head of the town council; but one is inclined to think that Sages were not as a rule welcome in such circles, partly because of their connection with the Sanhedrin and the Patriarch, and partly because their religious and ethical attitudes might prove uncomfortable to men of affairs.

On the other hand, the Sages had so much spiritual influence, and carried such moral weight with the common people, that the leading citizens could scarcely have kept them altogether out of the town councils even if they had wanted to. The Jewish town was what it was thanks in no small measure to the role played by the scholar-Sage in the religious and cultural life of the community. The plain people reposed their confidence in him. He was, in a sense, the defender and spokesman of the common man in relation to the ruling powers, whether those powers were Roman or Jewish.

There is another aspect to the role of the Sages in public life, and that is the actual assumption of headship in town councils. The possibility has already been raised that the Sanhedrin gave subventions to certain Sages in order to enable them to hold municipal office.[16] Whether that was so or not, there is clear evidence that Sages held the office of *Rosh* in some towns during the period we are studying. Thus, when Rabbi Akiba bequeathed advice to his son Joshua, he said:

> My son, do not make your home in a town where the head man of the council is a *talmid hakham*.[17]

We also find Sages acting as *parnasim* (wardens) for the distribution of charity, whether or not in combination with the office of

16 JLTA I, p. 251.
17 Pes. 112a; this is the correct reading, supported by mss, and by the older printed versions. (The current editions have *talmidei hakhamim*.) The same sentiment is expressed in Babylonia in the third century; see Pes. 113a, and Tosafot B.B. 110a, s.v. *v'lo tema*.

town leader. Examples are Rabbi Akiba,[18] Rabbi Haninah ben Teradyon (of whom it was said "A person should not contribute to the charity fund unless it is under proper supervision, by someone like, say, Rabbi Haninah ben Teradyon")[19] and Benjamin the Just, "who was appointed to look after the Tzedakah fund."[20]

It appears that Rabbi Ishmael, too, acted in that capacity, and that he made it a habit to supplement the fund he was administering out of his own pocket. The Mishnah, dealing with the ways in which a man or woman can be released from a vow, comes upon the case of one who tried to evade his social duty (in those days it was considered praiseworthy for a man to marry his niece) for reasons which will become apparent:

> A man once vowed that he would have no benefit from his sister's daughter. They brought her to Rabbi Ishmael's house and made her beautiful. Then Rabbi Ishmael said to the man: My son, is this the woman from whom you vowed to abstain? The man said: No! Whereupon Rabbi Ishmael declared the vow null (*in accordance with established procedure, on the ground that it was made in error*). Then the Rabbi broke into tears and said: The daughters of Israel are lovely, but it is poverty that mars their loveliness. When Rabbi Ishmael died the maidens wept for him, in words that echoed the lament for King Saul (*II Sam. 1 : 24*): "Ye daughters of Israel, weep for Rabbi Ishmael."[21]

An important branch of public assistance in the Jewish town was *hakhnassat kallah* — providing for the marriage of girls from needy families, particularly orphans. Obviously Rabbi Ishmael took a special interest in this activity.

THE SAGE AND HIS LIVELIHOOD

Practically all the Sages agreed that their rôle was compounded of two principal elements: *Torah* (study and teaching) and *gemillut*

18 See JLTA I, p. 250.
19 Av. Zar. 17b.
20 B.B. 11a.
21 Ned. IX: 10.

hassadim (deeds of lovingkindness — i.e. social action in the broadest sense). But which of these had priority? At this point there was a divergence of opinion. Some thought that the cardinal principal was *hesed;* they were the *anshei ma'aseh* (men of good works), the *hassidim* in the old sense of the word. One of them was Rabbi Haninah ben Dosa, of whom the Mishnah says: "When Rabbi Haninah ben Dosa died, the last of the *anshei ma'aseh* passed away."[22]

There were others who gave primacy to the study of Torah. That is why one finds certain Sages who took little part, or none at all, in public affairs. But of this, more later.[23]

We have spoken of certain Sages who were wealthy, and mentioned a few of them by name. Some, like Rabbi Tarphon, even contributed to the support of their students. On the other hand, many Sages were very poor, and eked out a meagre living by manual labor — like Rabbi Joshua ben Hananiah, who made needles by hand in a small forge. There were even some, like Rabbi Joshua ben Nuri, who had to take charity. Of him we are told that he would go out into the fields with the gleaners in order to pick up his subsistence.[24]

But the typical Sage of the period we are describing had to divide his time between his studies, his good works — and earning his daily bread. Those whose means were quite limited chose a very austere life-style, so that the time needed for attending to life's necessities would be reduced to a bare minimum.[25]

At the extreme end of the spectrum were ascetics like Ben Azzai, who did not take a wife. Said he: "I am in love with the Torah."[26]

22 Sot. IX: 15.
23 See below, p. 498 ff.
24 Yer. Peah VIII: 20d.
25 See Ber. 35b. where Rabbi Judah bar Ilai contrasts his own generation, after the Bar Kokhba War, with "previous generations." They, he says, made the Torah their principal occupation, their worldly occupations secondary; as a result they were successful at both. His own generation, he complains, gives primacy to worldly matters, and makes Torah a spare-time affair; as a result, it succeeds at neither.
26 Yev. 63b.

But he was very much the exception. The majority of the Sages were opposed to this attitude of self-denial. One of the more forthright expressions of the regnant view is given by Rabbi Ishmael:

> The Torah says: "Thou shalt gather in thy grain."*(Deut. XI:14)* What is this supposed to teach us? I might have thought that because it is written elsewhere (*Josh. 1:8*) "This Book of the Torah shall not stir from thy mouth" — I might have thought that was to be taken literally. Therefore the Torah teaches us here: "(No;) gather in thy grain." Live a normal life, after the way of the world.

In the same talmudic context the minority view is expressed by Rabbi Simeon bar Yohai, who protests:

> Is it possible that a man should plough at ploughing-time, and sow at seedtime, and reap at harvest time, and scatter the chaff when the wind blows (*and still have any time left*)? Then what becomes of the Torah?[27]

It is true that many of the Sages regarded labor as a virtue in itself — a *mitzvah;* but having to work so hard in order to make ends meet, and still find time to discharge one's obligations to Torah and one's fellow-man posed seemingly insuperable obstacles. The difficulties involved were echoed by Rabbi Nehunyah ben Hakaneh, late in the first century or early in the second:

> He who takes upon himself the yoke of the Torah will be relieved of the yoke of the government and the yoke of worldly care.[28]

I do not think it is correct to read in these words, as commentators mediaeval and modern do, the conclusion that the Jewish town supported the scholar-Sage and paid his taxes as well.[29] There is not the slightest hint in the sources that anything of the sort took place before the end of the second or the beginning of the third century.

---

27 Ber. 35b; comp. Sifre 42, Finkelstein p. 90.
28 Av. III:5.
29 See the discussion in Büchler's *Studies in Sin and Atonement,* 1928, p. 91 and note 3.

It seems to me that Rabbi Nehunyah's utterance is simply a pious hope — a message of faith and comfort to those occupied with the study of the Torah. Surely, he says, Heaven will shield them from worry by helping them earn their daily bread, and by keeping from their door the Roman tax-gatherer, to whose extra-curricular and unpredictable exactions the average Jew was exposed in those days shortly after the Destruction.

Since the Sage could not receive a salary from the public purse nor accept payment from individuals, neither in his role as judge nor in his capacity as teacher to the community, the position was economically problematical, the more so when times were hard. Some, as we have seen, met the situation by embracing a life of extreme poverty, although as has been pointed out, they were a small minority, and the course they chose was not recommended.[30]

We have already observed that the Sages dealt realistically with the need for judges in small towns, by leaving the courts in the hands of men who could afford to take the time to sit in judgment; taking care, naturally, to weed out the corrupt ones, and to give preference to decent citizens who would be likely to turn to them for guidance.[31] Of course, had this policy been pursued to its logical conclusion, it would have meant that the same class — the propertied class — would also have been the ones to be taught Torah. And indeed, there is a tradition that seems on the surface to say that one should teach only the well-to-do. But when the time comes for us to examine the source of this, we shall find that it is not authentic, but based on a text which has become garbled in transmission.

Nevertheless, the problem remained. The heirs of the Pharisees were left with a dilemma on their hands, an ethical-religious conflict of values. About a century earlier, Hillel the Elder had taught:

30 For more expressions of the majority view, see ARNA Chap. II, Goldin pp. 60–61, where Rabbi Akiba and Rabbi Tarphon and Rabbi Judah ben Bathyra and Rabbi Jose of Galilee are quoted in praise of physical labor. In the third century a compromise was formulated: "Let him who wants to enjoy the good things of life do so, as did Elisha; let him who wants to deny himself, do so, like Samuel of Ramah." (Ber. 10b.)
31 JLTA I, pp. 223f.

"He that maketh worldly use of the Crown (*of the Torah*) is doomed." Now, in the third decade of the second century, the Sages still believed that it was forbidden to let the Torah become a means to an end.[32]

The primary intent of this oft-repeated admonition was that one should not seek any personal honor or benefit from being a scholar, nor accept any monetary recompense in return for teaching either groups or individuals. After all, the Torah was given to Moses as a free gift for all mankind, and symbolically enough in the desert, which is no man's — and therefore everyman's — land. Hence, a person who has acquired a knowledge of Torah is under an obligation to impart it freely to others, whether they are his own disciples, or simply members of the public.

It is instructive to note some halakhic consequences of this "no recompense" doctrine. Regarding the Sage who acts as a judge, the Mishnah lays down this rule:

> He who accepts a fee for sitting in judgment — his decisions are null and void.[33]

With respect to the Sage-as-teacher, another tractate in the Mishnah yields the following:

> One who is bound by a vow not to derive any benefit from a certain person ... may (*nevertheless*) teach him *midrash, halakhot* and *aggadot*.[34]

But there is another side to this picture. Those dedicated souls among the Sages who chose a life of austerity, and devoted themselves to study and good works, felt that the good they were thus

---

32 For Hillel: Av. I:13. For the Hadrianic era: "R. Zadok says, make not the words of the Torah a crown wherewith to aggrandize thyself, nor a spade wherewith to dig (Av. IV:3)." It is said that R. Tarphon regretted all his life the fact that he had gotten some benefit from his learning. He said: "Woe is me, that I have made use of the crown of the Torah." (Ned. 62a; Yer. Shev. IV: 35b).

33 Bekh. IV:6.

34 Ned. IV:3. [The point is, he cannot take any reward for such instruction.] A baraitha quoted in both talmudim extrapolates from Deut. IV:5 "Behold I have taught you" etc. — even as I have taught without pay, so too do you. (Ned. 37a; Yer. ibid. IV: 35c).

freed to accomplish far outweighed the small violation of the "no recompense" principle involved in accepting their minimal subsistence needs from the community. There were probably many such scholars who, personally contemptuous of worldly comforts, were equally willing to forgo the spiritual self-satisfaction of simon-pure adherence to Hillel's principle, and were ready to accept their modest daily bread from others, if only that would enable them to pursue their holy tasks. There were even those who ruled as a matter of principle — and they were not necessarily *hassidim* — that it was *permissible* to be supported by people of means, in order to be free to serve the community. They did not think that this was using their learning as "a crown for self-aggrandizement", nor as "a spade to dig with".

Actually, we do find in the tradition words of praise for people of means who offer hospitality to scholars and their disciples, or extend help to them.[35] For the most part, the recipients of such generosity belonged to the class of itinerant scholars referred to in Berakhot 63b. Such men possessed nothing at all they could call their own; and whenever they came to a place, they would be put up by one or another of the better-off residents, who would see to their wants for as long as they stayed in that town.

A paradigm of this can be observed in the practice of Jesus and his disciples:

> Provide neither gold, nor silver, nor brass in your purses. Nor scrip for your journey, neither two coats, neither shoes, nor yet staves: for the workman is worthy of his meat. And into whatsoever city or town ye shall enter, inquire who in it is worthy, and there abide till ye go hence.[36]

35 To be sure, there is nothing to show that these references predate Bar Kokhba; and it seems certain that the practice itself became general only after the Revolt. But see the quotation attributed to Rabbi Simeon bar Yohai, a contemporary of Bar Kokhba, in Sifre Deut. Sect. I (Finkelstein p. 6). Comp. the following: "Rabbi Jose ben Haninah said in the name of Rabbi Eliezer ben Jacob: Whoever makes a scholar welcome in his home, and shares his possessions with him, Scripture accounts it as though he had brought the daily offering on the altar." (Ber. 10b). A similar passage occurs at the end of the same tractate (Ber. 63b).

36 Matt. 10, 9–11.

This seems to imply that the practice is not a mere compromise with principle. On the contrary, it is perfectly *legitimate* for the teacher of the word to be housed and fed. He is compared to a workman, and those for whom he toils actually owe him his room and board. Paul expatiates on this idea, when he says: [37]

> Let the leaders that rule well be counted worthy of double honour, especially they who labour in the word and doctrine. For the scripture saith, Thou shalt not muzzle the ox that treadeth out the corn. And, The labourer in worthy of his reward.

Here Paul is making it the duty of the community to support, not just the itinerant teacher, but even more, the settled one who lives in town permanently.

The wandering scholars were no doubt the most plebeian of the Sages, the plainest of the plain people, like Jesus and his disciples. But even the others, who had a fixed address, so to speak, and did not hold with the idea that the community ought to give them a living — even they ruled that it was permissible to accept the gifts of generous patrons, who not only supported them, but in some cases made them economically independent. One imagines that what the following story reflects is not entirely untypical: [38]

> Rabbi Jose ben Qisma said: Once as I was travelling along the road a man met me and gave me greeting, and I returned his greeting. Then said he to me: Rabbi, from what place are you? And I said, I come from a great city of Sages and *soferim*. Said he, Rabbi, would you be willing to live with us in our town? I would give you a thousand thousand dinars of gold, and many precious jewels besides. I answered him, Were you to give me all the silver and gold and precious jewels in the world, I would not live anywhere except in a place of Torah.

37 I Timothy 5. 17–18.
38 *Pereq Qinyan Torah*, Sec. 9. This chapter is a baraitha found in *Eliyahu Zuta*, 17, and in *Kallah Rabbati*, VIII. It was attached, liturgically, to the tractate Avot as a "sixth chapter" [in order to complete the six Sabbaths between Pesah and Shavuot.]

Rabbi Jose ben Qisma was active in the generation preceding the Bar Kokhba War. Now, it is true that there are versions of this text that attribute the story to Rabbi Jose ben Halafta, who belongs to a later time; it is also true that this tradition bears all the earmarks of legendary exaggeration. Then too, one must reckon with the possibility that the man who met the Rabbi was a visitor from some other country, and that what Rabbi Jose was refusing was a tempting offer to leave Eretz Israel. But in spite of all these reservations, it is fair to assume that there were scholars who would not have turned down an offer of this sort, but would have considered going to a place where the general level of education and culture was low — for the very reason that such a place needed them most.

Certain sources (not, to be sure, identifiable with any certainty as pre-Bar Kokhba) imply that some scholars became prosperous as a result of their learning, perhaps because they *did* accept offers like the one just quoted. There is a hint of that in the following:

"To love the Lord your God." (*Deut. XI : 13*). Because you might think: I will study Torah in order to become rich, or in order to be called Rabbi, or in order to be rewarded — therefore does the Torah teach you "Love the Lord your God." Whatever you do, do it purely out of love.[39]

The itinerant Sages — the proletarians, so to speak, — depended on the good-heartedness of charitable folk, but at least they remained free to teach the Torah as they understood it, without fear or favor. One cannot be so sure of the others, whose patrons supported them, sometimes in style. This could not but make them less independent, both in their teaching and in their public activities. Perhaps it was of some of these that it was said: "They could have spoken in protest, but they failed to do so;"[40] and of others that they became "mere wands for their bailiffs to wave at will,"[41] and worst of all, "lickspittles who ought to be denounced in public as profaners of the Holy Name."[42]

39   Sifre Deut. Sec. 41, Finkelstein p. 87.
40   Shab. 55a.
41   Ibid. 139a.
42   Yoma 86b.

But it must be said that within the time-frame we are examining the vast majority of Sages fall into one of the three following categories: those who earned their living by working at some manual trade; those with some independent means of their own; and those who chose to live a life of utter poverty, and so owed nothing to any affluent benefactor.

We have already referred to the possibility that the Sanhedrin and the Patriarch may have supported certain Sages out of funds collected from Jewish communities. The Yerushalmi tells of one such fund-raising "campaign" — apparently a forerunner of what was later to take on organized form as *d'mei kalilah*.[43] We also read of Rabbi Akiba and a colleague of his being sent on a fund-raising mission for the Sages to a property owner in Eretz Israel, so apparently the effort was not confined to the Jews of the Diaspora.[44]

It does seem that even in the days of Yavneh there were some very poor Sages who had to go abroad in order to earn a living. It was a phenomenon that became common in the third century. Apparently these Sages were actually sent on missions by the Sanhedrin, with instructions to counsel with the Diaspora communities, and to strengthen their ties with the mother country. While they were teaching and preaching abroad, the affluent members of the communities they were visiting would feed and house them, and sometimes give them valuable gifts, so that on their return home these Sages would be free for a time to devote themselves to study and teaching. The Talmud tells the following story:

> The Patriarch Rabban Gamaliel once travelled on the same ship with Rabbi Joshua. The only food Rabban Gamaliel had with him was some bread, while Rabbi Joshua had some bread and some flour. When Rabban Gamaliel's bread was all gone, he depended (*for food*) on Rabbi Joshua's flour. He said to him: Could you have known that we would be delayed to such an extent that you brought along (*extra rations of*) flour? He answered: There is a star that appears

43 See Yer. Hor. II: 48a and JLTA I, p. 251.
44 Yer. Pes. IV: 31b.

once in 70 years, and I thought that it might make its appearance and lead us off course. Rabban Gamaliel said: All this you know, yet you have to travel! [45]

The patriarch's exclamation is an expression of regret that so great a scholar as Rabbi Joshua should be reduced to the necessity of travelling in order to keep body and soul together. [46]

Finally, it should be noted that it was only later, during the third century or at the end of the second, that it became the established practice for the community to provide a living for its resident spiritual leader-scholar-judge. But incipient signs of the practice can be seen in the period we are discussing. [47]

LEARNING AND DOING

It was pointed out above that there existed a sort of division of the Sages into activists and pure scholars: between those who dedicated their lives to good works, and those who confined themselves to the study — and teaching — of Torah. The tension between the *anshei ma'aseh*, at one extreme, and those of whom it was said *toratam umanutam* at the other, had long existed. [48] There is a tradition that during the very period we are discussing — the reign of Hadrian — the issue was finally put to a vote. The majority gave priority to the study of the Torah, without necessarily implying a quietistic attitude to the performance of good works. Because it is my belief that this tradition has been incorrectly un-

---

45 Hor. 10a.

46 It seems that Sages in need volunteered to go abroad as emissaries of the Patriarch. I suggest that Rabbi Akiba, who started out as a poor man, became economically independent in this fashion. The Talmud offers a miraculous explanation for the rise in his fortunes (Ned. 50a–b). [It has been suggested that Rabbi Joshua knew about Halley's comet, some fifteen centuries before the birth of the astronomer Halley! The trouble with that suggestion is that the comet, whose period is 76 years, appeared in 66 C.E., whereas Rabban Gamaliel's voyages took place in the nineties. See JLTA I, pp. 124 ff. and the note in the Soncino Talmud ad loc.]

47 [Alon speaks of a source for this but I am unable to find it.]

48 [Comp. Urbach: The Sages, Vol. I pp. 603–620, "The Struggle Between Learning and Practice."]

derstood, I propose now to examine it very carefully. Here is the version in the Bavli:

> Rabbi Tarphon and the elders once sat together in the upper chamber of the house of Nithza in Lod. The question came before them: Is study more important, or is action? Rabbi Tarphon gave his answer and said, action is more important. Rabbi Akiba spoke up and said, study is more important. All of them answered and said, study is more important, because it leads to action.[49]

The usual explanation offered for this tradition is that the discussion took place during the Hadrianic persecutions after the Bar Kokhba Revolt.[50] According to this view, the Sages were confronting the Roman decree which made *both* the teaching of Torah and the practice of the principal mitzvot (circumcision, the Sabbath) punishable by death. The question before them was, for which of the two, Torah or practice, ought one to risk one's life? As is well known, Rabbi Akiba acted on his conviction, defied the ban on teaching, was caught and suffered martyrdom at a public execution.[51] The same course was chosen by Rabbi Haninah ben Teradyon, and he suffered the same fate.[52]

But there are serious difficulties with this interpretation. The principal one is chronological: Rabbi Tarphon died before the Revolt, and Rabbi Jose of Galilee seems to have done so too, since his name never appears after Bar Kokhba. Besides, the likelihood that the Sages would come together in the south (Lod) at that time seems very remote.

The simplest explanation of this tradition is that it reports a gathering of the Sages in peace time, before the Bar Kokhba Revolt, to tackle an old and vexed problem concerning the proper role of the Sage. The version in the Yerushalmi makes it clear that the matter was put to a vote, although there is some question

49 Kid. 40b; comp. Sifre Deut. 41, Finkelstein p. 85; Yer. Pes. III:30b; Yer. Hag. I:16c. [Among those present the Sifre mentions Rabbi Jose of Galilee.]
50 [See Weiss, *Dor Dor*, Vol. I, p. 125; Graetz, *Geschichte* IV. p. 429.]
51 Ber. 61b.
52 Av. Zar. 18a.

about the name of the upper chamber where the discussion took place.[53] But the decision is cited unequivocally: *talmud* (study) has priority over action, whether the latter means good works or ritual performance or any other activity. We read:[54]

> Rabbi Abbahu sent his son, Rabbi Haninah, to Tiberias to study Torah. People came and reported to him: He spends his time performing deeds of kindness. Whereupon he sent this message to his son: Are there no graves in Caesarea?[55] For they (long ago) decided in the upper chamber of Beth Arus in Lod, that learning is to be given priority to action.

There is a passage in "The Fathers According to Rabbi Nathan" which has a bearing on this matter:

> Once, as Rabbi Simeon ben Yohai went about visiting the sick, he found a certain man afflicted and laid up with bowel sickness, uttering blasphemies against the Holy One blessed be He. Wretch, the Rabbi said, you should be praying for mercy instead of cursing. The man replied, (Very well then), may the Holy One remove the sickness from me and lay it on you. Rabbi Simeon said: That serves me right, for I forsook the study of Torah and engaged in activities that use the time up.[56]

---

53 For a discussion of the various names given the location, see the exchange between I.N. Epstein and S. Klein in Tarbiz, I, 2, pp. 127 ff., 131 f., 133 f.

54 Yer. Pes. III: 30b; Yer. Hag. I: 6c. The decision is not to be understood in a rigidly literal sense. All the Sages agreed that learning which does not issue in action is sterile. Rabbi Eleazar ben Azariah spoke for his generation when he taught: "One whose wisdom exceeds his works, to what may he be compared? To a tree that has many branches and few roots. The wind comes and plucks it up and leaves it overturned ... But one whose works exceed his wisdom, to what may he be compared? To a tree with few branches and many roots. Even if all the winds in the world come and howl at it, they cannot move it from its place." (Av. III: 17).

55 A play on Exod. XIV: 11. Burial of the dead is the ultimate kindness, since it cannot be repaid; but if good works had been the goal, there was no need to leave home.

56 ARNA Chap. 41, Goldin p. 169, and notes ad loc. In the Hebrew text, the last two words quoted should be read as though they were *dibhre*

THE DEMOCRACY OF LEARNING

We have surveyed several questions related to the role of the Sages in the community at large. These have included their own socio-economic position, and some of the ferment of ideas which bore on their public activity, such as the tension between study and practice, or the choice between labor and poverty. But we must not overlook something else — a rather intense struggle which took place, in part, during the very decades of the second century we are dealing with. The outcome of this struggle determined, in large measure, the future development of what had been universal education for all Jews. The total accessibility of Torah-learning to everyman was quite possibly threatened during these critical years, but the threat passed.

Among the Sages of tannaitic and amoraic times, it is not at all difficult to name those who came from the poorest and most uneducated classes. For the Torah was no man's property; its "crown" was available to all. This had always been the great rule which made the Sages of Israel the popular and influential leaders of the common people.

But there are indications in the literature that over a period of generations there was a trend running counter to this popular tradition of openness. A sort of hereditary caste of scholars — and therefore of leaders — seemed to be emerging. A careful observer can detect the incipient signs of a spiritual aristocracy. Had this tendency continued unchecked, Judaism would have developed differently. But the tendency was strongly opposed, and it withered away.

As a rule, scant attention is paid to the references that reveal this phenomenon. One of them occurs in a context describing the protocol of precedence for entrance and seating in the academy presided over by the Patriarch: [57]

> *battalah; debharim betelim* is a term highly unsuited for such an act as visiting the sick. I would apply the same interpretation to the words of Pappus ben Judah to Rabbi Akiba (Ber. 61b), when both of them were in Roman custody: "Happy art thou, Akiba, for thou hast been arrested on account of the Torah; woe is me, Pappus, for I have been arrested for *debharim betelim*."

57 Tos. Sanh. VII:8–9 (426); Bavli Hor. 13b.

When the assemblage has need of them (for some point of halakhah) the sons of the Sages and the disciples of the Sages are brought ahead of the leaders of the people. ... Sons of the Sages and disciples of the Sages who are learned enough to follow the discussion sit facing the Sages (Gemara: they enter and sit in front of their fathers, with their backs to the public); but if they are not able to follow the discussion, they sit facing the assembled people. Rabbi Eleazar son of Rabbi Zadok says: At feasts, special places are reserved for them.[58]

So we discover that sons of the Sages, simply by virtue of their family connection, had the privilege of sitting in a special place of honor.[59]

The intrusion of the hereditary factor into what had been the utterly egalitarian world of Pharisaic Judaism is also reflected in the following, which comes from the end of the third century:

The Galileans sent to inquire of Rabbi Helbo: After the Kohen and the Levi, who is entitled to be called to the reading of the Torah? He did not know what to answer, so he sent and asked Rabbi Isaac Nappaha, and this was his reply: After those two, scholars appointed *parnasim* of the community are called, and after them, scholars qualified for that appointment, and then, the sons of those who have been appointed *parnasim;* after them, the heads of the synagogues and members of the public.[60]

The Church Father Origen, probably unaware that there was any issue here, and therefore all the more valuable as a witness, reports early in the third century that he had spoken to a Jew, "the son of a Sage" (*huios sophou*) who had been trained to suc-

---

58 Rashi: "They are seated alongside the Sages because of the respect due their fathers."

59 See Alon: "Sons of the Sages" in JJCW p. 436 ff. [The original Hebrew of that essay appeared in the Jubilee Volume in honor of Alon's teacher, I.N. Epstein. It was the last of his monographs that Alon lived to see in print.]

60 Git. 59b–60a.

ceed his father.[61] Adding Origen's testimony to that of the Tosefta and the Talmud, we may say there is evidence that for a time the sons of Sages constituted something of a caste, starting life with special privileges, and groomed to succeed their fathers.

Admittedly, these sources are from the third century, or at best from late in the second. For an earlier time we shall have to make do with the somewhat less explicit evidence of *Avot d'Rabbi Natan* :

> "Raise up many disciples," (*said the Men of the Great Assembly*. Av. I: 1). The School of Shammai say, one ought to teach only him who is talented and meek and of good famiily (*ben avot*) and rich. But the School of Hillel say: One ought to teach every man, for there have been many sinners in Israel who were drawn to the study of Torah, and from whom descended righteous, pious and worthy folk.[62]

First of all, as we intimated above, in this matter of being rich the text is questionable. In their riposte the Hillelites pay no attention to wealth or the lack of it, but speak only of sinners. Many years ago Jacob Reifman suggested that instead of '*ashir* (rich) the reading should be *kasher* (worthy).[63] This intuition of his was borne out later on when Schechter published version B of the same work, and there the corresponding passage reads:

> The School of Shammai say: One ought to give instruction only to those who are worthy (*k'sherim*) and to those of good family (*b'nei avot u-v'nei-b'nei avot*). But the School of Hillel say: Teach every man.[64]

61 P.G. 11. *Epistola ad Africanum*, p. 62.
62 ARNA Chap. 3, Goldin p. 26.
63 Bet Talmud, IV, p. 48. [What Alon says here rests on his lecture notes, dated in his own hand "Winter 5706" (1946). His monograph "The Sons of the Sages," which appeared in 1950, the year of his death, apparently represents his later thinking on the subject. There he explicitly rejects the idea that the silence of the Hillelites on the theme of wealth proves anything at all. See JJCW, p. 440, note 12. But his conclusion about what must have been the original reading still holds.]
64 ARNB, Chap. 4, ed. Schechter, p. 14.

These *b'nei avot* were simply students whose fathers were Sages. Thus we find a school of thought whose purpose was to create a scholarly caste. The motive was to maintain the ethical and religious purity of those circles who were to be the custodians of the tradition.

Additional evidence from a somewhat external source is provided by early Jewish-Christian literature. In the "Preachments of Peter" embodied in the pseudo-Clementine *Homilies* we learn something about the training of students in the early church in Eretz Israel, and of their appointment as teachers (*didaskaloi*.) Those who wished to study could only be accepted if they were

good and righteous (ἐυλαβής) and circumcised (ἐμπερίτομος) and faithful (πιστός = כשר) (P.G. II, 32).

After at least six years of study, during which they were repeatedly tested, they were appointed teachers. But there was an assumption that their fathers before them had been teachers, because we read of the problem of a teacher who might die childless; and of one whose son might be unsuited to be a teacher, or too young.

There can be little doubt that these Jewish Christians conducted themselves as Jews in this, as in other respects. And since the source of this information has been dated to about 140 C.E., the situation described must be that of the pre-Bar Kokhba era.[65]

From the various pieces of evidence here presented we can conclude somewhat as follows: while students, to be acceptable, had to be faithful and suitable, it was advantageous for them to be the sons of Sages as well. Additional sources, which we shall refrain from citing here, make it seem likely that this trend reached its apogee at the end of the second century and the beginning of the third. Perhaps it had something to do with the emergence at that very time of scholars in the role of appointed community administrators (*parnasim*) and it may be that the tend-

---

65 [See JLTA I, p. 301. But by the time Alon wrote "The Sons of the Sages," he was concerned that the consensus on the dating of the *Homilies* had been questioned (see JJCW p. 457). Again, this point was not enough to jeopardize his case. And it appears that the question is still moot: see *Theologische Realenzyklopadie*, Berlin-New York, 1980, VIII, pp. 118 ff.]

ency was abetted by the Patriarchs, who made such appointments. In any event, the whole development was resisted by the generality of the Sages, who protested against the concentration of halakhic authority into the hands of certain families.

This opposition to the intrusion of hereditary privilege into the house of study was expressed in many ways, some of which we shall quote:

1. Let not the son of an *'am ha-aretz* say: Torah is not innate in me (sc. *so why should I aspire to it* ... [66]

2. You might say, let the sons of the elders study, let the sons of the great study, let the sons of the prophets study! Therefore does Scripture teach us: "But ye shall surely keep all this commandment (*Deut. XI : 22*)" — telling us thereby that all of us are equal when it comes to (*the study of*) Torah.[67]

3. If one beholds a proselyte who wants to study Torah, one should not say: Look who has come to study! The very mouth that has been eating forbidden meats and crawling abominations! Be guided by what Scripture says (*I Sam. X : 12, when Saul broke into prophecy*) "A man of the place spoke up and said: Who is their father?" Does the Torah have a father? (*Saul himself has already been called "the son of Kish."*) Furthermore we read: "What is his name, and what is his son's name, if thou knowest" (*Prov. XXX : 4*) and it is written further: "House and riches are the inheritance of fathers, but a wise wife is from the Lord." (*ibid XIX : 14*)[68]

An echo of the issue — whether there should be hereditary rights to scholarship — may be detected in the dictum of Rabbi Jose Hakohen, one of the disciples of Rabban Johanan ben Zakkai:

4. Prepare thyself for the study of Torah, for it will not come to thee by inheritance.[69]

66 Midrash Tannaim, p. 21.
67 Sifre Deut. 48, Finkelstein 112.
68 Tos. B.M. III : 25 (378).
69 Mishnah Av. II : 12.

Finally, let us present an exhibit from the amoraic period, by which time the issue had been just about settled:

> 5. Why is it not usual for scholars to have sons who are scholars? Rabbi Joseph said, to keep people from making the error of thinking that the Torah is theirs by right of birth. Rabbi Shisha bar Ida said, so that scholars might not become arrogant.[70]

It was in the days of these very Rabbis, early in the fourth century, that the tendency to develop a scholarly aristocracy came to a final end. Torah-learning was and remained available to all comers, and one did not have to be a "somebody" to acquire it, together with the prestige and influence that went with it. In the power structure of the community the scholars became the spokesmen of the common people, constituting a counterpoise to those other elements whose influence derived from economic and social factors.[71]

THE GALILEANS

Since we have been examining the role of the Sages in the life of the community, it will now be in order for us to look into a widely held view which would limit that role to the southern part of the country (Judah) at least until the middle of the second century. In this view the northern region (Galilee) is perceived as the home of ignorant peasants, unlettered and non-observant provincials, backwoodsmen, so to speak.

This is the prism through which many historians have seen the Galilee of the early centuries of our era — a land innocent of the Torah and of its mitzvot, both before the Destruction and

70 Ned. 81a.
71 [More reserved in his judgment is Ephraim E. Urbach in his article *Class Status and Leadership in the World of the Palestinian Sages* (English) in the "Proceedings of the Israel Academy of Sciences and Humanities," 1966, II, No. 4. He says: "Gedaliah Alon is correct in stating that the dicta emphasizing that the Torah cannot be inherited allude to the tendency to bequeath Torah-learning and its status, including the perquisites attaching thereto, which manifested itself among the families of the Sages ... But to my mind, the phenomenon is not to be dated as late as Rabbi Yehuda the Patriarch." (p. 25)]

after, throughout the Yavneh period. It is a theory which has nourished a wide variety of far-reaching conclusions about social, religious and political history.

To cite one important example: there are those who find the simple non-observant farmers and fisherfolk of "Gelil ha-Goyim" (the district of the gentiles) a most natural seed-bed for Christianity. On this reading, Jesus and his disciples are the spokesmen of the *amei ha-aretz* in their struggle with the "doctors of the Law" (Sages of the Torah), i.e. the Pharisees, who are particular about the proper observance of the mitzvot. For present purposes it matters little whether the reading is that of a Christian historian, for whom "Pharisee" is a pejorative word; or that of a Jewish historian, who uses the theory in defense of Judaism.[72]

The fullest exposition of this thesis about the Galileans is the work by Abraham Büchler on "The Galilean Am ha-Aretz."[73] Büchler follows an analysis of his own, by which he traces the origins of this phenomenon to two distinct types: 1) the non-observant, who have no respect for ritual, especially for the rules of purity and of tithing; and 2) the "know-nothings," who have no respect for learning, and only contempt for the Sages. The latter kind were to be found in the South, while the non-observant ignoramus was characteristic of Galilee.

But Büchler goes further. He finds that this Galilean phenomenon manifests itself only *after* the Destruction; all the evidence comes from the disciples of Rabbi Akiba and their contemporaries — i.e. from the middle of the second century. In any event, according to Büchler's analysis Galilee remains the special locus of the *'am ha-aretz*, since non-observance goes hand in hand with ignorance in this case, and the North as he sees it was never much of a center of Torah.

The question before us is: are these conclusions supported by the evidence? It behooves us to make a fresh examination of the sources, especially as they relate to the period we are studying — the Hadrianic era.

---

72 From an entirely different perspective, the view of the Galileans as rough and ready backwoodsmen makes them the prime source of rebellion against Rome.

73 *Der Galiläische 'Am ha-'Arez̧*, Vienna, 1906.

Before we do that, however, it should be made clear that no one questions certain established facts. It is agreed that the main center of learning, before the Destruction, was Jerusalem; and that afterwards its place was taken by Yavneh. It is also unquestioned that during the years when one or the other of these two locations was predominant, the secondary centers of Torah were in the South, within a reasonable radius of Jerusalem or Yavneh respectively.

On the other hand, it can be shown that there is no real reason for labelling Galilee as the special abode of ignorance and crude impiety. On analysis, it turns out that the stereotype actually has nothing to back it up. Büchler's method, based as it is on the fact that sources dealing with the *'am ha-aretz* are predominantly of Galilean origin, is vitiated by one important weakness. Most of his citations come from the post-Bar Kokhba generation, when the center of gravity of Jewish life *in general* had moved to the North, and *everything* had become predominantly Galilean!

To be sure, there are a number of explicit statements about the ignorance, and antagonism to the Sages, characteristic of the "men of Galilee." But surely these are not to be taken as reflections of objective fact, but rather as exaggerated expressions of the kind of intramural antagonism that often arises between districts of the same country. Of course the South, in its day, was much more the intellectual center, and inclined to look down its nose at the provincials of the Galilee. Take for example the exclamation attributed to Rabban Johanan ben Zakkai: [74]

> O Galilee! O Galilee! You hated the Torah! In the end you will be fated to fall into the hands of the *meṣiqin*.

Rabban Johanan is supposed to have said this after he had spent 18 years in the Galilean village of 'Arab, and only twice in all that time had he been asked halakhic questions.[75]

Now this whole tradition is not very believable. For one thing, it is highly unlikely that Rabban Johanan spent so many years in 'Arab. And then, the idea that he foretold the *meṣiqin* (before the

---

74 Yer. Shab. XVI:16d. The attribution is by Ulla.
75 See Mishnah, Shab. XVI:7 and XXII:3.

Destruction) has a legendary ring. Besides, those extortionists were not at all confined to the Galilee![76]

So we should understand this tradition as the survival of an old local prejudice. The same can be said for such phrases as "thick-headed Galilean" uttered by Beruriah, herself of Galilean origin.[77] Such expressions tell us less about the level of culture in Galilee than they do about the level of snobbery in Judah.

How little real information is to be derived from such manifestations of prejudice based on place of origin (whether spoken banteringly or with serious intent) may be seen from the following:

> Rabbi Simlai came to visit Rabbi Jonathan, and said to him: Teach me some aggadah. He replied: I have a tradition from my forbears that discourages teaching aggadah to Babylonians or to Southerners, for they are gross in spirit and wanting in Torah, and you, sir, qualify on both counts: you come from Nehardea and live in the South.[78]

Now, these words come from the third century, when neither the Babylonians nor the Southerners could be faulted as far as learning was concerned. Indeed, it was the very time when the great Rabbi Joshua ben Levi was in his prime at Lod! So there is obviously no point in reading the words as an objective description. They are clearly a current, perhaps even a good-natured, dig.

The phrase *"bavlai tipshai"* ("foolish Babylonians") is fairly common in the Talmud.[79] It would be hard to find anyone who takes it as evidence of anything more than the competitive spirit between localities. It ought to be just as legitimate to treat the early tannaitic expressions which downgrade the Galileans, as belonging to the same genre — mere evidences of a rather durable human foible.[80]

---

76 See JLIA I, p. 62.
77 Eruv. 53b.
78 Yer. Pes. V:32a; comp. Bavli ibid. 62a. [In the Bavli, apart from a slight change in the cast of characters, the addresses seem to be switched: R. Simlai comes from Lod, but his home is Nehardea.]
79 E.g. Beẓah 16a; Yoma 57a; Zev. 60b.
80 The status of the three main districts of Eretz Israel with respect to

It would appear, then, that the case for Galilean ignorance is not proven. But that is not all. There is evidence on the positive side, which tends to show that during the period under study Jewish learning and observance in the North were at a quite respectable level. Let us briefly summarize some of that evidence.

First, there is the question of the mitzvot. The Galileans were supposed to be especially careless in matters of tithing, of ritual purity, and of sabbatical-year produce. Yet we find the people of Sepphoris asking Rabbi Johannan ben Nuri for direction on an issue involving fruits of the sabbatical year.[81] And the same Jews apply to Yavneh for guidance concerning the permissibility of growing two species of vegetable together.[82]

Furthermore, the farmers in the district of Sepphoris see to it that their vegetables are kept free of ritual impurity (the source seems to refer to a time before the Bar Kokhba War).[83] And the people of Meron ask Rabbi Akiba about a detail in the rules of tithing.[84]

From a place in the Galilee called Rom Beth 'Anat a question comes to Rabbi Hanina ben Teradyon of Sikhni asking for a ruling about a *miqveh*.[85] In another passage. we find the poor Jews of Kfar Shihin particular about the rules of *'eruv*.[86]

Torah-knowledge is expressed figuratively in the following: "It used to be said: In Judah there is grain, in Galilee there is straw, in Transjordan only chaff. But then they had to change it and say: In Judah there is no grain, only straw; in Galilee no straw, only chaff; and in Transjordan, neither the one nor the other." ARNA 27, Goldin, pp. 115–6. [Contrast Goldin's interpretation, p. 201, n. 23.]

81 Tos. Shevi, IV : 13 (66).
82 Tos. Kil. I : 4 (73).
83 Tos. Makh. III : 5 (675).
84 Tos. Dem. IV : 13 (51).
85 Tos. Miq. VI : 13 (658). It may be relevant to point out that, according to Josephus, who was of course dealing with pre-Destruction times, the majority of Galileans refused to settle in Tiberias when Herod Antipas founded it, because it was built over graves, and therefore ritually impure (Ant. XVIII : 37–38). Josephus also shows the Galileans giving tithes to *kohanim*. Indeed, a reading of Josephus or of the Gospels reveals the Jews of Galilee to be as observant of their religion as any other Jews.
86 Tos. Eruv. IV : 17 (143).

There are even instances when the Galileans prove to be stricter than their southern brethren in halakhic practice and religious customs. For example:

Once it happened that Rabban Gamaliel sat on the stools of gentiles in Akko on the Sabbath and (*the locals*) said to him. It is not customary to sit on the stools of gentiles on the Sabbath (*because of appearances — it looks as though one is engaged in business dealings*).[87]

Something similar seems to apply to the difference in custom between Judah and the Galilee with regard to working on the 14th of Nisan — the day before Passover. The Mishnah says:[88]

In Judah it was customary to work on the eve of Passover until the noon-hour; but in Galilee they did no work at all on that day.

A possible explanation for this difference is that the older practice, once followed universally, was not to work on the 14th of Nisan. The general tendency in halakhic development was in the direction of relaxing prohibitions, and so it came about that the central authorities made work permissible until noon. But outlying districts, like Galilee, were inclined to be more conservative, and were slower to accept the newer permissive rulings. At any rate, one thing certainly emerges from this difference between North and South: the Galileans were staunch in their observance of religious tradition.

Similar conclusions can be drawn from the report in the Tosefta about Judah and Hillel, two sons of Rabban Gamaliel, who scandalized the whole district of Kabul in the Galilee by entering the bathhouse together.[89] They were told: "We don't do that kind

---

87 Tos. M.Q. II:15 (231); Yer. Pes. IV:30d. In the Bavli we read: "Once it happened that Rabban Simeon ben Gamaliel (sic) sat down on the stools of the gentiles in Akko on the Sabbath, and the whole district was scandalized. They said, we have never seen such a thing in all our days" (Pes. 51a).

88 Pes. IV:5.

89 Tos. M.Q. II:15 (231). Instead of telling the Galileans that what they were about to do was licit (*mutar*), one of the brothers tactfully withdrew. Comp. Pes. 51a.

of thing in these parts — two brothers bathing together."

The Galileans were also stricter about greeting mourners on the Sabbath. In the South it was permitted.[90] There were also differences between the two with respect to a widow's rights. The Galileans gave her the right to continue living in her husband's home, and being supported by his estate, for as long as that was her wish (the same usage applied in Jerusalem). But in Judah the custom was to include in her marriage contract the clause: "until such time as the heirs are minded to give thee thy *ketubah*" — which meant that they could terminate their obligation at will, by paying her off with the amount of her marriage settlement.[91] It is in this context that the Yerushalmi remarks:

> The men of the Galilee were more concerned for their honor than for their property (*and this included the Jerusalemites as well*) while the men of Judah were concerned for their property more than they were for their honor.[92]

If one may generalize, it appears that the customs of Galilee with regard to marriage, where they differed, did so on the side of greater sensitivity.[93]

So much for the observance of the mitzvot. As for the state of learning in the Galilee, we know that many of the Sages of Yavneh who visited the North before the Bar Kokhba War taught extensively, and found large and eager audiences. We have already

90 Yer. Ber. II : 5b et passim.
91 Mishnah Ket. IV : 12.
92 Yer. Ket. IV : 24b.
93 Tos. Kel. I : 4 (261). Bavli ibid. 12a; Yer. ibid. I : 25a. Perhaps it will be instructive to compare variations between North and South in the area of ethical values. The Talmud reports: "Galileans say, perform deeds (*that will be eulogized*) before your bier; Judeans say, perform deeds (*that will be eulogized*) after your bier." This tradition may be explained in the light of Semahot III : 6 (ed. Higger 111–112) where the posture of the Galileans is represented by the Jerusalemites, and the further comment is given: "For in Jerusalem they spoke only what was true of the deceased, whereas in Judah they attributed to him virtues whether he has them or not." Compare the well-known difference between the Shammaites and the Hillelites about what praises to sing before a bride (Ket. 16b).

mentioned the memory of this reflected in the comment of a Babylonian Amora: "I feel like Ben Azzai (teaching) in the marketplaces of Tiberias."[94] Also in Tiberias, one comes upon Rabbi Jose the Galilean expounding the laws of the red heifer, with Rabbi Simeon ben Hananiah at his side.[95] Rabbi Eliezer ben Jacob delivers a *derashah* in the same city,[96] while not too far away Elisha ben Abuya (later to become infamous) teaches in the Vale of Ginosar.[97] It is reported that Rabbi Eliezer once spent the Sabbath in *Upper* Galilee (usually thought of as rather remote) and there he was asked no less than thirty questions about the laws of the *sukkah!*[98]

Apart from such instances, it should also be remembered that not a few Sages and scholars came out of Galilee. Some of them settled there. Others served in Yavneh, Lod and Bene Beraq. Rabbi Jose the Galilean has already been mentioned. (The Church Father Jerome speaks of him as one of the great wise men of the Pharisees who are referred to in the traditions of the Jewish Christians).

Another prominent figure was Rabbi Halafta of Sepphoris, who conducted a Beth Din in that town. In Sikhni there was Rabbi Hananiah ben Teradyon. It also seems likely that Rabbi Joshua ben Neri was a Galilean, and that in the very period we are discussing, Rabbi Eleazar ben Perata lived in Sepphoris.[99]

Among the Galilean scholars of the time that can be listed are Abba Jose Halikufri of Tivon,[100] Johanan ben Tarsha of Ginosar,[101] Rabbi Jose ben Thaddai of Tiberias[102] and possibly "Nehemiah of Shihin."[103]

We also find a certain Judah "of Kefar Akko" (perhaps *Agin?*)

---

94 E.g. Eruv. 29a.
95 Sifre Zuta, Huqqat, ed. Horovitz, p. 302.
96 Ibid. p. 305. See Epstein in Tarbiz I, p. 60.
97 Yer. Hag. II:77b.
98 Suk. 28a.
99 NumR. XXIII; Tanhuma, ed. Buber p. 159.
100 Mishnah Makhsh. I:3.
101 Tos. Kel. B.B. V:6 (595).
102 Derekh Ereṣ I.
103 Yer. Sot. II:18b. In the Bavli, ibid 18b, he is called "Nehunyah, ḥofer sihin."

discussing an aggadic midrash with Rabban Gamaliel.[104] Among the students of Rabbi Akiba there is one Simeon of Shiqmona.[105] Rabbi Eliezer visits his student Joseph ben Perida at Uvlin in the Galilee,[106] and the same Rabbi hears a report from another student of his who comes from Upper Galilee.[107] Then there is Rabbi Simeon, who tells us the following:

> Once when I spent a Sabbath in the village of Beth Page, I met a student of Rabbi Akiba ... and I reported what he had told me to my colleagues in Galilee ... and later I recited the matter to Rabbi Akiba himself.[108]

Apparently Rabbi Simeon had colleagues in the Galilee during the lifetime of his master — fellow-students of Rabbi Akiba.

Lastly, it may be in order to point out that at the funeral of Rabbi Akiba's son a great throng assembled, with mourners from both the Darom (South) and the Galil (Galilee).[109] This makes it apparent that in the northern province there was no dearth either of scholarship or of respect for scholars.

What has been said should be enough, it seems to me, to cast considerable doubt on the notion that the Galileans stood outside the sphere of influence of the Sages. Indeed, a reconsideration of the known facts must lead to the conclusion that there is no reason at all to draw religious and cultural boundaries between the centers of Jewish population in North and South during the first several centuries of the present era.

104 Mekhilta d'Rabbi Ishmael, ed. Horovitz p. 196. [Lauterbach II, p. 180.]
105 Sifre Num. 133, Horovitz p. 177; comp. B.B. 119a.
106 Tos. Eruv. I:2 (138); Bavli ibid. 11b; Yer. ibid. I:18d.
107 Tos. Kel. B.M. II:1 (579); Bavli Shab. 52b.
108 Tos. Me'ilah I:5 (557).
109 Semahot VIII:13, ed. Higger p. 160.

CHAPTER TWENTY-ONE

THE WORLD-OUTLOOK OF THE SAGES

There is no intention here of attempting a full-scale analysis of the thought-world of the pre-Bar Kokhba generation, nor of presenting a complete picture of the *Weltanschaung* of even a few of the leading teachers of the day — not even of one of them. Such an enterprise would require an effort of major proportions, and of no small difficulty.[1] Besides, we are now engaged in studying the history of the Jewish People, rather than the history of Judaism. What we shall try to do here is to elicit from the sources a few of the salient points about Jews and Judaism in the thought of the Sages, paying particular attention to those socio-religious concepts which were at the core of their influence on the people at large. In other words, we shall try to seek out those elements in their thinking which drew so many of the common people into their orbit, and transformed these teachers into popular leaders, almost to the point where the great majority of the masses identified with them.

But before we examine the sources, we must lay down certain guide-lines. First of all, not everything attributed to the Sages of a particular generation originated with them. Very often they were transmitting ideas received from their predecessors, even when that is not made explicit. Nevertheless, we will be right if we regard the form, the style and the accentuation as peculiarly their

1 [In the event, the enterprise was carried to completion almost two decades after the words above were spoken, when Ephraim E. Urbach published his two-volume work *Hazal* (Hebrew, Jerusalem, 1966). The English translation by Israel Abrahams is titled "The Sages, Their Beliefs and Concepts," Jerusalem 1976, 1076 pages; both Hebrew and English by the Magnes Press of the Hebrew University. Urbach's introductory chapter ("The Sages", I, pp. 1–18) and the notes thereon, are suggested here instead of the short bibliography in Tol. I. p. 323.]

own. Put in another way: the major contribution of the "Sages of Yavneh," those who occupied the stage between the years 70 and 135 C.E., from the Destruction to the Bar Kokhba Revolt, was the collection and ordering of the tradition as it had come down from preceding generations. It was they who brought together the scattered teachings, in both halakhah and aggadah, of the centuries that had gone before, casting the oral tradition into a mould, fashioning compilations which, by the very fact of their coming into being, proceeded to elicit further growth.

With this in mind, it will be natural for us to expect the generation we are studying to express its own creativity not so much in terms of new concepts as in terms of fresh formulations and new stresses. Indeed, this is exactly what we find. This is the way in which the teachers of the generation gave voice to their own thinking, and registered their reaction to the difficult social, national and political situation in which they found themselves.

Secondly, even when our cursory examination of the sources enables us to draw something of a composite portrait of the principal trends of the time, we shall have to remember that no blanket description will serve. Far from it. The age was one of extraordinary division of opinion in the academies over some very important issues. It was a generation rich in outstanding thinkers and men of action, some of whom appear to have been highly distinctive and independent in their doctrines and outlook. Considering as well the extent to which they diverged in social and economic background, it is not surprising that one finds some far-reaching differences in the religious and social thinking of the Tannaim.

Most exceptional, both in their religious ideas and in their way of life, were those extreme pietists among the Sages whose search for pure holiness, verging sometimes on asceticism, set them in sharp contrast to the teachers of the mainstream (who aimed to improve life, rather than to revolutionize it). In any event, we cannot here investigate the wide spectrum of religious ideologies. It is, however, important to stress that there was an essential unity in the thought-world of the Sages. The various schools all stood on common ground: the Torah, and its interpretation according to the Pharisaic tradition. And the ideal end which they shared was one and the same: the triumph of Truth in the world, and

of Peace, and of the Good — in short, the coming of the Kingdom of Heaven here on earth.

The most striking feature of the thought-world of the Tannaim,
particularly those of the Yavneh generation, is its earnest simplicity
in both substance and form. Every saying of the Sages is characterized by a high seriousness. There is a total absence of any
motive or purpose other than to get at the core of meaning, at
the compelling truth. There is nothing here of the intellectual
exercise, no hint of the aesthetic pleasure to be derived from
orderly thinking, no echo of the delight to be found in the ad-
venture of the mind.

More: the truth sought by the Sages was not conceived as an
end in itself. It was always intended to lead, directly or indirectly,
to a way, to a course of action. This resulted in part from the
fact that the whole outlook of the Sages was bounded by and
saturated with religious feeling. Their striving for holiness and
their sense of the imperative to which man is born made it impossible for them to conceive of the world of ideas as something
abstract, autonomous. Indeed, it is this that sets the ethical system of the Tannaim apart from that of many of the Stoic philosophers, both those who were their contemporaries and those who
lived before them.

The earnest simplicity in the thought of the Sages extends, as
we have noted, to form as well as to substance. Hence the absence,
to a very large extent, of any conscious artistry in their utterances,
of any of that individuality which is the hallmark, the signature
of the artist.

Here again we encounter a contrast with a type of Greek literature which came to the fore at the very time of the Tannaim —
the literature of rhetoric, in which content served as the vehicle
for style, and ideas yielded pride of place to beauty of form and
graceful expression. Certainly, the aggadah developed its own
forms, such as the parable, or the stylized use of scriptural texts
— but its power resides in honest conviction, and not in any verbal
or literary artifice.

A deep emotional commitment lies just below the surface of
tannaitic discourse, occasionally breaking through into expression.
When the tradition tells of Sages who "burst into tears" on con-

templating the decay of social morality, or confronting the fate of Jews and Judaism in their time — that is no mere figure of speech. Nor is the emotionally opposite outburst of the unquenchable Akiba, when he "laughs aloud" at the burdens of the time, and chides his masters and colleagues for weeping at Israel's sorrows.[2]

The Tannaim did not recognize the virtue of resignation, as taught by the Stoics. That elitist, individualistic mode of thought, which made such quietism the recommended goal for the wise man, was foreign to their outlook. This is one more key indicator of the folk-character of Pharisaism and its popular teachers. It was an outlook which could not conceive of a separation between thought and action; a world-view activist by definition.

And yet, one is struck by an air of serenity pervading the thought-world of the Sages. Sometimes this seems quite astonishing. Surely they must have accumulated a heavy load of pain and rage against the oppressive Roman occupation, on the one hand, and against the accompanying decay of social values and the deterioration of religious life on the other. And yet, they faced their world with controlled serenity. Even at those moments when their feelings showed through, the clarity and depth of their inner serenity remained untouched. This, indeed, may be what constitutes the real greatness of the Tannaim — the root-cause of their tremendous influence on the Jewish people: their extraordinary combination of moral vision, of exacting ethical standards in the prophetic tradition, coupled with humane practical wisdom and an understanding for human frailties; their capacity for personal greatness yoked to personal self-effacement; their lively intellectual awareness wedded to a deep serenity of spirit.

To be sure, these qualities had been developed within the Jewish tradition over the centuries. The Sages of Yavneh inherited them from their predecessors who had lived in the days of the Second Commonwealth, before the Destruction. Now, tested in the fires of adversity, the Judaism they had inherited grew more profound in its thinking, and acquired new dimensions.

2   Mak. 24b.

FREE WILL

The Pharisaic doctrine concerning man's power to choose, despite Divine prescience, found its classic formulation in Rabbi Akiba's famous paradox — in the very generation we have under review. This point of theology was crucial in separating Sadduceanism and Essenism from Judaism. The latter developed as a religion which gives man freedom of choice, and which makes him totally responsible for all his actions. This doctrine does not teach resignation; it leaves very little room for mere good intentions, or for faith without works. It goes without saying that it rejects the idea of instantaneous personal salvation achieved through the miraculous intervention of an external power, as in Christianity.

> Rabbi Akiba said: All is foreseen, but freedom of choice is given; and the world is judged by grace,[3] yet everything is according to the balance of deeds.[4] He used to say: Everything is given on pledge, and a net is cast for all the living: the shop is open: the dealer gives credit: the ledger is open: and whosoever wishes to borrow may come and borrow: but the collectors unceasingly make their daily rounds, exacting payment from man, whether he is aware of it or not, with or without his consent; for they are able to support their demand. The judgment is a judgment of truth, and everything is made ready for the feast.[5]

A companion-piece, spoken by Rabbi Tarphon, an older colleague and former teacher of Rabbi Akiba, is directed primarily to students and Sages:

> The day is short, there is much to be done, the workers are slothful, the reward is great, and the Master keeps urging. He used also to say: It is not your duty to finish the work, yet you are not free to desist from it. If you have studied much Torah you will receive great reward, for your Employer can be depended on to give you due recompense;

3 Avot III : 15.
4 Ibid.
5 Ibid. III : 16

but know that the reward of the righteous will be (given) in the time to come.[6]

"Service", which is seen as the performance of good works, contributing towards the totality of life and making the world more harmonious and complete, cannot really be achieved unless it is motivated by love and crowned by love. The Sages of that generation discussed at great length this problem of "serving God out of love," which they all agreed is the only genuine service. Perhaps the most pithy summation of the doctrine is the penetrating comment of Ben Azzai on the verse "Thou shall love the Lord thy God with all thy heart and all thy soul" (Deut. 6:5):

With all thy soul — to the point of self-effacement.[7]

Love is the only possible matrix for an inner faith powerful enough to disregard the limitations of reality and circumstance. It alone can breed that unmitigated trust which allowed Rabbi Akiba to say "Whatever the Merciful One does, is for the best."[8]

There are times when such faith leads men to abandon normal prudence, and to leave aside participation in the daily duties of life. We find Rabbi Eleazar of Modi'im actually proposing such a course, as he expounds the scripture concerning the manna (Exod. 16:14):

One day's portion every day — this means that a man may not gather on one day the portion for the next day, as is done on Friday for the Sabbath. For Scripture says "Each day's portion on that day." This led Rabbi Eleazar to say: He who has enough to eat today, and wonders, what will I eat tomorrow — he is a man of little faith. That is what Scripture means when it says (*ibid.*) "that I may test them, to see whether they will walk in my way or no.[9]

6 Ibid. II:15–16.
7 Sifre Deut. 32, Finkelstein p. 55. [One meaning of *nefesh* is "self," see Brown, Driver, Briggs *Dictionary* s.v.]
8 Ber. 60b.
9 Mekhilta d'Rabbi Ishmael, Beshallah II, Lauterbach II, p. 103. The Babylonian Talmud attributes to Rabbi Eliezer the Great: "He who has a piece of bread in his basket, and says, What shall I eat tomorrow? belongs to those of little faith" (Sot. 48b).

It is not surprising to find this comment coming from Rabbi Eleazar, who was one of the extreme pietists; nor to find a realist and religious moderate like Rabbi Joshua ben Hananiah interpreting the selfsame verse in the exactly opposite sense:

> *One day's portion every day* — so that a man might gather tomorrow's bread today, even as one (prepares) on the eve of the Sabbath for the Sabbath.[10]

This love of Providence and absolute trust in Him shows through in the short prayer recommended by Rabbi Eliezer for situations of emergency:

> Thy will be done in heaven above; grant peace of spirit to those who revere Thee here below; and whatsoever is good in Thine eyes, do Thou do.[11]

But it should be understood that the love of God is inseparable from His service, so to speak; from the subjugation of one's will and one's desires to the divine will, which is to be realized only by constant and consistent effort. Only in this way can human life be made both complete and secure. Man must learn to see himself in a dual capacity, as both the child of God and the servant of God. This is the meaning of the phrase commonly used by the Sages, "acceptance of the yoke of the kingdom of Heaven."[12] It is not to be equated with submission to the inevitable, or to a power greater than oneself. It is to be understood rather as the achievement of an inner conviction and integration, as though one had cast anchor in the Eternity of the Godhead and moored oneself to His Truth and His Power.

ISRAEL

The Sages of the pre-Bar Kokhba generation gave a great deal of thought to the meaning of Jewish existence, to the spiritual role and special destiny of Israel, to the fate of the people and to its

---

10 Ibid.
11 Tos. Ber. III:11(7); comp. Bavli ibid. 29b.
12 [Comp. *yozer* preceding morning *Shema;* "Authorized Daily Prayer Book" with commentary by J.H. Hertz, pp. 112–113.]

hopes. Their thinking finds expression in many utterances, some of them in sharp disagreement with others, yet all of them informed by much serious thought and by an abundance of love. Perhaps the best known of these sayings is, once again, by Rabbi Akiba: [13]

> Beloved is man, in that he was created in God's image; but it was by a special love that it was made *known* to him that he was created in God's image, as he can read in Scripture: "For in the image of God made He man." (Gen. 9:6).

> Beloved are Israel, in that they were called children of the All Present; but it was by a special love that it was made *known* to them that they were called children of the All Present, as they can read in Scripture: "Ye are children unto the Lord your God." (Deut. 14:1).

> Beloved are Israel, in that to them was given the precious instrument (the Torah); but it was by a special love that it was made *known* to them that to them was given the precious instrument by which the world was created, as they can read in Scripture: (Prov. 4:2): "For I give you good teaching; forsake ye not My Law."

In this pithy formulation Rabbi Akiba enunciates a view concerning humanity as a whole and its relation to the Creator, and a doctrine about the special position of the Jewish people within that constellation, a position due solely to the Torah, a unique gift of love from their Father in heaven. Once again it is this Sage who is the one best able to voice what is in the hearts and minds of his people. This is no structured creed or system of beliefs, but rather something much more meaningful — a plumbing of the depths and very roots of a people's many-faceted experiences. Akiba seems to have understood wonderfully well what his ravaged folk went through between the time of his birth (about 40 C.E.) and the time of his public execution (about 135 C.E.). Not surprisingly, the Mishnah chooses a saying of his with which to conclude its discussion of the Day of Atonement: [14]

13   Av. III:14.
14   Mishnah, Yoma VIII:9.

Happy are you, O Israel! Before whom do you purify your-selves, and who is it that makes you clean? Your Father in heaven! As it is written: *I will sprinkle clean water upon you, and you shall be clean* (Ezek. 36:28).

This joy, and this pride-without-arrogance are not diminished by the suffering which the people undergoes. On the contrary, mar-tyrdom for the glory of God awakens love of Him among the nations of the world, who envy, so to speak, the halo which suf-fering bestows on the martyr-people. Here again is Rabbi Akiba, commenting on Exodus 15:2 "This is my God, and I will glorify Him."[15]

In the presence of all the nations of the world I shall speak the glories and praise of Him who spoke — and the world came into being. Because all the nations ask Israel, saying: "What is thy beloved more than any other beloved, that thou dost so adjure us?" (Cant. 5:9) that is, that you are so ready to die for him, so ready to be killed for him, as it is written, "Therefore do the maidens (*'alamot*) love Thee,' which means, they love Thee even unto death (*'ad mawet*). Nay, but you are handsome, you are strong, why not come and intermingle with us? But Israel answers the nations thus: Do you know Him? Let us but tell you something of his praise: "My beloved is white and ruddy, preeminent above ten thousand (5:10)." When the nations of the world hear some of this they say, "Let us join hands with you," as it is written, "Whither is thy beloved gone, O fairest among women, whither is thy beloved gone that we may look for Him together? (6:1)" Whereupon Israel says to the nations, Oh no! for it is written, (2:16) "My beloved is mine and I am His;" and further is it written (6:3) "I am my beloved's and my beloved is mine."[16]

15 *Mekhilta d'Rabbi Ishmael*, Beshallah, Horovitz p. 127, Lauterbach II, pp. 26–27.

16 I do not think this homily can be assigned to the time of the Hadri-anic persecution following the Bar Kokhba War. This was scarcely a time to arouse "envy" of the Jews among the pagans. Apart from that, we have no quotations from Rabbi Akiba for the post-Revolt

The uniqueness of the Jewish people, according to this view, its special chosenness as a holy people set apart — these make it clear that the spiritual greatness of Israel does not derive from its great personalities and teachers, but from the people as a whole. At this point in the thinking of the Sages the concept of the election of the people of Israel combines with the concept of the essential equality and freedom of every individual Jew. The resultant blend of religious conviction and patriotic fervor in which faith in God's love for Israel intermingled with the belief in the equality of every individual and the hope for national liberation, was not new. It had been present for several generations before the Destruction, and had issued in a wide spectrum of ideologies, stretching from the various Zealot movements to *most* of the many trends among the Pharisees. (Here and there one finds expressions of Pharisaic opinion which do *not* accept the general principle.) In this instance, it is Ben Azzai, disciple and younger colleague of Rabbi Akiba, who voices the representative opinion: [17]

The Lord spoke unto Moses etc. saying: (Exod. 12:1).
Rabbi Akiba says: *Saying* means, go and say to them, it is only for your sakes that He is speaking to me. For during all the thirty-eight years after the golden calf He was angry with Israel and He did not speak with Moses; as it is written: "So it came to pass that when all the men of military age had died off, the Lord spoke unto me." (Deut. 2:16f).
Said Rabbi Simeon ben Azzai: I do not dispute the words of my teacher; I am merely supplementing them when I say that it was not only with Moses that He spoke because of Israel's merit; when He spoke to all the rest of the prophets it was only for the sake of Israel. In the case of Ezekiel we read, "I remained there appalled for seven days among

period, even though we do have a story about a communication from him in prison before his execution by the Romans. It seems more likely that the present passage echoes memories of the days following the Destruction of the Temple, or of the "War of Quietus" (see above chap. 3). I would opt for the latter possibility here, as well as in connection with the decision about the three sins which one may not commit even to save one's life.

17 *Mekhilta* Bo 1, ed. Horovitz p. 5, Lauterbach I, p. 13 f.

them;" and then these words follow: "It came to pass at the end of seven days that the word of the Lord came unto me saying..." (Ezek. 3:15–16). In the Book of Jeremiah it is written (4:27) "And it came to pass that after ten days the word of the Lord came to Jeremiah saying." You find the same thing in the case of Baruch the son of Neriah, who complained to God: "Thou didst say woe is me, for the Lord hath added sorrow to my pain (ibid. 45:3)." Why, he asks, have I been treated differently from all the other disciples of the prophets? Joshua ministered to Moses, and the Holy Spirit rested upon him; Elisha served Elijah, and the Holy Spirit rested upon him; but I, why have I been treated differently? "I am weary with my groaning and I find no rest (ibid.)." *Rest* means the spirit of prophecy (as in "the spirit *rested* upon them" Num. 11:26). Now notice what God answers him: "Thus shalt thou say unto him, thus saith the Lord: Behold, that which I have built will I break down, and that which I have planted will I pluck up; and this in the whole land; and seekest thou great things (*i.e.* prophecy) for thyself? Seek them not." What he was saying to him was this: Baruch son of Neriah! If there be no flock, what need is there of a shepherd? If there be no vineyard, what need of a fence? And why? Because (*ibid.*) "Behold, I am about to bring evil upon all flesh." Thus do we find in every context that the prophets prophesied only for the sake of Israel.

So it is not the great personality who sheds lustre on his people, and bestows greatness upon it. Rather it is the common people, the collective national genius, so to speak, that grants to the gifted ones the privilege of serving as the means of expression for the higher good that is implicit in the inner nature of the common man.

This conception finds its way into the halakhah in a number of cases, as in the instance involving day-laborers cited in the Mishnah:[18]

---

18 B.M. VIII:1; comp. JLTA I, pp. 159–160.

Once Rabbi Johanan ben Mathia said to his son: Go out and hire us some *po'alim.* He went and made an agreement with them that he would provide them their meals. When he came back, his father said to him: My son, even if you prepare them a banquet worthy of Solomon in all his glory you will not have discharged your duty, for they are the children of Abraham, Isaac and Jacob. So (if you want to protect yourself) go to them before they start work and get them to stipulate that they will not hold you responsible for anything more than bread and pulse.

The same principle comes into play in connection with damages for inflicting indignity: [19]

A person who cuffs another is liable for damages of a *sela* (four *zuz*); Rabbi Judah, quoting Rabbi Jose the Galilean says: One hundred *zuz*. If he slapped him, he must pay 200 *zuz*. If he did it with the back of his hand, he must pay him 400 *zuz*. If he tore at his ear, pulled at his hair, spat upon him and the spittle touched him, or pulled his cloak off him, or loosed a woman's hair in a public place, he must pay 400 *zuz.* The general rule is: all is in accordance with the honor and dignity of the offended person. (*A different standard, apparently, from the one just laid down.*)

(No,) Rabbi Akiba said, even the poorest in Israel are to be looked upon as freemen who have lost their properties; for they are children of Abraham, Isaac and Jacob. (*A case in point:*) Once a man pulled a woman's hair loose in the public street, and she haled him before Rabbi Akiba, who found the defendant liable for damages of 400 *zuz.* The man said: Rabbi, give me time. Akiba granted him time. The man saw her standing at the entrance to her courtyard, so he broke in front of her a cruse containing an *issar's* worth of oil. She unloosed her hair, scooped up the oil in her hand and put it on her hair. The man had set up witnesses to catch her. Now he appeared before Rabbi Akiba and said: "Rabbi, do I have to give 400 *zuz* to a woman like this"

19   Mishnah B.Q. VIII: 6.

(who sacrifices her own dignity for an issar's worth of oil)?
Rabbi Akiba answered him: "You have said nothing, since
(the law is that) he that harms himself, though he has not
the right, is not culpable; whereas if others have harmed him,
they are culpable."

In a similar vein, the Bavli quotes both Rabbi Ishmael and Rabbi
Akiba in the following: [20]

> If a man was being sued for 1,000 *zuz*, and was clad in a
> cloak worth only 100 *maneh*, the cheap cloak is to be re-
> moved, and he is to be clad in a cloak worthy of his stand-
> ing. It was taught in the name of Rabbi Ishmael, and the
> same was taught in the name of Rabbi Akiba: All Israel
> are worthy of (wearing) that cloak.[21]

The principle that all individuals are equal, for which we have
just given some halakhic examples, may well be reflected "theologically" in the following: [22]

> Abba Yudin of Sidon said in the name of Rabban Gamaliel:
> How do we know that a person ought not to say, 'I am un-
> worthy to pray for the Temple, or for Eretz Israel'? Be-
> cause the Torah says (Exod. 22:23) *I will surely hear their
> cry.*

Thus the ordinary person is encouraged to believe that his prayer
for the redemption of Israel counts, too. Simple folk were inclined
to believe that only the great or the saintly had the "right" to
speak up for the public welfare; it would be presumptuous of
them, the plain people, to think that they could affect the tragic
fate of their country and their nation. Therefore Rabban Gamaliel
taught: Not so! Every single person is a fit spokesman before
the throne of Mercy; the restoration, the redemption, depends so
to speak on him. What he is saying, in effect, is that the coming
of the Messiah is in the hands of everyman.

20 B.M. 113b.
21 At this point the Talmud introduces the Mishnah Shab. XIV:4, where
    kings' children are permitted on Sabbath what is normal for them,
    and Rabbi Simeon exclaims, "All Israel are princes!"
22 *Mekhilta d'Rabbi Simeon bar Yohai*, p. 151.

LEARNING AND LABOR

The egalitarian idea also underlies the very many statements attributed to the Sages of Yavneh in praise of physical work. These statements see labor as 1) a moral imperative for all men, fundamental to the personal spiritual health of each individual; 2) the indispensable basis for a viable social structure; and 3) a desideratum in the life of the Sage, since Torah needs work to bring it to fulfillment and to demonstrate its truths.

This doctrine of the interdependence of Torah and labor is deeply rooted in the old tradition of the Pharisees dating from the days of the Second Commonwealth. It is reflected as well in the literature of the Judaeo-Hellenistic world.[23] We referred to this earlier, in a discussion of "work ethic." It remains for us now to set forth some of the more striking sources from the period we are examining: first, *The Fathers According to Rabbi Nathan*, version A :[24]

> Shemaya taught : *Love labor and despise lordship* (Av. I : 10). How am I to understand that? It means that everyone should love work; no one should despise it. For even as the Torah was given as a covenant, so too was work given as a covenant; as it is written : (*Exodus 20:9*) *Six days shalt thou labor and do all thy work; but the seventh day is a Sabbath unto the Lord thy God.*[25] Rabbi Akiba said : There are times when a man does work, and thereby escapes death, and there are times when a man does no work and in consequence is sentenced to death by Heaven. ...
> Rabbi Tarphon said : The Holy One did not allow his Shekhina to rest upon Israel until they did some actual work, as it is written : *Let them make Me a sanctuary, then shall I dwell among them* (Ex. 25 : 8). ...

23 See e.g. Josephus, *Apion*, II : 39, 41; Philo, *De Spec. Leg.* II, 60 (Colson VII, p. 345); *Testaments of the Twelve Patriarchs*, Charles, Vol. I, p. 327. The same attitude towards work as a moral imperative is found in early Christian writers — by contradistinction to the contempt in which manual labor was held by aristocratic Roman society.

24 ARNA Chap. II, Goldin pp. 60f.

25 I.e. just as rest on the Sabbath is a mitzvah, so is work on the other six days a mitzvah.

Rabbi Jose of Galilee said: It is only through idleness that a person dies.

Version B of the same work contains the following:[26]

Rabbi Eliezer said: Great is work, for Adam tasted no food until he had done some work ... Further, said he: Great is work, for just as Israel was commanded concerning the Sabbath, so too were they commanded concerning (the duty to) labor, as it is written: *Six days shalt thou labor ,and do all thy work* ... Rabbi Eleazar ben Azariah said: Great is work; for every artisan takes pride in what he calls his 'craft' while the Holy one, Blessed be He, calls the world His 'work', as it is written: *He rested from all His work which He had wrought* (Gen. 2:2). How much more ought we human beings be proud of our labor.

Moving on in the sources we find the following in the Tosefta:[27]

Rabbi Eleazar ben Zadoq quoted Rabban Gamaliel: One who is equipped with a craft, to what may he be compared? To a vineyard with a fence around it. No cattle or wild animals can enter it; wayfarers cannot consume its fruit or even see what it contains. But one who has no trade or craft, to what may he be compared? To a vineyard unfenced. Every animal can come in and consume, every passerby can enter and help himself, for it is all exposed to view.

The Yerushalmi offers the following:[28]

On the verse (Deut. 30:19) *Choose life!* Rabbi Ishmael taught: This means, choose thyself a trade.[29]

A corollary of this attitude of the Sages to the value of labor in human life is their great respect for those who do the world's work — from field-hands to craftsmen. Perhaps there is no finer

---

26 ARNB Chap. 21, ed. Schechter p. 44.
27 Tos. Qid. I:11 (336).
28 Yer. Peah I:15c; Qid. I:61a.
29 There were, to be sure, those who differed with him, and were willing to forego the commandment to labor so as to devote themselves wholly to study and thought.

expression of this than the saying, so unaffected in its simplicity, attributed by the tradition to "The Sages of Yavneh:"[30]

> The Sages of Yavneh used to say: I am one of God's children, and he (*the farm-hand*) is one of God's children. I do my work in the town, while he does his work in the field. I rise early to my task, and he rises early to his task. Just as he does not boast about his work, so do I not boast about my work.[31] Would you say that I do much and he does little? Have we not been taught, it is all the same whether a person accomplishes much (Torah) or little, so long as he directs his heart to Heaven.

So the Sages see the ordinary farmer, the man with the hoe, as their comrade and equal, even though he has but little Torah learning. His rights and his status are in no way diminished. Rabbi Joshua ben Hananiah teaches this when he says:

> If a man reviewed but two halakhot in the morning and two in the evening, and was busy all day at his work — it is accounted to him as though he had fulfilled the whole Torah.[32]

SOCIAL ETHICS

During the last several centuries of the Second Jewish Commonwealth, Jewish religious thought devoted considerable attention to a search for the main principles of the Torah. The commandments were very numerous; but both Sages and people felt that at the core of this multiplicity there must be a "great rule" (*k'lal gadol*) or perhaps two, constituting the ultimate ground and purpose of all those imperatives in the Torah and the Prophets.

The motive for this search was not any intellectual need for

---

30 Ber. 17a.
31 [This translation differs from the one offered for the same passage in JLTA I, p. 154 — but so does Alon's treatment of the text. There he simply quotes the standard printed versions of the Bavli. Here he prefers the text used by the *Arukh*, and "certain mss." — yielding, incidentally, a better meaning.]
32 *Mekhilta*, Horovitz p. 161; Lauterbach, II, p. 103–4.

order and system. The enterprise had a very practical end in view. If one could discover the essential meaning underlying the commandments, one would come into possession of a fundamental guiding principle for living, a lodestar for man's thought and action, a purifying and integrating force capable of lifting one's whole life to a higher plane.

Two main formulations emerged out of this search. One of them based the whole Torah on the *Love of Man;* the other on the *Love of Man and Love of God.* Common ground to both schools was the belief that the foundation and goal of man's proper conduct is the good of society, of mankind.[32a]

The "Sages of Yavneh," engaged as they were in reconstructing the shattered life of their nation and reconstituting its religious institutions, continued this generations-old process of seeking to distill the moral essence of the Torah. Prime examples of this are the summations made by Rabbi Akiba and Ben Azzai:[32b]

> Said Rabbi Akiba: *Thou shalt love thy neighbor as thyself* (Lev. 19:1) — this is the great general rule in the Torah. Ben Azzai said: there is a greater principle, namely: *This is the book of the generations of man; in the l.keness of God made He him.* (Gen. 5:1)

Now, there are those who profess to see in this a dispute over whether the command to love includes the stranger, with Rabbi Akiba taking the narrow view (*re'akha* = thy neighbor, ergo thy fellow-Jew) and Ben Azzai stressing mankind (*adam*) thus including gentiles. However, this interpretation has no leg to stand on. In the present context neither Ben Azzai nor Rabbi Akiba were concerned about the question of universalism versus particularism. The issue between them here is something entirely different.

Rabbi Akiba sees the imperative to love one's fellow-man as a derivative of the inherent *natural* equality of all human beings — an equality which should by rights be built into all forms of society. Ben Azzai on the other hand, derives the duty to love

32a See Alon in Tarbiz XI, 1940, pp. 127–132, *Mehqarim* I, pp. 274 ff. (not in JJCW).
32b Sifra, ed. Weiss, 89b; Yer. Ned. IX:41c.

others from "the Book." Man is entitled to love and respect because he is made in God's image. The love of man is thus a derivative of the love of God, for there is a spark of the divine in man. The Midrash puts this very well: [32c]

> Do not say: Since I have been humiliated, I have a perfect right to humiliate the other person ... Said Rabbi Tanhuma: If you do that, do you realize Whom you are humiliating?

So then, the love of the other is an *absolute*, not discharged by merely granting him equality with one's self, or giving him only such rights as one is satisfied with. It becomes apparent that the difference between the Sages is more than merely theoretical; it has practical consequences. Rabbi Akiba would seem to be offering a yardstick for the fulfillment of the commandment: "as thyself." If you demand for your fellowman the rights that are yours, if you see to it that he has full equality with you, you have done your whole duty by him. This problem is dealt with in the famous argument between Rabbi Akiba and Rabbi Joshua ben Perata over the hypothetical case of the two men in the desert with just enough water for one to survive.[33] Both Sages quoted the same biblical verse: "That thy brother may live with thee" (Lev. 25:36), but they came to opposite conclusions. Ben Perata said: "Let both of them drink, and both die." Rabbi Akiba said: "Your first duty is to preserve your own life."[34]

Here we find Rabbi Akiba upholding a "realistic" ethic, as against the "idealistic" school, represented in this case by Ben Perata. In the Halakhah generally, the view that usually prevails is that of Rabbi Akiba.

The same principle lies behind the clash of opinions about an entirely different issue: a man's right to impoverish himself by giving to the poor:[35]

32c GenR XXIV (ed. Theodor pp. 236–7), where this statement is placed *after* Rabbi Akiba's formula.

33 Sifra, Behar, V:3, ed. Weiss 109c; comp. B.M. 62a.

34 A similar problem was discussed by the Stoics; see Pines in Tarbiz, XVI (1945), pp. 238–240.

35 Ket. 50a.

He who distributes his wealth to the needy may not give away more than a fifth (of all he has) lest he himself become the object of charity. Once it happened that a man tried to expend (more than a fifth) and his colleague held him back. Who was that? Rabbi Yeshevav. Some say: Rabbi Yeshevav (was the over-generous one) and his colleague held him back. Who was that (colleague)? Rabbi Akiba.

The second version of this tradition is no doubt the correct one, because the Yerushalmi too reports that Rabbi Yeshevav tried to give everything he had to the poor (although it has Rabban Gamaliel as the one who stopped him:)[36]

> There was the case of Rabbi Yeshevav who began to distribute all his possessions to the poor. Rabban Gamaliel sent him a message: Have not the Sages (*at Usha*) ruled that one may give only up to one fifth of one's property to *mitzvot*?[37]

The line taken by Rabbi Akiba and Rabban Gamaliel seems designed to keep the commandment to love one's neighbor on a socially practical level, and to avoid in the halakhah those tendencies which might be emotionally satisfying to the individual, but could prove socially harmful. If we were to translate the thinking of these Tannaim into modern terms, we would say that they wanted to see the love of one's fellow man harnessed to socially constructive ends.

There are questions involving the relationship between law and ethics where this practical morality enters into the discussion. The Mishnah poses a case:[38]

> A man died, leaving a widow, a creditor and heirs; and he had goods on deposit or loan in the hands of others. Rabbi Tarphon says: The property should be given to the one at the greatest disadvantage. Rabbi Akiba says: Pity has no place in the legal process (*eyn m'raḥamim ba-din*); rather,

36 Yer. Peah I:15b.
37 The word is apparently a synonym for "charity," a Palestinian usage, in the way that the root *zkh* does duty for *gemillut ḥasadim;* comp. Mishnah Sot. I:9 and Tos. ibid. IV:8 (300).
38 Ket. XI:2.

the property goes to the heirs, for all the others must substantiate their claim by oath, but not so the heirs.

Despite the other interpretations suggested by the Babylonian Talmud, the "disadvantage" referred to by the Mishnah must be economic and physical — which is the way the Yerushalmi understands it.[39] As far as Rabbi Tarphon is concerned, when there is a question of legal doubt, the matter is to be settled by invoking purely humane considerations. Rabbi Akiba, on the other hand, believes that if the law has been invoked, the decision should be made on purely legal grounds, for the good of society.

A statement attributed to Rabbi Hanina ben Dosa in *Avot*, and Rabbi Akiba in the Tosefta, speaks of an inseparable bond between religion and social ethics :

> A person in whom the spirit of his fellowmen takes pleasure, in him the spirit of the All Present takes pleasure; but one in whom the spirit of his fellowmen find no pleasure, in him the spirit of the All Present finds no pleasure.[40]

In a way, this saying gave autonomy to ethical conduct; interpersonal behavior was made independent from what is conventionally known as religion. God himself was, so to speak, powerless to forgive the wrongs committed against other human beings; only the wronged could do that. So it is that we read in the Mishnah : [41]

> *From all your sins before the Lord shall you be clear (Lev. 16:30).* This verse was expounded by Rabbi Eleazar ben Azariah as follows : (by deliberately attaching "before the Lord" to the preceding noun instead of the following verb) : Transgressions between man and God can be atoned for by Yom Kippur, but transgressions against one's fellowman cannot be atoned for by Yom Kippur until one has appeased (*i.e. gained the foregiveness of*) one's fellowman.[42]

39 Bavli ibid. 84a; Yer. ibid. IX:33a. Comp. Tos. Bekh. II:7, 8, 10. (536).
40 Av. III:9; Tos. Ber. III:4 (6).
41 Yoma VIII:9.
42 The Sifra, ed. Weiss 83a, puts it a little differently: "Things between

Rabbi Akiba achieved the same result by a different homiletic device. He took the phrase *v'naqeh lo y'naqeh* (Ex. 34:7) literally, pretending to overlook its idiomatic meaning ("he will not altogether remit all punishment"):

> First it says "he will remit," and then it says "he will not remit!" How do you reconcile these two? This is how: *He will remit* — what is between you and Him; *He will not remit* — what is between you and your fellowman.[43]

There can be little doubt that teachings such as these had a very real impact on life and religion in the troubled times when they were spoken. They must have been particularly meaningful in ameliorating the social problems of people in distress. At an earlier period, during the Second Commonwealth, a number of competing religious sects had given birth to a variety of social movements, each dedicated to realizing its ethical ideas (the Essenes are merely the most obvious example). The same sort of thing now took place as a result of the social dislocation that followed in the wake of the Destruction. This included the development of organized forms of social welfare and mutual assistance.

A brief symbolic summary of these constructive factors in the life of the generation we have been examining can be gathered from the midrashic comment of Rabbi Eleazar of Modi'im on verse 20 of chapter 18 in Exodus:

> *Thou shalt show them* — means, where they live;[44]
> *the way* — means, visiting the sick;
> *in which they shall walk* — means, burying the dead;
> *in it* — doing deeds of loving kindness

---

you and the All Present are forgiven; things between you and your neighbor are not forgiven until you appease him."

43 Sifre Zuta, ed. Horovitz, p. 248.
44 [Alon uses the current reading *beit hayyehem,* also found in B.Q. 100a; but Lauterbach has ample warrant for omitting *beit.* The explanation Alon gives below was suggested by Rashi in B.M. 30b.] The phrase means "livelihood," as when Rabbi Ishmael expounds "Choose life" to mean *umanut.* So too, EcclR. on the verse, "Enjoy life with the woman whom thou lovest" (Eccl. 9:9) = "acquire a trade along with Torah." See also Qid. 28a.

and the work — doing justice according to the law;
that they must do — the higher justice, beyond the letter of
the law.[45]

ATTITUDE TO ROME

Josephus in his time had concluded, after the Destruction of the
Temple, that the triumph of Rome was a sure sign of divine favor.
There was a new chosen people, so to speak. The selection had
passed from Israel to Rome, even if only in the temporal, political
sense, even if only in this world.

It need scarcely be said that this was not the way the Sages,
nor indeed the generality of Jews, read the history of their times.
As far as they were concerned, the Destruction was a punishment
for their sins, and the Roman occupation, which had preceded it
by a good many years and was to stay on for a good many more,
was simply another yoke placed around their necks. It was the
"fourth kingdom" spoken of in the apocalypse (see the Book of
Daniel) following on Egypt, Babylon and Greece. Roman rule was
a temporary state of affairs; it would pass away in due course. Its
end (*qetz*) was first of all in God's hands; but to some extent also
in theirs.

The Sages never tired of discussing that *qetz* — really the "end
of days" — nor did they weary of exhorting the people to prepare
themselves for the redemption. A counterpoint to this theme was
their incessant denunciation of the "wicked kingdom," and their
excoriation of the corrupt officials who administered that corner
of the Empire — the governors and lesser colonial functionaries in
Eretz Israel.

But the real issue of the moment was: just how "temporary"
was this temporary state of affairs? There were those who pressed
for it to end quickly — the impatient ones (*dohaqei ha-qetz*). For
them, redemption was surely just around the corner. "Speedily will
the Temple be rebuilt."[46]

---

45 Mekhilta, ed. Horovitz 198, Lauterbach II, p. 182; comp. B.Q. 99b–
100a, where the attribution is to Rabbi Joseph.

46 Note for example, the urgent sense of messianic expectancy in Fourth
Esdras, or the Syriac Baruch, two books closer in spirit to rabbinic
literature than any other apocalyptic works.

However, most of the Sages adhered to the clear-eyed Pharisaic tradition of facing facts, and had no wish to commit themselves or their followers to a desperate denial of reality, no urge to focus the emotional resources of the nation on unrealistic expectations about a world to be made over in the very near future. From this standpoint, the temporary state of affairs was going to last for quite a while. Even though, in the long view, it was abnormal and transient, it was nevertheless about to constitute a major period in history. One had, therefore, somehow to come to terms with it.

That is why we find the Patriarchate trying to open channels of communication with the Roman authorities, and to gain recognition from them. That is why a deputation of Sages sails to Rome for "diplomatic" talks. Even more striking: we find leading Sages taking part in discussions with Roman governors on cultural and religious questions like Judaism, Greco-Roman thought, and the like. Even in the area of halakhah there is a sort of de facto recognition by Jews of the Roman government, although it must be said that between the Destruction and the Bar Kokhba War the over-all tone is negative, with allowances made for certain inconsistencies.

This largely negative attitude finds expression in three principal areas: 1) Roman courts; 2) Roman taxes; and 3) Roman public works and welfare — in short, at exactly those points where the occupation was likely to touch the life of the average person.

ROMAN COURTS

Shortly before the Bar Kokhba War we find two prominent Tannaim stressing the principle that Jews ought to steer clear of "the courts of the gentiles," referring apparently to the tribunals established under the auspices of the Legate:

> Rabbi Tarphon used to say: Wherever you find tribunals (*agoriot*) of the gentiles, even if their laws are like Jewish law, you may not have recourse to them.[47]

> Rabbi Eleazar ben Azariah said: Now, suppose the gentile courts judge according to Jewish law, may I conclude that

47 Git. 88b.

their judgments are valid? I may not, for Scripture says, *These are the ordinances that thou mayest set before them* (Exod. 21 : 1). You may judge their cases, but they are not to judge your cases.[48]

These texts do not say explicitly that they refer to Roman courts, and it is of course possible that they mean the local tribunals of the Hellenistic towns in and around Eretz Israel. But it is more probable, especially in the light of Rabbi Eleazar's concluding words, that the passages really do deal with the courts of the kind called *conventus*, administered under authority of the *Legatus* by his *assesores*. In the patois of the Greek-speaking East, it would be natural for such tribunals to be called *agoriot*, just as the *assesor* was called *synkathedros*.[49]

This exhortation against the use of Roman courts does not of itself indicate a rejection of the legitimacy of Roman rule, any more than does a similar exhortation by Greek writers of the same time. In the identical way, Paul urges Christians to settle their disputes among themselves and to keep out of Roman courts, even though he, like Plutarch, cast no doubt at all on the legitimacy of Roman rule.

But in the case of the Jews there is a difference. There seems to be a principle at stake. It is hinted at in the emphatic "even if their law is like Jewish law." First of all, the thrust here seems to be the preservation of Jewish judicial autonomy. But the difference goes deeper. Plutarch complains that Greeks run to bring all sorts of inconsequential matters before Roman judges. From the Jewish side, apart from two rather dubious instances, there is scarcely any evidence of such a phenomenon. Jews kept away. There was something fundamental here — a rejection of the Roman right to sit in judgment. "Their judgment is not valid."

On the other hand, there was another legal area in which the Halakhah *did* come to terms with the realities of life, and that is the legality of documents. The Mishnah states:[50]

48 Mekhilta, Horovitz 246, Lauterbach III, pp. 1–2.
49 [See JLTA I, p. 213. For the terminology, see Krauss, *Griechische und lateinische Lehnwörter usw.* I, pp. 180, 86.]
50 Git. VIII:5.

If he dated it (*a writ of divorce*) according to an unaccustomed era, (such as) the era of the Medes, the era of the Greeks, or 'after the building of the Temple,' or 'after the Destruction of the Temple'... (the writ is invalid).[51]

I am not inclined to assign this ruling to the time and the conditions of the post-Bar Kokhba period, though of course that is possible. What does seem clear is that the Sages were very meticulous about preserving uniformity of styling in legal documents, especially writs of divorce. They therefore showed a greater readiness to accept the common, standardized dating, which was in Roman terms.[52] So there is something to the remark by Ulla (a Palestinian Sage of the third century): "Why did the Sages decree that the Caesar should be mentioned in divorce documents? For the sake of the peace of the kingdom."[53]

Actually, we learn that this was old Pharisaic practice, going back to the days of the Second Commonwealth:

A Galilean *min* once remarked: I have a complaint against you Pharisees, for you mention the Emperor along with Moses in the document of divorce.[54]

Apparently, then, there were Zealots who objected to the mention of "Caesar" (*e.g. in such and such a year of Nero Caesar*) in a document written "according to the Law of Moses and Israel." Nevertheless, that was the way the Pharisees did it. On the other hand, it is possible that there were disputes about this within the Pharisaic camp, and that all that has reached us are echoes of the argument; hence, the lack of absolute consistency in this matter.

CRIMINAL LAW

As we have seen, the tendency was to deny any civil jurisdiction to the Romans, "even when their laws are like our laws". But

---

51 The Bavli, ibid 80a, misses the point, which is that the irregularity consists in the *failure* to use *Roman* dating.
52 [There seems to be an interesting parallel here to Alon's remarks about the tendency to accept Roman standard weights and measures; see JLTA I, p. 165.]
53 Git. 80a.
54 Mishnah, Yad. IV:8.

what about criminal law? What about public safety? After all, the Halakhah itself denied authority in such matters to Jewish courts after the Destruction, quite apart from the fact that this whole branch of law was excluded by the Romans from their grant of judicial autonomy to the Jews. How, then, did the Sages view the Roman authority in such matters?

We have reasonably clear evidence to show that during the period *after* the Bar Kokhba War this very matter was the subject of dispute among the Sages. There were some who saw it as their duty to co-operate with the Romans, though only at the initiative of the latter, in the maintenance of public order. This can be illustrated by the cases of Rabbi Eleazar son of Rabbi Simeon, and of Rabbi Ishmael son of Rabbi Jose, who functioned as directors of public safety, aiding in the Roman drive against *listim.*[55] Apparently there were Tannaim who frowned on such co-operation with the authorities, and thought these gentlemen should have risked turning the appointment down.

Take Rabbi Eleazar ben Rabbi Simeon. The Talmud relates that when the appointment was laid upon him, he agreed to hand over such *listim* as the local police could lay hands on:[56]

> Rabbi Joshua ben Qorha sent word to him: Vinegar son of wine! (*unworthy son of a worthy father*) How long will you go on handing over the people of God to certain death? Back came the answer: I am weeding thorns out of the vineyard. Rabbi Joshua retorted: Let the Owner of the vineyard Himself come and weed out the thorns.

As for Rabbi Ishmael the son of Rabbi Jose:

> One day Elijah the prophet met him and said: How long will you go on turning the people of our God over to be executed? He answered: What can I do? I am under royal

---

55 Highwaymen, who sometimes combined robbery with murder; real bandits, not just Zealots-in-flight, as some would have it, although political and criminal motifs were sometimes hard to distinguish from one another.

56 B.M. 83b.

command. The prophet replied: Your father fled to Asia; you flee to Laodicea.[57]

Of course, since these sources derive from the post-Bar Kokhba era, we must not draw conclusions from them about the generation before the "last *polemos*", especially since resistance to Rome was greatly weakened by that war. But there is an earlier report which, for all its lack of clarity, does nevertheless afford us a glimpse of what Rabbi Tarphon thought about the matter under discussion:

> It was rumored that certain Galileans had killed a man. They came to Rabbi Tarphon and said: Will the master hide us? He answered: What can I do? If I do not hide you, you will be found out; if I do hide you, I will be acting contrary to the dictum of the Rabbis that "One should not believe a rumor, yet one may not altogether disregard it". The best thing would be for you to go and hide yourselves.[58]

This tradition, as the current editions of the Talmud have it, assumes that Rabbi Tarphon hesitated to hide these people for fear that they might be guilty. Had he been sure of their innocence, he would not have hesitated; on the other hand, had he been sure of their guilt, he would certainly have turned them in. That is the way Rashi understands the passage.

However, there was another reading of this text, preserved in the *She'iltot* of Rav Ahai Gaon,[59] which makes it appear that Rabbi Tarphon demurred, not because the men might be guilty, but because he himself might get into trouble! Otherwise, he was quite satisfied to see them escape from Roman arrest, as implied (in our text, too) by his advice: "Go and hide yourselves!" So the Rabbi appears to negate the validity of Roman jurisdiction in criminal, as well as in civil law.

It is, of course, impossible to say with any certainty that the text in the *She'iltot* is the correct one, though a good case can be made out for such a statement. It is also reasonable to credit the Gaonim with a high degree of accuracy in this area.[60]

---

57 Ibid. 84a.   58 Nid. 61a.   59 No. 129.
60 Attention was called to the different reading long ago by Tosafot ad loc. and by the *Rosh*.

On general grounds it can be stated that the Jews found Roman criminal procedure very drastic ("their laws are not like ours") and their penalties severe. Taking everything into consideration, the least that can be said in this area is that here, too, the Jews avoided co-operation with the occupying authorities wherever and whenever they could.

ROMAN TAXES

It need scarcely be said that the Sages, in common with the public at large, looked askance at tax-collectors, tax-farmers, customs officials and the like. The question whether Roman taxes are to be regarded as legally valid imposts had been argued even before the Destruction. This does not mean that those who claimed such taxation was illegal refused to pay it; that was a political question, not a legal one.

But the legal theory could have practical consequences when it came to withholding active help from the government in collecting its taxes, or to such passive steps as tax-avoidance. As far as Jewish taxgatherers and taxfarmers were concerned, their lowly status in both halakhah and aggadah is well known. The fact is that any Jew who served in these capacities could neither serve as a lay judge nor give testimony as a witness. Furthermore, a "*haver* who becomes a tax-collector is to be dropped from his *haverut*".[61]

This attitude goes back to a time long before the Destruction, as the Gospels make abundantly clear.[62] Publicans (taxfarmers) were looked on with contempt, regarded as corrupt extortionists.[63]

We have said that the antipathy to Roman taxation found expression in the Halakhah.[64] Apart from the disqualification of

---

61 Yer. Dem. II:23a.
62 E.g. Luke 7.34; Matt. 18.17. In the latter text, Jesus speaks of a "heathen" and a "publican" in the same breath. Nevertheless he was prepared to accept the legitimacy of Roman rule ("Render unto Caesar the things which are Caesar's"). Not so the Jewish Sages.
63 Comp. "the taxgatherer who has no fixed limit." (B.Q. 113a).
64 The extent to which Jewish taxgatherers were suspected of exceeding their authority can be gathered from the Mishnah, Tohorot VII:6

publicans in court, there was the legal propriety of non-payment of taxes and imposts. To be sure, this became the subject of dispute later on, after the Bar Kokhba War, when there were Sages who denounced "theft from the customs". But the Mishnah records the following:[65]

> One may swear to murderers, robbers or taxgatherers that it (one's property) is *terumah*, even if it is not, or that it belongs to the crown, even though it does not ...

It is possible that this tradition originated at a time before the Destruction. But the Yerushalmi attributes it to a distinctly post-Destruction authority:[66]

> We have learned (in the *Mishnah*!): Rabbi Ishmael says, when Scripture reads (Lev. 19:12) *Ye shall not swear by my name falsely*, it means, but ye may swear to murderers, robbers and taxgatherers.

In connection with this ruling, the Babylonian Talmud expresses astonishment: But did not Samuel establish the principle that the law of the land is law!? The Talmud resolves the contradiction by explaining that the Mishnah refers to "self-appointed taxgatherers", or to those who were not bound to a limited amount due — i.e. they could collect whatever the traffic would bear.[67]

In the Yerushalmi, however, we find the third century Rabbi Johanan quoted as coming to terms with the situation, and teaching that it is forbidden to swear falsely to evade a tax which is

(following the text of mss. Cambridge, Parma, the Munich Talmud, supported by Maimonides and the Tosefta): "If taxgatherers enter a house it becomes unclean (*i.e. its contents, as they are presumed to lay hands on everything*). If there was a gentile with them they are believed if they say, 'We didn't touch a thing'." See also the midrash on the verse (Lev. 26:17) *They that hate you shall rule over you.* "When the gentiles stand over Israel, they demand only that which is visible ... but when I put your own worst elements over you, they will rummage for what you have hidden away."

65 Ned. III:4.
66 Yer. Ned. III:38a.
67 Ned. 25a; B.Q. 113a.

davar shel yishuv — apparently, a levy for a purpose clearly in the public interest.[68]

The division of opinion over this question, with some indications pointing to the very period we are studying — early second century — is reflected in the following: [69]

> It is forbidden to smuggle (it) (them) past the customs.[70]
> Rabbi Simeon quotes Rabbi Akiba: It is permitted.

The Talmud concludes that the argument is about linsey-woolsey; but as for hoodwinking the customs, that is allowed. The question is immediately raised, but what about Samuel's ruling that the law of the land has the force of Jewish law? The problem is disposed of in the same manner as in the case of the Mishnah about publicans.

In sum, then, it seems reasonable to suppose that even in pre-Destruction days there were Tannaim who taught that it was forbidden to deceive the revenue authorities. But it is likely that the majority held, in theory at least, that the Romans had no *right* to impose these levies. It was therefore permissible to avoid paying them, if one could, and was no sin to violate one's oath in this connection. The situation was comparable to being held at knife's point by robbers. No wonder, then, that Jews who served the occupation in its revenue department were viewed with a jaundiced eye.

It need scarcely be added that all this applied with even greater force to those special exactions which the Romans laid on the subject population from time to time:

> Once it happened that the leading citizens of Sepphoris received some unwelcome letters from the government (*apparently demanding special payments from the boulē, the town council*). They came to Rabbi Eleazar ben Perata[71] and

68 [Yer. Ned. III:38a.]
69 B.Q. 113a.
70 "Them" is the preferred reading. On the theme, comp. Semahot II:9, ed. Higger p. 107: "He who steals (evades) the customs is (like) one who sheds blood."
71 Probably the first of that name, a colleague of Rabbi Haninah ben Teradyon; although Bacher thinks this story refers to the second

said: Rabbi, we have gotten evil letters from the crown. What do you say? Shall we flee? He was afraid to tell them to flee, so he answered indirectly: Why do you ask me? Go ask Jacob and Moses and David. He meant, *Jacob fled* (Hos. 12:13) and *Moses fled* (Exod. 2:15) and *David fled and escaped* (I. Sam. 19:18).[72]

But what alternative course of action did the Sages actually propose? They disapproved of Jews participating in the Roman system of tax collection. What did they suggest instead? We simply do not know the answer to that question. It sounds reasonable to guess that they would promote the decentralization of taxgathering, by making it a function of the local authorities; but we know that even at that level they avoided co-operation with the occupying power, though some of them served as heads of municipal councils. In other words, it was not their business to answer the question: How does one co-operate with the government. If conditions forced some of them to become reluctant cogs in the Roman administrative machinery, that was to be understood as nothing more than bowing to the force of circumstances.[73]

It is equally difficult for us to reconstruct from our sources the attitude of tannaitic "civil" law to matters arising out of acts of the Roman fiscal administration. For example, suppose the Romans confiscated the property of a Jew for non-payment of taxes, and then sold it to another Jew. Does the purchaser have valid title in Jewish law? After the Bar Kokhba War it seems that such transactions had legal status; but it is likely that before the War this was not the case.

Rabbi Eleazar ben Perata, who lived towards the close of the second century.

72 Num. XXIII:1. Comp. Tanhuma *Mas'ei* I ed. Buber p. 161.

73 Note the following: "Seek no intimacy with the ruling power. (Av. I:10). What does that mean? It teaches that one should not think, 'I shall be the ruler of the city' or 'I shall be the viceroy', for these are the ones that rob Israel. Another interpretation is: One should not think of accepting office, for in the beginning they open a door to his profit, and in the end they open a door to his downfall." **ARNA**, chapter 11, Goldin p. 181, n. 20.

PUBLIC WORKS AND WELFARE

The attitude of the Sages towards the achievements of the Romans in these fields calls to mind the famous discussion between Rabbi Simeon bar Yohai, Rabbi Jose and Rabbi Judah bar Ilai. When Rabbi Judah expressed admiration for the improvements made by the Romans, Rabbi Simeon retorted: "Everything they have built only to serve their own selfish interests. They have built markets in order to house brothels, baths in order to preen themselves, and bridges so that they can collect tolls."[74] Similar negative judgments can be found elsewhere in the literature — although to be sure there were some Sages who gave credit where credit was due, pointing out that Roman bathhouses could be used by rich and poor alike.

During the reigns of Trajan and Hadrian the Romans could certainly have pointed with pride to an extensive program of bridge-building and road construction in the Middle East. It is true that all these works were motivated basically by the needs of the Empire — strategic and economic. But at the same time they aided mightily in the development of trade and the suppression of banditry, to the general benefit. What did the Sages think of all this?

> Rabbi Gamaliel said: By four things does the Empire exist *(lit: eat)*: by tolls, and bathhouses, and theaters, and crop-taxes *(arnoniot=annona)*.[75]

There are problems about the reading of this text, but there can be little doubt that its tenor is negative. The Rabbi's antipathy to things Roman was so strong that it led him to overlook, rightly or wrongly, the positive aspects of the Roman contribution to civilization in the Middle East.

But is his an isolated statement? If it is, it will not entitle us to generalize about the attitude of the Sages at large. We need additional evidence. A passage from late in the second century provides it:[76]

74 Shab. 33b. Somp. JLTA I, p. 23, note 1.
75 ARNA chap. 28, Goldin p. 116. [See Goldin's notes ad loc.]
76 Midrash Hagadol, ed. Schechter p. 666.

He (*Rabbi Reuben ben Astrobulus*) used to say: The public squares and bathhouses and roadways that the wicked kingdom builds would justify their ruling the world (*dayyan linhol et ha-olam*) if they built them altruistically (*l'shem shamayyim*); but their whole intention is only for their own sake.[77]

<hr />

77 There is some evidence that this passage was at one time included in certain versions of the Mishnah Avot. See Tol. I, p. 342, note 124.

CHAPTER TWENTY-TWO

JEW AND NON-JEW

One of the more difficult problems in the study of Jewish history is the question of the relationship between Jews and gentiles.[1] It is a question that has many aspects — religious, national, social, economic, political and cultural. The question emerges full-blown in all these aspects during the days of the Second Commonwealth.

The issues involved were greatly aggravated by political conditions during the time of the Hasmonean monarchy, and especially later when the country came into the Roman sphere of influence.[2] For the present, however, we shall confine our attention to what we know about the period between the Destruction and the Bar Kokhba War.

The Great War against Rome, the War of the Ḥurban (66–74 C.E.) must certainly have affected the attitudes and relations between the Jewish people and the gentile world. But that is not to

1   Bertholet, *Die Stellung der Israeliten und der Juden zu den Fremden,* 1896; countered by Guttman, *Das Judentum und sein Umwelt,* 1927; Büchler, *The Levitical Impurity of Gentiles* in JQR n.s. 17; countered by Alon, *The Levitical Uncleanness of Gentiles,* in JJCW, pp. 146 ff. [See also Urbach, *The Sages,* pp. 541–554.]

2   Bear in mind that as a rule our sources draw attention to the irregular and the unusual, to episodes of friction and clash between Jew and non-Jew. This should not blind us to the probability that normal and even friendly relations were common between individuals of the two groups in Palestine. I am convinced that the Hasmonean kings tried to solve the problem of co-existence in their kingdom, and that they succeeded in large measure. Even the Herodian rulers sought the same end, although they adopted rather one-sided means. I would go further and say that even during the regime of the Roman Procurators and Legates, relationships between Jews and gentiles had their normal and constructive side, and were not confined to unfriendliness and friction.

say that the Jews retreated into their own shell, and cut themselves off from all contact with other peoples and cultures. It is true that this is just what most historians would have us believe. The majority of them portray this as the moment when religious and nationalistic exclusivism got the upper hand. Christian historians describe it as the ascendancy of a particularistic form of Judaism, called Rabbinism or Talmudism, everywhere among Jews, including the Hellenistic Diaspora. Jewish historians, like Dubnow, say that after the Destruction, the Jewish People found its very survival threatened, so that it became necessary to erect a defensive dike of separatist rules and regulations, so as to prevent Jewish identity being submerged.[3]

It is my contention that these two views are at bottom one and the same, and that they are both fallacious. I suggest that the principal factors at work during the years that followed the Destruction were political and economic. It must be remembered that during the war and its aftermath, the great majority of non-Jews in Judaea and the neighboring territories were *allied with Rome* against the Jews. The Roman War with the Jews created an enduring bond between the empire and the Hellenized pagans in Judaea. That meant that these pagans had a lot to fear from the Jews if the latter should ever succeed in mounting a successful revolt against their Roman masters.

Another element of major importance was the fact that in the aftermath of the war gentiles stood to gain economically — and did — from the defeat of the Jews. There were now tracts of deserted, unoccupied land in the country, and the Romans encouraged non-Jews to take them over. Other land, not deserted but confiscated, was given to new gentile owners even when Jews remained as tenant-farmers on land that had been theirs. In general the Romans treated the local pagans as a privileged class, giving them administrative positions, and using their help in keeping the conquered population in check.

It was conditions such as these which gave rise to the halakhic restrictions on the transfer of property to non-Jews which we dis-

---

3 ["Judaism secluded itself within its own boundaries." M. Avi-Yonah, *The Jews of Palestine*, New York, 1976, p. 13.]

cussed above.[4] These restrictions arose out of motives of Jewish national interest. Tradition, to be sure, is able to adduce purely religious reasons for them; but even the tradition is aware of the national motive. Furthermore, we may be reasonably sure that not too many years after the Destruction conditions became somewhat more normal, and ordinary day-to-day contact between Jew and gentile resumed its natural course.

As we pointed out earlier in this work,[5] the large Jewish communities that had existed in the Hellenistic cities along the Mediterranean coast had for the most part been wiped out at the beginning of the War of the Destruction; but had to a great extent sprung up again within a single generation. This is reflected in the visits of Rabban Gamaliel II and Rabbi Joshua ben Hananiah to Jewish communities at Ashkelon in the South and at Akko in the North.[6] What this means is that economic realities, the regenerative powers of the Jewish people and the old tradition of normal relations between Jews and their non-Jewish neighbors — all these had reasserted themselves, and had brought about the restoration of regular contact between the peoples.

The return of the Jews to the port cities along the Mediterranean coast indicates the resumption as well of commercial ties between them and the gentile world abroad. With respect to foreign trade we have evidence of co-operation between Jews and non-Jews in Judaea, especially as concerns nearby countries (but not excluding more distant lands). Thus, we learn that Tyre and Sidon imported most of their farm produce from the Jewish areas of Galilee.[7] On the other hand we learn of a market in Meron in the days of Rabbi Akiba, where most of the produce came from the gentiles.[8]

It was not the purpose of the Halakhah to inhibit economic

---

4   JLTA I, pp. 285–287. To be sure, there is no proof that these restrictions did not predate the Destruction; but then, there is nothing to show that they did. See, however, Ginzberg: "The Significance of the Halachah for Jewish History" in the collection *On Jewish Law and Lore*, Philadelphia, 1955, e.g. p. 80.

5   JLTA, pp. 135 ff.

6   See especially Av. Zar. 32a, and Tos. Miq. VI:3 (659).

7   Tos. Dem. 1:10 (45); Yer. ibid. I:22a.

8   Tos. Dem. IV:13 (51).

co-operation between Jews and non-Jews, although obviously there were situations when it did restrain trade because of the limitations imposed by the Jewish dietary laws. An example of this is the prohibition against eating cheeses manufactured by non-Jews.[9]

A much more serious brake on commercial relations was the ban on doing any business at all with gentiles during their religious festivals, including the three days preceding.[10] These were occasions of great opportunity for the merchant, but the Jews had to stay away. The same goes for the annual trade fairs, which were usually connected with some pagan shrine or some religious festival. The fear of contamination by idolatry was a powerful deterrent, and the halakhic rules in this respect were strict and explicit.

Nevertheless, one wonders whether all the prohibitions were always observed to the letter, even though it is only fair to say that the people at large shared the revulsion against anything that smacked of idolatry. Furthermore, during the subsequent centuries, the pressure of economic need was in the direction of easing some of these restrictions.

A stronger obstacle to free interchange between the peoples was no doubt the restriction on social contact. Because of the dietary laws, Jews could scarcely sit down to eat with non-Jews, although it was theoretically possible for a gentile to invite his Jewish neighbor to join him in a meal prepared in strict conformity with the rules of kashrut.

But there were other factors, perhaps more serious, which tended to constrict social contacts between Jews and pagans. There was, or was perceived to be, a profound difference in ideas about ethics and morality. To the Sages — and probably to the majority of the people — the average pagan was considered prone to violence and bloodshed. One was therefore warned not to be caught alone with him, nor to be treated for one's ailments by him.[11] In sum,

---

9 Mishnah Av. Zar. II:5, where Rabban Gamaliel and Rabbi Joshua ben Hananiah exchange some remarks on the subject.
10 Ibid. I:1–2. Rabbi Ishmael wanted the prohibition extended to the three following days as well.
11 *Ibid.*

one was to avoid his company in circumstances where he could cause harm.¹²

Similar suspicions centered on the supposed unbridled sexual proclivities of the pagans; Jewish women were therefore forbidden to be alone in their company.¹³ Probably there was some objective basis for this suspicion, although we cannot be sure how much it was colored by certain preconceptions. Put differently: the revulsion felt by Jews at the more obvious aspects of pagan society and worship in general — the idols, the cruelty, the uninhibited sensuality — apparently led to an emphasis, perhaps an overemphasis, on the dark side of ancient civilization, and to the formation of negative stereotypes.

In spite of all this, the Sages themselves engaged in a fair amount of social and intellectual interchange with non-Jews. The record reveals a surprising degree of personal warmth and sociability, not to speak of intellectual respect for classical thought. From Rabbi Johanan ben Zakkai onwards, Patriarchs and Sages can be found in conversation with Roman officials on such matters as Judaism, the Torah, the Jewish people, phenomena of nature, and other topics. What is more, such dialogues are reported with "philosophers" and with just plain "gentiles". The evidence points to an ongoing exchange of religious and philosophic ideas, con-

---

12 The extent to which the people of the period under review regarded the non-Jews in their midst as violence-prone, is evidenced in Mishnah Berakhot IX:4. (The word *kerakh,* when unspecified, usually refers to one of the coastal cities of Judaea, where the majority of the inhabitants were non-Jews): "He who enters a *kerakh* should offer two prayers, one on coming into town, and one on leaving. Ben Azzai says, four prayers, two on entering and two on leaving, offering thanks for what is (safely) past, and making supplication for what is yet to come." A baraita explicates: "He says, May it be Thy will that I enter this city in peace. Once inside, he says May it be Thy will that I leave this city in peace." (Berakhot, Tos. VII:'6 (16); Bavli 60a; Yer. IX:14b). This Baraita, which tells us something about life in the parts of Eretz Israel at the time, also reveals something about the non-Jewish population.

13 Mishnah Av. Zar. II:1. For the time we are discussing, see Tos. Ket. I:6 (261).

ducted over a period of generations in a friendly spirit of mutual tolerance.

As for the attitude of the Sages to the ordinary non-Jewish man in the street, there is an interesting contrast in the behavior of two famous scholars:

> Of Rabban Johanan ben Zakkai it was said that he was always the first to greet anyone, gentiles included, in the market place.[14]

On the other hand, Rabbi Ishmael was more reserved:

> Once a gentile met Rabbi Ishmael and greeted him with a blessing. He replied: Thou hast spoken. Another met him and cursed him. He replied: Thou hast spoken. His disciples said: Master, you answered the one the same as the other! He replied: Even so is it written, "They that curse thee shall be cursed, and they that bless thee shall be blessed."[15]

RELATIONS AT LAW

Trade inevitably gives rise to a certain amount of litigation. In the circumstances which we have been describing, where the parties might well have been a non-Jew and a Jew, and both might want to avoid appearing before the Roman authorities, they could make use of the Hellenistic municipal courts, which the Romans had left in place. Alternatively, they could have recourse to a Jewish Beth Din.

While we have no evidence of such mixed cases being tried in Hellenistic courts, we know that Jews did use the municipal institutions of non-Jewish cities for archival or notarial procedures. We shall deal with this matter soon. But apparently they would not consent to being litigants in such institutions. On the other hand, we do find gentiles frequently appearing in that capacity in Jewish courts. Sometimes they would ask that the case be tried according to Jewish law; at other times they specified a hearing "in accordance with non-Jewish law".[16] When the legal system had

14 Ber. 17a.
15 Yer. Ber. VII:12c.
16 Comp. Tos. B.Q. IV:2 (351); Yer. ibid. 4b: "The ox of one non-Jew

not been determined, Rabbi Ishmael suggested that the Jewish judge select whichever system would favor the Jewish litigant! Rabbi Akiba and Rabban Simeon ben Gamaliel disagreed and insisted on complete judicial impartiality.[17]

These matters are connected with a fundamental issue of principle, which came to the fore during the period we have under study. Put in simple terms, the question is: Does Jewish law apply to Jews only? There were some who conceived of the law laid down in the Torah and elaborated in the Halakhah as national-religious in character. Thus, even its social laws would apply to the Jewish citizen only, but not to those who did not come under that heading.

There were others, however, who maintained that at least the fundamentals of civil law in the Torah and the Halakhah, as they affect the individual were meant to be, and are, all-human, universal, and apply to everyone, Jew and non-Jew alike. This, then, was the conflict in legal theory. It was in the nature of things that the resolution of this conflict should be strongly influenced by actual conditions, and by the course of events.[18]

During the first generation of the second century this theoretical problem found expression in two different answers to a certain halakhic question. Both answers led to the same practical result: *gezel ha-nokhri asur* — it is forbidden to take, by any means whatsoever, that which rightfully belongs to a pagan. But although the net result is the same, the theoretical basis is different. Rabban Gamaliel ruled that it is forbidden to take (the term literally means "theft, robbery") the property of a non-Jew, because the act would disgrace the Jewish people. The gentile is protected de facto. De jure, however, the law does not shield him.[19] But Rabbi Akiba reasons differently:

How do we know that *gezel nokhri* is prohibited? From the

gores the ox of another non-Jew; even though both agree to have the case judged by Jewish law etc."

17 B.Q. 113a; comp. Sifre Deut. XVI, Finkelstein pp. 26–27.
18 A similar problem was faced by Roman law; the solution was the creation of *jus gentium*.
19 Yer. B.Q. IV:4

verse (Lev. 25:48) *After he has been sold, he may be redeemed,* which implies that the regular redemption procedures must be followed — no absconding, no cutting the amount, — for it says *He shall reckon with him that bought him* — let him be meticulous.[20]

It seems that Rabbi Akiba's view is the one that prevailed. This conclusion is supported by the fact that the tannaitic tradition about the universal religion of mankind, known as the seven Noachide Commandments, includes the administration of justice as one of the basic tenets of civilization.[21]

In effect then law, and the dispensation thereof, is something which the Jewish people shares with other peoples. The Halakhah developed its own equivalent of the *ius gentium* to govern dealings between gentiles and Jews, and also recognized that there were valid systems of law other than its own.

The interaction between legal systems was especially noticeable during the period we have been studying, and can be illustrated by the following halakhot: [22]

> Any writ is valid that is drawn up in the ערכאות (*MS Cambridge reads* ארכאות) of the gentiles, even if they that signed it were gentiles, excepting a writ of divorce or a writ of manumission. Rabbi Simeon says: these too are valid; the only ones declared invalid are those drawn up by such as were not authorized judges.

The *'archa'ot* spoken of here were not courts of law, but ἀρχεῖα i.e. registries, municipal institutions in the Greek-speaking cities where contracts and similar documents were not only deposited, but also officially registered. A document not duly registered in such an *archeion* was not really valid. It appears that these regis-

---

20 B.Q. 113a–b: comp. Midrash Tannaim p. 121. [Two different interpretations of this passage exist, neither of which changes the net effect. The translation incorporates both.]

21 ["The Laws of the Sons of Noah" (i.e. humanity) are based on Genesis IX:3–7. A thorough essay in English on the subject is a desideratum. See "The Pentateuch" by J.H. Hertz, ad loc., and *Encyclopedia Ivrit* s.v. *ben Noah*.]

22 Mishnah, Git. I:5.

tries sometimes served as centers for actually drawing up and signing the documents; in other instances the finished document was brought in to be registered.[23]

A baraita on the same subject quotes R. Akiba as teaching that any writ drawn up in the registries of the gentiles is valid (except for divorces and manumissions) even though it be signed by non-Jews; but the other Sages do not agree.[24]

> Rabbi Eleazar ben Jose reported: This is what Rabban Simeon ben Gamaliel said to the Rabbis in Sidon: There was no disagreement between Rabbi Akiba and the other Sages on the validity of documents drawn up in the registries of the gentiles. Their disagreement was confined to cases where the writs were drawn up by laymen ... (And) Rabban Simeon ben Gamaliel said, even writs of divorce and manumission are valid, in places where Jews do not sign.

Both talmudim find difficulty with the idea that documents with a religious aspect, such as divorces and certificates of emancipation, could be made legal by non-Jews. But that is a question for a history of the Halakhah, and need not detain us here. Our sole purpose has been to demonstrate the extent to which the Sages of the second century accepted and made use of certain non-Jewish institutions of public law in the Land of Israel and its environs.

But it must be remembered that the whole thing was purely voluntary. There is no hint of anything like coercion on the part of the Romans.[25] The fact that the Bavli cites in this connection the dictum of Samuel that "the law of the land is law", shows merely that the Romans recognized these registries — not that they made it compulsory to use them. The truth is, as we have already observed, that the Sages tended towards conformity in the

---

23 This institution was not universal in the Roman Empire. It was peculiar to the time and place being discussed. See Mitteis, *Reichsrecht und Volksrecht in den östlichen Provinzen des römisches Kaiserreiches*, pp. 95–96; 170–171. On the Halakhah here involved, see Gulak, *Letoledot ha-mishpat ha-ivri*, Vol. I, "Real Property", pp. 44–59.

24 Tos. Git. I:4 (323–4); Bavli ibid. 11a; [Alon explains why the passage must be read as interpreted here.]   25 Gulak, ibid. p. 59.

field of contracts. That emerged above, in connection with the dating of documents in accordance with Roman usage. Here again we find the tendency to normalize economic relations with non-Jews in Palestine and in the region generally.

As time went on this halakhah remained in force, but a thrust developed in the opposite direction. Certain baraitot indicate that the drawing up and registering of documents in gentile *'arkha'ot* came to be frowned upon, and regarded as a last resort, to be used in cases of emergency.

As for cultural relations — against these the Halakhah set its face consistently. Although not all the Sages were agreed that contact with gentile culture was bound to lead to assimilation, there was nevertheless general assent to the principal admonitions — not to teach one's children the Greek language, nor "Greek wisdom"; to keep away from gladiator shows (unless one went to save a gladiator's life); and in short, to avoid *te'atra'ot, kirk'sa'ot* and *itztadionim* — theaters, circuses and stadia.[26]

SOCIAL WELFARE

From a number of tannaitic halakhot we are able to conclude that the Sages mandated the inclusion of gentiles in the distribution of assistance to the needy. As it happens, none of these halakhot can be dated explicitly to the pre-Bar Kokhba generation. My own opinion is that this branch of the Halakhah became more inclusive from the *middle* of the second century onwards. Here are some of the sources:

> The poor of the gentiles are not to be prevented from foraging for gleanings, forgotten sheaves, or corners of the field...[27] This is for the sake of peaceful relations... They may be encouraged (to till their fields) in the Sabbatical year... and they are to be greeted with the word *Shalom*, in the interest of peaceful relations.[28]

In a town of mixed Jewish and gentile population the *par-*

---

26 See Alon, Kiryat Sefer 1943, pp. 91–92; and JJCW pp. 141–145.
27 For the Biblical laws, see Lev. XIX:9 and Deut. XXIV:19 ff.
28 Mishnah Git. V:8–9.

nassim are to collect charity dues from both, for the sake of peaceful relations, and to distribute to the needy of both communities equally, for the sake of peaceful relations. One pronounces eulogies over the dead of the gentiles, and comforts their mourners, and buries their dead, for the sake of peaceful relations (*mip'ne darkei shalom*).[29]

SALVATION FOR THE GENTILES

Finally, let us look at the theology of the matter: how various Sages conceived of the place of the "other" — the non-Jew in the Divine scheme of things.

> Rabbi Eliezer says: All gentiles are excluded from a share in the world to come ... Said Rabbi Joshua to him: ... but there are righteous people among all the nations who *do* have a share in the world to come![30]

This question — whether there is ultimate justification and salvation outside of Judaism — was one of the concerns of Jewish thinkers for several generations before the Destruction, and it continued to occupy the thought of Tannaim and Amoraim for a long time afterwards.

The question is a theological one, but it had practical consequences as well. What for example, was to be the status of the "God-fearers", those unconverted gentiles who nevertheless had renounced idolatry, accepted the seven Noachide commandments, or even observed the Sabbath rest? Some Sages welcomed such gentiles, while others remained antagonistic. There were those who went so far as to say that it was forbidden to teach Torah to a non-Jew, and others who taught that, in theory, it was a capital offense for a gentile to keep the Sabbath. Before the Destruction there was even a dispute as to whether it was permissible to accept free-will offerings donated by gentiles.

It does appear that during the years between the Destruction

---

29 Tos. Git. V:4–5 (328); comp. Bavli ibid. 61a. The phrase about burying their dead is absent from the Vienna ms. and from the current versions of the Tosefta.

30 Tos. Sanh. XIII:2 (434).

and the Bar Kokhba War, the moderate opinion represented by Rabbi Joshua gained more or less universal acceptance.[31] This is borne out by Justin Martyr in his *Dialogue With Trypho*, where he puts the following into the mouth of the Jewish protagonist:

> It would have been better for you to concentrate on the philosophy of Plato or some other philosopher, and thus achieve a life of constancy, of continence and moderation; you would have earned the perfect life. But now that you have put your faith in a man, and denied God, you are beyond redemption.[32]

Similarly, the author of Fourth Esdras speaks of righteous men among the nations of the world, even though he thinks of them as individuals rather than groups.[33]

But after making all due allowance for the range of opinion among the Sages, we must admit that most of the first Yavneh generation tended to minimize any humanitarian aspects of gentile behavior in their time.[34] It is a reasonable assumption that in this they were reflecting the popular mood of the day. It is also highly likely that there were considerable differences between social classes, and that people higher on the socio-economic scale had a much less antagonistic attitude toward their non-Jewish neighbors.

PROSELYTES

Various historians have drawn our attention to the large number of converts to Judaism in Rome and her provinces at the end of the first and the beginning of the second centuries. Some of these came from the highest levels of Roman society, not excluding the senatorial class.[35] We know about Domitian's persecution of such Judaizers during the nineties, towards the end of his reign, when

---

31 The opinion is echoed by Rabbi Akiba, who says: "The children of *wicked* gentiles will have no share in the world to come." Sanh. 112a.
32 Chapter VIII. Alon interprets this passage in accordance with the translation given here.
33 IV Esdras, I:36.
34 B.B. 10b.
35 [See EJ s.v. "proselytes", and bibliography listed in Smallwood, *The Jews Under Roman Rule*", p. 206. See also GLA II, pp. 382 ff.]

he went after members of the Roman aristocracy who were secret converts, and others who were merely "God-fearers" — fellow-travellers, so to speak. The phenomenon did not escape mention by important writers of the time, such as the historian Tacitus and the satirist Juvenal.

Modern papyrology has added to the evidence a fragmentary record of a hearing before Trajan about 111–113 C.E. when a member of the Alexandrian delegation could charge that "the Senate was full of Jews".[36] But there is no need to belabor the point. When we find Josephus saying that converts to Judaism are to be found everywhere in the world (it scarcely matters whether he means full *gerim* or only sympathizers) or when the Syriac Baruch, also in the first century, says something similar; or when Justin Martyr, a contemporary of those we have mentioned and a Christian to boot also refers to the same phenomenon –– then we may well believe that we are hearing reliable evidence of the situation as it really was.[37]

36 P. Oxy. 1243 = CPJ II no. 157; vide supra chap. I, note 86.
37 Josephus: *Apion*, II. 123–4, 282–6; Baruch: in Charles, II, p. 471, 41:4; Justin Martyr: in *Dialogue With Trypho*, 9:4; 23:3; 24:3. There are two main schools of thought regarding the spread of Jewish proselytism. One reasons that the end of the Temple cultus forced Judaism to become a *universalistic* religion, devoid of national or political characteristics. I do not think this explanation is sound. The other view, which may have something to recommend it, holds that the bravery of the Jews in resisting the Romans, both in action and in surviving defeat, won the admiration and adherence of many gentiles.

[Apparently Alon assumes that the spiritual inadequacy of ancient paganism is too obvious to mention. As a recent summary puts it: "During the late republic and early empire proselytism seems to have continued and accelerated. In a situation in which many Romans were finding that the formal state religion and the humble domestic cults failed to satisfy their spiritual and emotional needs, some turned for fulfilment to philosophy or the mystery cults of the East, while others were attracted by the lofty monotheism and high moral code of the Jews." Smallwood: *The Jews Under Roman Rule*, p. 205. However, while not minimizing the extent of this movement, Smallwood finds it difficult to believe that any significant number of those who were attracted to Judaism were able to accept *milah* (circumcision) and *tevillah* (immersion) "and the full rigors of the law". Maybe so, as

It will be of interest to mention some of the proselytes whose names occur in the literature of our period. Judah the Ammonite *ger* is one;[38] Minyamin, the Egyptian *ger,* a student of Rabbi Akiba, is another.[39] It seems that Niphates the proselyte lived at the very time we are studying;[40] and one of the best known proselytes, the wealthy Roman matron Valeria, was a contemporary of Rabban Gamaliel.[41] Rabbi Eliezer and Rabbi Joshua interviewed a proselyte lady of similar social standing whose name has not been preserved.[42] From whatever we can tell, the parents of Judah ben Gerim were also converted late in the first or early in the second century.[43] And last, but far from least, there was Aquila, an outstanding personality of the time, who is reputed by both Jewish and Christian traditions to have been related to the Emperor Hadrian.[44]

Many of the proselytes in the Land of Israel were immigrants from other countries. In fact, there are grounds for believing that *gerim* had always tended to gravitate towards Eretz Israel, if they could manage to do so. There were many reasons for this. In any event, Jewish Palestine was a ponderable factor in attracting converts to Judaism.

Certainly, not all Sages were equally enthusiastic about the entry of gentiles into the Jewish fold. At the time we are discussing Rabbi Eliezer was the one who was particularly vocal in expressing reservations. He may have had his doubts about the ability of these recruits to remain steadfast to the bitter end; he may have been dubious about their sincerity and the depth of their convictions.

far as large numbers of people were concerned; this is, of course exactly what underlies the Pauline position. But it does overlook the fact that, on the contrary, it is exactly the discipline of the mitzvot which has attracted many converts.]

38 Mishnah Yad. IV : 4.
39 Tos. Qid. V : 5 (342).
40 Yev. 98a.
41 R.H. 17b; Yev. 26a; in Hebrew her name looks like Bolariah.
42 EcclR. I : 8.
43 Shab. 33b.
44 Tanhuma, Mishpatim V; comp. above, Chap. four, n 16; [and see Umberto Cassuto in the (unfinished, German) *Encyclopedia Judaica* s.v. "Aquila".]

But his were the doubts of the skeptical minority. The generality of the Sages, and certainly the people at large, were happy to welcome new entrants into the Jewish fold, and even those sympathizers who stood on the fringe. This receptive attitude in turn encouraged the flow of converts into Judaism, a factor which must certainly be taken into account in any assessment of the situation on the eve of the Bar Kokhba War.

THE SAMARITANS

Since this chapter deals with the "external" relations of the Jews of Judaea at the beginning of the second century, it will be appropriate for us to include two groups not strictly defined as "others": the Samaritans and the Diaspora communities.

The attitude of the Sages to the Samaritans was probably a faithful reflection of popular feeling, and a mirror image of what the Samaritans felt about the Jews. The subject derives its importance from a question about which historians are in disagreement, and the sources unhelpful: what role did the Samaritans play during the Bar Kokhba War?

Post-biblical literature of the Second Commonwealth is almost unanimous in its rejection of the Samaritans and its antipathy to them. Wherever they are mentioned in the works of Josephus, in the Gospels, in the Apocrypha, the reader cannot help but feel that the Jews regarded them as an alien religion and a foreign people. Apart from that, there is a rather unrelieved sequence of clashes, conspiracies and bloody passages-at-arms between the Jews and the Samaritans. It would seem that the matter can be summed up as follows: throughout the Second Commonwealth period the Jews treated the Samaritans as aliens, as *nokhrim* in every respect.[45]

However, on closer study it turns out that this was not necessarily the *unanimous* opinion of Jews; nor was it *always* the opinion of Jews. In fact there were many areas in which friendly and cooperative relations existed between these two related peoples, even though it is natural that this truth is blurred in most of the documents that have come down to us.

45 See Montgomery, *The Samaritans*, pp. 125–246.

But post-Destruction talmudic sources show us Sages still wrestling with the problem: Are Samaritans halakhically Jews or gentiles? The truth is that it is impossible to find a consistent answer to this question.[46] In any event, those who held that the Samaritans were a species of Jews (who had wandered rather far afield) granted that for the most part they treated certain mitzvot quite carelessly; nor could the fact be ignored that some of their practices differed wildly from the Jewish norm.

After the Destruction we encounter a new phenomenon: places with mixed Jewish-Samaritan population. There is also a perceptible northward shift of the Samaritans, who had previously reached no farther than En Ganim. But the sources have preserved no incidents, episodes or remarks that might have enlightened us as to mutual attitudes during the several generations between the Destruction and the Bar Kokhba War. All we have is traces of economic and social contacts. Thus, Samaritans import grain from Judah; and a Jewish writ of divorce bearing the signature of Samaritan witnesses is ruled valid by Rabban Gamaliel.[47]

But even in the absence of cases, the literature of the Halakhah tells us a good deal about the attitude of the Tannaim to the Samaritans, and this enables us to draw certain conclusions. The fact that the old question still comes up — are the Samaritans Jews or gentiles? — certainly tells us something. There is no unanimity about the answer. Most Tannaim are inclined to think that they are basically Jews, albeit with certain reservations. The Mishnah just referred to is a case in point:

> Once a writ of divorce was submitted to Rabban Gamaliel at Kephar Othnai, bearing the signatures of Samaritan witnesses, and he pronounced it valid.

46　See *Seven Minor Treatises* (Hebrew) ed. Michael Higger, New York, 1930, "Masekhet Kuthim", I:1, p. ‎מ"א‎ (p. 42 in the translation): "The usages of the Samaritans are at times like those of the heathen, at times like those of the Jews." The same point lies behind the remark of Rav in M.Q .12a: "The halakhot of the festival are like the halakhot of the Samaritans."

47　Mishnah Git. I:5.

The fact that this happened is confirmed in the Tosefta by Rabbi Judah.[48] The subject is debated in the Babylonian Talmud by Abaye and Rava, and the final halakhic ruling is that the document is valid even if both witnesses are Samaritans.[49] In this instance, they are treated as Jews.

At issue was the trustworthiness of Samaritans, and it seems to be upheld by Rabban Gamaliel in another context:

> Rabbi Simeon says: There are three regulations regarding *demai* produce (*i.e. that which is suspected to be untithed*). Once it happened that our teachers entered certain Samaritan villages near the highway. Some green vegetables were set before them. Rabbi Akiba promptly tithed them. Rabban Gamaliel said: How can you take it upon yourself to contravene the words of your colleagues? Who gave you authority? He replied: Was I making a ruling for anybody? I simply tithed my own portion ... When Rabban Gamaliel came among them (*the Samaritans*) he declared their grain and legumes *demai* (*possibly untithed*) and all their other produce definitely untithed. And when Rabban Simeon ben Gamaliel visited them and saw that they had gotten into bad habits, he declared everything of theirs definitely untithed.[50]

Our conclusion must be that Rabban Gamaliel had basically equated the Samaritans with Jewish *amei ha-aretz*, at least in this respect. Rabbi Akiba, on the contrary, suspected them of neglecting the mitzvah to begin with; but he too included them within the parameters of the household of Israel.

A clear-cut expression of the fundamental difference of opinion regarding the status of the Samaritans can be found in the pithy — and opposing — definitions of them put forward by Rabbi Ishmael and Rabbi Akiba early in the second century. Rabbi Akiba said: They embraced the Torah out of conviction (*gere emet* — true proselytes). Rabbi Ishmael said: No, they took on the religion of Israel out of fear (*gere 'arayot* — because of "lions";

---

48 Tos. Git. I:4 (323).
49 Git. 10b.
50 Tos. Dem. V:24 (56).

that is, to save their skins).[51] The Yerushalmi, too, credits Rabbi Akiba with the view that they are *gere tzedeq* — i.e. fully Jewish.[52] The Tractate Kuthim has even Rabbi Ishmael agreeing that originally they were genuine proselytes.[53]

The same difference of opinion about the status of the Samaritans lies behind the following Mishnah:

> Moreover, they declared before him (*i.e. Rabbi Akiba*) that Rabbi Eliezer used to say: One who eats the bread of the Samaritans is like one who eats swine's flesh (*i.e. Samaritans are not Jews*). He replied: Be quiet! I will not tell you what Rabbi Eliezer taught concerning this.[54]

The fact that Rabbi Akiba silenced them implies that he tended to permit Samaritan bread. But it fails to tell us what Rabbi Eliezer's opinion was. A reasonable guess is that, according to Rabbi Akiba's information, Rabbi Eliezer permitted the bread of the Samaritans; but Akiba didn't want to say so, because his disciples had heard otherwise, and he did not want to parade a difference of opinion between senior Sages before them. He therefore silenced them, but deemed it unseemly to take the subject any further.

There are grounds, then, for detecting a tilt in favor of the Samaritans during the inter-war period. One possible reason for this might be that they had taken some part on the Jewish side in the first war against Rome. In any event there are many indications of an improvement in relations between the two peoples on the eve of the Bar Kokhba War. This is not to say that the long-standing quarrelsomeness and bad blood between the two peoples evaporated altogether. Still, a measure of drawing closer is seen to be possible. Under certain circumstances they would be able to make common cause against a common foe.[55]

---

51 Qid. 75b.

52 Yer. Git. I:43:c.

53 Higger, op. cit., Heb. p. ע״ס English p. 46.

54 Mishnah Shevi. VIII:10.

55 [The Samaritans are dealt with in some detail by Alon in his essay "The Origin of the Samaritans in the Halakhic Tradition", first published in 1947. For English translation, see JJCW pp. 354–373.]

THE COMMUNITIES ABROAD

Under the heading of external relations, there remain for consideration the Jewish communities in other countries.[55a]

There is a good deal of evidence for rather close connections between the Jewish leadership in Judaea in the first third of the second century, and the Jews of the Diaspora. It was pointed out above how ties between the center of the Jewish world and its periphery were renewed during the days of Rabban Gamaliel II, and how the reconstituted Sanhedrin at Yavneh functioned as the chief religious authority for the Jews abroad, even as it did for Jews living in the homeland.

The way in which this worked can be seen when we read how a question about the laws of Sabbath reached Rabban Gamaliel from Tripoli in Phoenicia (Syria)[56] or that Rabbi Ishmael discussed the laws of purity with the people of Madeba.[57] Similarly, the Jews of Sidon asked the Sages for a ruling in a matter involving the laws of divorce.[58]

The Jews of Assia (identified as Etzion Gever, or Aqaba, and thus outside the Holy Land) showed notable persistence in their efforts to get a question of theirs answered. Their delegates made the pilgrimage to Yavneh on *three* festivals, until finally they got a ruling.[59]

The story of Theodos, leader of the Jewish community of Rome, is a case in point. When the Sages disapproved of something he had done, they did not hesitate to rebuke him: "If you were not Theodos, we might well have excommunicated you!"[60] Apparently everyone involved took it for granted that their authority extended all the way from Yavneh to Rome.

There is a baraitha which records a discussion between Palestinian authorities and Jews far outside the boundaries of the Roman empire — off in the Parthian kingdom. It concerns a halakhic

---

55a [What follows may be regarded as an appendix to this chapter.]
56   Tos. Eruv. IX:25 (150).
57   Mishnah Miq. VII:1; the Rabbi may have been visiting there.
58   Mishnah Git. VII:5.
59   Tos. Hul. III:10 (504); Tos. Miq. IV:6 (656).
60   Tos. Yom Tov II:15 (204); Ber. 19a; Yer. Pes. VII 34a; comp. JLTA I, pp. 231–232.

question with practical consequences, and may be evidence of an attempt to impose the halakhah of Eretz Israel on the Jews of Mesopotamia.

> Rabbi Jonathan ben Bag(bag) sent (*a message*) to Rabbi Judah ben Bathyra at Nisibis: I have heard that you say that the daughter of an Israelite who is betrothed (*to a kohen*) may eat of the *terumah*.

Since sanctified food-offering may be eaten only by priests and their families, there is obviously an issue here. Rabbi Judah replied by demonstrating that the young lady was indeed legally entitled to the privilege:

> but what can I do, since the Sages have ruled that the daughter of an Israelite may not eat *terumah* until she has entered the marriage canopy.[61]

There was another factor which tended to preserve and strengthen the ties between the Diaspora and the mother country — authority over the calendar. This remained firmly in the hands of the Jewish authorities in the Holy Land. Notification of New Moons and Leap Years was made to the communities abroad by messengers (in the case of New Moons) and by missives (in the case of Leap Years). The rule that such acts can be performed only in the Holy Land, and the instances when exceptions were made to that rule — all this has been discussed earlier in this work.[62]

A notable mark of the interest and concern which the Sages felt for the Jews of the Diaspora was the special translation of the Hebrew Scriptures into Greek, made apparently under the guidance of Rabbis Eliezer, Joshua ben Hananiah and Akiba. The work was executed by Aquila, a convert to Judaism who had been born a pagan in Pontus, and had been a Christian before he became a Jew. Clearly, it was designed to provide the Jews of the Greco-Roman world with a Bible they could read which would be faithful to the Jewish tradition as interpreted by the Sages of Yavneh.

---

61 Qid. 10b; Yer. Ket. V:29d; Sifre Num. Korah 117, p. 137; Tos. Ket. V:1 (266).
62 See JLTA I, pp. 240 ff.

It seems that the much older Greek translation, the Septuagint, had been based on a Hebrew text not always in agreement with the norms established in the Land of Israel. It is also possible that the Sages wanted a Greek text that would avoid the Christian interpretations that had grown up around certain verses in the Septuagint.

Those portions of Aquila's translation which have survived give ample evidence of the extent to which he is faithful to the masoretic Hebrew, even when it means doing violence to proper Greek grammar and syntax. In some instances *halakhic midrash* finds its way into the translation — and so the Greek language is enriched by some rather peculiar neologisms. In any event, as far as we can make out, Aquila's translation circulated widely in the Diaspora, even though it never completely displaced the Septuagint.[63]

The organic bond between the Diaspora and Eretz Israel found tangible expression in the regular contributions for the support of the Sages which now replaced the half-shekel which the Jews abroad had used to send to the Temple before the year 70.[64] It went even further with the Jews of adjacent countries. Those in Egypt and Transjordan would actually send in the Poorman's Tithe (*ma'aser 'ani*) during the Sabbatical Year, "so that the needy in the Land of Israel might be sustained".[65]

The famous journeys of the Sages of Yavneh across the seas, as well as into Egypt and Mesopotamia, were no doubt part of a calculated program to renew and strengthen ties between the mother country and the Diaspora.[66] But quite apart from these longer journeys, we find Sages on briefer trips to towns along the coast of Phoenicia, as when Rabbi Simeon and Hananiah ben Hakhinai spend some time in Sidon,[67] and certain disciples of Rabbi Akiba are discovered on a journey down the coast, heading for Akhziv.[68]

63 On Aquila, see Burkitt in JQR os X p. 207; Krauss, *Steinschneider Festschrift* (German) p. 115. [Also Umberto Cassuto in the (unfinished, German) *Encyclopädia Judaica*, Berlin 1929, Vol. III, pp. 27–36.]
64 Yer. Hor. III : 48a.
65 Mishnah Yad. IV : 3.
66 For details see JLTA I, pp. 234 ff.
67 Tos. Nid. VI : 6 (647). This was during the lifetime of Rabbi Akiba.
68 Av. Zar. 15b.

Then there were students who came from abroad to study. Among them we can point out Abba Yudin (or Gurion) of Sidon, Hanan the Egyptian, Rabbi Johanan the Sandal Maker of Alexandria, and Rabbi Judah ben Bathyra from Nisibis.

We must conclude that the evidence we have tells only part of the story. But it is enough to prove that after the initial shock that followed the Destruction of the Temple, scattered Jewry was able to reunite as one people, centered on the ancestral land. Of course, there must have been some, both in Judaea and in the Diaspora, who despaired of a future for their people, and who were absorbed into the surrounding populations. But the majority seem to have remained steadfast, little realizing the magnitude of the new catastrophe that awaited them in the not too distant future.

CHAPTER TWENTY-THREE

THE GATHERING STORM

The fundamental question about the second war between the Jews of Judaea and the Roman empire — the War of Bar Kokhba — is this: did it break out all at once, in reaction to something specific the Romans did, such as building the pagan shrine Aelia Capitolina on the site of the Temple, or making circumcision illegal, or both acts combined? Or was the outbreak rather the culmination of a long process, the result of pressure that had been building up over many years?

An unequivocal answer to this question depends, of course, on certain factual information which we simply do not have. What, for example, was the date of Hadrian's edict against circumcision? The silence of our sources on this and other important details prevents us from settling the fundamental question in a really definitive way.

But we are not left completely in the dark. The literature hints at a certain amount of restiveness in the country during the pre-war years. These hints are buttressed by several newly discovered papyri which tell of the same kind of ferment.

Specifically, we learn from the Talmud that in the years before the Bar Kokhba War, armed bands of Jewish highwaymen roamed the countryside. One such report relates:[1]

> Certain disciples of Rabbi Akiba were once on the road to Kheziv when they were overtaken by some robbers who asked them where they were going. They replied: 'To Akko.' On reaching Kheziv (*about nine miles north of Akko*) they stopped. The robbers said to them: 'Whose disciples are you?' They answered: 'Rabbi Akiba's.' Whereupon the high-

1   Av. Zar. 25b.

waymen said: 'Happy are Rabbi Akiba and his disciples, for no evil person has ever done them harm.'

Here we see Jewish *listim* treating Sages and their disciples with great deference, causing the Gemara to exclaim: "Look, what a difference between the thieves of Babylonia and the *listim* of Eretz Israel!"[2]

Evidence of the same phenomenon — Jewish banditry during the period under discussion — is also provided by the following:[3]

We are told that the son of Rabbi Hanina ben Teradyon joined up with a band of highwaymen and learned their secret. So they killed him and filled his mouth with earth and pebbles. After three days they put him in a box and wanted to say a eulogy over him out of respect for his father; but the Rabbi would not allow them. He said: Let me be, and I will speak about my son. Whereupon he gave forth with the 13th and 14th verses of the fifth chapter of Proverbs: *Neither have I hearkened to the voice of my teachers, nor inclined mine ear to them that instructed me! I was well nigh in all evil in the midst of the congregation and assembly.* His mother quoted the 25th verse of chapter seventeen: *A foolish son is vexation to his father, and bitterness to her that bore him;* while his sister recited chapter twenty, verse seventeen: *Bread of falsehood is sweet to a man, but afterwards his mouth shall be filled with gravel.*

It is also possible that the Galileans who asked Rabbi Tarphon to hide them from the Romans because they had killed a Jew were a manifestation of this movement of *listim*.[4]

The following story as well may belong to this same period:[5]

Once it happened that a *listos* was caught (*by the Romans*) at Caesarea of Cappadocia. As he was being led to his execution, he called out: Send word to the wife of Simeon

2   Ibid. 26a.
3   LamR III:14, in a homily on Lamentations III:16: "He hath broken my teeth with gravel, and hath made me to wallow in ashes."
4   Nid. 61a; see above, p. 541.
5   Yer. Yev. II:4b; Bavli ibid. 25b; Tos. ibid. IV:5 (244).

ben Kahana that I killed him as he was entering Lod (i.e. *so thdt she could collect her widow's settlement and be free to remarry*). The case was brought before the Sages and they accepted his words as evidence. To this citation Rabbi Judah replied: What does that prove? All he said was, "We killed him." (*i.e. he was not a self-confessed murderer.*)

Now, it is a fact that highway robbery existed in Eretz Israel during various periods, even before the Destruction, and that Jewish travellers were victimized by them the same as any others. The phenomenon appeared, as far as we can judge, because of certain social and political conditions, such as insurgency movements and the like; or as the result of economic depressions (or for that mater, when these factors existed at the same time). In the present instance, it would be natural to assume that the pre-Bar Kokhba years, the twenties of the second century following the *polemos* of Quietus, were times of economic difficulty. True, we have no explicit evidence of this, but only certain indirect inferences.

But before we go any further, there is a broader question to be settled first. What were economic conditions like in the empire as a whole during the reign of Hadrian? The well-known regnant view is that almost the entire second century (until the last days of Marcus Aurelius) was a golden age of prosperity for the whole Mediterranean world. It was the time when trade with India rose to a peak, a time when great public buildings were put up in the eastern cities of the empire. This was a time when the very affluent tended to dispense largesse, and writers to depict in glowing colors the wealth and tranquillity of the Roman empire. Visible testimony to this prosperity in the vicinity of Eretz Israel can be seen in the ruins of Gerasa (Jerash) in Transjordan.[6]

Hadrian showed an especially active concern for the economic welfare of his domains. He travelled widely in the provinces, and had many stately buildings erected. His accession heralded an era of peace, and was a factor in the forward surge of world trade and commerce, and of a general growth in prosperity. Here and there he took economic measures, such as reducing taxes or easing their payment, or making special provision for people of limited means.

6 See Kraeling: *Gerasa*, 1938.

Some historians, however, point to the other side of the picture. Hadrian's extensive travels cost the people of the districts he visited a pretty penny, and reduced their treasuries significantly. The large bureaucracy that his projects entailed saddled the empire's taxpayers with an additional burden. And as for those stately buildings so generously "bestowed" on cities in the provinces — in the last analysis it was the citizenry that had to bear the enormous costs.[7]

These general considerations apply to the empire as a whole. When we come to consider the specific situation in Judaea, we need to examine evidence relating specifically to that country. And indeed, there are several tannaitic traditions which appear to reflect hard times, drought, or even famine, in the pre-Bar Kokhba years. The Tosefta reports : [8]

> A case involving Joshua, son of Rabbi Akiba, who took a wife and stipulated (*in the marriage agreement*) that she would provide his sustenance while he studied Torah. But when the years of want came, they decided to divide their property between them (*since the contract was now impossible*).

Another passage in the Tosefta tells us : [9]

> Rabbi Tarphon went through a marriage ceremony with 300 women and fed them *terumah,* for those were years of drought (*he was a kohen*).

Another passage in the Tosefta reads : [10]

> Rabbi Judah said: the family of Memel and the family of Gorion in Ruma used to distribute dried dates to the poor, for it was a time of drought.[11] The poor of Kfar Sikhin used at that time to go out and pace off the Sabbath limit (*so as to get some dates to eat.*

7   See especially Rostovtzeff: Social and Economic History of the Roman Empire, 2nd. ed. 1957, p. 371.
8   Tos. Ket. IV:6 (264); Yer. ibid. V:29d
9   Tos. ibid. VI:1 (266); Yer. Yev. IV:6b.
10 Tos. Eruv. IV:17 (143); Yer. ibid IV:22a; Bavli 51a.
11 Ruma is in Lower Galilee, south of the Vale of Beth Netofa. Ms. Erfurt reads, mistakenly, "*daroma.*"

Actually, drought is a perennial problem in Eretz Israel, and has been throughout recorded time. But for the period we are examining there seems to be evidence of an economic depression more severe than the ordinary belt-tightening caused by a lack of rain. The Mishnah reads: [12]

> Rabbi Eleazar ben Azariah thus expounded before the Sages in the vineyard at Yavneh: The sons inherit, and the daughters receive maintenance; but just as the sons inherit only after the death of their father, so do the daughters receive maintenance only after the death of their father.

The effect of this is to exempt fathers from the obligation to maintain their daughters. However, Rabbi Eleazar's contemporary Rabbi Johanan ben Baroqa disagrees completely: "A man is obliged to provide for his daughters."[13]

Another Talmudic tradition runs to the same effect: [14]

> Our Rabbis of Yavneh[15] expounded the verse "Happy are they who keep justice, who do righteousness at all times" (Ps. 106:3) — as a reference to one who provides for his sons and daughters when they are little.

It seems that this had become a problem in the years before the Bar Kokhba War, and the Sages at Usha discussed it during the difficult days that followed the war. Here, apparently, is what the discussion was about: there were people who tried to have their children fed at public expense, because they themselves simply could not afford it. A halakhic discussion arose: should the father be compelled to do his duty, and the community exempted from assuming the responsibility?

This problem may have arisen because of the Roman food-relief called *alimenta*, which was administered during the regimes of Nerva, Trajan and Hadrian, when food was distributed to poor children. In any event, these halakhot are a reflection of the hard

---

12 Mishnah Ket. IV:7.
13 Tos. Ket. IV:8 (264); Yer. ibid. 28d; Bavli ibid. 49a.
14 Ket 50a; comp. Midrash Tehillim ad Ps. 106, ed. Buber, p. 454.
15 Variae: Rabbi Eliezer, Rabbi Eleazar.

times that prevailed during the years preceding the Bar Kokhba War.

However, hard times alone will not suffice to explain the growth of highway robbery during these years, both in Galilee and in the South (in the vicinity of Lod). For one thing, we have already discovered the son of Rabbi Hanina ben Teradyon among the robbers — and his family was fairly affluent. Indeed, his father was a prominent citizen in charge of distributing charity funds![16] It is therefore only reasonable to assume that the son's involvement with a violent gang was not motivated by the need for money.

Secondly, there is the business of these gangs killing Jews. Granted, there is evidence for robbery and theft in the years following the Destruction; but this is the first time we hear of murders after the fall of Jerusalem — and what is more, of the assassination of prominent individuals like Simeon ben Kahana.[17] Consequently, we may regard this phenomenon as political in nature — a sign of the gathering storm.

DATE OF THE WAR

We are now about to examine two documents which have recently come to light, and which seem to show that a rebel movement was building up in Judea for some years before the war actually broke out. One of these is dated, beyond any shadow of doubt, at the year 128 C.E. As for the other, I disagree with those who have assigned it to a post-Bar Kokhba time. I am convinced that it is to be dated no later than 129 C.E. But before we go any further, we had better establish to our satisfaction the date of the Bar Kokhba War itself!

It is well known that the literary sources offer two contradictory accounts as to when the war took place. Some put it in the early

---

16 B.B. 10b; Av. Zar. 17b.

17 He seems to have been a student of Rabbi Eliezer ben Hyrcanus, and to have taught Rabban Simeon ben Gamaliel; see Yer. Hal. IV:60b; see also Hyman: *Toledot Tannaim va-Amoraim.* ["Simeon ben Kahana lived at the time of the Bar Kokhba Revolt... It is possible that the band killed him for political reasons and fled to Cappadocia and were apprehended there." Lieberman, *Tosefta Kifshuto,* VI, p. 29.]

thirties of the second century; others place it in the early twenties. This chronological problem was debated by historians during the nineteenth century. Some of them, especially among Jewish scholars, gave credence to the earlier dating.[18] But by now the issue seems to have been pretty well settled in favor of the thirties.[19] Because, however, there have been a few voices calling for a reconsideration in favor of the earlier date,[20] we had best review the evidence.

The principal ancient narrative sources give the date of the Bar Kokhba War as the early thirties. Dio Cassius does so by implication in his *Roman History*.[21] Eusebius, in his *Chronicle*, as transmitted by Jerome, fixes the date: 132 C.E.[22] However, Jerome himself says in a number of places that the Bar Kokhba War took place *fifty years* after the Destruction — which leaves us with the year 120. (Jerome was probably citing a tradition current among Jews). The *Chronicon Paschale*, which has no connection with Jerome, gives the year 119.

Turning to Jewish sources, we read in the Yerushalmi: "It was taught that Rabbi Jose said: Beitar survived for 52 years after the Destruction of the Temple."[23] On the other hand, a contrary tradition places the "War of Beitar" (a synonym for the Bar Kokhba War) some ten years later:[24]

From the war of Vespasian to the war of Quietus — 52 years; and from the war of Quietus to the war of ben Koziba — sixteen years.

18 See e.g. Rapoport, *Erekh Milin*, s.v. "Adrianus."
19 See esp. Schürer, ed. Vermes and Millar I, p. 540; Weber in Cambridge Ancient History, XI, pp. 300 ff.
20 Raphaeli: "Jewish Coinage and the Date of the Bar Kokhba Revolt," in JPOS 1923, pp. 193–199; Halevy: *Dorot Harishonim*, vol. V, pp. 586 ff.
21 Dio's *Roman History*, Epitome of Book LXIX, Cary VIII, p. 447 f.; comp. GLA II, no. 440.
22 Ed. Schoene II, 168–169.
23 Yer. Taan. IV:69a; LamR, II:2.
24 *Seder Olam Rabbah*, ed. Neubauer, II, p. 66, ed. Ratner, p. 145. There are other versions of this text, but the one given here seems to be the correct one.

It should also be pointed out that an inscription in honor of Severus, the commander who ultimately put down the Bar Kokhba Revolt, refers to his earlier service as a consul.[25] It so happens that we know exactly when he served in that office: it was in 127 C.E. Therefore, it must have been later than that when he commanded the legions that fought Bar Kokhba.[26] Then there is the numismatic evidence. Vogt points out that coins dated 131 show Hadrian, having returned from Egypt, dressed in the accoutrements of war — something not usual for this emperor.[27] This proves that trouble had already erupted in Judaea.[28]

Finally, we have known for some time that Hadrian was given a second "acclamation" as emperor no later than December of the year 135. This could only have happened at the end of the Bar Kokhba War, just as he was proclaimed *Imperator* the first time after his victory over the Dacians in 117–118.

The date of the second triumph is pinpointed further by the recent discovery of a Roman certificate of discharge from the army, bearing the date April 14th, 135. In such certificates the emperor's titles are always listed, and we can see that he had *not yet* been awarded his second acclamation. Ergo: the Bar Kokhba War must have ended between April and December of 135.[29]

In any event, the war took place in the thirties — not in the twenties.

DOCUMENTARY EVIDENCE

A Roman papyrus, first published in Florence in 1928, has a bearing on our subject.[30] It is a copy of a formal request, sent to the imperial *Legatus* by twenty-three veteran servicemen of the

25 Dessau: *Inscript. Lat. Select.* I, p. 231, no. 1056.
26 A fact mentioned later in the inscription; and the *cursus honorum* always listed a man's offices and honors in strict chronological order.
27 Vogt: *Alexandrinische Münzen*, I, 97.
28 Schehl agrees; see *Hermes*, 1930, pp. 177 ff.
29 See Heichelheim: "New Light on Bar Kokhba's War," in JQR n.s. vol. 34 (1943–44) pp. 61–63.
30 *Papiri Greci e Latini, Publicazione della Societa Italiana*, vol. IX, no. 1026, pp. 43–44. See Aegyptus 1929, 242–53; Rev. Arch. 1930, 333; Syria 1928, 268; J.E.A. 15, 118.

Xth Fretensian Legion. These men, all of them from Alexandria in Egypt, explain that they had originally begun their service as seamen in the fleet based at Misenum, Italy, during certain consular years (which we can identify as 125–126) but had soon been sent to serve as soldiers with the Tenth Fretensian (the chief garrison legion in Judaea from the year 70, and for several centuries afterwards.) This legion was beefed up with auxiliary cohorts and other legions whenever need arose. Its role is described by Josephus, and its presence in the country is amply attested by many inscriptions.

Now, write these veterans, "in these happier times, when we are being released from our oaths (of service) . . . having conducted ourselves as good soldiers in every respect for over twenty years . . . we are about to return to our native city of Alexandria which is in Egypt." They go on to request a certificate that they are being discharged from the army, not from the navy.

Added to the letter is a memorandum given at Caesarea (*Prima Colonia Flavia*) dated the 22nd of January in the year 150. The *Legatus* states that it is not customary to give such discharge papers; but he will sign in the nature of a notification to the prefect of Egypt that these men are indeed veteran *soldiers.*

The meaning of all this is that the veterans had spent most of their years in service (the normal Roman "hitch" was 25 years) as land-based troops; and since the benefits of an ex-legionary were much better than those of a former seaman, they did not want to be classified in their original status.

I suspect that their reference to "happier times" hints at their service in difficult days — the days of the struggle with Bar Kokhba. I suggest they are saying that having been through such action should count for more than their few years at the oars.

The point that interests us most is, just when were they attached to the Tenth Legion in Judaea? All the papyrologists who have dealt with this document are unanimous about one thing: these sailors must have been sent to reinforce the Xth at a critical time, when actual fighting was in progress. Vitelli, the scholar who published this papyrus, and the other scholars who have dealt with it, all agree that the transfer must have taken place in the year 132, when the Bar Kokhba War was in full force.

However, I am afraid I cannot agree. For one thing, when the veterans talk about having served for "more than twenty years," they certainly do not mean to include their years in the navy; for how can anybody call 25 years "more than twenty?" So the phrase must refer to their time in the Legion — and if they had been transferred in 132, they would have been in only 18 years. To be sure, you might say that 20 is just a round number, and not to be taken literally. That would be fine, had they not said *"more* than 20!" But since they did write that phrase, we must take them at their word. Twenty years before the date of this document brings us to the 22nd of January 130. "More than" that, yields a date no later than the year 129. It seems highly likely that these men were detached from the Italian navy to serve in the garrison in Judaea because of some emergency in the latter country. So it is reasonable to suppose that in 129 or 128 the state of insurrection in Judaea was such as to make it necessary to reinforce the troops stationed there.

Another earlier papyrus relates to the subject at hand. It is dated in the year 128, and is a rather prosaic receipt:[31]

> Dionysus son of Socrates and the associate collectors of public clothing for the guards have received from the weavers of the village of Socnopaei Nesus nineteen tunics for the needs of the soldiers serving in Judaea five white cloaks (or caps) . . . .

The requisitioning of supplies from the Egyptian population for troops stationed in other countries appears not to have been unusual.[32] A papyrus dated early in the third century (216–217) tells of camels being requisitioned in the Egyptian town of Philadelphia "for the needs of the noble soldiery in Syria of our lord and Emperor Severus Antoninus."[33] It is clear that these camels were needed for the large force which Caraculla mustered against the

31 Pap. Ryl. II 189 (Catalogue of Greek Papyri in the Rylands Lib. ed. Himt. II p. 237); see Johnson in *An Economic Survey of Ancient Rome,* by T. Frank, Baltimore 1936, vol. II, "Roman Egypt," p. 626.
32 Sometimes the military paid a fair price, sometimes less, sometimes nothing at all.
33 Wilcken, *Chrestomathie,* no. 245; BGU 266.

Parthians. By analogy, we can assume that the clothing referred to in the earlier document was for the reinforcements being deployed in Judaea; because, under more static circumstances, each eparchy itself supported the troops quartered on it. The local population paid a levy called *annona militaris*, making it unnecessary to import quartermaster stores from outside.

That is why any evidence of military supplies being brought from one country to another can be taken as a sign of some crisis. For example, a papyrus dated September 9th, of the year 138 (after Hadrian's death) tells of clothing being requisitioned in Philadelphia of Egypt for troops at Cappadocia.[34] Schehl suggested that this is proof of a particularly critical military situation in that area, resulting in a need for extra clothing for the reinforcements. He deduces consequently that there was a threat of war with the Parthians shortly after the accession of Antoninus Pius.[35] It should be noted that Cappadocia, like Syria, was always a staging ground for campaigns against the Parthians, whether offensive or defensive.

In order to support his deduction, Schehl sought to tie this document to the Rylands papyrus quoted above. He suggested that the tunics requisitioned for the troops in Judaea were also connected with a threat of war with Parthia.

Actually, we are told by Spartianus that war with the Parthians really was about to break out during Hadrian's reign, but that it was averted by the emperor himself, who settled matters by negotiation while he was on a trip in the East.[36] Most scholars, however, agree with Wilhelm Weber in attributing this episode to the year 123–4, when Hadrian was on a swing through the eastern provinces. But Schehl would have us believe that it took place during Hadrian's last trip to the East (128–132). In his opinion, there was a threat of war with Parthia beginning in 128, and that explains the concentration of troops in Judaea, as shown by the Rylands papyrus.

But I do not think he has made his case. I think we must accept

34 BGU 1564. See Johnson, in Frank, op. cit p. 627.
35 "Zur Geschichte des Kaisers Antoninus Pius" in *Hermes* Vol. 65 (1930) pp. 177 ff.
36 *Scriptores Historiae Augustae*, [translated by David Magie, Loeb Classical Library, Vol. I, p. 29.]

the report of Spartianus at face value, and not lift it out of context. Its position in the narrative show's that the author intended to refer to Hadrian's earlier trip. That leaves us with the unavoidable conclusion from the papyrus dated 128 that the garrison in Judaea was being strengthened just then (it seems it was already rather large) because at that very time there were noticeable disturbances and insurrectionary activities in *Judaea itself*.

So far, then, the Talmudic sources taken together with the papyri we have examined give us reason to believe that for quite some time before the outbreak of war there was a state of unrest in Palestine sufficient to require reinforcement of the regular garrison.[37] What produced this state of disturbance? That is the question we must ask ourselves.

One explanation that suggests itself is that after the atmosphere of detente that followed the draconic rule of Quietus, and the promising start made by Hadrian with his original plan of restoring Jerusalem, there was a tremendous let-down when those plans were abandoned. The resultant mood among the Jews was one of bitter disappointment.[38] Out of this resentment grew rebel bands, men who lived outside the law, harassing the authorities, sometimes engaging in robbery in order to sustain themselves, possibly taking action against Jews whom they judged to be too cooperative with the Romans.

On the other hand, it may be that a decision was taken in Rome, for imperial considerations, to shift policy sharply against the Jews, particularly those in Judaea. That would certainly evoke considerable unrest. Our problem is that we lack sufficient data to put these hypotheses to the test. But there are some hints.

For example, coins of the city of Tiberias minted there in the year 119–120 bear the outline of a pagan temple, apparently of Zeus, which may be the *Hadrianeion* spoken of by Epiphanius.[39] So that around the time these coins were minted, an idolatrous

37 A conclusion arrived at by Strathmann in Palästinajahrbuch XXIII (1927), pp. 92–123; and Gray in Am. Journ. Sem. Lang. 1922–3, p. 123.
38 See GenR 64, quoted above Chap. IV, note 9.
39 *Panarion* 30; comp. *Sefer ha-Yishuv*, p. 70. See Hill, "Catalogue of the Greek Coins of Palestine in the British Museum," 1914, p. 15; Watzinger, *Denkmäler Palästinas* II, 1935, p. 85.

shrine was dedicated at Tiberias to the chief god of Rome and to Hadrian, who functioned as his representative on earth. This parallels the (later) Jerusalem coins showing the shrine of Aelia Capitolina on the site of the Holy of Holies; so too for Mount Gerizim at Neapolis (Nablus) where the Samaritan Temple had stood.

From this evidence Jones reasoned that the city government of Tiberias (and according to his reckoning, of Sepphoris as well) had been taken out of the hands of the Jews and turned over to the gentile minority.[40] To be sure, Tiberian coins going back to the time of Trajan bear the likeness of Hygeia, goddess of health, probably in association with the local hot springs; but that is still not quite in the same class as a temple to Jupiter!

To sum up: we lack clear-cut information about Hadrian's attitude to the Jews of Judaea, so we can carry our speculations no further. We must now turn our attention to the immediate causes of the Bar Kokhba War.

THE HISTORICAL TRADITIONS

Two apparently conflicting traditions describe the outbreak of the Bar Kokhba War. First we present the account given by the Roman historian Dio Cassius:[41]

> At Jerusalem (Hadrian) founded a city in place of the one which had been razed to the ground, naming it Aelia Capitolina, and on the site of the temple of the god he raised a new temple to Zeus. This brought on a war of no slight importance nor of brief duration, for the Jews deemed it intolerable that foreign races should be settled in their city, and foreign religious rites planted there. So long, indeed, as Hadrian was close by in Egypt, and again in Syria, they remained quiet, except insofar as they purposely made of

40 Jones, *The Greek City*, 1940, p. 81.
41 *Dio's Roman History*, Epitome of Book LXIX, transl. by E. Cary, vol. VIII, pp. 447 ff. Dio is here describing Hadrian's journey to the Middle East, which apparently included an actual visit to Jerusalem. We know that he was in Syria, Palestine, Arabia (Transjordan) and Egypt during 129–131. Traces of his visit are especially evident at the ruins of Jerash.

poor quality such weapons as they were called upon to furnish, in order that the Romans might reject them, and they themselves might then have use of them; but when he went further away they openly rebelled.

This account, which puts the building of Aelia Capitolina before the war, seems to be contradicted by the Church Father Eusebius, who reports that the shrine was built after the war to punish the Jews for their rebellion.[42] However, it is possible to reconcile these two versions, and most historians do so, by suggesting that Aelia was begun before the war, and was therefore one of its causes; but that the bulk of the work was done after the war, so it came to be seen as one of its results.

But an account that really seems to be at variance with Dio's is presented in the 'Life of Hadrian" attributed to Spartianus.[43]

> At that point the Jews as well took up arms, because the mutilation of the genital parts (*i.e. circumcision*) had been forbidden to them.

Most historians give greater credence to the account by Dio Cassius, and with good reason; indeed, there are those who ignore any other version. A recent example is Domaszewski, who believes that it was only after the war that Hadrian prohibited circumcision.[44] However, a great many scholars still try to reconcile the two accounts. They do this by accepting the statement that the ban on circumcision preceded the war, while claiming that it was not directed specifically against the Jews.

I believe that there is substance to this view. In the first place, it makes sense to see the edict in the framework of Domitian's earlier empire-wide decree against castration and sterilization. And it is a conclusion that can be drawn from the Digests of Modestinus, (48:8,11) where, under a law of Antoninus Pius the Jews are expressly permitted to practice circumcision on themselves, and are forbidden to perform it on non-Jews, under pain of suffering the penalty for violating the law against castration.[45]

42 Ecclesiastical History IV:vi:4 (Lake I, p. 313.)
43 *Historia Augusta* XIV:2, Magie I, pp. 44–5; comp. GLA II, p. 619.
44 *Geschichte der römischen Kaiser*, 1909.
45 See Schürer I, p. 677, note 80, Vermes and Millar I, p. 537.

The same is implied by Origen when he speaks of the willingness of the Samaritans to suffer martyrdom rather than give up the practice of circumcision. They are persecuted, says Origen, not on account of their faith, but for violating the *lex Cornelia de Sicarii*, which, under Domitian and Hadrian included castration as a criminal act. Only the Jews had been exempted from it.[46] Based on the additional fact that a Roman ban on circumcision was also in effect in the second century in Arabia, Schürer established, rather convincingly, that we are dealing here with a general prohibition, rather than with a measure directed solely against Jewish rebels.[47] This would tend to prove that the prohibition antedated the Revolt.

On the other hand, Schürer does not seem to be right when he cites as evidence the fact that, according to certain papyri, in Egypt at the end of the second century each individual case of circumcision required the approval of a priest. Actually, the requirement does not prove that there was a general prohibition; it may have been nothing more than an administrative procedure. This may have been based on the fact that in Egypt, circumcision was for priests only, not for ordinary people![48]

In trying to prove that the ban on circumcision antedated the Bar Kokhba War, we are on firmer ground with the Jewish sources.

> Rabbi Ishmael ben Elisha said: Since the day the Temple was destroyed we should really have made it a rule for ourselves not to eat meat nor to drink wine; but one does not make regulations which most people cannot live up to. And since the day the wicked empire has taken over, laying upon us its evil decrees, keeping us from the (*study of*) Torah and (*the life of*) mitzvot, and not permitting us to gather for the "Week of the son," we ought to have ruled not to take a wife, and not to beget children; and so the seed of Abraham would die out of itself. But let the Jews be; let them live

46 Contra Celsum II:13.
47 Schürer, loc. cit.
48 I cannot agree with Elbogen's suggestion (Encyclop. *Eshkol*, s.v. "Adrianus" pp. 118 ff.) that the ban on circumcision applied only to potential converts to Judaism.

in error, rather than make rules which they will have to break knowingly.[49]

The corresponding passage in the Tosefta quotes Rabbi Ishmael as having said: "Because they have uprooted the Torah from our midst, shall we then decree that Jews refrain from marrying and from begetting children and from celebrating the 'Week of the son?' "[50]

The well known tradition about the ten martyrs who were executed by the Romans after the Bar Kokhba War includes the name of Rabbi Ishmael.[51] The historicity of this recollection is accepted by scholars in our day.[52] Earlier in this work we tried to explain that two men, whose identities are not altogether clear, suffered martyrdom during the repression under Quietus, and that their memory became entangled with that of two other prominent citizens who had been killed during the first war with Rome. Somehow the death of the second pair was transferred to the repressive days that followed the War of Bar Kokhba.[53] At any rate, the Rabbi Ishmael mentioned here is not the famous scholar of that name who was a contemporary of Rabbi Akiba.

It seems that the Rabbi Ishmael of this tradition did not live at the time of the Hadrianic persecution that followed the Bar Kokhba War. This is demonstrated by the passages which quote him as one no longer able to speak for himself, such as "in the name of Rabbi Ishmael, a disciple stated before Rabbi Akiba.[54] The Mishnah also describes Rabbi Akiba reporting a tradition

49 B.B. 60b. The "Week of the son" was a seven-day celebration of the birth of a boy, culminating with his circumcision on the eighth day. Apparently, the text which Nahmanides used read: "the week of the son and the week of the daughter." See Semahot, ed. Higger, p. 20.

50 Tos. Sot. XV:10 (322); ms. Erfurt attributes the statement to Rabban Gamaliel.

51 The oldest versions are LamR II:5 ("The Lord hath swallowed up"); and Midrash Tehillim on Ps. 29, ed. Buber 44b–45a.

52 Guttman in *Encyclopedia Judaica* (German) s.v. "Bar Kokhba"; Krauss in *Ha-Shiloah* 44 (1925). [Zeitlin in JQR ns 36 (1945–6) argues that the Ten Martyrs never were, but are purely legendary. He does admit, however, that an "Ishmael" was martyred during the revolt.]

53 Above, chapter 3, note 29: "Pappus and Lulianus."

54 Mishnah, Eruv. I:2.

told him by the people of Madeba "in the name of Rabbi Ishmael,"[55] These signs point to the fact that *this* Rabbi Ishmael died before Rabbi Akiba — which is to say, *at least* before the defeat of Bar Kokhba.

Consequently, we may say that the tradition we have quoted reflects conditions *before* the war. Now, Rabbi Ishmael spoke not only about circumcision, but more sweepingly about such things as the nullification of Torah-study and the performance of the mitzvot, about the "uprooting of the Torah from our midst" altogether. This can strengthen the assumption that even before the war, the Romans had interdicted the practices of Judaism, somewhat in the way in which we know they did after the war.

However, a more careful examination of the tradition reveals that the only specific practice mentioned is circumcision. All the other terms are general, except for "the Week of the son." The broad general terms can be interpreted this way: the oppressive burdens laid upon us by the occupying power deter us from living a proper Jewish life in accordance with the Torah. There had been, to be sure, temporary edicts of persecution, including a ban on circumcision during the regime of Quietus. But it does not seem to me that the words of Rabbi Ishmael should be assigned to that time. They are couched in terms that seem to deal with the "normal" oppressiveness of the occupying power, rather than with any critical or exceptional periods.

At this point we must deal with an attempt to call in the Tosefta as witness to a pre-war ban on circumcision. I am afraid the attempt fails. The Tosefta reads:

> The *mashukh* has to be re-circumcised. Rabbi Judah said no, that should not be required, for it is dangerous. They said: Many were circumcised in the days of Ben Koziba and they begat children and did not die.[56]

It was suggested by a scholar in the nineteenth century that the "many" referred to in the last sentence had been kept from observing the rite by a Roman ban on circumcision, and were able

55   Miq. VII : 1.
56   Tos. Shab. XV (XVI) : 9 (133); Bavli Yev. 72a; Yer. Shab. XIX : 17a.

to perform the mitzvah only after Bar Kokhba's initial victories had given them the freedom to do so.[57]

But there is a flaw in that theory. A ban on circumcision, if there was one, would not explain why men tried to efface its results. The situation was quite different with the hellenizers under Antiochus Epiphanes close to four centuries earlier. Their "plastic surgery" was voluntary, and was undertaken because they wanted to appear in the public games, and were ashamed of the mark of the Jew branded on their flesh.

The most probable meaning of the Tosefta in question is that there were assimilationists in Roman times as well, who tried to hide the effects of circumcision; and then later (when Bar Kokhba and his rebels gained the upper hand), returned to the fold — voluntarily or involuntarily.

This interpretation also has in its favor the virtue of explaining the inclusion of these people in the following list of miscreants:[58]

He who eats abominations is accounted an apostate (*meshummad*) as is one who eats carrion or crawling things or swine's flesh or drinks the wine of libation to idols, or desecrates the Sabbath or is a *mashukh* (*has drawn his foreskin*).

The Yerushalmi explains the phrase "a violator of the covenant" to mean "one who draws his foreskin" (*sc. over the corona, to hide the mark of circumcision.*)[59]

What our investigation adds up to is this: although some of the proposed evidence does not hold up, there is enough to con-

---

57 J. Derenbourg: *Essai sur l'histoire et la géographie de la Palestine,* Paris, 1867, p. 4'9 [Derenbourg is not really insistent: "... il se peut certainement que déjà avant le soulevement ... Adrien ou Rufus aient étendu les ordonnances sévères contre la castration, alors en vigueur dans tout l'empire romain, à l'opération qui était pour les juifs une prescription religieuse."] For Graetz's different theory, relating the matter to tax-evasion under Domitian, see MGWJ vol. I, p. 194. I do not myself think that motivation a sufficient one to explain such heroic counter-measures.

58 Tos. Hor. I:5 (474).

59 Yer. Sanh. X:27c and Peah I:16b; Bavli Sanh. 99a. For the phrase *mefir brit,* comp. Tos. Sanh. XII:9 (433) and Mishnah Avot III:11. [Danby (*The Mishnah,* p. 451) offers the felicitous rendering: "makes void the covenant of Abraham our father."]

vince us that two Roman actions, viewed by the Jews as inimical, had already been taken before the Bar Kokhba War — the edict against circumcision, and the building, in its initial stages at least, of Aelia Capitolina.

The question remains: what was the reason for these measures? This is an important question, and at the same time a very difficult one. Unfortunately, it is also one which we cannot answer with any kind of assurance, because we know too little about the situation.

But where certainty is lacking, there is room for hypothesis. Modern historians have offered two sharply opposed views of the deeper causes of the clash. The one most widely held is associated with such famous scholars as Emil Schürer and Theodor Mommsen, and is followed by some Jewish scholars as well.[60] According to this view, the Romans had no intention at all of interfering with the Jews or their religion when they issued their edict forbidding circumcision (along with castration). Nor were they out to harm anybody by building Aelia Capitolina. That measure was no different from what was done elsewhere in the empire, where places that had become the fixed encampment of legions were turned into cities — a process that can be observed in the West, within the *limes* of Germania. So the project on Mount Moriah was undertaken by the emperor in all innocence, and with the best of intentions.

As it happened, however, his measures were objectively a severe blow to the Jews, particularly the ban on circumcision, and they reacted violently. The emperor, "who had meant them no harm," was taken aback. He did not understand the Jews at all; he and they were on a collision course. Hence the persecution, the fierce war — and the massive suffering that it brought in its train.

There is an echo here of the line followed by some historians

60 [For example, and with qualifications, Joseph Klausner in "History of the Second Temple," (Hebrew) Vol. V. He expatiates on the idea that the Romans found the Jews incomprehensible. While criticizing Mommsen for relying too heavily on this as a cause, he does say: "This lack of understanding — something like that which poisoned our relationships with the Mandatory Power in the twentieth century — had a fateful outcome for the Jewish people and its land." (p. 132).]

in explaining the War of the Destruction — the First War with Rome. The Romans and the Jews never understood one another, so the explanation goes; hence the tragedy that was implicit in their confrontation; hence the bitterness of their clash. However, this view seems a little too naive. Hadrian, at any rate, had had plenty of opportunity to learn a good deal about the Jews. He had had first hand experience of the Jewish *tumultus* under Trajan; and he was a man "with a great thirst for knowledge" about lands and peoples. Surely he knew what circumcision meant in Judaism; surely he was aware of how the Jews would feel about a shrine dedicated to Jupiter on the very site of their most holy sanctuary.

The second, diametrically opposite view of the situation is the one espoused by Wilhelm Weber.[61] According to him, the Roman Empire took deliberate measures to protect itself against those eternal rebels, the Jews, who were constantly subverting the very existence of the state. Actually, they were such a nuisance that they left the Romans very little choice. Hadrian therefore decided to take the bull by the horns and to smite these rebels decisively, once and for all. Hence the ban on circumcision, hence the building of Aelia Capitolina. He knew exactly what he was doing. The Roman religion must displace that of the Jews; Rome's chief god must conquer the God of Israel, and drive him from his sanctuary.

Weber's theory is all very well, but it leaves unexplained the central question: What prompted Hadrian to vent his fury on these "eternal rebels" *at that particular time,* especially after he had begun his reign by showing them a very friendly attitude, by giving every indication of a benign policy towards them? Weber does nothing to explain the sharp reversal in Hadrian's policy. That such a reversal took place there can scarcely be any question, and it remains a riddle.

Purely from the point of view of sound historiography, it would probably be best for us to steer a middle course between the two theories stated above. It certainly seems unlikely that Hadrian started out with the idea of forcing the Jews to give up their religion; and equally unlikely that he was abysmally ignorant about

61 *Römische Herrschertum und Reich im 2ten Jahrhundert,* p. 172.

Jewish attitudes and national feelings. Yet he went ahead with his decrees, deliberately ignoring their deepest loyalties and the fundamental tenets of their faith.

When he outlawed castration and lumped circumcision with it he was by-passing the traditional status of Judaism in the Roman Empire as a *religio licita,* which had always been expressly exempt from any laws which might otherwise interfere with it. And when he decreed the creation of a Greco-Roman Jerusalem, centered on a temple of Zeus-Jupiter, he was disregarding a fundamental aspect of the Jewish people's existence, especially that part of the people that still lived in Judaea. What these steps amount to is neither forced assimilation, on the one hand, nor well-meant blundering on the other. They amount to a considered policy of *cancellation* of previous Jewish rights, plus an attempt to *erase the Jewish character* of the country, by pushing to the fore the Greek-Roman and other non-Jewish minorities in the population.

What lay behind this policy? Most historians attribute to Hadrian an affinity for all things Hellenic, which led him to prefer the Greek element in his domains, particularly in the Hellenistic East. Spartianus, in his "Life of Hadrian," says that this emperor was contemptuous of foreign cults, which in this context means oriental ones.[62]

The numismatic evidence points in the same direction. Coins commemorating Hadrian's visit to Judaea in the year 130 appear to have been struck some time after he had left the country, between the years 134 and 138. The usual practice in such commemorative coinages *(adventus augusti)* was to include in the design something of the special local flavor and character of the eparchy graced by the august visitor. In this case, however, the Jewish nature of the province is nowhere indicated. On the contrary, there are transparent hints that this is a hellenistic province, participating in a "Greco-Roman renaissance."[63]

It is possible that we are witnessing here another shift of Roman

---

62 [Historia Augusta XXII:10, Magie I, p. 69.]

63 Hill, "Catalogue of the Greek Coins of Palestine in the British Museum," 1914; Mattingly-Sydenham, "The Roman Imperial Coinage," II, pp. 331–340; P.L. Strack, "Untersuchungen zur Reichsprägung" II, p. 162.

imperial policy in that perennial balancing act between Judaism and Hellenism, those two important pillars in the structure of the empire. This time the balance shifted in favor of Hellenism. What we do not know is, what caused this about-face on Hadrian's part.

I find no cogency at all in Elbogen's suggestion that the break was caused by the Jews' disappointment with Hadrian's visit in 130, on which they had pinned exaggerated hopes.[64] Nor do I attribute any importance to the conversations supposed to have taken place between Rabbi Joshua ben Hananiah and the emperor.[65] These conversations must be regarded as legendary, echoing perhaps some negotiations at a time unknown to us. It may have been in 117, when Hadrian was first in Judaea; or perhaps on his visit to the East in 123.

Those who find some clue by referring to Hadrian's reputation as a man of changeable moods[66] may do so; but to my mind this does not explain very much.

Epigraphic evidence enables us to declare with a fair amount of certainty that early in his regime (at the beginning of the twenties) Hadrian took some very energetic measures in favor of Hellenic culture, not least in Greece itself. He it was who revived the panhellenic idea (in the year 125) and was later given the title *Panhellenios* along with the honorific *Olympios*.

So far as Palestine is concerned, we have already cited the Tiberian coins, and the statement by Epiphanius supported by other evidence about Greek temples in Tiberias, Neapolis and Jerusalem. So it is possible that those who suggest that the gentile minorities in those places were given control of the city government, are right; and it may be that the growth of insurrectionary movements in the country during the decade of the twenties is traceable to this policy of hellenization which seems to have characterized Hadrian's whole approach to the role of the empire at that time.

---

64 Encyclopedia Eshkol (Hebrew) s.v. *Adrianus*.
65 Shab. 119a; Hul. 59b; Bekh. 8b; et passim; *pace* Bacher, *Die Agada der Tannaiten*, Strassbourg, 1903, vol. I, p. 171.
66 E.g. Domaszewski, *Geschichte der römischen Kaiser*, 1909, II p. 177. [The reputation was probably established by Spartianus, when he described the emperor as "semper in omnibus varius."]

CHAPTER TWENTY-FOUR

THE BAR KOKHBA WAR

Before we survey the war itself, and the various problems connected therewith, it would be well to examine the two principal narrative accounts. First, Dio Cassius: [1]

> At Jerusalem he (*i.e. Hadrian*) founded a city in place of the one which had been razed to the ground, naming it Aelia Capitolina, and on the site of the temple of the god he raised a new temple to Jupiter. This brought on a war of no slight importance nor of brief duration, for the Jews deemed it intolerable that foreign races should be settled in their city and foreign religious rites planted there. So long, indeed, as Hadrian was close by in Egypt and again in Syria, they remained quiet, save insofar as they purposely made of poor quality such weapons as they were called upon to furnish, in order that the Romans might reject them and that they themselves might thus have the use of them; but when he went farther away they openly revolted. To be sure, they did not dare try conclusions with the Romans in the open field, but they occupied the advantageous positions in the country and strengthened them with mines and walls, in order that they might have places of refuge whenever they should be hard pressed, and might meet together unobserved underground; and they pierced these subterranean passages from above at intervals to let in air and light At first the Romans took no account of them. Soon, however, all Judaea had been stirred up, and the Jews everywhere were showing signs of disturbance, were gathering together, and giving evidence of great hostility to the Romans, partly by secret

1 *Roman History,* LXIX: 12, 1 ff; [Cary VIII, pp. 447 ff. Comp. GLA II, no. 440.]

and partly by overt acts; many outside nations, too, were joining them through eagerness for gain, and the whole earth, one might almost say, was being stirred up over the matter. Then indeed, Hadrian sent against them his best generals. First of these was Julius Severus, who was dispatched from Britain, where he was governor, against the Jews. Severus did not venture to attack his opponents in the open at any one point, in view of their numbers and their desperation, but by intercepting small groups, thanks to the number of his soldiers and his under-officers, and by depriving them of food and shutting them up, he was able, rather slowly, to be sure, but with comparatively little danger, to crush, exhaust and exterminate them. Very few of them in fact survived. Fifty of their most important outposts and nine hundred and eighty five of their most famous villages were razed to the ground. Five hundred and eighty thousand men were slain in the various raids and battles, and the number of those that perished by famine, disease and fire was past finding out. Thus nearly the whole of Judaea was made desolate, a result of which the people had had forewarning before the war. For the tomb of Solomon, which the Jews regard as an object of veneration, fell to pieces of itself and collapsed, and many wolves and hyenas rushed howling into their cities. Many Romans, moreover, perished in this war. Therefore Hadrian in writing to the senate did not employ the opening phrase commonly affected by emperors, "If you and your children are in health, it is well; I and the legions are in health."

Second, the early Christian historian Eusebius:[2]

The rebellion of the Jews once more progressed in character and extent, and Rufus, the governor of Judaea, when military aid had been sent him by the Emperor, moved out against them, treating their madness without mercy. He destroyed in heaps thousands of men women and children, and under

2 *Ecclesiastical History*, IV. vi1–4 [Lake I, p. 311 f.]

the law of war, enslaved their land. The Jews were at that time led by a certain Bar Cochebas, which means "star," a man who was murderous and a bandit, but relied on his name, as if dealing with slaves, and claimed to be a luminary who had come down to them from heaven and was magically enlightening those who were in misery. The war reached its height in the eighteenth year of the reign of Hadrian in Beththera, which was a strong citadel not very far from Jerusalem; the siege lasted a long time before the rebels were driven to final destruction by famine and thirst, and the instigator of their madness paid the penalty he deserved. Hadrian then commanded that by a legal decree and ordinances the whole nation should be absolutely prevented from entering from thenceforth even the district round Jerusalem, so that not even from a distance could it see its ancestral home. Ariston of Pella tells the story. Thus when the city came to be bereft of the nation of the Jews, and its ancient inhabitants had completely perished, it was colonized by foreigners, and the Roman city which afterwards arose changed its name, and in honour of the reigning emperor Aelius Hadrian was called Aelia. The church, too, in it was composed of Gentiles, and after the circumcised Jewish bishops the first who was appointed to minister to those there was Marcus.

These two principal sources seem to complement one another. Dio describes the war in broad outline — the dimensions of the uprising and its reverberations outside Judaea; the tactics of the opposing armies and the enormous casualties on both sides. Eusebius, on the other hand, fills in with certain details about the leader of the Jewish rebels and his messianic pretentions; tells something about the scene of the last battle at Beitar, and reports the exclusion of the Jews from the Jerusalem district in the aftermath.

But a second glance shows that neither of them tells us anything at all about the actual course of the war, although Dio is ostensibly writing a summary of it. A search of all other available sources leaves us equally without any real military history of the several years of hard fighting.[3] Keeping this in mind, we must still ask our ourselves what seem to be the *probable* answers to the following questions:

a) Where was the theater of war? In the whole country? Part of it?
b) Were the Samaritans involved?
c) What Roman forces were committed?
d) What was the course of the action?
e) Did Jerusalem change hands?
f) How were the rebels organized, militarily and politically?
g) What was the attitude of the Sages to the revolt?
h) What were the punitive Roman edicts after the defeat?[4]

THE THEATER OF WAR

Because the sources are not explicit on this point, there has been room for difference of opinion among scholars. Adolph Büchler made a thorough study of this question, using all the sources available to him.[5] He concluded that all the fighting took place in the south-central region — *Yehudah*, or Judaea proper.[6] The other two principal regions, Galilee and Transjordan, were, according to him, *not* scenes of action.

Some of Büchler's arguments seem to me quite definitive, others less so; but I believe that in the main he has been able to make

---

3 [The dramatic discoveries in the desert caves have illuminated many details of life during the Bar Kokhba War, and validated some facts which were suspected to be mere rhetoric (like the leader's real name, *bar Koziba*). But in the main, Alon's statement above still holds good. For a review of the state of Bar Kokhba studies to date, see the running commentary by Menahem Stern on Cassius Dio in "Greek and Latin Authors on Jews and Judaism," Vol. II, Jerusalem 1980, pp. 393 ff., especially p. 394.]

4 [Alon's notes indicate that he intended to discuss as well the demographic and economic aftereffects of the war; the traditions about postwar martyrdom among the Sages; and a number of related topics. He did not live to fulfill these intentions.]

5 *"Die Schauplatz des Barkokhbakrieges"* in JQR o.s. XVI (1904), pp. 143–205.

6 [We have adopted this term from Menahem Stern, to distinguish Judaea the region from Judaea the country.]

a case for the conclusion that the focus of military operations and their center of gravity lay in Judaea proper.[7]

Büchler's chief point of departure is the fact that Dio Cassius speaks only of war in "Judaea." The assumption here is that Dio uses this term in the specific, limited sense, meaning one of the three regions into which the country was divided — Judaea, Transjordan (Arabia) and Galilee. The country as a whole, by the time Dio wrote, was known by its new name "Palaestina."

But it must be objected, to begin with, that there is no proof at all that Dio uses the term in its limited sense. Actually, it can be shown that he uses the country's old name (Judaea) interchangeably with its new official one (*Syria Palaestina*). And it certainly seems reasonable to assume that he would revert to the old name when speaking of events that took place before the new one was decreed.

Another thing — the name "Judaea" for a region is a Jewish usage. If memory serves, there is no instance in the whole of non-Jewish literature where the word is used in that limited sense. You do find it so used in tannaitic literature; in Josephus; in the Gospels; in the Acts of the Apostles — all works emanating from Jewish circles. It is therefore difficult to ascribe the usage to Dio Cassius.[8]

On the other hand, Büchler presents some very solid arguments when he cites Jewish sources speaking of the "war in Judaea."[9]

---

7 Essentially the same view had been presented by Derenbourg in his *Essai* (1867) pp. 427 ff. The contrary opinion is put forward by Schlatter, who argues for a wider field of operations, including Galilee; see his *Die Tage Trajans und Hadrians,* and his article in ZDPV 1933, pp. 180–184.

8 [But Stern is able to cite one passage from Pliny (and a possible one from Mela) where Judaea is used in the restricted sense. See GLA II, p. 403.]

9 Sifre Deut. 322, Finkelstein p. 372: "Once during the war in Judaea (*pulmus she-bi-yehudah*) a Roman decurio on horseback was chasing a Jew." And in the next paragraph: "It happened in Judaea (*Yehudah*) that flies betrayed them (the rebels)." Sifre Deut. 323, Finkelstein p. 373. This must mean that Jewish fugitives or fighters during the Bar Kokhba War, hiding from the Romans in caves [or in the tunnels described by Dio?] were given away by flies swarming near the air-

And strikingly enough, with reference to the effects of the fighting, we find the phrase "When Judaea was devastated."[10] It is true that there are instances where "Judaea" (*Yehudah*) is used as a contrast to "Diaspora" (*Golah*), and in such cases it certainly does mean the country as a whole.[11] This fact, which Büchler does not mention, might be thought to vitiate his argument; but I do not feel it has a bearing on the examples he cites. In any case, there are tannaitic sources which can be read only in the sense of "Yehudah" = Judaea proper, and not "Yehudah" = the country as a whole.

Take the passages dealing with the Law of the *Sikarikon* (clearing the title of land whose owners had been killed in the revolt). The Mishnah says the law did not apply in *Yehudah* until the time when Jews were killed in the war;[12] the Tosefta says that in Galilee, the Law of Sikarikon never applied.[13] In this instance there can be no doubt. In this Mishnah, *Yehudah* means "Judaea proper."

This is further proven by a comment in the Yerushalmi on the same Mishnah:[14]

> At first they (*sc. the Romans*) decreed destruction (*shemad*) on Judaea, for they had it as a tradition from their forbears that the Patriarch Judah had slain Esau (*their ancestor*) as Scripture says, "Thy hand shall be on the neck of thy foes" (Gen. 49:8) so they proceeded to enslave them and to seize their fields etc. ...

Here there can be no doubt that the intent of the homily is to refer to the territory of the ancient tribe of Judah exclusively — Judaea proper. A slightly different version of the same tradition elsewhere in the Yerushalmi yields the same result.[15]

holes. [See now Amos Kloner: "The Subterranean Hideaways of the Judaean Foothills and the Bar Kokhba Revolt," in The *Jerusalem Cathedra*, no. 3, Ben Zvi Institute, Jerusalem 1983, pp. 113 et seq.]

10 Tos. Ter. X:15. (43)
11 E.g. Tos. Sot. VI:11. (306)
12 Git. V:6.
13 Tos. Git. V:I (328); also Yer. ibid. V:47b.
14 Ibid.
15 Yer. Ket. I:25c.

To be sure, most of the persecutory decrees that the Romans imposed after the revolt had been put down were applied to the entire country. But it seems that things were not quite so bad up in the north. The hand of the occupying powers was a little less heavy in that part of the country.

It is also true that the much-quoted tradition about "the *boula'ot* (*town councils*) in Judaea"[16] most probably refers to Judaea proper — a point which Büchler makes.[17]

Another significant consideration is the well-known removal of both the Sanhedrin and the Patriarchate to Galilee after the war. One can only conclude that the Galilee had not been ravaged by the war the way the South had. Then too, there is the evidence provided by Jerome, who describes devastated locations in the country which he himself saw (in the 5th century) — all of them in Judaea proper.

It has been suggested that the important Galilean city of Sepphoris *did* take part in the revolt, and was punished for this disloyalty by being turned into a Greek *polis* and renamed Diocaesarea[18] But it is obvious that this need not necessarily be so. The new name of the place can just as easily have been given to it *before* the war, the way Aelia Capitolina was given to Jerusalem. In fact, there is good reason to believe that Sepphoris took no part at all in the revolt. As Hill points out, the coins of that city minted during the reign of Antoninus Pius bear the legend (lacunae given their probable readings) : *DIO*(caesarea) *AUTO*(noma) *PIS*(te) *PHILE*[19] — "Diocaesarea, Autonomous, Loyal, Friendly."

In the sources which we do have, certain place names are mentioned in connection with battles which were fought during the war. Beitar and Jerusalem are the most obvious. Har Hamelekh and Tur Malka are also clearly terms for the central Judaean massif.

16 E.g. Git. 37a; comp. "the 24 *boula'ot* in Judaea which were destroyed" (Yer. Ned. IV:35d).
17 To be sure, there are those who maintain that these councils were wiped out in the first war with Rome, 66–70; see S. Klein in the Chayes Festschrift (Hebrew) pp. 279 ff. But note JLTA I, p. 146–7.
18 See Yeivin, Interim Report on the Excavations at Sepphoris.
19 [This is a transliteration of the Greek inscription.]

It is otherwise with an episode involving Kefar Haroba.[20] There is a place with that name eastwards of the Sea of Galilee. But there is also a place bearing the same name in Judaea, southeast of Lod. Then we have the names of three locations where Hadrian situated garrisons: Hamatha, Kefar Laqitia and Bethlehem of Yahud.[21] The third of these is obvious. Where to locate the second is uncertain. As for the first, Hamatha, its location has given rise to a certain amount of disagreement. Schlatter thought it was just another name for Emmaus, and Klein agreed.[22] Büchler, on the other hand, rejected this identification, and pointed instead to Hamath in Judaea, basing himself on another midrash. However, the text in Buber's edition of Lamentations Rabbah reads *Hamtha d'Gader* — which leaves the identity of the place pretty much up in the air. So too, the Vale of Beth Rimmon is problematical, although it might conceivably be located in Judaea.

As for those places mentioned as having been destroyed along with Beitar,[23] there is this to say: Kefar Shiḥlia, Kefar Bish and Kefar Dikhrin are all in Judaea proper. The same can be said for Gophna. Three other places mentioned in the same aggadot — Kevush, Shihin and Migdal Zevieh — are all in Galilee; but I agree with Büchler when he says there is no proof that the traditions about these places refer necessarily to the Bar Kokhba War. In both the Yerushalmi and Lamentations Rabbah traditions about the the two wars are recorded side by side. The Galilean place names may well go back to traditions about the earlier war, the war of Vespasian and Titus.[24]

Having presented evidence and arguments to prove that the war was fought out in Judaea proper, we must now weigh such evidence as there is to the contrary — namely, that Galilee too was the scene of action during the Bar Kokhba War.

20 LamR II:5. In *Yalqut Ha'azinu* the name has been changed, by error, to Kefar Hananiah.
21 LamR ed. Buber, p. 82; current editions read "Beth El of Yahud."
22 *Leshonenu* III, p. 270; *Sefer Ha-Yishuv* p. 47.
23 Yer. Taan. IV:69a; LamR ibid.
24 A similar line is followed by S. Klein in *Neue Beiträge zur Geschichte und Geographie Galiläas*, 1927, pp. 79–94; see also his *Eretz Ha-Galil*, pp. 52–54.

Our first witness is Sulpicius Severus, writing at the beginning of the fifth century, who states that the Jews attempted to rebel during the reign of Hadrian, and tried to wrest Syria and Palestine away (*Syriam ac Palaestinam diripere conati*).[25] From this it would follow that all of Palestine — and Syria as well — got involved in the fight.

Büchler was aware of the difficulty which this posed to his own contrary conclusion. He suggested, however, that the text of Sulpicius Severus had become garbled; that he had originally written "Syriam Palaestinam," using the official Roman name decreed by the Empire to replace the name "Judaea" after the suppression of the revolt. While this proposed emendation cannot be proven, it sounds very reasonable to me. But we are still left with Dio's testimony that non-Jews joined in the fight against Rome. Besides, there may well have been places in Syria where there were large Jewish populations who joined in the fray. The verdict on this evidence must be that it is inconclusive.

Another curious bit of testimony, not mentioned by Büchler, comes from Jerome. In one of his works he writes:

> Because the Jews *in the Galilee* rebelled again, he destroyed the remnants of that city (*Jerusalem*).[26]

But I am inclined to think that Jerome is not to be taken too literally on that point. He probably wrote in terms of the situation as it existed in his own days, when the Jewish population was concentrated in the Galilee. It is also possible that the Jewish anti-government riots of the year 351, under Gallus, which were definitely centered in Galilee, influenced Jerome's phrasing.

We turn now to a passage in the Yerushalmi dealing with the Biblical law of the produce forgotten by the harvester, which must be left for the gleaners.[27] The Mishnah cites Rabbi Jose, who says that this law does not apply to olive trees.[28]

---

25 *Historia Sacra*, II; 31; P.L. 30, 146.
26 "De Nativitate Domini" in Morin, *Anecdota Maredsolana*, vol. III, pp. 396–7.
27 Deut. XXIV:19.
28 Peah VII:1.

Rabbi Simeon bar Yaqim said: Rabbi Jose ruled thus only with respect to those early days when olive trees were rare, because Hadrian the Wicked had come and devastated the whole country.[29]

Faced with this tradition, which runs counter to his thesis that Hadrian destroyed only Judaea proper, and not the olive country of Galilee, Büchler suggests that Rabbi Simeon is not quoting a historical memory, but rather citing a legal argument advanced by Rabbi Jose to justify his position that olive trees are exempt from the law.

However, I do not find this convincing. I would doubt that Rabbi Jose, himself a Galilean of the second century, would say anything about his native region that did not conform in every detail to the realities in that section of the country.[30] What is more, Rabbi Jose appears in the Tosefta as a man very much aware of the deterioration of agriculture after the Bar Kokhba War, and very much concerned about it, and about the effect of meagre rainfall on crops.[31] Apparently, then, he is to be taken seriously when he speaks of the falling off of olive production in the Galilee as a result of the war. What we cannot conclude is that the damage in the north was as severe as it was in Judaea proper.

Rabbi Jose was born in Sepphoris. He has left us a deposition about what happened to that Galilean center of population and commerce.[32]

Rabbi Jose said: I saw Sepphoris in the days of its serene prosperity (*shalvatah*). It had eighty[33] dealers who sold only one kind of pudding.

29 Klein suggested reading "Vespasian" for "Hadrian" (*Eretz Ha-Galil*, p. 52) but without substantiating his proposal. It is true that the Bavli frequently confuses these two emperors, as do late midrashim; but that cannot be said of the Yerushalmi.

30 Büchler's attempt to make something out of the peculiar usage *Kol ha-'areṣ*, on the ground that the Hebrew phrase usually means "the whole world," — comes to nothing in the light of ms. Rome, which reads *kol ereṣ Yisrael*.

31 Tos. Shevi. VII:18 (72).

32 B.B. 75b.

33 Or "180 markets for. ..." The mss. vary.

What Rabbi Jose is telling us is that in his lifetime the once-flourishing center went downhill economically, and its population dwindled. It is reasonable to conclude that this deterioration followed on the heels of the Bar Kokhba war.

Evidence of a similar nature is presented by the following:

> Rabbi Simeon Shezuri said: My father's family were men of substance in the Galilee. Why were their holdings ruined? etc . . .[34]

Here again, a word of caution is in order. We cannot be absolutely sure that the economic ruin did not set in with the first war against Rome.

Turning to epigraphy, we can produce at least two inscriptions which seem to prove that the fighting *did* spread to Galilee. The first marks the burial place of a soldier of the XIVth Legion (Gemina) who died at Geder.[35] Since this legion was not normally stationed in Palestine, it must be assumed that it, or some elements of it, were detached for service in the Bar Kokhba war.

Another Latin inscription on a soldier's grave was found in Beth Shean. This man, a Macedonian, served in the XIth Legion (Claudia) which almost certainly saw action at Beitar. It would seem, then that a *vexillatio* of this legion was stationed at Beth Shean — from which it appears that there was some military activity in that northern part of the country around that time.[36]

This survey of all the available evidence leads to the conclusion that the war was not completely confined to Judaea proper. In Galilee as well as in Transjordan there were acts of rebellion and defiance of Rome. If that summation is accepted, then the state-

---

34 Tos. B.Q. VIII:14 (362). Shezur is on the border between Lower and Upper Galilee. The reading in ms. Erfurt (Rabbi Ishmael) is mistaken. Comp. Bavli B.Q. 80a; Yer. Sot. IX:24a.
35 Corpus Inscript, Lat. II. no. 1291; see Ritterling in Pauly-Wissowa vol. 12, s.v. *legio*, p. 1747; and Jeremias in ZDPV, 1932, p. 78.
36 The epitaph was published by Michael Avi-Yonah in the Quarterly of the Department of Antiquities in Palestine, vol. 8, 1938, p. 57. Avi-Yonah assumed that the soldier died in action; but that remains unproven. In any event, the inscription from Geder confirms the reading *Hamatha d'Geder* referred to above.

ment by Cassius Dio about the very large number of villages and fortresses destroyed in the fighting falls into place, and becomes believable.[37]

However, it seems that outside Judaea proper the revolt did not last very long; that it never became as concentrated elsewhere, nor as intense. And in the final, decisive stages, the whole brunt of the battle was borne by the South. Furthermore, the major Galilean cities — Tiberias and Sepphoris — apparently did not join in the fighting, so that such rebels as there were in that part of the country were left without large centers of population to serve as bases of operations.

It is also possible that socio-economic conditions made the Galilee less fertile soil for the rebellion. A considerable element of the population there seems to have been willing to accept Roman rule, and to co-operate with it. Hence, no doubt, the short duration of the Galilean phase of the revolt. Even so, the war did not pass without leaving economic and political scars on the Galilee, even if they were not as devastating as those which marked Judaea proper.

Did the Samaritans Fight?

Scholars have differed on this question, some claiming that the Samaritans did participate in the Second War against Rome, while others have come to the opposite conclusion. Perhaps we should review the evidence.

First, there is the well-known legend of the Samaritan at Beitar who brought about Bar Kokhba's downfall by insinuating that Rabbi Eleazar HaModai was guilty of treason.[38] It has been

---

37 ["It is scarcely conceivable that the Jews of Galilee held aloof from the revolt completely." Smallwood, op. cit. p. 442. This is her summation, after reviewing the evidence pro and con. Stern, GLA II, pp. 402–3, musters the arguments and evidence for activity outside Judaea, and concludes: "Nevertheless, the revolt only spread in a very limited way into other parts of the country, being centered mainly on Judaea proper." Thus, both Smallwood and Stern, from opposite perspectives, arrive at approximately the same conclusion as Alon. See also above, note 7.]

38 Yer. Taan. IV:68d; LamR II:12.

argued that this proves the Samaritans were on the side of Rome. On the contrary, say others; how could a Samaritan have come to Beitar and talked to Rabbi Eleazar unless the Samaritans were trusted allies of the Jewish fighters?

Actually, it is probable that neither argument holds water. The whole legend is doubtless just another of those folk stereotypes that label the Samaritans as traitorous informers and devious conspirators.

Then there is the fact that the Samaritans, too, suffered from the Romans. They were forbidden to circumcise their children, and a temple to Zeus (or Serapis) was erected on their holy Mount Gerizim. But these facts do not prove that they took part in the revolt. The ban on circumcision predated the war, while the pagan shrine could have been planned and built — like Aelia Capitolina — in the year 130. The work may have been completed later, but not necessarily as a punishment for rebellion.

The evidence provided by the Samaritan Chronicles is late, and contains inner contradictions. For example, the Samaritan *Book of Josua* says that when Hadrian returned from Egypt to "Arabia" and Palestine, he laid siege to Jerusalem. Two Samaritans from Kefar Yashuv entered the city by stealth and helped the Roman subdue it. That means that not only did the Samaritans not support the Jews in their revolt — they helped their enemies.

On the other hand, the same source has Hadrian planning to destroy Shechem. Furthermore, the Samaritans, in accordance with their ritual and custom purify by fire every spot where Hadrian had trod. It was the Jews, they say, who informed against them, leading the emperor to forbid circumcision, *tevillah* (immersion) and the observance of Sabbaths and festivals! Shechem, the Samaritan capital, is destroyed, and the Samaritans take refuge in the countryside. Their religious leaders are crucified and left unburied. Others are slaughtered in fortresses. This account of Samaritan suffering is substantially repeated in the Adler Chronicle.[39]

All this indicates that the Samaritans *were* allied with the Jews in the second revolt against Rome. A remark by the Church Father

39   See **REJ** vol. 49, pp. 49–81.

Eusebius seems to confirm this:

The temples in Jerusalem and on Mount Gerizim were both destroyed in the war of Vespasian and Hadrian.[40]

Since there is no other record that the temple on Gerizim was destroyed during the days of Vespasian,[41] it seems probable that Eusebius was in possession of a tradition about a Samaritan war during the reign of Hadrian, in the wake of which the shrine on Gerizim was razed, and a pagan temple put up in its place.

On the other hand, Theodoritus, writing in the 5th century, claims that the Samaritans were the eternal enemies of the Jews and fought against them on the side of Rome. He does not, however, specify the Bar Kokhba revolt. If indeed his remarks are based on anything historical, it may be the "Samaritan-Jewish War" at the time when Septimius Severus was embroiled with Pescennius Niger in the year 193.

One attempt to prove that the Samaritans did *not* take part in the revolt is based on the remark by Rabbi Abbahu: "Thirteen towns were absorbed by the Cutheans in the days of the *shemad* (Hadrianic persecutions)."[42] So apparently, the Samaritans did well at that time. But I don't think that is what Rabbi Abbahu meant. The tradition he transmitted should probably be explained in the light of the fact that after the war the Samaritan population gradually increased and spilled over into Jewish areas, which then became mixed areas. One primary cause of this was the reduction of the Jewish population after the Bar Kokhba War, especially in small towns bordering on Samaria. Because this happened in the aftermath of the war, the tradition connected it with the *shemad*.

If these conflicting literary witnesses leave the question unanswered, the epigraphic evidence gives us the right to conclude that the Samaritans *were* actively rebellious against the Romans, who were forced to station troops in centers of population in Samaria. There is, for example, the epitaph found just east of Shechem on the grave of a Roman soldier who belonged to a

---

40 Eusebius, *Theophany* (Syriac), ed. Lee, London, 1842.
41 Josephus, JW III:7:32 (307–15) does speak of a Roman massacre of Samaritans, but does not mention their temple.
42 Yer. Yev. VIII:9d and Qid. IV:65c.

centurio of the Vth Legion, Macedonian.[43] Abel is probably right in surmising that the inscription dates from the Bar Kokhba War, since that is the only time we have record of the Vth Macedonian being stationed in Palestine.[44] So we can assume that units of that legion had been quartered in Shechem to preserve order in a place where order needed preserving.

Samaria has also yielded a dedicatory inscription, which reads (after the missing letters have been filled in):

> To Jupiter the Most Beneficent, soldiers of the detachment of the Cohort from Upper Pannonia, citizens of Siscia and tribesmen of the Latobici and Varciani, have erected this altar.[45]

Paleography indicates that this inscription belongs to the second century. Vincent, who first deciphered it, rejected the possibility that it could have emanated from the Bar Kokhba War. His argument: Samaria (the city) was of no strategic importance; and the Samaritans, who populated the place, hated the Jews and could therefore not have participated in their war against Rome.

But Vincent's proof does not convince, and the opposite seems more likely. The inscription probably does date from the Bar Kokhba War, because that is when other soldiery from Pannonia were in the country. This conclusion is shared by Kubitschek and by Alföldi who studied the inscription at various times.[46]

The presence in Samaria of Roman troops brought in during a war from far-off places invites comparison with what had happened during the War of the Destruction. Then, as we know, there was a great concentration of Samaritans at Mount Gerizim, bent on rebellion. At that time, as Josephus tells us, "the whole of Samaria was already occupied by garrisons."[47] It makes sense, because from the very beginning of that war there were indications that the Samaritans were restive, until finally they came out in open insurrection. It is a reasonable assumption that those instan-

43 Revue Biblique, XXIV p. 421.
44 Ibid. p. 427.
45 See revision by Blackmann in ZDPV 1913, p. 223.
46 See Antiquité Classique 7 (1938) pp. 81–85 and ZDPV, 1913, p. 223.
47 JW III:7:32 (309).

ces of movement between Jerusalem and Galilee during the First War, such as the southward flight of John of Gischala and his rather large following to Jerusalem, or the journey northward of the emissaries of the Sanhedrin to the Galilee, accompanied by a Jewish military escort — such movement had to pass through Samaria, and required at least some degree of co-operation from the Samaritans.

So one must come to the conclusion that the old enmity between the Jews and the Samaritans was not enough to keep them from joining hands against their common enemy, the Romans. As we have already noted, the two peoples drew somewhat closer during the two generations between the War of the Destruction and the Bar Kokhba War. Most of the Sages were willing to classify the Samaritans as Jews — "righteous proselytes." Their role during the War of the Destruction may well have won them that confidence.

Even more telling is the statement by the Patriarch Rabban Simeon ben Gamaliel, leader of the Sanhedrin in the generation immediately after the Bar Kokhba War:

> Those mitzvot which the Samaritans observe, they observe much more carefully than we Jews do.[48]

This Patriarch reveals his positive attitude toward the Samaritans when he says: "The Samaritans are like Jews."[49]

As for Vincent's argument that Samaria has no strategic importance — the Romans were not there for reasons of strategy. They were there to keep the Samaritans in check — to keep them from bursting out of their hill-country and helping the Jews.

To sum up: it can be said that most of the Samaritans did not rebel. But there were not a few — "from among the youth," in the words of the Adler Chronicle — who took steps aimed at joining the Jewish rebels; something like what had happened in the earlier war, or perhaps a little more this time. For all practical purposes, however, their main contribution to the war effort was to keep a certain number of Roman troops tied down in Samaria.[50]

48 Tos. Pes. I:15 (156).
49 Tos. Ter. IV:14 (32); and frequently in the Yerushalmi.
50 ["The Samaritans may not have participated in the revolt, but they

THE ROMAN FORCES

Over and above the description of the war by Dio Cassius as "of no slight importance nor of brief duration," there is evidence of the magnitude of the conflict in the large number of military formations which the Romans committed to the struggle. All the evidence consists of Greek and Latin inscriptions, most of which describe the service records of Roman military personnel and list their decorations.[51]

It is often difficult to determine from a particular inscription whether the entire legion mentioned therein took part, or only a detachment (*vexillatio*) of it. There are even cases where it is possible to wonder whether any elements at all of the named legion participated, or only one "seconded" individual.

The Roman forces that participated in the war can be grouped as follows: A. Legions. B. Reinforcement Units (*Auxi'ia*), C. Naval Forces.

Under normal conditions, it was Roman military practice to keep a specific military formation in one or another part of the Empire on a permanent basis, moving it when required, and then returning it to home base as a permanent garrison. The legions and auxiliary units that were brought to Judaea in the Bar Kokhba War came from the following garrisons: 1) Local (= Judaea); 2) Arabia (= Transjordan); 3) Egypt; 4) Syria; 5) Africa; 6) The Danube Basin (Dacia, Moesia, Pannonia etc.); 7) Britain.

What follows is a listing of the Roman formations mentioned, by countries of origin — that is, by the countries which were normally their permanent stations.

1. Judaea: Legio X Fretensis. A centurion of this outfit was decorated for valor. The legion had long been, and continued to be, quartered in Judaea.

2. Arabia: Legion III Cyrenaica.

worshipped the Jewish God, on whose cult the revolt had centered. The desecration of their sacred place can be seen as a precaution rather than a punishment." Smallwood, op. cit. p. 462.]

51 [For a comparative table of the Roman forces on the Bar Kokhba front, according to 1) Schürer (Vermes-Millar pp. 547 ff); 2) Alon (here); and 3) Yeivin (The Bar Kokhba War, 1946) — see J. Meyshan in *Palestine Exploration Quarterly* (Hebrew 1958, pp. 19 ff.)]

3. Egypt: a) Legio II Traiana.
   b) Legio XXIII Deioteriana. (It is generally agreed that this legion was wiped out in the Bar Kokhba War, because from this time forward its name disappears from the roster of Roman military formations)[52]
4. Syria: a) Legio III Gallica
   b) Legio VI Ferrata (possibly). This legion was stationed in the Jezreel Valley after the war, so it may have participated.[53]
   c) Legio IV Scythica;
   d) Legio V Macedonica; (possibly).[54]

In connection with the involvement of the Roman garrison in Syria in the Bar Kokhba War, attention should be paid to inscriptions that put the Roman governor of Syria in Judaea during the war. It is a reasonable assumption that he led the troops from his eparchy under his command — the governor was also C-in-C — into action. A Greek inscription found at Ankara reads:

> In honor of Gaius Julius Severus, scion of Kings and princes . . . who served as legate in Asia by virtue of the missive and writ of appointment issued by the divine Hadrian; chief of the Fourth Scythian Legion; and who administered the government of Syria while Publicius Marcellus was out of the country on account of the Jewish war etc. etc. . . .

5. Africa: Legio III Augusta (Mauretania).
6. Danubia: a) Legio X Gemina.
   b) Legio XIII.
   c) Legio XIV.
   d) Legio XI Claudia.
   e) Legio VII (possibly).

As for lesser units, there is evidence that some of them came in as auxiliaries from as far away as Britain.

---

52 [For discussion of the fate of this lost legion, see Stern in GLA II, p. 398.]
53 [See GLA II, pp. 396–7.]
54 ["There is clear evidence for the presence in Palestine of *vexillationes* from . . . Legio V Macedonica . . . from an inscription found near Beitar." Stern, GLA II, p. 399.]

a) A cohort of cavalry from Britain, Cohors IV Lingonum, has left signs of having been stabled at Emmaus.[55]
b) From Arabia, there was a cohort called Cohors VI Ulpia Petr(?)
c) An inscription found in Nazareth, and dated in the year 139, lists men with honorable discharges. It mentions three different "wings" *(alae)* of cavalry and twelve cohorts of infantry that were encamped in Syria-Palaestina. Doubtless many of them took part in the war which had ended only four years earlier.
d) Cohorts from far-off Pannonia on the Danube are mentioned in an inscription from Sebaste (Samaria). At least three of them can be identified.

NAVAL FORCES

A well-known inscription mentions the *Praefectus classis Syriacae* who was decorated for service in the Bar Kokhba War. But we know of no naval action. If there was any, the rebels must have held a part of the coastline — say, around Jaffa — for about a year, and must have had some gentile allies.

Summing up, it appears that the Romans used twelve or thirteen legions, or elements thereof, in putting down the revolt, not to speak of numerous auxiliary troops. These were forces vastly greater than those used by Rome in the War of the Destruction, which amounted to three or four legions plus auxiliaries. The extent of military power now brought to bear has been remarked upon by modern historians.[56] It is a measure of the intensity of the revolt, and a testimony to the bravery and the fighting ability of the rebels.

THE COURSE OF THE WAR

The sources at our disposal do not provide us with enough data to map out the military campaigns, not even in the most general terms; neither from an operational nor from an administrative point of view. Consequently, we can only speculate about the most

---

55 A legion was normally divided into ten cohorts. A cavalry wing *(ala)* consisted of 500 or 1,000 horsemen, divided into 16 or 24 squadrons *(turmae)*.
56 E.g. Domaszewski, op. cit. II, p. 130. [In this connection, see Stern's note in GLA II, p. 400, especially his quotation from Mommsen.]

likely answers to certain specific questions which have given rise to some amount of confusion and disagreement.

How was the revolt organized? The report by Cassius Dio quoted at the beginning of this chapter indicates that the Jews made secret preparations over a long period of time. These preparations included the storing of arms, the fortifying of positions throughout the country, and the readying of communications and transit systems between these positions. What emerges from this description is the picture of a unified general plan, at least for the first stages of the war.

The account given by Eusebius makes it appear that the rebels had a unified, centralized command, under Bar Kokhba, from the very beginning. This would be in sharp contrast to the war of 66, which broke out completely unplanned and unexpected, and was quite disorganized in its early stages. It stands in even sharper contrast to the spontaneous, scattered uprisings put down by the Syrian legate Varus in the year 4 B.C.E., following on Herod's death. If the historical tradition passed on to us by the gentile historians reflects what really happened, then it will have to be admitted that the Jewish insurrectionary movement had learned some hard lessons during a century plus of resistance to Roman rule.

It is the opinion of a number of modern Jewish historians, especially Graetz, that the travels of Rabbi Akiba to many parts of the Diaspora were connected with preparations for the Bar Kokhba revolt. An itinerary of the countries he visited would include Cilicia, Cappadocia, Phoenicia, Arabia, Africa, Media and Mesopotamia. And since Rabbi Akiba turned out to be a strong supporter of Bar Kokhba, the idea suggests itself that his journeys must have had something to do with the coming struggle.[57]

But Halevy was probably right when he rejected this hypothesis.[58] Akiba's travels, he said, were for religious purposes: he had no political or military aims. All indications are that they took place even before the Trajanic uprisings, and a long time before the Bar Kokhba Revolt.

---

57 See Graetz, *Geschichte*, IV⁴ chap. 8, p. 135; comp. JLTA I, p. 236.
58 *Dorot Ha-Rishonim*, Part I, Vol. V, pp. 620 ff.

Indeed, there is room for doubt as to the complete accuracy of the reports provided by Cassius Dio and Eusebius. We can take it as correct, for example, that as the war progressed Bar Kokhba took overall command into his hands, without necessarily believing that he planned it in advance and directed all its operations from the start in a completely coordinated fashion. It is equally reasonable to be a little skeptical about Dio's description of the meticulously planned operations of the rebels. It seems much more likely that the whole thing started as a series of spontaneous local outbursts led by autonomous leaders, as had happened in previous wars. The difference this time was the early coalescence of all rebel forces under a unified general command, and especially the emergence of a charismatic leader — Bar Kokhba — who was able to gain control of the rebellion and of the rebels, and to direct them with a firm and decisive hand. Herein lies the principal explanation for the power and duration of this revolt. Centralization led to effectiveness in the planning and execution of operations, and helped create that discipline which is one of the products of sound organization.

This view of the revolt as having begun in a series of scattered acts of rebellion fits in well with the idea suggested earlier, namely that there were a lot of uncoordinated rebel movements in the country before the actual outbreak of war. The same conception seems to underlie the aggadic traditions in talmud and midrash. One such is the story about the two brothers in Kefar Haruba who conducted successful guerilla warfare against the Romans. People said: "We ought to put crowns on their heads!" An old man met them, and said: "May your Creator help you!" Said they: "Let Him not help nor hinder — 'For Thou, O Lord, hast forsaken us!' (Ps. 60:12)."[59]

Apparently, then, there were local "crowned leaders" just as there were, according to Josephus, during the riots under Varus and in the War of 66, Aggadot like the one about Tur Malka having been destroyed because of a fight between local Jews and a Roman patrol over a chicken and a rooster at a Jewish wed-

---

59 Yer. Taan. IV: 69c. The same retort is attributed to Bar Kokhba himself on the preceding page; cf. LamR II:2.

ding,[60] and about Bar Daroma, who is quoted as having uttered the same blasphemous remark attributed variously to Bar Kokhba and to the two brothers — these and other similar aggadot all point in the direction of many local outbursts and many local leaders. To be sure, legends are not solid historical evidence; but in this case, reason and experience point in the same direction. One thing is certain: the neatly fashioned accounts of Cassius Dio and Eusebius cannot be accepted altogether at face value; they are too reductionist, too simplified.

As far as the development of the war from a military point of view is concerned, there may well be something to be learned from a look at the countries from which Rome called in her troops to meet this emergency. It stands to reason that the first to make contact with the rebels were the troops already stationed in the country — the Xth Fretensian Legion, plus such auxiliary forces as had been brought in before the war to help with counter-insurgency measures. In command of these forces was Tinneus Rufus, Legate for Judaea and Commanding Officer of the Tenth Legion. His role as C-in-C when the war began, and then as governor after the war when stringent military government was in force, made his name the one most prominently associated with the war, both in talmudic literature and in the writings of the Christian Church Fathers.

The first stage of the war resulted in a crushing defeat for the Roman military. They were driven out of Judaea — all of it, Jerusalem included.

The second stage, it would seem, began with the arrival in the theater of war of Publicius Marcellus, the *legatus pro praetore* of Syria, with some of the legions stationed in that eparchy. Possibly at the same time, legions and supporting auxiliaries arrived from Egypt and from Arabia (Transjordan). It appears that these forces as well took a beating. This may have been when the XXIInd Deioteriana was cut up, if that is what happened to it.

Probably at this stage the rebels extended their hold down into the Shefelah and on to the Mediterranean coastal plain; because it seems quite clear that the Syrian navy engaged in actual combat

60 Git. 57a.

during the war. We are in no position to say whether this took the form of off-shore attacks, or involved engagements at sea with "pirate-ships" of the rebels.

The third and final stage would have begun with arrival of legions from the army of the Danube, no doubt synchronized with the arrival from Britain of the new commander-in-chief, Julius Severus, probably attended by a goodly detachment of his own headquarters troops. Severus immediately sought to put the rebels on the defensive. He avoided large-scale confrontations, but used his now considerable forces to push the Jews gradually back into their fortified positions, taking care to isolate these positions one from the other.

The Jewish insurgents were becoming exhausted. They no longer had the strength to mount concentrated attacks on the crack Pannonian soldiers, who were reckoned among Rome's finest. Now the rebels had to content themselves with self-defence, or at best with harrying the enemy by minor guerilla actions. Bit by bit the Romans whittled away the areas under rebel control, until at last Bar Kokhba's remaining forces were concentrated in the stronghold of Beitar for the final desperate battle.

This suggested outline for a military history of the Bar Kokhba War — [it might be called an informed hypothesis] — has not included Hadrian himself among the generals who fought in Judaea. The truth is that a fierce debate has raged around the question whether or not he was there in person at any time during hostilities. Recently, there has been an attempt to settle the question by numismatic evidence, based on coins issued at the end of the war or soon afterwards. But the new evidence has only produced new disputes. My own opinion is that there is nothing in the sources to indicate that Hadrian took a personal part in the war in Judaea, nor are there any reasonable grounds for supposing that he did.

THE CONQUEST OF JERUSALEM

During the course of hostilities did the rebels gain control of Jerusalem? There is no unanimity on this point. The problem is due to differing evaluations of the literary evidence and varying interpretations of the numismatic material.

To begin with, there is the literature of the Aggadah, which accepts unquestioningly the tradition that Hadrian conquered the city and laid it waste. The midrashim in which this aggadah are found are all late.[61] The aggadah itself has nothing to say about the role of Jerusalem in the war. It can scarcely be regarded as of much historical value.

Church Fathers and Christian chronographers beginning with Eusebius early in the fourth century consistently speak of Hadrian as the last conqueror of Jerusalem, after Vespasian. There is no real reason to disregard a tradition so explicit, but some sceptical historians would have us do so, on the basis of the fact that Cassius Dio, the principal historian of the war, makes no mention of Jerusalem changing hands. The reply to this might very well be that the argument *e silentio* is no argument, especially since Dio's report is given in the most sweeping, general terms.

The same sceptics cast doubt on the report by Appian of Alexandria (2nd century C.E.) and should probably be given the same answer. This is what Appian says:

> (Pompey) ... destroyed their greatest, and to them holiest city, Jerusalem, as Ptolemy ... had formerly done. It was afterward rebuilt and Vespasian destroyed it again, and Hadrian did the same in our time.[62]

So there is evidence enough from the literary sources that Jerusalem was conquered by the rebels during the Bar Kokhba War, and that then it was taken from them.

As for coins minted by the rebels, we have a number that specifically mention Jerusalem.[63] One type bears the legend *Leherut Yerushalayim* (Of the Freedom of Jerusalem). Another simply has "Jerusalem," and verso, "Year One (Two, Three) of the Freedom of Israel."

61 ExodR. LI:5; Tanhuma, Pekude IV (Buber 64b); DeutR 313. Comp. Samaritan Chronicle in REJ 48, pp. 49 ff.
62 *Roman History, Syriacus Liber* 50:152; see GLA II, p. 179.
63 In the ancient sources, these coins are called "rebel coins, like those of Ben Koziba." (Yer. Maas. Sh. I:52d). Ms. Leiden and ms. Rome read *she-marad,* an error for *shel mered.* In the Tosefta they are called *ma'ot kozbiot* (Tos. Maas. Sh. I:6 (86); also Bavli B.Q. 97b).

This looks like proof positive that the rebels controlled Jerusalem when these coins were struck. However, it has been suggested that these inscriptions represent war aims, slogans rather than realities. *"Leherut Yerushalayim"* should be taken to mean: *"For the liberation of Jerusalem."* According to this view, the coins were struck during the last stages of the war, when Jerusalem was once again in Roman hands, to show the resolve of the rebels to fight on until the holy city was freed from the enemy.[64]

Nevertheless, there are coins dated "Year One (or Two) of the Liberation of Jerusalem," bearing the word "Jerusalem" again on the other side. It seems incontrovertible that the other side signifies the place of coinage, or of the issuing authority. This would certainly mean that the rebels controlled the city. However, this too has been denied; the argument is that it is merely a declaration of intent.[65] But this argument is unconvincing. On balance, it seems probable that Jerusalem was captured by the rebels, and held by them for one or two years.

What role did the Diaspora play in the Bar Kokhba War? Cassius Dio, it will be remembered, had "the Jews everywhere" involved along with their brethren in Judaea. Some historians take this at face value, and assume that Jews fought Romans throughout the Empire. While Dio's language is not at all specific in this regard, there is no compelling reason to deny that it is entirely possible.

Indeed, that is exactly what happened during the War of the Destruction. While the fighting was going on in Judaea, there were short outbursts of rebellion by Jews in Egypt and Cyrenaica. According to Josephus, the Zealots sent emissaries to Babylonia at that time, urging the Jews there to open a front against the eastern flank of the Empire. There are also grounds for believing that

---

64 See Reifenberg in JPOS 1941, pp. 293–294.

65 Mildenberg: "The Eleazar Coins of the Bar Kokhba Rebellion" in *Historia Judaica* XI (April 1949) pp. 77–108. He goes further, and rejects the historicity of the personalities mentioned on the coins — Simeon, the Nasi and Eleazar the Kohen. [The papyri found in the caves prove that he was wrong, and Alon was right. Simeon was Bar Kokhba's real name; Eleazar was a real priest. See below, note 74.]

such emissaries tried to stir up a revolt of the Jews in the Syrian city of Antioch at that time.

Later, during the closing years of Trajan's regime, the identity of interest between the Jews of Judaea and those of the Diaspora was expressed quite unmistakably. A shorthand term for this phenomenon would be "pulmus shel qitos" — the War of Quietus.

But when we reach the Bar Kokhba War, it seems that we must agree with those historians who believe that the Jews of the Diaspora did *not* take part in the revolt. If they had, somebody would have made mention of it, however slight. What we do have is evidence to the contrary. Justin Martyr, a contemporary of the events themselves, writing in Rome some 15 or twenty years later, presents his interlocutor Trypho as a Jewish refugee from the war, arriving in Ephesus while the war was still going on, and conducting a dialogue publicly with the author in this large city in Asia Minor.[65a]

Granted, the Jewish Sage Trypho is surely a literary invention of the Church Father, himself a native of Sebaste in Samaria. But Justin would scarcely have set the scene for this calm public discussion in Asia Minor, unless it could be assumed that all was quiet in that quarter, and that Jews wanting out of the Bar Kokhba struggle could find a safe haven there.

As for Dio's comment, no doubt it should be taken to mean that Jews from the Diaspora took part in the war by actually coming to Judaea and joining up. We are led to the same conclusion by the aggadic tradition that has very large numbers of Jews fighting the Romans. The same derives from a weighing up of the precedents and the probabilities. It was also to be expected that the Jews of the Diaspora should lend their support by providing food, weapons and other military supplies. Dio's highly condensed account simply does not go into detail.

In support of this reading of the situation it may be pointed out that the extremely punitive Roman decrees that followed the war, making the study and practice of Judaism illegal, abolishing the Jewish courts, and so on — almost certainly did not apply

65a [Justin Martyr: *The Dialogue with Trypho,* trans. by A. L. Williams, SPCK, London, 1930, p. 2.]

to the Jews of the Diaspora. If the latter had really risen in revolt, it is scarcely conceivable that they would have escaped the same punishment.

Nevertheless, we can be sure that these same Jews followed the news from Judaea with bated breath, half-hoping, half-anxious. Their frame of mind finds a glancing reflection in Justin Martyr's "Dialogue with Trypho." One morning, while waiting to renew his discussions with the Jew, the author observes the young Jews of Ephesus withdrawn and fearful, immersed in discussion of the latest news from Judaea.[66] Thus suddenly the curtain is lifted for a fleeting moment, and we catch a glimpse of the inner world of the Diaspora Jews, desperate with anxiety for their brothers in Judaea who were fighting for their lives, now overcoming, now being overcome.

WARTIME LEADERSHIP

Whatever the immediate spark that ignited the popular uprising against Rome — whether it was a purely religious sense of outrage at the ban on circumcision, or a religio-national protest against the building of a pagan shrine on Jerusalem's Temple Mount — there can be no doubt that the Bar Kokhba War soon became a war of national liberation. Its goal became nothing less than complete independence from Roman rule. This is evident from Jewish as well as Christian literature. If additional evidence is needed, it can be read on the coins which the rebels minted, inscribed "Year One (or Two, or Three) of the Redemption (or Liberation) of Israel."

It seems, however, that to many of the rebels this "redemption" meant more than simply shaking off the foreign yoke. It meant "messianic redemption!" These eschatological overtones distinguish the Bar Kokhba War from the War of the Hurban. That war, too, was a war of national liberation. It too produced coins inscribed "The Freedom of Zion." But there was a difference. Despite the presence of certain millenarian trends and sects among the Jews who fought that first war, no single charismatic leader with messianic pretensions emerged. Civil and military leadership

66 [Ibid., p. 20.]

was a group affair, and there was no talk of kings or messiahs. Control remained in the hands of the Sanhedrin — at least until the coup of the year 68, when the Zealots seized power.

But things were different in the last great revolt. Bar Kokhba flashed upon the scene like a heaven-sent leader. Rabbi Akiba pronounced his famous accolade: "This is the King-Messiah!"[67] and one of Rabbi Akiba's disciples, Rabbi Simeon bar Yohai, even reported that his great teacher had applied to the situation the verse which had, by common consent, been reserved for the Messiah: "A star (*kokhav*) hath stepped forth out of Jacob."[68]

In the same vein there is the aggadic tradition which states:

> Bar Koziba reigned for two years and one-half. Said he to them (*the Sages*) I am the Messiah.[69]

To this can be added the statement by Eusebius, quoted above, that Bar Kokhba was seen by the Jews as a supernatural figure. Jerome, too, reports that Bar Kokhba was popularly perceived as a wonder worker, a miracle-man.

In this connection it is perhaps worth considering an early Christian document written no more than a few years after the Bar Kokhba War: "The Apocalypse of Peter," the full text of which has been known only since 1910.[70] The Master is speaking:

> "And ye, receive ye the parable of the fig tree thereon: as soon as its shoots have gone forth and its boughs have sprouted, the end of the world will come." And I, Peter answered and said unto him "Explain to me concerning the fig tree..." And he answered and said unto me: "Dost thou not understand that the fig tree is the house of Israel?" ....
> Verily I say unto you, when its boughs have sprouted at the end, then shall deceiving saviors come and awaken hope, saying: "I am the Savior who am now come into the world." And when they shall see the wickedness of their deeds (even

---

67 Yer. Taan. IV:68d; LamR II:2.
68 Nu. 24:17.
69 Sanh. 93b.
70 E. Hennecke: *New Testament Apocrypha*, SCM Press, vol. II, pp. 668–9.

of the false saviors) they shall turn away after them and deny him to whom our fathers gave praise, the first Messiah whom they crucified and thereby sinned exceedingly. And this deceiver[71] is not the messiah. And when they reject him he will kill them with the sword, and there shall be many martyrs...

There is a consensus among historians that Bar Kokhba persecuted the Christians. After all, they stood aside from the revolt, and treated him as a false messiah. Besides, the Church Fathers say so. The document just quoted adds to our picture of this leader as claimant to the mantle of the messiah; and it is a very early document.[72] This, despite the vague and clouded language — a quality not unknown to apocalyptic literature.

Nevertheless, it is greatly to be doubted that the short-lived "republic" which the rebels managed to set up was organized as a "messianic kingdom." On the contrary — such evidence as we have points in the opposite direction. Our primary data are the coins which the rebel state issued, and to these we must now give our attention.[73]

THE BAR KOKHBA COINS

The Bar Kokhba coins can be organized into three chronological groupings, according to the year of issue inscribed on them:
1) Year One of the Redemption of Israel.
2) Year Two of the Freedom of Israel.
3) (No Date) of the Freedom of Jerusalem. These bear the name of Simeon or Eleazar the Priest. Many scholars ascribe them to the third year of the war.

The coins can be organized differently, in accordance with the name of the issuing authority, thus:

71 [Alon renders this as *'ish kezabhim*, though without comment but perhaps interpreting it as a pointed reference to Bar Koziba.]
72 [... "the period of origin must be fixed at least in the first half of the second century." Hennecke, op. cit. p. 664.]
73 The principal studies in this field are those by Reifenberg, Mildenberg and Narkiss. [For an updated listing of studies of the numismatic material, see GLA II, pp. 394–5.]

1) Simeon, Nasi of Israel. (In some cases, just Simeon, or the first three letters of his name).
2) Eleazar the Priest. (One coin has both Simeon and Eleazar the Priest).
3) Jerusalem (simply).

First, let us deal with the theory proposed by Mildenberg, that the coins tell us nothing about the realities, but are merely wishful slogans. Simeon is merely a name fondly remembered out of the past (he may be thinking of Simeon the Just, 3rd century B.C.E.). Eleazar the Kohen is a sort of eponym for a High Priest; the same for Jerusalem. The whole thing is to be treated as symbolic, proclaiming war aims, not actualities.

This far-fetched theory scarcely requires refutation. Had the rebels really wanted slogans they could have found more impressive names. And if comparisons are in order, one may cite coins of an earlier war of liberation — the Hasmonean struggle. Those coins of the second pre-Christian century bear the names of real people, real authorities. It is therefore in order to conclude that these coins of the second Christian century do as well.

Who then is this "Simeon, Nasi of Israel?" Some say, Bar Kokhba himself. To be sure, we have no proof that Bar Kokhba was named "Simeon."[74] The passage in Lamentations Rabbah (II:2) which is sometimes cited as proof that this was his name, can be otherwise interpreted.

There are others who say that the coins refer to the Nasi (Patriarch) Simeon ben Gamaliel. This speculation must be rejected, not so much for chronological reasons, as for the fact that Rabban Simeon functioned as patriarch after the war. If he had been one of the leaders, the Romans could not possibly have allowed him to get off scot free, considering the severity with which they punished everybody who had anything to do with the revolt.

---

74 [When Alon delivered these lectures, the discoveries in the Judaean Desert had not yet been made. Now we *have* proof that the real name of the leader of the revolt was Simeon bar Kosba (or Koziba), and that Bar Kokhba was his *nom de guerre*. This makes much of the discussion above superfluous. At the same time, it verifies the soundness of Alon's historical judgment.]

We are forced, then, to conclude that the Simeon of the coins is none other than Bar Kokhba himself.

So it turns out that Bar Kokhba was neither messiah nor king, but simply Nasi — a title doubtless the equivalent of "Ethnarch," which is the way the first Hasmonean rulers were styled. Apparently the rebels took that early Maccabean regime as their model — a regime which recognized no monarchy, but rather *nesiut* — a principate. To press the analogy further, one recalls that Simeon the Hasmonean, the first *ethnarkhos,* was appointed "until such time as a true prophet shall arise in Israel." This provided the theological underpinning for withholding the crown from him. That — the renewal of the monarchy — would have to wait until the culmination of history, when prophecy would reappear, and a new revelation be given to mankind.

What we learn from the coins is that the people did *not* see in Bar Kokhba a messiah or a prophet. The title given him implies leadership with limited powers, not absolute monarchy. To those who profess to see the contrary idea symbolized on certain coins, which reveal a star ("A star hath stepped forth out of Jacob") surmounting, a four-column structure (the Temple?) — there are two answers. First, the star device was used by King Jannai, two centuries earlier — and he had no messianic pretensions. Secondly, the star is either a decorative device or a symbol of freedom — nothing more.

It must be added that Bar Kokhba must have served as chief of the high command of the revolt, although there is nothing explicit about this on the coins. This role was apparently part and parcel of his office as Nasi. In the same way, the original Simeon, the Hasmonean, who was acclaimed *ethnarkhos* by his people, was also given the office of national *strategos* (commander) at the same time.

What then was the nature of that messianic belief that so many of his contemporaries, Sages included, fastened onto Bar Kokhba? It must have been an expression of hope and faith that great things were about to happen. These surely included the downfall of the "wicked empire," the ingathering of the scattered Jewish exiles, the rebuilding of the Temple and the emergence of the "New World" that was to follow. The Jewish fighters believed that driving the Roman garrison out of Judaea and the liberation of Jerusalem were portents of the imminent advent of the Messiah. Who else would that be but Bar Kokhba himself, he who had led the victorious rebels, rallied the nation, given it back its country and wreaked vengeance on the Romans?

However, the "World to Come" which was believed to be just around the corner, bore no resemblance to the system of government that was being set up in the here and now — in the embattled, newly-freed Judaea. It was the will of the people that that system be constructed on the model traditionally associated with the first war of national liberation, back in the days of the Second Commonwealth — the Maccabean struggle.

The tradition associated with that struggle conformed to the main thrust of what the people wanted, namely a balanced political system. Its elements were: democracy (a popular council) coupled with authoritative leadership (the Nasi); and a parallel religious authority — the priesthood.

This brings us to the second imprint of the issuing authority on the Bar Kokhba coins: the name "Eleazar Ha-Kohen." Who was he?

Some say Rabbi Eleazar ben Azariah; others suggest Rabbi Eleazar ben Harson, while still others point to Rabbi Eleazar Ha-Moda'i. Of the first it can be said with some certainty that he died before the war broke out, as I have demonstrated elsewhere.[75] As for Rabbi Eleazar ben Harson, he is a rather shadowy figure of legend, to whom the Aggadah attributes 11 years in the High Priesthood before the Destruction![76]

That leaves us with Rabbi Eleazar Ha-Moda'i. There is no real evidence that he was a kohen, but no proof that he was not. And since tradition places him in Beitar at the time of the siege, and couples his name with the fateful final days of the war, we may surmise that he is the Eleazar of the coins — always remembering that this is no more than an informed guess.

Whatever the identity of that priestly figure, one thing is certain:

---

75 See "The Patriarchate of Rabban Johanan ben Zakkai" in JJCW, p. 321, note 24.

76 Yoma 9a.

he represents to the people a higher authority. One thinks back to the pre-Hasmonean period, after the end of Persian rule, and remembers that for several centuries the High Priest functioned as the sole supreme ruler of the nation. Even afterwards, the Hasmonean ethnarchs (*nesi'im*) always stressed their own role as High Priests. The coins of John the Hasmonean (*Yohanan Kohen Gadol*) bear no other title. Still later, when their decendants became kings, Jannacus, or Yannai, and Mattathias Antigonus imprinted on the Hebrew text of their coins the title *Kohen Gadol* (High Priest).

So it is almost a certainty that the inscription "Eleazar Ha-Kohen" on Bar Kokhba coins is a means of legitimization of the new Jewish authority, which the people would expect to consist of two supreme echelons: the civil and the priestly.

This is not, however, to be taken as proof that the Temple (or even a temporary altar) had been rebuilt, and the sacrificial cult restored. There is no shred of evidence for such a conclusion. However, it is quite possible that steps were taken to reorganize the upper priesthood in readiness for the devoutly anticipated restoration.

To my mind there is a third basis of legitimization and authority indicated on the coins. The word "Jerusalem" is not merely a reference to the place where they were minted. It means "The City and the People of Jerusalem," much like the inscription *"Hever Ha-Yehudim"* on the Hasmonean coins of the Ethnarch Johanan. There is, to be sure, a difference of opinion as to whether the phrase means the Council (Sanhedrin) or the people. If we are dealing with the early Hasmonean state I am inclined to think that there is not much constitutional difference between the two. Even if the phrase *hever ha-heyudim* means "the Jewish People," and the coins cite them as the juridical basis of the issuing authority (after the High Priest) — "The People" in realistic terms, means their representatives the Sanhedrin.

There is a parallel here with the earlier war against Rome, the one that began in 66 C.E. Josephus refers to the Jewish government of that day as *koinon ton hierosolomiton* — "the people of Jerusalem." The Jerusalemites acted on behalf of the whole nation, and kept an eye on what the leaders were doing. Executive power, it appears, was in the hands of a selected handful of leaders — and of the Sanhedrin, most of whose members, it seems, were Jerusalemites.

So it looks as though the coins struck during the War of the Destruction, with the legend "Jerusalem the Holy," were expressions of a juridical fact: Jerusalem as the issuing authority, not the place of minting. We can apply the same reasoning to the Jerusalem coins of the Bar Kokhba War. They proclaim the third echelon of legitimacy — the popular-democratic — to which the uprising laid claim.

THE SANHEDRIN

Talmudic sources tell us that the Sanhedrin sat in Beitar. First, the Bavli: [76a]

> Rav Judah quoted Rav: A town which does not have at least two (*sc. judges*) to speak and one to understand (*foreign tongues*) is no fit place for a Sanhedrin. Beitar had three, Yavneh had four.

It is quite true that the parallel passage in the Yerushalmi differs. It wants the entire membership to understand, and a minimum of two to be able to speak. Three is better; four makes it a superior tribunal. "And in Yavneh there were four."[77] But no mention of Beitar!

However, I do not think this vitiates the evidence of Rav, who after all did spend many years in Palestine only two generations after the war, and who transmitted many old and reliable traditions concerning past events in that country.

The famous epistle of Rabbi Sherira Gaon also repeats the tradition that the (or a) Sanhedrin sat in Beitar:

> After the Temple was destroyed they went to Beitar. Then Beitar too was destroyed, and the Sages were scattered in every direction.[78]

76a Sanh. 17b. Rashi: The idea is that there be judges who understand evidence without the need of interpreters.
77 Yer. Sheq. IV: 48d.
78 Iggeret Rav Sherira Gaon, ed. B.M. Lewin, p. 10.

The problem here is, of course, that Sherira may simply have been echoing the Talmud, rather than citing an independent source. That the former is more likely is indicated by his amazing sequence Jerusalem-Beitar, a clue that he was simply following the sequence in the Bavli passage quoted above.

In any event, we are entitled to ask: what sort of Sanhedrin was it that sat in Beitar? Was it composed, as before the *hurban*, of Pharisees plus representatives of the citizenry from across the land? Certainly, it no longer included any Sadducees. Or was it perhaps a replica of the Sanhedrin of Yavneh — an assembly of Pharisee Sages, including Pharisee priests? The latter, it will be recalled had become a permanent element even during Temple times.

No definitive answer to this question is available. But we can make reasonable suggestions, although these will involve us in further questions regarding the authority and status of the wartime Sanhedrin. What seems most likely is, that its authority covered all areas of public life in the state, exactly as before the Destruction. If, on the other hand, it was simply a Beth Din of learned Sages, it would not likely have had a real share in the governance of the country.

On balance, the probability is that the Sanhedrin *did* play a real role in the provisional administration established by the rebels. After all, the main thrust of rebel activity in almost every area was to re-establish the old regime — life as it had been before Jerusalem and the Temple were destroyed. Consequently, it makes sense to suppose that the Sanhedrin, too, was reconstituted in its old form. Of course, it was only to be expected that the Sages would now be the dominant element. In the intervening two generations — the Yavneh generations — it was they who had been the standard bearers of national consolidation and recovery; and in the present crisis most of them rallied around Bar Kokhba. It was therefore only natural that theirs should be the decisive influence in the revived Sanhedrin.

THE PATRIARCHATE IN BEITAR

Talmudic tradition places the family of Rabban Gamaliel, reputed to be a cousinhood with very many branches, in Beitar during the war. First, the Bavli:[79]

> Rav Judah quoted Samuel, who had a tradition attributed to Rabban Simeon ben Gamaliel: There were a thousand children in father's household. Five hundred of them studied Torah, and five hundred studied Greek wisdom. Only two of us survived — I here, and my brother's son in Assia.[80]

This does not say outright that the Patriarch's family was nearly wiped out, nor even that they lived in Beitar. But the corresponding, though not identical, tradition in the Yerushalmi does place the family in Beitar, and has them suffer an all but mortal blow. Again, the authority quoted is Rabban Simeon ben Gamaliel:[81]

> There were 500 scribal schools in Beitar, and the smallest of these had no less than 500 children. The children said: If the Romans come, we shall advance against them with our styluses and poke their eyes out. Finally, when for our sins (*the enemy broke in*) they wrapped each child in his book and burned him; and I alone am left of them all. He applied to himself the verse (Lam. III:51): "Mine eye affected my soul Because of all the daughters of my city."

Raban Simeon's concluding remark, taken in conjunction with the tradition mediated by Samuel, which also goes back to the same verse in Lamentations, leads us to the conclusion that the children of the Patriarch's family lived — and died — in Beitar.

Did the family take any part in the leadership? It is reasonable to assume that they had some connection with the Sanhedrin, perhaps even with its leadership. Beyond that we can say next to nothing, except to add that they were no doubt able to exert some degree of moral influence.

---

79 Sot. 48b.
80 For descendents of the Patriarch's family in Assia, see *Seder Tannaim va-Amoraim*, pp. 60–61.
81 Yer. Taan. IV:69a; LamR II; Bavli Git. 58a.

COMPULSORY MOBILIZATION

Despite the lack of direct and explicit information about forced enlistment in the ranks of the rebels, it stands to reason that this must have been one of the measures that enabled them to organize their army. This can be deduced from the statements frequently heard from the Church Fathers about Bar Kokhba's persecution of the Christians of his day. It is a tradition which comes in two versions, one of which explains that the Christians refused to recognize Bar Kokhba as the Messiah — which of course they could not do, since it would clash with their faith in Jesus. A number of modern historians, Jews included, give the same interpretation.

However, in the view expressed here, Bar Kokhba's messianic role was still entirely in the realm of the speculative, something unrealized, belonging to the post-war future. It was not on this basis that he commanded the revolt, or the obedience of the people. Actually, there is another tradition, recorded by Christian writers: Christians were punished, and suffered martyrdom, because of their refusal to join the fight against the Romans. For Bar Kokhba forced "every person" to ally with him in the war against Rome.[82]

This is probably an accurate reflection of what really happened. We do not need to interpret the persecution of the Christians in Palestine as religiously motivated. The likelihood is that they were proceeded against as draft evaders! This, of course, presupposes that a decree of general compulsory enlistment had been issued covering all citizens of the rebel state.

Obviously, then, we must ask, who were these Christians? Were they gentiles? If they were, then the mobilization order must have included non-Jews. This is unlikely, even though Cassius Dio speaks of non-Jews getting into the fight. No, these were doubtless Jewish-Christians who, despite their belief in Jesus, regarded themselves as Jews in every respect. Many Jews also still thought of them as Jews — somewhat peculiar, but still Jews.[83]

In any event, it comes as no surprise to learn that most (though

82 Michael Syrus, IV 105–6. [Yadin assumes that the Bar Kokhba letters ordering the arrest of certain individuals refer to "draft dodgers." See his *Bar Kokhba*, p. 125.]

83 The above-mentioned *Apocalypse of Peter* also regarded these victims of Bar Kokhba as Jews.

not all) of these people refused to join up with the rebels. The same thing had happened in the war of 66 C.E. The well-known tradition attributed to Eusebius, that has the community of Jewish-Christians in Jerusalem moving en masse to Pella in Transjordan in the year 68, while the capital was under siege, because of a vision that appeared to them, has become a symbol of the break between the early Church and the Jewish People fighting for its life.

When Church Fathers write about the persecution of Christians by the "murderous *listos*" Bar Kokhba, without mentioning that these were *not* gentile Christians, but Jews, they leave a false impression. These persecutees had insisted on being counted as Jews; but now, in a time of trouble, they refused to answer the call. To transmit this information in general terms, without a word of explanation, can only be regarded as clearly tendentious, intended to serve a polemical purpose. A parallel is the statement by Justin Martyr that the Jews curse the Christians in their synagogues — a slight but nonetheless harmful distortion of the *Birkat Ha-Minim*.[84]

The Book of Deuteronomy speaks of certain exemptions from military service, such as the newly-married, the new householder, and others (Deut. XX: 2 ff.). There is a difference of opinion in the Mishnah regarding these rules.[85] Purely as a surmise, it may be suggested that the dispute is connected with the call-up ordered during the Bar Kokhba War.

> These rules apply to a war of choice (*milhemet reshut*); but in a commanded war (*milhemet mitzvah*) all go forth, even the bridegroom from his chamber and the bride from her huppah. But Rabbi Judah says: These rules apply to a commanded war; but in a war of duty (*milhemet hovah*) all go forth, even the bridegroom etc. etc.

In tannaitic literature generally, only two terms are used in this connection: *milhemet hovah*, which is limited to the wars of con-

---

84 See JLTA I, p. 289.
85 Sot. VIII: 7; comp. Tos. ibid. VII:24 (309). Talmudic references to support this suggestion may be found in Bavli Sot. 44b and Yer. ibid. VIII: 23a.

quest under Moses and Joshua; and *milhemet reshut,* which applies to all other combat. The term *milhemet mitzvah* makes its appearance with the disciples of Rabbi Akiba, and is applied to wars of defence. It may be that it was in this connection that the difference of opinion recorded in the Mishnah arose, as a result of the compulsory mobilization decreed by Bar Kokhba.

THE ATTITUDE OF THE SAGES

Rabbi Akiba's outspoken backing of the Bar Kokhba revolt doubtless expressed the point of view of a great many — perhaps the majority — of the Sages. The fact that the Sanhedrin moved to Beitar, and that the Patriarch and his family did the same, points to the same conclusion. Rabbi Eleazar Ha-Moda'i, whether or not he is the Eleazar Ha-Kohen of the coins, was clearly an ally of Bar Kokhba, even though at the very end they had a falling out, according to tradition.

But it is apparent that not all the Sages agreed. There was Rabbi Johanan ben Torta, who said to Rabbi Akiba:

Akiba! Grass will be growing out of your cheekbones — and the son of David will not yet have come![86]

It seems that this was not merely the denial of Bar Kokhba's messianship by one who nevertheless supported the revolt politically.[87] It was more likely representative of a school of thought among the Sages opposed to this war from the very start. An echo of such a point of view may be found in certain midrashim which speak of those who try to "force the end of days" — among whom are numbered Bar Kokhba and his generation.

Perhaps the most striking of these midrashim is the aggadah recorded in the Bavli, which has Bar Kokhba proclaiming himself the Messiah, and the Sages examining him — and then executing him.[88] This is most certainly nothing but legend, emanating from circles antagonistic to Bar Kokhba. We have a contrary Palestinian tradition that Bar Kokhba did not meet his death at any human

86 Yer. Taan. IV:68a.
87 *Pace* J. Gutmann in *Encyclopedia Judaica,* (German) vol. 3, pp. 1081-82.
88 Sanh. 93b.

hands at all, neither Roman nor Jewish, but "by the hand of Heaven" (the bite of an asp). It seems certain that no one really knew how he died, and speculation on the subject was rife. He may have taken his own life when the Romans broke through in the last siege. But the notion that he was executed by a tribunal of Sages seems quite out of the question. No doubt it arose after his downfall, yet it seems quite likely that some of the Sages turned away from him even while the war was in progress. Is it probable that this happened in the very last stages of the struggle, as in the First War with Rome, when some of the Sages tried to stop further useless bloodshed? That apparently was the stand taken by Rabbi Eleazar Ha-Moda'i. In any event, for most of the war the Sages stood solidly with the rebels. This was an important factor in the national unity which held almost — if not quite — to the very end.

Before moving on to deal with the punitive decrees which the Romans imposed on the vanquished Jews, we must examine briefly the tradition that connects the disciples of Rabbi Akiba with the Bar Kokhba War.[89]

> Rabbi Akiba had 12 thousand pairs of students ... and all of them died at the same time ... leaving the world desolate until Rabbi Akiba came to our masters in the South, Rabbi Meir and Rabbi Judah and taught them ...

Sherira Gaon writes in his famous *Epistle:* "Rabbi Akiba raised up many disciples, but there was a destruction *(shemada)* upon the disciples of Rabbi Akiba."[90] Then he copies the above-quoted passage from Yevamot verbatim. The generally accepted interpretation of this tradition is that Rabbi Akiba's students went out to battle and were cut down en masse.

But there was a somewhat different version of the tradition, and it is recorded in the same talmudic context:

> Rabbi Hama bar Abba, and some say it was Rabbi Hiyya bar Abin, was reported to have said: They all died an evil death. What was that? *Askarah* (a plague).

89 Yev. 62b; EcclR XI: 10; GenR LXI: 3.
90 Iggeret, ed. Lewin, p. 13.

Even of this text there are varying versions; it may have reference to execution by the Romans. On reflection, it seems likely that some mass decimation of a group of Rabbi Akiba's students took place before the war, because we know that after the war the rabbi could not have had time to train Rabbi Meir and Rabbi Judah. His arrest and public execution must have taken place not long after the fall of Beitar.

THE DECREES

Immediately after the Bar Kokhba War — perhaps even before hostilities had ended — the Roman authorities introduced a sweeping series of prohibitory regulations. The purpose of these decrees was to crush the national spirit of the Jews, perhaps even to put an end to their presence in Palestine as a collective entity. Let us examine the various areas covered by these decrees, and look at the problems associated with each of them.

1) Closing the Jewish Courts: It is a fact established beyond question that the Romans abrogated the Jewish judicial autonomy in all its aspects. The tradition is related by Rav (2nd–3rd centuries):

> The wicked kingdom decreed *shemad* (annihilation) upon Israel, ordering death for anyone who ordained (a judge) or who accepted ordination, and decreeing that the city where the act was done was to be reduced to rubble and the boundaries of the local authority were to be obliterated. What did Rabbi Judah ben Bava do? He went and sat between two mountains, between two large towns, namely Usha and Shafr'am, and there he ordained five Sages: Rabbis Meir, Judah, Jose, Simeon and Eleazar ben Shamu'a ... When a Roman patrol caught sight of them he said: "My sons, run!" They said: "Master, what will become of you? He answered: "Here I lie before them like a useless thing (*lit: like a stone no one will turn over*)." It was said that the Romans did not leave the spot before they had sunk 300 iron lunkha'ot into his body, so that it became a veritable sieve.[91]

91 Sanh. 14a; *lunkha'ot* are lances, cf. Krauss: *Lehnwörter* s.v.

The Decrees

The decree making it a criminal offense, under penalty of death, to appoint Jewish judges is but one expression of a general abolition of Jewish autonomy. The Mishnah rules:

> If she produced a writ of divorce without a Ketubah, she is entitled to the amount of her Ketubah; but if she produced a Ketubah without a writ of divorce, saying 'My writ of divorce is lost,' while he claimed, '(I paid but) my receipt is lost,' the like of these may not be paid. The same applies to a creditor who produced a bill of indebtedness without a prozbol. Rabban Simeon ben Gamaliel says: Since the time of the *sakanah* (the Hadrianic persecution) a woman is entitled to her Ketubah without a writ of divorce, and a creditor, is entitled to his due without a prozbol.[92]

A similar conclusion can be drawn from the Tosefta:

> What was the original reason for the custom of marrying virgin brides on Wednesday? So that if the bridegroom wanted to charge non-virginity, he would find the court in session the following morning... From the time of the *sakanah* they began celebrating such marriages on Tuesdays, and the Sages raised no objection.[93]

Certain historians have cast doubt on the historicity of some of the other alleged Roman prohibitions. But in this area there seems to be complete certainty. The existence of "native" courts of local jurisdiction was a common phenomenon throughout the provinces and districts of the Roman Empire; nor was it confined to autonomous cities. Even in places with the status of "subjugated areas" the Romans tolerated the de facto continuation of such local judicatures.[94]

Since, however, this situation had no official legal standing, there is nothing surprising in the fact that it could be, and was, suspended after the revolt. No rescript was required, no legislative measures were needed. The whole thing could be attended to

92 Ket. IX: 9.
93 Tos. Ket. I:1 (260); comp. Bavli ibid. 3b, Yer. ibid. 24d.
94 See JLTA I, pp. 212–213.

administratively — and that, no doubt, was exactly the way it happened.

2) Closing the Synagogues. Public Torah Study made Illegal. The decree forbidding assemblies for the study of Torah is well known from aggadic sources.[95] The fact is also attested to in the Halakhah:

> Originally, they would announce it on the three pilgrim festivals ... After the Destruction, this was changed to thirty days in advance. But from the time of the *sakanah*, it was decided that each person should pass the information on to his neighbors and relatives and fellow townsmen — and that would suffice.[96]

There can be little doubt that in this passage, too, the *sakanah* — "danger-time" — refers to the period when the Hadrianic decrees were in force. Obviously, the only way for the news to get around was by word of mouth, for the synagogues had been shut down.

The decree forbidding public gatherings could readily have been based on a standing rescript issued by Julius Caesar, and affirmed by his successors. It made allowance for those organizations specifically exempted by the Senate. Julius Caesar and the emperors who followed had exempted the Jews, among others, from this restriction. What more simple than to remove this "privilege" from the Jews in Judaea after the revolt, and just let them fall under the general prohibition?

Here again, there was no need for any special legislation. True, Judaism had been treated as a *religio licita* for several centuries, so that de facto the change was enormous. But it could all be done simply by issuing a local order, without tampering with the law as it stood.

3) Specific Mitzvot: Many tannaitic sources tell us of a ban on Jewish religious practices during the Hadrianic persecutions.

---

95 Ber. 61b for the imprisonment and execution of Rabbi Akiba; Av. Zar 17b for Rabbi Haninah ben Teradyon, Rabbi Meir's father-in-law.

96 Tos. B.M. II:17 (374); Bavli ibid. 28b; Yer. ibid. II: 8c. The reading — and interpretation — in the Bavli (*misherabu ha-anasim*) should be disregarded. [The announcement concerned found objects.]

Specific mention is made of a) Hanukkah, b) Sukkah, c) Tefillin, d) Mezuzah, e) Terumah, f) The Sabbatical Year, g) Tevillah. A general tradition on the subject is contained in a homily attributed to a Rabbi who himself lived through this difficult time:

> Rabbi Nathan says: *Of them that love me and keep my commandments (Exod. XX:6)* — this refers to the Jews who live in the Land of Israel and lay down their lives for the mitzvot. "You, sir, why are you being led out to be executed?" "Because I circumcised my son." "And you, why to be burned at the stake?" "Because I read the Torah." "And why are you about to be crucified?" "For eating matzah." "And you there, why are they giving you 100 lashes of the flagellus?" "Because I performed the ceremony of the Lulav."[97]

It is important to deal squarely with the doubts that have been expressed about the historicity of this talmudic tradition about Roman persecution of the Jewish religion; doubts based on the well-known Roman tolerance in religious matters, and on the reluctance of imperial Rome to interfere with the cultic practices of peoples under her protection. Yet there can be no shadow of doubt that these traditions reflect historical reality. True, the persecutions varied in intensity from place to place and from time to time; it is reasonable to suppose that they were much worse in Judaea proper than in Galilee. Nor will it be helpful to attempt analogies with Christianity, which was persecuted steadily and relentlessly at this time. Christianity was a new religion, unprotected by the law, whereas Judaism had been legally recognized since the Romans first came to the Middle East.

What will help is a little reflection on some of the ups and downs in Jewish history. It will become clear that even a legally recognized religion could suffer intense local persecution in times of crisis. Josephus reports that, during the First War with Rome the legate of Syria, aided by the Greeks of the city of Antioch, made the observance of the Jewish Sabbath impossible throughout that province.[98] According to Philo, something quite similar was

97 *Mekhila d'Rabbi Ishmael, Bahodesh,* Lauterbach II, p. 247.
98 JW VIII:3:3 (43–53); see JLTA I, pp. 71 and 74.

tried by Felix in Alexandria at one point; and Jerome tells of like persecutions in Judaea during the First War.

In all these instances the act occurred in a specific political context, or in connection with war between the Jews of Judaea and the Romans. In no case was any imperial action involved. It was always something done by the local authority — at highest, the provincial legate.

It is highly unlikely that the Romans deliberately set out to obliterate the Jewish religion. Had that been their purpose they would have banned its observance throughout the Diaspora. But everything we know points in the contrary direction. The conclusion must be that the restrictions imposed in Judaea itself were not directed against Judaism per se, but were politically motivated. To the extent that Jewish religious practices acted as an ethno-cultural dynamic force, making the Jews a strongly cohesive national group, unruly and almost impossible to deal with, the Romans had to make their political counter-attack by striking at the Jewish religion.

As for the legal aspects of the so-called "Hadrianic" persecutions, it appears certain that they involved no imperial legislative acts. The only such law of which we know anything — and it predates the war — is the ban on circumcision. What happened in Judaea was made possible because of the status of the defeated Jewish population as *dediticii:* a mass of subjugated individuals stripped of the protection of public law, deprived of all collective civil rights. That gave the local governor, Tinneus Rufus, the power to deprive them of any of their religio-cultural practices, as he saw fit. It also explains why these restrictions did not apply to the communities of the Diaspora. At the same time, let it be remembered that the status of *dediticii* was normally a temporary phase of comparatively short duration.

With regard to the enforcement of pagan worship on the Jews, a word should be said in conclusion about those historians who make a distinction between Hadrian and the Seleucid ruler Antiochus Epiphanes several centuries earlier. As far as Hadrian personally is concerned they are certainly right; none of those decrees emanated from the emperor, as we have explained. But the persecutions themselves were quite similar, though they existed at the local level, as proven by many traditions.[99] It all goes back to the unprotected status of *dediticii,* which left petty officials and army officers on the spot free to deal with local subversives as they chose, without having to render account for their actions to their superiors in Rome.

99 Shab. 130a; Tos. Av. Zar. V:6 (468); Mishnah ibid. V:6; Yer. ibid. V:45a.

PART FOUR

DECLINE

CHAPTER TWENTY-FIVE

UNDER THE ANTONINES[1]

Hadrian died some three years after the end of the Bar Kokhba war. For the rest of the second century Rome was ruled by the Antonine Caesars: Antoninus Pius (138–161); Marcus Aurelius (161–180, part of the time with Lucius Verus); and Commodus (180–192).

Despite certain dark clouds on the horizon, the Antonine age is generally thought of as a rather benign period in the history of the Roman Empire.[2] But that does not hold good for Jewish Palestine, chiefly because the juridical status of the Jews did not revert to what it had been before the Bar Kokhba war. At some point during his reign Antoninus Pius set aside the Hadrianic decrees, but he did not restore the Jews to the autonomous position they had enjoyed before the war. Indeed, it is fairly certain that no improvement in their official status was effected during the entire Antonine period. That they were able to reactivate the Patriarchate and the Sanhedrin de facto was due entirely to their own efforts.

This means that the situation which had prevailed after the war of the Destruction in the first century now repeated itself. After the fall of Beitar, the Jews were once again reduced to the status of *dedliicii* — a group of subjugated individuals with no collective rights. That legal fact did not, to be sure, prevent them from gradually resuming most of the functions of an autonomous people, while the Roman authorities did not interfere. But the lack of official recognition certainly made a difference. It left

1   From this point on, Alon's lecture notes have been greatly condensed and edited.
2   Even though Gibbon begins "The Decline and Fall" with Marcus Aurelius.

the authority of the central Jewish institutions in a weakened posture, a situation that prevailed for the rest of the century. It must be admitted that many scholars take a different view of the Antonine period. They regard Antoninus Pius and Marcus Aurelius as great friends of the Jews, going so far as to identify the latter with the Roman emperor described in Talmudic tradition as the intimate friend and confidant of the Nasi, Judah I. However, I am not alone in the opinion that the major portion of Judah's term as Patriarch was in the days of the Severi.

The negative effect of the war on the political position in Judaea — now officially renamed *"Syria Palaestina"* — was matched by the deterioration of the country in social and economic terms. The struggle itself had wrought great havoc, and its consequences lasted for a long time. The general economic upswing in the Middle East at that time did not make itself felt in Eretz Israel for many years.

The same can be said for the morale of the people. Many Jews succumbed to despair and abandoned the fold, so that Judaism was left in a debilitated state for more than a generation. Indeed, the situation was worse than it had been after the first war with Rome. This time recovery was slower, and much more difficult.

It seems that this was the time when a fundamental change took place in the Jewish attitude to Roman rule.[3] The outright refusal to grant legitimacy to the occupation began to weaken. In its place arose the doctrine that rebellion against the ruling authority was contrary to God's will, except when Judaism itself was at stake.[4]

It also appears that the reduced circumstances of the Jews after the war made it necessary for them to work more closely with the non-Jewish element in the country. Out of this need arose a doctrine favoring coexistence and cooperation with gentiles in social and economic spheres.

---

3   Such respectful phrases as *kevod ha-malkhut* (the honor of the government) appear for the first time in baraitot of the third century.

4   "The Holy One adjured Israel not to go up en masse, nor to rebel against the nations. He also adjured the gentiles not to deal too harshly with Israel." Ket. 111a, per ms. Munich and others.

[642]

DECREASE IN POPULATION

Dio Cassius estimates the casualties of the Bar Kokhba war on the Jewish side at more than half-a-million, without including the victims of starvation and disease. While there is no guarantee that his figure is accurate, it need not necessarily be regarded as an exaggeration.

The loss in population must have been further compounded by extensive emigration, both forced and voluntary. Early Christian traditions report that the slave markets in Hebron and Gaza were flooded with Jewish captives for sale at bargain prices, because the supply was so plentiful.[5]

A tradition found in both Christian and Jewish sources refers Obadiah I:20 ("The captivity of Jerusalem which is in Sepharad...") to some of the Jews transported by Hadrian as captives.[6] Jerome, commenting on that verse, says that "the Hebrew who taught him Scripture" told him that "Sepharad" means "the Bosporus," where Hadrian sent the Jewish captives. The Church Father Eutychios reports that in the aftermath of the Bar Kokhba war, Jews fled to Egypt, Syria and the Aravah. Justin Maryr tells of Jewish war refugees in Asia Minor.[7] Rabban Simeon ben Gamaliel speaks of a nephew of his who remained behind in "Assia" after the war.[8] We also learn from a number of baraitot that certain Sages fled to such places as Babylonia, Laodicaea and Rome.[9] Not all of them stayed abroad; but not all of them came back.

One effect of the decrease in population was the abandonment of much farm land and other real property. This gave rise to legal problems concerning title to "abandoned property" whose owners might still be alive somewhere.[10] In any event, the drop in popula-

---

5   See Jerome on Zech. I:5 and Jer. XXXI:15; also the *Alexandrine Chronicle* (Vallarsi IV, 1065) and *Chronicum Paschale* ed. Dindorf I, 474.

6   Comp. the comment on Deut. XXIX:27 in *Midrash Haggadol*, Mossad Harav Kook, Jerusalem 1972, p.תרמ״ב.

7   *Dialogue with Trypho.*

8   Sotah 49a.

9   E.g. Rabbi Meir, Rabbi Jose, Rabbi Mathi ben Heresh and Rabbi Joshua's nephew, Hananiah.

10 Tos. Ket. VIII:3 (270); Bavli B.M. 38b; Yer. Yev. XV:15a. See also Gulak, *Toledot Ha-Mishpat Ha-Ivri*, I, pp. 2–5.

tion certainly had grave economic consequences, because of the accompanying decrease in agricultural production. In addition, the fierce fighting had already ravaged much of the countryside, leaving damage probably greater than that caused by the first war with Rome.[11]

The depressed state of farming is also reflected in the relaxation of certain halakhic rules pertaining to priestly offerings.[12] It finds an echo in the following homily on Lev. XXVI: 19:[13]

> *I will break your proud glory*: — Rabbi Joseph explained that these words refer to the town councils in Judaea.

What Rabbi Joseph is telling us is that the wealthy landed families who had dominated the local town and village councils *(boula'ot)* were wiped out by the war.[14]

Imperial legislation also played a role in reducing the Jewish population of Judaea. The edict excluding Jews from the Jerusalem district is one example.[15] The exclusion remained in force throughout the Antonine period.[16] Tertullian informs us that the Jews were

11 Comp. Rabbi Jose's remark on the destruction of olive-groves by "the wicked Hadrian," Yer. Peah Vii: 20a.

12 "Terumah of grains should not be mixed with that of legumes. But after Judah was devastated (God grant that it be rebuilt soon) they began to mix etc." Tos. Ter. X: 15 (43).

13 Git. 37a; comp. JLTA I, p. 147, Yer. Ned. 38.

14 See Alon in JJCW pp. 349 ff. To be sure, ARNA seems to attribute this tradition to Rabbi Hanina, Prefect of the High Priest (ed. Schechter p. 72; Goldin p. 95) but the attribution must be erroneous. *Semahot* states explicitly that the councils in Judaea were terminated at the time R. Akiba was executed (VIII: 9, ed. Higger p. 154). See Krauss in *Qadmoniot Ha-Talmud*, I, p. 45.

15 There is some skepticism about the historicity of this ban; see Marmorstein, "Eine eingebliche Verordnung Hadrians" in *Jeschurun,* Vol. XI (1924) pp. 149 ff; Krauss in the *Yediot* of the Jewish Society for the Exploration of Eretz Israel, Vol. IV, 3 (1936–7) pp. 52 ff.; Klein, in the introduction to *Sepher Ha-Yishuv*, p. 22. But the evidence in its favor cannot be dismissed. It comes from early Church Fathers (see the quotation from Eusebius, above Chap. 10, note 2) and is based on the testimony of contemporary witnesses.

16 Brief visits may have been permitted. There are indications that during the regime of the Severi, perhaps as late as Commodus, a small Jewish community was established in Jerusalem.

excluded from Bethlehem as well.[17]

These are some of the elements in the process which began after the Bar Kokhba war and continued for several generations — a process whereby the periphery of Jerusalem known as *Har Ha-Melekh,* that is, the hill-country of Judaea proper, was emptied or almost emptied of all its Jewish population.[18] The same applies to the area surrounding Hebron, which was colonized by non-Jews, and to places like Bethlehem, Emmaus and Timna, where visible evidences of the practice of Greco-Roman religion have survived. Other sites show archaeological indications that they were abandoned altogether.[19] In short, we may describe the second half of the second century as a demographic turning point, when the center of gravity of the Jewish population in Palestine shifted northwards, to Galilee.

A corresponding population movement southwards can also be detected, though its dimensions were much smaller. The Church Father Eusebius mentions certain "large Jewish villages" south of Beth Guvrin in his time, the fourth century.[20] It is a reasonable assumption that these places grew "large" in the years following the Bar Kokhba war.

Decisions of policy and administrative acts also contributed to the decline in population. According to Eusebius, Hadrian confiscated lands from Jewish farmers under the laws of war.[21] Without a doubt, this was no merely formal act, but a matter of deliberate policy. Just as after the Destruction large stretches of land were alienated from Jewish ownership, so now again many farmers lost title to their holdings, and became tenants of new owners, with an accompanying increase in the cost of working the soil. In many cases the government expropriated the land and leased large

17 Advers. Jud. 13, P.L. II 673.
18 See Yer. Dem. VI : 25b. Comp. below, pp. 736, 741.
19 R. Simeon bar Yohai, a survivor of the war, speaks of "villages in Eretz Israel that were uprooted" (Yer. Hag. I : 76c). Eusebius refers to once-inhabited sites that were ruins in his day. See his *Onomasticon,* entries 3, 10, and 945.
20 See E.Z. Mellamed : "The Onomasticon of Eusebius," in *Tarbiz,* IV, pp. 259–260.
21 *Ecclesiastical History,* IV : 6 : 1 [Loeb Classics I, p. 311.]

tracts to non-Jewish operators, to whom the Jewish farmers became sub-tenants.[22]

Another factor in displacing Jewish farmers was the confiscation of their land as punishment for violating any of the myriad Roman regulations.[23] This punishment was first used against Jews who ignored the ban on circumcision, but was soon imposed for other infractions as well. The practice persisted for many years, and the efforts made by the Sages to counteract its effects are apparent.[24]

RESTRICTIVE LAWS

The broad punitive measures imposed by the Romans during the Bar Kokhba war and after may be classified under two headings: 1) those which banned Jewish religious practices, and 2) those which suppressed the institutions of Jewish collective life. Both types of prohibition were based on the same legal principle: as subjugated rebels (*dediticii*) the Jews were deprived of all rights.

We have already rejected the view of Graetz, shared by Dubnow, that the Hadrianic decrees did not impose compulsory acts of pagan worship on the Jews.[25] The contrary is here maintained, namely that in this respect the Hadrianic decrees were an exact reprise of the acts of Antiochus Epiphanes in the second century B.C.E. This time, however, the emperor himself was probably not involved in specific prohibitions (apart from the ban on circumcision). It is quite possible that the legate on the spot received nothing more than a general directive to clamp down on the Jews.

---

22 These tenants could be removed from the land altogether without much difficulty; see JLTA I, pp. 61–62.

23 The practice was called *sikarikon;* see Mishnah Git. V:6; Tos. ibid, I:2 and Yer. ibid. V: 47b. The term itself is derived from *sicarius* (dagger) but not as Graetz thought, on account of the *sicarii* during the first War against Rome. It goes back to the law *lex Cornella de sicariis et veneficis,* which made castration (under Hadrian, circumcision too) punishable by death or exile, plus confiscation of property. The word later came to mean, any or all confiscation. See Tol. II, p. 122.

24 See JLTA I, pp. 286–7.

25 Above, pp. 635 ff.

The way that was implemented may have been entirely his own idea.

Possibly there is a parallel here with the persecutions suffered by the early Christians. The legal basis for these was uniform: the fact that Christianity was *religio illicita* (an illegal religion). But it was persecuted in a variety of ways at different times and places. Sometimes these acts were initiated by the emperor himself, but at other times they originated with the local prefect, acting on his own.

How long did these edicts remain in force? Our information is not precise, but one thing can be stated with certainty: the decrees involving religion were set aside earlier than those directed against Jewish communal life. However, the real question is, were *all* these decrees finally abolished in the year 138 when Antoninus ascended the throne? Many historians think so. But a careful analysis of the sources makes it appear otherwise. We find references in tannaitic literature *after* Bar Kokhba to Jews undergoing martyrdom for observing such mitzvot as circumcision or *tevillah*.[26] And when Rabbi Nathan speaks of "Jews living in the Land of Israel and defending the mitzvot with their very lives,"[27] it is scarcely reasonable to limit his words to the three years between the fall of Beitar and the accession of Pius.

There is, to be sure, the testimony of Modestinus that Pius permitted the Jews to circumcise their sons.[28] Obviously, when that permission was granted, all the other restrictions dealing with religion were lifted too. But that does not prove that Antoninus took this step at the very beginning of his reign.[29]

As for the second type of restriction, limiting the Jews' right of assembly, and making their institutions illegal — these restric-

26   *Masekhet Gerim*, I:1; see Higger: "Seven Minor Treatises," New York, 1930, p. 47, Heb. p.מ"ז.
27   *Mekhilta, Ba-Hodesh*, VI, ed. Lauterbach II, p. 24.
28   *Corpus Juris Civilis, Digesta*, 48.8.1.
29   The two traditions in the Bavli (R.H. 19a=Taan. 18a and Me'ilah 17a), one about "Sages who sought to convince a very influential Roman matron" to intervene against the decrees; and another about "Sages who journeyed to Rome" for the same purpose are not, in my opinion, to be dated to the immediate post-Bar Kokhba years (*shilfei ha-shemad*) but to a somewhat later time.

tions undoubtedly remained in force much longer. It seems that they lasted, de jure at any rate, throughout the Antonine period.

Evidence for the persistance of these prohibitions may be seen in several traditions. One of them, recorded in the Yerushalmi, says that the Jews were denied the right to judge their own civil cases in the days of Rabbi Simeon bar Yohai.[30] It would be far-fetched to assume that this applies only to the three years between the end of the war and the death of Hadrian.

The same can be said for the following:

> You will find that anything the Jews were willing to defend with their lives has survived, but anything they were not prepared to defend with their lives had not survived. Thus, the Sabbath, circumcision, the study of the Torah and *tevillah*, for which Jews laid down their lives — these have survived. But the Temple, the courts of law, the Sabbatical and jubilee years, for which they were not prepared to sacrifice their lives — these have not survived.[31]

This is a clear indication that the ban on Jewish courts continued in force after the war.

The matter can be summed up thus: As a result of the Bar Kokhba war, the legal basis for Jewish autonomy ceased to exist. All manifestations of Jewish collective life, whether national or religious, were now deprived of any official standing.

MORALE

By contrast to the divisiveness that marked the Jewish people during the first war with Rome (66–74), a strong sense of national unity was manifest during the war of Bar Kokhba. But in spite of this we may safely assume that the fall of Beitar, and the harsh suffering that followed, created a mood of despair among many of the survivors. There must have been large numbers who abandoned their Jewish identity and cast off their Jewish faith, for not everyone had the fortitude to resist the prolonged religious persecu-

30 Yer. Sanh. I. 18a and VII:24b.
31 *Mekhilta, Shabbata* I, Lauterbach III, p. 204 f.; comp. Sifre Deut. LXXVI, Finkelstein p. 141, where the attribution is to R. Simeon ben Gamaliel, and the days of the "*shemad*" are explicitly mentioned.

tion. Tradition has preserved a few example, such as Elisha ben Avuyah, the famous renegade Rabbi ("Aher") to whom legend has attributed not only apostasy, but also active assistance to the Romans in their persecutions.[32]

Perhaps more revealing is the midrash about the soldier in the occupying forces, apparently himself a former student of R. Joshua ben Hananiah:

> Two students of Rabbi Joshua ben Hananiah changed their raiment *(to avoid detection)* during the *shemad*. They were accosted by a certain soldier *(istratiot)*, an apostate. Said he to them : If you are sons of the Torah, you ought to be ready to give up your lives for her sake.[33]

A pervasive mood of depression endured for many years, even after the decrees of Hadrian had been relaxed. This was one factor among the many that made it so difficult to revive the spiritual life of the people. There were many side-effects. For example, it is widely believed that the Mandaeans originated as former Jews who had abandoned Judaism after the Bar Kokhba war. The fold was also abandoned by many Jewish Christians, who now gave up their Jewish identity and became Gentile Christians.

OCCUPATION FORCES

After the Bar Kokhba war, the Roman garrison in Palestine was increased from one to two legions, plus support troops. The Xth Fretensian stayed on, its headquarters still at Jerusalem (now called Aelia). A second legion, the VIth Ferrata, was stationed at Kephar Othnai.

Some of the smaller units are identified for us by a military diploma found in the vicinity of Nazareth and dated in the year 139.[34] It reveals that there were 12 *auxilia* of infantry and 3 of cavalry stationed in the country at that particular time. This adds up to a rather large army of occupation for so small a country.

Most of these troops were quartered in locations scattered across

32 Kid. 39b and Yer. Hag. II : 77b.
33 GenR. LXVIII, 9. Theodor-Albeck, p. 964.
34 See Alae in *Revue Biblique*, 1897, p. 599.

the face of the land. Their encampments, which were strictly out of bounds to all Jews, served as focal points for the control of the surrounding countryside; for collecting the supplies requisitioned from the inhabitants *(arnoniot* = *annona militaris)* by which the legions were provisioned; and for the administration of the strict military justice by which the country was governed during the first part of the Antonine period.

That one of these centers was Beitar itself we learn from an old midrash, apparently tannaitic in origin: [35]

> Scripture says: *He shall shut you up in till your towns (Deut. XXVIII: 52)*. This refers to the great towns in Eretz Israel, such as Beitar and Har Ha-Melech and the like.

The same situation is apparently what lies behind the following recollection: [36]

> It happened once that 60 men went down into the garrison[37] at Beitar, and not one of them returned alive.

Obviously, Roman military camps were places where Jews who had been caught violating the regulations could expect only the most summary kind of military justice, if any.

JURIDICAL STATUS

During the Antonine period the Jews were officially defined as *dediticii*, and from this status a number of consequences flowed. First of all, the right to organize their own corporate life was taken away. Hence the abolition of the Jewish civil courts *(n'tilat dinei mamonot)* and of Jewish local councils *(boula'ot)*. There is no indication that these instruments of Jewish autonomy regained *official* recognition at any time during the second century, although they did resume activity on an informal, tolerated basis.

Reversion to the status of a subjugated population also had its effect on the freedom of the conquered to practise their religion. Technically, the Jews had recovered full religious rights once Pius

---

35 *Midrash Haggadol,* Deut., Mossad Harav Kook, 1972, p.תרכ"א.
36 Tos. Yev. XIV: 8 (259); Bavli ibid. 122a.
37 Pace S. Klein, who interprets "Kharqom" as "the *siege* of Beitar" in *Horev* II, pp. 47ff.

had removed the ban on circumcision. But their inferior status exposed them to interference on the part of Roman officials, perhaps in punishment for acts disapproved of by the occupation authorities. Some of the sources dealing with religious persecution certainly must refer to post-Hadrianic times. Thus, in connection with the ruling in the Mishnah that the Book of Esther should get its public reading in certain towns on the Monday (market-day) *before* Purim,[38] Rabbi Judah says: [39]

> This applies to places which hold public prayers on Mondays and Thursdays, but in places where such assemblies are not held because it would be dangerous (read *mistaknin*) the risk should not be taken on any day other than the actual day of Purim.[40]

It seems obvious that the tanna was referring to unsettled times, but not to "the *sakanah*" in the limited sense of the Hadrianic persecutions.

The same applies to the decrees which Rabbi Simeon bar Yohai and Rabbi Reuven ben Istroboli tried to get rescinded.[41] Neither of the two was an adult at the time of the Hadrianic edicts, nor do the texts involved breathe a word about these well-known decrees. We must conclude that the two Rabbis were protesting one or another prohibition imposed on the Jews during the reign of Pius, or one of his Antonine successors.

The tradition reporting the other protest reads as follows: [42]

> On the 28th (of Adar) the Jews received the good news that the Torah was no longer forbidden.[43] For the (Roman) government had issued a decree forbidding them to study the

---

38 Mishnah, Meg. I:3.
39 Tos. ibid. I:4 (221); comp. Bavli 2a.
40 The preferred reading is that of ms. Vienna, and of ms. Munich for the parallel in the Bavli; also noted by Alfassi in his commentary ad loc. Current texts read *mitkansin* etc.
41 Above, note 39.
42 R.H. 19a = Taan. 18a; Megillat Ta'anit XII, ed. Lichtenstein, HUCA VIII. p. 350.
43 Lichtenstein (ibid. p. 279) and others assign this sentence to Second Temple times.

Torah, or circumcise their sons, or keep the Sabbath. What did Judah ben Shamu'a and his colleagues do? They went and took counsel with a certain (Roman) matron who used to advise all the notables of Rome. She told them: Go and protest aloud at night-time. They went and cried aloud at night, saying: Are we not children of the same father, children of the same mother? Why do you issue harsh decrees against us, such as you do against no other tribe or nation? The decrees were thereupon annulled, and that day was declared a feast day.

As the Talmud points out, Rabbi Judah ben Shamu'a was a student of Rabbi Meir's. It would hardly have been possible for him to have led a delegation to Rome in the year 138. It would also have been a highly unlikely time for Jews to ask why they were being singled out for harsh treatment. After all they had just thrown the entire Roman empire into turmoil by carrying on a revolt which most of the Jews of the empire had supported.

Halevy agrees with this reasoning, and proposes that the episode took place later, during the days of Antoninus Pius.[44] But when he suggests that the following *does* refer to the immediate postwar years, one must demur:

> Once the government had issued a decree forbidding the Jews to keep the Sabbath or circumcise their children, and compelling them to have intercourse with menstruants. Rabbi Reuven ben Istroboli went etc. ... They said: Who shall go and get the decrees annulled? Let Rabbi Simeon bar Yohai go, for he is adept at miracles. And after him who shall go? Let Rabbi Eleazar the son of Jose go etc. ...[45]

It is unlikely that Rabbi Jose's son Eleazar had reached manhood by the year 138, and as for Rabbi Simeon bar Yohai, that was the very time he was a fugitive from the Romans, living in a cave.

An indication of the reduced status of the Jews during the Antonine period is the fact that the Romans exacted the tax on land

---

44 *Dorot,* I, Vol. 5, p. 729 ff.
45 Me'ilah 17a. Graetz assigns this event to the sixties, the time of Lucius Verus.

even for the Sabbatical years. Since the days of Julius Caesar they had been exempted from that tax on the sabbatical, and for obvious reasons. Yet we read in the Mishnah:

> Rabbi Simeon says: Beforetime they used to call them "gatherers of Seventh Year produce." But when the extortioners became numerous they changed that, and took to calling them "traffickers in Seventh Year produce."[46]

Both Bavli and Yerushalmi explain the phrase about extortioners this way: "from the time when the government officials ordered the payment of the *arnona* on the Sabbatical Year."[47] We have no reason to reject the testimony of the two talmudim, even though the term used (*annasim*) usually refers to corrupt government officials who exact extra-legal payments.

The comment quoted above about the lapse of courts of law and sabbatical years, attributed to Rabban Simeon ben Gamaliel II, should be read in this light.[48] These institutions lost ground because of the unfavorable political situation. The right of the Jews to their own courts was no longer recognized, neither was their exemption from land taxes on the sabbatical year.

That unfavorable situation should be seen as the background for the warning to prospective proselytes.[49]

> An applicant for conversion should be addressed thus: Why do you want to become a Jew? Don't you know that these days Jews are persecuted and downtrodden and driven from pillar to post and made the victims of suffering etc. ...?

The tractate *Gerim*, which probably reflects the situation after the Hadrianic persecutions, also has a version of the warning to would-

---

46   Sanh. III:3; comp. Tos. ibid. V:2 (423).
47   The situation recurs later, when Rabbi Yannai in the third century permits Jews to cultivate their fields on the sabbatical, because of the *arnona* (Sanh. 26a; comp. Yer. ibid. III:21b); and early in the fourth century, which Rabbi Isaac praises those farmers who leave their fields fallow on the seventh year, even though they have to pay the *arnona* (see LevR I:1).
48   See above, note 31.
49   Yev. 47a.

be proselytes, in which they are told that Jews cannot practise their religion openly.[50]

The fact that it is Rabban Simeon ben Gamaliel, of the post-war generation, who says what he says in the following passage, is surely another indication that the old troubles did not come to end with the death of Hadrian:

> The question was asked: Who wrote *Megillat Ta'anit*: The answer was, Hanania ben Hezekiah and his circle, who cherished their sufferings. Said Rabban Simeon ben Gamaliel: We too cherish our sufferings, but what shall we do? Even if we tried to write them down, we should never be able to record them all.[51]

Apparently, then, the original "troubles" listed in *Megillat Ta'anit* were back again. The situation was uncertain; the screws could be tightened at any moment.

One might even read the words of Marcus Aurelius, quoted by Ammianus Marcellinus, as just one more example of this unfavorable atmosphere:

> For Marcus, as he was passing through Palestine on his way to Egypt, being often disgusted with the malodorous and rebellious Jews, is reported to have cried with sorrow: "O Marcomanni, O Quadi, O Sarmatians! At last I have found a people more unruly than you!"[52]

It is, of course, possible to argue that the prolongation of Jewish rightlessness by the Romans was due to the spirit of rebellion that was still alive among many Jews; or that Marcus was offended by the aid which the Jews of Palestine, along with other peoples of the region hod given to the attempted coup by Avidius Cassius just before the emperor's trip to the East in 175. But it is more

---

50 In *Seven Minor Treatises,* edited and translated by Michael Higger, New York 1930, page ע״ה translation p. 47. [The phrase pointed out is *v*e*inan nohagin b*e*farhessia,* Higger renders "they do not assume an air of ostentation," which, it is suggested, rather misses the point.]

51 Shab. 13b. [Rashi: cherish the anniversary of relief from the troubles].

52 XXII:5:5. Comp. GLA II, no. 506.

probable that the Jews were reacting to the severely repressive measures taken by the Romans after the fall of Beitar, and then to the harsh military government which characterized the occupation.

Perhaps we can find in this repression some of the background for a report in the *Historia Augusta* about a Jewish revolt in Judaea during the reign of Antoninus Pius, which had to be put down forcibly by the imperial *legatus*. In their attempts to fathom this isolated report, historians differ. There are those who suggest a tie-in with Jewish hopes for a Parthian victory, supporting the suggestion by citing certain aggadic passages. The trouble with this suggestion is that there was no war with Parthia during the reign of Pius! (To be sure, such a war was fought early in the reign of his successor, Marcus Aurelius.)

Others see in this report some aftershocks of the Bar Kokhba war. In this view, the fall of Beitar did not wholly extinguish the great rebellion of Hadrian's day. Embers continued to flare up under his successors. However, this interpretation has nothing to offer by way of proof. That does not mean that there was not an *indirect* connection between the Bar Kokhba war and the uprising under Pius. The war led to a harsh regime of occupation; the occupation bred an attempted revolt.

Another factor may have been the spread of outlawry in the postwar decades, as Mommsen suggests. No doubt the difficult economic conditions contributed to the proliferation of highwaymen at that time. But it also seems quite likely that there were men who had fought, or were suspected of having fought, against Rome, and who were unwilling or unable to resume civilian life. Such men may well have banded together in groups whose motives were a mixture of zealotry and banditry.[53] This unsettled situation could have provided the background for an outbreak, sparked off by causes which have since become obscure. In any event, the Roman retribution would have made considerable trouble for large numbers of people.

There is no intention here of claiming that the denial of legal status to the Jews of Palestine throughout the Antonine period

53 [Comp. the American West following the Civil War.]

meant that they were *altogether* unable to maintain the organs of their national and religious life. As we shall see, they did in fact manage to renew those institutions step by step, and without Roman interference. In fact, they even achieved a sort of de facto, if incomplete, recognition of those institutions

But before we go into that aspect of the situation on the national level, we must address ourselves to the organs of local government. Although in principle these, too, had been abolished as part of the revocation of all rights of the Jews as a people, in practice the Romans could not get along without the town and village councils. They needed them in districts where there was a large Jewish population, to help with administrative details, and most particularly for dealing with fiscal matters.

Obviously, such councils could only be led by men who were "in good odor with the government" (*m⁰quravim la-malkhut*), men who had not taken active part in the revolt under Bar Kokhba. But it must be said on their behalf that at least they made possible some residual form of Jewish public life. This is best observed in the two large cities of the Galilee; Sepphoris and Tiberias.

We know that both these places retained the municipal status that had been theirs before the war.[54] Each had been a *polis;* both continued to be. Certainly each had had a non-Jewish element among its citizenry, as both had had before the war. The percentage of gentiles in each may even have increased. But there is no room for doubt that the great majority of their inhabitants were still Jews. Granted: the civic institutions probably became rather more Hellenistic in style. Nevertheless, it is not correct to say, as Büchler and Jones do, that control of these cities was taken altogether out of Jewish hands, and entrusted entirely to gentiles.[55]

It has already been pointed out that most of the Tiberians and Sepphorites probably took no part in the Bar Kokhba revolt. That very probability makes it all the more likely that these Jews retained the position they had held in those cities before the war. This includes a role — diminished, perhaps, but still a role — in

---

54 See JLTA I, pp. 147 ff.
55 Jones: "The Greek City," p. 51. [Büchler: "The Political and Social Leaders etc." London, 1909, p. 10].

city government. The statement is made despite the fact that, officially, the two cities were not listed as "Jewish," but rather as "pagan."

The postwar era found the Jews of Tiberias and Sepphoris in a socio-economic position of considerable strength, probably because they had been noncombatants. So they were able to contribute in no small measure to the revival of Jewish public life in the country, and to play a role in the reestablishment of the nation's institutions. It is true that neither of these cities became the seat of the Sanhedrin or the Pariarchate in the first generations after the war. It is equally true that there was a prolonged struggle between the Sages and the ruling elites of the two cities, a struggle calculated to delay the emergence of a nationally recognized leadership. Nevertheless, the very fact that two large urban centers had survived the Hadrianic era, and were still serving as economic and social foci for the Galilee as a whole — this in itself was a powerful stimulus towards the revival of Jewish public life in the country.

Later on, during the regime of the Severi, the Sanhedrin and the Patriarchate did move to these two cities. But during the Antonine period conditions for such a move were not yet ripe. Those conditions were, however, already in the making. Important personalities began to take up residence in the two towns, significant groups began to coalesce there, and institutions that were destined to provide national and spiritual leadership began to take root.

In order to understand how some elements of social structure at the local level were able to survive the war, we must bear in mind that the Hadrianic edicts, even at their worst, did not strike at the entire Jewish population. The repressive measures of the Romans were, in practice, directed against prominent and influential persons. It was the same method as that employed in persecuting the Christians. The Romans went after individuals who defied their orders openly, and who led large numbers of people "astray." Such famous martyrs as Rabbi Akiba and Rabbi Haninah ben Teradyon were executed because they openly gathered large numbers of people together for the study of Torah. The crime of Rabbi Judah ben Bava was that he ordained a group of disciples. All three were guilty of violating the Roman laws prohibiting Jewish collective life. They were flying in the face of edicts which made Jewish autonomy illegal.

On the other hand, in those localities where community leaders and men of substance did not rebel against the Romans, it was possible for a semblance of normal life to survive. This includes not only the wealthy and powerful Tiberians and Sepphorites, who became participants in the administrative machinery of government after the war (some of them, no doubt, rather unhappily); it includes others as well. One need only mention the father of Rabbi Simeon bar Yohai. Besides, there were those among the Sages who were "close to the authorities" to the extent of counselling compliance with the ban on Jewish public activities. Take for example Rabbi Jose ben Qisma, who chided Rabbi Haninah ben Teradyon for risking his life by teaching Torah to large public gatherings; or Rabbi Eliezer ben Parta who, when caught in the same act, was willing to deny it.[56] Of this Rabbi it was said that "the prominent men of Rome" attended his funeral.

So we see that there were even Sages who maintained contact with the Roman authorities. They tried to accommodate to the situation as it was, seeking thereby to minimize the damage and the suffering caused by the defeat of their people. They must be credited with a contribution towards the reestablishment of the institutions of Torah, and with helping to rally the people around the leadership of the surviving scholars and teachers.

One interesting development in co-operation with the Romans was the emergence, apparently towards the end of the Antonine period, of Sages in official positions as directors of public safety. We know specifically of Rabbi Eliezer son of Rabbi Simeon, and of Rabbi Ishmael ben Jose, in that office.[57] Such positions were, to be sure, imposed on the appointees as *liturgeia*, or compulsory service, a means by which the local gendarmerie was recruited in many countries, including Palestine. We have evidence dating from the Antonine era for the existence in Asia Minor of civilian

56 Av. Zar. 18a and 17b.
57 B.M. 83b. and Pesikta d'Rav Kahana, ed. Buber 91b. In the Talmud the office is called *prohagona* while in the Pesikta it is called *arkhiliporin* (pl.) according to Buber's emendation.

police, headed by an *eirenarches*. For Palestine there is similar evidence from Byzantine times.

In the case of the Rabbis mentioned above, it is possible that their families were traditionally responsible for the office of local chief constable.[58] In any event, we see that there were times when Jews had relationships with the governing authorities, and even accepted official positions. But his does not indicate any improvement in their status. The public office was no honor, but a burden imposed on the subject, avoidable only by taking flight.[59]

One piece of Hadrianic legislation had effects which out-lasted his reign by many centuries. This was the law forbidding Jews to circumcise non-Jews, including any slaves they owned. Although the original thrust of the edict was not directed against Judaism, its enforcement after the Bar Kokhba revolt focused on preventing Jewish missionary activity. The net effect was to stem the flow of proselytes into the Jewish fold. The law remained in force throughout the Antonine and Severan periods, and we have no evidence that it was ever rescinded; so that when Constantine, the first Christian emperor, forbade the conversion to Judaism of Jewish-owned slaves, he was simply confirming a prohibition of long standing. Originally, of course, the law had been part of a rearguard action in defence of classical pagan civilization. But as things turned out it was a severe blow to the Jewish religion, even though it was never completely effective.

SOCIAL AND ECONOMIC CONDITIONS

Reference has already been made to the extremely bad economic conditions which prevailed in Palestine for many years after the Bar Kokhba war. At the same time, it should be borne in mind that there were some surviving elements of economic strength.

For the hard times that characterized the latter half of the second century, there is plentiful evidence in the Talmudic sources.

---

58 Simeon bar Yohai says to Rabbi Akiba: "If you don't teach me, I shall report you to Yohai my father, and he will turn you over to the Romans!" (Pes. 12a). As for Rabbi Ishmael ben Jose, he and his father were prominent and respected citizens of Sepphoris.
59 See JLTA 30–31, and below p. 702.

We are told, for example, of the want endured by the disciples of Rabbi Akiba and their contemporaries.[60]

It was said that six of the students of Rabbi Judah bar Ila'i had to cover themselves with a single cloak while they sat studying Torah.

When Rabbi Judah remarked that his generation, unlike its predecessors, gave more time to making a living than to study, he was, of course bemoaning the neglect of spiritual matters.[61] But implicit in his remark is the fact that people were finding it hard to make a living! In the same vein, when Rabbi Judah rails at the fact that in his day, by contrast to preceding generations, people used all kinds of devices to avoid paying their tithes, one understands that the decline in piety was caused in part by an increase in poverty.[62]

The economic situation was no doubt a factor in the emigration of certain scholars. The Sifre relates : [63]

Rabbi Eleazar ben Shamu'a and Rabbi Johanan the Sandlar were on their way to Nisibis (*in Mesopotamia*) to study under Rabbi Judah ben Bathyra. When they got as far as Sidon they bethought themselves of Eretz Israel and raised tear-stained eyes to heaven, rending their garments and reciting the verse, "Ye shall possess it, and shall dwell therein" (Deut. XI : 21). Said they: "It is a commandment to live in the Land of Israel, a mitzvah equal to the sum of all the other commandments in the Torah." Whereupon they turned around and went back home.

60 Sanh. 20a. Of that Rabbi himself, we are told that he and his wife had one cloak between them, so that they had to take turns going out; and when Rabban Simeon ben Gamaliel declared a public fast, Rabbi Judah could not attend the prayer gathering because he had nothing to wear (Ned. 49b). We also hear of a meeting of a calendar committee of seven sages some years after the Bar Kokhba war, when "those who had cloaks cut off one half and gave it to the colleagues who had none" (Yer. Hag. III : 78d).
61 Above, p. 490, note 25.
62 Ber. 35b.
63 Sifre Deut. 80. Finkelstein p. 146.

A similar point is made by a story about Rabbi Simeon bar Yohai. Certain of his disciples went abroad, earned a goodly sum, and returned home. Seeing this, others of his disciples wanted to do the same. In order to keep them from leaving the country the Rabbi, it was said, performed a miracle, exposing a hidden treasure of golden dinars.[64]

For the period in question we find Tannaim expressing disapproval of people who go abroad, even temporarily, in order to improve their economic position. Rabbi Simeon sets a rather strict halakhic norm:

> One ought not leave the country before the price of wheat has risen to one *sela* for two *seah*. Said Rabbi Simeon: That applies only if there is none to be had even at that price. But if one can find any at all even at twice that price he should not emigrate. He used to say: Look at Elimelech in the Book of Ruth. He was a prominent citizen, a leader of his community. But because he emigrated to Moab, he and his sons died of hunger, while back in Bethlehem the whole town survived on the lands Elimelech had left behind.[65]

Other Sages of the time expressed similar sentiments, for example Rabbi Meir:

> Anyone who has his fixed abode in Eretz Israel, and eats his daily bread in purity, and speaks the holy tongue, and recites the Shema morning and evening — he can rest assured that eternal life will be his.[66]

No doubt it was the desperate economic situation that impelled the Sages assembled at Usha to rule that a man was duty bound to feed his minor children, both sons and daughters.[67] The same situation probably explains the ruling that forbids transportation out of the country of grain, wine and oil. The regulation must have

---

64 Yer. Ber. IX:13d; GenR XXXV:2, Theodor p. 128. for a fuller version see Midrash Tehillim 92:8 and ExodR III:3.
65 Tos. Av. Zar IV:4 (466). Cf. Ruth I:19. "The whole city was astir."
66 Yer. Shab. I:3c.
67 Ket. 49b; Yer. ibid. IV:28d. See above, p. 574.

been introduced after the Bar Kokhba war, because in normal times these products were the leading export items.[68]

It is in this light that we probably should interpret Rabbi Jose's concern about the deterioration of farming in his day.[69] Agriculture was the very foundation of the economy, and a decline in agricultural production would have been quite enough to bring about a general depression in both town and country.

These hard times were probably a major cause for the spread of that banditry which is revealed by the literature of the period. Warnings not to go out alone at night and not to take to the road by oneself originate from this time. Against such a background, the appointment of Rabbis as directors of public safety becomes understandable.

The poverty of Palestinian Jews at this period is no doubt the basis for the remark attributed to Marcus Aurelius that they were "malodorous."[70] Corresponding evidence of their destitution can be seen in a third-century description of a theatrical performance in the wealthy cosmopolitan city of Caesarea. The non-Jewish audience consists of affluent merchants and men of rank, Greeks, Romans and Levantine Hellenists. For their amusement the pantomimists make fun of the Jews, a beggarly lot whose staple food is the carob bean, and who have to chop up their beds for kindling wood, so that they have nothing to sleep on but the bare earth. As for clothing, one tattered cloak must last them for a lifetime.[71]

Clearly, the non-Jewish element in the country was not at all badly off. The general improvement in trade throughout the empire brought its benefits to the seaports and commercial cities of Palestine, with their largely gentile populations. The imperial government made its contribution by improving the network of roads and bridges. The initial purpose may have been to facilitate the

68 Tos. Av. Zar. IV : 2 (465); B.B. 90b.
69 Tos. Shevi. VII : 18 (72).
70 See above, p. 654.
71 LamR, Proem 17, and III : 12. [The source does not mention Caesarea; but the version of the midrash in the proem attributes it to Rabbi Abbahu (ca. 279–320). Since he was the leader of the Jewish community in the port city, Alon's tacit assumption that the *mimos* mentioned in the midrash appeared at the famous amphitheatre of Caesarea makes perfect sense.]

movement of troops and military supplies, but at the same time these improved communications could not but stimulate the growth of trade and commerce. During the Antonine period there was also an upsurge in urban public works. Various public buildings, market-places, storage-granaries and the like were added to the landscape of many cities.[72] Jerash in Transjordan, a city which flourished in the Antonine period, has left tangible evidence of this efflorescence.[73] One is reminded of the famous argument between Rabbi Judah and Rabbi Simeon about the motives of the Romans for all this construction.[74]

Despite the general poverty of the Jews, it appears that a small upper crust among them shared in the new prosperity. The evidence we have relates specifically to merchants in Tiberias and Sepphoris. Regarding the first of these cities, two Greek-language inscriptions found in Rome indicate that there were well-developed trade relations during the second century between Tiberias and Italy.[75]

As for Sepphoris, the tonsorial elegance of some of its rich men comes out in this description: [76]

Rabbi Nehorai said: Absalom used to shave once every 30 days. (cf. II Sam. XIV:26). Rabbi Jose said: No, every Friday, for that is what royalty do, though the men of Tiberias and Sepphoris do not limit themselves to that.[77]

SANHEDRIN AND PATRIARCHATE

During several decades after the Bar-Kokhba war, efforts to re-establish a focus for Jewish national and religious life centered chiefly on the activities of Rabban Simeon ben Gamaliel II and his circle. Neither of the two main central institutions — the Patriarchate and the Sanhedrin — was restored immediately after the end of Hadrian's reign. The first steps consisted of isolated

---

72 See Watzinger: *Denkmäler Palästinas,* 1933, p. 94; ZDPV 1909, 270; 1911, 112.
73 Kraeling: *Gerasa,* p. 46.
74 Shab. 33b; comp. JLTA I, p. 23, note 1.
75 See JLTA I, p. 148, n. 44.
76 Tos. Sot. III:16 (297).
77 For care of the hair and beard as a sign of wealth, see Ned. 51a.

efforts to take care of the most pressing religious and social needs of the people. For the time being, there were no institutions, and no fixed place where the leadership was located.

One immediate need was the Jewish religious calendar. Thus we read:[78]

> Once seven Sages came together in the Vale of Beth Rimmon in order to intercalate the calendar, and these were they: Rabbis Meir, Judah, Jose, Simeon, Nehemiah, Eliezer ben Jacob and Johanan the sandalmaker. ...

Note: there is no Patriarch present, even though it is ordinarily the exclusive prerogative of the Patriarch to initiate this procedure and to invite members of the Sanhedrin to ratify his decision. Therefore it seems certain that the meeting described took place at a time when Rabban Simeon ben Gamaliel was not functioning, and had probably not yet come out of hiding. The sequel to this episode shows how stop-gap and temporary the gathering was, for the Sages proceeded to other agenda as well — they engaged in Torah-study.

Another such gathering, specifically for the study of Torah, is said to have taken place about this time. According to the Bavli, "our Sages" gathered at the "Vineyard in Yavneh." Those present were Rabbis Judah, Jose, Nehemiah, Eliezer son of Rabbi Jose the Galilean etc.[79] These were all disciples of Rabbi Akiba, so the time must have been right after the Hadrianic persecutions.

A different version of what appears to have been the same meeting is to be found in the Midrash Rabbah:[80]

> In the aftermath of the *sh'mad* our Sages gathered at Usha, and these were they: Rabbis Judah, Nehemiah, Meir, Jose, Simeon ben Yohai, Eliezer son of Rabbi Jose the Galilean, and Eliezer ben Jacob. They sent a message to all the elders of the Galilee: Let everyone who is learned come and teach, and everyone who is not learned come and learn. So they

78 Yer. Hag. III: 78a.
79 Ber. 63b–64a.
80 CantR II:16, on Song II:5. The reference to Rabbi Judah in this midrash seems to contradict Ber. 63b (= Shab. 53b) where he is described as "the leading authority on all subjects."

gathered and studied together and disposed of various matters of public importance (lit: *did whatever needed to be done*). When it was time for them to leave they said: Ought we to leave the place where we have been guests without a word (of appreciation)? So they paid due deference to Rabbi Judah by asking him to expound, not that he was their superior in Torah, but because they were assembled in his home-town, etc. etc. . .

The contradiction between the two reports regarding the location of this assembly has aroused a good deal of scholarly discussion. As it happens, this is not the only reference in the Babylonian Talmud to "Yavneh" or "The Vineyard at Yavneh" as the scene of events occurring after the Bar Kokhba war.[81]

I am convinced that the tradition quoted in the Bavli has no basis in fact. If we accepted it at face value we would have to believe that conditions in Judaea proper immediately after the war were rather benign, and that the political situation at that moment was particularly favorable for the Jews. Otherwise, how could the Sages have returned to the town which had been the seat of the Sanhedrin and the Patriarch, so soon after the *sh°mad*?

Besides, the Babylonian tradition contains an inner contradiction regarding the place of the meeting. Somewhere in transmission a geographical error must have crept in, because the Bavli agrees with the Midrash that Rabbi Judah opened the proceedings by speaking in praise of the Sages who had travelled great distances to be present, while in response the Sages paid honor to their host, ass to "all who open their homes to scholars, and give them food and drink." This shows that Rabbi Judah was at home, and was playing host to his colleagues. But we know the name of Rabbi Judah's home town. It was Usha.

This gathering at Usha has all the earmarks of an unscheduled emergency meeting. It was not convened by the Patriarch, indeed no Patriarch was present. Apparently there *was* no Patriarch, nor

---

81 See Büchler's study of this problem in the Chayes Memorial Volume, (Abhandlungen usw. Wien 1933) pp. קל"ז ff. His conclusion: It is highly improbable that the Sages ever assembled in Yavneh after the war. On the other hand, Halevy defended the tradition of the Bavli; see his *Dorot*, I: 5, chap. 26, pp. 740–744.

any regularly constituted Sanhedrin. This is not surprising; the absence of Rabban Simeon ben Gamaliel calls for no special explanation. It was too soon after the war for the Patriarchate to raise its head, even unofficially. Indeed, it is more than likely that Rabban Simeon and other members of the Patriarch's family were high on the "wanted" list of the Roman authorities, on account of their role in the revolt. The tradition attributed to Rabban Simeon comes to mind, regarding the numerous children of his father's household, of whom only two survived the fall of Beitar.[82]

Perhaps there is additional evidence in the following tradition that the Romans were out to arrest the Patriarch, although there are some difficulties with the text:[83]

> When the wicked Turnusrufus ran a plough over the Sanctuary[84] an order was issued condemning Rabban Gamaliel to death. A certain *hegmon* (*see variae*) came and stood in the Academy and proclaimed: "Wanted, the man with the nose! Wanted, the man with the nose!"[85] When Rabban Gamaliel heard this, he went into hiding.

The difficulty is that Rabban Gamaliel (the Younger) was Patriarch after the first war with Rome, in the first century, while "Turnusrufus" in Talmudic literature always means Tineius Rufus, *Legatus pro praetore* of Judaea at the time of the Bar Kokhba war, in the second century. Some scholars have tried to solve the contradiction by suggesting that in this one instance Turnusrufus means Terentius Rufus, who was, according to Josephus, Commander-in-Chief Roman forces in Judaea after the first war, the War of the Destruction.[86]

---

82 Sot. 49b; B.Q. 83a. See also Yer. Taan. IV:69a where it appears that Rabban Simeon definitely was in Beitar all through the siege.
83 Taan. 29a.
84 Mishnah: "and the city was ploughed under;" Yerushalmi: "Rufus, may his bones rot, ran a plough over the Sanctuary."
85 Various explanations have been offered for this phrase, e.g. the Latin *nasus* may be a play on the Patriarch's title *"nasi."* The simplest explanation would be that this Patriarch had a prominent nose!
86 JW VII:2:2 (31); comp. Alon in *Sefer Klausner* p. 167, n. 65 [=JJCW p. 337 n. 73].

However, this solution seems somewhat forced. Everywhere else in the literature, Turnusrufus is the Roman who presided over the post-Bar Kokhba persecutions. Besides, the ploughing under of the Sanctuary is mentioned nowhere except in the time of Hadrian. Jerome, too, reports a Jewish tradition that the Romans ran a plough over the Temple site *after the fall of Beitar.* All this leads most scholars to conclude that the names of two patriarchs, father and son, became garbled in transmission, and that the tradition quoted here should read "Rabban Simeon ben Gamaliel;" that it was he who was forced to flee from the Academy, and hide from the Romans.

There is therefore every reason for supposing a prolonged period of uncertainty and improvisation on the part of the Sages in their attempts to reactivate the institutions of Jewish life, and to resume the organized study of Torah. It was only after the passage of considerable time that the Sanhedrin was re-established in a fixed place (Usha) and the Patriarchate began to function again.

This long hiatus may well have been a factor in the restraint with which Rabban Simeon ben Gamaliel exercised his authority later, when he did take up the reins of office. It may also underlie his reputation for moderation and humility. In any event, the situation militated against strong leadership; cautious circumspection was the order of the day. Perhaps this weakness at the national center lies behind certain attempts made at this time in Babylonia to break away from the religious authority of the mother country.

But it was to the character of Rabban Simeon ben Gamaliel that what ensued was in large measure attributable. The renewal of the national institutions, their gradual growth from weakness to strength as the resultant of forces not always working in harmony, was guided by the new Patriarch with a blend of sagacity, moderation and resilience combined with a capacity for decisive action at moments of crisis. He seems to have been blessed with a friendly disposition, the ability to work with others, a strong awareness of the need for consensus, and at the same time the will to assert his authority and to insist on the prerogatives of his office. He was the right man in the right place to guide his people, to give it a renewed sense of unity, and to regain for the Sanhedrin a large measure of the social and religious leadership of the nation. When Rabban Simeon ben Gamaliel became Nasi, that office was in a weak posture vis-à-vis the Sanhedrin.[87] The latter body was governed by a triumvirate: the Patriarch himself; Rabbi Nathan as *Av Beth Din* (President of the Court); and Rabbi Meir as *Hakham* (chief jurisconsult).[88] After a time, according to the same source, Rabban Simeon ordered a change in protocol: when the Nasi entered the assembly, everyone was to rise and remain standing until he said, "Be seated." The other two officials were to be received with lesser measures of deference.

There can be little doubt as to what this was all about. The dignity and authority of the Patriarch were being emphasized. He was *primus;* his colleagues were not quite *pares.* The necessity for this step arose from the fact that the Sanhedrin had exercised sole authority while the Patriarch had been unable to appear at Usha. When he did arrive, and had become firmly ensconced in office, he took measures to re-establish the seniority of his position.

It was not long, however, before he ran into trouble. Rabbi Meir and Rabbi Nathan tried to unseat him — almost certainly with the help of other members of the High Court. But apparently he had his supporters, and the attempt failed. At the same time, his own effort to retaliate against his opponents came to nothing, because of opposition from the Sages.

The net effect of this struggle for authority was to restore the office of Nasi to something like its prewar eminence.[89] But it must not be thought that the Sages emerged from this struggle completely stripped of their power. On the contrary, from this time forward the Patriarch shared a large measure of his authority with the Sanhedrin. Indeed, of all the Patriarchs Rabban Simeon ben Gamaliel is the one most often seen in consultation with his col-

87 See the account in the Babylonian Talmud, Hor. 13b–14a.
88 The nature of this office is uncertain. It appears again later when Judah I directs in his will: "Simeon my son is to be *Hakham,* Gamaliel my son is to be *Nasi*." (Ket. 103b).
89 See the version in *Halakhot Gedolot,* Venice ed. p. 124. Echoes of this struggle seem to reverberate in the traditions about the Sages collected in the tenth century by Sherira Gaon; see Schechter in JQR o.s. 14 (1902) p. 490. [For Alon's exposition of these materials, not reproduced here, see Tol. II pp. 72–3.]

leagues of the High Court. He gives a ruling conveyed to him by Rabbi Jose, and in various contexts quotes Rabbi Johanan the Sandalmaker, Rabbi Judah, Rabbi Meir, the latter's disciple Rabbi Judah ben Shamu'a, and Rabbi Judah ben Yair.[90] It would be hard to find any other Sage — not to speak of a Patriarch — so given to citing other scholars as authority for his dicta.

There can be little doubt that this phenomenon derived from the personal modesty and pacific nature of Rabban Simeon. There is telling evidence of this in the Mishnah which shows him consulting the Sages of his Beth Din about the laws of "firstlings." What is striking is the fact that this area of ritual Halakhah had always been regarded by the Patriarchs as their own special preserve.[91]

This genial approach of his led to the fullest co-operation between Rabban Simeon and the Sanhedrin, as witness the following

> Rabbi Ammi ben Qorḥah quoted Rav: Why does the Halakhah always follow the rulings of Rabban Simeon ben Gamaliel? Because he used to deliver in summary form decisions already arrived at by his Beth Din.[92]

What this means is that Rabban Simeon never declared a ruling on his own, but sought the consensus of his Beth Din. Therefore his opinions had the force of law.[93]

The decision taken at Usha not to invoke the ban against any Sage doubtless reflected the growing power of the members of the Sanhedrin.[94] Rabbi Meir was involved in one such episode:

---

90 Tos. Suk. II:2 (193) = Bavli ibid. 26a, Yer. ibid. 53a; Tos. Maas. Sh. III:18 (92); Tos. Ber. V:2 (12); Tos. Kel. B.Q. IV:2 (572); ibid V:4 (574); Tos. Ket. VI:10 (268) Tos. Yev. X:16 (252); Mishnah B.M. VIII:8; Bavli Shab. 15b; R.H. 19a.

91 See JLTA I, p. 318.

92 Yer. B.B. X:17d.

93 His respect for the majority extended to public opinion. Thus: "Rabbi Simeon ben Gamaliel and Rabbi Eliezer ben Zadoq say that the promulgation of Leap Years and all matters affecting the public should be acted on only with the consent of the majority of the community."

94 Yer. M.Q. III:81d; Bavli ibid. 17a.

There were some who sought to impose a ban on Rabbi Meir. Said he to them: I shall pay no attention to you until you present a bill of particulars to justify your action.[95]

A clash is indicated here between Rabbi Meir and the leaders of the Sanhedrin, who were prevented from banishing him by the decision just mentioned. This instance does not necessarily imply any restriction on the powers of the Patriarch, because the issue was after all between a member of the High Court and the Sanhedrin as a whole. But since in the last analysis the authority to put anyone under a ban rested with the Patriarch, it does point to a climate of tolerance of the independent rights of the individual Sage vis-a-vis the Patriarch.

The High Court at Usha originally had three heads, as noted above: The Nasi, the *Av* (Chairman) and the *Hakham* (Chief Counsel). But it seems that after the confrontation, Rabbis Nathan and Meir vacated their positions. After that, it is likely that those posts remained vacant. The sources indicate that two other Sages — Rabbi Jose and Rabbi Judah — became the intimate counsellors of the Patriarch, as though performing the functions of the absent two without taking over their positions.[96]

By combining the firm exercise of his prerogatives with a willingness to share authority Rabbi Simeon ben Gamaliel was able to restore the dignity of the Patriarch and to win the confidence and support of the Sanhedrin. The same policy stood him in good stead in his efforts to re-establish the religious hegemony of Eretz Israel over the Jews of the Diaspora.

The years of turmoil under Hadrian had made for a weakening of the ties that bound the Diaspora to the mother country. One major cause of this trend was the emigration of many Sages to Diaspora communities, where they took charge of local religious leadership. It stands to reason that when community life in the old country was at a standstill, the Jews in the Diaspora were forced to fend for themselves. Such independence established precedents

95 Yer. M.Q. III:81c.
96 See especially the account of the three of them at Akko in Tos. Ber. V:2 (12). For the special role of Rabbi Jose and Rabbi Judah, see Tos. Suk. II:2 (193) or Bavli ibid. 26a; Yer. Sheq. III:47c and VIII:51a; Bavli Men. 104a.

which threatened to dissolve the religious primacy of the old homeland once and for all.

The most vivid description of this problem, and of the attempt to cope with it, has been preserved in the tradition about Hananiah, Rabbi Joshua's nephew, who took it upon himself to promulgate a Leap Year in Babylonia: [97]

Hananiah, the son of Rabbi Joshua's brother, conducted the procedure for intercalating a calendar year outside the Holy Land. Rabbi[98] sent him three missives by the hand of Rabbi Isaac and Rabbi Nathan. The first letter contained greetings, addressing Hananiah with great deference. The second contained this message: "Those whom you left behind in Palestine as mere striplings have become full-grown rams." The third letter declared: "If you do not subordinate yourself to our authority, then get yourself out into the wilderness and offer sacrifices, and let Nehuniah be your acolyte." When Hananiah read the first letter, he paid public honor to the two messengers. When he read the second letter, he honored them again. But when he read the third, he wanted to scorn them. "You can't do it," said they, "for you have already honored us publicly." Whereupon Rabbi Isaac stood up and addressed the assembled Jews: "Does the Torah say: these are the appointed seasons of Hananiah, Rabbi Joshua's nephew?" "No," they chorused, "these are the appointed seasons of the Lord" (Lev. XXIII:4). "That," said Rabbi Isaac, "is determined by us in the Holy Land." Then Rabbi Nathan arose for the prophetic lesson: "Is it written that out of Babylonia shall go forth Torah, and the word of the Lord from Nehar Peqod?" "No," came the answer, "for out of Zion shall go forth Torah, and the word of the Lord from Jerusalem" (*Isaiah II:3*). etc. etc . . .[99]

97 Yer. Ned. VI:40a (= Sanh. I:19a); also Bavli Ber. 63a, with certain variations. Comp. JLTA I, p. 241.

98 The meaning is no doubt "Rabban Simeon ben Gamaliel;" comp. Halevy, *Dorot*, II, p. 199 plus notes. There are times when the Yerushalmi uses this locution for "The Patriarch" — any Patriarch.

99 For notes on the variant versions of this episode, see Tol. II p. 76; comp. Mann, "The Bible as Read, etc." p. 555 ff.

According to this tradition, the Patriarch sent two *Babylonian* Jews who had been living in Palestine to foil the breakaway attempt by a *Palestinian* Sage who had settled in *Babylonia*! The collection of funds in Babylonia at this time is additional evidence of the drive to restore the authority of the mother country over the Diaspora. The same may possibly be said of the contributions mentioned in the Stobi inscription from the Balkans, if we accept the dating proposed by Frey.[100]

But the Jewish authorities were not only concerned to preserve their authority; they were also sensitive to the needs, and careful of the dignity, of their fellow-Jews in other lands. It is in this light that we should view the promulgation of a Leap Year in Assia by Rabbi Meir.[101] The same applies to Rabbi Akiba's journey to Nehardea for official calendrical purposes, and to the similar action in the following century by Rabbis Simeon ben Yehotzadaq and Hiyyah bar Zarnoqa.[102] By associating Diaspora Jewish leaders and communities with procedures that were properly the province of the Patriarch and the Sanhedrin, these authorities in the homeland were showing concern for the Jews abroad, and demonstrating awareness of their requirements.

This awareness and concern also found expression at home, through the appointment of Sages from outside the country to senior positions in Eretz Israel. It is proper, says Rabban Simeon ben Gamaliel, that Rabbi Nathan, a son of the Babylonian Exilarch, should be appointed *Av Beth Din* (President of the High Court), because of the deference due his distinguished father.[103] In the same way, the Patriarch Judah I deferred to Rabbi Hiyya and appointed Rabbi Haninah the Babylonian as *"yoshev b^{e}rosh"*.[104]

The renewed ties between Babylonia and Palestine are reflected in still another way: the flow of Babylonian scholars to the academies in the homeland, some to visit, some to stay. Examples

---

100 See JLTA I, pp. 249–50.
101 See JLTA I, pp. 243 ff.
102 Sanh. 27a.
103 Hor. 4b.
104 Ket. 103b.

are Rabbi Nathan, Rabbi Josiah and his son Rabbi Ahi, Rabbi Isaac, Jose the Babylonian (Issi ben Judah) and Yadu'a the Babylonian. Travel in the opposite direction includes the journey of Rabbi Jose to Nisibis,[105] of Rabbi Simeon to Sidon,[106] and especially of the Patriarch himself, whose travels out of the country were almost certainly intended to strengthen the bonds between the Diaspora and the center of Jewish life in Eretz Israel. We can document the presence of Rabban Simeon ben Gamaliel at Akko and Achziv,[107] as well as at Sidon and Laodicaea.[108]

IMPEDIMENTS FROM WITHIN

Among the factors which impeded the restoration of the national religious institutions to their former state of activity, not the least was the unfavorable political situation. When the Sanhedrin and the Patriarchate began to function again after the war, it was without official recognition by the Romans, albeit there was no interference from that quarter. There is no doubt that the "withdrawal of Jewish civil jurisdiction"[109] remained in effect for many years, and that the efforts to renew Jewish judicature in the form of *batei din* manned by Sages encountered many obstacles. Even after such courts began to operate unofficially, they were not alone in the field. Litigants could take their business to the civil courts provided by the government.[110]

This situation, it is true, was an abiding feature of the occupation, even later when the Patriarchate and the Sanhedrin enjoyed full official recognition. But now, during the decades after the Bar Kokhba war, was when the competition hurt most, because Jewish autonomy was suspended, and the *batei din* were powerless to en-

---

105 Yer. Yev. XII:12c; Bavli ibid. 102a; XII: comp. Tos. ibid. XII:11 (255).
106 Tos. Ter. VII:12 (38); Zev. I:5 (479); Par. IV:9 (633).
107 Tos. Ber. V:2 (12) and Mass. Sh. III:18 (19). [Both places were then considered "over the border."]
108 Yer. Sheq. VI:50a et passim; and Midrash Tannaim p. 205, where *Rabbenu* apparently means Rabban Simeon ben Gamaliel, not Judah ha-Nasi.
109 Yer. Sanh. I:18a.
110 See JLTA I, p. 213.

force their decisions, indeed were under threat of punishment if they sought to do so.

However, this was not the only competition faced by the courts of the Jewish Sages. The Jewish tribunals manned by laymen *(hedyotot)* which had long been a function of the town councils, were also available to litigants. And particularly now the importance of the town councils was enhanced, because the Romans needed them in the efforts of the administration to put the country together again.[111]

It cannot be denied that these lay tribunals, regardless of their usefulness to the Romans, were also a national asset to the Jews. After all they were *Jewish* courts, which was better than having none at all. As a matter of fact, the tannaitic tradition grants them a certain legitimacy. Nevertheless, from the aspect of long-term national interest, they cannot be mentioned in the same breath as the courts of the Sages. The reason is that those "lay magistracies" were not integrated into a unified national legal system. They were by nature ad hoc and temporary.

Viewed objectively, they were also a hindrance to the reanimation of the national judicature. In working towards the latter goal. the Sanhedrin and the Patriarch found these local tribunals something of a stumbling-block. But they had to come to terms with them somehow (as with the courts of arbitration, or *borerim*). This they did by limiting their powers, and by trying to bring them into their own sphere of influence. From the latter half of the second century onward we hear loud complaints from certain Sages about the deficiencies of certain "judges in Israel," and it is probably these lay magistrates who are meant.[112]

On the other hand, Büchler explained the matter differently. He proposed that these were Jews appointed by the Romans to administer *Roman* law. Without expatiating here on the improbability that the Romans ever made such appointments, or on the even more unlikely notion that Jews ever tried cases in accordance with Roman law, we must register our conviction that those

111 See above p. 658 and JLTA I, pp. 222 ff.
112 Shab. 139a, and JLTA I, ibid.

"Judges in Israel who bring retribution on the world" were Jews, appointed by Jews.

When Büchler applies his theory to "the dayyanim of Sepphoris," and suggests that they were Jews functioning as Roman judges, he is overlooking the fact that the sources call them *"ziqᵉnei av bet din,"* and that their halakhic opinion is cited in the Mishnah.[113]

His case is equally unproven when he quotes as evidence the following passage in the Yerushalmi:[114]

> In the days of Rabbi Simeon ben Yohai *(the reading "ben Shetah" is an obvious error)* jurisdiction over civil matters was prohibited to the Jews. Rabbi Simeon ben Yohai said: I thank Heaven that I know not how to judge.

Büchler proposes that the Rabbi was about to have an appointment as a Roman civil court judge thrust upon him, and was pleased because his ignorance of court procedure enabled him to get out of the assignment.

In this instance, Büchler's case depends on there being a logical connection between the two sentences in the Yerushalmi passage. But if their juxtaposition is merely fortuitous, due to the association with a certain Sage, then we arrive at a much more credible explanation for Rabbi Simeon's sense of relief. We know that he was one of those Sages who preferred to avoid involvement in public affairs, but rather to devote themselves to study and teaching.[115] He is relieved simply because he does not have to serve as a *dayyan* in a Jewish court. Like some others, he believes that even good works can be a distraction from man's true vocation.

THE OPPONENTS OF THE SAGES

Our examination of the difficulties encountered by the scholars in their efforts to restore the central institutions of Jewish life has led us to the question: who actively opposed them? The question arises because the literature speaks of *sin'at hakhamim* (hatred of the Sages). Are the haters to be identified simply with the pro-

113 B.B. VI:7.
114 Yer. Sanh. I:18a.
115 Shab. 11a; and see the quotations from Rabbi Simeon above, Chap. 6 p. 491.

fiteers denounced under a variety of names in halakhah and aggadah: the rich and powerful who were "close to the authorities," the "tax-collectors" "publicans" "usurers" and even some who "allocate charity funds but do not contribute?" Are those the ones who are meant, the antipathy being mutual? Büchler is inclined to think so.

On the other hand, it does not appear that antagonism to the Sages was confined to any one social class. It was also rooted in ideas and principles, not just in economic self-interest. Witness the following dictum of Rabbi Jose:

> Those who calculate the coming of the Messiah have no share in the world to come. The same applies to one who hates the Sages and their disciples, and to the false prophet, and to the delator . . . .[116]

It would be difficult to find any economic factor common to this heterogeneous group of individuals. On the contrary, there is some evidence for dislike of the Sages on the lower rungs of the social ladder. We hear of a man whose wife came home late from the synagogue one Sabbath night, after listening to a talk by Rabbi Meir. The angry husband refused to let her into the house, insisting that she go back and spit in the teacher's face. (For the sake of domestic harmony, Rabbi Meir co-operated).[117]

Similarly, it was told that a certain man said to his wife:[118] "I swear that I will have no relations with you until Rabbi Judah and Rabbi Simeon have tasted your cooking."

> Rabbi Judah tasted *(although it was demeaning)* for he reasoned thus: If God ordered that His holy name be erased *(in the ordeal of the Bitter Waters, Nu. V:23)* simply in order to allay the doubts of a suspicious husband, and restore harmony between man and wife, all the more ought I set my

116 Derekh Eretz, chap. II, Bacher suggested that the entire passage refers to Jewish Christians; see MGWJ 1898, pp. 505–7. This seems to be unsupportable.
117 Yer. Sot. I:16d.
118 Ned. 66b.

dignity aside. Rabbi Simeon would not taste. He said: I certainly will not comply and demean myself.

It would be far-fetched to see the people who figure in these and similar incidents as members of the wealthy and influential class. Obviously they belong to the common folk. Are they to be classified as *amei ha-aretz*? Is that what is meant by the term?

The question of the identity of the *amei ha-aretz* is one of the most vexed and controversial in the whole history of the period. There is as yet no satisfactory theory to account for the division between the *haver* and the *am ha-aretz*, nor any consensus as to the identity of the latter. In the present context we shall confine ourselves to a few generalizations, without going into details or presenting the evidence.

Let us begin by disagreeing with some of the analyses which have been proposed. The first of these, based on certain New Testament passages, is advocated by many German Christian scholars, in which they are joined by some Jewish historians.[119] In this view the *amei ha-aretz* are simply the people at large — everyone who is not a *haver*, not one of the inner circle of religious elite.

If that were a true picture, it would be difficult to explain the great popularity of the Pharisaic teachers among the masses of Jews. Josephus is quite explicit on this point, in his *Antiquities* and elsewhere. And the folk-quality of Pharisaic teaching is eloquent testimony to the close bond between the Sages and the common people.

Then there is the view of Büchler, which tends to see the phenomenon as regional and time-specific, limited to the Galilee and to the post-Bar Kokhba generation. We have already dealt with these theories.[120]

The fact is that the term *am ha-aretz* has more than one meaning. Sages in the post-Bar Kokhba era disagree about how to

119 [E.g. M. Avi-Yonah, in "The Jews of Palestine," Schocken 1976, p. 63; in the Hebrew original *Biyemei Roma U-Vizantion*, 4th ed. Jerusalem 1970, p. 37.]

120 See above, pp. 507 et seq., and JJCW, "The Bounds of Levitical Cleanness," pp. 190 ff.

define it.[121] As a result, they disagree in their attitude to the *am ha-aretz.*

There is one chief distinction to be made in the use of this term. On the one hand it refers to the person who disregards the mitzvot connected with agriculture (tithes, heave-offerings, the sabbatical year, etc.); and on the other hand it means the person who disregards the study of Torah and the recitation of the Shema. Obviously, there must have been, especially among the latter, those who "hated the Sages" because they were the spokesmen and bearers of the Torah-culture, especially the Oral Torah.

It is true that we find the Sages expressing impatience with the *amei ha-aretz.* No doubt they viewed with distaste (1) the *deliberate* neglect of the mitzvot related to agriculture; (2) the *deliberate* disregard of Torah-study — that study which had been central to the Pharisaic way of life before the Destruction, and which the Sages had persistently promoted ever since;[122] and (3) a certain grossness and vulgarity bred by the neglect of learning. Possibly too, the Sages sensed a measure of antagonism to their role as leaders of the people, based perhaps on antipathy to the oral tradition of which they were the spokesmen.

Who then were these "principled" *amei ha-aretz,* and what was the nature of their opposition to the Sages? Some of them must have opposed the idea that the Torah has absolute dominion over the life of the individual. This in turn would breed non-observance of certain mitzvot, and an equal disregard of the imperative of Torah-study. After all, there were elements in the population, not confined necessarily to the upper class, who had never associated themselves with the trend initiated by the Sopherim during the early days of the Second Commonwealth and developed thereafter by the Pharisees, whereby the Torah was made central to the life of the people and to the life of the individual Jew. From this point of view, the *amei ha-aretz* must be regarded as a reactionary force.

They must also be seen as continuing certain strains of Sad-

---

121 Ber. 47b = Sot. 22a; also Tos. Av. Zar. III:11 (464).
122 Rabbi Simeon bar Yohai declares that towns and villages were destroyed in punishment for their refusal to retain "scribes and teachers." (Yer. Hag. I:76c.)

duceanism. To be sure, the Sadducees nere essentially members of the upper class. But the possibility remains that their world-outlook, with suitable variations, found a responsive echo among the lower classes. The exchanges between Jesus and the Pharisees reported in the Gospels tend to confirm this suggestion.

That is not to say that socio-economic factors played no role at all. To be sure, most of the Sages were plebian, but there also were those among them who came from wealthy patrician families, including members of the priesthood. In addition, there was the tendency towards the consolidation of a scholarly elite, which has been discussed above;[123] and although the process was not allowed to mature, while it lasted it might have been an additional factor in alienating some of the common people from the religious leadership claimed by the teachers of the Torah.

Add to this the universal human tendency to resent intellectuals, a tendency which comes to the fore especially in times of crisis, and you have a situation which might readily have brought some of the lower classes to share the resistance to the leadership of the Sages.

All this said, it is still maintained that the great majority of the common folk were loyal followers of the Pharisees and their successors, the Sages. The latter in turn were staunch defenders of the masses against the depredations of the wealthy and the influential.

In sum, the men who strove to re-establish the Sanhedrin and to renew Jewish public life had their hands full, and the very difficult economic conditions did not make their task any easier. One cannot but admire their efforts, and appreciate the results they achieved. They were working with a generation which included numbers of people who had despaired of a Jewish future and turned away from Judaism. They also had to cope with new sectarians, including the Christians, who confronted the Jewish spiritual leaders with new problems, especially after the Bar-Kokhba war.

Naturally enough, it is the academic activities of the Sages about which we know most. Despite the economic depression, they

123 Chap. 6, pp. 501–506.

maintained a great many centers for the study of Torah throughout the country. Apart from the Beth Midrash at Usha, there were academies elsewhere headed by Rabbis Simeon, Judah, Jose, Eleazar ben Shamu'a and Meir (though the latter was really a peripatetic scholar). There were also academies run by the disciples of Rabbi Ishmael and of Rabbi Eliezer ben Jacob.

The discussions in these academies ultimately bore fruit in the Mishnah, and in the tannaitic literature associated with it. To be sure, this literature was not actually put down in writing until the following generation and the one after. But the bulk of its content in both Halakhah and Aggadah goes back to the disciples of Rabbi Akiba and their contemporaries. Theirs was the last generation involved in the heroic and doomed struggle to regain political independence. It was also the first generation that turned its attention to the task of fashioning a way of life capable of surviving in a world that afforded no prospect whatsoever of liberation in any foreseeable future.

CHAPTER TWENTY-SIX

THE SEVERAN CAESARS
(193—235)

The assassination of Commodus in 192 brought the Antonine line to an end. There followed a short sharp struggle in which the chief contenders for the throne were the generals Pescennius Niger and Septimius Severus. In the event the victory went to the latter, and for the slightly more than forty years that followed, the empire was ruled by Septimius Severus (193–211) and his son Caracalla (211–217); Macrinus (217–218), Heliogobalus (218–222), and Alexander Severus (222–235).

This regime, which Rostovtzeff called "The Military Monarchy," marks the opening of the final chapter, in broad terms, of the history of Imperial Rome. By revamping the power structure in favor of the army, at the expense of the Senate and the aristocracy, Septimius took the step which led in the long run to the elimination of the last vestiges of the old republican institutions. Within less than a century after his accession the *principatus,* which had endured at least nominally since Augustus, had given way to the *dominatus* of Diocletian and Constantine the Great, and autocracy was in the saddle. It took scarcely one hundred years more for the process to be completed whereby the Roman Empire was transformed, during the reign of Theodosius I (379–395), into a completely Catholic Christian state, with everything that that implies.

The same span of years — from the Severi to Theodosius II — can be seen as a major transition in the history of the Jews in their native land, and indeed of Jewry throughout the Roman Empire. At the outset of those two centuries the Patriarchate, under the Severi, achieved the maximum of its power and prestige. Before the two centuries had passed it was engaged in a losing struggle for its very existence. It must be remembered that this institution was the mainstay of Jewish life not only in

Palestine but throughout the Roman Empire, and to some extent beyond its borders as well. The abolition of the Patriarchate in 425 C.E. was a severe blow to the Jewish People at large.

The same sort of thing can be said about the civil status of the Jews in Palestine and elsewhere. Under the Severi their rights were confirmed by the regime, both in theory and practice. By the time of Theodosius they had become a barely tolerated minority, deprived by law of their rights, and persecuted zealously by the new Christian masses and the newly powerful clergy.

It may be even more important to note that the same 200-year span is marked by major milestones in the literature of the Jewish People. The first classic work in Halakhah — the Mishnah — was created at the beginning of this epoch, during the Severan period. And when the two centuries were drawing to a close the last classic work in the Halakhah of Eretz Israel was completed — the so-called Palestinian Talmud, the Yerushalmi.

An attempt to examine Jewish history during the Severan period encounters certain difficulties. The first of these is chronological, but of some importance: when did the Patriarch Judah I die? Some say, in the last days of the Antonines; others think that he lived into the beginning of the Severan period. There are even some who believe that he flourished as patriarch during the first two decades of the third century. The problem is connected with the identity of that "Antoninus" who is described by the Aggadah as the friend and frequent interlocutor of "Rabbi" (presumed to be Judah I).

Without entering into a thorough analysis of this question, we shall vote with those scholars who identify the "Antoninus" of the Talmud as Caracalla (211–217) and the "Rabbi" associated with him as Judah I.[1]

A second difficulty arises from our uncertainty about the date of origin and reliability of one of the principal sources for the history of the times — the *Scriptores Historiae Augustae* ("Lives

---

1 [The emperor's full name was Marcus Aurelius Antoninus Caracalla. For a summary of the literature on the question, see Stern in GLA II,. pp. 626 f.]

of the Caesars").[2] The other two main sources are Dio Cassius, whose *Roman History* was finished in the year 238; and Herodianus, whose work in Greek covers the years from 180 to 244.

REPORTED DISTURBANCES

There are indications in the sources of disturbances in Palestine during the early years of Septimius Severus. Graetz postulated two such outbreaks: 1) a clash between the Jews and the Samaritans in the years 193–4, against the background of the civil war, with the Jews siding with Septimius, and the Samaritans supporting Niger; and 2) a revolt of the Jews against Severus in the years 198–200.[3]

There is definite evidence for some political or military violence during the years 193–4.[4] However, a careful examination of all the sources leads one to conclude that it is highly improbable that it ever came to outright war between the Samaritans and the Jews. The theory that these two related peoples chose that particular moment to settle long-standing accounts, because rival claimants for the imperial purple were just then locked in combat — seems far-fetched. In all of history, there is no known instance where Jews or Samaritans actively aided the enemy of the other in time of war. On the contrary, many Samaritans joined the Jews in fighting against the Romans in the War of Destruction, as well as later during the Bar Kokhba revolt. In the same way, Jews helped the Samaritans later on during the Byzantine period, when the Samaritans rose up in rebellion.

Certainly it is possible that most of the Samaritans sided with Niger, and since most of the Jews supported Septimius, there may well have been clashes between them. But these were more in the nature of intense political squabbles over the expected outcome of the struggle between the Roman generals. Because of the intensity of this political excitement, and the sharp reaction of the competing Romans, the memory of these events loomed large. Christian

2   [For a survey of the conflicting views and unresolved questions, see GLA II, pp. 612 ff.]

3   Graetz, *Geschichte*, IV⁴ p. 206, and GLA II, pp. 623 ff.

4   For Alon's extended analysis of the evidence, not reproduced here, see Tol. II. pp. 96–101.

chronographers in particular recorded them as an internal Samaritan-Jewish war.

So that what took place in 193–4 is not to be interpreted as a war or an uprising, but as the sort of thing that was happening at the time all over the Middle East. Antioch threw in its lot with Niger, while Laodicea backed Severus; Beirut was for Niger, Tyre was for Severus — and so on. It was only natural for the Jews to participate in the general turmoil. Perhaps they hoped thereby to improve their position, and if so, perhaps they were right. One wonders whether their support for Septimius was not a factor in their improved status under the regime which he established.

As for the purported uprising of the Jews *against* Severus in the year 198, the sole evidence is a passage in the *Historia Augusta*, where the following occurs in connection with the wind-up of the Parthian War of 197–199 :

> Notwithstanding this, he gave permission that his son should celebrate a triumph; for the Senate had decreed to him a triumph over Judaea because of the successes achieved by Severus in Syria.[5]

Graetz supposed that this triumph was granted to Caracalla for suppressing a revolt by the Jews in Palestine. He was not too concerned by the reference to "Syria;" the term is a broad one. However, in the present context there is a reference to "Palestinians," so the difficulty remains. Various efforts have been made to explain this triumph, but none of them seem to succeed.[6] Our conclusion must be that the thing never happened. It is nothing but a legend, like so much else in this particular source.[7]

---

5 "Life of Septimius Severus"; see GLA IL p. 623. The other evidence adduced by Graetz does not really prove anything.

6 [Stern offers a resume of the opinions (GLA II. p. 264) and suggests the possibility "that some military achievements in Judaea are indeed implied here, but that these were not necessarily connected with the Jews, who no longer at that time constituted a majority of the population of Judaea proper."]

7 [For a concurring opinion, see Avi-Yonah: "The Jews of Palestine," p. 79.]

IMPROVED RELATIONS

It is generally accepted that the rule of the Severi (193–235) was the high-water mark in friendly relations between Rome and the Jews. True, the many traditions about the "benevolent Emperor Antoninus" are almost certainly folk-tales.[8] Nevertheless, they do reflect the fact that Antoninus Caracalla and his father Septimius Severus treated the Jews well.[9]

But there is more solid and reliable evidence in the form of inscriptions naming synagogues after emperors of this dynasty. A principal example is the one from Kasyoun in the Upper Galilee. It is in Greek, dated 197, and it prays for the welfare of Septimius Severus and his sons Caracalla and Geta.[10] Additional evidence pointing in the same direction is the midrashic reference to an "Asverus" synagogue in Rome.[11]

There does not appear to be a single example of this sort of thing — naming a synagogue for an emperor, or putting up a plaque in his honor — between the Destruction of Jerusalem in the year 70, and the accession of Severus in the year 193.[12] For the relations between Rome and the Jews, it was a little as though the good old days of Augustus Caesar were back again. A witness to this fact is Jerome, who speaks of a special relationship between the Severi and the Jews.[13]

LEGAL POSITION

From the political thaw we turn to the improved legal status of the Jews under the Severi. In this connection the basic document is an edict issued jointly by Septimius and Caracalla:

8 The Aggadah has Antoninus converting, or almost converting to Judaism (Yer. Meg. I:72b and Bavli Av. Zar. 10b.)
9 [See GLA II no. 517, with commentary; also ibid. nos. 521, 524.]
10 Klein in *Yediot* of the Faculty of Jewish Studies, II p. 25; also idem, *Sepher Ha-Yishuv*, (cited hereinafter as *Yishuv*) 151–152. For a Latin inscription found in Hungary which may have a bearing on the subject, see CIJ, no. 977.
11 Bereshit Rabba, Theodor-Albeck, p. 209; see also Kimhi's commentary on Gen. I:31.
12 For such inscriptions in pre-Destruction times, see CIJ nos. 284, 365, 416, 496, 503.
13 In his commentary on Daniel XI:34. See JLTA I, p. 26.

The Emperors Severus and Antoninus declare municipal honors to be open to those who follow the Jewish religion, while at the same time requiring of them such obligations as are not inconsistent with their faith.[14]

The obvious implication is that prior to this decree Jews were barred from municipal honors in Greek and Roman cities. Just when they had been reduced to that position is not clear. It seems probable that it was in the wake of the Bar Kokhba war, because we find Jews running the municipalities of Tiberias and Sepphoris between the years 70 and 135. In any case, this edict restored them to all the rights possessed by other citizens of the Empire.

The statement that this happened during the reign of the Severi is supported by the mention of Jewish *bouli* and *istrategi* (which I take to mean municipal officers) in talmudic literature, at a time coinciding with the Patriarch Judah I.[15] The absence of any such mention during the generation before that, coupled with the frequency with which Jewish *bouleutin* are referred to during the following years, seems to round out the picture.

The edict by the joint Emperors speaks of both the "honor" and the "duty" of serving in municipal office. Actually this fits in with what we know about the Severan period. It was a time of transition with respect to service on city councils. What had been an honor was gradually becoming a burden to be avoided, so that Jews no doubt increasingly availed themselves of the privilege of exemption on religious grounds — something implied at a later time by the legislation of Christian Emperors.[16] And it would appear that when the Historia Augusta says that Alexander Severus "respected the privileges of the Jews," the reference is to the privilege of exemption from municipal office for religious reasons.[17]

What, then, are we to make of the statement that Septimius Severus promulgated a law forbidding conversion to Judaism (as well as

14 Dig L.2.3.3.
15 B.B. 143a and Yer. Yoma I: 39a; the Greek-derived words are rendered here in accordance with manuscript readings.
16 [The note here in Tol. (II. p. 106, no. 97) seems to arise from a misunderstanding.]
17 Life of Alexander Severus; GLA II. no. 520.

Christianity)?[18] There are those who see this as a sign of animosity
to the Jews, and others who discern a punishment for a supposed
revolt in Palestine. However, the soundest approach is to view this
act as nothing new, but rather a simple confirmation of the edict
of Pius, forbidding the circumcision of gentiles as a violation of
the *Lex Cornelia* against castration.[19] There are no grounds for
assuming that the law was motivated by anything more than a
desire to preserve and defend the ancient Roman religion.

CONSTITUTIO ANTONINIANA

A very important and highly problematic source relative to our
present discussion is the so-called "constitution" promulgated by
Caracalla in the year 212, extending Roman citizenship to all free
subjects of the Empire. As Ulpian reports the matter:

> Those who live in the Roman world were made Roman citi-
> zens by virtue of the constitution of the Emperor Antoninus.[20]

What appears to be an actual Greek text of the edict somewhat
mutilated, has been found in papyrus form. The relevant portions
as reconstructed by Paul Meyer, reads as follows:

> I grant Roman citizenship to all aliens (*xenois* = *peregrini*)
> in the civilized world (*i.e. the Empire*), all peoples retaining
> their former status; but excluding the *dediticii*.[21]

In interpreting this law, the most difficult problem revolves around
the specific meaning of the *dediticii*.[22] Apparently the concept had

---

18 GLA II, 515,
19 Comp. the punishment detailed by the jurist Paulus, *Sententiae*, V, 22;
    3 f: [and the commentary by Stern, GLA ibid.]
20 *Digesta*, 1.5.17. Dio Cassius (78.5) also reports this legislation.
21 Pap. Giessen 40. [The article by Jones: "Another interpretation of the
    Constitutio Antoniniana" in JRS 26 (1936) pp. 223 at seq. makes
    readily available the two main suggestions about how to read the
    missing words. In the version proposed by Adolph Wilhelm, the
    middle clause would yield: "....no one remaining outside the citizen
    bodies..." This is the reading preferred by Jones. Naturally, the
    present editor has adhered to the reading and interpretation given by
    Alon (Tol. II, p. 107).]
22 There is a voluminous literature dealing with the interpretation of this
    papyrus. See especially Stroux: "Die Constitutio Antoniniana," in

never been clearly defined in Roman law of the classical period, so that there were variations and contradictions in the way it was applied administratively. Modern scholarly opinion on the subject divides into three main schools of thought.

First, there is the view represented by Mommsen, according to which all the provincials were legally *dediticii,* so that this law did not do much for them. The fact that they were permitted to create ostensibly autonomous cities did not alter their status in law as second class subjects. The permission was granted on sufferance, not as of right; it could be revoked or withdrawn at any time. Mommsen believed that somewhat later the Romans deliberately withheld the *lex provinciae* from conquered lands, keeping their populations permanent *dediticii.* It was his opinion that the only people who obtained Roman citizenship under the Edict of Caracalla were the inhabitants of fully autonomous cities.

Jones disagrees. He thinks that the term applies only to the inhabitants of those territories where the Romans had not allowed the creation of organized municipal governments — of *poleis* or *civitates.*[23] These areas were directly under Roman administration, and did not constitute corporate public bodies in the legal sense. Wherever the Romans had allowed the formation of autonomous urban government, the people were not called *dediticii,* but *peregrini.* It was the latter, says Jones, already citizens of *civitates* even if they were payers of the poll-tax, who now became Roman citizens. All others remained mere subjects, as heretofore.

A third view is that the *Constitutio* gave Roman citizenship to all the inhabitants of the whole Empire. Who then were the exceptions, the *dediticii?* Simply those barbarians who had been settled in frontier areas; plus foreigners who were in temporary residence, no matter how prolonged; plus freedmen whose manumission was legally clouded in some way.

My own view is closest to that of Jones. That would mean that the Jews of the Diaspora were full beneficiaries of the new citizen-

Philologus, 1933, p. 272; Jones: art. cit. in JRS 1936; and Kübler's article in PW vol. V, s.v. *peregrini.*

23 Such as the countryside of Egypt (before Severus) or Cappadocia; to which we may add Jewish Palestine, except for Sepphoris and Tiberias.

ship law. But in Palestine, where there were extensive areas without a city (*polis*) in the formal legal sense, there was no improvement in the status of the Jews.

This may help explain the trend toward "urbanization" — the incorporation of Greek-form municipal bodies — which was so marked a feature of life in Palestine under the Severi.[24]

TAXES

The question arises whether the act of Caracalla relieved the Jews of the discriminatory "Jewish taxes," especially the *didrachmon* (two dinarii per person per annum) imposed by Vespasian after the fall of Jerusalem almost a century and a half earlier. The sum was not large, but the tax was morally degrading, not merely because it was discriminatory, but especially because it was intended to replace the half-shekel, the Jews' own Temple tax.[25]

In answer, we have the unequivocal testimony of Origen that the Jewish tax remained in place. Writing in the year 240, the Church Father was replying to a question by Julius Africanus, who wanted to know how the Book of Susannah could speak of a Jewish court in Babylonia trying a capital case. Origen writes:

> Even today, when the Romans rule the whole world, and the Jews pay them the two drachmas etc. etc.[26]

The persistence of the special Jewish tax may be due to the conservatism characteristic of the regime, as exemplified by Caracalla's statement that the existing *politeumata* (if the reconstruction of the text is correct) are to continue in *statu quo*, despite the newly added Roman citizenship. On the other hand, there may have been a fiscal motive. The total of all the special taxes from all the Jews in the Empire at two dinarii a head must have represented a considerable sum, which the imperial treasury may have been loath to give up.

24 There is a high degree of probability that the jurisdiction of a city was in practice extended to a wide surrounding area. [On the meaning of "Urbanization," see below pp. 748 ff.]

25 See JLTA I, p. 64 ff.

26 Schürer II, p. 248, n. 28, reproduces the text (Vermes and Millar II, p. 209, n. 32). See P.G. 11, 41 ff.

THE DIASPORA

How did the grant of Roman citizenship affect the Jewish communities in the Empire at large? Ostersetzer believes that it diminished the autonomy of the Jewish communal courts.[27] Although there is some logic in his surmise, the fact is that Jewish judicial autonomy survived, unaffected by the edict. The same holds good for the rights of other ethnic groups, wherever provincial autonomy remained in place. Indeed, that is probably the meaning of the clause in the Constitutio (as reconstructed) where it speaks of leaving the *politeumata* unchanged — which must refer to provincial self-rule, including local courts and systems of law. In any case, it is clear that the right of provincials throughout the Empire to retain their own courts and follow (within limits) their own laws, remained undisturbed.

Now it is true that there is an edict of Caracalla of the year 213 which seems at first blush to cast doubt on this statement. The edict disallows a bequest made by one Cornelia Salvia to the Jewish community of Antioch.[28] Since the Emperor Marcus Aurelius had permitted legally constituted corporations (*collegia*) to receive bequests (*legata*) this suggests that the Jewish community was not recognized as a *collegium*.[29]

But that conclusion does not necessarily follow. The likelihood is that the testator in this case was not Jewish, but rather a gentile Roman citizen, one of those sympathizers with Judaism called "God Fearers." Gifts and bequests from such "fellow-travellers" were apparently not uncommon, if one may judge from references in the Talmud and in contemporary Christian literature, as well as from inscriptions that have survived in Asia Minor. Thus, the edict of 213 can be regarded as an isolated instance. All it proves is that Caracalla was following his father's policy of discouraging gentile attraction to Judaism.

THE POLITICAL POSITION

The many legends about the intimate and friendly contacts be-

27 REJ 97 (1934) pp. 65–96.
28 Justinian Code I, 9, 1.
29 For a discussion of this matter, see Juster: *Les juifs etc.*, II, pp. 432–434.

tween the Emperor and the Jewish Patriarch should be seen as just that — legends (except for the tradition about the large tracts of land which the Romans leased to the Jewish leader).[30] But legend or no, the tradition is emphatic in reporting that relations between the Roman administration and the Jewish Patriarchate were very good at this time. Take the midrash on Leviticus XXVI : 44 : "Yet for all that, . . . I will not reject them, nor spurn them, nor destroy them, nor annul my covenant with them."

> *I will not reject them* — in the days of the Chaldeans, when I provided (Daniel) Hananiah, Mishael and Azariah (to save them);
> *nor spurn them* — in the days of the Greeks, when I provided Simeon the Just and Mattathias the Hasmonean and his sons
> *nor destroy them* — in the days of Haman, when I provided Mordecai and Esther;
> *Nor break my convenant with them* — in the days of the Romans, when I provided "Rabbi" and his circle of Sages.[31]

There are many *variae lectionis* for the text of this passage.[32] But whatever the reading, it is clear that the tradition dates from the time when the Patriarch was Judah I, or his son Gamaliel III, or possibly in the first years of his grandson Judah II Nesia. It undoubtedly reflects the lofty position vis-a-vis the Roman authorities enjoyed by the Patriarch and his associated Sages. The Patriarch had become the shield and buckler of his people in their relationship with the government; just as Daniel's friends stood high at the court of Nebuchadnezzar, and as Simeon the Just had saved his people in the reputed encounter with Alexander, and later on the Hasmoneans had played that role in the clash with Antiochus Epiphanes.

Another homily which reflects the official status of the Patriarch in the Roman colonial administration, and the frequent contact between them, is one that comments on the encounter between

30 Yer. Shevi. VI : 34d; see below p. 713.
31 Meg. 11a.
32 The only one that goes to the substance, is the reading in the printed versions "Persians" instead of "Romans." That is no doubt due to the censorship of the (Roman) Catholic authorities.

Jacob and Essau (Gen. xxxiii:15). Essau offers Jacob a military escort; Jacob tactfully declines. Says the Midrash:

> Whenever Rabbenu had to go to see the Roman authorities, he would think of this passage, and travel without a Roman military escort. Once he failed to pay attention to this passage, and took along a Roman escort. (The consequences were dire.)[33]

This shows not only that Judah Ha-Nasi maintained regular official contact with the Roman colonial administration, as his grandfather Gamaliel II had done,[34] but also that a troop of Roman soldiers was assigned to him.[35]

Probably the most telling evidence of the status of Jewish autonomy in Palestine comes from the letter written by the Church Father Origen to his friend Julius Africanus in the year 240. His comment about the didrachmon was quoted above, in connection with taxes. But his remarks about autonomy are also relevant.

---

33 GenR 75, Theodor-Albeck, p. 935.
34 See JLTA I, pp. 120 et seq. The relationship established at that time was almost certainly suspended by the Bar Kokhba war, but the question is, when was it restored? The answer here proposed is that Judah obtained Roman recognition only after he was already in office. On the other hand, some historians believe that his father Rabban Simeon II was officially "Patriarch" in Roman eyes (see Zucker *"Studien z. jüdischen Selbstverwaltung*, pp. 140–41; Baron: *The Jewish Community*, I, p. 114, III, p. 28). But there is no real evidence to support this conclusion. It seems more likely that he was simply tolerated de facto.

As to the idea put forward by Juster that the Romans were impelled to restore the Patriarchate by their need to defuse the threat of further Jewish military and political resistance [cf. Avi-Yonah: "... a healthy respect for the military prowess of the Jews ..." op. cit. p. 36] — it is scarcely likely that such a threat was credible after the Bar Kokhba war. What is more probable is that the staunch persistence of the Jews in maintaining their separate identity led enlightened Roman rulers to restore autonomy to the Jews of Palestine, as well as to their brethren throughout the Empire.
35 Interesting is the comment by Rashi (eleventh century) that the Patriarch was a "ruler" (*shalit*) recognized by the government. See his commentary on Shab. 122a, top of the page.

At the present time their chief[36] has authority over them by consent of the Emperor, as though he were exercising the prerogatives of their own former ruler. Thus, they maintain legal procedures in accordance with the Torah, even judging capital cases unofficially, albeit the Emperor is aware. This we observed when we dwelt in their country for many years.[37]

Apart from the questions raised by his mention of capital jurisdiction, Origen's testimony shows how real were the autonomous powers then exercised de facto by Palestinian Jewry under Roman rule.

Certain Jewish sources imply that the Romans enforced the rulings of Jewish courts. This would indicate complete official recognition of such courts. Even though the dating is uncertain in two out of the three texts below, the overwhelming probability is that they come from the Severan period:

> A bill of divorce given under compulsion is valid if ordered by a Jewish court; but if by a gentile court, it is invalid. However, if what the gentiles do is, beat the man and say: "Do what the Jews tell you!" then it is valid.[38]
>
> Rabbi Hiyya (third century) taught: when the gentiles enforce decisions of Jewish courts, the results are valid.[39]
>
> A *halitzah* imposed on a man by a Jewish court is valid, but if by a gentile court it is invalid (unless) the gentiles beat him and say: "You do as Rabbi N. told you!"[40]

This does not mean that the Romans gave up their authority to hear Jewish litigants, or to overrule the decisions of Jewish

---

36 "Ethnarch;" elsewhere Origen uses the term "Patriarch" (PG 12, 1055).
37 Origen's sojourn in Palestine ended at the latest in the year 230. Therefore Avi-Yonah cannot be right when he attributes the fact that the Romans turned a blind eye to such "flagrant disregard of Roman law" ... to the anarchy that enveloped the Empire after 235 ("The Jews of Palestine" p. 49.) The issue of capital punishment raised by Origen has been discussed in JLTA I, p. 210. To the references cited there, add Ostersetzer, in REJ 97 (1934); and Alon, JJCW, p. 123.
38 Mishnah, Git. IX:8.
39 Yer. Git. IX:50d.
40 Tos. Yev. XII:13 (256).

courts.[41] But it does testify to the strength the latter had achieved fairly early in the third century. So that when we find the Jewish Patriarch entrenched in his authority in *Roman* law during the fourth century, both within Palestine and beyond its borders in Jewish communities throughout the Empire, it appears highly likely that this was the culmination of a process begun under the Severi. To suggest that it began under the Christian Emperors (from Constantine onwards) leads to a number of improbabilities. To recall that Rabban Gamaliel of Yavneh had probably achieved that status by the end of the first century is irrelevant, since the war of Bar Kokhba cancelled all that. Therefore we find ourselves, by a process of elimination, in the days of the Severi.

One theory adhered to by a number of important historians must be submitted to a critical examination. This is the idea that the Romans made the Patriarch responsible for collecting taxes from the Jews throughout the country.[43] The theory is based on passages in Talmudic literature which do make it appear that Judah I was in charge of getting the revenue from Jewish taxpayers to the Roman exchequer.[44] If this were so it would be proof of the legal status of Jewish autonomy, and would have major implications for the collective fiscal "independence" of Palestnian Jewry, not to speak of the power of the Patriarch.

But there is one striking difficulty with this theory. It casts the Patriarch in an unsavory role. Tannaitic literature unvaryingly treats those who collect Roman taxes with contempt, comparing them to thieves and robbers. "A *haver*," it was said, "who becomes a tax-collector is to be dropped from the *havurah*."[45] Furthermore, there does not seem to be any evidence for tax-collection on a province-wide basis anywhere else in the Empire. And another thing: If the Patriarch were responsible for collecting Roman taxes, he would normally have been paid for such a

---

41 See JLTA pp. 215f; pace Juster II, pp. 96 ff.
43 Gulak, in *Tarbiz* I, pp. 121–122; Zucker, *Studien*, p. 159; Baron, *The Jewish Community*, I, p. 143.
44 Yer. Ket. X: 34a; Yer. Yoma I: 39a; Bavli B.B. 143a. See Gulak: *Roman Taxes in Palestine* in Sefer Magnes, pp. 97–104.
45 Tos. Dem. III: 4 (48).

service. But there is no hint anywhere that he had income from that source.[46]

More: there is no mention anywhere of the bureaucracy which the Patriarch would have needed to perform this function for him. In short, the theory must be abandoned.[47]

JERUSALEM

It is quite possible that the improved position of the Jews in the third century led to the renewal, on a small scale, of a Jewish community in Jerusalem. The prohibition against settling there had been imposed in the aftermath of the Bar Kokhba war.[48] But in the third century there is mention of many Sages visiting the old capital. Rabbi Ishmael ben Jose went there to pray,[49] and so did Rabbi Jonathan.[50] The latter Sage, together with Rabbi Joshua ben Levi and Rabbi Haninah, appears in Jerusalem on a joint visit.[51]

More telling than any of this, however, is the reference to a settled "community" (*kehillah*) in the Holy City, in whose name certain halakhot are cited. One of these is put on record by a third century Amora, Rabbi Jose ben Eliakim, "in the name of the Holy Kehilla in Jerusalem."[52] Another is attributed to a long chain of authorities, harking back to Judah I himself.

Said Rabbi Simeon ben Pazi, quoting Rabbi Joshua ben

46 Even John Chrysostom who attacks the Patriarchs as "hucksters" and "traders" never once accuses them of making money as tax-collectors.
47 The real role of the Patriarch with respect to taxes was that of supreme Jewish judge, supervising intramurally the equitable distribution of the burden imposed collectively by the occupation.
48 See p. 644. There is some doubt as to whether visits, including extended ones, were also prohibited. Certain disciples of Rabbi Akiba are said to have prayed in the streets of Jerusalem (Ber. 3a) and the Tosefta (Ned. VI:1 (280) speaks of a man who enjoined his wife not "to go up to Jerusalem," — but she went. The reading in the Bavli (ibid. 23a: "to go up on pilgrimage") does not destroy the sense. It is true that later on Constantine renewed the ban; but Jews still managed to make furtive visits.
49 GenR 81, Theodor-Albeck p. 974; Yer. Av. Zar. V:44a.
50 GenR 32, Theodor-Albeck, p. 296.
51 Yer. Maas. Sh. III:54b.
52 Ber. 9b.

Levi, who cited Rabbi Jose ben Saul, who had it from "Rabbi" in the name of the Holy Community in Jerusalem.[53]

There are also traditions transmitted by Amoraim "in the name of the men of Jerusalem."[54]

One way of dealing with this evidence, which flies in the face of the received notion that there were no Jews in Jerusalem between the Destruction and the Arab conquest, is to explain it away. Büchler (and others following in his footsteps) have suggested emending these passages, by changing "in Jerusalem" to *"from* Jerusalem."[55] He would then postulate a community "from Jerusalem" in Sepphoris! But such forcing of the text seems to me quite unacceptable. The surgery would have to be carried out on other references to that Holy Community, in the Yerushalmi and in the Midrash.[56] There is also a reference to one "Shebna of Jerusalem" two generations after the fall of Beitar.[57] We even know the names of the leaders of the Jerusalem community: Rabbi Simeon ben Menassia and Rabbi Jose ben Hameshullam — men close to Judah Ha-Nasi.

Apparently, then, there was such a community, probably founded in the days of Judah I. But that does not give grounds for assuming that the edict of Hadrian banning all Jews from Jerusalem had been officially rescinded. It seems that it was still on the books.

HALAKHAH

The improved political position of the Jews appears to have had some effect even on the Halakhah. For example, Judah Ha-Nasi took steps to abolish the fast of the 17th of Tammuz, and according to one tradition, the fast of the 9th of Av as well.[60] He

---

53 Bez. 14b and 27a.
54 Pes. 113a,
55 Büchler; *Die Priester usw.;* Klein, in *Eretz Yehudah* p. 183; and the introduction to *Sepher Ha-Yishuv,* p. ‏ב"א‎.
56 Yer. Maas. Sh. II:53d; EcclR. IX:7; see *Otzar Ha-Geonim, Berakhot,* p. 23.
57 Shab. 12b. For other evidence, proposed but disqualified, see Tol. II, p. 117, note 185.
60 Meg. 5a–b; Yer. ibid. I:70c.

was acting in accordance with the tradition that the four fast days mentioned by Zechariah (VIII: 19) are obligatory only when there is no peace, or when the Jewish People is in the midst of a time of troubles.[61] Apparently, then, Rabbi Judah regarded his day and age as one of serenity — a time of no troubles.

It is possible that this attitude lies behind the Mishnah on wedding celebrations:

> During the last war they forbade the bride to be carried through the town in a litter, but our Rabbis have permitted the bride to be carried through town in a litter.[62]

The expression "our Rabbis" *(rabbotenu)* often refers specifically to the two immediate successors of Judah Ha-Nasi — his son Gamaliel III, and his grandson Judah II Nesiah. What concerns us here is that the permission must have been granted near the end of the Severan regime, because an older prohibition — that of "bridal crowns" — was still in force during the lifetime of Rabbi Simeon ben Eleazar, a contemporary of Judah Ha-Nasi,[63] and it is reasonable to suppose that both restrictions were set aside at the same time. Does it not then seem likely that conditions were so far improved as to make these tokens of national mourning seem no longer appropriate?

If we add to all this the comment by Jerome that Septimius and Caracalla were "especially fond of the Jews,"[64] we will be justified in interpreting Rabbi Hiyya's early morning remark to Rabbi Simeon bar Halafta against the background of their times. As they watched the dawn unfolding over the Vale of Arbel, he turned to his companion and said:

> So it is with the redemption of Israel: at first a little light, growing greater bit by bit, step by step, but all the time with an increasing intensity.[65]

---

61 R.H. 18b. [The four fasts are 3 Tishri (Gedaliah), 10 Tevet, 17 Tammuz and 9 Av.]
62 Mishnah Sot. IX:14.
63 Tos. Shab. IV:7 (115); in ms. Erfurt, erroneously, "Rabbi Eleazar".
64 Commentary on Daniel, XI:34; see JLTA I, p. 29.
65 Yer. Ber. I:2c.

One may well conclude that Rabbi Hiyya believed the condition of the Jewish people had so far improved in his day as to constitute the first stage of a new dawn.

RECOGNIZING ROMAN RULE

It is possible that this newly benign attitude of Rome to her Jewish subjects may have been a major factor in the development of a more positive stance towards Roman rule on the part of the Jews. This is not to say that the Jews became enthusiastic supporters of the imperial system. Rome was still seen as "the wicked kingdom." But it may well be that the Severan period gave an important impetus to the process whereby the conquered became adjusted to their conquerors, learned to accept the legitimacy of the regime, and made a sort of peace with the fact that their country would remain occupied for quite some time to come.

The long drawn-out, stubborn refusal of the Jews to come to any kind of terms with Roman rule had been weakened by the defeat in the Bar Kokhba war. Now, in the third century, there emerged a sort of policy of accommodation, which may be stated as follows: no more armed resistance, and recognition of the validity of government laws and measures, except for those which interfered with the Jewish religion. One well-known formulation of this is the comment by Rabbi Jose ben Rabbi Haninah on the threefold repetition of the adjuration in the Song of Songs ("I adjure ye, O Daughters of Jerusalem") one of which is taken to mean that Israel is put under oath "not to rebel against the gentiles."[66]

This accepting attitude finds expression in the halakhah permitting *kohanim* to contract ritual impurity if necessary in the course of paying deference to the Emperor. Rabbi Hiyya bar Abba (late third century) went through the cemetery at Tyre to reach the Emperor Diocletian, in order to pay his respects.[67] His teacher, Rabbi Johanan, is quoted as having said:

It is a mitzvah to go to see the ruler. One need not be concerned at the implied recognition of sovereignty. When the

66 Ket. 111a, referring to Cant. II:7, V:8, and VIII:4. Comp. CantR II:18.
67 Yer. Ber. III:6a and Naz. IV:56a.

time comes, and the House of David is restored, there will be no problem in telling one sovereignty from the other.[68]

The qualifying sentence does not detract from the total acceptance in the non-millenial present of the facts of life. While the evidence we have quoted comes from late in the third century or early in the fourth, it can be shown that this attitude was already being expressed during the Severan period. Rabbi Yannai, for example, taught: "Always have due respect (actually, *eimah* = fear) for the crown."[69] He derived this teaching from the respectful language used by Moses in addressing Pharaoh. The idea is elaborated in the Mekhilta in a homily on the verse, "All these thy servants shall come to me, and bow down to me." (Exod. XI : 8).

The extra word "these" teaches us that Moses really meant *"You* will come and bow down;" but he did not say so baldly, because of the deference due a king. ... So too, we find that Joseph spoke respectfully to Pharaoh ... as Hananiah, Mishael and Azariah addressed the King of Babylon with respect.[70]

What we have here is a kind of religious sanction for deferring to royalty per se.

The doctrine of submission to duly constituted authority had not been unknown earlier, during the days of the Second Commonwealth, but it had had few adherents then. Josephus reports that the Essenes used to make applicants swear to keep the faith with all men, especially with rulers, on the theory that the latter would not be in power unless God approved of them.[71] So too, Paul teaches that "the powers that be are ordained of God."[72]

Prior to the Bar Kokhba war there is no evidence of such ideas among the Sages. It may be conjectured that two factors combined after the fall of Beitar to make this doctrine more acceptable.

68 Yer. ibid.; comp. Ber. 9b.
69 Zev. 102a and Men. 98a.
70 *Mekhilta*, Lauterbach I, p. 101.
71 JW II : 8 : 7 (140). To be sure, we do not know whether this was meant to include foreign rulers.
72 Romans, 13.I.

First, there was not much choice: the Jewish People was greatly weakened, its will to resist at a low ebb. Second, the newly favorable political conditions under the Severans may have made cooperation with the Romans now seem more reasonable. Especially noteworthy is the emergence of a changed attitude with regard to the legality of the Roman power to tax. The older dispensation made it permissible to swear falsely to "murderers, robbers, taxgatherers" and the like.[73] In striking contrast is the teaching of the school of Rabbi Yannai, in the third century, explaining away the older rule: "They meant unauthorized 'taxgatherers' (extortioners)," not proper agents of the government.[74]

The newer teaching was expressed by the Patriarch Judah I, in his testament to his son: "Do not try to evade the *mekhes.*"[75] Elsewhere this admonition is put in even stronger terms:

He who cheats ("steals") the *mekhes* (government revenue) is like one who sheds bloods; not only that, but he is comparable to an idolator, an adulterer, and one who violates the Sabbath.[76]

The same point is made by the midrash on Daniel III: 16, where Shadrach and his friends address King Nebuchadnezzar:

Having said 'O King!' why did they have to add his name? Or if they said 'O Nebuchadnezzar!' why did they say 'O King!' This is what they meant: You are our king when it comes to the payment of imposts and *arnoniot* and capitation taxes; but when it comes to religion, you are no more to us than yon barking dog.[77]

THE LIMITS OF CO-OPERATION
However, it should be remembered that this "recognition" of Roman rule fell short of complete submission to it. In a number

73 Mishnah Ned. II:14; Yer. ibid. III:38a; see above p. 543. The teachin is associated with the school of Rabbi Ishmael.
74 Ned. 28a and B.Q. 113a.
75 Pes. 112b.
76 Semahot II: 9, Higger p. 107.
77 LamR 33.

of respects the original negative attitude, including denial of legitimacy to acts of the colonial administration, remained alive under the surface. If flared up whenever Roman rule became excessively burdensome or high-handed — or when questions of life and death were at stake.

Proof that there were limits to Jewish co-operation with the Romans comes from evidence dealing with public security and political crimes. We have already pointed out that there was no unanimity among the Sages on this score.[78] In the second century, when Rabbi Eleazar ben Simeon and Rabbi Ishmael ben Jose accepted Roman appointment as directors of public safety, Rabbi Joshua ben Qorḥa condemned them for not fleeing the country.

In a distinctly third century source we find a similar difference of opinion about cooperation with the Romans in matters arising from political crime. A hypothetical situation was posed:

> A group of people are travelling along the highway when they are accosted by gentiles (the subsequent discussion makes it plain that these are government troops) who say: Give us one of your number that we may execute him, otherwise we shall kill all of you. What to do? Let them all be killed, rather than surrender a single soul. But if they are asked for a specific person, as Joab asked for Sheba the son of Bichri, then let them surrender him, so that the rest not be killed. Rabbi Simeon ben Laqish said, that applies only if he was guilty of a capital crime, as Sheba ben Bichri was. Rabbi Johanan said, no, even though he was not proven guilty, the order must be respected.[79]

At issue is obedience to an official order of the occupying authority. Resh Laqish is willing to obey only if the party concerned would have been guilty under Jewish law. Rabbi Johanan disagrees. An official order must be obeyed — but only in the circumstances described. Even Rabbi Johanan counsels compliance only when there are many lives at stake, in an emergency. Therefore, his doctrine does not imply unequivocal acceptance of Roman rule.

78 See above, p. 540 f.
79 Yer. Ter. VIII: 46b; comp. Tos. Ter. VII:20 (36). For Shebna, see
    II Sam. XX:22.

The same point is at issue in the parallel passage in the Tosefta, where the disputants are men of an earlier generation — Tannaim. Rabbi Judah takes the position adopted later by Rabbi Johanan, while Rabbi Simeon foreshadows the view to be espoused by Resh Laqish.

In the same context we read of an episode in the third century when a man wanted by the Romans hid out in Lydda. Troops came and surrounded the city, and issued an ultimatum: give us the man, or we destroy the city. Rabbi Joshua ben Levi talked to the fugitive, and convinced him to give himself up. Before that, the Rabbi had been having visitations from Elijah the Prophet, but these now ceased. So Rabbi Joshua fasted several times, until Elijah appeared to him once more, and said: "What! Shall I reveal myself to an informer?" To which the Rabbi answered: "But I was only following a mishnah." Said the prophet: "Do you call that a mishnah for *ḥassidim*?" Apparently it was still considered somehow indecent to turn over a person accused of what appears to have been a political offence, even though a whole community was in jeopardy.[80]

That there continued to be limits to cooperation with the Romans, especially when they imposed unusual and unreasonable burdens, becomes apparent from the counsel by Rabbi Johanan (third century):

> If you are drafted to serve on the boulē, let the Jordan be your boundary *(that is, get out of the country).*[81]

(The "honor" or serving on the council made one liable to make up any shortfall in taxes.)

A similar attitude is expressed by the Midrash in expounding Psalms XLV:2 and Isaiah LVIII:9.[82]

It is true that not all these sources can be placed without question in the third century. But at least those that can show the last of the Tannaim still wrestling with this question: what is the moral and legal position of the fiscal demands of the governing Roman administration?

80 Yer. ibid.
81 Yer. M.Q. II:81b and Sanh. VIII:26a–b.
82 LevR XXXIV:1 and 15.

That the question continued for some time to be moot can be seen by the downright contradiction between the Babylonian Talmud and the Tosefta in the matter of the slave seized by the Imperial *fiscus*. The Gemara teaches that that slave does not automatically gain his freedom (should he e.g. escape) as he would have done if the original owner had deliberately sold him to a non-Jew.[83] Thus, the seizure does not constitute a legally valid act. But the Tosefta teaches the exact opposite![84] Nor will it do to try to overcome the contradiction by emending the text. What we have here is two conflicting opinions. Apparently the confiscation is for unpaid land-taxes. The Gemara does not equate this with a deliberate sale, even though the non-payment was deliberate. The Tosefta, on the other hand, treats the unpaid taxes as a valid debt. The owner of the slave is like any other defaulting debtor. The seizure removes his debt, and he has lost all future claim to the slave.

Similar conclusions can be drawn from passages that concern the seizure of produce by agents of the government. In dealing with the halakhic consequences of such acts, one question is whether they are in the same class as transactions deliberately entered into, or not. Again, we are confronted with divergent traditions. One of these treats the confiscations as *force majeure*, not to be compared to agreements contracted with free will and intent. The Tosefta, however, is prepared to treat such seizures as having the consequences of normal legal transactions.[85]

The same question seems to lie behind the divergence between the Tosefta and the Mishnah regarding the rations of troops billeted on Jewish families (a practise called *akhsania* = *hospitium*). May one give them forbidden produce, i.e. *demai* (doubtful as to tithes etc.) or seventh-year fruits? The Tosefta says explicitly that one should not feed Sabbatical year produce to such troops, while

---

83 Git. 44a (top) and Mishnah Git. IV:6,
84 Tos. Av. Zar. III:16 (464).
85 Bavli Git. 44a; Tos. Dem. VI:3 (56); comp. Yer. ibid VI:25a. [Alon devotes considerable space to an analysis of the halakhah; see Tol. II, pp. 123–124.]

the Mishnah is equally explicit, saying: "One may feed *demai* produce to the poor and to billeted troops."[86]

If the obligation to feed the troops is legitimate, then it is like any valid debt, and cannot be discharged with forbidden produce. Otherwise it can.[87]

It becomes apparent that the status of the occupation in Jewish law was still being debated at the end of the tannaitic period. But one thing is obvious: by the time of the Severan Caesars a breach had been made in the long-standing wall of complete non-recognition.

The causes for this change were, as we have intimated, twofold. On the negative side, the Jewish people was now too weak to continue its stiff-necked resistance to the Roman occupation, what with the failure of the Bar Kokhba revolt and the ensuing persecution and economic breakdown.

On the positive side, the newly benign rule of the Severi and the great improvement in the political atmosphere made it possible for the Jews to become more accepting of Roman rule. Although this changed attitude never achieved universal acceptance — there were still "unreconstructed rebels" in the generations that followed — it did in fact gain the upper hand, influencing the whole future course of Jewish history.

86 Tos. Shevi. V:21 (69); Mishnah Demai. III:1. [Alon's statement that the Mishnah and the Tosefta diverge is based on the reading of the Tosefta in ms. Erfurt. However, ms. Vienna and the editio princeps *agree* with the Mishnah, and Lieberman accepts their reading. Some mediaeval halakhists quote one, some the other. See *Tosefta Kifshuto*, Zera'im II, p. 560.]

87 [Feeding the poor is another matter. In dealing with that, we leave the area of contracts, and enter the field of social legislation.]

CHAPTER TWENTY-SEVEN

HIGH NOON OF THE PATRIARCHATE

During the third and the fourth centuries of the current era the President of the Sanhedrin (*Nasi*) was recognized by the Romans as "Patriarch," or Chief of the Jews. Jewish tradition traces the office much further back, to Hillel the Elder, leader of the Pharisees at the end of the first century B.C.E. Some thirteen descendants of his, the various Gamaliels and Simeons and Judahs were reckoned as "the *Nesi'im*" of the dynasty of Hillel.

However, it seems unlikely that the office in pre-Destruction times was the same as it became later. After all, before 70 the Pharisees were only one party in the Sanhedrin, sharing power with the largely Sadducean priesthood, and with the elders — the aristocracy representing the important families of town and country. Back then the Pharisees had not yet become the sole shaping force in the spiritual and social life of the nation.

On the other hand, those scholars who reject out of hand the tradition about Hillel and his descendants are equally wide of the mark. What seems most likely is that Hillel and his heirs after him acted as leaders of the Pharisaic bloc in the Sanhedrin before the Destruction. Even then this bloc carried decisive weight in a number of matters, so that their chief was perceived as a leader of quite some consequence — a sort of *nasi*.

For all practical purposes, the defeat of the year 70 removed the other parties from the scene. Without the Temple, the priesthood had lost its principal source of influence and power. Besides, the conquerors were not prepared to allow this elite to continue its leadership of the nation. The same Roman attitude blocked the return of the elders to positions of importance, not to speak of the fact that the social upheaval caused by the war had left the old aristocracy ruined.

For these reasons the "High Court" which Rabban Johanan

ben Zakkai convened at Yavneh must be seen as only partially the heir of the Great Sanhedrin of Jerusalem. The Beth Din at Yavneh dealt only with those items on the agenda of the Jerusalem Sanhedrin which were of a purely religious nature, especially those which were urgent, such as fixing the religious calendar. Apparently it had already become the practice for those matters to be dealt with by the Pharisaic bloc anyway.

STRUGGLE FOR POWER

When Gamaliel II became Nasi, after the interregnum of Johanan ben Zakkai, the revived Sanhedrin broke out of these narrow confines. Especially after the Romans (during the regimes of Nerva and Trajan) recognized the Sanhedrin and its President as the official leaders of the Jews, these institutions expanded the scope of their authority, particularly in the legal area. Perhaps it was natural that this growth in power should have brought about a certain amount of rivalry between the Patriarch and the Sanhedrin.[1] Basically, this struggle can be understood as the outcome of differing conceptions about the relationship between the two. The Sages regarded the Nasi as technically head of the Sanhedrin. Such powers as he had were derived from the body over which he presided. The Patriarchs, on the other hand, believed their office to be a separate and independent entity, indeed in some senses superior to the Sanhedrin. The latter they viewed as a partner of the Nasi, designed to aid him in the exercise of his authority.

It may well be that the rivalry between these two was in actuality a continuation of the tension that had existed in earlier times between the Sanhedrin and the High Priests. The latter had exercised autonomous authority, in a quasi monarchical fashion, while the lay members of the council had always striven to maintain their independence from priestly domination. In the post-Destruction situation, the Patriarch no doubt saw himself as the legitimate heir and successor to the High Priest, while the Sanhedrin still strove to preserve its own rights and prerogatives.

In practice, the dispute between these two centers of authority narrowed down to three main areas of jurisdiction. The question

1   See JLTA I, pp. 315 et seq.

was, who had authority over the calendar, over the appointment of judges, and over halakhic decisions.

THE CALENDAR

The authority to declare ("sanctify") the New Moon, and thus to determine the dates of Holy days, was a highly important one in the religious and social life of the Jewish people. It was a principal factor in creating a sense of unity between all the communities in the Homeland, and to a certain degree in the Diaspora as well. Consequently, whoever controlled this aspect of Jewish life possessed immeasurable influence over the nation as a whole. No wonder the Patriarchs fought hard to retain this authority, and to resist efforts in the Diaspora to have this function performed by "local option."

The authority over *minui* or *semikhah* (ordination of judges) also became a bone of contention.[2] In principle, ordination was the equivalent of admission to the Sanhedrin as a full member (*zaqen*). The question was, who had this power of admission? Obviously, if the *Nasi* had it, he could pack the Sanhedrin, and make it subordinate to his will. What is more, since the ordained leaders could then be sent to local communities as spiritual leaders and judges, (alongside the local lay judiciary and arbitrators) this ordination and appointment centralized a good deal of power in the hands of those who controlled these procedures. Here too was a prize worth struggling over.

Lastly, there was the power to make halakhic rulings. When a vote was taken (*nimnu ve-gamru*) on some question of major importance, was the voice of the Patriarch simply one among many? Or did he have a special status and carry special weight? At stake was the spiritual and religious direction in which Judaism was to be guided.

As things worked out, all these issues were decided by compromise and cooperation. But that does not mean that power and authority were divided equally. Take, for example, control of the calendar. During the term in office of Gamaliel II it had led to a serious confrontation. In the end, even the Sanhedrin agreed that

---

2   See also JLTA I pp. 226 ff.

the primary authority in this field belonged to the Nasi. The initiative was in his hands. He summoned the meetings of the calendar commission; they functioned as his assistants and advisors. As for the appointment of judges, there is no evidence that before Judah I, the Patriarch was recognized as having any special authority to ordain. Nevertheless, we find him in fact doing so. This seems to point to a compromise of a different sort — yielding de facto but not de jure.

But when it came to purely religious matters the Sanhedrin was unwilling to yield one iota of halakhic authority. The opinion of the Patriarch would be listened to, but it carried no special weight against the decision of the majority. On the other hand, the Sanhedrin gave the Patriarch the courtesy of refraining from putting a question to the vote unless he was present and participating. In sum, the Patriarch was granted the upper hand in the conduct of public affairs, wherever the organized forms of Jewish life were concerned; but in the area of religion, including both teaching and practice, the Sanhedrin remained supreme.

These developments are quite understandable against the background of the situation in which the Jewish people found itself. There was need for a centralized and stable focus of authority. Amidst the anarchy and confusion that followed the Destruction in the year 70, such a focus was provided by the *nesi'im* descended from Hillel the Elder. They served as a rallying point for all who wanted to see the nation recover some sense of unity and resist the tendency, encouraged by the Romans, to split up into a congeries of small local groupings.

On the structural-administrative level, the compromise between the Patriarch and the Sanhedrin has been described above in general terms as the emergence of a collective leadership involving, alongside the Nasi, the President of the Court (*Av Beth Din*) and perhaps the Hakham (Chief Counsel?). So too, the modus operandi of the Sanhedrin has been dealt with.[3] An unanswered question is this: could the "junior" members of the collective leadership

---

3   JLTA I, pp. 317 f. and p. 312. It seems that in practice the Av Bet Din presided in both the Court and the Academy when the Patriarch was absent. The role of the Ḥakham is not clear. Perhaps he served as number three — a sort of deputy Vice-Chairman.

summon the plenum on their own initiative, perhaps even without the knowledge of the Patriarch? We have no evidence one way or the other.

The very struggle for power between the Sanhedrin and the Patriarchate underscores the interdependence of these two institutions, as does the fact that it never came to a complete break between them. Besides, the Patriarchate had its own separate and historic role to play. The Nasi served as leader and spokesman of the Jews of Palestine, and indeed of world Jewry. He was so regarded by the Romans, and so accepted by the Jews. He embodied memories of past glories — the crown of David, so to speak — and dreams of its future restoration at the end of days. It was this quality, this aura of royalty, which gave the Patriarchate a comparative advantage in its struggle with the Sanhedrin during the Roman period following the Destruction.

At first, during the days of Rabban Gamaliel of Yavneh, the struggle came to rest in a fairly stable equilibrium. Then, after his death, the Patriarchate went into eclipse. The dynasty of Hillel was shunted off to one side by political and military events during the regime of Hadrian. Thereafter, following the end of the Bar Kokhba war, some time had to elapse before the legitimate heirs of Hillel could return to office.

That is why Gamaliel's son Simeon had such an uphill struggle to reestablish the primacy of the office he had inherited. During the years before he reappeared on the scene the nation had looked to leaders like Rabbi Eleazar ben Azariah and Rabbi Tarphon. The Sanhedrin that gathered in Usha had the authority all to itself.

What this means is that in the aftermath of the war there was a kind of vacuum in the central leadership of the nation. Men of property and influence in various localities gained power by cooperating with the Romans at the expense of national cohesion. In short, the years between the fall of Beitar (135) and the advent of Judah I Ha-Nasi towards the end of the century were years when the fortunes and the morale of the nation were at a very low ebb. The forces of disintegration had an almost free field.

JUDAH THE FIRST

Of all the Patriarchs, Rabban Simeon's son Judah is the only one regularly referred to as "Ha-Nasi" (the Patriarch par excellence) and as "Rabbi" (tout court). He embodied in his person and his activities the culmination of one period and the beginning of another. His regime capped a process begun by his grandfather Gamaliel of Yavneh whereby the Patriarch emerged as the titular leader of all Jewry. And it ushered in a period of two centuries during which the office he held was fully established in Roman law as the actual and legal headship of the Jews in Palestine and throughout the Empire.

Judah ben Simeon ben Gamaliel was the Patriarch who in his public personality combined most completely the two elements which characterized the office in its classical period — spiritual greatness and scholarly stature, on the one hand; strong political leadership on the other. This combination started to unravel immediately after his death; none of his successors quite came up to his level in both areas. A separation set in between what might be called (though the analogy is inexact) the "spiritual" and the "temporal." One of his contemporaries summed it up in a phrase often quoted:

> From the time of Moses until the time of "Rabbi," Torah and worldly greatness have never been combined in one person.[4]

Certainly, the historic circumstances had prepared the ground for the appearance at the helm of Jewish leadership of a man possessed of these qualities. On the other hand, the fact that Judah was this kind of man made it possible for him to fill the role which the times called for.

According to tradition he was his father's firstborn child, and saw the light of day towards the end of the Hadrianic persecutions. It seems that he spent his childhood away from his father Rabban Simeon, who had to keep out of sight of the Romans. His teachers were the leading Sages of the day, disciples of Rabbi Akiba (like Rabbi Simeon and Rabbi Eleazar ben Shamu'a) and of Rabbi Judah ben Ila'i. Later on he studied with his father and with

---

4 Git. 59a; Sanh. 36a. "Greatness" is here taken to mean "political leadership," as per Rashi in Sanhedrin, not "wealth," as per Rashi in Gittin.

Rabbi Joshua ben Qorḥa. His special teacher, it seems, was Rabbi Jacob ben Qorsha'i.[5]

The fact that he was exposed to so many teachers and influences may have been one cause for his eclectic tendency in matters halakhic, and his ability to synthesize varying traditions. At the same time, it may explain his tendency to settle moot questions decisively.[6]

It is quite likely that the same educational background contributed to his tactful treatment of his colleagues, never presuming on his rank when involved in scholarly discussion. An example of this can be seen in a discussion between him and Rabbi Ishmael, the son of Rabbi Jose. The Patriarch stated that a certain act was prohibited on the Sabbath. Rabbi Ishmael said: "But father permitted it." Rabbi Judah replied: "The Sage has ruled" (i.e. it is *res judicata*).[7] In this connection Rav Pappa remarked:

> Note the respectful affection with which those Sages treated one another. Had Rabbi Jose still been alive at that time, he would have sat at the feet of Rabbi Judah. Now his son and successor actually does sit at the feet of Rabbi Judah, yet the Patriarch yields!

In another matter where opinions conflicted, Rabbi Judah is quoted as saying: "I am a member of the Academy, and he is a member of the Academy. I have my opinion and he has his."[8]

This acceptance by the Patriarch of the fact that, in interpreting the Torah, he was an equal among equals certainly had its roots in the insistence by the Sanhedrin that each of its members had the right of independent judgment, and that the Nasi had only one vote. At the same time, one senses Rabbi Judah's political skill. In the case of Rabbi Ishmael ben Jose, the Patriarch knew how to retain the loyalty of the leaders of the Beth Din of Sepphoris.[9]

---

5 For these biographical details, see Qid. 72b ("As R. Akiba breathed his last, 'Rabbi' was born"); Yer. Pes. X:37b; ibid. III:30a; B.M. 84b; Yer. Shab. X:12c.
6 See Frankel, *Darkhe Ha-Mishnah*, Warsaw 1923, p. 206.
7 Shab. 51a.
8 Yer. Av. Zar. II:41d–42a.
9 Comp. Yer. Git. VI:48b: "Shall we poor creatures question the judgments of Rabbi Jose?"

At any rate, the manner of his growing up, and the multiplicity of teachers he had, were calculated to prepare him for the role of a leader whose main task was to get many gifted people to work together.

This ability of his may account for the tradition that he was a very humble man, as we read: "When 'Rabbi' died, true humility and the shunning of sin vanished from the world."[10] This tradition, so frequently echoed, is the more remarkable because we know that in his personal quality he was one of the most imperious of men, especially in his role as leader of the nation. Indeed, some people found him intimidating.[11]

This apparent paradox can be explained by his extraordinary strength of character. He knew how to discipline himself when the situation demanded it, when the task to which he had been called required him to enhance the office he had inherited, and to fortify Jewish self-rule in Eretz Israel. So that when the occasion called for it, he could be gracious and forgiving. In short, he was a natural-born leader, confident, assured and in control of himself, by common consent head and shoulders above his colleagues in the Sanhedrin. He could afford to be "humble" at times, and generous even more frequently.

In this constellation his great wealth was a not inconsiderable factor. His economic resources, and his style of living, are described as nothing short of regal. The sources, with aggadic hyperbole, put his wealth on a par with the Roman Emperor "Antoninus" and claim that the supervisor of his stables was better off than King Sapur of Persia.[12]

The wealth of the Patriarch was based on his extensive landholdings. It might be supposed that he had inherited these estates, because his grandfather Rabban Gamaliel of Yavneh was also a

---

10 Mishnah Sot. IX:15.
11 He instructed Gamaliel III, his son and successor: "Strike fear into the hearts of the students!" (Ket. 103b). It seems that while he treated the Sages with all due respect, he was inclined to be rather hard on students. Of one he remarked: "I doubt he has a brain in his skull!" (Yev. 9a). Of another he exploded: "Is Bar Kipaḥ still insisting on his nonsense?" (Yer. Naz. IX:57d.)
12 Ber. 57b and Av. Zar 11a; B.M. 85a and Shab. 113b.

landowner. But the sources indicate that the holdings of Judah I were all in Galilee, whereas those of his grandfather were almost certainly in Judaea proper. We are left to wonder whether the family had lost its properties in the South after the Bar Kokhba war, especially as there is no mention of any land at all owned by the intervening Patriarch, Rabban Simeon ben Gamaliel II.[13]

There is evidence that the agricultural produce of these lands war, especially as there is no mention of any land at all owned ducts mentioned are wine and balsam, while some areas were used for cattle-raising.[14]

The economic position of this particular Nasi was probably enhanced by the fact that Judah married into wealth. His father-in-law was enormously rich, if somewhat deficient in learning.[15]

We know that later Patriarchs were the recipients of gifts and contributions from Jews in all parts of the country and abroad. The question is, did Judah I also receive such gifts? The answer must be that it is entirely possible, although we have no evidence. In any event, that was not the source of his wealth. That came, as we have noted, from his estates (some of which were worked by tenants) and from the marketing of the products raised on them. This economic independence made it easier for him to draw the wealthy into his circle. However, the well-known saying: " 'Rabbi' used to honor the rich" should not be misunderstood.[16] The context makes it obvious that the Patriarch was interested in raising contributions for the public good. No doubt he also wanted to have the socio-economic elite, as well as the scholarly elite, on his side. The following episode, in the same context, is instructive:

> Ben Bunais came into the presence of 'Rabbi' who said: "Make way for a man worth 100 *maneh*." Another man entered, and the Nasi said: "Make way for one worth 200 *maneh*." Rabbi Ishmael ben Jose spoke up and said: "That

13 For details about the Patriarch's estates, see Tol. II, p. 132.
14 Yer. Av. Zar. V:44d; Bavli Shab. 52a; Hor. 7b; Yer. Dem. I:22a; GenR XX, Theodor-Albeck, p. 190; Yer. Yev. IV:6a; Nid. I:49b.
15 Ned 51a = Sanh. 22b.
16 Eruv. 86a.

fellow's father has 1,000 ships at sea, and owns 1,000 villages on land." The Patriarch replied: "When next you see his father, tell him not to send his son to me so improperly dressed."

A generation later we find this elite — the *bouleutin* who controlled the local communities — on very good terms indeed with the *nesi'im*. In the antechamber of the Patriarch they were given precedence over ordinary folk waiting to see the Nasi. A certain rivalry arose between the "important" people and the humble scholars. This must have been what prompted Rabbi Johanan to reassert an old Pharisaic principle: "A learned man, though he be a *mamzer*, takes precedence over an ignorant High Priest."[17]

There can be little doubt that all this was strongly influenced by the socio-political structuralization that was taking place in the Roman world at the time. The emergence of a hereditary class of property owners, *the honestiores*, who were eligible, and at the same time required, to run the municipalities on behalf of the imperial government could not but have its effect upon the Jews.

The phenomenon is observable in largely Jewish towns like Sepphoris and Tiberias, and more indirectly elsewhere. Men of property tended to take over the power structure on the local level, along with the attendant responsibilities for the needs of the community. One result of this was the growth of an aristocratic ambience around the Patriarchate, something which aroused a measure of resentment in certain scholarly circles.

It seems that Judah Ha-Nasi lived in the style — and sometimes adopted the attitudes — of a grand seigneur. This is illustrated by his disdain for the colloquial Aramaic speech of the common folk:

> In the land of Israel, who needs the Syrian tongue? One ought to speak either the Holy tongue — or Greek.[18]

It is highly unlikely that Judah held any brief for Greek. What he really wanted was for everybody to speak Hebrew. It was said

17 Yer. Hor. III:45c; Shab. XII:13c.
18 B.Q. 82b–83a.

that his housemaid spoke excellent Hebrew, and was even consulted by scholars as to the meaning of certain words in the Mishnah.[19]

Of course, the motivation for Hebrew came in part from nationalistic feelings. This is well illustrated by the remark of Rabbi Jonathan of Beth Guvrin:

> There are four principal languages, each suited for a particular purpose: Greek for poetry and song; Latin for military subjects; Aramaic for lamentation — and Hebrew for speaking.[20]

Incidentally, the same prejudice in favor of Hebrew is expressed by a third century Babylonian teacher when he tells people not to pray in Aramaic. His view is supported by the Palestinian Rabbi Johanan,[21] and no doubt underlies the following difference of opinion:

> The daily Shema ought to be recited as written (*i.e. in Hebrew*) — so says 'Rabbi.' But the Sages say, any language will do.[22]

Nevertheless, the preference for Greek over Aramaic does indicate a certain elitism on the part of Judah I. Note also his harsh words when referring to *amei ha-aretz*.[23] Granted, that antagonism may have been directed against illiteracy, and against those "know nothings" who stubbornly refused to study even *ḥumash*. But the sharp epithets he used do show how far he had distanced himself from the common folk.

As for his wealth, one aspect of it was that it enabled him to support many students and Sages. At the same time, this added to the prestige and power of the Patriarchate, and gained the support of these recipients of largesse. Certain favored Sages, like

---

19   R.H. 26b; Meg. 18a; Yer. Meg. II:73a.
20   Yer. Meg. I:71b; Yer. Sot. VII:21c; EstR IV, end [where "Persian" is substituted for "Aramaic"].
21   Shab. 12b.
22   Ber. 13a.
23   B.B. 8a.

Rabbi Hiyya, were semi-permanent guests at Rabbi Judah's table.[24]

There are numerous references to the generosity of 'Rabbi.' For example, he supported the daughters of the heretic renegade Elisha ben Abuyah ('Aḥer') out of respect for their father's learning.[25] But even in distributing charity, his bias in favor of scholarship comes out strongly.[26]

The fact that Judah Ha-Nasi was able to bring under his authority both the scholarly element and the wealthy merchants and landowners constitutes a significant achievement. The former were centered around the Great Beth Din. The latter were scattered strategically around the country. They had been entrusted by the Romans with financial and administrative authority at the municipal level, so that Judah's success in gaining the adherence of this class is especially important.

The time came when he moved the seat of the Patriarchate (and of the High Court) to Sepphoris, that most "Hellenistic" (but Jewish) of Galilean cities.[27] The move put the seal on the acceptance of his authority (after some initial resistance) by the Jewish power structure of this important town. At the same time it symbolized the submission of the local Jewish spiritual leadership, established by Rabbi Jose ben Halafta, to the superior authority of the Nasi and his Great Beth Din.[28]

In short, Judah I was able to unite Palestinian Jewry into one organic whole under the political, social and religious leadership

24 Eruv. 73a; Ber. 43a; Bezah 25a. This practice became standard in the third century, although some Sages declined the the honor (and the dependence) for example Rabbi Pinhas ben Yair (Hul. 7b) and Rabbi Eleazar ben Pedat (Meg. 21a).

25 Hag. 15b; Yer. ibid. II:77c.

26 Comp. B.B. 5a; Ket. 10b; Yer. Yev. IV:6b.

27 According to tradition, it was there that he spent the last 17 years of his life (Yer. Kil. IX:32d). Büchler's surmise that he made the move in order to be near the Roman governorate of the Galilee is not acceptable. The Romans never had anything more in Sepphoris than a garrison stationed in the town fortress, the *kaṣra*. The town itself was governed by the boulē.

28 For Alon's disagreement with Büchler about the dayyanim of Sepphoris, see Tol. II p. 136, note 326.

of the Patriarch and the Sanhedrin. That structure was to endure for something like two hundred years.

THE AURA OF ROYALTY

It was not only his wealth that enabled Judah to exercise such strong leadership. A certain air of grandeur had been gathering about the office of Nasi since the days of his grandfather Gamaliel II. But it was only in Judah's regime that people began to talk in terms of "royalty." It was then that the claim was made that Hillel's family were descended, through the maternal line, from King David himself.

Once, on the eve of Tish'a be-Av, the Patriarch was leaving the Academy, accompanied by Rabbi Hiyya and by Rabbi Ishmael ben Jose, when he stubbed his toe. He promptly applied to himself the words of the Psalmist (XXXII: 10) "The pains of the wicked are many."

> Rabbi Hiyya said to him: It is for *our* sins that you are punished, as the Book of Lamentations says: "The *anointed of the Lord* is entrapped in our corruption" (IV:20). To which Rabbi Ishmael ben Jose added: That would have been an apt quotation even if we had not just been studying the passage.[29]

Certain scholars even see the same glorification of the Nasi in the words used by Rabbi Hiyya to signal the Patriarch that a certain mission had been accomplished. The code-phrase he chose was: "David King of Israel liveth!"[30]

Most telling of all is the halakhah which permitted *kohanim* to attend the funeral of a Patriarch. It makes its first appearance at the death of Judah I:

> Rabbi Hiyya said: On the day that 'Rabbi' died, the laws of priesthood were suspended.[31]

The concentration of spiritual and temporal power into the

29 Yer. Shab. XVI:16c.
30 R.H. 15a.
31 Ket. 103b, per ms. Munich. The current editions read *kedushah* instead of *kehunah*. See Tosafot ad loc. and Yer. Ber. III:6a.

hands of one man characterized the Patriarchate of Judah I, and some if not all of the same rubbed off on his immediate successors. Rabbi Simeon ben Halafta went so far as to declare:

> The words of Scripture: "Cursed be he who doth not carry out the words of this Torah" apply to the decision of the Beth Din here on earth.[32]

But perhaps the strongest terms are those used by the Tosefta:

> Beauty and power, wisdom and wealth, ripe old age, dignity and worthy children — these rewards are appropriate to the righteous, and a good thing for society... Rabbi Simeon ben Manassia added: All of these qualities characterized 'Rabbi' and his sons.[33]

When necessary, the Patriarch was able to enforce his judgments and those of his court by despatching certain of his retainers who acted as a sort of police force — probably the *qaṣuṣi* mentioned in the Talmud.[34] This method of enforcement was used later in the third century, when these retainers apparently got the name *balushi*.[35]

THE SMALLER COMMUNITIES

Like his father and his grandfather before him, Judah I concerned himself with the needs of the lesser towns and villages in Eretz Israel. Like them, he made pastoral visits to many communities in different parts of the country.[36] The purpose of these visits was to strengthen the bond between the outlying communities

32 Yer. Sot. VII : 21d.
33 Tos. Sanh. XI : 8 (432).
34 Ber. 16b; see EcclR X : 3.
35 Ber. 45a; Yer. Ket. IX : 33a; compare the comments of Origen about the powers exercised by the Patriarchs. However, the Patriarch imposed his rule more often by the use of the ban (*niddui*) than by the power of his police.
36 Comp. JLTA I pp. 232 ff. Alon places him in Akko (Yer. Shevi. VI : 36b); Lod (Tos. Nid. VI : 3 (647) and Ahil. XVIII : 18 (614) Bavli Nid. 47b); and on the road (Hag. 5b; GenR 76, p. 906; Shab. 125b; Av. Zar 35b; and B.M. 85a). Regarding his visit to Simonia see GenR. 81, p. 969; Yer. Yev. XII : 13a; Tanhuma 96 : 5.

and the central institutions, as well as to instruct the people in the rulings of the Patriarch and the Sanhedrin.

More frequently than not he did not go himself, but sent out members of the Sanhedrin to act as his emissaries.[37] There can be no doubt that many of these representatives, acting on behalf of the Nasi and the Great Beth Din, were sent out during the regime of Judah I and his successors for the purpose of supervising schools in the local communities, and of setting up schools where necessary. It is interesting to find the practice still being followed by the grandson of Judah I, namely the Patriarch Judah II Nesiah.[38]

THE POWER TO APPOINT

What happened to *minui* — the authority to ordain judges — during the time of Judah I? It was pointed out above that at one time this authority was exercised by certain Sages apparently on behalf of the Sanhedrin; but that at a subsequent stage, the Sanhedrin delegated its authority to the Patriarch. Finally it came to be exercised by either, with the advice and consent of the other.[39] The intermediate stage, when the Patriarch had full authority, is identified by some scholars as the time in office of Judah I, and they appear to be right. The fact is that any such appointments mentioned as having been made during his regime and that of his son Gamaliel III are described as having been made in the sole discretion of the Patriarch.[40]

To be sure, this concentration of authority greatly enhanced the power of the Patriarchate. But at the same time it helped elevate the status of those Sages who were thus appointed to local leadership as *parnassim* and *dayyanim*. It certainly strengthened them in their rivalry with the local lay power structure.

Thus we may say that the Patriarchate of Judah I was the time when the Sages came into their own as *the* leaders of the Jewish communities. It is almost certain that they gradually took over not only the spiritual and cultural leadership, but also the management of all organized community life. This was made possible

37 For source references, Tol. II, pp. 139–140.
38 Yer. Hag. I : 76c.
39 JLTA I. pp. 276 ff.
40 E.g. Sanh. 5a; Yer. Hag. I : 76c; Ned. X : 42b; Taan IV : 68d.

because Rabbi Judah was able to yoke together under his strong leadership the two main rivals for control of the community — the Sages, to whom he belonged by virtue of birth, education and the office he held; and the socio-economic elite, among whom he moved easily by virtue of his wealth and breeding, not to speak of his excellent connections with the Roman rulers.

This harmony between the "temporal" and the "spiritual" did not survive Judah I by more than a generation. The two rivals for authority resumed their contention in the days of his grandson, Judah II Nesiah. On the religio-cultural side the competition between the Patriarchate and the Sanhedrin was also renewed. Nevertheless, the situation that had been created during the Patriarchate of the great Judah Ha-Nasi was not completely reversed. Spiritual leadership had come to be regarded as overall leadership; witness the role of the "Sage" — as *moreh hora'ah, hakham* or *rav* in the Jewish communities of all subsequent generations.

The enhanced status of the Rabbis under Judah I was attended by certain changes he introduced which had the effect of strengthening the authority of the Patriarch. For one thing, he decreed that no *talmid* (unordained scholar) was permitted to rule (*lᵉhorot*) on ritual matters.[41] If we adhere to the version of this decree in the Yerushalmi, its plain meaning is this: just as no one can be a *dayyan* (judge) without ordination, so no one can be a *moreh hora'ah* (ritual authority) without ordination. Judah Ha-Nasi thus took into his hands, and institutionalized, what had hitherto been a matter for the free judgment of the individual learned scholar.[42] It is noticeable that in the ordination formula he used, (and it has remained in use through the centuries) *yoreh* precedes *yadin*.[43]

It would seem that he also undertook to bring order into what had hitherto been the unfettered freedom of each scholar to interpret the Torah, on the theoretical level, according to his own lights

41 Yer. Shevi. VI: 36b–c; Git. I:43c; comp. Bavli Sanh. 5b.
42 See JLTA I, pp. 309 ff.
43 Sanh. 5a. It seems obvious that it was he who decided when one or another individual should be invited to take a seat in the Sanhedrin, he who determined the order of precedence. For his role in convoking sessions, see Midrash Tannaim 213 and Sifre Deut. CCCIV (403); "...when the Patriarch seats the Elders at an earthly session etc."

and the traditions he had received from his teachers. "Rabbi" ordered that instruction should be made official — it could no longer be given "in the shuq".[44] But this decree of his met with opposition, even from his intimate Rabbi Hiyya. It was apparently the same issue that had arisen when his grandfather tried to keep certain people out of the academy. At that time, one of the first things the Sages did after they had deposed Gamaliel II was to dismiss the doorkeeper and throw open the gates of the Beth Midrash.[45]

The dominant position of Judah I in the Sanhedrin is illustrated by the fact that there is no mention during his years in office of any Av Beth Din or Hakham. His father had shared authority with these two officials (in his case, Rabbi Nathan and Rabbi Meir) and according to the Yerushalmi, so too had his grandfather Rabban Gamaliel — at least after the uprising against him. But Judah I seems to have gotten along without any official "Chairman of the Court" or "Deputy Nasi."

Perhaps this should be viewed as another indication of the method used by the strongest of the Patriarchs to surmount the chronic tension between his office and the body of which he was technically president. The roots of that tension undoubtedly lay in two differing perceptions of the nature of the Patriarchate. Originally, in the Great Sanhedrin of pre-Destruction times, the High Priest had held a special position, with special prerogatives. Another official of importance was the Nasi, leader of the Pharisees at that time.[46]

In the reconstruction that followed the first war with Rome, Rabban Gamaliel of Yavneh may have seen himself as inheriting the mantle of both — as the legitimate heir of the High Priest as well as leader of the Pharisees. The High Priest had been for centuries the head of the nation, with a separate authority of his own. The Sages, on the other hand, preferred to see their head as the

44 M.Q. 16a.
45 Ber. 28a; Yer. ibid. IV:4d. It should be borne in mind, however, that when a halakhic issue was put to the vote, the Patriarch had no special standing. He was an equal among equals; he was one man with one vote.
46 See JLTA I. pp. 192 ff.

continuator of the old *nesiut* — their leader to whom *they* had delegated authority. Then, after these differing views had led to a rupture, subsequently healed, the reconciliation was in a sense a recognition by the Sages of the new historic circumstances. After all, they seemed to conclude, the Nasi was now the embodiment of national unity and identity, a surrogate sovereign, so to speak. That role was played to its fullest by Judah I. For two centuries after him — as long as the Patriarchate lasted — his successors did their best to live up to his standard.

We have noted that he did without official deputies. But in practice he surrounded himself with intimates and advisors. Among these were Rabbi Ishmael ben Jose, Rabbi Hiyya and his sons, and apparently also his secretary, Rabbi Aphes. It seems that these men were not chosen purely on grounds of personal preference. Considerations of policy were no doubt also a factor. For example, Rabbi Hiyya and his sons were Babylonians, and surely served the purpose of cementing the Patriarch's ties with that great Diaspora community. (Rabban Gamaliel of Yavneh had also chosen a Babylonian — Rabbi Nathan, son of the exilarch — as his Av Beth Din.) A similar motivation may explain the appointment of Rabbi Haninah to be Head of the Academy (*Rosh Yeshivah*). The preferment given to Rabbi Ishmael ben Jose, chief of the Beth Din at Sepphoris, was probably not unconnected with recognition of the overall authority of the Patriarch by the leaders of that important Galilean community.

Rabbi Aphes and Bar Kappara were both southerners — from the *Darom*. It might have been considered important to have that section of the country represented in the Patriarch's entourage.

OPPOSITION TO JUDAH I

Although most members of the Sanhedrin appreciated the advances made under the strong leadership of Judah Ha-Nasi, it was inevitable that he should have had his critics. We have mentioned his clash with Rabbi Hiyya, one of his closest collaborators, on the issue of whether to confine instruction to the Academy. Although the Patriarch punished this breach of "discipline," there is no evidence that Rabbi Hiyya, and those who agreed with him, ever gave way on this issue.

Another of Judah's intimates, that many-sided man Bar Kappara — halakhist, fabulist and coiner of epigrams — once earned the displeasure of the Patriarch by satirizing the wealthy ignoramuses who surrounded the Patriarch's "court" — including the latter's own father-in-law.[47]

A very different type of Sage, much less a man of the world, much more given to piety and humility and good works, was Rabbi Pinhas ben Yair, an even more severe critic of the Patriarch's regal life-style and authoritarian manner.[48] There are echoes of a real clash between the two of them, told in veiled terms out of deference to both sides.[49] Rabbi Pinhas refused to be a guest at the Patriarch's establishment. He railed against the conspicuous affluence ("white mules!") and would not lend his name to a proposed halakhic enactment. People with his austere outlook doubtless viewed the development of the Patriarchate as contrary to the tradition of humility and the simple life which they believed to be at the heart of the Torah as interpreted by the Pharisees.

These divergences of outlook never came to an outright split. But their manifestations must not be thought of as merely stray episodes. The opposition they expressed was inherent in the whole situation.[50]

Once an interesting contretemps took place at the Patriarch's own table. Rabbi Hiyya's two sons, Judah and Hezekiah, had been unusually silent, and the Patriarch suggested that wine might loosen their tongues. The expedient worked rather too well, for the young men gave forth with these oracular words:

> David's son will not arrive until two families who now hold hereditary power have vanished from the scene, and these be they: The Exilarchs in Babylonia and the Patriarchs in Eretz Israel.[51]

47 Yer. M.Q. III:81c; see Bacher: *Aggada der Tannaiten,* II pp. 500 ff. For Bar Kappara see, inter alia Ber. 62b; Sifre Num. 30; Taan. 11a.
48 Hul. 7a; Yer. Shab. I:3c = Sheq. III:47c = Mishnah Sot., end.
49 Hul. 7b; Yer. Dem. I:22a.
50 It seems that both Bar Kappara and Rabbi Pinhas ben Yair were Southerners.
51 Sanh. 38a [The young men were sober enough to back up their words with a fitting scriptural quotation (Isaiah VIII:14). Rabbi Hiyya tried

Note: The young men coupled the Patriarch with the Exilarch (*Resh Galuta*) a purely temporal official in the Persian Empire. They were probably hinting at the resentment aroused among scholars by the authoritative way in which Judah I enforced his will in administrative matters. Indeed, there is evidence that he used his power of withholding *minui* as a means of disciplining scholars who had incurred his disfavor. Of Bar Kappara he said: "He will not be appointed while I am alive."[52]

The reaction in scholarly circles to such highhandedness may possibly be reflected in the following:

> Rabbi Zeira said: There were men of piety and scholarship who should have been ordained, such as Judah and Hezekiah. In time to come the Holy One will ordain his own group of *tzaddikim*, and will seat them around Him in the Academy on High.[53]

This may be an oblique protest against the monopoly on appointments exercised by Judah I, not only because he denied the nod to some, but because he favored others. Witness the following:

> Rabbi Simeon ben Eleazar said: In every Assembly (*Yeshivah*) there are always some who deserve purgatory; but in the latest Assembly they are all of that ilk.[54]

Doubtless there was some objective justification for complaints like that. But it would be a mistake to attribute this situation simply to an autocratic Patriarch with a strong will to power. Rabbi Judah was motivated by the needs of his people and the opportunities of his day. He seized upon the chance offered by current political conditions to reorganize and strengthen the position of the Jewish people in Palestine. In the process, he did things that

to appease the Patriarch by pointing out that *yayyin* (wine) and *sod* (secret) have the same numerical equivalent — hence "In the wine and out the secret" (*in vino veritas*).]

52 Yer. M.Q. III:81c.
53 EcclR. II:30; see Zori: *Shilton ha-Nesiut ve-ha-Vaad*, I, Bk. 3, part 1, p. 194. The correct reading of the midrash yields the names given above — the very sons of Rabbi Hiyya who were so indiscreet at the Patriarch's table.
54 *Midrash Tannaim*, Hoffman, p. 8.

did not always sit well with the Sages, were not always in harmony with their world-outlook, and sometimes even ran counter to their interests. But he did succeed in reinvigorating the Patriarchate on both the socio-political and the spiritual planes.

The question is, could the monarchical quality which he infused into his office endure? Could the Pharisaic tradition (Torah, ethics, folk wisdom and approachability) fused harmoniously with strong leadership and a regal life-style — could this combination survive the man who had blended its parts into a whole?

The answer rested with those who came after him.

THE SUCCESSORS

Scarcely one generation after the death of Judah I, the Patriarchate and the Sanhedrin parted company. From the time of Rabbi Johanan (late third century) when the Va'ad, as it came to be called, moved to Tiberias, the Patriarchs no longer functioned as heads of the Great Beth Midrash, nor of its associated Great Beth Din. The "temporal" and the "spiritual" leadership were separated from one another (even though the separation was never quite complete).

The acid test for this separation is what happened to the power of appointment (*minui*). Several sources indicate that Rabbi Johanan ordained his own students, and that Rabbi Joshua ben Levi did the same.[55] That does not mean that the Nasi was no longer involved in ordination. As we have seen, according to one tradition, the two authorities had equal rights in this respect; while according to a different tradition, each required the advice and consent of the other. The fact is that, whatever the theory, in practice they continued to need each other, and to cooperate. But the "personal union" between the two elements, the spiritual-academic and the socio-political — that was finished. The Patriarchate became more and more a temporal authority, much like the Exilarchate in Babylonia. People were no longer able to look to the descendants of Hillel for authoritative information about Torah and religious practice. The address for such questions became almost exclusively the Sages of the Vaad.

55 Sanh. 14a, 5b, 30a; Yer. Hag. I: 76c, Ned. X:42b.

This separation may have contributed to the preservation of that atmosphere of popular openness, even folksiness, that surrounded the circles who pursued the study of Torah. It certainly arrested any tendency towards the institutionalization of the scholar-class as an intellectual elite. It helped keep the Sages in close contact with the masses of plain people.

It is not entirely clear what the situation was during the interval between the death of Judah I and the separation of the Sanhedrin from the Patriarchate in the days of Rabbi Johanan. Some scholars think that the separation took place almost immediately after the great Nasi passed away. Others believe that his successors continued for a time to serve as heads of the Yeshivah. The reason for this difference of opinion is that the traditions in the talmudim about the succession appear to disagree with one another.

In the Bavli, the famous deathbed directive of Judah Ha-Nasi is reported this way:

> Let my son Simeon be *Ḥakham,* my son Gamaliel, *Nasi;* and let Haninah bar Hamma sit at the head . . . Rabbi Simeon entered the bedchamber and the dying Patriarch instructed him in the duties of the *Ḥakham.* . . . Then his son Gamaliel entered, and was told how a Nasi should behave. His father said to him: My son, conduct your *nesiut* with a firm hand, and keep the students in awe of you . . . .[56]

According to this version, Rabbi Haninah was to become *Rosh Yeshivah* of the Great Academy — and we do find him in that position later on.[57] The fact that he refused the appointment for a time, until a certain Rabbi who had seniority had served, does not alter the fact that this office, which Judah I had occupied, was now separated from the Patriarchate.

But the Yerushalmi tells it differently:

> As 'Rabbi' lay dying he directed his son . . . Give *minui* to all of them at one and the same time . . . but appoint Rabbi Haninah bar Hamma first ('at the head') . . . When he had breathed his last, and his son wanted to carry out his

56 Ket. 103b.
57 Ber. 18b; Shab. 59b.

instructions, (Rabbi Haninah) declined the appointment. He said: I will not accept the office until you have appointed Rabbi Aphes the Southerner before me (*qama'i*). There was an old Sage there who said: If Haninah goes ahead of me (*qᵉdammi*), I am Number Two (*tinyen*); and if Rabbi Aphes goes ahead, I am still Number Two. So Rabbi Haninah allowed himself to be appointed third.[58]

Again, the fact that the Yerushalmi has Rabbi Haninah stepping aside for *two* others does not matter; the real difference is that in this version, he is merely granted *minui*, not made Head of the Academy. The new Patriarch Gamaliel III is still the Head; it is he who makes the appointments.

Graetz dealt with the contradiction between the two talmudim by deciding in favor of the Yerushalmi; and Halevy followed his lead.[59] Weiss tried to defend the Bavli, while Ginzberg left the question (whether there were Heads of the Academy at that time other than the Patriarch) unresolved.[60]

If we attempt a fresh examination of the problem, our starting point should be this: nothing in the Yerushalmi contradicts the statement in the Bavli that Rabbi Simeon was made *Ḥakham*. Although the Babylonian Talmud does not seem to understand the nature of that office, it is clear that it was occupied by the third member of the triumvirate which headed the Sanhedrin. This three-headed leadership had functioned during the regime of Rabban Simeon ben Gamaliel, and now his son Judah I, about to depart from the scene, intended to have it revived. Obviously, then, some-one must have been nominated to be the other member of the trio — the *Av Beth Din*.

Another point to be remembered is that the order, or sequence, in which Sages were ordained was a matter of importance. It de-

---

58 Yer. Taan. IV:68a; comp. EcclR. VII:16. The Midrash gives Rabbi Haninah's name correctly; the Yerushalmi has the name and the patronymic reversed.

59 Graetz *Geschichte* IV p. 282 and idem in MGWJ 1852, p. 440; Halevy in *Dorot*, II:2, pp.ה"ני‎et seq. The latter, unwilling to discount the Bavli altogether, tries to harmonize it with the Yerushalmi.

60 Weiss, *Dor Dor*, III, 8th ed. p. 40, n. 2; Ginzberg: *Perushim vᵉHiddushim*, III, p. 192 f.

termined seniority with regard to eligibility for higher office.[61] In the present context, the following episode is especially germane:

> Rabbi Akiba gave *minui* to Rabbi Meir and Rabbi Simeon. He said: Let Rabbi Meir take his seat first. Rabbi Simeon's face clouded over. Rabbi Akiba said to him: Let it be enough for you that I know, and your Creator knows, how great is your strength (in Torah).[62]

Is it not probable that the priority thus given to Rabbi Meir had something to do with his becoming *Ḥakham* under Rabban Simeon ben Gamaliel?[63]

Furthermore, there is evidence that in the Yavneh days, Rabbi Eleazar ben Azariah was called "*tinyen*," (number two) and that he was *Av Beth Din*.[64] The reason he was so called is that he acted as deputy to the Patriarch. It would not be surprising if, considering the Patriarch as a separate entity, the deputy should be referred to intramurally as "the head."

In the light of this, it becomes possible to reconcile the Yerushalmi with the Bavli. Rabbi Haninah, or whoever was ordained first, became ipso facto the *Av Beth Din*.[65] It is indisputable that the *Av Beth Din* presided over the High Court *and* the Academy even in earlier times, although he may have been technically supposed to be acting on behalf of the Patriarch.

By reconciling the two talmudim we are able to discover what Judah I was about. He was restoring the tripartite collective leadership of Patriarch, *Av Beth Din* and *Ḥakham*; but restoring it with a difference. Before his time, the other two had been elected by the Sanhedrin; now he was telling his son and successor to appoint them. Not only that, but he himself was selecting his other son to be *Ḥakham*. This has the appearance of a compromise between the old-style of collective leadership, which gave a lot of

61 Yer. R.H. II: 58b; Sanh. I: 18c.
62 Yer. Sanh. I: 19a. In the group ordination when Rabbi Judah was martyred (Sanh. 14a) Rabbi Meir's name also comes first.
63 Hor. 13b; Yer. Bik. III: 65c.
64 Yer. Pes. VI: 33a, coupled with Ber. IV: 7d and Taan. IV: 67d.
65 See Zechariah Frankel in MGWJ I, p. 349, and M. Guttman in *Mafteah Ha-Talmud*, I, p. 90.

power to the Sanhedrin, and the one-man rule of Judah I, which put the Nasi in the saddle. In any event, it is obvious from the intrusion of Rabbi Haninah as Head of the Academy that Judah's successors would no longer be exercising his monarchical style of leadership. A process of the separation of powers had set in, and it would lead to the almost exclusive jurisdiction of the Sanhedrin in the areas of legal decision, Halakhah and academic study.

This process was only at its beginnings during the interim period that followed the departure of Judah Ha-Nasi. His son Gamaliel III, and his grandson Judah II Nesiah were still accounted heads of the Great Beth Din, and at times even took the lead in the deliberations of the Great Beth Midrash. At the same time, they could be overruled in matters of Halakhah. We find this happening to Gamaliel III. "His colleagues" called him to order on a point of Sabbath observance; and Rabbi Hoshiah vetoed a halakhic proposal of his.[66]

Perhaps just because it was a time of collegiality and shared authority, this transitional generation accomplished much in tackling the practical problems of religious life, as well as in dealing with theoretical issues in the Academy. Both Gamaliel III and Judah II Nesiah were scholars of a high order, gifted in addition with sagacity and executive ability. By associating the Sanhedrin with their activities on behalf of the general welfare, they were able to achieve results that endured.

Not the least of these achievements were in the field of literature. Most of the works that we call "tannaitic," except for the Mishnah, were put together during the post-Judah I generation or immediately thereafter. We shall not describe them here, but attempt rather to deal with several matters that appear to need clarification.

First of all, it should be noted that a number of *taqanot* attributed by the tradition to "Rabban Gamaliel and his Beth Din," refer to Gamaliel III; and others attributed to " 'Rabbi' and his Beth Din" refer to Judah II Nesiah. There are also references to *"minyanim,"* that is, "votes taken" (i.e. assemblies convoked by the Sanhedrin with the participation of the Patriarch). Many of these synods clearly took place during the last years of the Severan

66   Yer. Shab. VI: 8a; Yer. Hal. IV: 60a.

period. Thus, in three different places Rabbi Jannai says: "They voted and decided in the Havurah."[67]

Even more important is the fact that in many cases where the tradition speaks of *"Rabboienu"* in connection with halakhic decisions, the term refers to actions taken by the Sanhedrin in conjunction with either Gamaliel III or Judah II Nesiah. Halevy pointed out three places where *"Rabbotenu"* means Judah II.[68]

There is a problem created by references to a conference at Usha involving certain personalities who could not have been born in time to have encountered participants in the original famous gathering at Usha. We also hear from Amoraim about *"taqanot* of Usha,"* and about a vote taken there, apparently in amoraic times.[69]

It is scarcely likely that Rabbi Johanan bar Nappaha (3rd. cent.) could ever have been in touch with members of the post-Bar Kokhba synod of Usha. A way out of this difficulty that suggests itself is to postulate a special session at Usha convoked by Gamaliel III, perhaps because of the historic memories associated with that Galilean town.

TAQANOT

The Severan period was especially prolific in measures enacted by the Jewish authorities to meet the social and economic circumstances of the times. The leaders of the day, especially the Patriarchs, showed themselves responsive to the needs of the people, and displayed the courage to discard time-hallowed traditions when that was what had to be done.

In the present context we can do no more than glance at some of the reforms that were introduced during the Severan period. First

---

67 Mak. 21b; Yev. 92b; Tem. 7a; Yer. Yev. I:2c.
68 *Dorot,* II. 48, ref. Yer. Av. Zar. II:41d; Git. VI :48d and Nid. III: 50d. See Zori op. cit. (note 53). Examples of the use of *Rabbotenu* where the dating is almost certainly the end of the Severan period, are Tos. Nid. V:3 (694); Par. V:1 (634); Ket. VIII:1 (270); comp. Bavli Ket. 38b; Yer. ibid. VIII:32b; Tos. ibid. V:7 (267); Bavli ibid. 63b; Yer. ibid. V:30b.
69 B.B. 28a; Yer. ibid. II :13d; Tos. Shevi. IV:21 (67); R.H. 15a; Ket. 49b.

and foremost among those who faced up to the changes that were
needed was Judah Ha-Nasi himself. The main thrust of his activity
was in the direction of normalizing the life of the people. In some
instances he was merely putting the final seal on a process which
had been long in the making, and had just been waiting for someone in authority with enough courage to make it official. In this
respect, he set the pace for his son Gamaliel III and his grandson
Judah II. His sense that the time had come to recognize the ob-
solescence of certain procedures is epitomized by the Yerushalmi
when it states that "Rabbi" abolished the bonfires that had sig-
nalled the New Moon, and also relaxed the strict rules of evidence
that had governed testimony of sighting the lunar crescent.[70]

The fact is that the whole ritual of "witnesses" to establish the
beginning of a new month had been vestigeal for some time. Astronomical calculations had determined the matter at least since the
time of Rabban Gamaliel of Yavneh. Yet the Sanhedrin was still
going through the motions one generation before Judah I.[71] Even
he did not altogether abolish the ritual, probably because it was
thought to be a valuable symbol of the Patriarch's authority, especially with respect to the Jews of the Diaspora.

In another of his enactments, Judah I dispensed Caesarea, Beth
Guvrin and Beth Shean from the payment of tithes.[72] The motivation for this was undoubtedly the decrease in the number of Jewish
farmers in those areas, and the desire to enable those who remained
to cling to their holdings. The measure also had sound theoretical
underpinnings, and had been discussed earlier. Nevertheless 'Rabbi' met with considerable opposition. There were even those in
his own circle who chided him: "A thing which your fathers
and forefathers said was forbidden — how can you make it permitted?"

Another ancient practice which 'Rabbi' tried to abrogate was
the sabbatical year in agriculture. No doubt he was moved in this
case too, by a desire to protect the public. The biblical command
to let the land lie fallow (*shemitta*) every seventh year had been
observed throughout the period of the Second Commonwealth as

70 Yer. R.H. II : 58a.
71 Tos. R.H. II : 1 (210); Yer. ibid. II : 57d; Bavli ibid. 22b.
72 Yer. Dem. II : 22c; Hul. 6b.

"a mitzvah confined to the Holy Land." After the Destruction it was assumed to be still in force, but many Jews simply disregarded it, and the sources are full of references to "those suspected of neglecting *shevi'ith*."[73] The reasons for this are not far to seek: the difficult economic situation, coupled with the fact that the government now frequently ignored the traditional Roman practicè of forgiving taxes on farm produce during sabbatical years.

The Halakhah had already shown the effects of these conditions.[74] As for Judah I, his thinking on the subject is revealed by the following incident. A teacher of small children was brought before him, accused of dealing in *shemitta* produce.

> Rabbi Judah said to them: What do you want of the poor fellow? That's how he keeps body and soul together.[75]

This attitude of the great Patriarch was not due to light-hearted carelessness of halakhic norms, or disregard of proper legal methods. On the contrary, it was based on well thought-out legal grounds. "Rabbi" was able to demonstrate that the Torahitic law of *shemitta* had lapsed with the Destruction, and was by his time being preserved only by authority of the Rabbis (*mi-divrei sofe- rim*).[76]

In this particular instance his attempt to update the halakhah met with considerable opposition, led by Rabbi Pinhas ben Yair.[77] It seems that those Sages who were closest to the common folk, most 'proletarian' in their outlook, felt strongly about preserving this time-hallowed tradition, just because it symbolized the willingness of plain Jews to make sacrifices for the sake of the Torah.[78]

---

73 Especially Mekhilta, Lauterbach III, p. 204 ff.: "Sabbatical and Jubilee years, for which they were not prepared to sacrifice their lives." Comp. above p. 648.

74 "They used to call them 'harvesters of Seventh Year produce,' but when the oppressors became many, they called them merely 'traffickers in Seventh Year produce' " (Mishnah, Sanh. III:3.)

75 Yer. Taan. III:66c; comp. E.Z. Melammed in *Ta᷉biz* XXII, p. 119.

76 Git. 36a; Yer. Shevi. X:39c.

77 Yer. Dem. I:20a; Yer. Taan. III:66c.

78 Cf. LevR. I, where the words of the Psalmist (103:20): "Ye mighty heroes who fulfil his word" are applied to people who observe the Seventh Year, and quietly accept the losses involved.

To many Sages, "commandments connected with the Land" had now become especially important; their observance was regarded as a kind of *"kiddush ha-shem."*

In the event, Judah retreated from his proposal to abolish the sabbatical year. But his son did succeed in easing its restrictions to a certain degree:

> Rabban Gamaliel and his Beth Din issued a *taqanah* permitting farmers to work their land right up to Rosh Hashanah of the Seventh Year.[79]

Another important reform instituted by Judah I concerned the ownership of land. With his characteristic motive of restoring some degree of normality into social and economic life after the stormy years of the second century, he moved to regularize title to property which had been confiscated by the Romans and subsequently disposed of by them:

> "Rabbi" set up a Beth Din and they decided by vote that after the field had been in possession of the usurping occupant for twelve months, the first comer to buy it thereafter obtained secure title; but he must give the original owner one quarter.[80]

The original halakhah had treated land confiscated by the Romans as stolen property. If anyone then acquired such land he was regarded as a 'robber', and the transaction was void.[81] The net effect of this was that Jews hesitated to buy such property, leaving it to be snapped up by gentiles.

The Mishnah just quoted describes the stages whereby the effects of this "law of the *sikarikon*" were mitigated, while leaving the principle (the original owner, wherever he might be, still had title) intact. But finally, as we have seen, a way was found to make the new title valid. The original owner, if one showed up, would be

---

79 Tos. Shevii. I:1 (61); Yer. ibid. I:33a; Bavli M.Q. 3b. The older rule had been that planting must stop at the preceding Passover or Shavuot, depending on the nature of the field or orchard (Mishnah Shevi. II:1).
80 Mishnah Git. V:6.
81 See Git. 58b.

compensated; but stability of land ownership would be maintained, in the public interest.

Another rather surprising *taqanah* had a similar thrust. It dealt with the usurer (*malveh b'ribbit*) or robber (*gazlan*) who repents, and wants to make restitution. The Tosefta says:

> The Sages look with disfavor (*ein ru'ah hakhamim nohah*) on anyone who accepts the repayment proferred by these.

Rabbi Johanan, at the end of the third century, explains that this 'Mishnah' was taught in the days of "Rabbi," and demonstrates the need for it by the following case in point: [82]

> A certain man wanted to repent (*for shady acquisition*). His wife said to him: 'Don't be a fool — if you repent you'll have to give everything back, and you'll be left without even the girdle around your waist'. He thought it over and changed his mind about repenting.

Here again we find Rabbi Judah in search of stabilization, even at the price of circumventing a fundamental religio-legal principle. The biblical prohibition against lending at interest was proving too difficult to maintain. Later in the century Rabbi Johanan was asked:

> Can interest already taken be recovered by litigation? He answered: If we allowed that, all our leading citizens would be stripped of everything they own! [83]

In other words, the whole socio-economic structure would become a shambles. There can be little doubt that this was the reason for the *taqanah* of Judah Ha-Nasi.

The word *gazlan* used in this context is not to be taken literally. It does not mean "robber," but rather a person who had acquired possessions without making sure that the seller was the rightful owner. In the unsettled circumstances of the years — more than a hundred of them — that had seen so much violence and social dislocation, from Vespasian and Titus through Quietus to Hadrian

---

82 B.Q. 64b; for the *taqanah* itself, Tos. Shevi VIII: 11 (37).
83 Yer. B.M. V: 10a; comp. Yer. B.B. III: 14a.

and after, all sorts of chattels had changed hands in all sorts of shady ways, such as the purchase from looters, or the "finding" of abandoned goods. At some point special measures were called for in order to restore normal and stable economic relationships, without invalidating fundamental principles of law.

The successors of Rabbi Judah were responsible for a *taqanah* with respect to a wife who refused marital intercourse. The Mishnah had quoted a law making her liable to a progressive reduction in the amount of her *ketubah*. But the Tosefta reports:

> *Rabbotenu* made a *taqanah* according to which she was put on notice once a week for a series of four weeks, after which she was to forfeit her entire *ketubah*.[84]

The intent of this *taqanah* may have been to protect wives from having to submit to unwanted intercourse.[85] It may even have been deliberately designed as a means of enabling women to initiate divorce proceedings, albeit at the price of waiving their marriage settlement.

Another halakhah of long standing banned the consumption of oil produced by non-Jews. The prohibition was well-known to Josephus, and is recorded by the Mishnah about 150 years after him; but the Mishnah goes on to say that "Rabbi" and his Beth Din lifted the ban. The Tosefta puts it this way: "Rabbi Judah and his Beth Din permitted the oil of gentiles."[86] Both Talmudim make it clear that the "Rabbi" referred to was Judah II Nesia, grandson of the Patriarch of that name.[87] His act set aside a prohibition deeply rooted among the Jews of both the homeland and the Diaspora.

---

84 Mishnah Ket. V:7; Tos. ib. V:7 (267); Bavli ib. 63b; Yer. ib. V:30b.

85 [Something expressly forbidden by the later Jewish codes: see *inter alia* Maimonides (12th cent.), *Yad*: *Deot* V:4 and *Issure Bi'ah* XXI: 12; Moses of Coucy (13th cent.) *SeMaG, Lavvin* 156; and Jacob ben Asher (14th cent.) *Tur. Even Ha-Ezer* 55, and *Orah Hayyim* 240. After the Geonim, the law made divorce mandatory in case of *moredet;* see Menahem Elon: *Ha-Mishpat Ha Ivri*, pp. 541–546]

86 Mishnah Av. Zar. II:6; Tos. ibid. IV:1 (467). For Josephus, Ant. XII:120; JW II:591; Life XIII:74. Comp. JJCW pp. 156 f.

87 Av. Zar. 36a; Yer. ibid. II:41d.

A highly plausible explanation for this *taqanah* is put forward by Rabbi Joshua ben Levi in the context in the Yerushalmi. He says that Jews used to risk (and lose) their lives to get kosher olive-oil from the Judaean hill region, now largely out of Jewish hands. Apparently this was felt as a problem in Judaea proper, but not in Galilee; which explains why it was Rabbi Simlai, a southerner from Lod, who was so active in getting the prohibition rescinded.

Actually, it was the same Rabbi Simlai who tried to get another prohibition abolished — the one against eating bread baked by gentiles. But Judah II was wary of further antagonising those Sages who had already dubbed his Beth Din "the permissive court."[88]

It is possible to discern two parallel lines of development behind these reforms. Along with changes in the socio-economic conditions of the age, there had also been a process of change in halakhic theory. The older view that pagans were levitically impure because of their idolatrous practices had been undergoing critical scrutiny.[89] It is not necessary for us to determine whether the theory came before or after the fact; surely there was interaction between the two. But it does seem most probable that the process of halakhic thinking that led to halakhic change was an outcome of the situation in the third century which had brought Jews and gentiles into much closer contact with one another.

There are other symptoms of this breaking down of barriers. For example, the older prohibition against trading with pagans on their festive days was somewhat relaxed.[90] Going still further, Jews running town or village councils were instructed that social services should be a joint venture: charity was to be collected from Jew and gentile alike, and distributed to all the needy; burial of the dead and comforting of the mourners was to be practiced without discrimination.[91]

This survey shows that the Patriarch Judah I, his son Gamaliel III, and his grandson Judah II Nesia were the authors of major

88 [Yer. Shab. I : 3d.]
89 See Alon: "The Levitical Uncleanness of Gentiles," in JJCW, pp. 146 ff.
90 Yer. Av. Zar. I : 39b.
91 Tos. Git. V : 4 (328); Yer. ibid. V : 47c.

reforms in the social, religious and economic life of their people. In most of these actions they stand revealed as courageous leaders, men of action with progressive outlooks. It is safe to say that they paved the way for a whole new era in the relationship between the Jewish people and the nations of the world.

CHAPTER TWENTY-EIGHT

A DWINDLING COMMUNITY

[It may be necessary at this point to remind the reader that Gedaliah Alon did not live to finish his work. At the outset, he had divided the six centuries before the Arab invasion into three stages, and had proposed to study them all. In the event, he only managed to complete his lecture notes for the Jewish history of the first stage, the years 70 to 235 C.E. He then went on to present a synopsis of Roman history up to Constantine the Great (4th century), in preparation for the Jewish history of the second stage, which — along with the third stage — remained unwritten.

Fortunately, however, he did write his introduction, containing a broad resume of these remaining two stages, so that it is possible to round out the picture by a re-reading of "The Age of the Amoraim (235–420)," and of "Byzantine Palestine (420–640)."[1]

This concluding chapter, therefore, will merely lift from volume II of the author's *Toledot* two extracts that add historical data (or historical judgment) to what has already been said. The first of these is taken from prefatory remarks to a lecture series that was intended to reach Theodotius II — but never did. The second is an abridged version of what appears to have been an independent lecture on the demography of Palestine during the whole span of the Roman period.]

Christian Rome*

The victory of Constantine at the Milvian bridge in 312 and his subsequent conversion to Christianity is generally thought of as the time when the Roman Empire became Christian. Certainly, it was a watershed; but it should be remembered that the process

1   See pages 29 to 38 above.
*   From Tol. II, pages 91 to 94.

of the Christianization of the state had been going on for several centuries, and would not be completed for nearly another hundred years.

In the meantime, remnants of the old Roman religion survived, even in the organs of government, and so did elements of the old Roman tradition of religious tolerance. And although legislation aimed at the Jews already made its appearance, there was still room for Judaism and its institutions to function. Indeed, with the resurgence of tolerance under Julian and his successors, in the middle of the fourth century, the Jewish Patriarchate enjoyed a brief infusion of prestige and importance, a sort of sunset glow before the dark set in.[2]

However, the Catholic Church gradually secured its hold on the Roman State, and the Hellenistic religions were vigorously eliminated. The Church had undergone several centuries of persecution; now the tables were turned and Christianity, armed with the power of the state, became the persecutor. There was now only one *religio licita;* no room was left for the various pagan cults, no patience with heretical doctrines.

This intolerance is undoubtedly connected with the very essence of the monotheism from which Christianity derived, and can therefore be seen as something it inherited from Judaism. However, Christianity outdid the mother religion in this respect. For Judaism had reached the point of recognizing the right of other religions to exist; it did not see it as mandatory to wipe them out; they were "licit" so to speak. Christianity, on the other hand, had set out to conquer the whole gentile world. In that world, it could brook no rivals.

In any event, an intense period of catholization of the Roman Empire set in at the end of the fourth century, and especially at the beginning of the fifth. But from this process of uprooting other religions, one religion was exempt — and that was Judaism. Why this was so is usually explained in theological terms, based on the thinking of the early Church. The Church Fathers, St. Augustine in particular, saw it as part of the divine plan that the Jews

2   In the year 358 Hillel II published the system for calculating the Jewish calendar in use to the present day. His successors were Judah IV (385–400) and the last Nasi, Gamaliel VI (400–425).

should survive, as bearers of the "Old Covenant," a part of the Christian story to which they would thus bear living witness.

This explanation, though widely held, is not necessarily correct. The toleration that early Christianity granted to Jews and Judaism may more convincingly be attributed to two other causes. First, the Jews were seen as having a valid tradition of their own. They were not part of that world of the gentiles which it was Christianity's mission to conquer. True, there never was a time when Christians stopped trying to convince the Jews; and individual instances of forced conversion can be cited even from these early days. But fundamentally, the conversion of the Jews was left to God's own good time, in the same way that the Jews believed the whole world would ultimately come to accept Jewish teaching — but only in the days of the Messiah.

Secondly, there was the very practical consideration that the unshakeable loyalty of the Jews to their own Torah made it *impossible* to convert them en masse. That this was a factor in their survival can be proven by examining the case of the Samaritans whose religion, unlike Judaism, was never recognized by the Church. Yet they too survived, because of their loyalty to their own tradition, and in the teeth of strenuous efforts by church and state to win them over.

But although Judaism was not suppressed during these first years of Christian triumph, it did suffer a number of severe restrictions. The winds of change were blowing, and they were to have a profound effect on the fate of the Jewish people. For example, the ban on building new synagogues was a very large straw in the wind. So too was legislation which diminished the civil status of the Jews. An especially hard blow was the termination of the Jewish Patriarchate in the year 425, after a series of measures restricting its powers. With the loss of that office, the Jewish people lost the chief external symbol of its unity centered on its homeland, the Land of Israel.

Nevertheless, Jewish history in the fourth, fifth and sixth centuries also presents another face. In the midst of the struggle to survive, in a world of kaleidiscopic change, the Jewish people continued to weave its own design on the tapestry of life and events. With all its ups and downs, achievements and defeats,

Jewry succeeded in preserving its organic unity, its collective mental health and world-outlook, refining in the process the values by which it lived, and fashioning the tools for group living with which it would face the future.

II. SOME POPULATION TRENDS*

We have already had occasion to observe the demographic effects of wars and depressions on the Jewish population of Palestine during the first two centuries after the Destruction.[3] The area hardest hit by the wars against Rome and by the postwar emigration was the Judaean hill-country. As for Jerusalem itself, the report by Christian writers that the Jews were barred from the city and from a narrow strip around it seems to be reliable. On the other hand, there is some doubt about Tertullian's statement that they were excluded from Bethlehem as well.[4]

The literature contains a number of references to *Har Hamelekh* as an area where only a handful of Jews continued to cling to their farms.[5] The exact geographical meaning of this term has been a matter of discussion.[6] It is true that the name, especially in its Aramaic form (*Tur Malka*) seems to refer to a particular town or village. But in general, it appears to mean a whole region, namely "The Mountains of Judah," with special reference to the territory north and west of Jerusalem.

Emigration from areas like this was not always to foreign lands. Some of it was internal movement, to other parts of the country. For example, we may take it for granted that when the governing institutions of Jewish life moved to the Galilee after the Bar Kokhba war, a great many ordinary people also made the same move, either because of political conditions, or under the pressure of adverse social and economic circumstances.

Another area to which people apparently moved from the Juda-

---

* From Tol. Vol. II, Appendix B, pages 242–262.
3 See JLTA I, pp. 5–6, 56, II pp. 53–56.
4 *Advers. Jud.* 13, P.L. II, 673.
5 Yer. Dem. VI:25b; ibid. V:24d; Yer. Av. Zar. I:40b; see above pp. 645, 736.
6 Klein in *Tarbiz* I pp. 136–144; idem, *Eretz Yehudah*, pp. 229–247; also *Yerushalayim*, 1928, p. 21.

ean hills was the southern Shephela. It seems that many towns in that area (and perhaps also the coastal cities of Jaffa and Caesaraea) received an access of Jewish inhabitants at that time, and the likelihood is that these were migrants from the hill-country. The fact that a number of new synagogues were built at Lod during the Severan period, and a number of old ones refurbished, may be due to this internal migration. We hear of two Sages of the time touring the "synagogues of Lod" — Rabbis Hoshaya and Hama bar Hanina.[7]

Apart from this reference, we know that Lod continued to serve as the venue for official proclamations of the New Moon right through the time of Judah I. Even later, the procedure was still carried out in the South, and not only because of the greater sanctity of Judaea proper. What happened was that the southern region had reasserted its claim to leadership over the new center in Galilee. Apparently the Jewish population in the South had increased to the point where it could make its voice heard.

THE SAMARITAN EXPANSION

A demographic phenomenon of considerable importance was the movement of Samaritans to parts of the country outside Samaria. The direction of this flow was initially towards the Shephela, the lowlands of Philistia, and from there on down to the coastal regions, both north and south. There was also some movement out of Samaria northwards beyond Ein Ganim, which had once marked the northern limit of the land of the Samaritans. Here, however, the movement halted at the valleys of Jezreel and Beth She'an.[8]

In this connection it is instructive to examine the following aggadah dating from the second century:[9]

> Once Rabbi Simeon ben Eleazar came to a city in the South (darom). He went into a synagogue and there he found a teacher, of whom he asked: Where can I find wine for sale? The other answered: Rabbi, this has become a Samaritan

7   Yer. Peah VIII:21b; Yer. Sheq. V:49b.
8   For a survey of Samaritan settlements, see Yitzhak Ben Zvi: *Sefer Ha-Shomronim*, 1935, pp. 64–132; and S. Klein: *Eretz Ha-Cuthim* in *Yerushalayim* (Lunz), no. X, pp. 133–160.
9   DeutR, II:24; comp. Yer. Av. Zar. V:45d; Bavli Hul. 6a.

town, and they do not make their wine in a state of purity
as my forefathers used to do. . . . .

Apparently this was a town where Jews and Samaritans lived side
by side. Rabbi Simeon, who was from Galilee, did not know
whether the place was now predominantly Jewish or Samaritan.

It is also relevant to cite the statement by Rabbi Abbahu (late
third century) that "during the *shemad* thirteen villages were settled
(among?) (by?) the Samaritans."[10] This is usually taken to mean
that Jews, seeking refuge from the Hadrianic persecutions, settled
among the Samaritans and were absorbed by them. But in view
of the context, I am more inclined to read this in the opposite
sense: that the Samaritans moved into Jewish territory to escape
the Roman ban on circumcision. Let it be remembered that even
when the Jews were released from that ban, it still remained in
force against the Samaritans.[11] Either way, the tradition speaks of
an intermingling of the two communities.

Apart from seeking refuge among the Jews at a time when it
was easier to be a Jew than a Samaritan, the latter had another
reason for moving. Economic opportunity was greater in the
wealthy towns of the Shephela, and even more promising along the
coastal plain. Samaritans with capital and initiative were drawn
in those directions, as evidenced by the well-established Samaritan
community in third-century Caesaraea. It can scarcely be doubted
that by that time the Samaritans had penetrated to Yavneh and
Gaza. In the fourth and fifth centuries there was an entirely Samaritan settlement at Kastra, near Haifa.[12]

The classic boundaries of the Samaritans are set forth by Josephus.[13] The Sages were well aware of the expansion of the Sam-

10 Yer. Yev. VIII:9d; Yer. Qid. IV:65c.
11 Origen reports that in his day, Samaritans were punished for practicing
    circumcision; and that their religious teachers fought for the preserva-
    tion of that rite, and for the Mosaic law. See *Contra Celsum* II, ed.
    Koetschau, p. 142; and *Commentary on Matthew*, X, ed. Klostermann,
    p. 666.
12 Antoninus of Placentia calls it *Castra Samaritanorum;* see also LamR
    I:17 and Midrash Samuel 16, 26a; also *Yishuv I*, s.v. "Onon" n. 9; and
    Ben Z'vi, op. cit. p. 103.
13 JW III, 48.

aritans beyond those boundaries. Commenting on the statement by Rabbi Simeon ben Gamaliel that the Samaritans were more meticulous than Jews in observing those mitzvot which they regarded as binding:

> Rabbi Simeon (*read*: *ben Laqish*) said: That was all very well as long as they lived in their own villages; but nowadays they haven't a shred of a mitzvah left.[14]

This shows that Rabbi Simeon ben Laqish believed that the main migration of the Samaritans took place between the middle of the second century and the middle of his own century, the third. There is every reason for accepting this as reasonably accurate.

On the other hand, those Samaritan legends which picture them controlling large segments of the country in the fourth century are not to be taken seriously.[15] The supposed areas include the following: from Gaza to El Arish; from Rosh Haniqrah to Tyre; from the Carmel to Akko; and from the hills of Galilee to Mount Lebanon. This is undoubtedly fiction — fiction based, however, on fact. The fact is that the Samaritans did indeed spread out during the second and third centuries.

This fact is testified to by the documented presence of Samaritans during the second century in Kefar Othnai, Antipatras, and several coastal points.[16] And although the evidence for their close settlement in Emmaus and Lod comes from a later time, it is fairly certain that they had moved in during the second century. The same applies to Caesaraea, where our earliest evidence comes from the third century.[17]

As for Yavneh, we know that it had a large Samaritan population in the fifth century. But the Tosefta shows that they were already there in the second century.[18]

14　Yer. Pes. I:27b. For the reference to Rabban Simeon ben Gamaliel, Tos. Pes. I:15 (156).

15　E.g. Adler Chronicle, REJ 45, (1902), pp. 91 ff.

16　Mishnah Git. I:5; Tos. Dem. V:23 (56) (first cent.); ibid. I:11 (46); Av. Zar. 31a.

17　Yer. Av. Zar. V:44d.

18　*History of Petrus the Iberian* (Syriac) ed. Raabe, pp. 126 ff. The original Greek of this work is lost; see *Yishuv* I p. 77, note 11. For

What caused the Samaritans to spread out from Samaria in this fashion? We have already suggested two causes: the push of religious persecution and the pull of economic opportunity. Perhaps we should add a third reason: the fact that the Jews had become too weak to resist the influx; indeed, in some areas there were no Jews left to resist.

Under the circumstances, it was only to have been expected that the Jews and the Samaritans should now find themselves allies in resisting the incursion of alien neighbors (Syrians and Greeks) as well as the depredations of the government. On the other hand, they were now trade competitors, and this could not but sharpen the ancient antagonism between the two peoples. These contradictory forces, one positive and the other negative, are reflected in the traditions of both groups.

The Sages had always been of two minds about the Samaritans. It is a striking fact that during the first generation after the Bar Kokhba war, Rabban Simeon ben Gamaliel said, "Samaritans are to be classified as Jews;" while one generation later his son Judah I said the exact opposite: "Samaritans are to be classified as gentiles." Finally, his grandson Gamaliel II issued a ruling: meat slaughtered by Samaritans is not kosher.[19]

What was the reason for this sharp change in attitude? Perhaps Rabbi Simeon ben Laqish gave us the answer when he said that the Samaritans were spoiled when they moved out of their own villages. Perhaps contact with the big bad world did make them less strict about their religion, so that Jews could no longer feel safe in eating their food.

But I would venture to suggest another reason for increased antagonism on the part of the Jews. The Samaritans posed a new economic threat: they were competitors. This may be the significance of the exchange between them and Rabbi Abbahu of Caesaraea.

the Tosefta, Dem. I:13 (46), where ms. Erfurt is defective due to a homoeoteleuton.
19 Tos. Ter. IV:12 (31) and 14 (32); Yer. Ber. VII:11b; Tos. Pes. I (II):15 (156) et passim; Hul. 5b, where the Talmud reads simply "Rabban Gamaliel and his Beth Din," but obviously means Gamaliel III.

They said: Your fathers used to be satisfied with our products. Why do you refuse what we offer? He replied: Your fathers were not spoiled in their behavior (*lo qilqᶜlu ma'aseihem*) but you have spoiled yours (i.e. you are no longer observant).[20]

FROM 235 TO 324 C.E.

More than anything else, it was the economic situation that shaped the destiny of the Jews in Palestine during these post-Severan years. There is every reason for believing that the great depression that characterized the times was a major cause of the reduction of the Jewish population of the country. There were a number of causes for the economic breakdown which was empirewide. First and foremost was the almost constant state of war, as Rome tried to fend off attacks from all sides — from the Persians and the Palmyrenes in the east, from the Goths in Europe itself. This violence was compounded by the internal wars between rivals for the throne of the Caesars.

The result was an enormous increase in the burden of levies and taxes, something which opened the door to a great deal of extortion by government officials, not the least active of whom were the common soldiers billeted all over the Empire. In Palestine there was an additional factor: the incursion of Arab marauders into the border areas.[21]

All this dislocation did much to disrupt public safety and the security of travel on the highways, and perforce had a seriously limiting effect on trade. High prices, especially for processed goods, and the grave deterioration of the currency did much to interfere with the proper cultivation of the soil, and agricultural productivity sank to a new low.

Jewish sources of the period reflect this situation to a considerable extent. There is talk about the difficulty of making a living, as illustrated by the following:

20 Yer. Av. Zar. V:44d.
21 Kräling: *Gerasa* provides excellent archaeological evidence for the economic deterioration as it affected the Middle East in the third century; see especially pp. 60–61.

A man once sold himself to the *ludarii* (*gladiator agents*). Then he came to Rabbi Abbahu and said: Redeem me! The Rabbi remarked: What can I do? He only did what he did so as to have something to eat! [22]

The atmosphere of the times is conveyed by an exchange between Rabbi Johanan and his son-in-law, Resh Laqish:

Rabbi Johanan said: Let him (the Messiah) come, but let me not see him (i.e. I fear the pangs of the Messiah). Said Resh Laqish to him: Do you refer to Amos V:19?[23] Let me prove to you that we are just as badly off right now. For nowadays a man goes into his field and finds a bailiff there... He enters the town, and is accosted by a tax-collector... He goes into his house, only to find his children suffering the pangs of hunger.[24]

For centuries agriculture had been the mainstay of the national economy of Jewish Palestine. Its loss of that position is strikingly reflected in certain third century traditions. Rabbi Johanan once said: "The *sifsuf* which we ate in our youth was better than what passes today for first-grade (*pankhrisin*)," to which the Gemara adds, "because in his days the world changed,"[25] and the soil dried up. A contemporary of Rabbi Johanan, Rabbi Eleazar ben Pedat, commented: "You can't find a worse occupation than farming."[26]

It is fairly certain that during the third century agriculture was the hardest hit branch of the economy. And since farming was the

22 Yer. Git. IV:46b. The Mishnah had expressly forbidden the use of community funds to redeem anyone who sells himself to heathen. [For the translation of *luda'i* (Lydians) as *ludarii*, see Sancino Talmud ad loc.]

23 "As if a man did flee from a lion, and a bear met him; and went into the house and leaned his hand on the wall, and a serpent bit him."

24 Sanh. 98b.

25 Yer. Peah VII:20a and Sot. I:17b. "*Sifsuf*" is fruit not good enough for the market; as for "*pankhrisin*," the Talmudic dictionaries differ widely about its derivation and meaning.

26 Yev. 63a.

principal pursuit left to the Jews, they suffered from the series of depressions in the third century more than the non-Jewish population. An additional reason for this was the fact that crop taxes were collectel in kind, particularly the levies from which the Roman troops were fed, so that the burden fell on agricultural villagers more than on townsfolk. Besides, the depredations of the soldiery were felt in the countryside more than in the cities.

This was a potent cause for people leaving the country, even if it was more often than not with the intention of coming back. Most of the source-references to this phenomenon concern Sages who went abroad to earn a living; but surely the same factors drove ordinary folk to emigrate.

Of course, we must not lose sight of a partially balancing factor — Jews coming into the country from abroad. From Babylonia a great many students came to study at the academies in the Land of Israel.[27] Other countries, too, were represented in this immigration. We find a reference to a community of Cappadocians at Sepphoris; and in the ancient, mainly third-century cemetery at Jaffa, Jews from Asia Minor, North Africa and Armenia are buried.[28] One must hasten to add, however, that this immigration came nowhere near balancing the emigration. The outflow was markedly greater.

URBANIZATION

The third century in Palestine was marked by the incorporation of urban areas as Greek-style cities (*poleis*) with accompanying changes of nomenclature.[29] The places involved were: 1) *Beth Guvrin*: became Eleutheropolis in 199–200, when Septimius Severus visited the country; 2) *Lod* (*Lydda*): became Diospolis at the same time; 3) *Emmaus*: became Nikopolis about the year 222; 4) *Ono*: became a polis with a boulē some time before 291;[30] 5) *Dio-*

27 [See Joshua Schwartz: "Aliyah from Babylonia in the Amoraic Period," in *Jerusalem Cathedra* 3, pp. 58 et seq.]
28 Yer. Shevi. IX:39a; *Yishuv* I, 80–88.
29 See Jones: "The Urbanization of Palestine," in JRS 1931, pp. 78 et seq.
30 Pap. Oxy. IX, pp. 239–240 of the year 291 mentions a Jew called Justus as a member of the boulē of Ono.

cletianopolis: was set up alongside Ashkelon, probably during the reign of Diocletian;[31] and 6) Maximinianopolis, in the Valley of Jezreel.[32]

What was the effect of this process on the Jewish population of Palestine? Some scholars believe that the Jewish inhabitants of the cities were simply uprooted. Schlatter, for example, says that that is what happened when Septimius Severus founded Diospolis and Eleutheropolis.[33] However, such a conclusion seems to be greatly exaggerated. To be sure, incorporation as a *polis* meant giving a distinctly pagan Hellenic cast to a city, as we can see from the coins minted by Diospolis and Eleutheropolis. But these places already had a considerable pagan element; while on the other hand, those pagans did not gain absolute control of the new municipalities — witness Justus, the city-councillor of Ono just mentioned. So there is no reason to believe that the Jews were completely driven out of these cities.[34]

Indeed, the evidence shows that Lod remained an essentially Jewish town throughout the third century; and a number of Midrashim tell us that Ono was still populated by Jews quite some time later. In fact, the new municipal situation was considered desirable by both Jews and Christians. It had its advantages, for it gave the municipality a degree of self-rule, especially in the collection of taxes and the administration of local services. Hence the eagerness of non-hellenic citizens to achieve "urbanization," in spite of some of the external features that accompanied the change. Christian sources tell us that Julius Africanus, the well-known Christian writer, led the deputation from Emmaus that petitioned the Emperor to incorporate the town under the new name of Nikopolis. This, despite the pagan symbols that adorned the coins of that city from its very start. A similar pragmatic motivation may

31 See Abel, *Emmaus* II, p. 306.
32 Ibid.
33 *Zur Topographie und Geschichte Palästinas,* Büchler takes the same line in JQR 1901, pp. 683–740.
34 [Alon's earlier statement in this connection that the Jews of these cities were "elbowed aside" and became a minority does not contradict what is said here. The translation "displacement" for *deḥiyat ragleyhem* (JLTA I, p. 32 n.) is perhaps misleading.]

lie behind the tradition that Judah I was pleased at the prospect that "Antoninus" might turn Tiberias into a *colonia*.[35]

THE DEMOGRAPHIC BALANCE

Before looking at the sources dealing with this subject, it should be pointed out that evidence from the immediately following period, the Byzantine, can help illuminate the situation in the generations preceding, since it is unlikely that any changes in that short period sent the Jewish population curve upwards. Secondly, the Halakhah relating to tithes and other such offerings can be revealing as far as the Jewish farming population is concerned, since only produce raised by Jews in the Land of Israel is liable for *terumot* and *ma'aserot*.

It was in connection with the latter that the Jerusalem Talmud, probably late in the fourth century, attributed to Rabbi Eleazar, a contemporary of Rabbi Johanan, the opinion that most of the land in Eretz Israel was already in non-Jewish ownership. Rabbi Johanan held the opposite view.[36] What this proves is that Sages in Palestine in the third or fourth centuries were not quite sure how to answer the question whether most of the rural population was still Jewish.

In the same context, Rabbi Zeira (early fourth century) was unable to get a clear-cut estimate as to whether the famous "Nicholas" dates were being cultivated in his day by more Jewish fruit-farmers than gentile ones. On the other hand, it was clear that Jews were in a minority in Caesarea; but then, neither of the other two main elements in that city was in the majority.[37] Indeed, we may be justified in taking that tripartie division as characteristic for the country as a whole — neither Jews nor Samaritans nor gentiles constituted a majority by themselves.

GALILEE

As far as the Galilee is concerned, there can be no doubt that its population was still solidly Jewish in the fourth century. The Church Father Epiphanius testifies that in Sepphoris and Tiberias

35   Av. Zar. 10a. A *colonia* would get tax-freedom.
36   Yer. Dem. II : 22b–c.
37   Ibid.; see JLTA I, p. 140.

and Capernaum and Nazareth "gentiles were not wanted".[38] He was obviously exaggerating, because we have explicit evidence that gentiles lived in Tiberias at that time, and doubtless in Sepphoris as well.[39] But in a broad sense he was right — Jews *were* the overwhelming majority in those towns.[40]

Many proofs can be culled from Jewish sources to show that at the time in question, Galilee was heavily populated by Jews. Rabbi Haninah (third century) found a slaughtered kid between Tiberias and Sepphoris, and it was declared kosher on the presumption that it had been properly slaughtered, since Jews were in majority in those parts. Later in the same century, Rabbi Ammi found some slaughtered chickens in the same area, and was given a similar ruling.[41] The same sort of thing happened with a roast kid that was found on the road to Gufta (also known as Govavta of Sepphoris). One of the reasons for declaring it permitted was that most travellers on that road were Jews. As it turned out, it had been dropped by someone on the staff of the Patriarch himself![42]

A like problem arose when a wheel of cheese was found at the inn of Lavi.[43] The same reasoning was applied to make it kosher.

THE DAROM

As far as "Judaea proper" is concerned, it is instructive to refer once more to the *Onomasticon* of Eusebius. He names "Jewish villages" and "large villages of Jews" south of Beth Guvrin in the fourth century.[44] The places he mentions are 1) Bethanim, 2)

---

38 The passage is quoted below, p. 753.
39 E.g. Yer. Shab. XVI:15d: "R. Ammi announced in the *shuq* of the gentiles ... "
40 Comp. Yer. Ket. II:26c: "Rabbi Yudin spoke of two who came from a town with a gentile majority, like Sussita." A town in Galilee with a gentile majority was, apparently, the exception rather than the norm.
41 B.M. 24b.
42 Yer. Sheq. VII:50c; see *Yishuv* p. 29.
43 So ms. Munich. Today the name belongs to a kibbutz. The spot was formerly called Lubia. Ed. Venice reads "Levi."
44 See the translation by E.Z. Melammed in *Tarbiz*, IV, pp. 259 ff. [And see now the dissertation by Joshua Schwartz (Hebrew University 1981, to be published) "A History of Jewish Settlement in Southern Judaea After the Bar Kokhba Revolt etc."]

Eshtamoa, 3) En Gedi, 4) Yuta, 5) Carmela, 6) Ayena, 7) Ein Ramon.

LOD

As for Lod (Lydda) there is an interesting passage in a work by Eusebius which has reached us only in a Syriac translation:

> There is a large city (*medinta hada rabta*) in the land of Palaestina, teeming with population, of which all the inhabitants are Jews. In the Aramaic tongue it is called Lud, and in the Greek speech it is known as Diocaesaraea.[45]

Of course there is something wrong here. Diocaesaraea is not Lod. Klein (*Yishuv* p. 131) thought that Eusebius really meant Sepphoris, and that the words "in the Aramaic tongue" and so on were a scribal insertion. In my own opinion, "Diocaesaraea" is a scribal error for "Diospolis." At all events, when Jerome speaks of Jewish cities in the context of the revolt against Gallus (351), he refers explicitly to Tiberias, Sepphoris and Lod-Diospolis.[46]

THE BYZANTINE PERIOD

In the history of Palestine the two centuries from Constantine the Great to the Arab conquest (324–636) are known as "the Byzantine Period." During those years the overriding factor was that the state was officially Christian, and the generality of the country's population was Christian. The question we must ask ourselves is, to what extent did this make for the reduction of the Jewish population? That the number of Jews in the country dwindled there can be no doubt. The only question is, to what degree?

It has already been pointed out that the early Christian emperors did not introduce any really persecutory legislation against the Jews. Nevertheless, the favored position of Christianity gave that religion great practical advantages. The activities of the Emperor Constantine and his mother Helene in building churches in Jerusalem, Bethlehem and elsewhere in the country were a highly

---

45 "History of the Martyrs in Palestine," by Eusebius (Syriac), edited and translated by W. Cureton; Syriac p. 29, English p. 27.

46 *Yishuv*, p. 33.

visible sign of the intention to impart a distinctly Christian character to the Holy Land. It scarcely mattered that the enormous costs of this building program were undoubtedly borne by the local inhabitants, a large proportion of whom were Jews and Samaritans.

The main importance of the new situation was that it helped Christianity spread its influence in the country, where before that time it had been accepted by only a small minority. This help was not confined to building churches at holy sites. Epiphanius tells us how Constantine took such steps as making a Christian settlement on the borders of Gaza an independent municipality. And the Theodosian Code decrees the dread penalty of death by fire for Jews who harm Jewish converts to Christianity.[47] That the Jews did not take this sort of thing lying down is the claim of the Church Father Epiphanius, in his long account of the Jew Joseph, who converted to Christianity, and was given a title by the Emperor:[48]

> Now the good Emperor, being a true servant of the Saviour, bestowed (*upon Joseph*) the honor of *comis,* and bid him ask for whatever his heart desired. Whereupon he asked for a very great privilege, namely the Emperor's permission to build churches of the Saviour by royal command in the towns and villages of the Jews, where hitherto no one had been able to build churches. For they have among them neither Hellene nor Samaritan nor Christian. This is a matter about which they are very particular, especially in Tiberias and in Diocaesaraea — which is Sepphoris — and in Nazareth and Capernaum, desiring that no gentile should be found there. ... Then Joseph took the letters and the writ of authority showing his title and went to Tiberias, bearing with him also the authority to draw funds from the government treasury ... and he began to build in Tiberias ... and the terrible Jews, who will stop at nothing, began to practice their usual witchcraft. ...

It seems that Joseph was not particularly successful. But there were

47 Cod. Theod. XVI 8.5.
48 *Panarion haer.,* Greek text in *Yishuv,* p. 70, Hebrew p. 72.

other occasions when the power of the state helped the new religion make inroads into regions populated by Jews. The razing of synagogues or turning them into churches was not uncommon in the fifth and sixth centuries, even in the land of Israel. Christian tradition claims also that Heraclius issued anti-Jewish edicts after his victory over the Persians.

To what extent, then, did the Christianization of the Empire, and with it the gentiles of Palestine, affect the demographic position of the Jews in the country in relation to the rest of the population?

One factor to be considered is Christian pilgrimage. The new status of Palestine as The Holy Land created a flow of pilgrims which abated somewhat at the end of the second century, but picked up appreciably after Constantine had made Jerusalem a magnet for the pious. There can be no doubt that some of these pilgrims stayed on. We know that by the end of the Byzantine period there were communities of Christians in the country from other lands, such as Armenians and Iberians. Monasteries, some of which still dot the landscape, began to be built in the fourth century and proliferated during the next two hundred years, drawing numbers of pious Christians to settle in their precincts.

But there is no reason for thinking that immigration was a serious factor in increasing the Christian population. It did increase, but largely through the conversion of pagans to the new religion. The question arises whether any large numbers of Jews and Samaritans also converted.

About the Samaritans we know that they rebelled against the Romans repeatedly at the end of the fifth century and through the sixth, and that they were the targets of some very severe edicts, including decrees of forcible conversion. In spite of this, they provided very few converts to Christianity. It stands to reason that the Jews, even more fiercely resistant to missionizing, provided even less. Such evidence as we have gives us no grounds for assuming that there were more than a handful of Jewish converts to Christianity during the Byzantine period. In the meantime, the movement of converts in the other direction — into Judaism — had not yet entirely disappeared.

There is a theory we should examine that seeks to explain the origin of the Christian literature in Syriac, most of it translated from the Greek. This literature, it is suggested, was intended for Jewish converts around the time of Constantine. But there does not seem to be any real basis for this suggestion. On the other hand, large segments of the gentile population of the country and its environs were Aramaic speaking, and the likelihood is that the Syriac literature was intended for the use of new Christians recruited from their ranks.

The persecutions from which Jews in Palestine suffered during the fifth and sixth centuries gave an additional impetus to Jewish emigration. Much of this movement was directed eastwards, towards the large and growing Jewish community of Babylonia, now come under Persian rule. But we lack proof of a migration of really large dimensions at this time. For that reason we must reject the suggestion that a great many Sages left Palestine for Babylonia during the reign of Constantius (337–361), even though Sherira already speaks in those terms. The supposed evidence most probably refers to the regular movement of scholars to and fro between the two countries.

Despite the negative factors at work, it can be stated that most of the Galilee retained its Jewish character through the sixth century. This applies as well to the principal cities of the region, Tiberias and Sepphoris. Theodoretus tells us that

> because there was nothing else that could be done, eleven bishops from Egypt were expelled to Diocaesaraea (Sepphoris), that city which is inhabited by Jews, the killers of our Lord.[49]

A passage from the Church Father Eutychius about the Byzantine Emperor Heraclius (610–640) is instructive in this connection:

> When Heraclius got to Tiberias he was greeted by the Jews living in Tiberias and in Mount Galilee and in Nazareth and in every village in that region.[50]

---

49 Theodoretus, *Hist. Eccl.*, in *Yishuv*, p. 132.
50 *Annales;* in *Yishuv*, p. 66, Hebrew p. 67. For the fact that Nazareth was solidly Jewish, see the *Itinerarium* of Antoninus of Placentia, *Yishuv*, p. 110.

Another area that was a center of Jewish population was the district around the Bay of Acre, including Haifa, Shiqmona and Akko.[51] For what it is worth, Eutychios reports that during the brief Persian invasion of Palestine in the seventh century there were 4,000 Jews in Akko, and a like number in Haifa.

When the midrash comments on the verse in Lamentations (I : 17) "The Lord hath commanded concerning Jacob that they that are round about him should be his adversaries," the listing of non-Jewish settlements impinging of Jewish areas is revealing:

> For example, Halamish next to Navah, or Kastra near Haifa, or Susita next to Tiberias, or Jericho hard by Na'aran, or Lod a few mile from Ono.[52]

Still another area where Jews lived in the fifth and sixth centuries was, surprisingly enough, Jerusalem and its environs.[53] A traveller from Italy who was in Hebron said that a great number of Jews (*innumerabilis multitudo*) came there to worship at the tomb of the patriarchs and matriarchs.[54]

As for the Samaritans, they must have been numerous during the fifth and sixth centuries. Otherwise they would not have been able to mount so many rebellions, nor to spread out as they did from their center at Nablus (Neapolis) to Caesaraea and beyond.[55] The same thing applies to the Jews who made their presence felt politically during the Persian invasion of Palestine.

There is much to interest us in the words of the eleventh century Karaite Sahl ben Maṣliaḥ :

> After they (the Jews) left Jerusalem the place remained a place of desolation for 500 years, and no Jew was able to go there. When they wanted to make a pilgrimage, the Jews of the East would come to Ma'aziah (Tiberias) to pray, while

51 *Yishuv*, p. 156 and p. 63.
52 LamR I:60 and CantR II:8. [Klein suggests that the garrison at Lod made life difficult for the Jews of Ono, *Yishuv*, p. 3.] For the other places mentioned, see entries in *Yishuv* s.v.
53 About Jews in Zo'ar during the Talmudic period, see Alon in *Kedem* II, 129–130; also Sukenik, ibid. 83–88.
54 *Antonini Placentini Itinerarum*, quoted in *Yishuv*, p. 41.
55 Ibid. p. 164.

those of the West would come to the city of Gaza, and those of the South would go to the city of Zoar.[56]

Another Karaite writer tells us:

Before the Muslim conquest they (the Jews) were unable to enter Jerusalem. They came from the four corners of the earth to Tiberias and to Gaza, out of their longing to be near the site of the Holy Temple.[57]

To sum up: in spite of the diminution of the Jewish population in the country during the Byzantine period, I do not think that they dropped below the level of a rather considerable proportion of the total. In my opinion the Christians, while they became the largest single element, never achieved an absolute majority. It seems that they were outnumbered by the Jews and the Samaritans, taken together. I believe that if we assume that the Jews dropped to about one quarter of the total, we shall not be far from the truth. That, roughly, was the situation when the Arabs won the battle of the Yarmuk in 636, and ended the rule of Byzantium in the Holy Land.

56 *Kedem* II, p. 129, note 1.
57 JQR n.s. vol. 12, p. 519.

INDICES

INDEX A. GENERAL INDEX

---

* Titles (e.g. Rabbi) are omitted except where indispensable.

Index

Index

Index

Index

Index

Index

INDEX B. HEBREW SCRIPTURES (O.T.)

Index

INDEX C. TALMUDIC SOURCES

Index

Index

Index

[787]

Index

Index

Index

Index

Index

Index

[796]

[797]

Index

Index